A Right to Housing

A Right to Housing

Foundation for a New Social Agenda

EDITED BY

Rachel G. Bratt, Michael E. Stone and Chester Hartman

TEMPLE UNIVERSITY PRESS

Philadelphia

Temple University Press
1601 North Broad Street
Philadelphia PA 19122
www.temple.edu/tempress

⊗ The paper used in this publication meets the requirements of the American
National Standard for Information Sciences—Permanence of Paper for Printed
Library Materials, ANSI Z39.48-1992

Library of Congress Cataloging-in-Publication Data

A right to housing : foundation for a new social agenda / edited by Rachel G. Bratt,
  Michael E. Stone, and Chester Hartman.
      p. cm.
   Includes bibliographical references and index.
   ISBN 1-59213-431-9 (cloth : alk. paper)—ISBN 1-59213-432-7 (pbk. : alk. paper)
   1. Housing policy—United States.   2. Right to housing—United States.
   3. Housing—United States–Finance.   4. Equality—United States.
   5. Social justice—United States.   I. Bratt, Rachel G., 1946–   .
   II. Stone, Michael E., 1942–   .   III. Hartman, Chester W.

   HD7293.R46 2006
   363.5'0973–dc22   2005050671

2   4   6   8   9   7   5   3   1

Contents

We dedicate this book to two extraordinary leaders in the fight for a Right to Housing:

DAVID BRADY BRYSON (1941–1999) was a brilliant legal advocate and a truly stalwart figure in the struggle to advance decent, affordable housing for all. We and many others will remember and treasure David's long and valued service at the National Housing Law Project. We are proud to include his last written work in this volume.

CUSHING N. DOLBEARE (1926–2005), the founder and long-time director of the National Low Income Housing Coalition, was a passionate advocate, policy analyst and organizer. Her creative ways of communicating how housing is "Out of Reach" to millions of households and her strong support of a National Housing Trust Fund are but two of her numerous contributions to realizing a Right to Housing.

Acknowledgments

FIRST, WE WANT to thank the authors of this volume. They were professionally adept and personally supportive as we worked through the many stages involved in compiling this book. We are especially grateful to Florence Roisman for selflessly taking on the task of updating David Bryson's chapter. We also acknowledge and thank Mary Ellen Hombs, who participated in the book's original conceptualization. We greatly appreciate her efforts and insights into a Right to Housing.

The book benefited from a significant amount of technical support. We are enormously grateful to several staff members of the Poverty & Race Research Action Council—Rebekah Park and Daniel Fleischmann in particular—for their work in entering the many revisions and copyediting marks accrued during the back-and-forth as each chapter went through several versions and updates during the book's lengthy gestation period. Maria Nicolau at Tufts University also provided support in the final stages of this project by processing a number of the communications with authors; we gratefully acknowledge her assistance. Teri Grimwood did her usual outstanding work in assisting with the creation of the index.

Peter Wissoker, our editor at Temple University Press, was supportive throughout our process, and we thank him for his expertise in shepherding this large book into production. Joanne Bowser and those she supervised in the copyediting process—always a more difficult task when many writers are involved—were wonderful to work with.

We also thank our families, who have patiently and lovingly supported this effort: Michael Bratt and Joanna and Jeremy Bratt; Ursula Stone; Amy Fine and Jeremy and Benjamin Hartman.

Most collaborative efforts involve a considerable amount of give-and-take among the participants, and individual efforts often vary along the way. In producing this volume, we acknowledge the work that was done by one or more of the editors at a number of critical points:

MES thanks CH and RGB for launching the project (along with Mary Ellen Hombs) more than a decade ago, and for providing the initial conceptualization of the book's basic premise.

CH and RGB thank MES for joining the project after it had started and for providing a series of fresh and critical insights.

MES and CH thank RGB for her key role in managing the overall project.

CH thanks MES and RGB for providing thoughtful and careful feedback to the authors prior to the drafting of the near-final chapters.

And RGB and MES thank CH for carrying an enormous load of work during the final year before the book went to press. CH's attention to detail and involvement in bringing each chapter to completion constituted a significant contribution for which we are extremely grateful.

The non-alphabetical sequencing of the editors' names was agreed to for reasons internal to the process and in no way reflects unequal contributions to the book.

Rachel G. Bratt, Michael E. Stone
and Chester Hartman

Why a Right to Housing Is Needed and Makes Sense: Editors' Introduction

IT IS UNCONSCIONABLE that in the 21st century, upwards of 100 million people in the United States live in housing that is physically inadequate, in unsafe neighborhoods, overcrowded or way beyond what they realistically can afford. Yet it could be quite different. We could and should guarantee high-quality, truly affordable housing in "good" neighborhoods for all and thus finally achieve the National Housing Goal of "a decent home and a suitable living environment for every American family," as articulated by Congress over a half-century ago in the 1949 Housing Act and reaffirmed in subsequent legislative initiatives.[1] This book embraces the view that a commitment to a Right to Housing should be the foundation not only for housing policy but also for a new social agenda.

The call to adopt and implement a Right to Housing not only has an ethical basis in principles of justice and ideals of a commonwealth. It is also based on a highly pragmatic perspective—the central role that housing plays in peoples' lives. Given the many ways in which housing is, or can be, the basic building block for a range of related benefits—personal health and safety, employment opportunities, a decent education, security of tenure, economic security—a host of new social relationships and economic opportunities would emerge if a Right to Housing were realized, and the extensive negative impacts of poor housing would largely disappear. A Right to Housing would also go a long way toward countering the pernicious trend toward our society's extremes of material well-being and opportunity—a trend that is creating larger and

larger fissures between the nation's richest and most of the rest of us—but most especially the poorest among us—disparities that have a clear racial dimension as well and that make true democracy impossible.

Just over 60 years ago, in his 1944 State of the Union address to Congress, President Franklin Delano Roosevelt declared that economic security is a necessary ingredient for a democratic society. He further asserted that there was a need for a whole series of economic and social rights, including a Right to Housing. This is part of his message:

> We have come to a clear realization of the fact that true individual freedom cannot exist without economic security and independence. "Necessitous men are not free men...." These economic truths have become accepted as self-evident. We have accepted, so to speak, a second Bill of Rights under which a new basis of security and prosperity can be established for all—regardless of station, race, or creed. Among these are: the right to a useful and remunerative job ... the right to earn enough to provide adequate food and clothing and recreation ... the right to adequate medical care ... the right to a good education [and along with several other enumerated rights] the right of every family to a decent home. All of these rights spell security. And after this war is won we must be prepared to move forward in the implementation of these rights, to new goals of human happiness and well-being. (Roosevelt 1944; see also Sunstein 2004)[2]

A bold, fresh approach to solving the nation's housing problems is timely because three-fourths of a century of government interventions and a multiplicity of strategies, both public and private, have not been devoted to truly solving the problem. To be sure, gains have been made, and millions of households have been assisted, but the gains and assistance have been partial, piecemeal and transitory at best. Any examination of the array and scale of housing and housing-related problems reveals clearly how painful, pervasive and persistent are these problems. Let us thus finally get past the illusion that merely tinkering with current policies and even appropriating more money will be sufficient to solve our housing problems. Fundamental change is necessary and long overdue.

This is not a new or original insight and call. Back in 1989, the Washington, DC-based Institute for Policy Studies assembled a Working Group on Housing (in which this book's co-editors Chester Hartman and Michael Stone as well as several of its contributors—Emily Achtenberg, Peter Dreier, Peter Marcuse and Florence Roisman—participated) that crafted a detailed housing program, put forward in *The Right to Housing: A Blueprint for Housing the Nation.*[3]

That document provided an analysis of the failures of the private market and of government programs similar to what is put forward in this book. And it included a detailed program for preserving affordable rental housing; promoting affordable homeownership; protecting the stock of government-assisted housing; and producing/financing new affordable housing. First-year program costs—estimated for each element of the program, with administrative costs added—at that time ranged from $29 billion to $88 billion, depending on how rapidly and fully specific program elements were introduced; by way of comparison, at the same time, the highly regressive income tax system for housing provided at least $54 billion in tax breaks for high-income households. The thrust of the various elements was to move substantial portions of the existing housing stock, as well as new additions, into the nonprofit sector (public as well as private)—"decommodifying housing" was the catchword. Annual costs would steadily decrease

as this fundamental shift in the nation's housing stock progressed. Congressman Ron Dellums of California introduced the program in the 101st Congress as H.R. 1122 (A Bill to Provide an Affordable, Secure and Decent Home and Suitable Living Environment for Every American Family). Needless to say, it did not pass. At the end of a hearing on the Bill, Congressman Henry Gonzalez of Texas, then Chair of the Banking, Finance & Urban Affairs Committee and Chair of the Subcommittee on Housing and Community Development, remarked, "What your group has presented is inevitably going to happen. . . . It is imaginative, it is seminal, it is creative." We agree and hope this book will hasten that day.

THE PHYSICAL IMPORTANCE OF DECENT HOUSING

Where one lives—particularly if one is poor, and/or a person of color—plays a critical role in fixing a person's place in society and in the local community. Living in substandard housing in a "bad" neighborhood may limit people's ability to secure an adequate education for their children, reduce chances of finding a decent job and deprive them of decent public services and community facilities. The quality of one's housing may also be an outward sign, as well as part of a person's self-image, that in some profound and important ways one has not succeeded.

Housing has always been viewed as one of the necessities of life—a critical element of the "food, clothing and shelter" triumvirate. Stories of homeless people freezing to death each winter provide stark reminders that housing is a fundamental need. In earlier eras, events such as the great Chicago fire of 1871 and the cholera epidemics that swept densely populated urban areas in the early and mid-19th Century dramatically made the link between poor housing conditions and health and safety (Friedman 1968). The public response was enactment of tenement house laws, first in New York City and followed by other large cities. The explicit goal was to regulate the "health, safety and morals of tenants" (Wood 1934) as well as to protect the nonpoor who were living in nearby neighborhoods.

Although housing conditions have improved dramatically since the 19th Century, poor quality is still a problem facing millions of Americans. Fires due to inadequate wiring or faulty furnaces are still commonplace, and many households are plagued by infestations of vermin and inadequate heating systems. In recent years, there have been compelling demonstrations of the links between health and housing. For example, a project undertaken under the auspices of the Boston Medical Center underscored that poorly maintained housing is closely linked to childhood injuries and lead poisoning, and that damp, moldy interiors are associated with elevated incidences of respiratory disease and asthma (Sandel et al. 1999, 25–26; see also *Scientific American* 1999, 19–20; Bernstein 1999; Pérez-Peña 2003).

Over the past 30 years, we have learned a great deal about the impact of lead on children's health. Lead poisoning has been called "the most common and devastating environmental disease of young children" (U.S. General Accounting Office 1993, 2). The Centers for Disease Control and Prevention estimates that 434,000 children younger than age six have blood-lead levels above the federal guideline (Avril 2003).[4] Hazards due to lead paint are most serious among poor, nonwhite households, who have a far higher incidence of lead poisoning than their higher-income white counterparts (Leonard et al. 1993, 8; National Low Income Housing Coalition 2003). St. Louis, which has the nation's fourth oldest housing stock, has childhood lead poisoning rates about six times the national average. In 1999, the city's lead poisoning prevention program was scheduled to decontaminate about 500 low-income apartments. However, "at that rate, it will finish deleading St. Louis in about 200 years" (Grunwald 1999).

Additional evidence on the connections between poor housing and health comes from a controlled study carried out in England, which revealed that residents living in high-quality public housing in West London were far less likely to become sick than those living in low-quality public housing in East London. Further,

researchers concluded that "the costs of failing to provide decent homes in stable environments to families—in the forms of ill health, underachievement, crime and vandalism—will far exceed the investment in adequate maintenance and repair of housing" (cited in Hynes et al. 2000, 35–36). Although there may be room for improving our ability to measure the cost-effectiveness of improved housing, physical problems caused by poor housing should not persist.

THE EMOTIONAL AND SYMBOLIC IMPORTANCE OF HOUSING

In addition to protecting people from the elements and providing (or not providing) physical safety, housing fulfills a variety of critical functions in contemporary society.[5] A landmark study prepared in 1966 for the U.S. Department of Health, Education and Welfare (predecessor to the Department of Health and Human Services) investigated what was known about the relationship between housing and the feelings and behavior of individuals and families. It concluded that "The evidence makes it clear that housing affects perception of one's self, contributes to or relieves stress, and affects health" (Schorr 1966, 3).

A decade later, a study of middle-income people affirmed that an important aspect of the meaning of one's house is

> the sense of permanence and security one could experience. . . . In this regard, people spoke of "sinking roots," "nesting," and generally settling down. The house . . . seemed to be a powerful symbol of order, continuity, physical safety, and a sense of place or physical belonging. . . . Closely connected . . . was [another] aspect of the house's meaning—the common notion that the house was a refuge from the outside world or even a bastion against that world . . . : a desire to escape from other people and from social involvement, the establishment of a place from which others could be excluded, and where, consequently, one could truly be oneself, in control, "more of an individual," capable of loving, and fully human. (Rakoff 1977, quoted in Stone 1993, 15)

Feminist architectural historian Dolores Hayden has also emphasized the emotional importance of housing: "Whoever speaks of housing must also speak of home; the word means both the physical space and the nurturing that takes place there" (1984, 63). If housing is overcrowded, dilapidated or otherwise inadequate, it is difficult, if not impossible, for family life to function smoothly. Empirical evidence demonstrating the importance of housing for emotional well-being comes from a recent study of the impacts of housing quality on mental health; better-quality housing was related to lower levels of psychological distress (Evans et al. 2000, 529).

Jonathan Kozol's poignant account of homeless families in New York City shelters underscores the extent to which grossly inadequate housing conditions contribute to family dysfunction:[6] A lack of privacy creates stress for all family members; the inability to have guests vastly constricts normal social access; children are unable to do homework and adults live in constant fear that their children will be endangered by the harsh social and physical environments (Kozol 1988).

Further, recent research on impacts of homelessness on children has revealed that while "only 5 percent of children entering shelters had a developmental delay requiring specialist evaluation, . . . half of the children living in homeless shelters had one or more developmental delays." In addition, although nearly one-half the school-age children in homeless shelters needed special education evaluation, only 22 percent actually received this testing. Children living in shelters also missed far more days of school than did housed children. And, finally, one-half of all children in shelters showed signs of anxiety and depression and demonstrated significantly more behavioral disturbances, such as tantrums and aggressive behavior, than did poor housed children (cited in Sandel et al. 1999, 39).

Although it may be difficult to prove that these and other types of problems are *caused* by poor or no housing,[7] it is undeniable that, at the very least, inadequate housing (including long-term residence in shelters) can exacerbate an already problematic situation. A key aspect of family well-being necessarily involves the provision of decent, affordable housing (Bratt 2002). As a bi-partisan task force report declared:

> [A] decent place for a family to live becomes a platform for dignity and self-respect and a base for hope and improvement. A decent home allows people to take advantage of opportunities in education, health and employment—the means to get ahead in our society. A decent home is the important beginning point for growth into the mainstream of American life. (Report of the National Housing Task Force 1988, 3).

More recently, this assertion was echoed by the Congressionally-appointed bi-partisan Millennial Housing Commission:

> Decent and affordable housing has a demonstrable impact on family stability and the life outcomes of children. Decent housing is an indispensable building block of healthy neighborhoods, and thus shapes the quality of community life. . . . Better housing can lead to better outcomes for individuals, communities, and American society as a whole. (2002, 1)[8]

Housing has also been credited as providing a significant boost on the economic ladder due to the opportunity it can present to build assets. Although a key argument of this book is that housing need not be viewed as the only or best vehicle for promoting savings and wealth accumulation (see Stone 1993,195–196, for a discussion of a social alternative to wealth creation through homeownership), and that much more housing can and should be socially and publicly owned, we acknowledge that, at least since the end of World War II, millions of households have been able to gain a foothold in the economy through their ability to become homeowners. However, recent research points to several important concerns and risks related to low-income homeownership, including the possibility of financial losses (see Retsinas and Belsky 2002:Part 3). And of course a central defect of the homeownership push is the enormous racial disparities that exist in homeownership rates and in the wealth-generating potential and actuality of home purchase (see Chapter 3 and Shapiro 2004).[9] Beyond the effects of housing itself, where people live, in terms of neighborhood setting and locational advantage, has a great deal to do with access to both educational opportunities and employment and social networks (see Chapter 18).

IMPORTANCE OF HOUSING IN A NEIGHBORHOOD CONTEXT

Even a cursory overview of this country's community development initiatives reveals that housing has consistently been given a central position. In the urban renewal program, for example, the earliest focus was on "slum" clearance. Later, the emphasis was on housing rehabilitation. As part of the Model Cities program of the mid-1960s, enforcing housing codes, developing "in-fill" housing on vacant land and rehabilitating housing were key components. The Community Development Block Grant (CDBG) program, in existence since 1974, has supported a variety of housing initiatives, with housing responsible for the largest share of CDBG expenditures (The Urban Institute 1995, iv).

During the 1980s and 1990s, nonprofit development organizations proliferated across the country and have become central players in community revitalization efforts. Here, too, there is a significant focus on housing, with the vast majority of these groups involved with housing production or rehabilitation (Vidal 1992, 5). The National Congress for Community Economic Development (NCCED) has estimated that there are more than 3,600 community development corporations (CDCs), which is the dominant type of nonprofit development organization (NCCED 1999). Moreover, housing produced by CDCs "is often a foundation for such activities as business enterprise, economic development, job training, health care and education" (NCCED 1999, 11).

Although many CDCs are acknowledging that their housing initiatives should be viewed in the broader context of comprehensive community revitalization—including the provision of social services, employment training and referrals, health care and substance abuse programs, and enhancing educational opportunities (U.S. General Accounting Office 1995)—the quality of housing is one of the most

visible and concrete signs of neighborhood well-being. Housing is, and will continue to be, a central component of virtually any community's rebuilding efforts, and CDCs are likely to continue to play a significant role (see Chapter 16).

OVERVIEW OF HOUSING NEEDS IN THE UNITED STATES

Despite the universal physical need for shelter, as well as the symbolic and emotional importance of decent housing, housing problems across our nation are serious and widespread. The U.S. Department of Housing and Urban Development (HUD), at the request of Congress, submits occasional reports on "worst case housing needs." These are renter households who have incomes of 50 percent or less of area median income, pay more than 50 percent of their income for rent and utilities and who may also live in severely inadequate quarters,[10] yet do not receive federal assistance. Slightly over 5 million of the nation's approximately 103 million households fall into this category (HUD 2003), with about 15 percent of them living in nonmetropolitan areas (National Low Income Housing Coalition 2001). Yet this figure does not include many of those with serious housing problems, such as the homeless. While estimates of the total number of homeless vary widely—in part a function of the inherent difficulty of counting these people—an often-cited figure is that there are 800,000 homeless people in the United States on any given night. And, over the course of a year, some 3.5 million people may be homeless for varying periods of time (National Low Income Housing Coalition 2005; see also Chapter 15).

In addition to the literally and virtually homeless are tens of thousands of people who are "pre-homeless" or nearly homeless. In New York City (and doubtless in many other cities with large immigrant populations), there have been numerous illegal conversions of basement space in single-family homes and apartment houses into small (typically, $5' \times 8'$) cubicles, with common kitchens and bathrooms, which present serious fire and health hazards. Officials are reluctant to clamp down on these living arrangements—even if they could systematically find them (estimates range from 10,000 to 50,000 units in New York City alone)—knowing that the consequence of enforcing housing codes would be serious increases in the homelessness population (Wolff 1994). Moreover, illegal units of this sort are not confined to central cities and immigrant populations (Lambert 1996). Among the worst housed of the nearly homeless are migrant farmworkers (Greenhouse 1998).

Owning one's home is of course no guarantee that a family's residence will be problem-free. About 2 million homeowner households lived in housing with moderate or severe problems in 1999,[11] and more than 6 million homeowner households paid more than 50 percent of their income for housing. About 84 percent of all homeowners facing severe housing problems earned less than 80 percent of area median income (National Low Income Housing Coalition 2001).[12]

Further, in 1999, about 2.6 million households lived in units with more than one person per room (the official measure of overcrowding); about one-half of this group faced overcrowding problems in conjunction with problems of costs and quality (National Low Income Housing Coalition 2001). Finally, and perhaps most depressing of all, the "worst case housing needs" figure does not include the approximately 1.7 million households with severe problems living in subsidized housing (National Low Income Housing Coalition 2001).[13] Included here are public housing units that are waiting to be repaired or substantially rehabilitated as well as thousands of units of privately owned subsidized housing that have a similar backlog of maintenance problems (see National Commission on Severely Distressed Public Housing 1992; England-Joseph 1994; Finkel et al. 1999).

Three additional factors are relevant when considering the scope of our housing problems: First, in terms of quality, HUD and Census Bureau criteria for "severely substandard" ignore the stricter, more relevant, legally enforceable local housing code standards. Incorporating such standards into definitions of adequacy would considerably increase the numbers of households living in "inadequate units."[14] Second,

a residence that is in decent condition, of the proper size for the household and within their financial means may nonetheless be unacceptably dangerous, isolating and unpleasant—hence substandard—if the surrounding residences and streets fail to meet minimal standards. And third, the affordability criterion embodied in HUD's "worst case" data fails to recognize the severe budgetary problems faced by renter households with incomes above 50 percent of the area median who must spend more than one-half their income for rent. In addition, many other lower-income renter households who pay less than 50 percent of their income for rent may still be paying way too much. This is explored more fully in Chapter 2, which argues that any fixed "proper" rent-to-income ratio standard ignores the realities that household size, income level and the need to pay for non-shelter basics all go into determining whether a given unit is "affordable" for a given household.[15]

What is the best estimate of the bottom line for all of the above housing problems? The National Low Income Housing Coalition (2001) estimates that some 18.5 million homeowner households and 17.2 million renter households are facing either moderate or severe housing problems. Of these 35.7 million households, about 19.5 million earned less than 50 percent of median income,[16] and another 7.5 million earned 50 to 80 percent of median income.[17] The Joint Center for Housing Studies has reached a similar conclusion, presented somewhat differently:

A staggering three in ten US households have housing affordability problems. Fully 14.3 million are severely cost-burdened (spend more than 50 percent of their incomes on housing) and another 17.3 million are moderately cost-burdened (spend 30–50 percent of their incomes on housing). Some 9.3 million households live in overcrowded units or housing classified as physically inadequate. And a disheartening 3.7 million households face more than one of these problems. (2003, 25)

Using his shelter poverty concept, Michael Stone has found a similarly massive number of households (about 15 million renters and

17 million homeowners in 2001) facing serious housing affordability problems. However, his analysis underscores "a significantly different distribution of the problem: Not all households shelter-poor are paying over 30 percent of their incomes for housing, and not all households paying over 30 percent are shelter-poor."[18] Most strikingly, his approach shows that families with children are more likely to have affordability problems, and that small middle-income households are less likely to have affordability problems, than is suggested by the conventional standard (see Chapter 2).

Another way of looking at housing needs is via estimates of the number of poor households eligible for housing assistance who do not receive it. About two out of three renters with incomes below the poverty line do not receive any housing assistance (Daskal 1998, 35). And, using HUD's higher income limits of eligibility for housing assistance, far more low-income households could receive housing if such funding were available. At the very least, the 5 million households who have "worst case housing needs" would be eligible for a subsidy from HUD.

Housing needs can also be examined by comparing the housing situation of those with the least housing opportunities and resources and those with the most, which are far from evenly distributed. Housing needs among our poorest citizens, discriminated-against racial groups and women heads of household are much more serious than among the population at large. For example, "regardless of income, the incidence of burdens is higher among minorities than whites..." (Joint Center for Housing Studies 2005, 25). Thus, housing is America's Great Divide. How and where one lives is *the* marker of one's socioeconomic and, to a large extent, racial status in the society and the local community. Moreover, this divide runs through all our major systems: education, health care, employment, criminal justice—in other words, we have developed into a "have/secure" and "have-not/insecure" society. (See Chapter 1 on income inequality, Chapter 2 on housing affordability, Chapter 3 on racial discrimination, Chapter 13 on the elderly and Chapter 14 on housing challenges facing women.)

The extremes of housing consumption are staggering. On the one hand, housing is the most conspicuous form of conspicuous consumption. Mega-mansions are commonplace in affluent suburbs, often replacing more modest dwellings that are demolished. And these are not the exclusive domains of the "rich and famous," as large numbers of households rode the wave of economic growth and expansion during the 1990s. A *New York Times* article described this Memphis scene:

> The beige, three-story mansion fills a one-acre lot.... Roof turrets, tall windows, columns that frame the front door at the head of a majestic, sloping driveway all heighten the impression of a palace.... The ranch house next door seems, by comparison, like a shack. "Such houses," observes Kenneth Rosen, who heads the University of California's Fisher Center for Real Estate, "are conspicuous proof that a family has achieved a level of wealth way beyond its physical needs. A mansion, more than luxury cars or anything else, shows everyone in the community that you are rich." (Uchitelle 1999)

On the other hand, millions of households are facing serious problems securing and paying for decent shelter. The most extreme situation is exemplified by the hundreds of thousands of Americans who, at any given point in time, are without any private domestic space at all—the country's homeless population.

As a society, we seem content to permit such disparities. And the problems can only get worse, as housing costs have been rising faster than incomes for most of the past 30 years. The Joint Center for Housing Studies has noted that "home prices and rents have continued to outpace general price inflation" (2003, 25). (See also Chapter 1 on income distribution trends and Chapter 2 on housing affordability trends.)

Moreover, "welfare reform," introduced in 1996, is having a nontrivial impact in the housing area, although its full effects remain to be seen. While a great many TANF recipients (Temporary Assistance for Needy Families, formerly known as AFDC) have entered the workforce, the pay levels for the majority of these jobs still is considerably below what is needed to cover the cost of market rents for apartments. In addition, millions of families who have never been on welfare, and who earn minimum wages or somewhat above, are still unable to afford decent housing (see Chapter 18).

The alarming loss of unsubsidized low-rent units is another important factor contributing to high rental housing costs. Between 1991 and 1997, the number of unsubsidized rental units affordable to extremely low-income households (those with incomes 30 percent or less of area median income) dropped by 370,000—a 5 percent reduction. At the same time that the low-rent stock has been decreasing, the number of households earning 30 percent or less of median income has been increasing (HUD 2000, 22). According to the Joint Center for Housing Studies, "In 2001, the 9.9 million renters in the bottom quintile [of income, which was no more than $17,000] outnumbered the supply of these [unsubsidized] units by fully 2 million. Reducing the pool even further, higher-income households occupied 2.7 million of the 7.9 million lowest-cost units" (2003, 28).

Beyond these important trends, there are deeper causes behind the staggering situation we are observing.

THE ROOTS OF HOUSING PROBLEMS

Housing problems are deeply ingrained in the operation of our economic system and in the ways in which society functions, and they have not emerged in just the past few decades. Rather, this country has a long history of such problems (see, for example, Stone 1993, Chapters 3, 4), the consequence of certain basic institutional arrangements and characteristics of our society. The most important factors include the workings of the private housing market; widening income inequality; persistent and pervasive housing discrimination; overdependence on debt and capital markets to finance housing; and public policies that are inadequate to counter these trends and, at worst, exacerbate them.

The Illusions of "the Market"

Throughout this nation's history, there has been a struggle between those who believe that we have a collective responsibility, through, but not limited to, government, to "promote the general welfare" and those who assert that the general welfare is and should be best achieved by all pursuing their own self-interest via "the Market," with government doing as little as possible, apart from providing for the common defense. From the Great Depression through the 1970s, the former view predominated, albeit often tempered with ritual apologies for interfering with the alleged virtues of the market. Over the past quarter-century, though, the idealization of the market as the answer to nearly all social and economic problems has emerged as the dominant ideology, with government portrayed not only as outrageously wasteful of "your money," but indeed as the very *cause* of poverty, anti-social behavior, declining educational performance and so forth.

Nowhere has this shift been greater than with regard to housing and housing policy. (A few of the most rabid examples of attacks on government interventions in housing are Salins 1980 and Husock 2003.) Public housing has been attacked as an integral part of the culture of welfare dependency as well as the worst of modern urban design. Never mind that most public housing does not fit the stereotypes and that relentless opposition from private real estate interests largely accounts for the failures of design and siting that do exist. Government assistance for housing the poor, to the extent that it is not opposed entirely, has largely shifted away from housing production to vouchers that ostensibly give recipients the freedom to shop in the "free" housing market. Yet this market tends, in many places, to have little or nothing available, forcing recipients to return their vouchers unused, while in other places, it consists of exploitative landlords who reap windfalls from the vouchers. Rent control has been discredited as allegedly destroying market incentives for landlords and developers to maintain and produce unsubsidized low-rent housing, thus (so the argument goes) causing decay and abandonment of great swaths of urban America. Government is blamed for runaway housing costs and inadequate housing production, through imposition of exclusionary zoning and strict subdivision and permitting regulations. Ironically, to the extent that this latter critique has some legitimacy, the governments responsible are under the control of and acting on behalf of high-income people seeking to protect their wealth from the market.

It is our view that the ideology of the virtuous market is largely a cynical and hypocritical rationalization for selfish individualism and widening inequality. Simplistic theories have been used to divert attention from the underlying causes of housing and other social problems by focusing instead on admittedly flawed, inadequate and often contradictory government responses to those problems. It appears that we have forgotten that markets are social creations, operating on the basis of legal and economic incentives and disincentives established and enforced by governments. The biggest and most profitable businesses get that way by ruthlessly driving out or buying up competitors in order to escape from the strictures of the competitive market whose virtues they proclaim. And they resist mightily government attempts to rein in their monopolistic depredations (cf. Microsoft). But when they fail, to whom do they turn to be bailed out? Why of course, the government via the taxpayers (see discussion of the savings and loan bailout and the crisis of Fannie Mae and Freddie Mac in Chapter 4).

Furthermore, the efficiency that in theory attaches to competitive "free markets" is at best a one-dimensional efficiency that has no place for distributive justice and neighborhood effects. For example, sharply escalating housing prices in many parts of the country are in fact the response of the free housing market to demand from ever-richer households at the top of the increasingly unequal income distribution (see Chapter 1 and Chapter 4). While taxing away some of this speculative wealth would dampen price increases, thereby making housing generally more affordable, and generate some revenue that could be used for low-income housing, such redistribution would ostensibly reduce the efficiency of the housing market. Yet, to add insult to injury, the tax system actually provides incentives for such speculation (see Chapter 5). Inefficiency on the upside of the market (for instance, windfall profits that the market would not generate without public assistance) does not seem to bother free-market ideologues.

As for so-called neighborhood effects, or externalities, free-market ideology/theory either sees them as beneficial or ignores them. For example, if tearing down smaller, older houses to build mega-mansions results in higher property values and hence higher property taxes and greater economic stress for older homeowners, free-market ideology sees this as a positive externality (the latter are better off because their property values have risen), not as a negative externality because their quality of life has diminished due to increased costs. If the free market produces massive houses on large lots sprawling across the landscape, the costs to natural habitats and watersheds, as well as the costs of increased traffic and air pollution, are largely externalized, imposed on others in the present and future rather than being part of the calculus of efficiency.

The housing market also treats housing as a commodity—an item that is bought and sold for profit. For the low-income renter or homebuyer, this creates problems at every step of the housing production, development, distribution and financing processes. The final cost of housing is the total of all the many costs involved—including land, building supplies, labor, financing, distribution and conveyance. At each phase of the process, the goal is to maximize profits, which in turn increases costs and reduces affordability.

KEY CAUSAL FACTORS OF HOUSING PROBLEMS—BEYOND THE MARKET

In addition to our view that the private housing market works at cross-purpose with the needs of providing decent, truly affordable housing for all, a number of other factors are at the root of our housing problems. Since each of these is developed more fully in the chapters of the book, the following offers an overview of these critical themes.

Widening Income Inequality

Our housing problems are directly and closely connected with the overall structure of our economic system. In contrast with several decades post–World War II, when the gap between the rich and the poor was shrinking, for the past 30 years this trend has changed. We have been mired in a period of sustained and growing income inequality, where the disparity between the upper and lower tiers of the income distribution has become ever wider. Moreover, various subgroups of the population (such as persons of color and single-parent families) are experiencing this disparity with a disproportionate frequency.

Beyond the inequality in income, for most households, the income side of the housing affordability equation is not keeping pace with the escalating costs of housing. Without adequate income, the ability of households to cover the costs of housing is simply impossible. These trends have not "just happened." Instead, as discussed in Chapter 1, they are the outcome of specific policies, goals and initiatives of both government and the corporate sector.

Persistent and Pervasive Housing Discrimination

Not only do people of color have lower incomes than their white counterparts, they are less able to compete in the housing market due to persistent discrimination.[19] Housing discrimination is nothing new (Loewen 2005). While it was a "given" before direct government intervention in housing during the Great Depression, it became codified through the guidelines of the Federal Housing Administration. Indeed, the agency's 1938 underwriting manual advised FHA inspectors who were assessing properties for mortgage insurance to do their job, as follows:

> Areas surrounding a location are investigated to determine whether incompatible racial and social groups are present, for the purpose of making a prediction regarding the probability of the location being invaded by such groups. If a neighborhood is to retain stability, it is necessary that the properties shall continue to be occupied by the same social and racial classes. A change in social and racial occupancy generally contributes to instability and a decline in values. (1938, Section 937)

While it took several decades for the FHA to change both its guidelines as well as its mode of operation, the legacy of housing discrimination and, indeed, various ongoing discriminatory practices, is still a grim fact of American life. Much more often than not, neighborhoods are characterized by occupancy by one racial group or another. Moreover, the activities and conscious decisions that have created these patterns are still widely practiced today. This critical issue is explored in Chapter 3. But the role of race and the reality of discrimination is a theme that runs throughout the book.

Overdependence on Debt and Capital Markets

Due to the intrinsic nature of housing (bulky, durable, tied to land) and the system of private ownership of almost all housing in this country, the housing sector is extraordinarily dependent on the cost and availability of borrowed money. Mortgage-lending institutions have thus been a dominant force in the housing sector for the past century. Their interests and evolution, including their periodic crises and consequent public policies, have had an enormous impact on the physical landscape of this country and on economic distribution and the stability of the overall economy. On the one hand, the mortgage system has facilitated the construction of vast amounts of housing and the spread of homeownership but has also widened housing inequality, fostered debt entrapment, destroyed neighborhoods and made the nation's economy increasingly unstable and vulnerable to the vagaries of global capital markets. Chapter 4 explains how these dilemmas have emerged and points toward some of the alternatives, which are discussed in Chapter 12.

Flawed and Inadequate Public Policies

Despite and perhaps because of these trends, in recent years, housing equity issues have receded from public and political concern. This has been accompanied by declines in government support for housing programs and subsidies relative to the growing need for such support. As journalist Jason DeParle concluded in 1996 (and little has changed since), "The Federal Government has essentially conceded defeat in its decades-long drive to make housing affordable to low-income Americans. . . . Housing has simply evaporated as a political issue." Almost no office holder or candidate for office, at any level of government, gives prominent attention to housing. The current Administration's view was expressed in the astounding comment made by HUD Secretary Alphonso Jackson at a May 2004 hearing of the House Committee on Financial Services. In response to a question from one of the committee members, Secretary Jackson "stated that he doesn't talk about housing the poor because 'being poor is a state of mind, not a condition'" (Committee Members Decry HUD Secretary's Comments on the Poor 2004).

But a lack of federal interest in housing was not always the case. Although this interest often grew out of a desire to use housing as a vehicle to attack nonhousing problems (Marcuse 1986), for decades the federal government was a major player in promoting housing for low-income households. What was historically the principal approach—low-rent housing developments built and managed by local housing authorities, with heavy federal subsidies—has been under relentless attack since the 1960s. And the two-decade-long emphasis (from the early 1960s through the early 1980s) in producing subsidized housing through the private sector has also lost favor among federal officials. "Shallower" subsidies provided through the Low Income Housing Tax Credit (LIHTC) and the HOME Investment Partnership program have added some new units but address only a very small fraction of the overall needs for housing affordable to low-income households—they fail to reach far enough down the income distribution, and very few units are permanently affordable.

Since its creation in 1986, the LIHTC has contributed to the production of about 1.8 million units, but many of these units are not available to those with incomes below 30 percent of median income (National Low Income Housing Coalition 2005).[20] The HOME program has funded the acquisition, construction and rehabilitation of about 800,000 units of housing since its inception in 1990, but again, many of the residents are not the most needy, and most of the units are not permanently affordable (National Low Income Housing Coalition 2005).

Between 1977 and 1994, the number of HUD-assisted households grew by 2.4 million. But this number camouflages a troubling trend: During the period from 1977 to 1983, the annual average increase was 215,000 units; however, between 1984 and 1994, the average annual increase fell to 82,000. From 1995 to 1998, no new funds for assisted housing were provided by Congress. Finally, however, starting in 1999, there was again modest recognition of the need for additional housing assistance, with the appropriation of funds for 50,000 new vouchers in that year, followed by 60,000 and 79,000 in FY2000 and FY2001, respectively (Bratt 2003, based on Dolbeare and Crowley 2002). In FY2002, funding for 26,000 new vouchers was appropriated, but Congress approved no new vouchers in FY2003, FY2004 and FY2005, and HUD requested none for FY2006 (National Low Income Housing Coalition 2005).

It is no surprise that these dismal numbers concerning new households being assisted reflect reductions in the inflated-adjusted level of appropriations for new housing units. Between 1976 and 2004, net new annual federal budget authority for assisted housing dropped from $56.4 billion to $29.25 billion (in constant 2004 dollars)[21] (Dolbeare, Saraf and Crowley 2004). In dramatic contrast, the largest form of federal housing aid—the indirect and highly regressive subsidy the tax system provides to homeowners via the homeowner deduction (the ability to deduct from one's taxable income base all property tax and virtually all mortgage interest payments)—was worth over $84 billion in 2004, with the majority of these subsidies going to households in the top two-fifths of the income distribution; nearly 37 percent of housing-related tax subsidies go to those earning over $86,000 (Dolbeare, Saraf and Crowley 2004; see also Chapter 5). Including investor deductions, in 2004 housing-related tax expenditures totalled $119.3 billion, four times the budget authority for housing assistance (Dolbeare, Saraf and Crowley 2004). In so many ways, the nation's housing system reflects and undergirds the extreme and growing class and race divisions that characterize the society as a whole.

Our flawed public policies are also causing a net loss of subsidized units. Various sources estimate that since the late 1980s, some 200,000 units have been removed from the inventory of assisted housing. This has been due to the loss of over 100,000 units through demolition of some severely deteriorated subsidized housing and as a result of the HOPE VI public housing redevelopment program (National Housing Law Project et al. 2002; see also Chapter 11), as well as the "expiring use" problem: There has been a loss of 60,000 units in some older subsidized housing developments where the owner has prepaid the mortgage and converted the buildings into market-rate dwellings, and a loss of about 40,000 units where owners have opted out of Section 8 contracts (Achtenberg 2002; see also Chapter 7 text and box).

The result of all of this is a chronic insufficiency of subsidized low-rent units. A recent estimate of housing needs comes from the Millennial Housing Commission, whose final report stated that "The addition of 150,000 units annually would make substantial progress toward meeting the housing needs of ELI [extremely low income; at or below 30 percent of area median income] households, but it would take annual production of more than 250,000 units for more than 20 years to close the gap" (2002, 18).

One impact of these shortages is long waits for subsidized housing. Based on data collected between 1996 and 1998, HUD estimated that, nationally, the average wait for a public housing unit was 11 months, and for a Section 8 rental assistance voucher, it was 28 months. For the largest public housing authorities (those with over 30,000 units), the wait for a public housing unit was 33 months, and 42 months for a Section 8 certificate. In New York City, the wait for either a public housing unit or a Section 8 voucher can be as much as eight years. Between 1998 and 1999, the number of families waiting for assistance increased substantially. The combined waiting list for a Section 8 voucher in 18 cities sampled grew from just under 500,000 to 660,000 households. The 40

waiting lists from those cities examined in the HUD study included about 1 million families. And HUD cautions that these figures may be an underestimate because many housing authorities have closed their waiting lists due to their overwhelming size (HUD 1999, 7–10).

The failings of our housing policies are, in part, due to the government's desire to fulfill a number of economic, social and political goals, beyond the desire to provide housing for the poor. In addition, housing policies are always greatly influenced and shaped by the needs of the private for-profit housing industry—an industry that has a sophisticated and well-financed lobbying component and that has been successful in gaining federal support for their agenda (see Chapter 5). It is little wonder, therefore, that housing policies have fallen short of the goal of providing decent, affordable housing for those most in need. While Chapter 6 asserts that our record of federal intervention in housing has been disappointing, regardless of the political party in power, it is acknowledged that somewhat more has been accomplished under Democratic than under Republican Administrations.

ORGANIZING FOR A RIGHT TO HOUSING

Achieving the ambitious vision and goals put forth in this book certainly will require a housing strategy and a movement well beyond what has been seen heretofore in this country. For the most part, housing organizing and activism in the United States have been modest and constrained in time, place and vision. Even in those periods where housing activism has reached a national scale and included aspects of a Right to Housing in its vision, the strategic approach has fallen far short (see Chapter 10; see also Stone 1993, Chapters 11, 12).

Past social movements have resulted in substantial expansions of basic rights far beyond what has been achieved with regard to housing. Emancipation, women's suffrage, the many gains of the labor movement, and the Civil Rights Movement particularly stand out. The women's movement, the gay and lesbian movement and the disability rights movement are also notable for what they have achieved, however imperfect and incomplete. Indeed, that these are all widely recognized as "movements" and referred to with the definite article "the" attests in some measure to their potency, in striking contrast with housing.

Any viable strategy to achieve a Right to Housing must emerge through a dynamic and participatory process that includes the following principles: understanding and confronting fundamental causes of housing problems; putting forth a vision of truly social housing provision; participating in alliances across issue lines; building organizations committed to leadership development and broadly inclusionary decision-making; generating independent funding for skilled organizers and organizing; and building alliances with trade unions.

AN OVERVIEW OF THE BOOK'S CHAPTERS

This book argues that what is needed is the legal mandate of a Right to Housing and institutional changes to make this mandate become reality.[22] In the first portion, which includes Chapters 1 to 7, we present an array of analyses demonstrating that beyond the litany of housing needs and problems, there exist key structural determinants of housing injustice. Critical changes in the labor market and the resulting widening income inequality and insecurity are discussed in Chapter 1. Chapter 2 reveals one of the most damaging impacts of our economic inequality, in demonstrating how shelter poverty afflicts tens of millions of American households, especially the most vulnerable groups in society. The following three chapters explain how key aspects of society and the housing system contribute to our housing problems. The role of race/racism is explored in Chapter 3; the faulty structure of our housing finance system is explored in Chapter 4 and the ways in which our federal housing subsidies have consistently favored the wealthy over the poor are detailed in Chapter 5. The sometimes perverse but nearly always inadequate housing policies promulgated over the last 70 years are discussed in Chapter 6. Chapter 7 and its accompanying box explore how one

federal policy around the issue of "expiring use restrictions" has evolved and has impacted poor residents of subsidized housing. Taken together, these chapters present a clear picture of the ways in which inequality and housing problems are an outgrowth of the nation's economy, financial structure, and flawed government and private market practices.

The second portion of the book opens with Chapter 8, which makes the "case for a Right to Housing." It continues by highlighting broad principles and strategies to achieve a Right to Housing, including Chapter 9, on the past and potential contributions of the courts, and Chapter 10, discussing organizing strategies for incorporating a Right to Housing into the political agenda. Chapters 11 and 12 offer proposals concerning how social ownership of housing and a more socially oriented finance system could contribute to that goal. The following three chapters provide insights on how our current housing system creates problems for three subgroups of the population—the elderly (Chapter 13), women (Chapter 14) and the homeless (Chapter 15)—as well as specific proposals for how a Right to Housing could substantially alleviate the suffering of these vulnerable groups of people.

Chapters 16 to 18 present further policy initiatives that could contribute to the implementation of a Right to Housing. Chapter 16 underscores the accomplishments and potential of community development corporations, and the box provides an overview of this activity in rural areas. Chapter 17 presents a detailed account of state and local government initiatives. And Chapter 18 examines the relationship between housing and economic security. The chapter concludes with the argument that a Right to Housing and a new social contract between residents and government could, indeed, form the basis for a new social agenda.

It is beyond question that as a society we have the resources to provide housing for all that is decent, truly affordable and in supportive communities. What is required is an activist government that has social justice as a prime goal. As well, it requires that housing policy and programs become central concerns and activities beyond the narrow field of housing providers and housing advocates. What is needed is a social movement, in which housing justice becomes linked in an integral way with the many other struggles for justice, opportunity and democratic participation.

Of course, we recognize that in advocating a Right to Housing, there are a host of issues and concerns that need to be addressed and resolved. For example, how much housing, of what quality and in what locations should constitute each person's minimum "right"? Should a Right to Housing include universal design features that would make all units both accessible to people with physical infirmities, as well as to visitors who are physically challenged?[23] What responsibilities should be borne by recipients, and how would those expectations be enforced?

Without diminishing the importance of such questions, we believe that the time is ripe to revisit a serious dialogue about the underlying rationale for a Right to Housing. More than 60 years after FDR asserted that the country needs a second Bill of Rights—one that includes a Right to Housing—it is time to make that promise come true.

As this book goes to press, we acknowledge that the realization of a Right to Housing may seem further away than ever. With hundreds of billions of dollars going to fight wars in Afghanistan and Iraq, terrorism in the U.S. and abroad, as well as to repair the damage left in the aftermath of the August and September 2005 hurricanes on the Gulf Coast, the expenditure of large sums of money to implement a bold new domestic social policy agenda may be off on a distant horizon.

We believe that the health of a society can be judged by the quality and affordability of its housing for the one-third of a nation least well-off. A society professing deep concern for human needs should not be so profoundly deficient in this area. At the start of a new century, the United States is still facing serious and deeply ingrained housing problems. Housing is so fundamental to human life and well-being that meaningful progress toward achieving a Right to Housing provides an excellent springboard for launching closely related social and economic reforms. The logic is sound. But the call to action has

been muffled, and key political actors have, for the most part, been unswayed and missing in action. This book is aimed at changing the prevailing mind-set and stimulating innovative, aggressive and far-reaching responses to our persistent housing problems.

NOTES

1. The Quality Housing and Work Responsibility Act of 1998 amended the National Housing Goal. It is arguable as to whether the new language constitutes a major or a modest retreat from the original goal, which was to be realized "as soon as feasible." The 1998 Act states "that the Federal Government cannot through its direct action alone provide for the housing of every American citizen, or even a majority of its citizens, but it is the responsibility of the Government to promote and protect the independent and collective actions of private citizens to develop housing and strengthen their own neighborhoods." And further, "that the Federal Government should act where there is a serious need that private citizens or groups cannot or are not addressing responsibly" and "that our Nation should promote the goal of providing decent and affordable housing for all citizens through the efforts and encouragement of Federal, State, and local governments, and by the independent and collective actions of private citizens, organizations, and the private sector." Title V, Section 505, Sec. 2 (2), (3) and (4).

2. While we have never come close to fully implementing FDR's second Bill of Rights, recent proposed legislation suggests that a Right to Housing still has political muscle. The Bringing America Home Act (H.R. 2897), filed in 2003, would provide affordable housing, job-training, civil rights protections, vouchers for child care and public transportation, emergency funds for families facing eviction, increased access to health care for all and Congressional support for incomes high enough so that families can support themselves. It would also provide the resources to enable local and state governments to end homelessness. Also introduced in 2003, the National Affordable Housing Trust Fund Act (H.R. 1102) would establish within the Treasury Department a fund to promote the development, rehabilitation and preservation of affordable and safe low-income housing through grants to states and local jurisdictions. The goal is to build and preserve 1.5 million units of rental housing for the lowest-income families over a ten-year period. Initial sources of revenue for the Trust Fund would come from excess Federal Housing Administration insurance reserves and from

excess funds generated by the Government National Mortgage Association (Ginnie Mae), a government-sponsored enterprise created in 1968 to support subsidized mortgage lending.

3. The 69-page document, written by Dick Cluster, is available from Community Economics, Inc., joel@communityeconomics.org.

4. A recent study published in the *New England Journal of Medicine* suggests that "lead poisoning might impair children's intelligence at far lower levels than current federal health guidelines. . . [N]ot only do small amounts of the toxic metal lower a child's intelligence, but each additional unit of lead has a more dramatic effect than at higher levels of exposure" (Avril 2003).

5. According to psychologist Abraham H. Maslow's hierarchy of human needs, the basic, "lowest" need that housing provides is shelter or protection. "Higher" level needs provided by housing include safety or security, a sense of belonging, self-esteem and self-fulfillment. "Lower needs" must be met before "higher needs" (discussed in Meeks 1980, 46–49).

6. Of course, it hardly needs mentioning that even worse than "grossly inadequate housing" is no housing or shelter at all—the most dire form of a housing problem.

7. Even in the case of lead poisoning, where lead-based paint can be found in peoples' homes, other sources of lead in the environment can pose health risks (such as lead in the soil, gasoline, old school buildings, water contaminated by old lead pipes). Thus, one can never be certain which contaminated source is producing the elevated lead levels that may be observed.

8. Empirical evidence underscores this point. In a longitudinal study of poor and homeless families in New York City, researchers found that "regardless of social disorders, 80 percent of formerly homeless families who received subsidized housing stayed stably housed, i.e., lived in their own residence for the previous twelve months. In contrast, only 18 percent of the families who did not receive subsidized housing were stable at the end of the study" (Shinn et al. 1998, as cited by National Coalition for the Homeless 1999).

9. There are huge differences in how housing ownership creates unearned wealth. Minority homeowners, who often live in areas with little value appreciation, are sometimes fortunate if they can sell their home for what they paid ten or twenty years earlier (Oliver and Shapiro 1995; Conley 1999; Shapiro 2004). White, middle-class homeowners frequently see their houses rise in value over the years by a factor of five, ten and even more, producing equity that can be drawn upon to provide comfortable retirement and numerous benefits to their offspring: higher education, a substantial inheritance and, most tellingly, financial aid so they can buy they own homes, thus perpetu-

ating, intergenerationally, the widely disparate racial gaps that inhere in homeownership.

10. Defined as units with any one of several serious physical deficiencies, such as plumbing—lacking piped hot water or a flush toilet or lacking both bathtub and shower, for the exclusive use of the residents of the unit; heating, including major systems breakdowns or inadequacies; electrical—either completely lacking or major problems such as exposed wiring and lack of outlets. Other inadequacies that would place a unit in the "severely inadequate" category pertain to serious upkeep problems and significant physical defects in building hallways. A housing unit is termed "moderately inadequate" if it has none of the defects associated with a severely inadequate unit but has significant plumbing breakdowns; unvented heating units; fewer upkeep or hallway problems than in the "severely inadequate" category but still has significant deficits, and if it lacks a kitchen sink, range or refrigerator for exclusive use of the residents of the unit (HUD 2000, A28–A29.

11. A moderate housing problem consists of a cost burden between 30 percent and 50 percent of income, occupancy of a unit with moderate physical problems, or overcrowding (more than one person per room); people who are homeless or who have been displaced are viewed as having a severe housing problem. Also included in the latter category are those with cost burdens above 50 percent of income, or occupancy of housing with serious physical problems (National Low Income Housing Coalition 2005).

12. This does not include homeowner households with less serious problems. More than 10 million homeowner households earning 80 percent or less of area median income have nontrivial problems with their unit, ranging from open cracks in walls or ceilings, inadequate heat and heating units, and water leaks inside the house (Joint Center for Housing Studies 1998, 68).

13. According to the Joint Center for Housing Studies, adding those households with severe and moderate problems who live in assisted housing, the figure comes to some 3.7 million households (2003, 27).

14. A government report published over 30 years ago still has relevance today: "It is readily apparent that even the most conscientious user of Census data. . . would arrive at a total 'substandard' housing figure which grossly underestimated the number of dwelling units having serious housing code violations. To use a total thus arrived at as a figure for substandard housing is grossly inadequate and misleading, because it flies in the face of extensive consideration given by health experts, building officials, model code drafting organizations, and the local, state and federal court system to what have become over a period of many

years, the socially, politically, and legally accepted minimum standard for housing of human beings in the United States.... Even if public and private efforts eliminate all housing which is substandard under most current federal definitions, there will still be millions of dwelling units below code standard" (Sutermeister 1969, 83, 102).

15. The term "affordable housing" is widely used and generally understood to imply affordable to households with limited income, but, as described more fully in Chapter 2, we regard affordability not as an inherent characteristic of housing but as a relationship between housing cost and the income of the user household: A multimillion dollar mansion is affordable to a multi-millionaire, a $200 per month apartment is not affordable to someone with monthly income of $300. Nonetheless, the term "affordable housing" appears throughout many of the book's chapters, given its prevalence in housing studies, popular writings, legislation, program titles and the like.

16. This is calculated as follows from NLIHC (2001): (1) 87 percent (percent of renter households earning below 50 percent of area median income with severe housing problems) × 7.9 million (number of renter households with severe housing problems) = 6.87 million renter households. (2) 46 percent (percent of renter households earning below 50 percent of area median income with moderate housing problems) × 9.3 million (number of renter households with moderate housing problems) = 4.28 million renter households. (3) 70 percent (percent of owner households earning below 50 percent of area median income with severe housing problems) × 7.6 million (number of owner households with severe housing problems) = 5.32 million owner households with severe housing problems. (4) 28 percent (percent of owner households earning below 50 percent of area media income with moderate housing problems) × 10.9 (number of owner households with moderate housing problems) = 3.05 million households with moderate housing problems. Total (1) + (2) + (3) + (4) = 19.52 million households earning less than 50 percent of area median income with moderate or severe housing problems.

17. This is calculated as follows from NLIHC (2001): (1) 7 percent (percent of renter households earning between 50 to 80 percent of area median income with severe housing problems) × 7.9 million (number of renter households with severe housing problems) = .55 million renter households. (2) 34 percent (percent of renter households earning between 50 to 80 percent of area median income with moderate housing problems) × 9.3 million (number of renter households with moderate housing problems) = 3.16 million renter households. (3) 14 percent (percent of owner households earning between 50 to 80 percent of

area median income with severe housing problems) × 7.6 million (number of owner households with severe housing problems) = 1.06 million owner households with severe housing problems. (4) 25 percent (percent of owner households earning between 50 to 80 percent of area median income with moderate housing problems) × 10.9 (number of owner households with moderate housing problems) = 2.73 million households with moderate housing problems. Total (1) + (2) + (3) + (4) = 7.5 million households earning between 50 to 80 percent of area median income with moderate or severe housing problems.

18. Stone (1993) has calculated that, utilizing conservative estimates of costs for nonshelter basics (such as food, clothing, transportation), a staggering 14 million U.S. households (almost three times the number with worst case housing needs) cannot afford to spend a single cent for housing if they are to have enough income to cover these other basic living costs. Among the forty-five major metropolitan areas analyzed in a Center on Budget and Policy Priorities study, the percentage of poor renters paying more than 30 percent of their income for housing—HUD's payment standard for families living in subsidized housing—ranged from a low of 65 percent to a high of 92 percent; all but five locales fell in the 70 to 90 percent range; using the 50 percent of income yardstick, the range was from a low of 39 percent to a high of 81 percent; all but eleven locales fell in the 50 to 70 percent range. (Note that in this study the author uses a definition of "poor" pegged to the official poverty line as opposed to HUD's definitions of income, which are in relation to area medians. In 1995, the poverty line for a family of three was $12,158 [Daskal 1998:Table A-1]). By 2005, the poverty line for a family of three had risen to $16,090.

19. The editors have chosen to allow each author to use whatever racial terms he or she feels most comfortable with (including issues of capitalization, hyphenation and such) rather than imposing a single style, given the complex and personal/political considerations that underlie such choices.

20. The LIHTC program requires that either 20 percent or more of the units in a given development be occupied by individuals whose income is below 50 percent of the area median income, or at least 40 percent of the units must be occupied by individuals below 60 percent of the area median income (National Low Income Housing Coalition 2005).

21. Another important measure of the level of federal assistance for housing is total dollar outlays. These are payments to maintain and operate the total subsidized housing inventory. This figure has grown significantly since 1976, as the total stock of assisted housing grew during much of this period. However, between 2000 and 2007, assisted housing outlays are projected

to drop by nearly $1 billion (Dolbeare, Saraf and Crowley 2004).

22. All the chapters, with one exception, were written specifically for this volume. Chapter 8 is an update of an earlier published article.

23. The Fair Housing Amendments of 1988 amended the 1968 Fair Housing Act, adding prohibitions against discrimination in housing on the basis of disabilities; requiring that multifamily dwellings constructed after March 13, 1991, be accessible to persons with disabilities; and establishing construction requirements concerning accessibility with regard to building entrances, common and public spaces, doors, kitchens and bathrooms as well as other dwelling components. There is question as to whether HUD abides by these guidelines.

REFERENCES

Achtenberg, Emily P. 2002. Stemming the tide: A handbook on preserving subsidized multifamily housing. Washington, DC: Local Initiatives Support Corporation.

Avril, Tom. 2003. Study sees increased lead-paint risk. *Boston Sunday Globe*, April 20.

Bernstein, Nina. 1999. Asthma is found in 38% of children in city shelters. *New York Times*, May 5.

Bratt, Rachel G. 2002. Housing and family well-being. *Housing Studies*, Vol. 17, No. 1, 13–26.

———. 2003. Housing for very low-income households: The record of President Clinton, 1993–2000. *Housing Studies*, Vol. 18, No. 4, 607–635.

Committee Members Decry HUD Secretary's Comments on the Poor. 2004. Press release from Rep. Barney Frank (Dem. MA), Ranking Democratic Member, May 24.

Conley, Dalton. 1999. *Being black, living in the red: Race, wealth, and social policy in America*. Berkeley and Los Angeles: University of California Press.

Daskal, Jennifer. 1998. In search of shelter: The growing shortage of affordable rental housing. Washington, DC: Center on Budget and Policy Priorities.

DeParle, Jason. 1996. Slamming the door. *New York Times Magazine*, Oct. 20.

Dolbeare, Cushing N., and Sheila Crowley. 2002. Changing priorities: The federal budget and housing assistance, 1976–2007. Washington, DC: National Low Income Housing Coalition.

Dolbeare, Cushing N., Irene Basloe Saraf and Sheila Crowley. 2004. Changing priorities: The federal budget and housing assistance, 1976–2005. Washington, DC: National Low Income Housing Coalition.

England-Joseph, Judy A. 1994. Federally assisted housing: Condition of some properties receiving Section 8 project-based assistance is below housing quality standards. Testimony before the Employment, Housing and Aviation Subcommittee, Committee on Government Operations, House of Representatives. Washington, DC: U.S. General Accounting Office, GAO/T-RCED-94-273.

Evans, Gary W., Hoi-Yan Erica Chan, Nancy M. Wells and Heidi Saltzman. 2000. Housing quality and mental health. *Journal of Consulting and Clinical Psychology*, 68 (3):526–530.

Federal Housing Administration. 1938. Underwriting and valuation procedures under Title II of the National Housing Act. Washington, DC.

Finkel, Meryl, Donna DeMarco, Deborah Morse, Sandra Nolden and Karen Rich. 1999. Status of HUD-insured (or -held) multifamily rental housing in 1995. Prepared for U.S. Department of Housing and Urban Development by Abt Associates. Contract HC-5964. Washington, DC: U.S. Department of Housing and Urban Development.

Friedman, Lawrence M. 1968. *Government and slum housing*. Chicago: Rand McNally & Co.

Greenhouse, Steven. 1998. As Economy Booms, Migrant Workers' Housing Worsens. *New York Times*, May 31.

Grunwald, Michael. 1999. Housing crunch worsens for poor. *Washington Post*, October 12.

Hayden, Dolores. 1984. *Redesigning the American Dream: The future of housing, work, and family life*. New York: W. W. Norton & Co.

Husock, Howard. 2003. *America's trillion-dollar housing mistake: The failure of American housing policy*. Chicago: Ivan R. Dee.

Hynes, H. Patricia, Doug Brugge, Julie Watts and Jody Lally. 2000. Public health and the physical environment in Boston public housing: A community-based survey and action agenda. *Planning Practice and Research*, Vol. 15, No. 1–2, 31–49.

Joint Center for Housing Studies. 1998. A decade of miracles: 1988–1998. Christmas in April Tenth-Year Anniversary Report and 1998 Housing Study. Cambridge, MA: Harvard University.

———. 2003. *The state of the nation's housing, 2003*. Cambridge, MA: Harvard University.

———. 2005. *The state of the nation's housing, 2005*. Cambridge, MA: Harvard University.

Kozol, Jonathan. 1988. *Rachel and her children*. New York: Fawcett Columbine.

Lambert, Bruce. 1996. Raid on illegal housing shows the plight of suburbs' working poor. *New York Times*, December 7.

Leonard, Paul A., Cushing N. Dolbeare and Barry Zigas. 1993. Children and their housing needs. Washington, DC: Center on Budget and Policy Priorities.

Loewen, James W. 2005. *Sundown towns: A hidden dimension of American racism.* New York: The New Press.

Marcuse, Peter. 1986. Housing policy and the myth of the benevolent state. In *Critical perspectives on housing,* eds. Rachel G. Bratt, Chester Hartman and Ann Meyerson, 248–258. Philadelphia, PA: Temple University Press.

Meeks, Carol B. 1980. *Housing.* Englewood Cliffs, NJ: Prentice Hall, Inc.

Millennial Housing Commission. 2002. Meeting our nation's housing challenges. Washington, DC.

National Coalition for the Homeless. 1999. Homeless families with children. NCH Fact Sheet #7. http://nch.ari.net/families.html

National Commission on Severely Distressed Public Housing. 1992. The final report. A report to the Congress and the Secretary of Housing and Urban Development. Washington, DC.

National Congress for Community Economic Development. 1999. Coming of age: Trends and achievements of community-based development organizations. Washington, DC.

National Housing Law Project, Poverty & Race Research Action Council, Sherwood Research Associates, Everywhere and Now Public Housing Residents Organizing Nationally Together. 2002. *False hope: A critical assessment of the HOPE VI Public Housing Redevelopment Program.* Oakland, CA: The Project.

National Low Income Housing Coalition. 2001. Low income housing profile. Washington, DC. http:www.nlihc.org

———. 2005. *2005 Advocates' guide to housing and community development policy.* Washington, DC. http:www.nlihc.org

Oliver, Melvin, and Thomas Shapiro. 1995. *Black wealth/White wealth: A new perspective on racial inequality.* New York: Routledge.

Pérez-Peña, Richard. 2003. Study finds asthma in 25% of children in Central Harlem. *New York Times,* April 19.

Rakoff, Robert M. 1977. Ideology in everyday life: The meaning of the house. *Politics and Society,* 7(1):85–104.

Report of the National Housing Task Force. 1988. A decent place to live. Washington, DC.

Retsinas, Nicolas P., and Eric S. Belsky, eds. 2002. *Low-income homeownership: Examining the unexamined goal.* Washington, DC: The Brookings Institution.

Roosevelt, Franklin Delano. 1944. *Unless there is security here at home, there cannot be lasting peace in the world.* Message to the Congress on the State of the Union. January 11. In *The public papers and addresses of Franklin D. Roosevelt, 1944–45. Victory and the threshold of peace,* ed. Samuel I. Rosenman. 1950. New York: Harper and Brothers.

Salins, Peter. 1980. *The ecology of housing destruction: Economic effects of public intervention in the housing market.* New York: Center for Economic Policy Studies.

Sandel, Megan, Joshua Sharfstein and Randy Shaw. 1999. There's no place like home: How 'America's housing crisis threatens our children. San Francisco: Housing America and Boston, Doc4Kids Project.

Schorr, Alvin L. 1966. *Slums and social insecurity.* Prepared for the U.S. Department of Health, Education and Welfare. Research Report No. 1. Washington, DC: U.S. Government Printing Office.

Scientific American. 1999. The invisible epidemic. November, 19–20.

Shapiro, Thomas M. 2004. *The hidden cost of being African American: How wealth perpetuates inequality.* New York: Oxford.

Shinn, Marybeth, Beth C. Weitzman, Daniela Stojanovic, James R. Knickman, Lucila Jimenez, Lisa Duchon, Susan James and David H. Krantz. 1998. Predictors of homelessness among families in New York City: From shelter request to housing stability. *American Journal of Public Health,* 88, 1651–1657.

Stone, Michael E. 1993. *Shelter poverty: New ideas on housing affordability.* Philadelphia: Temple University Press.

Sunstein, Cass R. 2004. *The second Bill of Rights: FDR's unfinished revolution and why we need it more than ever.* New York: Basic Books.

Sutermeister, Oscar. 1969. Inadequacies and inconsistencies in the definition of substandard housing. In *Housing Code Standards: Three Critical Studies,* Research Report No. 19, National Commission on Urban Problems, Washington, DC.

The Urban Institute. 1995. Federal funds, local choices: An evaluation of the Community Development Block Grant Program, Vol. 1. Prepared for the U.S. Department of Housing and Urban Development. Washington, DC. HUD-PDR-1538(I).

Uchitelle, Louis. 1999. More wealth, more stately mansions. *New York Times,* June 6.

United States Department of Housing and Urban Development. 1999. *Waiting in vain: An update on America's rental housing crisis.* Washington, DC.

———. 2000. *Rental housing assistance—The worsening crisis. A report to Congress on worst case housing needs.* Washington, DC.

———. 2003. *A report on worst case needs for housing, 1978–1999: A report to Congress on worst case housing needs. Plus update on worst case housing needs in 2001.* Washington, DC.

United States General Accounting Office. 1993. Lead-based paint poisoning: Children not fully protected when federal agencies sell homes to public. GAO/RCED-93-38.

————. 1995. Welfare programs: Opportunities to consolidate and increase program efficiencies. GAO/HEHS-95-139.

Vidal, Avis C. 1992. Rebuilding communities: A national study of urban community development corporations. New York: Community Development Research Center, New School for Social Research.

Wolff, Craig. 1994. Immigrants to life underground: New York illegal roomers live one rung above homeless. *New York Times*, March 13.

Wood, Edith Elmer. 1934. A century of the housing problem. Originally printed as part of a symposium, "Low cost housing and slum clearance," *Law and Contemporary Problems*, Vol. 1. Reprinted in *Urban housing*, eds. William L. C. Wheaton, Grace Milgram and Margy Ellin Meyerson, 1–8. 1966. New York: The Free Press.

Chris Tilly

1   The Economic Environment of Housing: Income Inequality and Insecurity

HOUSING AFFORDABILITY depends crucially on household income, not just on the price and availability of housing. Given that almost all housing is purchased in a private market, the distribution of income is the most important determinant of the quantity and quality of housing obtained by the rich, the poor and those in between. The average level of income; degree of income inequality between high- and low-income families; and income differences by race, gender and age all translate directly into how well different groups are housed. Understanding trends and disparities in income is essential for understanding the same with regard to housing.

The reverse is also true. Housing is the largest single expenditure for most U.S. families. This means that for housing, income is both chicken and egg: Income determines housing affordability, but the evolution of housing prices is the largest factor determining inflation—thus determining the purchasing power of income.

Basic income patterns reported in this chapter are straightforward:

- After controlling for inflation, average wages have fallen over the last 20 years.
- Household income has stagnated, and households have had to put more members to work for more hours.
- Income instability has grown: Job displacement and other sources of earnings losses have become more common.

- Income inequality has grown: The rich have become richer and the poor, poorer.
- Income gaps between white households and those of color have persisted.
- Single-mother families suffer a particularly severe income disadvantage, and recent cutbacks in welfare have sharpened this disadvantage.

All of these changes mark the reversal of post-World War II trends toward broader prosperity, reductions in poverty and inequality and construction of a stronger, more inclusive welfare state. This is the downside of the much-touted "new economy." While the new patterns are straightforward, the reasons behind them have been hotly debated. Many analysts hold that relatively impersonal, nonpolitical and inexorable forces of globalization; technological change; and evolving family structure have driven these income changes. I will argue instead that conscious business strategy and, to a lesser extent, public policy have greatly shaped globalization and technical change, and have had additional direct effects on wages and income. Employment strategies used by businesses have squeezed housing affordability by way of wages. Chapters 2 and 4 explore how business strategies in terms of finance and housing development have reduced housing affordability and security by other routes. To the extent that we can push business and government to adopt other strategies and policies, the results in terms of housing affordability and security could be quite different.

THE GROWING DIVERGENCE BETWEEN BUSINESS AND WORKER FORTUNES

The U.S. economy has changed markedly over the last 30 years. Two large-scale shifts have radically altered the ways that prosperity is shared in the United States. The first concerns the relative fortunes of business and workers; the second concerns the relative fortunes of the rich and poor.

Business and Workers Part Ways

The first big shift: A business boom no longer means prosperity for working people. From the early 1900s to the 1970s, business and worker fortunes rose and fell more or less in tandem. The Great Depression was difficult for capitalists and workers; the boom during World War II and the early postwar years buoyed profits and wages alike. When President John Kennedy declared that "a rising tide lifts all boats," he summarized the experience of the times. Of course, not all persons benefited equally from the rising tide: People of color and women of all racial and ethnic groups lagged behind in wages, and families with limited ability to take part in the labor market (notably, elders and single mothers of young children) depended on social welfare generosity rather than on labor market dynamism. In general, however, business cycle booms brought with them significant upsurges in wages and employment.

No more. The divergence between business and worker prosperity, which began to appear in the 1970s, was particularly apparent during the most recent completed economic expansion, which ran from 1991 to early 2001. This upturn saw business activity and profits lift despite, and to some extent because of, stagnant wages and initially slow employment growth. In fact, in the first two years of this "boom," virtually all job growth was accounted for by involuntary part-time employment, leading some to call it the "jobless recovery"—a label that applies equally to the first few years of the expansion that began in late 2001. Even after actual job growth began in 1994, wages remained flat until 1997 after controlling for inflation. Business analysts attributed the "health" of the expansion to low labor costs. "From the perspective of business," pointed out economist John Miller (1995:9), "it is lagging wage growth that sustains the boom. Modest wage increases guarantee that rising labor costs will not cut into profit margins even as the economy expands."

Low labor costs resulted not just from stationary wages but also from corporate America's new habit of continuing to downsize even as sales rose. Over 8 million U.S. workers were displaced from their jobs during the economic expansion years from 1993 to 1995—not far different from the 9 million who were laid off during the recession years from 1991 to 1993 (Uchitelle 1996). Although white-collar lay-offs captured headlines—and have indeed become more common—the bulk of those displaced remain rank-and-file workers, not managers (Farber 1997).

The profit rate is the ratio of annual profits to accumulated business investment in plant and equipment—much as an interest rate is the ratio of annual interest to principal. The bottom line for business: In the mid to late 1990s, U.S. profit rates reached their highest level in decades. U.S. corporations received a dazzling $876 billion in profits in 2000, or about one dollar in nine of total national income, although the recession that followed took some of the shine off profit figures (U.S. Bureau of Economic Analysis 2002). The 1990s profit rate surge did not mean that businesses were claiming a larger share of the economic pie but rather that businesses took home about the same share despite investing less to generate these profits. Businesses have continued to reap profits even though there have been fewer additions to productive investment, which has pushed the ratio upward. As well, corporations have won decreased corporate income tax rates (Baker 1995). But U.S. workers and their households are paying the price in terms of wages, income and employment.

Wages and Household Income

The failure of businesses to make productive investments, along with their underinvestment in worker training (Marshall and Tucker 1992), help to explain why wage levels have remained flat—and have even fallen somewhat over the long run. Productivity has grown slowly, especially in comparison with other industrialized countries. U.S. real output per worker (a measure of productivity) grew only about two-thirds as fast as output in Western Europe and one-third as fast as in Japan between 1979 and 1990 (Freeman 1994:26). Productivity growth did perk up at the end of the 20th century, driving overall growth in output per hour for all businesses from 1990 to 2001 up 2.2 percent per year, well above the 1.4 percent per year crawl of 1979 to 1990 (U.S. Bureau of Labor Statistics 2002a). Growth in U.S. manufacturing output per hour still lagged behind that of France, Sweden, Korea and Taiwan, among others, during the 1990s (U.S. Bureau of Labor Statistics

2002b). Thus, the per worker "slice of pie" available to be shared between labor and management has expanded relatively little.

Figure 1.1 shows one set of consequences for U.S. workers and households. The average real (inflation-corrected) hourly wage, periodically beaten down over the 1970s, 1980s and 1990s, stood in 2002 at only 95 percent of its 1973 value (a drop from $15.94 to $15.17 in 2002 dollars). This ended an unbroken string of real wage advances from the 1950s through 1973. Median real annual household income (the level of income in which exactly one-half of U.S. households stand above, the other one-half below) also sputtered until the early 1990s yet grew significantly during the 1990s expansion, only to stall again when recession hit in 2001. Overall, household income gained only 14 percent

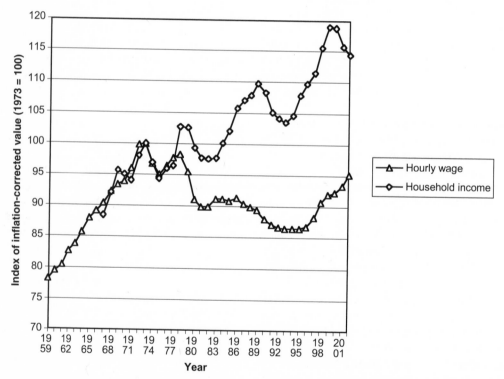

FIGURE 1.1. Losing ground: Average hourly wage and median household income, adjusted for inflation, 1959–2002 (Index: 1973 value = 100).

Note: To put wages and income on the same scale, the figure uses an index of 1973 = 100, so an average wage of 200 would mean two times the 1973 wage, whereas a wage of 50 would mean one-half of the 1973 wage.

Source: Average hourly wage is for production or nonsupervisory workers in private industry (U.S. Council of Economic Advisors 2003, Table B-47). Median household income is from U.S. Census Bureau (2003, Table A-1).

between 1973 and 2002 (rising from $37,092 to $42,409 in 2001 dollars, growing an average of 1 percent per year)—again, ending a "golden age" of far more rapid income growth.

Several aspects of Figure 1.1 deserve comment. For instance, why should there be so much attention to wages? After all, households receive income from a variety of other sources: property income, such as dividends, interest, rent and pensions; government transfers, such as Social Security, unemployment insurance and welfare; and transfers from other households, such as alimony, child support or gifts. Nonetheless, the labor market is by far the preponderant source of household income, accounting for 78 percent of the total (Albelda and Tilly 1997, Table 3.2). Except for small groups of households that depend primarily on other income sources, wages are decisive in setting income.

If wages are so decisive, why has household income advanced (if modestly) over the past 30 years while wages have regressed? The key is that households have put more members—especially mothers—to work, partly in an attempt to overcome wage declines (though growing numbers of women have also entered the workforce because of changing roles and attitudes). The percentage of women working for pay (or actively looking for work) rocketed from 38 percent in 1960 to 60 percent in 2002 (U.S. Council of Economic Advisors 2003, Table B-39). As of 1999, 45 percent of all U.S. households deployed two or more earners (U.S. Census Bureau 2000a, Table 2). In short, U.S. households have managed to win small increases in real income only by what some observers have called a "family speed-up" (Currie, Dunn and Fogarty 1980).

Unemployment and Underemployment

In addition to growing slowly, income has become more unstable in a variety of ways. The unemployment rate, which averaged 4.8 percent in the 1960s, climbed to an average of 6.2 percent in the 1970s and to 7.3 percent in the 1980s (Figure 1.2). These are documented as averages because the unemployment rate swings up and down over the business cycle. The 1990s were considerably kinder, averaging 5.7 percent

unemployment. In fact, as the economic expansion continued, businesses complained of a labor shortage, as they did in the late 1980s. The *Wall Street Journal* even lamented "Dilbert's revenge," using the well-known comic strip character's disgruntled worker persona to label a growing feeling among workers that bargaining power was beginning to shift back their way (Lublin and White 1997). Another recession struck in 2001, however, driving unemployment above 6 percent by 2003 and casting an uncertain shadow over the future. In any case, the 1999 rate of 4 percent, which many economists at the time termed "full employment," still exceeded the low point of 3.5 percent in the late 1960s.

The official unemployment rate, moreover, understates the true level of joblessness, leaving out several groups of the "hidden unemployed":

1. "discouraged workers," who still want a job but have recently given up looking because of a poor job market for their particular skills or in their particular location
2. involuntary part-time workers, who would prefer full-time hours (over 4 million workers in 2002, according to the U.S. Bureau of Labor Statistics! [*Employment and Earnings,* January 2003])
3. those who are available for work but are not looking due to family, school or health issues
4. those who want a job but have not looked for one in the last year
5. the enormous U.S. prison population, currently around 2 million—we incarcerate people at ten times the rate of European countries, temporarily keeping them off the unemployment lines (Baxandall 1996).

In October 2003, for example, the official unemployment rate was 6 percent. However, by adding in only those profiled in numbers 1 and 3 above, unemployment would have jumped to over 12 percent, more than doubling the official rate (National Jobs for All Coalition 2003).

Of course, even the official unemployment rate is much higher for some than for others. Additional data from October 2003 revealed that Latinos were more than one-fifth more likely to be unemployed than the average worker, blacks were nearly twice as likely to be jobless and teens were almost three times as likely. (The

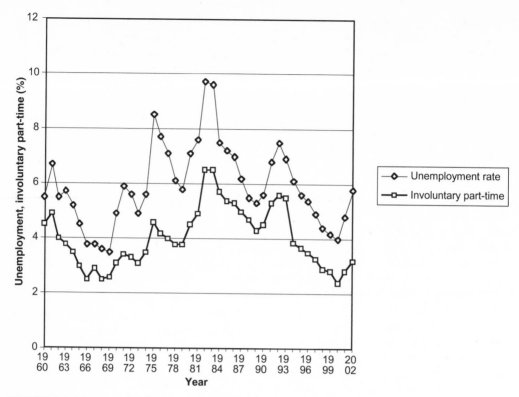

FIGURE 1.2. Not enough jobs: Unemployment and involuntary part-time employment rates, 1960–2002.
Note: The Bureau of Labor Statistics changed the definition of involuntary part-time employment in 1994, resulting in a one-time drop. (For a discussion of this changed definition, see Tilly 1996.)
Source: Unemployment from U.S. Council of Economic Advisors 2003, Table B-42. Involuntary part-time employment from 1960 to 1993 from data provided by Thomas Nardone, U.S. Bureau of Labor Statistics, updated from the U.S. Bureau of Labor Statistics, *Employment and Earnings*, various years.

unemployment rate of women was close to the national rate.) Joblessness followed a patchwork pattern across the country. In September 2003, unemployment rates ranged from a low of under 3 percent in the Dakotas to a high of 7.3 percent in Oregon and 12.2 percent in struggling Puerto Rico, with depression levels of 10 percent and higher in agricultural communities of California, Texas and Arizona—reaching an astounding 30 percent in Yuma, Arizona (U.S. Bureau of Labor Statistics 2003a).

Downward Mobility

While unemployment offers one window on income instability, we can also look at income instability by examining how many people lost jobs or experienced dramatic earnings declines. Economy-wide, downward mobility has become markedly more common. Tracing the trajectories of individual prime-age adults, Stephen Rose (1994) found that about one-fifth experienced declines of 5 percent or more in real earnings over the decade of the 1970s; that proportion rose to one-third during the 1980s. Men and women crisscrossed: Men's likelihood of losing annual earnings increased, whereas women became less likely to lose earnings. However, in terms of hourly wages (factoring out the effect of changes in weeks and hours worked, which enter into annual earnings), both groups became more likely to experience declines in the 1980s.

Annette Bernhardt and co-authors (2001) found similar results when they followed two cohorts of teenage white males—one group from 1966 to 1981 and another group from 1979 to 1994. Permanent wage growth was 21 percent lower for the later group.

What reduced average wage growth and heightened the probability of downward mobility? Rose (1995) accounts for one-half of men's greater probability of an earnings drop by the increased frequency of job changes. Bernhardt and co-authors (2001) also found that even after taking into account the changing characteristics of young white men, their odds of changing jobs in a two-year period jumped by 43 percent between the earlier and later periods. Particular symptoms of heightened job insecurity are starkly visible. Temporary employment has exploded: Employment in temporary help agencies has grown twenty-fold since the 1960s (though it still amounts to only 1 percent of the workforce; other forms of "contingent" work bring the total up to 9 percent—U.S. Bureau of Labor Statistics 2001, Table 5). The Census Bureau's Displaced Worker Survey shows that permanent layoffs have become more common (Farber 1996). Displacement rates from 1991 to 1993, nominally years of recovery from a mild recession, were higher than those during the deep recession years from 1981 to 1983. Middle-age men took the biggest hit. In turn, displacement rates from 1980 to 1992 exceeded job loss rates from 1968 to 1979, according to research based on the Panel Study of Income Dynamics (Boisjoly, Duncan and Smeeding 1998). Between those two periods, the percentage of workers who were laid off increased by one-third, and the percentage of workers who were fired doubled.

While the frequency of job changes increased, the benefits of job stability decreased at the same time. The payoff to accumulating seniority with a single employer, long a standard feature of compensation (Abraham and Medoff 1980), diminished sharply during the 1980s (Chauvin 1994; Marcotte 1998). Both the opportunity for long-term job attachment, and the rewards for that attachment, have declined.

In short, workers' wages—on average—continued to stagnate, and household income recovered only modestly, even though the 1990s were bountiful years for business. Rising prices combined with flat incomes made housing purchase or rental less affordable to the average family. Growth in unemployment, contingent employment and downward mobility fed insecurity in housing tenure.

GROWING INCOME INEQUALITY

All of the evidence so far spells out the results of the divergence between business and worker fortunes. However, there has been a second large economic shift as well—the growth of inequality among the rich, those with middle income and the poor. Figure 1.3 shows the shares of total income obtained by the richest 5 percent, the next-richest 15 percent, the middle 60 percent and the lowest 20 percent of U.S. households.[1] In the mid-1970s, the richest households began to gain, at the expense of middle-income households and to a lesser extent of the poorest. This upward shift of income accelerated during the 1980s, with the richest cashing in and everybody else—including the next-richest 15 percent—losing out. As with the U-turn in wage levels, this marked a significant reversal: During the 1950s and 1960s, income shares remained relatively stable, with a slight trend toward greater equality.

Figure 1.4 translates income shares into (inflation-adjusted) dollar figures to illuminate the scope of the new wave of income inequality. In 1970, on average, a household in the top 5 percent garnered $129,086 in income, 14 times as much as the average household in the bottom 20 percent, who received $8,930 (figures are expressed in 2002 dollars). By 2002, households in the richest 5 percent had moved ahead to a handsome $251,078—putting them 25 times as high as the poorest one-fifth of households, who inched forward to $10,124. The middle 60 percent achieved a modest advance over this 20-year period, with income starting at $31,774 and ending up at $45,221. We see that although, on average, real household income advanced slightly, much of the population shared little in this step forward.

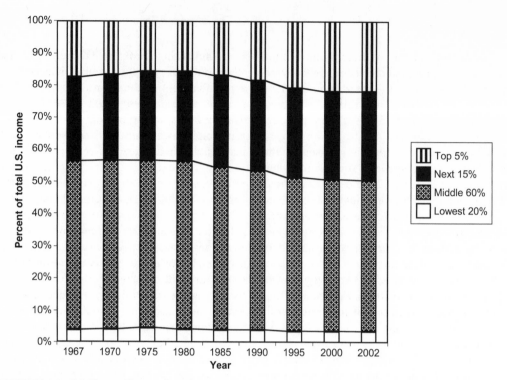

FIGURE 1.3. Trickle up: Shares of total U.S. income received by families at different income levels, selected years 1967–2002.
Source: U.S. Census Bureau 2003, Table A-3.

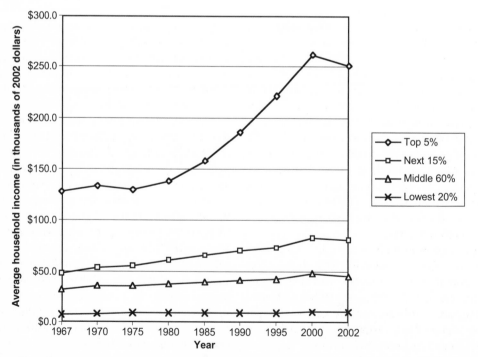

FIGURE 1.4. Unequal gains: Average income levels (in thousands of 2000 dollars) for high-, middle-, and low-income households, selected years 1967–2002.
Source: Calculated by author from U.S. Census Bureau 2003, Table A-1.

Figures 1.3 and 1.4 tell the story of income, the amount of money received in a given year, not wealth, which is the total value of assets possessed by a household. Wealth is even more unequally distributed: In 1998, the top 5 percent of U.S. households controlled 68 percent of net financial assets and 59 percent of total wealth, including homes and other assets (Wolff 2000).[2] Furthermore, inequality in wealth has been widening apace (although it did moderate slightly in the late 1990s). The richest 1 percent, who held 20 percent of the nation's net worth in 1976, had nearly doubled their share to 38 percent—almost the same share as the bottom 95 percent of households—by 1998 (Wolff 1996, 2000). In the early 1980s, 200 years after the United States threw out the British aristocracy, the U.S. distribution became more unequal than that in Britain (Wolff 1996). Moreover, racial differences in wealth loom large. Whites have an enormous wealth advantage over blacks, mostly because of unequal inheritances. In 1994 (the most recent year that researchers have examined), the median net worth of white households was more than 50 times as great as that of blacks ($52,000 vs. $1,000), and the ratio has not changed since the early 1990s (Gittleman and Wolff 2004).[3]

For most U.S. families, a home is their only significant asset. Of course, this leaves most of the one-third of U.S. households who are tenants without *any* significant assets. While housing is the main form of wealth for the typical family, total wealth figures are dominated by the super-rich, whose financial holdings dwarf their home values. As a result, homes only account for 29 percent of total wealth, and lower-income homeowners have considerably less home equity, on average, than do high-income homeowners (Wolff 2000).

Differences in homeownership rates underlie racial differences in wealth. White households are more than one-half as likely to own a home as are blacks, and on the average, white-owned homes are worth almost one-half more than those that are black-owned (Oliver and Shapiro 1995, Table 5.3). Even more startling is the difference in holdings of financial assets such as stocks and bonds. Whereas the median white household possesses $7,000 in net financial assets, the

median black household has precisely zero—in other words, for one-half of black households, debts equal or exceed financial assets (Oliver and Shapiro 1995, Table 4.4; Shapiro 2004).

It is tempting to suppose that growing income and wealth inequality simply represent another facet of the divergence between business and workers. To some extent, this is true: Given the ebullient stock market from the 1990s to 2001, dividends and capital gains have enriched the richest. Yet, income polarization involves more than labor-capital polarization for two reasons. First, a key determinant of household income is the composition of that household. More adults in a household can contribute additional income (particularly earnings). A higher rate of Americans are living alone or as single parents whose earning potential is curtailed by the time demands of child care (Albelda and Tilly 1997), therefore swelling the number of low-income households. At the same time, rising rates of paid employment by wives and mothers create more two-earner households, frequently (though by no means always) at the upper end of the income distribution. Family structure itself shapes the contours of income.

A second reason why income polarization goes beyond the labor-capital divide is that even among the rich, most are working people. In 89 percent of married-couple households with incomes of $100,000 or more, either the husband or wife works full-time year-round. Nearly one-half the time, both work full-time year-round (calculated by author from U.S. Census Bureau 2000a, Table 6). Therefore, most of the worsening of income inequality represents an increase in earnings inequality. Between 1979 and 1999, the hourly earnings of a worker at the 90th percentile (earning more than 90 percent of other workers) relative to a worker at the 10th percentile increased by 21 percent for men and by 45 percent for women (Mishel, Bernstein and Schmitt, 2001, Tables 2.7, 2.8). Indeed, earnings inequality has increased in multiple areas, such as among occupations, industries, racial and ethnic groups, and levels of educational attainment (Freeman 1986).

As with household income, widening disparities in earnings mean that the average hourly wage loss of 6 percent conceals enormous variation. Among men, for example, earners at the 90th percentile saw wages increase from $27 to $29 per hour (in 1999 dollars) between 1979 and 1999; wages at the 10th percentile tumbled by one-tenth, from $7.34 to $6.59 (Mishel, Bernstein and Schmitt 2001, Table 2.7). Men with a high school education or less suffered even sharper wage setbacks. Not all wage earners lost, but those at the bottom lost a lot. Low-wage workers did regain some lost ground as the economy heated up and Congress boosted the minimum wage in the late 1990s, but not enough to offset earlier wage declines (Tilly 1998).

Wage earners who were at the 10th or 90th percentile in 1999 are not necessarily those who were at those levels in 1979. Comparing one-year data over time overlooks the fact that workers' wages fluctuate. In fact, if everybody's earnings varied from year to year but each worker averaged the same income as every other over the long haul, there would be far less cause for concern about earnings inequality. However, most earnings mobility is quite limited: Even averaging wages of young adults (whose wages are expected to be most volatile) over ten years only reduces overall inequality by about one-fourth. Also, wage mobility over time decreased between the 1970s and 1980s, meaning that high and low earners became more likely to be frozen at a given wage level—and that the increase in wage inequality captured in a series of snapshots understates the rise in inequality among workers (Buchinsky and Hunt 1999).

In summary, income and wealth disparities have widened. Those at the top have flourished, those in the middle have struggled to stay even, and those at the bottom have suffered major setbacks. Worsening income inequality translates directly into growing inequality in housing affordability. More concentrated wealth-holding has serious implications for housing as well. Housing itself is one major form of wealth, and financial assets or inherited housing are the prerequisites for homeownership. Wealth constitutes the cushion preventing a household's short-term income losses from undermining housing security. As a small number of super-rich claim a growing share of income and wealth, housing affordability and security diminish for the rest of the nation.

REASONS FOR BUSINESS-WORKER DIVERGENCE AND GROWING INEQUALITY

Why have the rules of the economic game changed so dramatically? Many analysts point to the importance of globalization and technological advancement. These two factors are indeed important contributors to the growing economic divergences. But they are neither neutral nor unalterable; rather, they are shaped to a large extent by business strategy. Nor do these factors offer a complete explanation of the current economic distress. Instead, shifts in business strategy have broader effects extending beyond these two drivers. U.S. businesses have predominantly pursued a "low road" strategy designed to keep wages and other costs low, rather than investing in higher productivity.

The context for all of these changes is the breakdown of the post–World War II "golden age" for U.S. capital and labor. That rosy era was based on U.S. domination of global financial and goods markets. It also incorporated a "capital-labor accord," in which unions in the central mass production industries exchanged labor peace for growing wages, and a "capital-citizen accord," bartering social peace for an array of social programs such as Social Security and unemployment insurance (Gordon, Edwards and Reich 1982). By the 1970s, all three elements of the golden age were crumbling. At a global level, the U.S. industrial rivals, Europe and Japan, had rebuilt from wartime destruction. The Third World, from Vietnam to the Organization of the Petroleum Exporting Countries (OPEC), began to assert itself as well. The two domestic accords came under attack both from those who had been excluded—such as African Americans, other people of color and women of all races—and from businesses displeased that the concessions had been made at all. As the postwar economic order sputtered, then, three specific mechanisms reshaped the U.S. wage structure: globalization, technological change and shifting business strategy.

Globalization has two overlapping dimensions that are crucial for U.S. employment and earnings. First, U.S. (and other) corporations have found ways to produce goods—but even more importantly, to subcontract or outsource parts of the production process—in low-wage countries such as Mexico, Guatemala, Haiti, Thailand, Malaysia and dozens of others. As Bluestone and Harrison (1982) pointed out, new technologies of transportation and communication facilitated the international coordination needed for this shift. The move to offshore production has particularly revolutionized light industries such as apparel but has also had its effects in electronics, motor vehicles and numerous types of heavier manufacturing industries. Service industries are not immune to the effects of globalization, as many U.S. companies rely on data entry performed in the English-speaking Caribbean countries or software programming in India (Harrison 1994). All of these processes shift growing numbers of jobs abroad.

The second, even more important, dimension of globalization is that producers based in the industrialized countries of North America, Europe and Asia are far more aggressively contesting each other's markets for a variety of items. In addition to Western Europe and Japan, the newly industrialized countries of Asia, such as Taiwan and Korea, increase the number of those involved in the renewed struggle over markets. In everyday life in the United States, import growth is most visible in the automotive and home appliance markets, but it extends to a variety of markets (as does export growth).

The first shift, to offshore production, offers companies more geographic choices. The second offers consumers more product choices. However, both remove the former protected status of many companies and workers: Workers are subject to more competition from both low-wage and high-wage countries, and this competition exerts downward pressure on wages. The first shift represents a strategic change for U.S. companies—one that businesses take for granted but is by no means the only option. The second represents a large and long-term strategic change by corporations the world over—something far less within the control of U.S. businesses themselves. Both shifts have been facilitated by international trade treaties, such as the North American Free Trade Agreement (NAFTA) and the World Trade Organization (WTO), that diminish trade restrictions, as well as laws that strictly constrain international labor migration but leave capital migration unfettered.

Overall, both changes in the global economy are relatively small contributors to the changing structure of U.S. earnings. Despite the uproar over perceived effects of globalization, the sum of U.S. imports and exports still amounts to less than one-third of the nation's total domestic output; exports and imports each make up about one-half of this fraction (U.S. Council of Economic Advisors 2003). Though some analysts claim that globalization has had large effects on the wages of workers in industrialized countries, the general consensus among economists is that these effects have so far been relatively small (Freeman 1995).

Technological change has also rocked the boat. Businesses have worked hard to replace labor with machines, whether by mechanizing tasks completely (as with robots) or by using machines to make workers more productive (as with personal computers or supermarket scanners). Over the last 30 years, many businesses have been disproportionately successful in eliminating lower-skill jobs while creating more high-skill jobs, many of which involve interacting with new tools, such as computers, that require new know-how. The result is that over this time period, both the mix of jobs in the workforce and the task composition of particular jobs have shifted in the direction of greater education and skill requirements (Howell and Wolff 1991; Osterman 1995; Moss and Tilly 2001). This displaces workers at the low-skill end of the labor market and shrinks the pool of jobs for which they compete while heightening demand for high-skill workers, stretching wages further apart. The technological twist can then help to explain rising earnings inequality; it has no obvious connection with the general lag in wages and incomes.

Although technological change significantly affects income trends, as does globalization, its importance should not be overstated. As Howell (1994) pointed out, the shift toward higher-skill jobs essentially halted after 1982, while inequality between low- and high-education workers continued increasing. A much-noted economic study (Krueger 1993) found a substantial wage premium associated with working with computers. A more recent study (DiNardo and Pischke 1997, using German data), however, discovered that approximately the same premium accrues to workers who use hand-held calculators, pens or pencils, or who work while sitting down. Economist Steven Allen (2001) found that technological change accounted for less than one-third of the growth in the wage gap between college and high school graduates during the 1980s—the piece of wage inequality that one would expect to be most related to changes in technique. In short, the mixed evidence on the link between technological and wage changes suggests that we must look elsewhere for the main forces behind the new income trends (Mishel, Bernstein and Schmitt 1997).

Indeed, the rest of the industrialized world has experienced increased global competitiveness and speedier technological change. Yet despite significant stress on their industrial relations systems, no other rich country has experienced the extent of collapse in job quality and surge in wage and income inequality experienced by the United States (Freeman 1994). Explaining this difference is a third factor: U.S. businesses have largely responded to new competitive pressures by cutting costs rather than by enhancing quality. This translates into a concerted effort to keep wages low and minimize long-term commitments to the workforce. Another corollary of this "low road" strategy is the slow productivity growth already noted, resulting from sluggish investment in both physical and human capital. Furthermore, for many U.S. businesses that have attempted to raise productivity, this attempt has been based on fear and speed-up rather than on loyalty and training.

The new cost-cutting strategy incorporates keeping wages low, relentless downsizing and expanding part-time and contingent labor. In fact, although the number of workers in explicitly contingent statuses, such as temporary workers, still only amounts to about one-tenth of the workforce, employers are increasingly classifying all workers as contingent. As AT&T prepared to lay off an estimated 40,000 workers in early 1996, Vice President for Human Resources James Meadows told the *New York Times,*

"People need to look at themselves as self-employed, as vendors who come to this company to sell their skills." He added, "In AT&T, we have to promote the whole concept of the workforce being contingent, though most of the contingent workers are inside of our walls." Instead of "jobs," people increasingly have "projects" or "fields of work," he remarked, leading to a society that is increasingly "jobless but not workless" (Andrews 1996:D10).

Cost-cutting strategy also targets government-imposed expenditures, such as taxes and regulation. Corporate taxes as a percentage of profits, 40 percent in 1971, were only 31 percent in 2002 (U.S. Council of Economic Advisors 2003). Deregulation has loosened government controls on industries such as telecommunications, airlines and trucking, and has weakened the implementation of other regulations, ranging from environmental protection to occupational safety and health.

This newly dominant strategy accelerates the erosion of institutions such as unions, the minimum wage (which remained far below its 1970s level of buying power even after the 1996 increase and erodes every year with inflation), and job ladders within companies. Yet these are precisely the institutions that historically have defended worker wage levels, particularly those of workers with less individual bargaining power, and have provided avenues for upward mobility.

The "low road" is, at least to some extent, self-perpetuating. Cutting wages and taxes restrains consumer and government spending (although both consumers and government have done their best to borrow in order to continue spending). However, since exports still absorb only a small fraction of output, businesses count on domestic demand from consumers and government. Weak demand spurs firms to seek more ways to cut costs, and the cycle continues. To U.S. business as a whole, the strategy is irrational. Yet to individual businesses calculating their individual advantage, it makes perfect sense. Even more important, it is bolstered by the triumph of "free market" ideology in U.S. politics, which has helped to sweep away the policies and institutions that might discourage the low road.

TWO KEY DIMENSIONS OF INCOME CHANGES: RACE AND GENDER

As globalization, technological change and the low-road strategy transform the economy, not all groups in the population are equally affected by crumbling wages, sluggish income growth and heightened economic polarization. Indeed, in the United States, high and low wages and high and low household incomes have never been sprinkled randomly among the populace. Historically, people of color and women of all racial groups have earned lower wages (when they have received wages at all). Single-mother households as well as those headed by people of color also have received lower incomes. As such, these groups have most often been poorly housed. The new changes in income reflect this legacy, preserving the divisions of race and gender.

In income terms, race and ethnicity continue to divide America. Stagnant incomes and rising income inequality have struck particularly hard at blacks and Latinos. Figure 1.5 shows median household income by the racial or ethnic group of the household head, and Table 1.1 lists family poverty rates by race, ethnicity and family structure.

Some elements of the racial-ethnic hierarchy are immediately clear from Figure 1.5 and Table 1.1; others require further elaboration. The incomes of black and Latino households lag far behind those of white households, and the last 25 years have not brought them appreciably closer. Asians have a higher median income than whites. The Census Bureau does not publish equally detailed information on Native Americans, but other Census data reveal that the group had a median income only $1000 above that of black households, and lower than any other racial group, in 1999 (U.S. Department of Commerce 2005).

Table 1.1 confirms that black and Latino poverty rates are highest. Despite having a

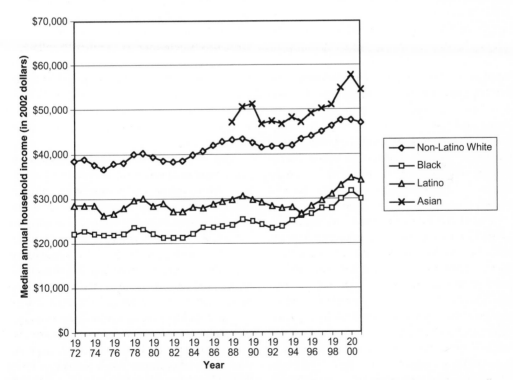

FIGURE 1.5. Persistent gaps: Median annual household income by race and ethnicity, 1972–2001 (in 2002 dollars).
Source: U.S. Census Bureau 2003, Table A-2. Race definitions changed in 2002, so 2002 data are not included.

TABLE 1.1 Poor, Poorer, Poorest: Percentage of Families in Poverty, by Race, Ethnicity and Family Type, 1999

	All Families	Single-Mother Families
White, non-Latino	5.5%	25.4%
Black	21.9%	46.1%
Latino	20.2%	46.6%
Asian	10.7%	—
Total	9.3%	35.7%

Source: U.S. Census Bureau 2000b, Table B-3.
Note: Latinos can be of any race. Single-mother families refers to female householder, no husband present with children aged under 18. Families (unlike the households appearing in Figures 1.1 and 1.3 to 1.5) are limited to groups of two or more people living together and related by birth, marriage or adoption. Data with this level of detail were not reported in later years.

higher median income, Asians are more likely to be poor than whites. Analysis of unpublished Census data from earlier years shows that Native American poverty rates fall between those of whites and blacks (Albelda and Tilly 1997, Table 2.1).

The median incomes of Latinos and Asians are somewhat deceptive, since incomes are highly polarized within both populations. The Asian population, for example, includes high-income Japanese-American professionals but also low-income recent immigrants and refugees from Southeast Asia and China. So, although the median income of Asians exceeds that of whites, a greater proportion of Asians fall below the poverty line. Such income differences within racial groups are also highly correlated with differences in housing tenure.

Of particular interest are the changes in relative incomes over time. Over the past 20 years, as the epochal shifts in the economy took place, Latinos have lost ground relative to non-Latinos. Black household incomes have actually caught up slightly with white incomes, but the full picture is more troublesome. Over the same period of time, a 30-year trend of black hourly wages catching up with white wages was reversed. In terms of hourly wages, controlling for education and labor market experience, black men fell further behind white men, and black women lagged behind white women (Bound and Dresser 1998; Bound and Freeman 1992; Corcoran

1998; author calculations based on U.S. Bureau of Labor Statistics 2003b and U.S. Bureau of Labor Statistics *Employment and Earnings*, January 2003). The black-white employment gap has also widened: In business cycle peak year 1973, black males were 88 percent as likely to be employed as white males, and black women were 105 percent as likely as white women (that is, more likely than white women). Two business cycle peaks later, in 1989, these percentages had slipped to 85 percent and 95 percent, respectively. Even in the 2000 business cycle peak, with unemployment at its lowest since the 1960s, the percentages rose to only 86 percent for men and 101 percent for women (U.S. Council of Economic Advisors 2003, Table B-41). Latinos also fell further behind non-Latinos in wages, though not employment (Borjas 1994; Corcoran, Heflin and Reyes 1998; Hinojosa-Ojeda, Carnoy and Daley 1991; Melendez 1993; author calculations based on U.S. Bureau of Labor Statistics 2003b and U.S. Bureau of Labor Statistics *Employment and Earnings*, January 2003).

Why? Part of the income story is one of family structure. Single-mother families have become more common among all race and class groups but has grown most rapidly among black families. Single mothers are also particularly common among Puerto Ricans, though not among most other Latino groups. As well, since single mothers have less opportunity to earn wages, they receive, on average, lower incomes than any other type of family (Albelda and Tilly 1997). As Table 1.1 shows, single-mother families are nearly four times as likely to fall below the poverty line as the average family. The prevalence of this family structure is in part the result of limited economic opportunities available to black and Puerto Rican men and to the higher risks of imprisonment and early death in these populations (Wilson and Neckerman 1986).

The widening gaps in hourly wages and employment tell us that another important part of the problem derives from the labor market. In fact, blacks were hit particularly hard by the three drivers of economic change: globalization, technological change and revised business strategy. Globalization represents one aspect of increased capital mobility within as well as between countries. As jobs have moved to the suburbs within metropolitan areas, to Sunbelt regions within the country as a whole, and to new locations around the world, African-American communities have been likely to end up stranded (Squires 1994). Given the continuing power of racial residential segregation, African Americans have also been singularly unable to move where jobs were growing (Jencks and Mayer 1990; Massey and Denton 1993; see also Chapter 3).

As technological change increases the demand for skills, the good news is that blacks are slowly catching up with whites in educational attainment and achievement. But the bad news is that, on average, blacks (and Latinos) still have lower levels of skill and education at a time when the penalty for limited skills is growing. Employers are also placing growing emphasis on "soft" or social skills—attitude, ability to relate well with customers and so on. And employers' assessments of the soft skills of blacks and Latinos are tainted by discrimination (Moss and Tilly 1996, 2001).

Blacks have also been hard hit by business restructuring. A *Wall Street Journal* study found that among a sample of over 35,000 corporate employers during the 1990 to 1991 recession, black employment was reduced by 59,000 workers. Despite the recession, net employment for whites, Latinos and Asians grew; whites, for example, gained 71,000 jobs (Sharpe 1993). Although black-white gaps in wages and employment did narrow at the peak of the 1990s boom (Cherry and Rodgers 2000), they expanded once again in the subsequent recession (author calculations based on U.S. Bureau of Labor Statistics 2003b and U.S. Bureau of Labor Statistics *Employment and Earnings*, January 2003).

The reasons for growing Latino disadvantage have not been studied as extensively as those for blacks. One major factor in the low wages of Latinos is the influx of immigrants (many of whom earn low wages). There is evidence as well that many of the same trends are at work for blacks (Ortiz 1991; Melendez 1993).

In addition to race and ethnicity, gender powerfully stratifies incomes and wages. The gender gap is one area in which wage inequality is falling rather than rising. In 1955, a woman

working full-time and year-round earned on average 64 percent as much as her male counterpart. In the 15 years that followed, women lost ground, languishing at 60 percent in the 1970s. But from the late 1970s onward, women recouped their losses, advancing to 77 percent in 2002—still not earnings equality, but a step in the right direction (Albelda and Tilly 1997, Figure 1.3; U.S. Census Bureau 2003, Figure 3).

While a smaller gender gap in wages is a welcome development, the problem is that this change has taken place primarily not because women's real wages were rising, but because men's real wages were falling. With—on average—men's wages lower and women's wages little higher, two earners have become increasingly necessary to support a family. This family speed-up is not an improvement in the standard of living. Indeed, the fact that more women are working for pay cuts in two directions. The paycheck is empowering for women, but with it come the stresses and costs of the "double shift"—one shift at the workplace and another caring for the home (Hochschild 1990, 1997). Part-time jobs are available as one option for women (or men) carrying out this balancing act, but part-time schedules typically come as part of a package that includes low wages, few or no fringe benefits, and reduced job security (Tilly 1996).

The group squeezed hardest by the continuing gender wage gap and the family speed-up is single mothers. Single motherhood has become more common, affecting 11 percent of U.S. children in 1970 but 20 percent of U.S. children (and 23 percent of mothers) in 2000 (calculated from U.S. Department of Commerce 1996, Tables 76, 79; 2001, Table 60). The reasons are many: Women have more hope of economic self-sufficiency, men have less to offer economically and values have changed to make it easier for women and men to separate. However, between the time demands of child care, the low wages of working women and the minimal level of welfare benefits, single-mother families end up with extremely low incomes: In 1999, 36 percent of single-mother families were in poverty (see Table 1.1); percentages were even higher for single mothers of color. As single parents and their children grew to make up a larger share of the poor population, sociologist Diana Pearce (1978) described the process as the "feminization of poverty." Economist Nancy Folbre (1984) later suggested that a more apt term might be the "pauperization of motherhood."

In this context, recent waves of state and federal "reform" have slashed away at a critical lifeline for single mothers, the program popularly known as welfare (traditionally known as Aid to Families with Dependent Children [AFDC] and renamed Temporary Assistance for Needy Families [TANF] in 1996). Even before the most recent round of cuts and restrictions, welfare had already become distinctly less generous. The typical state's average monthly AFDC benefit for a family of three tumbled from $690 in 1970 to $366 in 1994 (in 1994 dollars; Parrott and Greenstein 1995). AFDC covered 80 percent of poor children in 1973 but only 59 percent in 1990 (U.S. House of Representatives 1994:399).

In fact, for years the United States has stood out among industrialized countries for the stinginess of its welfare benefits. A 1990 study (Smeeding, O'Higgins and Rainwater 1990; see also McFate 1991) adopted an internationally consistent definition of the poverty line (one-half of a nation's median income) and asked, of nonelderly families in poverty before government aid and taxes, what percentage were lifted above poverty by government assistance. In the late 1980s, the government programs of France, the Netherlands, Sweden and West Germany pulled about 50 percent of these potentially poor families out of poverty. U.S. government action, embarrassingly, pushed a small number of added families into poverty: Taxes pushed more people below the poverty line than transfers lifted above it.

Unfortunately, the U.S. antipoverty policy record is becoming even worse. The 1996 federal welfare "reform" put into place lifetime limits, harsh work requirements and an end to the federal guarantee to provide full funding for the program (Albelda and Tilly 1997). The impact of cutting welfare extends well beyond welfare recipients themselves. It weakens the safety net under all mothers, reducing their bargaining power with bosses and spouses alike. As well, it floods the labor market with women who have limited skills and few alternatives. The predictable effects are job displacement and erosion of wage standards, particularly among vulnerable workers who are already concentrated at the low end of the labor market—although the late 1990s economic boom offset these effects for a time. At the time of this writing (late 2005), Congress appears likely to pass an even more draconian version of welfare reform with stricter work requirements, at a time when economic boom has turned to labor market bust.

Housing patterns echo these income patterns, sometimes in intensified fashion. As other chapters in this text explore in detail, people of color and single mothers suffer particularly acute housing problems. Because on average they earn lower wages and receive less total income, people of color and single mothers disproportionately struggle with housing affordability. Because they are more likely to endure irregular income and employment, African Americans, Latinos, Native Americans and single mothers of all races face greater risks for housing insecurity—in many cases leading to homelessness. As politicians chip away at the parts of the welfare system that have most aided single mothers and low-income people of color, they also have cut back or eliminated the programs that subsidize *housing* for those with low income.

CONCLUSION: THE DOWNWARD SPIRAL

Recent economic trends in the United States tell a story of income stagnation, growing income insecurity and widening income inequalities. These income setbacks worsen the built-in difficulties and inequalities in the nation's for-profit housing system. They also form part of a self-perpetuating economic cycle. Businesses feeling competitive pressure curb wages, thereby shrinking consumer income and tightening competition still more. Businesses underinvest in knowledge and equipment upgrading, thereby slowing productivity growth and reducing the surplus available for reinvestment.

Housing economics also feed into this cycle. When incomes do not keep up with housing costs, families must devote more work time and money to paying for housing, thus reducing any surplus of time or money that could be invested in education or training. This heightened housing insecurity increases the chance of homelessness or frequent relocations, making participation in the labor market all the more difficult for adults and disrupting education for children.

As troubling as this economic cycle may be, the political cycle is even more discouraging. The experience of sharpening income and housing inequality, abetted by ubiquitous pro-market ideology, divides low- and moderate-income people as they scramble to get closer to the haves and to distance themselves from the have-nots. Those running to keep up on the economic treadmill, unable to counteract the changed rules of the game, too often direct their resentment at those still worse off—immigrants, recipients of welfare or housing subsidies, Mexican workers—who are seen as competitors or undeserving beneficiaries of taxpayer-funded aid. However, in the national and global market, weakening one's competitors simply hastens the process of bidding down wages and job security; undermines any notions of universal rights to housing, employment or income; and divides the coalitions that could potentially resist the dangerous economic trends.

Stopping this downward spiral requires building politics and economics based on solidarity rather than division. Politically and economically, the target must be policies protecting the weakest and bolstering living, housing and work standards for all workers. Without such policies, worsening economic inequality and insecurity is certain to continue.

NOTES

1. Income distribution numbers used here and throughout the chapter are based on the Current Population Survey (CPS), in which the U.S. Census Bureau annually surveys income. Because the CPS undercounts property income, it understates income inequality. An alternative source, the Survey of Consumer Finances (SCF), indicates that income is actually more unequally distributed. For example, according to the CPS, the richest one-fifth of households received 45 percent of total income in 1983 and 47 percent in 1989; according to the SCF, the figures were 52 percent and 56 percent. However, the CPS offers more detail and is available on an annual basis (and is the data source conventionally used for income analyses).

2. These figures are based on the U.S. Federal Reserve System's Survey of Consumer Finances. Another source of wealth data, the Survey of Income and Program Participation, shows somewhat more equal—though still very lopsided—distributions of wealth (Oliver and Shapiro 1995, Table 4.1).

3. I have adopted the shorthand of calling households headed by black people "black" households, and so on. Given the limited degree of intermarriage among racial groups in the United States, this shorthand is relatively accurate though is becoming less so.

REFERENCES

Abraham, Katharine G., and James E. Medoff. 1980. Experience, performance, and earnings. *Quarterly Journal of Economics* 95:703–736.

Albelda, Randy, and Chris Tilly. 1997. *Glass ceilings and bottomless pits: Women's work, women's poverty.* Boston: South End Press.

Allen, Steven G. 2001. Technology and the wage structure. *Journal of Labor Economics* 19(2):440–483.

Andrews, Edmund L. 1996. Don't go away mad, just go away: Can AT&T be the nice guy as it cuts 40,000 jobs? *New York Times*, February 13, D1–D10.

Baker, Dean. 1995. The "profits = investment" scam. *Dollars and Sense*, September/October:34–35.

Baxandall, Phineas. 1996. Jobs vs. wages: The phony trade-off. *Dollars and Sense*, July/August:8–11, 42.

Bernhardt, Annette, Martina Morris, Mark S. Handcock and Marc A. Scott. 2001. *Divergent paths: Economic mobility in the new American labor market.* New York: Russell Sage Foundation.

Bluestone, Barry, and Bennett Harrison. 1982. *The deindustrialization of America.* New York: Basic Books.

Boisjoly, Johanne, Greg J. Duncan and Timothy Smeeding. 1998. The shifting incidence of involuntary job losses from 1968 to 1992. *Industrial Relations* 37(2):207–231.

Borjas, George J. 1994. The economics of immigration. *Journal of Economic Literature* 23:1667–1717.

Bound, John, and Laura Dresser. 1998. The erosion of the relative earnings of young African American women during the 1980s. In *Latinas and African American women at work*, ed. Irene Browne, 61–104. New York: Russell Sage Foundation.

Bound, John, and Richard Freeman. 1992. What went wrong? The erosion of relative earnings and employment for blacks. *Quarterly Journal of Economics* 107:201–232.

Buchinsky, Moshe, and Jennifer Hunt. 1999. Wage mobility in the United States. *Review of Economics and Statistics* 81(3):351–368.

Chauvin, Keith. 1994. Firm-specific wage growth and changes in the labor market for managers. *Managerial and Decision Economics* 15:21–37.

Cherry, Robert and William M. Rodgers III, eds. 2000. *Prosperity for all? The economic boom and African Americans.* New York: Russell Sage Foundation.

Corcoran, Mary. 1998. The economic progress of African American women. In *Latinas and African American women at work*, ed. Irene Browne, 35–60. New York: Russell Sage Foundation.

Corcoran, Mary, Colleen M. Heflin and Belinda I. Reyes. 1998. Latino women in the U.S.: The economic progress of Mexican and Puerto Rican women. In *Latinas and African American women at work*, ed. Irene Browne, 105–138. New York: Russell Sage Foundation.

Currie, Elliott, Robert Dunn and David Fogarty. 1980. The new immiseration: Stagflation, inequality, and the working class. *Socialist Review* 54:7–31.

DiNardo, John E and Jorn-Steffen Pischke. 1997. The returns to computer use revisited: Have pencils changed the wage structure too? *Quarterly Journal of Economics* 112(1):291–303.

Farber, Henry S. 1997. The changing face of job loss in the United States, 1981–1995. *Brookings Papers on Economic Activity: Microeconomics* 297–333.

Folbre, Nancy. 1984. The pauperization of motherhood: Patriarchy and public policy in the U.S. *Review of Radical Political Economics* 16(4): 72–88.

Freeman, Richard B. 1986. Factor prices, employment, and inequality in a decentralized labor market. Cambridge, MA: National Bureau of Economic Research and Corporation for Enterprise Development.

———. 1994. How labor fares in advanced economies. In *Working under different rules*, ed. Richard B. Freeman, 1–28. New York: Russell Sage Foundation and National Bureau of Economic Research.

———. 1995. Are your wages set in Beijing? *Journal of Economic Perspectives* 9(3):15–32.

Gittleman, Maury and Edward Wolff. 2004. Racial differences in patterns of wealth accumulation. *Journal of Human Resources* 39(1):193–227.

Gordon, David M., Richard Edwards and Michael Reich. 1982. *Segmented workers, divided work: The historical transformation of labor in the United States.* Cambridge: Cambridge University Press.

Harrison, Bennett. 1994. *Lean and mean: The changing landscape of corporate power in the age of flexibility.* New York: Basic Books.

Hinojosa-Ojeda, Raul, Martin Carnoy and Hugh Daley. 1991. An even greater 'U-turn': Latinos and the new inequality. In *Hispanics in the labor force: Issues and policies*, eds. Edwin Melendez, Clara Rodriguez and Janis Barry Figueroa, 25–52. New York: Plenum.

Hochschild, Arlie Russell. 1997. *The time bind: When work becomes home and home becomes work.* New York: Henry Holt and Company.

Hochschild, Arlie Russell, with Anne Machung. 1990. *The second shift.* New York: Viking Penguin.

Howell, David. 1994. The skills myth. *The American Prospect*, 18:81–90.

Howell, David, and Edward Wolff. 1991. Trends in the growth and distribution of skill in the U.S. workplace, 1960–1985. *Industrial and Labor Relations Review* 44(3):481–501.

Jencks, Christopher, and Susan Mayer. 1990. Residential segregation, job proximity, and black job opportunities. In *Inner city poverty in the United States*, eds. Laurence E. Lind and Michael McGeary, 111–196. Washington, DC: National Academy Press.

Krueger, Alan B. 1993. How computers have changed the wage structure: Evidence from microdata, 1984–89. *Quarterly Journal of Economics* 108: 33–60.

Lublin, Joann S., and Joseph B. White. 1997. Dilbert's revenge: Throwing off angst, workers are feeling in control of careers. *Wall Street Journal*, September 11, A1, A6.

Marcotte, Dave E. 1998. The Wage Premium for Job Seniority During the 1980s and Early 1990s. *Industrial Relations* 37(4):419–439.

Marshall, Ray, and Marc Tucker. 1992. *Thinking for a living: Work, skills, and the failure of the American economy.* New York: Basic Books.

Massey, Douglas S., and Nancy A. Denton. 1993. *American apartheid: Segregation and the making of the underclass.* Cambridge, MA: Harvard University Press.

McFate, Katherine. 1991. *Poverty, inequality, and the crisis of social policy: Summary of findings.* Washington, DC: Joint Center for Political and Economic Studies.

Melendez, Edwin. 1993. Understanding Latino poverty. *Sage Race Relations Abstracts*, Vol. 18, No. 2, 3–43.

Miller, John. 1995. Hard times roll on: Growth and well-being on different tracks. *Dollar and Sense*, May/June, 8–9, 38–39.

Mishel, Lawrence, Jared Bernstein and John Schmitt. 1997. Did technology have any effect on the growth of wage inequality in the 1980s and 1990s? Washington, DC: Economic Policy Institute.

———. 2001. *The state of working America, 2000–2001.* Ithaca, NY: Cornell University Press.

Moss, Philip, and Chris Tilly. 1996. "Soft" skills and race: An investigation of black men's employment problems. *Work and Occupations* 23(3): 252–276.

———. 2001. *Stories employers tell: Race, skill, and hiring in America.* New York: Russell Sage Foundation.

National Jobs for All Coalition. 2003. Web site. http://www.njfac.org/jobnews.html

Oliver, Melvin L., and Thomas M. Shapiro. 1995. *Black wealth/white wealth: A new perspective on racial inequality*. New York: Routledge.

Ortiz, Vilma. 1991. Latinos and industrial change in New York and Los Angeles. In *Hispanics in the labor force: Issues and policies*, eds. Edwin Melendez, Clara Rodriguez and Janis Barry Figueroa, 119–134. New York: Plenum.

Osterman, Paul. 1995. Skill, training, and work organization in American establishments. *Industrial Relations* 34(2):125–146.

Parrott, Sharon, and Robert Greenstein. 1995. *Welfare, out-of-wedlock childbearing, and poverty: What is the connection?* Washington, DC: Center on Budget and Policy Priorities.

Pearce, Diana. 1978. The feminization of poverty: Women, work, and welfare. *Urban and Social Change Review*, February.

Rose, Stephen J. 1994. *On shaky ground: Rising fears about income and earnings*. Research Report 94-02. Washington, DC: National Commission on Employment Policy.

———. 1995. *Declining job security and the professionalization of opportunity*. Research Report 95-04. Washington, DC: National Commission on Employment Policy.

Shapiro, Thomas M. 2004. *The hidden cost of being African American: How wealth perpetuates inequality*. New York: Oxford University Press.

Sharpe, Rochelle. 1993. Losing ground: In latest recession, only blacks suffered net employment loss. *Wall Street Journal*, September 14, A1, A12.

Smeeding, Timothy, Michael O'Higgins and Lee Rainwater, eds. 1990. *Poverty, inequality, and income distribution in comparative perspective*. London: Wheatsheaf.

Squires, Gregory D. 1994. *Capital and communities in black and white: The intersections of race, class, and uneven development*. Albany: State University of New York Press.

Tilly, Chris. 1996. *Half a job: Bad and good part-time jobs in a changing labor market*. Philadelphia: Temple University Press.

———. 1998. Good news: The minimum wage works. *Dollars and Sense*, September/October: 11.

Uchitelle, Louis. 1996. Despite drop, rate of layoffs remains high. *New York Times*, August 23, A1, D2.

U.S. Bureau of Economic Analysis. 2002. National Income and Product Accounts Tables, Table 1.14, National Income by Type of Income. http://www.bea.doc.gov/bea/dn/nipaweb/TableViewFixed.asp (accessed May 2002).

U.S. Bureau of Labor Statistics. 2001. Contingent and Alternative Employment Arrangements. News release, May 24. http://www.bls.gov/news.release/conemp.nr0.htm

———. 2002a. Web site. http://stats.bls.gov; series PRS84006092 (output per hour, all business, quarterly percentage change), accessed May 2002.

———. 2002b. International comparisons of labor productivity and unit labor costs in manufacturing, 2000. Report 962. http://stats.bls.gov

———. 2003a. Metropolitan area employment and unemployment. News release, December 4. http://stats.bls.gov/news.release/metro.t01.htm

———. 2003b. Median weekly earnings by sex, age, race, quarterly and annual 1979–2001. Unpublished data file based on Current Population Survey.

———. Various years. *Employment and Earnings* (monthly). References are to annual averages, tabulated in the January issue of each year.

U.S. Census Bureau. 2000a. *Money income in the United States: 1999*. Current Population Reports, Consumer Income, P60-209. Washington, DC: U.S. Government Printing Office.

———. 2000b. *Poverty in the United States: 1999*. Current Population Reports, Consumer Income, P60-210. Washington, DC: U.S. Government Printing Office.

———. 2003. *Money income in the United States: 2002*. Current Population Reports, Consumer Income, P60-221. Washington, DC: U.S. Government Printing Office.

———. 2005. American FactFinder web page. 2000 Census, Summary File SF-3, Tables P152A-P152I. http://factfinder.census.gov

U.S. Council of Economic Advisors. 2003. *Economic report of the president 2003*. Washington, DC: U.S. Government Printing Office.

U.S. Department of Commerce. 1996. *Statistical abstract of the United States, 1996*. Washington, DC: U.S. Government Printing Office.

———. 2001. *Statistical abstract of the United States, 2001*. Web site. http://www.census.gov/statab/www

U.S. House of Representatives, Committee on Ways and Means. 1994. *Overview of entitlement programs, 1994 Green Book*. Washington, DC: U.S. Government Printing Office.

Wilson, William J., and Kathryn M. Neckerman. 1986. Poverty and family structure: The widening gap between evidence and public policy issues. In *Fighting poverty: What works, what doesn't*, eds. Sheldon Danziger and Daniel Weinberg, 232–259. Cambridge: Harvard University Press.

Wolff, Edward. 2000. Recent trends in wealth ownership, 1983–1998. Working Paper No. 300. Annandale-on-Hudson, NY: Jerome Levy Economic Institute.

———. 1996. *Top heavy: The increasing inequality of wealth in America and what can be done about it*. New York: The New Press.

Michael E. Stone

2   Housing Affordability: One-Third of a Nation Shelter-Poor

IN HIS SECOND Inaugural Address, March 1937, President Franklin D. Roosevelt uttered his now-famous lament: "I see one-third of a nation ill-housed. . . ." During the half-century following the Great Depression and World War II, the proportion of the nation ill-housed was dramatically reduced, but the United States became and has persistently remained one-third of a nation "shelter-poor." Even after the 1990s brought the longest period of economic growth in the nation's history, the new century began with more than 32 million households in the United States unable to meet their nonshelter needs at even a minimum level of adequacy because of the squeeze between their incomes and housing costs.

When one-third of a nation is shelter-poor, it is impossible to claim that those affected are an unfortunate few left behind by pervasive and sustained prosperity. When the official unemployment rate is under 6 percent, yet more than 90 million people live in shelter poverty,[1] it is impossible to claim that the labor market can provide "good" jobs for all who are willing to work. When 32 million households cannot afford the homes they are living in, it is impossible to claim that the housing market has the capacity to provide "affordable housing" for all who are shelter-poor with just a little more subsidy or a little less regulation. Persistent and pervasive shelter poverty challenges us to acknowledge the structural flaws in our institutions of housing provision and income distribution.

How is the problem of housing affordability any different from that of health care, food and other necessities? Housing has a pervasive impact on all aspects of our lives. If it is adequate, housing provides privacy and security against unwanted intrusions, both physical and emotional. It defines our community and determines our access to jobs, services, stores and networks of support. The residence is the principal locus of family and personal life, in which our personality, values and many of our social roles are defined, shaped and experienced. In its complexity and contradictions, the housing environment may be the setting of anguish, abuse and violence, yet it nonetheless continues to offer the hope of security, love, and expressive and aesthetic fulfillment.

Despite its intimate and profound significance, adequate housing in the United States is not assured to all as a right. Rather, for most of us, the housing we need has to be purchased in the marketplace. What we are able to pay for housing determines not only the quality of our dwelling but also the quality of our residential community and indeed whether we have housing at all. The cost of housing is by far the largest single expenditure in most families' budgets. Not only is the cost large, it is inflexible. Housing is usually the first thing paid for out of disposable income. Other expenditures have to be adjusted to fit whatever income is left over. To be sure, in extreme emergencies, we will feed our kids even if it means not paying the rent. If this continues, however, eventually we will be evicted—lucky to find another place but otherwise homeless. That is, it is not our income alone but income in relation to the cost of housing that is decisive in determining our standard of living. Housing affordability is central to the dilemmas of inequality and insecurity confronting our society. The affirmation and realization of a Right to Housing would thus mean, most basically, the guarantee of true affordability, with pervasive benefits and implications far beyond housing.

This chapter examines the housing affordability problem in the United States through the lens of the shelter poverty concept. "Shelter poverty" challenges the conventional standard claiming that every household can reasonably afford up to a fixed percentage of income—currently 30 percent—for housing. It offers instead a sliding scale of affordability that takes into account differences in household composition and income. In the aggregate, the shelter poverty measure does not reveal a more extensive housing affordability problem than shown by the conventional approach. It does, however, suggest a rather different distribution of the problem. Some very-low-income households and larger households who pay less than 30 percent of their incomes are nonetheless shelter-poor because they still do not have enough left over after paying for their housing to meet their nonshelter needs at a minimally adequate level. By the same token, high-income households and many small households (especially the elderly) of middle income can afford to pay more than 30 percent of income for housing yet are still able to obtain adequate levels of nonshelter necessities and thus are not shelter-poor. The conventional percentage-of-income measures understate the affordability problem of families with children and other larger households in comparison with households of one and two persons as well as understating the affordability burdens of lower-income households in comparison with those of higher income. The shelter poverty approach is a more finely honed tool for identifying which segments of society are most vulnerable and where attention is most needed.

Before presenting the contours of shelter poverty in the United States, some of the confusing and inconsistent ways in which housing affordability is often understood and discussed will be examined. This leads to explication of the logic and methods underlying the shelter poverty standard of affordability. The balance of the chapter then summarizes the housing affordability situation at the start of the 21st century as well as trends since the 1970s. The major findings are not especially surprising but perhaps are more dramatic than might be expected; *viz:*

- Large and growing numbers of shelter-poor: The number of shelter-poor households has exceeded 30 million since the early 1990s, an increase of more than 70 percent since 1970.
- Worse for larger households: Among families with children, rates of shelter poverty are much higher and over the past several decades have risen faster than among households with just one or two persons.
- Worse for renters (but still bad for homeowners): Nearly one-half of all renter households are shelter-poor, victims of low incomes and rising rents; most are headed by a woman and/or a person of color. Nearly one-quarter of homeowner households are shelter-poor; most are single-parent families or elderly.
- Widening differences between renters and homeowners: Renters have experienced much greater increases than homeowners in their affordability problems; nearly two-thirds of the increase in shelter poverty since 1970 has been among the one-third of all households who are renters.
- Worse for households headed by a person of color: Renter households headed by a person of color have about a 25 percent higher rate of shelter poverty than renter households headed by whites, with a smaller but still significant racial gap among homeowners.
- Worse for households headed by a woman: More than one-half of all shelter-poor renter households are headed by a woman, and two out of five shelter-poor homeowner households are headed by a woman.
- Wide inequality among elderly households: Shelter-poor elders are predominantly very poor women living alone, renters and homeowners; elderly married couples, by contrast, have low rates of shelter poverty.

Other chapters in this text examine the underlying sources of persistent and pervasive shelter poverty in the economy and the housing system. Taken together, these analyses convincingly demonstrate that realization of a Right to

Housing will require changes in the prevailing ways of thinking about housing ownership, production and financing, along with strategies to narrow income inequality.

CONFUSION ABOUT THE MEANING OF HOUSING AFFORDABILITY

In both academic and policy discussions, the notion of housing affordability is often imprecise and inconsistent along a number of dimensions:

- Housing affordability versus housing standards
- Housing affordability versus "affordable housing"
- A conceptually sound standard of affordability versus the practical policy implications of such a definition
- A normative standard of affordability versus empirical analysis of housing costs in relation to incomes
- Diverse and incompatible definitions of housing affordability

Housing Affordability versus Housing Standards

Housing deprivation can take a variety of forms, of which lack of affordability is only one. People may live in housing that fails to meet physical standards of "decency," in overcrowded conditions, with insecure tenure, or in unsafe or inaccessible locations. While each of these other forms of deprivation is logically distinct from the lack of affordability, in reality, most households who experience one or more of these other forms of deprivation do so because they cannot afford satisfactory housing and residential environments.

If other forms of housing deprivation are largely due to the affordability squeeze, how should affordability assessments account for those households who seem *not* to have an affordability problem (as measured on some standard of affordability) yet *do* experience one or more other forms of housing deprivation? If the cost of obtaining satisfactory dwellings and residential environments within the same housing market area exceeds what such households

could afford, then they reasonably should be considered to have an affordability problem even though not revealed by application of an economic affordability standard. Only if such a household actually *could* afford adequate housing might it reasonably be considered to be living in inadequate housing by choice. Thus, while housing deprivation is complex and can take various forms, the measurement of other forms of deprivation and their relationship to affordability is, in principle at least, reasonably tractable.

On the other side, can it not be argued that those households that *do* appear to have an affordability problem yet are "overhoused" might not have an affordability problem if they were not overhoused? This question is the obverse of the one in the above paragraph and could in principle be answered by a similar analytical technique. The difficulty is of course arriving at a reasonable, broadly acceptable operational definition of "overhoused." Although the relationship between the number of persons in a household and the number of rooms or bedrooms in the dwelling is widely used as an operational definition, in its simplicity this definition tends to be simplistic. For example, an apartment consisting of two tiny bedrooms, a tiny living room and dining room, and a minuscule kitchenette could easily have less than one-half the usable space of a unit with one large bedroom, a good-sized living room and an eat-in kitchen. Is it reasonable to consider a widow living in the former to be overhoused because the apartment has five rooms, including two bedrooms, but not in the latter because it has three rooms, including just one bedroom? Of greater subtlety, but as significant for assessing affordability, should households be considered overhoused if they have rooms for anticipated additional children, for overnight visits from family and friends, for study or hobbies, or for home-based business or employment? That is, the number of households that appear to have an affordability problem, but would not have such a problem were they not overhoused, is likely to be considerably lower based on application of some flexible standard rather than a simplistic person/room or person/bedroom definition of what it means to be overhoused.

In sum, housing affordability is not really separable from housing standards. An analysis of the extent and distribution of housing affordability problems that takes into account the indirect effects of affordability on other forms of housing deprivation would increase the number, while adjustment for overhousing would decrease the number of households determined to have a "true" affordability problem. Because of these offsetting tendencies, and the difficulties of definition, housing affordability studies ideally should be iterative—such as applying an economic affordability standard in the first instance while exploring ways of enhancing the precision of the analysis to account for underhousing and overhousing.

Housing Affordability versus "Affordable Housing"

Affordability is quite often expressed in terms of "affordable housing." But this term is at best meaningless and at worst misleading, as affordability is not a characteristic of housing—it is a *relationship* between housing and people. For some people, all housing is affordable, no matter how expensive; for others, no housing is affordable unless it is free. "Affordable" housing only can have meaning (and utility) if three essential questions are answered: Affordable to whom? On what standard of affordability? For how long? Indeed, in light of the discussion in the section above, one might also add meeting what physical standard?

Prior to the 1980s, subsidized housing (public and private) was referred to as "low-income housing" and "low- and moderate-income housing," with explicit definitions of "low-income" and "moderate-income." Although such terms and definitions are still used in determining eligibility under various housing policies and programs in the United States,[2] in the 1980s, "affordable housing" came into vogue as part of the retreat from public responsibility for the plight of the poor and as affordability challenges moved up the income distribution. The term has since achieved international stature yet still lacks precise and consistent definition. As well, it has come to encompass not only social housing and low-income housing but also housing that includes financial assistance to middle-income households that find it difficult to purchase houses in the private speculative market. While the latter is touted as "affordable housing," in reality, it is affordable only to a narrow spectrum of households (depending upon the definition of affordability and local housing market). Such housing is frequently only "affordable" to the initial residents, after which it may be sold, not with restrictions to maintain affordability but into the speculative market where even a semblance of affordability is lost.

It thus seems that a far more accurate and honest term than "affordable housing" would be "below-market housing." The latter properly denotes identifiable segments of the housing stock, without making any unjustifiable general claim of affordability.

A Conceptually Sound Definition of Affordability versus the Practical Policy Implications of Such a Definition

There seems to be some confusion between, on the one hand, the importance of formulating a conceptually sound affordability standard for analytical purposes and, on the other, the potential consequences of adopting such a standard wholesale for purposes of policy. Although some people in the field recognize the conceptual weaknesses of the conventional ratio (percent-of-income standard), most of those who do retreat from fully embracing alternative approaches, declaring, for example, that such approaches are "clearly more sophisticated, and therefore more difficult to apply" (London Research Centre 1996:19; see also, for example, Budding 1980; Wilcox 1999).[3]

Acknowledgment that housing subsidy policy inevitably will and should be shaped by factors other than conceptual clarity of the affordability standard (such as potential perverse incentives, fiscal constraints, political interests) should not result in avoidance of intellectual responsibility for rigorous and sound conceptualization, both for purposes of analysis and as an important consideration (if not the sole consideration) in the formulation of policy.

A Normative Standard of Affordability versus Empirical Analysis of Housing Costs in Relation to Incomes

Studies of consumer expenditures have been carried out in Europe and North America since the late 19th century, yielding considerable information about how households have spent their incomes for housing and other items. One way of summarizing the data on housing costs has been to calculate the mean or median ratio of shelter expenditures to income. It has then been assumed that because households on average actually spend such a fraction of their incomes for shelter, ipso facto this percentage is justified as a standard of what is reasonable to spend.

In reality, what most households actually pay for housing is not what they realistically can afford: Many pay more, while some pay less, whether measured in money or as a percent of income. Who pays more and who pays less than they realistically can afford is not random. An affordability *standard* is a normative concept, which must have some independent logical or theoretical basis, against which households' actual circumstances can be measured. Otherwise, the standard is tautological or arbitrary, or affordability is purely subjective, as discussed in the next section.

Diverse and Incompatible Definitions of Housing Affordability

In practice, there appear to be six different approaches to defining housing affordability or lack thereof:

1. *Tautological*—ability or inability of households to pay for market-rate housing;
2. *Relative*—changes in the relationship between aggregate central tendency measures (medians or means) of house prices or costs, on the one hand, and summary measures of household incomes, on the other;
3. *Subjective*—whatever individual households are willing or choose to spend;
4. *Behavioral*—standards based on aggregate or average housing expenditure patterns, or

alternatively on the characteristics of households in arrears;
5. *Ratio*—normative standards of a maximum acceptable housing cost:income ratio;
6. *Residual*—normative standards of a minimum income required to meet nonshelter needs at a basic level after paying for housing.

Statements manifesting the first of these approaches, the *tautological*, are not unusual. For example: "[Affordability is] people's ability to secure housing, to rent or to buy, based on their ability to pay either the rent or the mortgage...." Or, households with an affordability problem are those "who cannot meet the market cost of buying or renting housing from their own resources, i.e., those whose housing costs have to be subsidized...."[4] Such statements, however, are circular and of no practical use, as they imply a standard of affordability but fail to provide any.

The *relative* approach is widely used by the mortgage lending and real estate industries to assess the residential sales market. It is simply an empirical summary that enables two or more points in time to be compared as to whether, on average, dwellings for sale have become relatively more or less affordable. The technical sophistication of such affordability measures does vary, with considerable discussion as to the most appropriate definitions of housing cost and income to use in constructing the measure as well as the implications of different definitions (see Linneman and Megbolugbe 1992; Pannell and Williams 1994). This approach provides no normative standard for assessing how much households realistically can afford and thus for determining how many and which kinds of households can and cannot afford those properties that are for sale. Nor does it provide any basis for assessing possible affordability stresses of households in their current situations as owner-occupiers or renters.

The *subjective* approach rests on the assumption of *Homo economicus:* Because households are rational utility-maximizers, every household is by definition paying just what it can afford for housing. Some households may live in undesirable conditions or some may have low incomes that give them few choices, but they make the choice that is best for them within their constraints. Thus, from this perspective, housing affordability per se has no generalizable meaning: It is neither rationally possible nor socially desirable to establish a normative standard of affordability other than individual choice.

More sophisticated versions of this perspective do recognize that the degree of financial flexibility does increase with income. Kempson, for example, has argued (1993:26–27) that:

> [P]eople differ in the way they allocate their money. Some choose to spend more on their housing and cut back on other expenditure; while others keep their housing costs low in order to spend more on other things. The higher the income the less need there is for such choices. . . .

Linneman and Megbolugbe (1992:388) have expressed this perspective particularly pointedly. While they acknowledge a "real" affordability problem among low-income households—claiming, though, that it is "primarily a problem of income inadequacy"—they assert, in response to widespread anguish about the cost of achieving homeownership, that housing affordability is "an issue manufactured by middle-class and affluent young adults with ever growing expectations. . . ."

While no one could disagree that higher-income households have considerable discretion about how to allocate their resources between housing and other items, and hence for them affordability may be quite subjective, at the lower end of the income distribution, households are not simply choosing freely between housing and other needs. Rather, since housing costs tend to make the first claim on a household's disposable income, lower-income households have little discretion in what they can spend for nonhousing items. Thus, "subjectivity" of affordability is not only not universal, it is not even a continuum that increases with income. Instead, there is a threshold above which affordability may become increasingly subjective. The important questions are what is that threshold or transition zone below which affordability is *not* subjective

and how to define and measure objective affordability below that threshold? These questions are not addressed within this perspective.

The fourth approach to conceptualizing housing affordability—the *behavioral*—has had two strands. One has focused on what households actually spend; in practice, this has formed the basis for the ratio approach, although in principle a residual income standard could also be defined behaviorally. This strand embodies perfectly the confusion between empirical analysis and normative standards discussed in the preceding section.

The other strand has focused on payment arrearage and involuntary displacement resulting from the financial squeeze between incomes and housing costs, with analysis of household characteristics and circumstances potentially providing a basis for assessing risk. Mortgage default and foreclosures, and rent arrearage and evictions for nonpayment, are the most proximate manifestations of such affordability stress. Homelessness (including doubling-up as well as shelter demand and street sleeping) is certainly the ultimate consequence for many families and individuals.

However, while these latter phenomena are complex and have aspects that may be difficult to measure, for the most part they are extreme behavioral responses to dire circumstances. Indeed, families with severe financial stress often continue to pay for their housing but live in substandard housing and/or have inadequate nutrition, with resulting threats to health and child development (see Doc4Kids 1998 and the sources cited therein). As Kearns has similarly put it (1992:539): "A static rate of incidence of rent arrears could hide the fact that households may be adjusting their expenditure priorities in order to meet their housing costs, and as a result be suffering hardship in other areas. . . ." Thus, at best, measures of payment arrearage and loss of housing due to financial stress are useful indicators of some of the consequences of extreme lack of affordability but do not in themselves provide a sufficient basis for establishing a normative standard of affordability.

The *ratio* approach recognizes that what many households pay for housing in relation to their income is the result of difficult choices among limited and often unsatisfactory alternatives. It asserts that if a household pays more for housing than a certain percentage or fraction of its income, then it will not have enough income left for other necessities. It usually specifies an explicit ratio of housing cost to income as a norm against which households' actual circumstances can be measured. This approach to a normative standard has the longest history and widest recognition and acceptance for assessing affordability throughout most English-speaking countries—even though there is no theoretical or logical foundation for the concept and the particular ratio or ratios that are used.

How can one account for the existence and persistence of the fixed ratio or percent-of-income affordability concept? Apart from the mathematical simplicity of the percent-of-income standard, the rationale for the conventional standard (and the rationalization for raising the acceptable level in the United States from 25 to 30 percent in the 1980s) has been built upon interpretations of empirical studies of what households actually spend for housing, as noted above. Because ratios are pure numbers, they can be compared across time and space, and thus are susceptible to being reified as universal and lawful. Such "laws" then become legitimated as standards. (See Feins and Lane 1981; Pedone 1988:9; Yip 1995:Chapter 7; for a critique of such alleged "lawfulness," see especially, Chaplin et al. 1994:13–14.)

Surely this is specious reasoning. Since a housing affordability standard is intended to measure whether housing costs make an undue claim on household income in relation to other needs, basing such a standard on what people actually pay provides no way of assessing whether they are in fact able to achieve some minimum standard for nonshelter necessities. Furthermore, the notion that a household can adequately meet its nonshelter needs if it has at least a certain percentage of income left after paying for housing implies that the lower the income of a family, the lower the amount of money it requires for nonshelter needs, with no minimum whatsoever. These logical flaws in the ratio approach lead inexorably to the residual

income approach to affordability, the only truly logical normative approach, as taken up in the next section.

THE SHELTER POVERTY STANDARD

The Residual Income Logic of Housing Affordability

The residual income approach to affordability—including the shelter poverty standard I have developed[5]—arises from the recognition that housing costs tend to be inflexible and for most households make the first claim on after-tax income—for instance, that nonhousing expenditures are limited by how much income is left after paying for housing. This means that a household is "shelter-poor" if it cannot meet its nonhousing needs at some minimum level of adequacy after paying for housing. That is, shelter poverty is a form of poverty that results from the squeeze between incomes and housing costs rather than just limited incomes. On this basis, only if a household would still be unable to meet its nonshelter needs if shelter costs were reduced to zero should its condition between regarded as *absolute* poverty rather than *shelter* poverty. Even in the latter circumstance, as long as housing costs are in fact not zero and do make the first claim on such a household's meager income, the depth of their absolute poverty is determined by the squeeze between their income and housing costs.

What are the implications of this logic for the amount and fraction of income that households realistically can afford? Consider, for example, two households with comparable disposable incomes. Suppose that one consists of a single person, while the other is a couple with three children. Obviously, the larger household would have to spend substantially more for its nonshelter necessities than would the small household in order to achieve a comparable material quality of life. This implies that the larger household can afford to spend less for housing than the small household of the same income. Now compare two households of the same size and composition but different after-tax incomes. Both would need to spend about the same amount to achieve a comparable standard of living for nonshelter items. The higher income household could thus afford to spend more for housing, in percentage of income as well as in monetary terms.

Generalizing from these examples, since the nonhousing expenses of small households are, on average, less than those of large households (to achieve a comparable basic standard of living), smaller households can reasonably devote a higher percentage of income to housing than can larger households with the same income. Since low-income and higher-income households of the same size and type require about the same amount of money to meet their nonhousing needs at a comparable basic standard of living, those with lower incomes can afford to devote a smaller percentage of income for housing than otherwise similar, higher-income households can afford. In this way, the shelter poverty scale emerges as a sliding scale of housing affordability—with the maximum affordable fraction of income varying with household size, type and income—that is logically sound and more realistic than the widely used ratio approach. The residual income logic reveals that any attempt to reduce affordability of housing to a single percentage of income, or even a set of ratios, simply does not correspond to the reality of fundamental and obvious differences among households.

The Shelter Poverty Scale

Operationalizing the shelter poverty standard involves use of a conservative, socially defined minimum standard of adequacy for nonshelter necessities, scaled for differences in household size and type. It takes into account the actual cost of a standardized, basic "market basket" of nonshelter necessities in determining the maximum amount of money households can afford to spend for housing and still have enough left to pay for this basic market basket of nonshelter necessities.[6] Thus, while the logic of shelter poverty has broad validity, a particular shelter poverty scale is not universal; it is socially grounded in space and time.

To illustrate, suppose a family of four persons has a disposable income of $2,000 a month. Their out-of-pocket expenses for rent and utilities are, say, $800 a month. They then have $1,200

a month available for nonshelter expenses. If the basic minimum cost standard for nonshelter items at some point in time were to be $1,500 a month for a household of four, then this family is "shelter-poor": They are unable to meet their nonshelter needs adequately at even a basic level because they have a deficit of $300 a month due to the squeeze between their income and their shelter cost. That is, shelter poverty is ascertained by considering actual income and actual shelter costs against a monetary normative standard for nonshelter items, not a normative standard for shelter costs.

The practical issue in translating the shelter poverty concept into an operational affordability scale is how to specify the monetary level of a minimum standard of adequacy for nonshelter items. Although every household has its own unique conditions of life, there do exist historically and socially determined notions of what constitutes a minimum adequate or decent standard of living. They represent norms around which a range of variations can be recognized and about which there certainly may be some philosophical debate. While the experience of "poverty" is recognized as more than just the inability to secure a socially determined minimum quantity and/or quality of essential goods and services, measurable material deprivation is certainly a central element in poverty. Furthermore, in societies where most basic goods and services are commodities, it is possible (at least in principle) to determine the monetary cost of achieving such a basic material level. This budget standards approach to poverty and income adequacy has a long and honorable history (see Bernstein et al. 2000; Bradshaw et al. 1987; Bradshaw 1993; Citro and Michaels 1995; Ruggles 1990).

There are, however, conceptual problems in the treatment of housing costs in the budget standards methodology due to the inherent nature and variability of housing costs. If the budget amounts for housing specified in the standard budgets really do represent the amount of income needed for essentially any household to obtain physically adequate housing, then housing affordability has no independent meaning; for instance, in principle, any household with an income no less than the total budget should be able to meet all of its basic needs, including housing, at the physical quantity and quality represented by the budget standard. However, while the budget standard methodology is well conceptualized and operationalized for other items, it is flawed with regard to housing. The issue is revealed by contrasting the budget standard approach and its implications for food with that of housing.

For both food and housing (and most other items), some combination of expert opinion, social surveys and focus groups is used to establish a minimal standard of type, quantity and quality, in a given social context at a given point in time. (The physical standard will of course vary by household type, and this qualifier applies to all of the following.) The food standard can then be priced, resulting in a monetary standard. Then, given the nature of food items—low price variance and high supply elasticity—essentially any household could in principle meet the physical food standard with the amount represented by the specific monetary standard, at least within a particular geographical region.

Housing, by contrast, is highly inhomogeneous. Because it is bulky, durable and tied to land, it shows high price variance and low elasticity of supply—even within a given market area. How then to price the minimum standard for housing? If prices are determined for a sample of housing units meeting the minimum physical standard, the price distribution has a large variance. Which point on the distribution should then be selected for the monetary standard for housing? If the very lowest cost is selected (say, the tenth percentile), then most housing is more expensive, and therefore most households, despite their best efforts, will not be able to obtain physically adequate housing at the monetary standard. That is, most households would need income above the total specified by the monetary budget standard in order to meet the minimum physical standard. If, on the other hand, the monetary standard for housing were to be set closer to the midpoint of the price distribution (say, the fortieth percentile, which is the definition of "Fair Market Rent" computed by the U.S. Department of Housing and Urban Development and used in recent U.S.

budget standards; see Bernstein et al. 2000), then some households are able to spend less than the monetary standard for housing and hence need less income than the total budget, through no virtue of their own, while others would have to spend more (though not as many as with a standard located at a lower point on the cost distribution). In sum, housing is unique; the budget standard methodology may be able to specify a reasonably precise *physical* standard for housing, but it cannot establish a precise *monetary* standard.

Thus, the budget standards concepts and methodology provide an appropriate basis for establishing a normative standard for *residual* income, but not for total income, given the distinctive nature of housing and housing costs. For operationalizing the shelter poverty scale for the United States, I have utilized as the normative standard for residual income the nonshelter costs (other than taxes) in the Bureau of Labor Statistics (BLS) Lower Budgets, appropriately scaled and updated.[7] This approach reveals, for example, that in 2001, a married couple with two children and a before-tax income of $30,000 a year could afford just 21 percent of their income for housing on the shelter poverty standard. They would have needed an income of at least $38,000 to be able to afford to spend 30 percent of their income for housing and still meet other necessities at a minimal level of adequacy. If their income were $20,000 or less, they could afford nothing for housing. A single parent with two children, working at a full-time job paying $10 an hour, could barely afford to spend 25 percent of her income for housing in 2001— and only if her job included health benefits and she had subsidized childcare; without these benefits, she could afford only a much lower percentage for housing. An elderly couple with an income of $15,000 could afford just 25 percent of their income for housing; but with an income of $17,000, they could afford 35 percent.

The following sections summarize the results of applying the shelter poverty standard to national data on housing expenditures to determine the extent and distribution of housing affordability problems, in the aggregate and for various subsets of the population, over time and in comparison with the conventional percent-of-income measures of affordability.

SHELTER POVERTY IN THE UNITED STATES[8]

Large Numbers of Shelter-Poor

In 2001, there were about 106 million households in the United States. Over 32 million were shelter-poor. Strikingly, about 2.5 million more households were paying 30 percent or more of their incomes for housing (Figure 2.1). That is, the shelter poverty approach does not overstate the extent of the housing affordability problem in comparison with the conventional measure. But, as we shall see, it does suggest a significantly different distribution of the problem: Not all shelter-poor households are paying over 30 percent of their incomes for housing, and not all households paying over 30 percent are shelter-poor.

There were 90 million persons living in shelter-poor households in 2001, compared with 84 million people living in households paying 30 percent or more of income.[9] The reason why the number of persons in shelter-poor households was 6 million greater than the number of persons in households paying 30 percent or more—despite the number of shelter-poor households being 2.5 million fewer—is the sensitivity of shelter poverty to household size and hence the relatively larger size of the typical shelter-poor household. The median size of shelter-poor households was 2.5 persons, compared with just 2.1 persons on the 30-percent standard. Thus, while 30 percent of all households were shelter-poor in 2001, 33 percent of all persons lived in households that were shelter-poor.

Increasing Shelter Poverty

Between 1970 and the mid-1990s, the number of shelter-poor households grew by more than 70 percent. From under 19 million households in 1970, shelter poverty grew slowly during the 1970s and then rose sharply in the long, deep recession of the late 1970s to early 1980s, to a

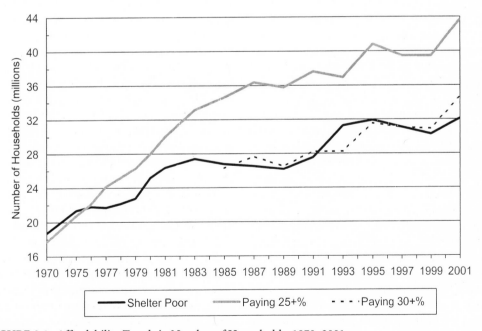

FIGURE 2.1. Affordability Trends in Number of Households, 1970–2001.

temporary peak of a little over 27 million house-holds in 1983. During the following six years of economic growth, shelter poverty actually de-clined by 1.2 million households. It then soared again in response to the recession of the early 1990s, reaching a new high of nearly 32 million in 1995. Over the next four years, sustained eco-nomic growth brought shelter poverty down to just over 30 million households. With the sub-sequent decline in the economy, shelter poverty climbed past 32 million households by 2001, again surpassing the previous peak (Figure 2.1). Over this period, the *rate* of shelter poverty has also fluctuated with the ups and downs of the overall economy. In 1970, 30 percent of house-holds were shelter-poor; the rate showed lit-tle variation from 1970 through 1979, then in-creased steadily to nearly 33 percent in 1983 before declining to 28 percent in 1989.[10] It in-creased dramatically over the next four years, reaching a record high 33 percent in 1993, fol-lowed by only a slight decline in 1995, before dropping to almost 29 percent in 1999, after which it again climbed past 30 percent in 2001 (Figure 2.2). The share of the population (as distinguished from households) living in shel-ter poverty has fluctuated between a low of about

31 percent in the early and late 1970s and late 1980s and highs of 36 percent in the early 1980s, 38 percent in the early 1990s and 33 percent as the decade turned.[11]

Shelter poverty is thus seen to be sensitive to business cycle fluctuations, with swings up and down as employment and incomes shift with the overall economy. It is important to keep in mind, though, that underlying these ups and downs, there has been a persistent, long-term shelter poverty rate of about 30 percent of all households—a rate that actually shows a slight upward trend of about two percentage points over the last three decades of the 20th century, as Figure 2.2 reveals. About one-sixth of shelter poverty can be considered cyclical—households who drop into shelter poverty when the economy turns down, suffering job loss and income decline, but who emerge from shelter poverty with economic upswings. The remain-ing five-sixths of shelter poverty is structural—households for whom growth in the overall economy does not provide the way out of shelter poverty.

Strikingly, in comparison with the tradi-tional percent-of-income measure, the shelter poverty approach actually shows far less growth

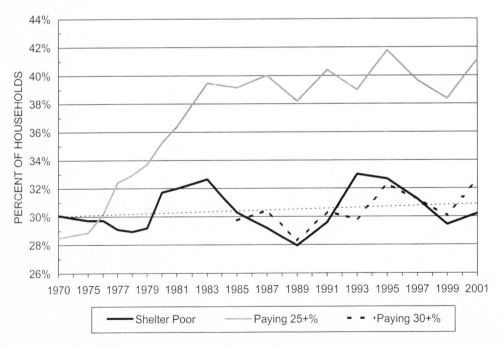

FIGURE 2.2. Affordability Trends in Percent of Households, 1970–2001.

in affordability problems since 1970. Note that prior to the 1980s, the conventional affordability standard was 25 percent of income, so this standard provides a long baseline comparison with shelter poverty, supplemented by comparison with the newer 30-percent-of-income standard since the mid-1980s. In 1970, the number of shelter-poor households exceeded the number paying over 25 percent their incomes for housing by over 1 million. Since 1976, however, the number of shelter-poor households has been less than the number paying over 25 percent, with the difference being 8 to 10 million households since the late 1980s (Figure 2.1). As this gap opened up, the proportion of households paying over 25 percent of income has exceeded 40 percent since the late 1970s, fully 10 percentage points higher than the rate of shelter poverty (Figure 2.2). These trends suggest that, as housing costs rose and the 25-percent standard was jettisoned as the basis for public and private decision-making, more households have had to accept paying over 25 percent of their incomes for housing as a permanent state of affairs. While many of these households are shelter-poor, those of higher income are not, as they can afford more than 25 percent of their incomes for housing without neglecting other needs.

Unlike the gap that opened up with the 25-percent standard, there has been fairly close correspondence in the aggregate number and percent of households shelter-poor and those exceeding the newer 30-percent-of-income standard—at least since the mid-1980s (Figures 2.1 and 2.2). However, as has already been suggested and will be further explored in the next section, this remarkable coincidence in the aggregate extent of the problem as measured by these two affordability standards masks sizable differences in the experience of large and small households.

Worse for Larger Households

The relative stability in the underlying long-term rate of shelter poverty masks a growing affordability problem over the past three decades for families with children. This is because the overall incidence is a mixture of trends in shelter poverty for small (one-person and two-person) households—for whom there has been a significant downward trend in the underlying rate of shelter poverty since 1970—and larger households (containing three or more people) for whom the basic shelter poverty rate has risen substantially during the same period. In 1970, small households had a 3 percentage point higher rate of shelter poverty than larger households. By 1975, these rates had reversed, and since then, the incidence of shelter poverty among larger households has remained consistently above that of small households—a differential reaching 8 percentage points by the late 1980s, then soaring to 15 percentage points in the mid-1990s before narrowing to 10 to 11 points later in that decade (Figure 2.3).

Of households containing three or more persons, the number who were shelter-poor rose by 86 percent—from a little over 9 million in 1970 to over 17 million by 1995, after which it dropped to the 15 to 16 million range. Meanwhile, their rate of shelter poverty rose from a low of 29 percent in 1970 to a relative peak of 36 percent in 1983. The rate declined just a few percentage points in the mid-1980s but surged to over 41 percent from 1993 to 1995, after which it declined to about 36 percent (Figure 2.3). That is, shelter poverty among households with three persons or more—nearly all of which contain children—has risen to where close to two out of every five are shelter-poor.

In comparison, the number of small households (one or two persons) who were shelter-poor rose 66 percent between 1970 and 1997, from slightly over 9 million to nearly 16 million, then declined a bit before rising to 16.5 million in 2001. However, because this increase was exceeded by enormous growth in the number of small households of relatively high income, the *rate* of shelter poverty among small households actually declined during the 1970s and remained less than 30 percent even in the recession of the early 1980s. It reached a low of 24 percent in 1989 before turning up to 27 percent during the recession of the early 1990s, fluctuating between 25 and 27 percent thereafter (Figure 2.3).

The conventional measures, by contrast, show no reversal in the affordability situations

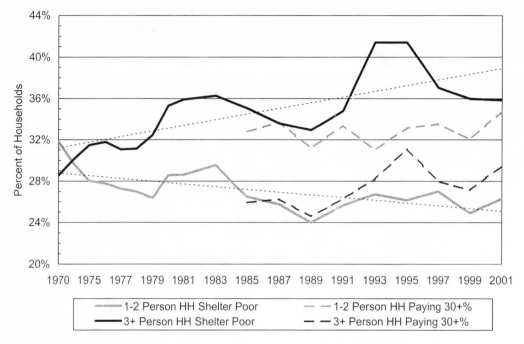

FIGURE 2.3. Affordability Trends by Household Size, Percent of Households, 1970–2001.

of small and larger households. The percent-of-income standards have consistently suggested that small households are substantially worse off than larger households, although the difference narrowed considerably in the early 1990s (Figure 2.3). The reason the conventional measure continues to suggest that smaller households are more likely than larger ones to have affordability problems is that it gives undue weight to the growing number of small middle-income households, many of whom are not necessarily shelter-poor, even if they are paying more than 25 or 30 percent of their incomes for housing. In revealing the disproportionate growth of affordability problems among larger households, the shelter poverty approach reveals much more clearly than the conventional approach how housing affordability is one of the principal causes and manifestations of the economic strains on families with children.

Worse for Renters (but Bad for Homeowners)

Nearly one-half of all renter households are shelter-poor, the incidence averaging about 45

percent since the early 1990s. By contrast, approximately one-fourth of all homeowner households are shelter-poor, averaging about 24 percent over the same period (Figure 2.4). The primary reason for renters' much higher rate of shelter poverty is that they are poorer on average than homeowners: median income in 2001 of about $25,000 for renter households compared with over $49,000 for homeowners. Also, unless they are protected by rent control or housing subsidies, renters do not have the benefit of relatively stable housing costs, unlike those many homeowners who have fixed-rate mortgages and have not recently bought their homes or borrowed against their equity.

In addition, shelter-poor renters are somewhat poorer than shelter-poor homeowners on average: Shelter-poor renters had a median income of $11,300 versus $16,300 for shelter-poor homeowners in 2001. Indeed, 56 percent of shelter-poor renters (8.4 million households) can actually afford *nothing* for housing compared with 42 percent of shelter-poor homeowners (7.1 million households). However, homeowners are far more diverse economically

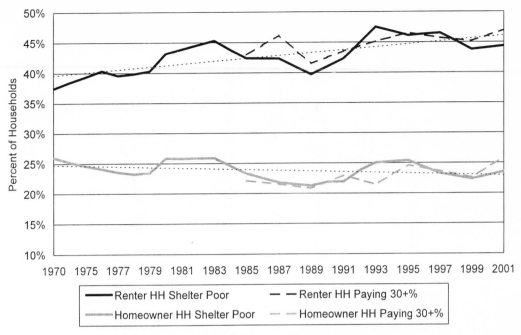

FIGURE 2.4. Affordability Trends by Tenure, Percent of Households, 1970–2001.

than are renters: For example, single home-owners have a median income of only $25,000; those with three or more persons have a median income of about $65,000. Homeowner shelter poverty also reflects wide social inequality among homeowners, with shelter poverty differences by income and household size correlating strongly with gender, race and age differences.

More than 15 million renter households were shelter-poor in 2001. More than four out of five had incomes of less than $20,000. Indeed, nearly 80 percent of all renters with incomes under $20,000 were shelter-poor. Shelter poverty rises sharply with household size, ranging from 31 percent of one-person renters to nearly 73 percent of renter households with six persons or more (Figure 2.5). This disproportionate burden on larger households means that the rate of renter shelter poverty measured in terms of persons was 52 percent in 2001 (41 million people) compared with 44 percent of households. More than one-half of all shelter-poor renter households are headed by a woman, and more than two-fifths are headed by a person of color.

By way of comparison, on the 30-percent-of-income standard, about 47 percent of renters

had an affordability problem in 2001 (with a median income of $13,900). As we have seen, though, the aggregate similarity in the extent of the problem on the shelter poverty and 30-percent standards masks significant differences by household size. Unlike shelter poverty, the conventional measure suggests virtually no difference in the rates of affordability problems among renters by household size, thereby understating the problems faced by families with children while exaggerating the problems of small households. For renters with incomes below $10,000, the two approaches show nearly all households to have severe problems. At higher incomes, however, shelter poverty remains quite serious among the largest households with incomes all the way up to $40,000 but among one-person households is not serious above $15,000. The conventional approach shows no such differences and hence, to repeat, is a much coarser instrument for understanding the problem and focusing resources where they are most needed.

A little over 17 million homeowners were shelter-poor in 2001. Homeowner shelter poverty disproportionately afflicts households headed by someone who is a woman and/or

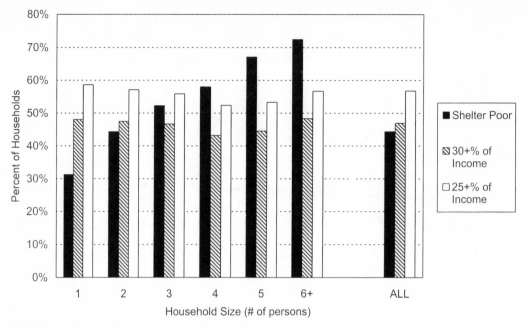

FIGURE 2.5. Renter Affordability by Household Size, Percent of Households, 2001.

elderly and/or a person of color. The rates of shelter poverty among one- and two-person homeowner households were slightly above 20 percent in 1997 but were much higher among larger households—26 to 28 percent for three-, four- and five-person households and 39 percent for six-or-more-person households (Figure 2.6). That is, once again, the shelter poverty approach reveals the greater affordability problems faced by larger households, although the rate rises much more steeply for renters. Among one-person households, the incidence of shelter poverty among renters is 10 percentage points higher than for homeowners. For three-person households, renters have a shelter poverty rate 26 percentage points higher; for six-or-more person households, the differential is 33 percentage points.

Widening Differences between Renters and Homeowners

Nearly two-thirds of the rise in shelter poverty since 1970 has been among the one-third of all households who are renters. In 1970, shelter-poor renters accounted for 45 percent of all shelter-poor households; since 1985, they have been a majority nearly every year. From 1970 through 1993, the number of shelter-poor renter households increased by 90 percent, from 8.4 million to 15.8 million, and has since fluctuated between 15 and 16 million. The incidence of shelter poverty among renters grew from 37 percent in 1970 to a temporary peak of over 45 percent in 1983. Renter shelter poverty then fell steadily to just under 40 percent by 1989, but with the onset of recession, it then soared to nearly 48 percent in 1993 and declined to a little under 44 percent in 1999 before turning upward again with the new century (Figure 2.4).

Single renters have experienced a substantial increase in the number who are shelter-poor yet a long-term downward trend in the percent shelter-poor. This trend is due primarily to striking differences in shelter poverty between elderly and nonelderly singles, and the enormous increase in the total number of nonelderly singles. Elderly singles, who are overwhelmingly female, have long been the poorest of all households and have faced rents increasing faster than incomes; by the mid-1980s, nearly one-half of such households were shelter-poor. Meanwhile, there has

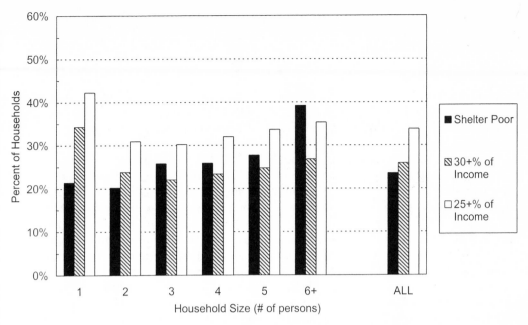

FIGURE 2.6. Homeowner Affordability by Household Size, Percent of Households, 2001.

been a rapid increase in the number of middle-income and higher-income nonelderly singles, nearly all of whom are not shelter-poor.

The majority of renter households containing three persons or more are shelter-poor and have had enormous increases in their rates of shelter poverty. Their incidence of shelter poverty rose from 44 percent in 1970 to 61 percent in the early 1980s, followed by some improvement through the rest of the 1980s. Their plight again worsened with the recession in the early and mid-1990s, when their rate of shelter poverty surpassed 66 percent. It fell slowly thereafter to 58 percent in 2001.

Meanwhile, the number of shelter-poor homeowners grew by 64 percent between 1970 and 2001—from slightly more than 10 million to 17 million households. Homeowner shelter poverty has been more volatile than that of renters, reflecting fluctuating homeownership rates, rising mortgage debt burdens and widening inequality among homeowners. There was an increase of nearly 4 million shelter-poor households from 1970 through the early 1980s, followed by a decline of 1.5 million households from 1983 through the late 1980s, and

then another surge of over 3.5 million households from 1987 through 1995. This was followed by a decline of under 1 million in the late 1990s, followed by another sharp increase of over 1.5 million in the number of shelter-poor homeowners between 1999 and 2001 as the economy again headed downward. The incidence of shelter poverty among homeowners has shown fluctuations with the economy, ranging between about 21 and 26 percent, against a background of a modest, long-term downward trend (Figure 2.4).

Homeowner households with one and two persons experienced sizable decreases in their rates of shelter poverty during the 1970s, with the rates remaining nearly unchanged at about 20 percent since the mid-1980s. Yet the number of small homeowner households who are shelter-poor rose by 45 percent from 1970 to 1997. The resolution of this apparent inconsistency is to be found in the more rapid increase in the number of small homeowner households who are not shelter-poor. Some of the latter are "empty-nesters," long-term owners who benefit from relatively low housing costs plus incomes rising with inflation; many others are younger, higher-income households without children. By contrast, it is primarily elderly and middle-aged female-headed households who account for the increase in the number of shelter-poor small homeowner households.

Larger homeowner households (three persons or more) have seen their rates of shelter poverty fluctuate with the economy. However, the variations are correlated with household size. Homeowner households with three and four persons have had fairly consistent shelter poverty rates of about 20 percent since the mid-1970s. Only the relatively small proportion of homeowners with five persons or more have experienced high and rising shelter poverty rates since the mid-1970s.

Shelter poverty patterns by tenure suggest the need for particular attention to the problems of renters—almost one-half of whom are shelter-poor and who, for the most part, are suffering simultaneously from the depredations of the private rental market along with low and stagnating incomes. They therefore need extensive and effective strategies from both sides of the affordability squeeze. Homeowners, by contrast, are only one-half as likely to be shelter-poor, and those who are shelter-poor mostly are afflicted by one side of the housing cost/income squeeze or the other. Specifically, one major segment of shelter-poor homeowners consists of older, long-term owners who have relatively low housing costs but very low incomes. Another group is single-parent families, for whom dissolved relationships left them with houses but with less income and hence mortgage and property tax payments that are much less affordable than before. The third major group consists of younger, more recent buyers of moderate to middle income who are carrying huge mortgage burdens.

Worse for Households Headed by People of Color[12]

The majority of shelter-poor households are white, but shelter poverty is disproportionately borne by households headed by a person of color. While about 77 percent of all households were headed by a white person in 1997, 66 percent of shelter-poor households were headed by a white. Conversely, about 23 percent of all households were headed by a person of color, but 34 percent of shelter-poor households were headed by a person of color.

Among households of color, the highest rates of shelter poverty have been experienced by Latinos, the next highest by non-Latino Blacks, followed by Asians. In 1997, 50 percent of Latino-headed, 45 percent of Black-headed (non-Latino) and 35 percent of Asian-headed households were shelter-poor, compared with 27 percent of white-headed households.

When examined by tenure, the same relative severity in the incidence of shelter poverty by race/ethnicity is found for both renters and homeowners. Among renter households, 58 percent of Latinos, 52 percent of Blacks and 46 percent of Asians were shelter-poor in 1997, compared with 42 percent of white renters. Among homeowners, 39 percent of Latinos, 36 percent of Blacks and 25 percent of Asians were shelter-poor compared with 21 percent of white households.

Notice that the differences in the rates of shelter poverty by race/ethnicity are somewhat smaller, controlling for tenure, because of differences in the proportions who are renters and homeowners. That is, households headed by a person of color are more likely to be renters, and renters have higher rates of shelter poverty. Over 57 percent of Latino households, 54 percent of Black households and 49 percent of Asian households were renters in 1997 compared with just 28 percent of white households. In addition, Black, Latino and Asian households are a steadily increasing proportion of all renter households of three persons or more and an even greater share of those who are shelter-poor.

Certainly, one of the major factors accounting for differential rates of homeownership between households headed by a person of color and by a white person are differences in income. But within tenures, are the higher rates of shelter poverty among households headed by a person of color due to lower average incomes and larger average household size, or are they perhaps also due to households of color paying more for housing? Analyses of shelter poverty among Blacks and Latinos (Stone 1993:52–53) and Asians (Stone 1996:10–12) demonstrate that, controlling for income and household size, differences in the rates of shelter poverty by race/ethnicity are not statistically significant for both renters and homeowners (and the same holds true for the conventional affordability standard). That is, a household of a given tenure, income and household size that is headed by a person of color is not more likely to be shelter-poor than is a white-headed household of the same tenure, income and household size.

However, the fact that Latinos, Blacks and Asians of a given tenure, income and household size pay, on average, comparable amounts for housing as do whites of the same characteristics does not mean that they obtain housing of comparable quality. Analyses of rates of physical problems by race/ethnicity, controlling for income, among Blacks, Latinos and Asians, reveal that race/ethnicity is a highly significant factor in determining the quality of housing occupied by a household of a given income or paying a given amount. They further reveal that the situation is worse for Blacks than Latinos and worse for Latinos than Asians; Blacks continue to be most victimized by racism in the housing market (Stone 1993:52–53; Stone 1996:10–12; see also Chapter 3). Combining this with the analysis of affordability demonstrates that there is not direct but instead indirect price discrimination against households of color: Although households headed by people of color are not more likely than white households of the same tenure, income and size to be shelter-poor, the former often get poorer quality housing for their money. This means that even though elimination of housing discrimination would, all else being equal, have little direct impact on shelter poverty among households of color, it would at least increase their chance of obtaining decent housing.

Worse for Households Headed by Women

Households headed by women comprised 38 percent of all households in 1997. Yet they accounted for 47 percent of all shelter-poor households and 48 percent of households paying more than 30 percent of income. Nearly 39 percent of all households headed by a woman were shelter-poor compared with a little over 31 percent of all households.

Among renters, 8.4 million female-headed households were shelter-poor in 1997—a little over 50 percent, compared with under 47 percent of all renters. Among homeowners, 6.2 million household headed by women were shelter-poor—30 percent—compared with slightly more than 23 percent of all homeowners. As with households headed by a person of color, the differences are smaller within tenure categories because households headed by women are more likely to be renters—44 percent of female-headed households are renters versus 34 percent of all households.

However, unlike households headed by a person of color, the differences in shelter poverty rates for female-headed households in comparison with other renters are explained entirely by differences in average incomes, not at all by household size differences. Despite the fact that there is no difference in median size, the median income of female-headed renter households was $17,000 in 1997 compared with $21,000 for all renters. Indeed, for every category of household size, households headed by women are poorer than other renters. Looking at shelter poverty by household size, female-headed households have shelter poverty rates 3 to 6 percentage points higher than for all renters of the same size, except for two-person renters, for whom the rates are comparable. Of those who are shelter-poor, the median income of female-headed households was just $8,900 in 1997 versus $9,600 for all shelter-poor renters. Among one- and two-person shelter-poor households, the income differences are small, but among all larger household sizes, shelter-poor female-headed households have median incomes about $2,000 lower than that of all shelter-poor renters of the same size.

Household size does matter for female-headed homeowners. Among homeowners, households headed by women are smaller on average than all households (1.8 vs. 2.4 persons). Fewer than two-thirds of all homeowners who live alone are women; yet more than three-fourths of shelter-poor homeowners who live alone are women; 27 percent of female homeowners who live alone are shelter-poor, nearly twice the 14 percent of male homeowners living alone. Indeed, women living alone are the modal type of female homeowner household: Approximately 40 percent of all female-headed homeowner households and almost 36 percent of those shelter-poor consist of a woman living alone.

Nonetheless, the majority of homeowner households headed by a woman have more than one person. The difference between female-headed and other household types is the smallest among two-person homeowner households (about 5 percentage points). Among larger households, by contrast, the differences are enormous: Female-headed homeowner households containing three or more persons have shelter poverty rates that are more than 10 percentage points higher than for other household types. Furthermore, these 2.5 million larger shelter-poor households account for about 40 percent of shelter poverty among female homeowners, and they account for nearly one-third of all shelter poverty among all homeowner households with three persons or more. This group of households is comprised mostly of women with children who are suffering financially as they try to support their families and avoid foreclosure. (See Chapter 14 for further discussion of the housing experiences of households headed by women and appropriate policies and strategies.)

Wide Inequality among Elderly Households

There were about 21 million households headed by a person at least 65 years of age in 1997. Of these, nearly 6.5 million, or 31 percent, were shelter-poor—just about the same percentage of all households who are shelter-poor. Seniors do, however, have a higher rate of homeownership (79 percent in 1997) than do younger households (62 percent). So when disaggregated by tenure, elderly households are slightly more likely to be shelter-poor than are younger households.

Far more significant, though, for understanding shelter poverty among seniors is the much smaller average size of elderly households. One-person seniors—most of whom are women—have about twice the rate of shelter poverty as do younger people living alone:

49 percent of senior renters are shelter-poor versus 25 percent of nonseniors; 30 percent of elderly homeowners are shelter-poor versus 15 percent of nonelderly households. Two-or-more person senior households—most of whom are married couples—show far less difference in their likelihood of being shelter-poor: indeed, among renters, 45 percent of the elderly and 45 percent of the nonelderly are shelter-poor; among homeowners, 24 percent of the elderly are shelter-poor versus 16 percent of the nonelderly.

These differences by household size are suggestive of the wide inequality among elderly households. There is one group with incomes of under $15,000, most of whom are shelter-poor: It includes the great majority of one-person renters (75 percent) and homeowners (60 percent); this group also includes a little under one-half of married-couple renters and about a one-fourth of married-couple homeowners. The other, relatively high-income group of seniors consists mostly of married-couple households: Among renters, about one-fourth of elderly households with two or more persons have incomes of $30,000 or more; among homeowners, close to one-half of elderly households of two or more persons have incomes of $30,000 or more. (See Chapter 13 for further discussion of the housing challenges of the elderly and policies for addressing them.)

The Housing Affordability Gap

In 2001, shelter-poor households faced a gap of about $450 a month, on average, between what they were paying for housing and what they could afford. By contrast, the average affordability gap was about $345 a month if one uses the 30-percent-of-income standard of affordability. Among renters, the shelter poverty affordability deficit averaged about $460 a month (about $5,500 a year), ranging from $370 a month for one-person households up to $530 for those of five-plus persons. The average affordability gap for shelter-poor homeowners was about $450 a month (nearly $5,400 a year), ranging from $390 a month for one-person households up to $800 for households of six-plus persons.[13]

Of course, these figures in no way measure the physical adequacy of the homes that shelter-poor families occupy or the quality of their residential environments. Some may be housed quite well but are financially squeezed; others are housed quite poorly but would have a considerably larger affordability gap if they were to obtain better housing in the private market. In addition, this figure does not include the tangible and intangible costs of homelessness.

The sum of the affordability gaps for all shelter-poor households is the national affordability deficit. In 2001, it was about $170 billion when using the shelter poverty standard and about $140 billion when using the 30-percent standard. By way of comparison, at the end of the 1980s economic boom, in 1989, the national shelter poverty affordability deficit was about $95 billion—$136 billion if measured in 2001 dollars. That is, over the 12 years from 1989 through 2001, the national housing affordability deficit grew 25 percent when measured in constant (inflation-adjusted) dollars.

While the national affordability deficit is staggering in terms of its economic and policy implications, it is less than 2 percent of the gross domestic product (GDP) of the United States, less than 10 percent of total federal budget outlays, less than three-fifths of military spending and less than one-half of Social Security outlays (U.S. Census Bureau 2001:Table 463).

CONCLUSION

This nation has a long history of ambivalence at best toward the poor. Periods such as the beginning of the 20th century, the 1930s and the 1960s, during which there was fairly widespread support for some efforts toward reducing inequality and assuring a minimum adequate standard of living, have been followed by periods of retreat from such concern. Each era of reform has, of course, not only been in response to incontrovertible human needs, but in response to political insurgency by those in need, with support of those in sympathy. The policies and programs adopted have provided a measure of relief for systemic economic and political stresses as well

as real benefits for some people in need. Yet at best the programs have been partial and piecemeal, and at worst stigmatizing and demeaning in practice if not in design.

If one were to believe in simple historical cycles, he or she might have predicted that the 1990s would have been a time of slowing and even of reversing some of the widening inequality that began in the early 1970s. However, the 1990s turned out to be a harsh extension of the 1980s' war on the poor. The suffering and the injustice are real and ultimately will be overcome only through broad and sustained political action. Nonetheless, we need to uncover, understand and publicize the nature and extent of this injustice and suffering if there is ever to be the moral and political strength for truly responsible reform and institutional change.

The now-platitudinous National Housing Goal of "the realization as soon as feasible of a decent home and a suitable living environment for every American family" makes no mention of affordability. Since these words were enshrined in the 1949 Housing Act, most of the U.S. population has come to occupy what would be called "a decent home," but the ability to afford a decent home has become more elusive. In recent decades, a considerable amount of effort and an even greater amount of rhetoric have been expended in pursuit of affordability for the promised "decent home" and "suitable living environment." The dilemma is that prevailing private practices and public policies have not only failed to bring about its realization, they have widened the gap between hope and reality even while ostensibly addressing the problem. Public action and social responsibility must move beyond the hollow promise of past policy to the establishment of a legally enforceable and publicly secured *right* to "a decent home and a suitable living environment."

Yet the persistence and scope of shelter poverty—one-third of the nation—and the magnitude of the housing affordability gap—$170 billion a year—reveal not only this society's failure to meet the housing needs of so many but also the folly of imagining that a Right to Housing for all could be realized if only there were more subsidies, additional construction and a bit of tinkering with the existing housing system. For if this society were to declare a Right to Housing, and were to interpret that right primarily to mean the right not to be shelter-poor, pouring $170 billion a year into the private housing market would not eliminate shelter poverty. Much, if not most, of the funds would be swallowed up by higher prices and higher profits. Dimensions of affordability not captured by the $170 billion affordability gap—such as elimination of homelessness—would also add to the price tag. Many households would opt to move to more satisfactory homes and communities that cost more than their current places of residence. The total claim on public resources would spiral upward, raising legitimate issues about the efficiency and cost-effectiveness of such an approach.

More realistically, recognition of the scope and persistence of shelter poverty, who is disproportionately afflicted by shelter poverty and the magnitude of the affordability gap should compel us to confront the roots of this problem in widening inequality of income, high and rising housing costs generated by the prevailing institutions of housing ownership and finance, and perverse public policies. Neither more nor less government tinkering can solve a problem that is rooted in the very structure of the housing and labor markets and the inextricable weaving of private profit and power with public policy. The resolution of this dilemma lies in a transformation of both the role of government and the mechanisms of housing provision. Rather than idealizing the market and providing endless subsidies and bailouts to private capital, public policy must transcend the limits of the market and truly serve social purposes. The chapters in the second half of this book suggest some of the ways in which this can happen.

NOTES

1. The 32 million shelter-poor households contained about 90 million people actually residing in housing units. This number does not include the literally homeless.

2. The term "moderate income" is one for which there is no longer a precise definition for national policy in the United States, although some state governments do have explicit definitions. But "low income," "very low income," and "extremely low income" are defined by federal statutes and regulations. Each year, the U.S. Department of Housing and Urban Development (HUD) publishes the income limits for each of these categories, adjusted for household size, for every geographical area of the United States. See Stone 1994, for a critique.

3. For extensive discussion of debates about affordability concepts in the United States from the late 1960s to early 1990s and in the UK since about 1990, see Stone 2003.

4. The two quoted statements have appeared in the public record in Britain (UK Parliament 2002), but similar statements are not unusual in the United States. The authors of these quotations shall nonetheless remain anonymous to avoid any embarrassment to them. While the authors might claim that I have taken their statements out of context, the contexts from which they have been taken do not dispel the essentially tautologic character of the statements.

5. The shelter poverty concept was formulated in the early 1970s and first appeared in print a few years later (Stone 1975). Ways in which it could be adapted for use in housing subsidy formulas first received attention in Stone (1983), and the most extensive discussion of the methodology and its implications may be found in Stone (1993). See Hancock (1993) for an independent, theoretically grounded formulation of the residual income logic of affordability.

6. Household size is the most decisive element of household composition in distinguishing affordability. Other elements, particularly ages and relationships, are also significant, though somewhat less so than household size. The shelter poverty scale presented in this chapter has been derived for nonelderly married-couple households, nonelderly single-adult households and elderly households in order to take into account elements other than just household size.

7. See Stone (1993), Appendix A, for details. See Stone (2003) for a detailed discussion of the derivation of a shelter poverty scale for the United Kingdom.

8. The extent and distribution of shelter poverty and conventionally defined affordability burdens have been computed from American Housing Survey data for every year from 1975 through 2001 and from decennial census data for 1970. See Stone (1993:Appendix B) for discussion of methods used to analyze these data.

9. The population base for determining the percentage of people who are shelter-poor is the population in households—-that is, the population occupying housing units. By definition, this excludes the population living in group quarters (such as penal and custodial institutions, nursing homes, boarding houses, military barracks, college dormitories,

fraternity and sorority houses, monasteries, convents and ships) as well as the homeless.

10. The mid-1980s decline in shelter poverty was not, however, merely a consequence of the recovery from the recession of the early 1980s. Another significant factor was the dramatic decrease during the mid-1980s in the total number of homeowners with incomes under $20,000 and hence in the number shelter-poor. This was an ironic way for shelter poverty to decrease because it was really a result of worsening affordability for many people. For example, in some cases, adult children moved back in with their parents because they could not afford to live on their own but in the process somewhat increased the household income. In other cases, foreclosures and forced sales in the face of job losses or other income problems led to former homeowners moving in with others or into apartments costing less than what they had paid as homeowners.

11. The reason for higher incidence among persons than households is that larger households are more likely to be shelter-poor than smaller ones. Obviously, the larger the household, the greater the number of people it houses in shelter poverty.

12. As of this writing (mid-2004), it has not yet been possible to update detailed analyses of shelter poverty by race/ethnicity, gender and age. Therefore, the results presented in the following three sections are for 1997.

13. Unfortunately, the American Housing Survey does not identify Native Americans, and even if it did, the subsample would be too small to draw statistically valid conclusions. Even the Asian/Pacific Islander subsample is quite small, meaning that sampling errors are quite large for the figures given for Asians. (See Stone 1996 for further discussion of this issue.)

14. The average affordability gap is so similar for renters and homeowners, yet the range is so much greater for homeowners by household size, because one-half of all shelter-poor households among both renters and homeowners have only one or two persons, while those with five persons or more account for just 14 percent of those shelter-poor among both renters and homeowners. Large homeowner households have large affordability gaps because of the burden of mortgage payments, yet the average gap for all homeowners is primarily a reflection of the situations of small, older homeowners with low housing costs but low incomes.

REFERENCES

Bernstein, Jared, Chaina Brocht and Maggie Spade Aguilar. 2000. *How much is enough: Basic family budgets for working families.* Washington, DC: Economic Policy Institute.

Bradshaw, Jonathan, ed. 1993. *Budget standards for the United Kingdom.* Aldershot: Avebury/Ashgate.

Bradshaw, Jonathan, Deborah Mitchell and Jane Morgan. 1987. Evaluating adequacy: The potential of budget standards. *Journal of Social Policy* 16:2, 165–181.

Budding, David W. 1980. *Housing deprivation among enrollees in the housing allowance demand experiment.* Cambridge, MA: Abt Associates.

Chaplin, Russell, Simon Martin, Jin Hong Yang and Christine Whitehead. 1994. *Affordability: Definitions, measures and implications for lenders.* Cambridge, UK: Department of Land Economy, University of Cambridge.

Citro, Constance, and Robert Michael, eds. 1995. *Measuring poverty: A new approach.* Washington, DC: National Academy Press.

Doc4Kids. 1998. *Not safe at home: How America's housing crisis threatens the health of its children.* Boston: The Doc4Kids Project, Boston Medical Center and Children's Hospital. http://www. boston-childhealth.org/research/Research/Doc4Kids/docs4kids_report.pdf.

Feins, Judith, and Terry Saunders Lane. 1981. *How much for housing?* Cambridge, MA: Abt Associates.

Hancock, Karen E. 1993. Can't pay? Won't pay? The economic principles of affordability. *Urban Studies* 30:1, 127–145.

Kearns, Ade. 1992. Affordability of housing association tenants. *Journal of Social Policy* 21:4, 523–547.

Kempson, Elaine. 1993. *Household budgets and housing costs.* London: Policy Studies Institute.

Linneman, Peter D., and Isaac F. Megbolugbe. 1992. Housing affordability: Myth or reality. *Urban Studies* 28:3/4, 369–392.

London Research Centre. 1996. *Getting the measure of affordability.* London, UK: London Research Centre.

Pannell, Bob, and Peter Williams. 1994. House prices and affordability. *Housing Finance* (UK) No. 23, August.

Pedone, Carla. 1988. *Current housing problems and possible federal responses.* Washington, DC: Congressional Budget Office.

Ruggles, Patricia. 1990. *Drawing the line: Alternative poverty measures and their implications for public policy.* Washington, DC: Urban Institute.

Stone, Michael E. 1975. The housing crisis, mortgage lending, and class struggle. *Antipode* 7:2, 22–37. Reprinted in *Radical geography*, ed. Richard Peet, 1978:144–179. Chicago and London: Maaroufa Press.

———. 1983. Housing and the economic crisis: An analysis and emergency program. In *America's housing crisis: What is to be done?*, ed. Chester Hartman, 99–150. Boston and London: Routledge and Kegan Paul.

———. 1993. *Shelter poverty: New ideas on housing affordability.* Philadelphia: Temple University Press.

———. 1994. Comment on Kathryn P. Nelson, "Whose shortage of affordable housing?" *Housing Policy Debate,* 5:4, 443–458.

———. 1996. *Shelter poverty among Asian-Americans.* Boston: Institute for Asian-American Studies, University of Massachusetts.

———. 2003. *Shelter poverty and social housing in the UK and US.* London, UK: The Foreign and Commonwealth Office, Atlantic Fellowships in Public Policy.

The United Kingdom Parliament. Select Committee on Transport, Local Government and the Regions. 2002. Affordable housing in the UK. Memoranda submitted in testimony. http://www.publications.parliament.uk/pa/cm200102/cmselect/cmtlgr/809/809m01.htm.

U.S. Census Bureau. 2001. *Statistical abstract of the United States, 1999.* Washington, DC: U.S. Government Printing Office. http://www.census.gov/prod/2002pubs/01statab/fedgov.pdf.

Wilcox, Steve. 1999. *The vexed question of affordability.* Edinburgh, UK: Scottish Homes.

Yip, Ngai Ming. 1995. *Housing affordability in England.* D.Phil. Thesis. York, UK: Department of Social Policy and Social Work, University of York.

Nancy A. Denton

3   Segregation and Discrimination in Housing

OVER A HALF-CENTURY has passed since the 1949 Congress promulgated the National Housing Goal: "The implementation as soon as feasible of a decent home and a suitable living environment for every American family." More recently, Chester Hartman has renewed the argument for a Right to Housing that "would include affordability, physical quality of the unit, and the social and physical characteristics of the neighborhood environment" (Hartman 1998:237; see also Chapter 8). While the overall quality of housing has improved greatly in the last 50 years, many lower-income people are faced with the shortage of low-cost units and the problematic conditions of the neighborhoods where they are located. Even critics of the concept of "housing as a right" concede that there remain substantial numbers of U.S. residents for whom "a decent home and a suitable living environment" is not a reality (Salins 1998). At low-income levels, particularly for people of color, it cannot be assumed that "a decent home" will automatically imply "a suitable living environment" because of the long history of residential segregation and discrimination in the housing market (Massey and Denton 1993).

Housing segregation and discrimination define and determine much of what happens in neighborhood housing markets as well as what happens to neighborhood residents. Dramatic differences in homeownership by race and ethnicity persist in the United States despite the fact that the overall level of homeownership, over 66 percent, is at an all-time high. (U.S. Bureau of the Census 2000). In 2000, 72.4 percent of non-Hispanic whites compared with 46.3 percent

of blacks and 45.7 percent of Hispanics owned their own homes, as did 53.4 percent of Asians, 55.5 percent of Native Americans, 45.0 percent of Native Hawaiians and Other Pacific Islanders, and 46.3 percent of those who identified with more than one race.[1] By 2002, homeownership was almost at 68 percent, and both whites and blacks had seen their ownership rates increase by 2 percent (JCHS 2003). Since people who do not own homes must rent them, these figures indicate that people of color are more likely to be renters, and affordability and poor quality issues are a severe problem for renters (NLIHC 2003).

These well-documented differentials in housing affordability and homeownership (cf. Bratt et al. 1986; Denton 2001; Hughes 1991, 1996; Stone 1993b) are linked to underlying patterns of housing segregation and discrimination via neighborhoods. Neighborhoods determine school quality, job opportunities, safety, exposure to crime and asset accumulation, among a host of other things (Denton 2001; Jargowsky 1994, 1997; Massey and Denton 1993; Wilson 1987, 1996). That the location of a house is as important as its characteristics and condition has long been a real estate broker's axiom. That individuals' opportunities for success are at least in part a function of the kind of neighborhood in which they live (and by implication the opportunities found there) has long been a common-sense notion referred to when people give their reasons for moving.

However, when discussing the poor, particularly racial and ethnic minority poor, popular discussions focus on their personal characteristics and see neighborhood conditions solely as the *results* of individual behavior, ignoring the role that these neighborhood locations may have played in *causing* a group's economic and social status. Particularly for those who are "shelter-poor," Stone's term for those who cannot afford both housing and other necessities of life (Stone 1993b and Chapter 2), the patterns of housing segregation and discrimination result in limited opportunities for personal advancement. Focusing on the *individual* characteristics of the poor rather than the *structural* effects of segregation and discrimination too often enables politicians and the public to assume that little can or should be done. This reversal of the causal logic has dramatic implications for housing policy and for activists concerned about housing for the poor. People confined to segregated neighborhoods have been denied the opportunities to amass resources, via housing appreciation, that would have helped them get ahead. Segregation has persisted for so long that not only does it hamper the efforts of those working in segregated communities for which it is hard to acquire resources, it is too often accepted by people of color who use it as a basis for building support for community-based housing programs (Stone 1993b:299). In short, issues of housing affordability and a Right to Housing are inextricably tied to questions of housing discrimination and segregation because patterns of segregation and discrimination in housing have led to the race/ethnic differentials in people's access to high-quality housing.

This chapter expands upon these preliminary points in a number of ways. First, for the three largest minority groups, African-Americans, Asians and Hispanics, it provides an overview of contemporary patterns of residential segregation from non-Hispanic whites by comparing segregation by race with segregation based on other characteristics and across groups to explain the uniquely high levels of African-American segregation. Second, it reviews the current state of discrimination in the housing market. Most of the discussion in this section looks at African- Americans and Hispanics, since Asians were not included in the last national study of discrimination. Third, both the causes and consequences of racial segregation and discrimination are examined, relating

them to attitudes toward interracial contact and exploring the linkages between neighborhoods and individual outcomes in terms of housing, family, education, work and politics. African-Americans are most often used as the example in this section because they are the group most often identified with the problems associated with concentrated poverty. Fourth, the contemporary dynamics of neighborhood racial change are discussed, focusing on the decline in all-white neighborhoods and the increase in multiethnic neighborhoods containing blacks, Hispanics and Asians in addition to whites. These neighborhood changes provide for some optimism, since they decrease the number of all-white places to which whites may flee. At the same time, they allow many whites to feel that housing segregation and discrimination are no longer problems, a more pessimistic implication. Finally, my implications from these analyses are drawn as they relate to future housing research and policy aimed at making a Right to Housing and Congress' 1949 promulgation realities.

PATTERNS OF RESIDENTIAL SEGREGATION

Residential segregation by race in U.S. metropolitan areas and cities is high, has been high in the past and shows little sign of quickly abating in the future, particularly for African-Americans (Harrison and Bennett 1995; Lewis Mumford Center 2001a; Massey and Denton 1993; Farley and Frey 1994; Frey and Farley 1996; Taeuber and Taeuber 1965; Lieberson 1980). While such a sweeping generalization obviously is subject to many specific qualifications, discussed below, the truth of this statement demands emphasis. Our collective refusal to acknowledge segregation as a serious problem, to talk about it and to seek strategies to combat it poses a challenge to anyone concerned with the future of our nation, our cities and our citizens. To talk about housing policy and the housing market without considering how past and present segregative practices have structured them is particularly misleading. We combine our myopia regarding segregation with a tendency to view it as somehow normal, as part of the growth of cities, the result of free choice, an experience that all groups have passed through as they blended into the melting pot of American life. Unfortunately, none of these statements is true, and they are best regarded as excuses or rationalizations for the current situation and the current unmet housing needs of the poor (Denton 1996).

RESIDENTIAL SEGREGATION BY RACE IN 2000

To begin to appreciate patterns of residential segregation in U.S. metropolitan areas, it is necessary to understand the measurement of segregation. Table 3.1 presents the 2000 segregation

TABLE 3.1 Dissimilarity Index of Segregation Indices for Selected Metropolitan Areas, 2000

Metropolitan area	Non-Hispanic whites versus		
	Blacks	Hispanics	Asians
Northern areas			
Boston	65.8	58.7	44.8
Chicago	79.7	61.1	42.4
Cleveland	76.8	57.7	37.8
Detroit	84.6	45.6	45.6
Los Angeles–Long Beach	66.4	63.1	47.7
New York	81.0	66.7	50.5
Newark	80.1	65.0	35.5
Oakland	61.8	46.9	40.5
Philadelphia	72.0	60.1	43.6
Riverside	44.9	42.5	36.0
St. Louis	73.1	27.3	42.5
San Francisco	60.0	53.5	48.4
SanJose	39.9	51.3	52.5
Southern areas			
Atlanta	64.5	51.1	45.2
Baltimore	67.5	35.8	38.9
Charlotte	55.2	50.4	43.3
Dallas	58.7	53.7	45.0
Ft. Lauderdale	60.8	31.0	28.2
Houston	66.3	55.1	48.4
Memphis	68.7	47.9	37.7
Miami	69.4	43.9	31.3
New Orleans	68.4	35.8	48.0
Norfolk–Va. Beach	46.0	31.5	33.9
Washington, DC	62.5	48.0	38.2

Sources: The dissimilarity index values come from Iceland, Weinberg and Steinmetz 2002. Since that report did not provide them for all metro areas, the missing numbers were filled in from the Lewis H. Mumford Center, http://mumford1.dyndns.org/cen2000/data.html.

indices for African-Americans, Hispanics and Asians in selected metropolitan areas with the largest black populations as well as those with the most Asians and Hispanics. For each group, their segregation from non-Hispanic whites is measured. The groups are defined to be mutually exclusive: Thus, black Hispanics are counted as Hispanics, not as blacks.[2] To calculate the segregation index shown, racial data for all the census tracts in a metropolitan area are used. Census tracts are small, nonoverlapping geographic units, about 5,000 people in size, that completely cover the metropolitan area and therefore can be thought of as neighborhoods (U.S. Bureau of the Census 1991). The index in Table 3.1 is the index of dissimilarity,[3] which varies between 0 and 100 and can be interpreted as the percent of either group that would have to change neighborhoods in order to be evenly distributed across the neighborhoods in a metropolitan area. Thus, in a metro area that is 20 percent black, each neighborhood would be 20 percent black in an even distribution, and the index of dissimilarity would be 0. Though a perfectly even distribution is seldom found, nor would it necessarily be desirable given the wide variety of individual housing and neighborhood preferences, highly uneven distributions, particularly by race, have been shown to result from social structural constraints on movement (Massey and Denton 1993). Values below 30 are considered low, those between 30 and 60 moderate and above 60 high.

A number of points are clear from an examination of the data in Table 3.1. First, in every metropolitan area with the exception of Riverside and San Jose (areas included because of their large Hispanic and Asian populations), the *level* of residential segregation of African-Americans is substantially higher than that of Hispanics or Asians. For example, in the New York metropolitan area, African-American segregation is 81.0, Hispanic segregation is 66.7 and Asian segregation is 50.5, so blacks are about 20 percent more segregated than Hispanics and 60 percent more segregated than Asians. Second, *all* of the segregation scores in the column for African-Americans in metro areas in the North (again with the exception of Riverside and San Jose) and eight of the eleven in the South are at or above the cutoff of 60, indicating high segregation. Among Hispanics, only five are that high, and none is that high for Asians. In fact, one of the Hispanic scores and one of the Asian scores is below 30, indicating low segregation. It is clear that the three major race/ethnic groups experience different patterns of residential segregation in these metropolitan areas. Finally, the table shows a difference between patterns of segregation in northern areas and southern areas, with the latter likely to have lower segregation, particularly for blacks. Segregation is also lower in metro areas in the West. This regional pattern is a long-standing phenomenon that reflects the age of the metropolitan area, the way the city grew, the force of industrialization and the pattern of southern living, where large boulevards were backed by smaller alleyways where servants lived (Massey and Denton 1993:41).

Having established the basic segregation patterns for 2000, the most recent year for which segregation indices can be computed,[4] we turn now to an examination of past changes in segregation in order to form an opinion of the current situation and the potential for future change. We would expect that, especially in the years since the Civil Rights Movement, the segregation of African-Americans would have declined. To the extent that the movement affected all persons of color, then it would be expected that segregation for Hispanics and Asians would have declined as well. (This is less easy to predict, however, given the large number of immigrants since the 1965 change in the immigration preferences and quotas [Edmonston and Passell 1994] and the practical advantages of living near members of one's own group when one first arrives in a foreign country.) Unfortunately, these expectations are not borne out by the research.

All analyses of the trends in segregation since 1970 agree that the declines in segregation for African Americans have been modest, at best, confined to areas outside the Northeast and Midwest, and to areas with relatively small black populations (Iceland, Weinberg and Steinmetz 2002; Lewis Mumford Center 2001a; Massey and Denton 1993; Farley and Frey 1994; Harrison and Bennett 1995). For Hispanics and Asians, segregation basically remained the same from 1970 to 1980, increased somewhat from 1980 to 1990 and increased again between 1990 and 2000, reflecting the continued population growth of those groups (Farley and Frey 1994; Frey and Farley 1996; Iceland, Weinberg and Steinmetz 2002). Analyses completed in 1980 and 2000 show that, while there is substantial within-group variation in segregation among Hispanics and Asians, the foreign-born are more segregated than the native-born, and all groups are more segregated in center cities than in suburbs. Thus, the conclusions reached above remain the same. (See Massey and Denton 1993:67–74, 84–88, 112–113 for a summary and references to the 1980 studies; see Logan 2003 for similar information about 2000.)

To put segregation by race/ethnicity into context, we need to know how groups are segregated by other characteristics. Examining segregation by income in 1990, Abramson, Tobin and VanderGoot (1995) report that in the 100 largest metropolitan areas, the average level of dissimilarity for the poor from the nonpoor is 36.1, a moderate level of segregation. Segregation is at a similar average level for high school dropouts versus non—high school dropouts, welfare recipients versus nonwelfare recipients and people with limited English proficiency versus proficient English speakers. Female-headed families versus non–female-headed families and foreign-born versus native-born dissimilarity indices are around 30, while the index for blue-collar workers versus non–blue-collar workers and the unemployed versus the employed is about 20 (Abramson, Tobin and VanderGoot 1995:53; White 1987:113). It is clear from the low values of these indices that the degree of segregation by race/ethnicity is unique in the U.S. urban landscape.

Segregation research shows two trends in urban areas: First, there is a tendency toward convergence as black segregation declined in all metro areas between 1980 and 2000, while it increased slightly for Latinos and somewhat more for Asians (Iceland, Weinberg and Steinmetz 2002). Second, the decreases in the segregation of African-Americans are small, and though the pace of change is often called slow,[5] these small changes are cumulating over time. Analyses done by the Lewis Mumford Center for Comparative Urban and Regional Research at SUNY Albany show that "at this pace it may take forty more years for black-white segregation to come down even to the current level of Hispanic-white segregation" (Lewis Mumford Center 2001a:1). Though this is a decided improvement over the 77 years that Massey and Denton reported it would take for those in the northern areas to fall below 60 (1993:221–223), the average is undoubtedly pulled down by the inclusion of the southern areas, which have lower segregation indices in general. While the segregation of Latinos and Asians tends to be much lower, the direction of change is currently upward and thus in need of monitoring to determine whether it is the result of immigration pressure or true increasing segregation of these groups.

Hypersegregation

Thus far, we have been using the index of dissimilarity as the measure of segregation. It provides a conceptually simple way to think about residential segregation, namely how "evenly" the population is distributed across the neighborhoods in a metropolitan area, with higher values indicating less "evenness" (really greater "unevenness" or more segregation) in the distribution of people across neighborhoods. In reality, however, the phenomenon of segregation is more complex. To capture this complexity, we can think

of five separate dimensions of segregation, of which *evenness* is the first. In addition to evenness, one can measure segregation as a group's *isolation* within neighborhoods, a group's *concentration* into densely packed neighborhoods, *centralization* of a group's neighborhoods near the downtown of a metropolitan area and the *clustering* of a group's neighborhoods into a large, contiguous ghetto (Massey and Denton 1993:74–78). The pattern of high segregation for African-Americans is unique because it persists when segregation is measured in these more complex ways. In areas where blacks are highly segregated on four or all five of these dimensions of segregation, the ensuing pattern is called "hypersegregation." Prior to 2000, this condition was found only for African Americans in certain metro areas (Denton 1994; Massey and Denton 1993), a condition that persists in 2000. However, in 2000, Hispanics are hypersegregated in Los Angeles and New York, though Asians are not hypersegregated in any metro area.

Table 3.2 shows the metro areas that can be classified as hypersegregated in 2000 and gives the score for each of the five dimensions of segregation. In accordance with the criteria for determining hypersegregation, all five or at least four of the five indices are above 60 for each of these areas. All of these metropolitan areas were

TABLE 3.2 Hypersegregated* Metropolitan Areas in 2000

Metro area	Evenness	Isolation	Concentration	Centralization	Clustering
Hypersegregated for blacks					
Atlanta	64.5	66.7	69.9	71.7	42.0
Baltimore	67.5	68.0	81.1	81.9	52.2
Chicago	79.7	77.6	84.4	66.3	73.4
Cleveland	76.8	72.1	87.4	85.6	66.0
Detroit	84.6	81.3	86.5	84.8	82.1
Houston	66.3	64.9	77.5	78.4	38.2
Los Angeles	66.4	65.2	78.7	72.1	55.8
Miami	69.4	78.2	83.1	67.7	43.5
Milwaukee	81.8	72.0	89.3	86.4	65.2
New Orleans	68.4	73.8	83.3	84.7	40.2
New York	81.0	82.7	83.4	76.5	46.9
Newark	80.1	78.1	88.6	63.9	81.4
Philadelphia	72.0	68.7	81.6	80.7	67.0
St. Louis	73.1	66.0	88.1	88.5	45.8
DC	62.5	65.4	77.9	72.4	45.7
Hypersegregated for Hispanics					
Los Angeles	63.1	78.1	77.0	71.8	35.0
New York	66.7	70.8	79.3	81.2	34.7

Source: Iceland, Weinberg and Steinmetz 2002.

*Hypersegregation is defined as a score greater than 60 on four or five of the dimensions of segregation.

also hypersegregated in 1990,[6] and though their segregation in general declined between 1990 and 2000 on all dimensions, many of the declines were modest. Blacks in Miami and New Orleans experienced slight increases in evenness and isolation; those in Atlanta, New York and Washington, DC, saw increases in isolation as well; while the black population of Houston, New Orleans, New York, Newark, and St. Louis experienced increases in clustering. This pattern implies that while African Americans were able to move to a larger number of neighborhoods, possibly more suburban ones, there is little evidence of dismantling of the ghetto. The fact that two metro areas now show patterns of hypersegregation for Hispanics is an ominous sign.

The meaning of hypersegregation comes from the combination of high scores for each dimension of segregation. Hypersegregation means living in large, contiguous, densely inhabited neighborhoods packed tightly around the urban core, with almost no residential contact with non–African-Americans within the neighborhoods themselves or in nearby neighborhoods—implying little personal contact with the larger world of U.S. society. "Ironically, within a large, diverse and highly mobile postindustrial society such as the United States, blacks living in the heart of the ghetto are among the most isolated people on earth" (Massey and Denton 1993:77).

Measures of segregation and hypersegregation tell us much about where people are but nothing about the process of how they got there. The next section considers contemporary patterns of discrimination in the housing market that help maintain these segregated patterns over time.

CURRENT PATTERNS OF HOUSING MARKET DISCRIMINATION

Discrimination in the sale and rental of housing in the United States was once complete, accepted and must have been close to 100 percent. A white person only needs to ask older relatives or do the slightest amount of archival research to find that it was once considered per-

fectly acceptable to tell someone that you did not rent or sell to blacks. In 1933, the federally created Home Owners' Loan Corporation (HOLC) created maps that coded areas as creditworthy based on the race of their occupants and the age of the housing stock. These maps, adopted in 1934 by the Federal Housing Administration (FHA), established redlining, preventing residents in black neighborhoods from obtaining long-term mortgages for their homes. Used together with restrictive covenants, violence and blockbusting, they served to finalize the construction of the ghetto (Jackson 1985:190–218; Squires 1992, 1994). Racial effects of these governmental policies were well summarized by Charles Abrams (1955:229–230):

A government offering such bounty [in the form of unconditionally insured mortgages] to builders and lenders could have required compliance with a nondiscrimination policy. Or the agency could at least have pursued a course of evasion, or hidden behind the screen of local autonomy. Instead, FHA adopted a racial policy that could well have been culled from the Nuremberg laws. From its inception, FHA set itself up as the protector of the all-white neighborhood. It sent its agents into the field to keep Negroes and other minorities from buying houses in white neighborhoods. It exerted pressure against builders who dared to build for minorities, and against lenders willing to lend on mortgages. This official agency not only kept Negroes in their place but pointed at Chinese, Mexicans, American Indians, and other minorities as well.

While all-black areas still exist in most of our urban areas, the official government sanction of redlining and discrimination in the housing market has been attacked in the courts and by statute. The 1948 Supreme Court decision outlawing the enforcement of racial covenants was followed by the 1968 Fair Housing Act (subsequently amended in 1988), the 1975 Home Mortgage Disclosure Act and the 1977 Community Reinvestment Act. While none of these had immediate effects, and enforcement has always been far from adequate, they did serve to move discrimination from the completely overt situation that had previously existed (Massey and Denton 1993:96–109, 195–205). Despite delays between passage and implementation of decisions and laws, and the fact that the U.S. Department of Housing and Urban Development (HUD) was as often a hindrance as a help in implementing the Fair Housing Act, overt discrimination in the housing market has decreased dramatically in the last 30 years, but subtle discrimination remains (Feins and Bratt 1983; Turner et al. 2002b). As a result, though the official and legal policies are long gone, the large black ghettos they helped to create remain, and whites still remember how quickly neighborhoods turned all-black under these policies. We could think of these as vestigial effects of these official policies that continue to exert their influence in the way housing is allocated today.

Research shows that despite having become more subtle, discrimination in the sales and rental of housing remains significant and important (Yinger 1998), and unlike segregation, discrimination is basically at the same level for blacks and Hispanics. The most recent national study of discrimination, using matched pairs of home seekers who differed only on race to inquire about housing, showed that both blacks and Hispanics experienced declines in unfavorable treatment during the 1990s, being treated unfavorably compared with whites in similar situations about 20 percent of the time on *each* visit to a realtor (Turner et al. 2002b). The exact figures for the discrimination index in rentals are 21.6 percent for blacks and 25.7 percent for Hispanics, with rates of discrimination in sales at 17.0 and 19.7 percent, respectively (Turner et al. 2002b). Compared with the Housing Discrimination Study ten years earlier, these numbers represent declines of almost 5 percentage points for black renters but no declines for Hispanic renters, and declines of 12 and 7 percentage points for black and Hispanic buyers. Discrimination against Asians, a group not covered in the earlier study, is 21.5 in rentals and 20.4 in sales (Turner and Ross 2003). Since for most people obtaining housing involves multiple visits to realtors or rental agents, even these relatively small probabilities of discrimination quickly cumulate to high probabilities of discrimination over the course of those visits. However, these national discrimination studies were not targeted to housing for the poor. Stone has shown that

lower-income blacks, Hispanics (1993b:50–54) and Asians (1996) nationally, as well as Latinos in the Boston area (1993a), experience greater difficulty in gaining access to physically adequate housing than do whites of comparable incomes. Stone's work clearly suggests that the problems of discrimination get worse at the bottom of the income distribution, something reflected in the addition of "source of income" as a protected class in the 1988 Fair Housing Amendments. It is clear that even today whites have far more opportunities in their housing search than do persons of color.

It is interesting to ask how this differential treatment arises, given the fact that the law expressly forbids it. The answer is that in the years since passage of the Fair Housing Act, housing discrimination has become extremely subtle (Feins and Bratt 1983). For the most part, housing, banking and insurance providers treat people of color politely and courteously. Discrimination occurs because whites are routinely given more information, more help or more options, all of which enable them to find housing faster. Likewise, realtors will tell minorities that rents are higher, downpayments are higher or that there are no other units available, and they are not called back as often as whites (Turner et al. 2002b; Turner and Ross 2003; Yinger 1995:33–42; Feagin and Sikes 1994:223–252; Hamilton and Cogswell 1997).

Furthermore, substantial evidence of discrimination in the mortgage and home insurance markets continues to exist (Turner et al. 2002a; Squires 1994:71–76; 1997; Yinger 1995:63–85). Banks are stricter about minority credit histories, quote higher down payments and less favorable mortgage rates as well as refuse to make loans on low-valued properties (Turner et al. 2002a; Squires 1994, 1997). The last is something that affects particularly the black poor, as their homes have not appreciated as much as those of whites, and they are twice as likely as whites to own homes valued at less than $50,000 (Squires 1997). Passage of the Home Mortgage Disclosure Act (HMDA) in 1975 and the Community Reinvestment Act (CRA) in 1977 have provided the data for measuring these forms of discrimination. The CRA in particular has been helpful in getting banks to service their entire customer base, but significant problems remain in all of these areas (Schwartz 1998; Squires 1992). Campen (1992) documents the extensive amount of effort that a community must exert in order to pressure banks into complying with the CRA, and recent reports that he has completed for the Massachusetts Community and Banking Council (Campen 2003) show that predatory lending by companies not subject to CRA has increased in Boston in recent years.

Black mortgage loan applicants are rejected at least twice as often as whites with comparable incomes (Dedman 1989; Munnell et al. 1996; Squires 1992), and a replication of the Dedman (1989) study of Atlanta a decade later showed no change (Wyly and Holloway 1999). Other research has shown that mortgage rejections for blacks and Hispanics are influenced by segregation in the mortgage industry's workforce (Kim and Squires 1998). As well, homeowner insurance, a necessary condition of mortgages, is often harder for minorities to get due to redlining, agent location and a host of other subtle discriminatory practices (Squires 1997). HUD is beginning to collect paired testing data on mortgage discrimination, and a recent HUD pilot study conducted in Chicago and Los Angeles focused on the initial stages of the process: the cost of the home, the loan amount and the loan products for which a buyer would be eligible. It found significant patterns of unequal treatment for both blacks and Hispanics as compared with whites. In some cases, minorities received no information at all because the loan officer would not deal with them until after a credit check had been made, something not required for whites. Though the differences varied across city and group, across the six topics that were studied,[7] both groups were treated significantly worse than whites on all but one topic in at least one of the two cities. For blacks, the topic on which they were treated the same as whites was "loan amount and price," while for Hispanics, it was no difference in "FHA encouragement" (Turner et al. 2002a). While the FHA can help low-income people qualify for loans, FHA loans should not be recommended for those who do not need them, as they carry higher fees.

In short, the process of seeking housing is often long and complex for everyone, particularly so for people of color and poor people in general. Obtaining rental housing often involves multiple visits to realtors or ads answered as well as credit checks and references. But this process pales in comparison to the number of steps involved in the sales of housing, which include not only dealings with realtors but also with banks, appraisers, mortgage agents and insurers. At each point in the process, there is the opportunity to discriminate, and the result of discrimination at any stage too often is denial of housing. Moreover, discrimination at the early stage, when basic mortgage information is taken (Turner et al. 2002b), can discourage minorities from continuing their housing search. Even if housing is obtained, the discrimination means that black and Hispanic households pay a "discrimination tax" that averages $4,000 every time they move (Yinger 1997).

The subtlety of discriminatory practices means that while the Fair Housing Act is primarily aimed at solving individual-level discrimination complaints (though this is less the case since the 1988 amendments), discrimination is difficult for an individual home-seeker to detect. It also means that whites do not see any examples of overt racism, and based on their own relative ease in finding housing, they are able to persist in their belief that housing discrimination is not a problem.

Whites also persist in the impression that once a few blacks enter a neighborhood, the neighborhood begins the process of rapid racial transition, an impression that is not without consequences, particularly the migration of whites out of cities (Adams et al. 1996). Whites do not see the practice of steering people to neighborhoods already containing people like them. For example, one African-American couple interviewed by Hamilton and Cogswell (1997:111) reported that they were shown at least 15 homes in primarily African-American areas, despite saying that they wanted a home in a different area that was mostly white. While overt steering is illegal, steering still occurs informally by realtors advising people that they would or would not "like" or "be comfortable in" a particular neighborhood. The latest HUD discrimination study found that although other forms of discrimination have declined, there was evidence that geographic steering was rising (Turner et al. 2002b; Turner and Ross 2003). Steering also occurs in the way that housing is advertised. Studies have shown that housing for sale or rent is less likely to be advertised if it is in integrated or minority areas (Turner and Wienk 1993:204–210; Turner et al. 2002b), but advertised units are ones that realtors are willing to show anyone (Yinger 1995:51–61). Manipulation of those units that are advertised and those that are not works to the advantage of whites and to the disadvantage of minorities. As a result, whites can be confident that they will mainly be shown housing in mainly white areas, and the opportunity to live in more integrated settings is seldom presented to them.

From even this brief overview, it is abundantly clear that discrimination is still a fundamental problem in the metropolitan housing markets of the United States. Even though discrimination has shifted from overt to covert and, as a result, is much more difficult for individual blacks to detect, its power in structuring access to housing opportunities remains.[8] We are a long way from achieving the National Housing Goal that was set by Congress over 50 years ago and also a long way from having a Right to Housing.

CAUSES AND CONSEQUENCES OF RESIDENTIAL SEGREGATION AND DISCRIMINATION

Despite the evidence presented with regard to the persistence of segregation and discrimination, contemporary rhetoric about them, from people of color as well as whites, often downplays their importance. Though sometimes these arguments raise important issues of equity or fairness—maintaining that minority neighborhoods have problems because they have been denied resources (Calmore 1993)—segregation and discrimination have consequences that go beyond mere resource needs. That these neighborhoods have been systematically denied resources of every imaginable kind is well worth noting, as is the success that many community development corporations (CDCs) have had

in improving neighborhood conditions (Brown 1996; Keyes et al. 1996; Squires 1992). But by focusing on resource denial, or neighborhood-based initiatives to reverse them, one ignores the underlying structure that initially caused the denial, namely the segregative and discriminatory processes of the real estate industry and government described earlier. Enforcement of the Fair Housing Act has long been inadequate (Massey and Denton 1993), a situation that persists to this day. A recent analysis by the Citizens' Commission on Civil Rights reveals that HUD is processing fewer complaints despite an increase in their number; compensation to victims has declined; the time it takes to resolve complaints has increased and the use of administrative law judges has declined (Relman 2002). Thus, current versions of segregation and discrimination still operate, serving to undermine the efforts and effect of resources given to poor neighborhoods.

A complete inventory of the causes of residential segregation and discrimination, and the historical documentation to back it up, is beyond the scope of this chapter but has been documented elsewhere (Farley et al. 1993; Massey and Denton 1993; Jackson 1985; Turner and Wienk 1993; Yinger 1995). While discussion and debate abound about the amount of segregation accounted for by each factor, there is considerable agreement among researchers that contemporary segregation is the result of four factors: discrimination (discussed in the preceding section), differences in suburbanization, income and attitudes.

Suburbanization is thought to be an underlying cause of segregation because of the postwar homebuilding boom in the suburbs, which benefited whites more than blacks due to discriminatory practices of the time (Jackson 1985; Massey and Denton 1993:53; Oliver and Shapiro 1995:22). Suburban areas, by virtue of being independent municipalities, have also enacted a large variety of "snob zoning" ordinances, such as minimum lot size and restrictions on multifamily or low-cost housing, which add to segregation and discrimination (Squires 1994; Schill and Wachter 1995). In 1990, the African-American population was less suburbanized than other groups (Phelan and

Schneider 1996), and with 39 percent of their group in the suburbs, compared with 58 percent of Asians, 49 percent of Hispanics and 71 percent of non-Hispanic whites, they are again the least suburbanized in 2000 (Lewis Mumford Center 2001b). In the suburbs, African-Americans tend to be in lower-income, less desirable locales (Alba and Logan 1993; Logan, Alba and Leung 1996). Since the segregation measures presented above are computed across the entire metropolitan area, if blacks are unable to move to the suburbs, they will necessarily be more segregated than other groups. Leaving aside the issue of access to the suburbs, black segregation remains high in the suburbs, albeit lower than that seen in the central cities (Lewis Mumford Center 2001b; Massey and Denton 1993:69). Hispanics and Asians are both more likely to be in suburban areas and to experience lower segregation there.

Income differences certainly account for some of the differences in segregation levels because housing in the suburbs, more often owner occupied and single family, tends to be more expensive than housing in the cities. However, in one way, discussions about how much segregation is accounted for by income differences miss the point. Certainly, there are more blacks who could afford to live in suburban areas than currently do, but in 1980, blacks at all levels of income were highly segregated, as opposed to Hispanics and Asians, whose segregation declined as their income rose (Denton and Massey 1988), a pattern that was also found in 1990 (Massey and Fischer, 1999). Furthermore, research from 1980 showed that poor whites tend to live among everyone else to a greater extent than do poor blacks (Massey and Eggers 1990) and in 2000 Fischer (2003) found that poor blacks are uniquely segregated. Taken together, these studies indicate that the role of income is at best modest compared to that of race in explaining segregation.

Attitudes, as expressed in residential preferences, are often cited as a cause of segregation. White attitudes toward blacks in their neighborhoods have become much more positive over time, but there remains a substantial difference between attitudes in "principle," which have improved a lot, and attitudes in "practice," which

have improved more slowly (Massey and Denton 1993:92; Farley et al. 1993; Bledsoe et al. 1996). However, in the most recent period, more whites have favored implementation of an open housing law (Schuman et al. 1997:134–135, 191–192). What this means is that whites agree in principle that blacks have the right to live anywhere they want and can afford to, but they are not in favor of laws that would enforce this principle in practice (Schuman et al. 1997).

Attitudinal data also reveal whites' expectations of neighborhood transition in studies that ask whites if they would be comfortable in neighborhoods with varying numbers of black neighbors and if they would move out of or into such neighborhoods. Results from studies in Detroit, Los Angeles, Atlanta and Boston confirm that whites are uncomfortable with even a small number of African-American neighbors, though they say they would not move out as quickly as they would refuse to move in (Farley et al. 1996). In Detroit in 1992, 56 percent of whites said they would feel comfortable in a neighborhood where 5 out of 15 homes were occupied by African-Americans, whereas only 35 percent said they would be comfortable in one where 8 out of 15 homes were occupied by blacks. Correspondingly, 29 percent said they would try to move out of a 5 black-home neighborhood and 53 percent from an 8 black-home neighborhood, while 58 percent and 71 percent, respectively, would not move in (Farley et al. 1994:756).

Black attitudes toward integration are also mixed, but studies in Detroit, Los Angeles, Boston and Atlanta show that blacks remain willing to live in neighborhoods that are between 90 percent and 10 percent white. However, their first preference would be for neighborhoods that are 50:50 white and black (Farley et al. 1996).

It is worth questioning the validity of both black and white preferences, however, since many blacks report that they would prefer to be in largely black neighborhoods or do not want to pioneer in all-white neighborhoods because of the fear of overt racial hostility (Feagin and Sikes 1994:252–264). Further, hardly any whites have actually had the experience of living with black (or Asian or Hispanic) neighbors, and black exposure to integrated neighborhoods is likewise limited (Bobo and Zubrinsky 1996). It is impossible to know now what peoples' attitudes would be in a more integrated world, but there is little reason to assume that they would remain as currently expressed.

More important than these studies of the *causes* of discrimination and segregation are the *consequences* of segregation. Too often, we discuss the severe consequences of segregation in underclass or poverty neighborhoods and on housing quality (Wilson 1987, 1996), as segregation concentrates poverty and other factors that lead to the development of these areas (Massey and Denton 1993:124). But housing segregation and discrimination also have disastrous individual, family, wealth and political consequences that affect the lives of all who experience them, not just the poor, and cost the society as a whole as well (Yinger 1995:89–103; Feagin and Sikes 1994). Lower segregation is also associated with better economic growth in both cities and suburbs during the 1990 to 1996 period (Wyly, Glickman and Lahr 1998; Rusk 1999).

One hidden cost of housing segregation and discrimination comes from the accompanying lack of wealth accumulation by people denied full access to the housing market. For many Americans, particularly those in the lower-middle and working classes, most of their wealth is accumulated through increases in the value of their home, their largest asset. A study by Oliver and Shapiro revealed that during the period from 1967 to 1988, white homes increased in equity by $21,900 more on average than did black homes. This amount can be directly attributed to bias in housing markets, and that accounts for about one-third of the black:white wealth difference among mortgage-holders (Oliver and Shapiro 1995:148). Housing prices tripled in the 1970s, enabling white homeowners who took advantage of discriminatory FHA financing policies to receive vastly increased equity in their homes. Those excluded by such policies, primarily African Americans, found themselves facing higher costs of entry into the housing market (Oliver and Shapiro 1995:150). Whites often use home equity loans to pay college tuition or help children with the down payment on their first homes. The Oliver and Shapiro study estimated the cost of the combined effects of mortgage discrimination and housing appreciation to the current generation of blacks at $82 billion, 71 percent of which is due to the failure of their homes to appreciate (Oliver and Shapiro 1995:151). Denial of this home equity money not only limits blacks' human capital attainments, but the cost of that lack of accumulation is paid by the rest of society in terms of loss of productivity.

While lack of wealth accumulation via housing is frequently overlooked, where one lives determines a wide array of other aspects about one's life and contributes to the costs of segregation (Galster and Killen 1995). Neighborhoods determine school districts, and the crisis in the public school systems of our nation's cities is reported almost daily in the media. In a society where low-skilled jobs are rapidly disappearing (Wilson 1996), the quality of one's education will determine one's life chances even more so than in the past. Youth, in particular, are disadvantaged by the lack of opportunity in poor neighborhoods (Galster and Mikelsons 1995). Segregated neighborhoods are also subject to higher rates of unemployment and lack of access to job networks and transportation (Hughes 1995), making it harder to find out about available jobs, even allowing for the effects of discrimination in the workplace (Wilson 1996). Persons living in highly segregated neighborhoods also face higher mortality risks and poorer health services, higher rates of teenage pregnancy and single motherhood, and higher crime rates (Massey and Denton 1993:165ff). To the extent that one becomes the victim of these effects, one's life chances are worse. To the extent that neighborhoods are homogeneous—that is, occupied by members of only one group— political leaders have safe seats but little power with which to form coalitions or make deals to improve the situation for their constituents (Massey and Denton 1993:156–158). In short, the forces of segregation ensure that its main costs will fall on the victims themselves.

All of these consequences lead to and reinforce something I term the "segregative system" (Denton 1996). The best empirical research to demonstrate this is that done by George Galster. In many articles, he has repeatedly shown the interactive, self-reinforcing nature of residential segregation in the United States (Galster 1992, 1993; Galster and Keeney 1988). In what Galster (1992) calls the "vicious circle of prejudice and inequality," segregation increases racial inequalities, which in turn reinforce segregation. Racial inequalities lead to prejudice, which also supports segregation as well as leads to housing discrimination, which supports continued segregation. The weight of our past history of segregation and the processes that led to it loom large, but it is constantly buttressed by the social, organizational and behavioral structures we have erected and within which we continue to operate. These structures occur in all areas of the housing marketing process—and in common-sense rules that govern individual behaviors regarding neighborhood choice and abandonment—and are reinforced by the political system at all levels of government. Clearly, beating the "segregative system" is going to be a long, uphill, protracted battle.

DECLINING ALL-WHITE NEIGHBORHOODS: INTERRUPTING THE SEGREGATIVE SYSTEM

One of the factors maintaining the "segregative system"—the set of discriminatory attitudes in the population, the discriminatory practices by organizational actors and the carryover of past segregation itself and past discrimination by individuals and organizational actors—is the presence of all-white neighborhoods. These neighborhoods provide a place where whites can flee as well as provide the "evidence" that when neighborhoods integrate, they do not remain as nice as the all-white ones. In a reverse manner, all-black or all-Hispanic neighborhoods are often used as examples of the potential dangers associated with integration.

It is thus important that we follow the experiences of these all-white neighborhoods over time. If they are maintaining themselves despite changes in attitudes, the law and the arrival of large numbers of new immigrants, then the future of integration is indeed as bleak as the segregation indices themselves seem to indicate. On the other hand, if these "sentinel" white neighborhoods are becoming fewer in number, then

we have evidence of the fact that at least one of the structural props supporting our separate societies is breaking down.[9]

In research done with my colleagues at SUNY Albany, I have updated some of my earlier work on patterns of neighborhood change in the large metropolitan areas of the United States (Denton and Massey 1991). Findings for the period from 1970 to 1990[10] for six of the largest metropolitan areas (New York, Philadelphia, Chicago, Miami, Houston and Los Angeles) mirror the pattern in all metropolitan areas for the period from 1970 to 1980: All-white neighborhoods are declining greatly in number (Alba et al. 1995; Denton and Anderson 1995). In short, integrated neighborhoods, though still relatively rare, are becoming more common, a finding that parallels other research on this topic (Ellen 1998; Nyden, Maly and Lukehart 1997).

The measurement issues behind that statement are complex. The research uses census tracts, the units commonly used for measuring segregation, as proxies for neighborhoods. While these may not correspond to anyone's ideal, personal or experiential sense of what a neighborhood is, their statistical properties of mutual exclusivity, coverage of the entire metropolitan area and relatively small size make them appropriate for this use. Categorizing a neighborhood as "all-white" involves defining whether or not a group is present in the neighborhood. Denton and Massey (1991) use an absolute rather than proportional cutoff of 30 persons to indicate a group's presence or absence in the neighborhood. The most recent work, using the 1990 Census, specifies that cutoff at 100 persons, arguing that this number is large enough that the persons would be visible in a group that averages 5,000 persons, as census tracts do. In a related paper on all-white suburban neighborhoods in the 50 largest metro areas in 1990, defining all-white neighborhoods as at least 95 percent white yields results that follow the same patterns as those presented here (Denton and Alba 1998).

Table 3.3 presents some of the key statistics for the metropolitan areas of New York, Philadelphia, Chicago, Miami, Houston and Los Angeles. The interpretation of these findings varies by area, and the process of neighborhood change is

TABLE 3.3 Summary of Neighborhood Race/Ethnic Composition Changes, 1970–1990, in New York, Philadelphia, Chicago, Miami, Houston, and Los Angeles

	New York	Philadelphia	Chicago	Miami	Houston	Los Angeles
Panel A: Fate of all-white neighborhoods						
No. tracts in area	3536	1043	1292	196	296	1404
All-white in 1970	1007	576	396	6	52	44
Percent remaining all-white in 1990	22.6	61.8	18.9	16.6	28.8	18.2
Panel B: Growth of multiethnic neighborhoods						
No. multiethnic W-B-H-A*						
in 1970	267	24	34	3	17	189
in 1990	925	111	193	50	107	691
Percent of total in 1990	26.2	10.6	14.9	25.5	36.1	49.2
Panel C: 1990 Center City and suburban multiethnic neighborhoods (W-B-H-A)						
Center City	26.1	14.7	10.5	5.9	47.7	49.4
Suburban	26.3	8.8	22.0	32.4	27.6	49.0
Panel D: 1990 all-minority neighborhoods						
Percent of total	14.7	4.9	20.7	6.6	3.9	10.6
Percent all black	3.1	3.6	18.9	2.0	1.0	0.1

Source: Denton and Anderson 1995, Alba et al. 1995.
*"W-B-H-A" refers to whites, blacks, Hispanics and Asians, who are each counted as present in the tract if their population is at least 100 persons.

affected by the larger structural context of the metro area itself: Is its population growing? Is it a destination for many of the new immigrants or not?

Several points are relevant. First, the decline in the number of all-white neighborhoods is substantial as shown in Panel A. In Chicago, Miami and Los Angeles, fewer than 20 percent of the neighborhoods that were all-white in 1970 remained so in 1990. In New York, just 22.6 percent of those remained the same as did 28.8 percent of those in Houston. Only in Philadelphia did a substantial 61.8 percent of the all-white neighborhoods in 1970 remain so in 1990. From more detailed analyses not shown, it is clear that many of these 1970 all-white neighborhoods by 1990 found themselves with African-American, Asian and Hispanic residents, along with their white residents. In fact, the entry of multiple groups was more common than the entry of a single group into the formerly all-white neighborhoods, suggesting that once a neighborhood "opens up," all groups are welcome. If a group is excluded, however, it is most often blacks.

Second, the emergence of four-group multiethnic neighborhoods, shown in Panel B, is equally dramatic. By 1990, nearly one-half of Los Angeles neighborhoods contained at least 100 of each of the four population groups, as did over one-third of Houston's neighborhoods and over one-fourth of those in New York and Miami. The relative presence of Asians in the metropolitan area as a whole is particularly important in this regard: Metropolitan areas like Philadelphia, Chicago and Miami that have low overall Asian proportions cannot have many neighborhoods that house at least 100 Asian residents. It is noteworthy that substantial white population remains in these multiethnic neighborhoods: They are almost always on average over 50 percent white and in suburban areas may be as high as 70 percent or 80 percent white. They are by no means all-minority neighborhoods with only a few white residents. Yet since the cut-off was 100 persons in each group, we know that they have at least 300 blacks, Hispanics and Asians. Only time will tell whether these neighborhoods are starting a racial transition to all-minority. But the large number of them, combined with the lack of evidence of particularly rapid race/ethnic turnover in the decade from 1970 to 1980 (Denton and Massey 1991), bodes well for the prospects of greater integration overall because it is hard to imagine this many neighborhoods undergoing racial transition.

Third, the number of all-white neighborhoods is declining in the city as well as the suburbs (Table 3.3, Panel C). Multiethnic neighborhoods are emerging in *both* central cities and suburbs. It is not just the neighborhoods within the city limits that are seeing population diversification. To the extent that suburban neighborhoods offer better schools, less violence, more job opportunities and the like, the emergence of these more diverse neighborhoods in suburbs is an indication that at least some people of color are able to avail themselves to these new opportunities. Research indicates improved life chances and outcomes for poor blacks who are able to move to low-poverty neighborhoods in the suburbs (Denton 2001; Goering and Feins 2003; Rosenbaum 1995).

Finally, the neighborhood world of 1970 in the six metropolitan areas shown in Table 3.3 could be characterized as either all white or all black, largely due to the small proportions of Hispanics and Asians in these areas at that time. Since these groups have grown substantially, it is reasonable to expect a corresponding rise in the number of neighborhoods that these groups claim, but the data do not reveal this. In general, Hispanics and Asians in 1990 tended to live in neighborhoods with whites. The group that remained in racially homogeneous neighborhoods in 1990 is blacks, as can be seen in Panel D of Table 3.3. It is impressive that the percent of all-minority neighborhoods is as low as it is, ranging from just over 20 percent in Chicago to just under 4 percent in Houston. However, the last row reveals that in Chicago and Philadelphia, most of these all-minority neighborhoods are all black, though in the other cities

they are not. Multiethnic but nonwhite neighborhoods are a possibility, of course, and the research did find a tendency for the number of black-Hispanic neighborhoods to increase, particularly in center city areas, especially in New York, Philadelphia and Chicago. This tendency was most likely the result of the continued concentration of poverty that occurred during the 1980s, with its concomitant geographic expansion of poor areas (Jargowsky 1997). While this trend is cause for serious concern, it must be emphasized that these neighborhoods, classified solely by race/ethnicity and not income as well, comprise only a small percent of the total number of neighborhoods in each metropolitan area, and both the number of high-poverty neighborhoods, as well as the size of the population living in them, have declined substantially since 1990 (Jargowsky 2003). Despite arguments that self-segregation is a natural tendency found among all groups, these data point instead to the existence of a segregative system that is particularly operant for blacks.

As noted previously, these analyses cannot be updated with 2000 data until neighborhood boundaries are matched over time. However, it is worth noting that my examination of census tracts in 2000 by their race/ethnic composition shows a continuation of these trends. In 2000, only one-fourth of the tracts in the 50 largest metro areas had only white residents (or were white with less than 5 percent of Hispanics or Asians or blacks), and almost one-third had at least 5 percent of their members from three or more groups, one of which was non-Hispanic white. All-minority neighborhoods, in any combination, made up just 7.5 percent of the total neighborhoods found in these metro areas. Therefore, it is clear that at the neighborhood level, increasing diversity continued through the 1990s.

This summary of analyses of race/ethnic compositional changes certainly shows the need for more detailed work on this topic and for study of a larger number of metropolitan areas. However, given the history of racism and discrimination in housing, and the slow change in the segregation indices reported earlier, the results are indeed intriguing, though hard to interpret. On the one hand, more integrated neighborhoods are a sign that the segregation in our urban areas is abating—a positive outcome. Given how high levels of racial segregation were and are, one would expect that any change in those patterns would at first be visible as very low levels of integration. Multigroup neighborhoods also decrease the number of all-white neighborhoods to which whites can flee. On the other hand, it is mathematically possible for every neighborhood to contain a few nonwhite residents while the majority of the nonwhite population remains highly segregated. The integrated neighborhoods, by allowing more and more whites to live in minimally integrated ones, could provide whites with the evidence to believe that segregation is no longer a problem, even though the research presented documents its ongoing presence in our society.

IMPLICATIONS FOR FUTURE HOUSING POLICY

What are the implications of patterns that show high levels of segregation and discrimination, combined with an increase in multiethnic neighborhoods, for a volume arguing that housing should be a fundamental right for everyone, including the poor? The prevalent policy implication is the importance of defining the right to a good house to embrace a good neighborhood as well, as is the opinion of Hartman (1998 and Chapter 8). Any social agenda that includes housing must pay particular attention to the location of the house. Research on segregation and discrimination makes abundantly clear that the best quality, most adequate house in a neighborhood with a high crime rate, bad schools, no jobs, no access to public transportation or other amenities does not fit the ideal of a good home. To ensure that a Right to Housing includes the right to a decent neighborhood will require that housing policy aimed at increasing the supply of low-cost housing pay attention to more than just the number of units. Given the limited success in increasing the supply of low-cost housing in recent decades, well documented in other chapters of this text, this chapter's emphasis on race and neighborhood amenities further complicates an already difficult task. However, ignoring the neighborhood dooms the housing efforts to long-term failure, as the concentration of poverty in some of the nation's most infamous public housing projects can more than attest. As a result, paying serious attention to the neighborhood imposes conditions on housing policy:

1. **Housing policies and programs should not increase income and racial segregation.** Housing policies or programs must demonstrate that they will not increase income and/or racial segregation *before* they can be implemented. Recognizing that there are many housing policies, especially those that seek to increase the supply of low-cost or low-rent housing, which result in small numbers of units, housing policies must evaluate both their own effect on income and/or racial segregation and the totality of their proposed effect when combined with other projects previously completed in the same area. Researchers can help policy makers by determining the best way to measure these effects and by monitoring them once a policy is implemented. Linking approval for construction or rehabilitation of low-cost housing to levels of income and residential segregation is the only way to guarantee that we will not alleviate the low-cost housing shortage at the expense of raising levels of income and racial segregation. Put another way, all housing programs must further the aims of the 1968 and 1988 Fair Housing Acts, and housing assistance must be dispersed throughout the metro area.

2. **Housing policy concerned with low-cost housing must explicitly consider race/ethnicity.** Programs for low-cost housing for specific groups (poor, elderly, female-headed families) or certain types of housing (owned, rental) must consider how profoundly the U.S. housing market is structured by race/ethnicity. While it may be harder to garner political support for race-targeted or place-targeted programs because they violate the assumptions of a "public good" (Vidal 1995), not taking race/ethnicity into account increases the likelihood that previous mistakes will be repeated. In one discussion surrounding the public housing bill in 1949, it was proposed that racial or ethnic discrimination be forbidden in any public housing project, a measure that would have defeated the housing

bill. Jackson (1985:226) describes how Senator Paul Douglas, whom he describes to be "as decent a man as ever served on Capitol Hill," urged "his liberal colleagues to put aside their principles temporarily" rather than defeat the chance of re-housing 4 million persons. Douglas had the short-term interests of black Americans in mind and felt strongly that no persons of any race should be treated as second-class citizens. However, the disastrous long-term effects of the location of public housing and slum clearance for blacks are precisely the issues we are dealing with today. The mechanisms of the housing market and peoples' expectation of how the market works are affected by race in all areas. One of the fundamental underlying structures of the low-cost housing submarket is race itself. A good part of the reason that, as a society, we have such a low-cost housing crisis can be traced to the fact that we do not particularly value the provision of housing for the poor, especially for blacks and other minorities, and especially not in good neighborhoods.

3. **National audits to measure discrimination in housing rental and sales, as well as by mortgage and insurance providers, should be carried out on a regular schedule. These should also include a component that specifically measures discrimination against the poor.** Funding to conduct audits in such a way that they provide evidence of the overall level of discrimination needs to be regularly allocated by HUD. Since audit and testing data are used to prove discrimination in court cases, most metro areas have people and organizations well qualified to conduct them, a fact that was used to great advantage in the last two rounds of discrimination studies. Furthermore, Yinger (1995) proposes that in addition to regular testing of the entire housing market, we also need representative audit studies targeted to specific types of neighborhoods—for example, integrated ones or lower-income ones that would serve to show if discrimination was the same across the income distribution.

4. **Better enforcement of the Fair Housing Act and strengthening the Community Reinvestment Act to include mortgages companies is essential.** Laws against discrimination in all aspects of the sale and rental of housing need to

be aggressively enforced. HUD's record in processing Fair Housing complaints (Relman 2002) combined with the fact that nonbank mortgage lenders are not subject to CRA (Campen 2003), both discussed above, are defeating the efforts of local housing and community development groups all over the nation. HUD needs to allocate money to these efforts if we are ever to see improvements in the way in which housing is allocated, particularly now that housing discrimination is such a subtle process that most whites do not even notice. The lack of affordable housing must be viewed as a structural problem of the housing market and the discrimination therein. It cannot be seen as a sign that poorly housed or unhoused individuals have somehow failed to work hard enough to be able to afford adequate housing for themselves and their families.

5. **Place-based *and* people-based strategies are both important, and they complement each other.** Improvement of places, as revealed by the notable accomplishments of numerous CDCs in recent years, is a necessary remedy for the lives of those who have been denied resources by the segregative system. At the same time, people-based mobility strategies offer choices to the poor that the middle class already have (Turner 1998), and Gautreaux and Moving to Opportunity (MTO) programs, which assist poor families to move to integrated and low poverty neighborhoods, provide successful models for this approach (Rosenbaum 1995; Turner 1998). Despite the fact that competition for declining resources too often pits advocates of one approach against the other, the magnitude of the problem is such that both are needed. Mobility programs will probably never be introduced on a scale large enough to help all of those in need, nor is it reasonable to assume that every place in need will have an active enough community group to deal with its problems. Further, interventions in places run the severe risk that their efforts in one place will be quickly overwhelmed by the surrounding social and political structures that currently support income and racial segregation. Debating this point allows persons not concerned with housing for the poor at all to do nothing, citing the internal conflicts and the fact that what should be done is not known.

6. **More publicity regarding successfully integrated neighborhoods is vital.** The presence of functioning racially and economically integrated neighborhoods must be highlighted and their characteristics made widely known. They cannot remain what Nyden, Maly and Lukehart (1998) call "one of our Nation's best-kept secrets." While local newspapers sometimes carry stories about this, reports on the evening news programs too often feature horror stories about the poor. To the extent that housing policy advocates and researchers are able to focus attention on successful models of integration and the beneficial outcomes of good housing in good neighborhoods, it can only help. Too much of what happens in contemporary housing markets is the result of people's ignorance of how neighborhoods change now as opposed to how they changed in the blockbusting heydays of 1955 or 1960 (Levine and Harmon 1992). Contemporary housing choices do not reflect preferences so much as they reflect a structural system that was built on racism. Housing choices today reflect fear of racial succession and fear of integration. While this is most often thought of from the white perspective, it is increasingly becoming true of blacks as well, adding yet another to the long list of costs we have paid for residential segregation in this country.

7. **Local programs should be models for national programs.** In some areas, local solutions to provide low-cost housing and local neighborhood renewal initiatives seem to be working and may be the only option in the current political climate. However, this chapter has shown that the segregation of African Americans is high in all areas, even where they are not numerous, indicating that race operates in the housing market on a national, not local, basis. The impetus to segregation from the HOLC/FHA redlining maps and the realtors code of ethics were also national, not local. It was the federal government, in complicity with local governments, that created the segregated housing system we see today (Gabriel 1996). Local efforts to deal with the issue of housing are taking on a national-level apparatus, and the ultimate challenge is to design national policies in the 21st century that will undo the errors of national policies of the 20th century.

In closing, this chapter points to the structural nature of segregation and discrimination in the current housing market. As john powell (1995:905) has pointed out, civil rights efforts focused on individuals and individual discrimination, and their remedies were and are also individuated. In a world where segregation is high and discrimination is subtle, individual remedies are not enough. Lawyer john powell argues that the goal of the post–civil rights agenda must be to attack the system of racial hierarchy and racial subordination in a group-based manner that addresses power disparities between groups. His concluding words are worth quoting:

> The post–civil rights agenda must focus on subordination and exclusion. The key to this focus is understanding that racial discrimination and economic deprivation are not only oppressive, but they are also structural and institutional. Without characterizing oppression as structural, and without developing an agenda that is oriented toward destabilizing and disturbing this structure, any formal or individual progress will be largely rendered impotent by the greater institutional mechanisms. (powell 1995:910)

The implication of powell's words for low-cost housing are clear. Increasing the supply of low-cost units without paying attention to the structural context responsible for the shortage and the disadvantaged neighborhood location of the units is a short-term solution leading inevitably to a long-term crisis. Via mortgage interest and property tax deductions, the government subsidizes housing for the wealthy. The poor and people of color deserve equal treatment so that they can enjoy good housing in a good neighborhood.

NOTES

1. Census 2000 was the first census where people could identify with more than one race. This choice was made by 2.4 percent of the population.

2. It should be noted that these groups are internally highly heterogeneous, including native-born and recent immigrants, and combine Mexicans, Cubans, Puerto Ricans and other persons from

Spanish-speaking countries under the umbrella term "Hispanic." Likewise, Chinese, Japanese, Thais, Indians, Filipinos, Vietnamese and many other groups are combined in the Asian category. That we would see distinctions in the segregation index if we measured it for each group separately is undeniable, but we can also learn about residential patterns by looking at the broader groups shown, which correspond to the race/ethnic classification used by the U.S. Census Bureau.

3. The formula for the index of dissimilarity is $D = .5* \sum |(x_i/X)(y_i/Y)|*100$, where x_i and y_i are the tract level totals for groups x and y, X and Y are the metropolitan area totals for the same groups, and the index is summed across all tracts.

4. Since segregation indices require data for all parts of the metropolitan area, they can only be computed for years when the decennial census of population and housing is conducted.

5. Note the subtitle of Farley and Frey's 1994 article: "Small steps towards a more racially integrated society."

6. According to the Iceland, Weinberg and Steinmetz report (2002), Hispanics were hypersegregated in Los Angeles and New York in 1990, though this was not reported earlier.

7. The six topics were information requested; loan amount and house price; number of products; coaching to deal with credit problems; follow-up contact and encouragement of FHA mortgage.

8. I have focused on white preferences because of their greater influence and control in the real estate market due to their larger population size. Black preferences show a much different pattern from those of whites. Blacks are considerably more likely to prefer neighborhoods where the racial mix is closer to 50:50, to dislike being pioneers in an all-white neighborhood, but they also indicate a willingness to move into neighborhoods with all but the most extreme racial compositions (Farley et al. 1994:763). Thus, it is unlikely that black preferences alone are creating the all-black neighborhoods we see.

9. It should be noted that this focus on neighborhoods as the units of analysis is complementary to that of segregation indices, which focus on the population in an entire MSA or city. The former looks at segregation from the point of view of a typical neighborhood, the latter from the point of view of a typical person. Theoretically, it is possible for *all* neighborhoods to be integrated at low levels—for instance, to have some nonwhite residents—at the same time that the segregation indices remain high—that is, the bulk of the nonwhite population lives in segregated neighborhoods.

10. It is not yet possible to present these patterns for 1970 to 2000, as the process of matching the census tract boundaries is quite time-consuming.

REFERENCES

Abrams, Charles. 1955. *Forbidden neighbors: A study of prejudice in housing.* New York: Harper & Brothers.

Abramson, Alan J., Mitchell S. Tobin and Matthew R. VanderGoot. 1995. The changing geography of metropolitan opportunity: The segregation of the poor in U.S. metropolitan areas, 1970–1990. *Housing Policy Debate* 6:45–72.

Adams, Charles F., Howard B. Fleeter, Yul Kim, Mark Freeman and Imgon Cho. 1996. Flight from blight and metropolitan suburbanization revisited. *Urban Affairs Review* 31:529–543.

Alba, Richard D., and John R. Logan. 1993. Minority proximity to whites in suburbs: An individual-level analysis of segregation. *American Journal of Sociology* 98:1388–1427.

Alba, Richard D., Nancy Denton, Shu-yin J. Leung and John R. Logan. 1995. Neighborhood change under conditions of mass immigration: The New York City region, 1970–90. *International Migration Review* 29(3):625–656.

Bledsoe, Timothy, Michael Coombs, Lee Sigelman and Susan Welch. 1996. Trends in racial attitudes in Detroit, 1968–1992. *Urban Affairs Review* 31:508–528.

Bobo, Lawrence, and Camille L. Zubrinsky. 1996. Attitudes on residential integration: Perceived status differences, mere in-group preference, or racial prejudice? *Social Forces* 74:883–909.

Bratt, Rachel G., Chester Hartman and Ann Meyerson, eds. 1986. *Critical perspectives on housing.* Philadelphia: Temple University Press.

Brown, Prudence. 1996. Comprehensive neighborhood initiatives. *Cityscape: A Journal of Policy Development and Research* 2:161–176.

Calmore, John O. 1993. Spatial equality and the Kerner Commission Report: A back-to-the-future essay. *North Carolina Law Review* 71:1487–1495.

Campen, Jim. 1992. The struggle for community investment in Boston, 1989–1991. In *From red lining to reinvestment: Community responses to urban disinvestment,* ed. Gregory D. Squires, 38–72. Philadelphia: Temple University Press.

———. 2003. *Borrowing troubles.* Report for the Massachusetts Community and Banking Council, Boston. Accessed at www.mahahome.org.

Dedman, Bill. 1989. Blacks denied S&L loans twice as often as whites. *Atlanta Journal and Constitution,* January 22.

Denton, Nancy A. 1994. Are African Americans still hypersegregated? In *Residential apartheid: The American legacy,* eds. Robert D. Bullard, J. Eugene Grigsby and Charles Lee, 49–81. Los Angeles: CAAS Publications.

———. 1996. The persistence of segregation: Links between residential segregation and school segregation. *Minnesota Law Review* 4:795–824.

————. 2001. Housing as a means of asset accumulation: A good strategy for the poor? In *Assets for the poor: The benefits of spreading asset ownership*, eds. Thomas M. Shapiro and Edward N. Wolff, 232–266. New York: Russell Sage Foundation.

Denton, Nancy A., and Bridget J. Anderson. 1995. A tale of five cities: Neighborhood change in Philadelphia, Chicago, Miami, Houston and Los Angeles, 1970–1990. Paper presented at the annual meetings of the Population Association of America, San Francisco, April 6–8.

Denton, Nancy A., and Douglas S. Massey. 1988. Residential segregation of blacks, Hispanics and Asians by socioeconomic status and generation. *Social Science Quarterly* 69:797–817.

————. 1991. Patterns of neighborhood transition in a multi-ethnic world: U.S. metropolitan areas 1970–1980. *Demography* 28:41–63.

Denton, Nancy A., and Richard D. Alba. 1998. The decline of the all-white neighborhood and the growth of suburban diversity. Prepared for the Suburban Racial Change Conference, Harvard University, March 28.

Edmonston, Barry, and Jeffrey S. Passell. 1994. Ethnic demography: U.S. immigration and ethnic variations. In *Immigration and ethnicity: The integration of America's newest arrivals*, eds. Barry Edmonston and Jeffrey S. Passell, 1–30. Washington, DC: Urban Institute Press.

Ellen, Ingrid Gould. 1998. Stable racial integration in the contemporary United States: An empirical overview. *Journal of Urban Affairs* 20:27–42.

Farley, Reynolds, Elaine L. Fielding and Maria Krysan. 1996. The residential preferences of blacks and whites: A four metropolis analysis. Paper presented at the annual meetings of the Population Association of America, New Orleans, May 9–11.

Farley, Reynolds, and William H. Frey. 1994. Changes in the segregation of whites from blacks during the 1980s: Small steps towards a more racially integrated society. *American Sociological Review* 59:23–45.

Farley, Reynolds, Charlotte Steeh, Tara Jackson, Maria Krysan and Keith Reeves. 1993. Continued racial residential segregation in Detroit: "Chocolate city, vanilla suburbs" revisited. *Journal of Housing Research* 4:1–38.

Farley, Reynolds, Charlotte Steeh, Maria Krysan, Tara Jackson and Keith Reeves. 1994. Stereotypes and segregation: Neighborhoods in the Detroit area. *American Journal of Sociology* 100:750–780.

Feagin, Joe R., and Melvin P. Sikes. 1994. *Living with racism: The black middle-class experience*. Boston: Beacon Press.

Feins, Judith D., and Rachel G. Bratt. 1983. Barred in Boston: Racial discrimination in housing. *Journal of the American Planning Association* 49:344–355.

Fischer, Mary J. 2003. The relative importance of income and race in determining residential outcomes in U.S. urban areas, 1970–2000. *Urban Affairs Review* 38:669–696.

Frey, William H., and Reynolds Farley. 1996. Latino, Asian and black segregation in U.S. metropolitan areas: Are multiethnic metros different? *Demography* 33:35–50.

Gabriel, Stuart A. 1996. Urban housing policy in the 1990s. *Housing Policy Debate* 7:673–694.

Galster, George C. 1992. The case for racial integration. In *The metropolis in black and white: Place, power and polarization*, eds. George C. Galster and E. W. Hill, 270–285. New Brunswick, NJ: Center for Urban Policy Research.

————. 1993. Polarization, place, and race. *North Carolina Law Review* 71:1421–1426.

Galster, George C., and W. Mark Keeney. 1988. Race, residence, discrimination, and economic opportunity: Modeling the nexus of urban racial phenomena. *Urban Affairs Quarterly* 24:87–117.

Galster, George, and Maris Mikelsons. 1995. The geography of metropolitan opportunity: A case study of neighborhood conditions confronting youth in Washington, D.C. *Housing Policy Debate* 6:73–102.

Galster, George C., and Sean P. Killen. 1995. The geography of metropolitan opportunity: A reconnaissance and conceptual framework. *Housing Policy Debate* 6:7–43.

Goering, John, and Judith D. Feins, eds. 2003. *Choosing a better life: Evaluating the moving to opportunity social experiment*. Washington, DC: The Urban Institute Press.

Hamilton, Susan, and Stephen J. H. Cogswell. 1997. Barriers to home purchase for African-Americans and Hispanics in Syracuse. *Cityscape: A Journal of Policy Development and Research* 3:91–130.

Harrison, Roderick J., and Claudette E. Bennett. 1995. Racial and ethnic diversity. In *State of the Union: America in the 1990s, volume two, social trends*, ed. Reynolds Farley, 141–210. New York: Russell Sage Foundation.

Hartman, Chester. 1998. The case for a right to housing. *Housing Policy Debate* 9:223–246.

Hughes, James W. 1991. Clashing demographics: Homeownership and affordability dilemmas. *Housing Policy Debate* 2:1217–1250.

————. 1996. Economic shifts and the changing homeownership trajectory. *Housing Policy Debate* 7:293–325.

Hughes, Mark Alan. 1995. A mobility strategy for improving opportunity. *Housing Policy Debate* 6:271–297.

Iceland, John, Daniel H. Weinberg and Erika Steinmetz. 2002. *Racial and ethnic residential segregation in the United States: 1980–2000*. U.S. Census

Bureau, Series CENSR-3. Washington, DC: U.S. Government Printing Office.

Jackson, Kenneth T. 1985. *Crabgrass frontier: The suburbanization of the United States.* New York: Oxford University Press.

Jargowsky, Paul A. 1994. Ghetto poverty among blacks in the 1980s. *Journal of Policy Analysis and Management* 13:288–310.

———. 1997. *Poverty and place: Ghettos, barrios and the American city.* New York: Russell Sage Foundation.

———. 2003. Stunning progress, hidden problems: The dramatic decline of concentrated poverty in the 1990s. Report in the Living Cities Census Series, The Brookings Institution. http://www.brookings.org/dybdocroot/es/urban/publications/jargowskypoverty.pdf.

JCHS. 2000. *State of the nation's housing: 2003.* Cambridge, MA: Joint Center for Housing Studies, Harvard University. http://www.jchs.Harvard.edu/publications/ markets/son2003.pdf

Keyes, Langley C., Alex Schwartz, Avis C. Vidal and Rachel G. Bratt. 1996. Networks and nonprofits: Opportunities and challenges in an era of federal devolution. *Housing Policy Debate* 7:201–230.

Kim, Sunwoong, and Gregory D. Squires. 1998. The color of money and the people who lend it. *Journal of Housing Research* 9:271–284.

Levine, Hillel, and Lawrence Harmon. 1992. *The death of an American Jewish community: A tragedy of good intentions.* New York: The Free Press.

Lewis Mumford Center. 2001a. Ethnic diversity grows, neighborhood integration lags behind. Report of the Lewis Mumford Center, SUNY Albany. http://mumford1.dyndns.org/cen2000/WholePop/WPreport/page1.html

———. 2001b. The new ethnic enclaves in America's suburbs. Report of the Lewis Mumford Center, SUNY Albany. http://mumford1.dyndns.org/cen2000/suburban/ SuburbanReport/page1.html

Lieberson, Stanley. 1980. *A piece of the pie: Blacks and white immigrants since 1880.* Berkeley: University of California Press.

Logan, John R. 2003. America's newcomers. Report of the Lewis Mumford Center, SUNY Albany. http://mumford1.dyndns.org/cen2000/ NewComersReport/NewComer01.htm.

Logan, John R., Richard D. Alba and Shu-Yin Leung. 1996. Minority access to white suburbs: A multiregional comparison. *Social Forces* 74:851–881.

Massey, Douglas S., and Nancy A. Denton. 1993. *American apartheid: Segregation and the making of the underclass.* Cambridge, MA: Harvard University Press.

Massey, Douglas S., and Mitchell L. Eggers. 1990. The ecology of inequality: Minorities and the concentration of poverty, 1970–1980. *American Journal of Sociology* 95:1175–1177.

Massey, Douglas S. and Mary J. Fischer. 1999. Does rising income bring integration? New results for Blacks, Hispanics and Asians in 1990. *Social Science Research* 28:316–326.

Munnell, Alicia, Geoffrey M. B. Tootell, Lynn E. Browne and James McEneaney. 1996. Mortgage lending in Boston: Interpreting HMDA data. *American Economic Review* 86:25–53.

NLIHC. 2003. *Out of reach 2003.* Washington, DC: National Low Income Housing Coalition. http://www.nlihc.org

Nyden, Philip, Michael Maly and John Lukehart. 1997. The emergence of stable racially and ethnically diverse urban communities: A case study of nine U.S. cities. *Housing Policy Debate* 8:491–534.

———. 1998. Neighborhood racial and ethnic diversity in U.S. cities. *Cityscape: A Journal of Policy Development and Research* 4:1–17.

Oliver, Melvin L., and Thomas M. Shapiro. 1995. *Black wealth/white wealth: A new perspective on racial inequality.* New York: Routledge.

Phelan, Thomas J., and Mark Schneider. 1996. Race, ethnicity, and class in American suburbs. *Urban Affairs Review* 31:659–680.

powell, john a. 1995. An agenda for the post-civil rights era. *University of San Francisco Law Review* 29:889–910.

Relman, John. 2002. Federal fair housing enforcement at a crossroads: The Clinton legacy and the challenges ahead. In *Rights at risk: Equality in an age of terrorism,* eds. Diane M. Piché, William L. Taylor and Robin A. Reed, 99–113. Washington, DC: Citizens Commission on Civil Rights. www.cccr.org.

Rosenbaum, James E. 1995. Changing the geography of opportunity by expanding residential choice: Lessons from the Gautreaux program. *Housing Policy Debate* 6:231–269.

Rusk, David. 1999. *Inside game/outside game.* Washington, DC: Brookings Institution Press.

Salins, Peter D. 1998. Comment on Chester Hartman's "The Case for a Right to Housing": Housing is a right? Wrong! *Housing Policy Debate* 9:259–266.

Schill, Michael H., and Susan M. Wachter. 1995. Housing market constraints and spatial stratification by income and race. *Housing Policy Debate* 6:141–167.

Schuman, Howard, Charlotte Steeh, Lawrence Bobo and Maria Krysan. 1997. *Racial attitudes in America: Trends and interpretations,* Revised Edition. Cambridge, MA: Harvard University Press.

Schwartz, Alex. 1998. From confrontation to collaboration? Banks, community groups, and the implementation of community reinvestment agreements. *Housing Policy Debate* 9:631–662.

Squires, Gregory D., ed. 1992. *From redlining to reinvestment: Community responses to urban disinvestment.* Philadelphia: Temple University Press.

———. 1994. *Capital and communities in black and white: The intersections of race, class, and uneven development*. Albany: State University of New York Press.

———, ed. 1997. *Insurance redlining: Disinvestment, reinvestment and the evolving role of financial institutions*. Washington, DC: The Urban Institute Press.

Stone, Michael E. 1993a. Latino shelter poverty and housing strategies. In *Latino poverty and economic development in Massachusetts*, eds. Edwin Melendez and Miren Uriarte, 177–200. Boston: University of Massachusetts Press.

———. 1993b. *Shelter poverty: New ideas on housing affordability*. Philadelphia: Temple University Press.

———. 1996. Housing affordability among Asian Americans. Institute for Asian American Studies, University of Massachusetts, Boston.

Taeuber, Karl E., and Alma F. Taeuber. 1965. *Negroes in cities: Residential segregation and neighborhood change*. Chicago: Aldine Publishing.

Turner, Margery Austin. 1998. Moving out of poverty: Expanding mobility and choice through tenant-based housing assistance. *Housing Policy Debate* 9:373–394.

Turner, Margery Austin, and Ron Wienk. 1993. The persistence of segregation in urban areas: Contributing causes. In *Housing markets and residential mobility*, eds. G. Thomas Kingsley and Margery Austin Turner, 193–216. Washington, DC: Urban Institute Press.

Turner, Margery Austin, Fred Freiberg, Erin Godfrey, Carla Herbig, Diane K. Levy and Robin R. Smith. 2002a. All other things being equal: A paired testing study of mortgage lending institutions. http://www. huduser.org/Publications/PDF/aotbe.pdf.

Turner, Margery Austin, Stephen L. Ross, George Galster and John Yinger. 2002b. Discrimination in metropolitan housing markets: National results from Phase I of HDS2000. Published November 7, 2002. http://www.huduser.org/Publications/pdf/Phase1_Report.pdf.

Turner, Margery Austin, and Stephen L. Ross. 2003. Discrimination in metropolitan housing markets: Phase 2—Asians and Pacific Islanders. http://www.huduser.org/publications/pdf/phase2_final.pdf.

U.S. Bureau of the Census. 1991. Census of population and housing, 1990: Summary tape File 1 technical documentation, A-5. Washington, DC: The Bureau.

U.S. Bureau of the Census. 2000. Census of population and housing, 2000: Summary File 3 Tables H11, H12, H13. Washington, DC: The Bureau.

Vidal, Avis C. 1995. Reintegrating disadvantaged communities into the fabric of urban life: The role of community development. *Housing Policy Debate* 6:169–230.

White, Michael J. 1987. *American neighborhoods and residential differentiation*. New York: Russell Sage Foundation.

Wilson, William J. 1987. *The truly disadvantaged: The inner city, the underclass, and public policy*. Chicago: University of Chicago Press.

———. 1996. *When work disappears: The world of the new urban poor*. New York: Alfred A. Knopf.

Wyly, Elvin K., Norman J. Glickman and Michael L. Lahr. 1998. A top 10 list of things to know about American cities. *Cityscape: A Journal of Policy Development and Research* 3:7–32.

Wyly, Elvin K., and Steven R. Holloway. 1999. The new *Color of Money*: Neighborhood lending patterns in Atlanta revisited. *Housing Facts and Findings* 1:2(Summer). http://www. fanniemae-foundation.org/programs/ hff/v1i2-color_money.shtml.

Yinger, John. 1995. *Closed doors, opportunities lost: The continuing costs of housing discrimination*. New York: Russell Sage Foundation.

———. 1997. Cash in your face: The cost of racial and ethnic discrimination in housing. *Journal of Urban Economics* 42:339–365.

———. 1998. Housing discrimination is still worth worrying about. *Housing Policy Debate* 9:893–927.

Michael E. Stone

4 Pernicious Problems of Housing Finance

THE SYSTEM OF housing provision and finance erected in the 1930s and fully implemented after World War II was one of the pillars of the postwar prosperity, sustaining and stabilizing the economy as well as transforming the nation's social and physical geography. However, during the 1960s, this postwar stability began to crumble. Inflation took hold, competition for credit increased, interest rates rose and the housing sector suffered disproportionately.

Attempts to deal with these problems have contributed to worsening housing affordability, from both the income side and the housing cost side. On the one hand, responses by business and the government to increasing globalization and the associated squeeze on corporate profitability have generated widening income inequality: Those at the bottom have experienced declining real incomes; those in the middle have, at best, barely kept up with inflation; while those at the top have substantially improved their standard of living (see Chapter 1). Meanwhile, housing costs have been driven to dizzying heights, caused in part by demand for housing from ever richer households at the top of the income distribution, but also by runaway speculation in housing markets in many areas, perverse housing policies and a restructured national mortgage system.

Since the late 1960s, the system of housing finance in the United States has undergone profound transformation. Once a relatively separate, protected and locally based system, housing finance has become integrated into the national and global capital markets, with massive institutions becoming the controlling intermediaries between distant capital markets and local housing markets. Why and how has the residential finance system been transformed, and what have been the consequences? The chapter begins with an examination of the structural changes in the housing finance system and then explores several major areas of impact: first, the shift of housing production toward more expensive houses, associated with widening income inequality as well as with standardization of lending; second, the recent, modest increase in middle-income homeownership, fueled not only by economic growth but also by special programs in response to advocacy and anxiety about discrimination and diminished affordability in the mortgage system; and third, greater risk-taking by households and lenders, leading to greater household debt burdens, an upward trend in residential mortgage foreclosures and instability at the nation's (and the world's) largest mortgage institutions.

While the 1990s and early 2000s have been celebrated as a period of low inflation and low interest rates, the enthusiastic hucksters of the era rarely acknowledge where these conditions came from: draconian cuts in government social spending, diminishing job security and globalization of corporate capitalism. The concentration, centralization and rationalization of housing finance may have been inevitable with the new economic order. But the consequences have been mixed, at best, for housing, households and communities. Understanding the structure and dynamics of the mortgage system is thus essential for understanding the extent, depth and persistence of housing problems—and the need for new models of housing finance in order to realize a Right to Housing.

HOUSING FINANCE AND THE ECONOMY

While new housing is of course costly to produce, most housing is not new. Yet because housing is a commodity in this society, the market value of well-maintained older housing is typically of the same order of magnitude as similar new housing, and most housing is sold and resold and refinanced repeatedly over its lifetime. For most of these transactions, the bulk of the cost is financed through mortgage loans. The financial burden of repaying these loans with interest constitutes by far the largest component of residents' housing costs for both renters (indirectly) and homeowners. Most rental housing is mortgaged, with exception of public housing and nonprofit elderly/handicapped housing, and over 65 percent of all homeowners have mortgages on their homes (Kennickell, Starr-McCluer and Surette 2000:Table 11B). On average, two-thirds of total monthly housing costs for homeowners with mortgages goes for their mortgage payments; the share of rents going toward mortgage payments is probably at least as great.[1] The institutions and mechanisms of mortgage lending thus have a contradictory role: They have been essential to the functioning of the private housing market but have also been primary sources of persistent and pervasive housing affordability problems.

Historical Background on Institutional Mortgage Lending[2]

During the first three decades of the 20th century, mortgage lending by financial institutions moved to the center of the U.S. housing system, facilitating expansion of residential construction and sales but also imposing a rigidity on housing costs and making the stability of the overall economy vulnerable to the ability of people to afford their housing payments. Thus, when the economy collapsed at the end of the 1920s, the mortgage system was a big part of the debacle. Millions of households lost their homes

to foreclosure because they did not have the incomes to pay off their mortgages. Millions lost their savings because the banks had invested in home loans that were not being repaid. With no new funds available for investment, private residential construction practically came to a halt, and the private housing market nearly ceased functioning, adding to the depth and duration of the Great Depression.

When a new framework for housing finance was erected in the 1930s, it was still built around mortgage lending by private financial institutions—reflecting the power of those institutions and the general philosophical commitment to have the government assist rather than replace private investment. The major and most profound and pervasive forms of federal support for housing put into place in the 1930s were therefore designed to stimulate and protect private institutional lending. They consisted of the system of central banking and deposit insurance provided by the Federal Home Loan Bank system (FHLB); the mortgage insurance program of the Federal Housing Administration (FHA) and, a decade later, the mortgage guarantee program of the Veterans Administration (VA); and the secondary mortgage market facilities of the Federal National Mortgage Association (FNMA, known as "Fannie Mae").

Strategically, the rebuilt mortgage system focused on wide promotion of debt-encumbered homeownership through the creation of low down payment, long-term loans to replace the earlier type of large down payment, short-term mortgage loans that had restricted the market to relatively well-off groups in the population. The new type of loan reduced monthly payments for a given size loan and lessened the personal savings needed to purchase a home. But in doing so, it created the illusion of ownership through the reality of debt. Furthermore, by making loans more easily available, the effective demand for houses was expected to increase, thereby contributing to overall economic growth as well as supporting the lending and construction industries in particular.

Of course, it took World War II to restart the economy and generate the savings needed to set the reconstructed mortgage system into operation. Savings that had accumulated during the war, along with housing needs virtually unmet since the start of the Great Depression, provided the impetus for what became the postwar housing boom, facilitated by federal support for financial institutions to make the new long-term, low down payment loans. The postwar suburban boom produced some 30 million new housing units in two decades, increasing the nation's homeownership from about 40 percent at the end of the war to over 60 percent by the 1960s. Housing construction accounted for one-third of all private investment and nearly one-half of all public and private construction during this period. Housing debt represented the biggest single component of a vast explosion of private borrowing. Yet despite the success of the new mortgage system in dealing with the housing needs of a majority of Americans and contributing to prosperity, the system contained some inherent flaws and weaknesses.

First of all, even though mortgage lending contributed to economic growth, it grew much faster than the overall economy, hence faster than consumers' ability to repay the debt. Between 1946 and 1965, residential mortgage debt grew about three times as fast as gross domestic product (GDP) and disposable personal income. As more and more current income goes to paying past debts, the potential for profitable new lending to support continued economic growth without inflation becomes constrained. The mortgage system has thus been an important factor in the ups and downs of the business cycle.

Second, while the expansion of mortgage credit has contributed immensely to the growth and profitability of the entire housing industry, the increasing dependence on credit made production of new housing and the cost of buying and occupying both new and used housing increasingly sensitive to the supply and cost of mortgage money. No other major industry is as dependent on borrowed funds, and for no other major consumption item is price as sensitive to interest rates.

The third problem with the new mortgage system has arisen from the promotion of (debt-encumbered) homeownership as the essence of "the American Dream." Following World War II, homeownership became more than ever the mark of full citizenship, the essential symbol of status in American society. However, with wider accessibility of homeownership, the insecurity and low social status of renting became sharper: Tenure became an increasingly defining part of the great divide between the haves and have-nots, strongly correlated with race and marital status, and masking—if not truly replacing—class differences (Dean 1945; Perin 1977; Heskin 1983). Even for many who have made it across the divide, the struggle to achieve and sustain mortgaged homeownership can impose heavy costs—including family stress and exclusionary and snobbish attitudes as well as financial hardship and the risk for mortgage foreclosure—without necessarily yielding the promised fulfillment and satisfaction (Rakoff 1977; Stone 1993:Chapter 1).

The fourth major weakness built into the mortgage system created in the 1930s was the financial vulnerability of "thrift institutions"—savings and loan associations (S&Ls) and mutual savings banks—which were the mainstays of residential lending. Since they put nearly all of their funds into long-term mortgage loans, if interest rates on these loans were constant for the term of the loan, these lenders received a fairly stable and predictable rate of return year after year, regardless of what happened to interest rates after the loans were made. On the other hand, thrifts obtained most of the funds they loaned from savings deposits that could be withdrawn with little or no notice. As long as interest rates on savings accounts were competitive with other investments and substantially higher than the rate of inflation, the risk in "borrowing short and lending long" was not great. Thus, for two decades following World War II, thrift institutions were fairly successful at sustaining a steady inflow of funds into savings accounts, which they then used to support their own growth and a large fraction of the expansion of mortgage credit. As the major suppliers of housing funds, the thrifts were relatively insulated from the rest of the capital markets and not dramatically affected by economic fluctuations. In the 1960s, however, conditions changed, exposing the inherent flaw in the financial structure of thrift institutions, generating two decades of instability and bringing forth another set of transformations in the housing finance system—changes that overcame the weakness in the structure of thrift institutions but not in the housing finance system's other problems.

Problems in the Late 1960s[3]

The onset of sustained inflation and intense competition for credit in the second half of the 1960s had profound implications for the housing finance system. Prior to the 1960s, savings and loan associations (which were the principal suppliers of mortgage credit), mutual savings banks and other mortgage lenders had sufficient funds from savings deposits and mortgage repayments to meet the demand for new mortgage loans. So government-supported capital infusions through the Federal Home Loan Banks and the Federal National Mortgage Association were only a minor part of the total supply of housing credit. In the early 1960s, though, as the economy and housing construction expanded sharply, middle-income households were saving less and spending more. With growing housing demand, but savings accounts not correspondingly expanding, S&Ls turned to borrowing from the Federal Home Loan Banks in order to provide the funds needed for making new mortgage loans. The Federal Home Loan Bank system, in turn, raised the necessary funds by selling securities in the national capital markets.

As credit competition intensified after the mid-1960s, thrift institutions began to suffer from the imbalance caused by "borrowing short and lending long," described above. In order to keep mortgage rates low, savings institutions were limited by federal regulators in the rate of interest that they could pay on savings accounts. As long as there was little inflation and other interest rates were also low, this posed no problem for thrifts. But in the tight-money period of 1966, wealthier households diverted more than $16 billion of their savings into other types of investments paying higher rates of interest; in 1969, they diverted nearly $35 billion from savings accounts (U.S. League of Savings

Associations 1979:11). This sudden withdrawal of large amounts of money from savings institutions is termed "disintermediation." In order to raise money to offset deposit withdrawals, S&Ls turned increasingly to the Federal Home Loan Banks for capital advances, while other lenders sold off their FHA-insured and VA-guaranteed mortgages to Fannie Mae. Mortgage interest rates, which had rarely exceeded 6 percent prior to the 1960s, surpassed this level in 1966 and by 1970 reached nearly 8.5 percent (U.S. Savings and Loan League 1972:41).

The weakening of the traditional, locally based housing finance system led mortgage lenders and their supporters in the federal government to launch a two-pronged strategy. The first component, which was largely put into place between 1968 and 1970, involved the reconceptualization and expansion of government-sponsored secondary mortgage market institutions. The second element, which was only fully implemented in the early 1980s, was deregulation of the financial system. With these changes, the housing finance system embarked on a new era of enormous complexity that served to channel more funds and profits into the industry— but at a cost. Higher interest rates for mortgages, stimulation of real estate speculation and house price inflation, and worsening economic instability were among the consequences of these changes in housing finance (McIntyre 1991; MacDonald 1995, 1996).

Government-Sponsored Secondary Mortgage Markets

Under the pressure of the times, lenders and policy makers became increasingly interested in expanding residential financing through secondary mortgage markets, so as not to be as dependent on savings accounts for funds. Secondary mortgage markets provide a way for locally based originators of mortgage loans (primary lenders) to sell off some mortgages instead of holding them in their own portfolios.[4] This provides primary lenders with additional funds to make more loans. The buyers of mortgages in secondary mortgage markets are large institutions that seek the financial benefits of mortgage lending but do not want to be bothered with investigating the capabilities of borrowers and appraising the values of the properties prior to loans being made, nor with collecting mortgage payments after loans have been made. Secondary market investors traditionally have included insurance companies, large commercial banks, pension funds and government-sponsored entities (GSEs) like Fannie Mae.

In order to stimulate more secondary mortgage market investing, the 1968 Housing Act provided the authority to privatize Fannie Mae over a two-year period. By 1970, Fannie Mae was to become a profit-making corporation, with its own board of directors and the authority to sell stock and issue securities. Fannie Mae was to remain subject to some federal supervision and had financial privileges available only to federal agencies; for example, even though Fannie Mae securities would not be backed explicitly by the federal government, it was assumed that the U.S. Treasury would repay investors if ever Fannie Mae itself could not do so (Tuck 1979:406–408; FNMA 1972).

The 1968 act also created the Government National Mortgage Association (GNMA, "Ginnie Mae"), a government agency within the Department of Housing and Urban Development that retained Fannie Mae's more risky functions, such as financing for subsidized housing. More importantly, though, Ginnie Mae was authorized to provide the federal government's full financial guarantee to mortgage-backed securities (MBSs) issued by private companies holding FHA and VA mortgages. Mortgage-backed securities are like shares in a mutual fund. Groups of mortgages are batched together into "pools." Buyers of securities in a given pool of mortgages are entitled to a share of the aggregated principal and interest payments from all of the borrowers whose mortgages are in the pool. Private investors in these new Ginnie Mae securities would put up money that would be invested in mortgage loans, and they would be guaranteed profitable repayment, first by the FHA/VA protection on the individual mortgages and second by the full faith and credit of the U.S. government on the securities (Tuck 1979:408–409).

The Emergency Home Finance Act of 1970 added the final ingredients in this expanded public-private secondary market framework. Until this point, Fannie Mae had been limited to purchasing government-backed FHA/VA mortgages, which had been a large share of mortgages in the immediate postwar era (Stone 1993:107–108). By the 1960s, however, that proportion had dropped significantly, mainly because the interest-rate ceiling on these loans remained below the market rate for long-term uninsured mortgages. This led to pressure for a secondary mortgage market for conventional mortgages so that lenders could sell off some of their growing number of mortgages lacking FHA or VA backing. The 1970 act authorized Fannie Mae to purchase uninsured mortgages meeting certain standards.

In addition, the 1970 act created another secondary mortgage market agency, the Federal Home Loan Mortgage Corporation (FHLMC, known as "Freddie Mac"), within the Federal Home Loan Bank system to purchase both conventional and insured mortgages from S&Ls and other members of the system (Tuck 1979:415). S&Ls had pushed for creation of their own federally sponsored secondary market institution because historically most of the mortgages purchased by Fannie Mae had been originated not by S&Ls but by mortgage companies. Unlike thrift institutions and commercial banks, mortgage companies have no depositors; they sell into the secondary market every loan they originate and are not part of the Federal Home Loan Bank system.

Despite these major policy changes establishing a greatly expanded framework for secondary mortgage market activity, thrift institutions continued to be the dominant element of the residential mortgage system through the 1970s. At the end of the decade, they still held more than one-half of all outstanding mortgage debt on one- to four-family houses and well over one-third of multifamily mortgage debt—nearly all of it in long-term fixed-rate loans (U.S. League of Savings Associations 1981:26–27). Part of the reason for this was that Freddie Mac got into operation very slowly during the decade, and so it did not yet provide substantial new funds to thrift institutions through buying up older long-term mortgages in thrifts' portfolios.[5]

The Push for Deregulation in the 1970s

As mentioned above, in the period of tight money and rising open-market interest rates during 1966, higher-income households diverted billions of dollars in savings to more lucrative investments, including savings accounts at commercial banks. Commercial banks could attract savings deposits because they made mostly short-term business and construction loans and hence were not locked into long-term fixed-rate sources of income as were the thrifts with their portfolios of low-interest mortgages. Although the interest rates the commercial banks could offer depositors on savings accounts were subject to regulation, the regulators raised the rates with the market, so savings accounts at commercial banks were an attractive (and safe, due to government deposit insurance) alternative to savings accounts at thrifts. As a result of the disintermediation problem that this created for thrift institutions, in 1966, federal regulators put tighter controls on commercial bank interest rates, setting rate ceilings slightly lower for commercial banks than for thrifts, thereby giving thrifts a slight edge in obtaining and retaining deposits. However, in order to keep mortgage interest rates down, the interest rate ceilings on saving accounts were usually set below open-market rates for nonbank investments (Carron 1982:5). Evidence that this new level of regulatory assistance did not solve the thrifts' stability problem is revealed by the large-scale withdrawals of savings deposits during 1969 to 1970, noted above, and a further round of disintermediation during 1973 to 1975. Interest rate ceilings may have protected thrifts from commercial bank competition for the savings of relatively wealthy households but not from the financial alternatives offered by brokerage houses, corporations and the U.S. Treasury.

The intensified competition for savings and competitive disadvantage faced by regulated institutions like thrifts (and to a lesser degree commercial banks) in the new era of inflation accelerated a movement toward financial deregulation that had begun in the late 1950s and received a big boost in the wake of the disintermediation crisis of 1969 to 1970 (Florida 1986: 209–212; Meyerson 1986:471). The argument was that if interest rates on savings accounts were not subject to government regulation, thrifts could offer whatever competitive rates were necessary to attract and retain deposits. But the only way in which thrifts could afford to offer higher rates to savers would be to raise mortgage interest rates because mortgage payments were, of course, their primary source of income. Thus, deregulation had the potential to help depository institutions but could have dire consequences for housing affordability.

Three major deregulation bills were introduced into Congress in the mid-1970s but were not enacted due to successful opposition from small financial institutions—fearing that they would be swallowed up—and real estate interests—fearing greater competition for credit and higher interest rates (Florida 1986:212–213). However, the momentum was clearly toward deregulation—although it took the economic collapse of the early 1980s to bring about enactment of the necessary legislation.

The Triumph of Deregulation in the 1980s

From 1980 until 1983, the United States experienced a recession much deeper and longer than that of the mid-1970s—so severe that even mainstream economists and business people called it a depression. It was in fact a double recession, as the 1980 economic decline was followed by a slight expansion despite rising unemployment in 1981, which was followed by a full across-the-board drop in 1982. It was so severe that all of the institutional changes of the late 1960s and early 1970s were not sufficient to protect the housing finance system from the devastatingly tight money and high interest rates. First, housing production collapsed—largely (but not entirely) because construction interest rates rose to nearly 20 percent, while demand dried up with rising unemployment and falling real incomes. Although the new financial mechanisms were helpful in getting some high-cost money into housing, credit availability was still part of the problem.[6] Furthermore, with lots of old lower-rate mortgages still on their books, the residential finance industry as a whole suffered a severe earnings squeeze in 1980. And in 1981 and 1982, the industry experienced its first operating losses since the Great Depression (U.S. League of Savings Associations 1989:52). Due to insolvencies and mergers, the number of federally insured S&Ls, which had been nearly constant at about 4,000 from 1975 through 1980, declined 22 percent from 1980 through 1983 (U.S. League of Savings Associations 1989:47; Carron 1986:211ff.).

The crisis of the thrifts, together with depressed earnings of commercial banks and the weak international position of the dollar, overwhelmed remaining resistance to financial deregulation. In 1980, the Depository Institutions Deregulation and Monetary Control Act (DIDMCA) was passed, providing, among other things, for phased decontrol of interest rates on deposits and permission for thrifts to diversify gradually out of mortgages (Florida 1986:217–218; Vartanian 1986:141; Fraser 1986:243ff.). The provisions of DIDMCA were too gradual to have much immediate impact on the thrift crisis, however. Also, Federal Home Loan Bank Board advances of nearly $60 billion a year were no more than stopgaps. As well, the Reagan Administration had little inclination to provide special assistance to housing finance (Florida 1986:219–220). The continuing crisis and long-developing deregulation agenda thus led to a second landmark financial deregulation law, the Garn–St. Germain Act of 1982. The law accelerated and expanded the process in the following ways: moving quickly toward eliminating restrictions on the interest rates that institutions could offer depositors; facilitating variable-rate mortgages, with interest rates that go up and down with the rates paid to attract deposits; allowing thrifts to diversify into all sorts of non-housing investments; permitting conversion of mutually owned (i.e., depositor-owned) thrifts to stock ownership; and providing emergency financial assistance to distressed S&Ls (Meyerson 1986:467–469; Vartanian 1986:147ff.).[7]

With deregulation, many thrift institutions moved aggressively into alternative investments. Many others remained active in housing finance, but more as mortgage bankers—for instance, originating loans that were immediately sold to secondary market institutions, buying mortgage-backed securities and swapping old mortgages for mortgage-backed securities. In 1970, 86 percent of the assets of federally insured thrifts were in the form of mortgage loans. In 1979, mortgages were still 82 percent of assets but thereafter dropped below 80 percent and kept declining, reaching 54 percent by 1988. The thrifts' fastest growing class of assets became mortgage-backed securities, growing from less than 4 percent at the end of the 1970s to nearly 16 percent by 1988. Nonmortgage loans and other assets (including direct equity participation in real estate but excluding cash and non-housing investment securities) grew from about 6 percent at the end of the 1970s to over 16 percent by 1988 (U.S. League of Savings Associations 1989:49). Furthermore, during the 1980s, over 40 percent of mortgage loans for the purchase of single-family homes had adjustable instead of fixed rates, including about 60 percent in 1984 and 1988 (U.S. Office of Thrift Supervision 1989:D-1). That is, by the mid-1980s, the financial imbalance of the thrifts had largely been eliminated, in part because they were diversifying out of primary residential lending, but even more because they were passing many of the risks of lending onto borrowers, other investors and, as we shall see, taxpayers.

Some thrifts responded to the phase-out of ceilings on the rates that they could pay for deposits by competing aggressively for funds; they then put the money into highly speculative projects in order to pay the high rates and make profits. These institutions were quite successful at attracting "hot money" depositors, wealthy investors who sought big returns yet were protected by federal deposit insurance. By and large, these were the thrifts that ended up collapsing in the next and bigger crisis of the late 1980s—at public expense. Most thrifts did not so actively pursue deposits in this way but instead filled the gap between their deposits and their desire to invest by borrowing from the Federal Home Loan Banks. FHLB advances, which had helped to sustain the savings institutions through the tight money periods of 1970, 1974 to 1975 and 1980 to 1982, actually tripled in the 1982 to 1988 period, growing to nearly $300 billion, or 22 percent of thrift liabilities (U.S. League of Savings Associations 1989:50).[8] That is, while deregulation meant that thrifts were no longer required to provide moderate-rate mortgages for middle-income homeownership, it did not mean that they gave up government protection: They still had the security of federal deposit insurance and Federal Home Loan Bank advances.

Mortgage Lending in the 1980s

In the broad financial explosion that began after 1982, residential mortgage lending managed to hold its own. With savings institutions moving away from their traditional role as originators of residential mortgages for their own portfolios and into mortgage banking and nonmortgage investing, all sorts of other financial and nonfinancial companies got into the business of originating mortgage loans—the so-called primary mortgage market (Guttentag 1984:243–247; Kane 1986:266). As thrifts themselves and these other institutions sought to turn over these loans and obtain new funds for profitable lending, federally sponsored housing credit grew exponentially, and the government-sponsored secondary mortgage market institutions (Fannie Mae, Freddie Mac, Ginnie Mae) became the principal sources of housing finance. In 1986, thrift institutions yielded their century-long role as the dominant providers of home-mortgage credit, when for the first time the residential mortgage debt held by federally supported agencies (directly) and their mortgage pools (indirectly) exceeded the total held by S&Ls and savings banks (U.S. League of Savings Associations 1989:29).

Of the federally sponsored secondary-market institutions, Freddie Mac grew rapidly during the 1980s. Acting as a true secondary-market agency, it retained only a small portion of the mortgages that it bought; it aggregated the rest into pools and issued mortgage-backed securities against these pools, thereby bringing other investors into the world of housing finance. Fannie Mae, by contrast, continued its traditional role as buyer of insured mortgages for its own portfolio during this period while also taking on a new role in the 1980s as an issuer of mortgage-backed securities. Fannie Mae's total contribution to the residential finance system was slightly greater than that of Freddie Mac but grew more slowly and involved somewhat less activity in mortgage-backed securities. Finally, the volume

of privately issued securities backed by pools of FHA/VA mortgages and guaranteed by Ginnie Mae grew at the fastest pace of all, since these MBSs had the lowest risk, due to federal guarantees, as explained above.[9]

A vast array of new programs, institutions and techniques were thus created and put into place to tap the national and international capital markets for housing, both directly and indirectly, and to provide thrift institutions with more flexible asset and liability structures. In addition to financial deregulation and expansion of federally sponsored secondary mortgage markets, many state and some local governments also sought to draw funds for housing from the national capital markets by creating housing finance agencies and issuing mortgage revenue bonds.[10] Also, deregulation led many types of financial entities to become involved in housing finance, even outside of the government-sponsored agencies, through the creation of sophisticated mortgage-backed securities sold to wealthy private investors and institutions. Even the commodities markets became involved, setting up mortgage "futures" trading to enable hedging and speculation in mortgage interest rates.

The Savings and Loan Crisis and Bailout

As the 1980s drew to a close, hundreds of thrifts collapsed because they had invested in speculative land development projects and high-risk junk bonds that did not yield their promised high profits, which had been the basis for offering very high interest rates on savings accounts and certificates of deposit. Because these institutions now had on their books large volumes of nonperforming and even worthless assets, not only could they not pay high interest rates, they could not even return the deposits themselves to the unhappy savers who wanted their money back. The institutions were insolvent, and as members of the Federal Home Loan Bank System, they were taken over by the Federal Savings and Loan Insurance Corporation (FSLIC). Because the savings accounts were insured, FSLIC had to pay off the depositors and itself soon ran out of funds. The crisis revealed all too clearly that deregulation had not only failed to provide much help to the housing industry; it had even failed to save much of the thrift industry.

In 1988, the S&L collapse became a source of daily headlines, but there was little action from the Reagan Administration. Congress also moved gingerly, as it too had enthusiastically backed deregulation, and many members of the banking committees had benefited from financial industry ties and campaign contributions. With FSLIC insolvent and demands being made for general appropriations to pay off depositors, Congress finally began to move (U.S. General Accounting Office 1988a, 1988b), and soon after his inauguration, President Bush (senior) announced his bailout plan (White House 1989).

The S&L bailout legislation was debated for six months, with most attention devoted to questions of who would pay and how. Finally, on August 6, 1989, the Financial Institutions Reform, Recovery, and Enforcement Act (FIRREA) was signed (Hershey 1989; Barth and Wiest 1989:1). The law's most significant feature was that most of the hundreds of billions of dollars for the bailout of (mostly wealthy) depositors at failed thrifts would be paid for by the public through our taxes. FIRREA also essentially eliminated the 55-year-old Federal Home Loan Bank system through the following changes: FSLIC was dissolved, and deposit insurance for thrifts was placed within the solvent but shaky Federal Deposit Insurance Corporation (FDIC); the independent Federal Home Loan Bank Board was replaced by an Office of Thrift Supervision (OTS) within the Treasury Department; the regional Home Loan Banks, owned by member thrifts, were allowed to continue, but all regulatory functions were placed directly within the federal government. The law established new restrictions on thrift institutions and gave regulators stronger enforcement powers; as well, it mandated some small-scale measures to support slightly below-market housing (Barth and Wiest 1989; Low Income Housing Information Service 1989). It was all, of course, much too little and much too late.

The estimated cost of the S&L bailout continued to rise after FIRREA was passed, doubling by the spring of 1990 to an estimated $325 to $500 billion over a 10-year period (Gosselin 1990a). The S&L scandal generated understandable public anger about the fraud, political payoffs, lax oversight and costs to the taxpayers but too often missed the deeper and longer-term roots of the crisis. As we have seen, the processes of deregulation and resulting chaos represented the response to very real weaknesses in the housing finance system—the contradiction between providing long-term mortgages with relatively low and fixed rates, and the need to offer high rates on savings accounts to attract funds to lend. It was a bad response, but it was to a very real problem rooted ultimately in the inability of U.S. capitalism to solve the problem of housing affordability through a system of profit-driven mortgage-debt financing, which inevitably passes much of the costs and risks of financial instability and insecurity onto housing consumers and the government.

Furthermore, the public bailout itself proved highly inefficient and inequitable (Campen 1991). Considerable attention was focused on the regional redistribution of wealth resulting from the bailout, from the Northeast and Northwest to the Southwest, especially Texas (Bailey 1990). Less attention was focused on the upward redistribution of wealth: This involved, at the first level, the hundreds of billions of dollars lent to developers, speculators and financial manipulators that will never be repaid by them; but at the second level, within the failed institutions, much of the deposit funds were in large "hot-money" accounts, so taxpayers were forced to bail out depositors far wealthier, on average, than themselves (Gosselin 1990b). This massive two-level process of redistribution has only exacerbated widening economic inequality.[11]

The Illusion of Stability in the 1990s

At the end of the 1980s, the economy spiraled into another deep recession. It was the inevitable result of the immense gap that had developed between soaring speculative values and mountains of debt on one side and stagnant household incomes and the underlying weaknesses of the U.S. economy on the other. The official unemployment rate rose to about 7 percent by 1991, but the real impact was far worse, as millions of people gave up looking for work and therefore stopped being counted in the official unemployment rate. The federal deficit jumped to $220 billion in FY1990, and then to a new high of $270 billion in FY1991, as government tax revenues plummeted with the recession (U.S. Office of Management and Budget 1992). In 1991, assets of failed banks (commercial banks and thrifts) set a record as well—$64 billion—and another record of over $100 billion in 1992, as more big banks collapsed under the weight of nonperforming real estate loans. Continuing bank failures of this magnitude sent the Federal Deposit Insurance Corporation into bankruptcy by late 1991; it was itself bailed out only with new taxpayer-backed borrowing authority (Skidmore 1991).

The recovery from the early 1990s' recession was much slower than in previous cycles, with housing/real estate/banking problems and federal budget deficits as major drags on growth during the first half of the decade. From 1992 through 1994, the economy grew at an average rate of less than 3 percent a year, about one-half the rate of other recoveries over the past half-century. In the second half of the decade, growth did accelerate, averaging 3.7 percent a year from 1995 through 1999, but even this was modest by historical standards (Henwood 1999). Furthermore, economic growth during that decade was associated with the lowest rate of investment in real productive capacity and the highest rate of investment in financial assets—the Wall Street mania and debt-financed housing and consumer spending binge—of the past five decades (Henwood 1999; Moseley 1999).

Yet the economic expansion of the 1990s and early 2000s was the longest on record, facilitated by remarkably low interest rates and low inflation, even though the official unemployment rate fell to 6 percent in the fall of 1994 and below 5 percent in the middle of 1997 through the start of the new millennium. How was this possible? The answer is to be found in increasing economic insecurity that kept wage pressures down and widened income inequality (see Chapter 1; see also Henwood 1999, placing U.S. inequality in an international context). Associated with what was occurring in the labor market, government social spending continued to be cut drastically: On the one hand, budget cuts exacerbated the deterioration of

living conditions for those at the bottom; on the other hand, tight spending and rising revenues caused steady reductions in federal budget deficits and by late in the decade turned into surpluses, thereby limiting competition for credit and helping to keep interest rates down. Furthermore, weaknesses in the economies of most other nations meant that imported goods were relatively cheap, facilitating high rates of consumer spending with low inflation in the United States.

Housing finance was deeply enmeshed in the course of the economy during the 1990s. While the mortgage-backed securities (MBSs) market had been fully developed by the end of the 1980s, economic conditions of the 1990s brought the full fruition of MBSs, resulting in even greater integration of housing finance with the global capital markets. In the early 1990s, new computer-based techniques of investment analysis mated with relatively low interest rates and high housing demand to spawn a complex array of attractive mortgage-backed securities. During the period from 1991 through 1993, interest rates on MBSs were higher than corporate and Treasury bonds and seemed virtually risk-free, due to the explicit government guarantee on Ginnie Mae securities and implicit guarantee on Fannie Mae and Freddie Mac securities. In response, many major investment houses bought MBSs issued by these government-sponsored entities and then issued and promoted another type of security, called collateralized mortgage obligations (CMOs), backed by these securities. CMOs, which had first been introduced by Freddie Mac in 1984, divide the expected interest payments and principal repayments from pools of mortgages into slices called "tranches." Each type of CMO, which is very much like a bond, corresponds to a particular tranch; each has a unique combination of interest rate, term to maturity, rate of repayment of principal and risk. Because different kinds of investors have different financial goals, tax situations and tolerance for risk, the diversity of CMOs has opened up housing finance to a whole array of wealthy individual and institutional investors, including pension funds, insurance companies, banks and Wall Street firms themselves (Benson 1996; Lea 1996:167).

The market for these sophisticated mortgage-backed securities is, however, quite complex and unregulated, and even elaborate computer models cannot anticipate all the possible risks. Thus, in the mid-1990s, when the economy and mortgage interest rates did not behave as predicted, there was chaos in the MBS markets. With the economy recovering slowly early in the decade, mortgage rates dropped below 8 percent at the beginning of 1993 and below 7 percent briefly at the end of the year (FHLMC 1999), triggering a rash of mortgage refinancings by homeowners. In turn, this led to a greater rate of prepayments of mortgage-backed securities than had been anticipated. Then, in 1994, economic growth accelerated, leading to concerns about inflation, causing mortgage rates to climb to over 9 percent in late 1994 and early 1995 (FHLMC 1999). While such higher rates would have been attractive to investors buying newly issued MBSs, pessimism regarding inflation and potential reduction in mortgage demand from consumers, as well as declining market values for previously issued MBSs, led the MBS market to dry up. Suddenly, lots of investors were trying to bail out. There was a liquidity crisis in the market when buyers could not be found, and many investors sustained substantial losses. What should have been obvious, but perhaps did not get much attention from promoters and high-flying investors, is that government backing associated with MBSs issued by GSEs only protects investors against losses due to homeowners not paying their mortgages, not fluctuations in the market value of MBSs resulting from interest rate fluctuations in the capital markets. So what had looked like very safe, high-yield investments turned out to be almost like junk bonds in terms of risk (Benson 1996:62–64). Eventually, after several years of lower and relatively stable mortgage rates, the MBS market recovered but was no longer as profitable or as exuberant. This experience reveals how very sensitive to interest rates the housing finance system remains and how unanticipated behavior by consumers can be transmitted to the capital markets.

While the discussion here and in most of the literature has focused on the development of the secondary mortgage market institutions and financing vehicles, the 1990s were also a period of continuing changes at the "retail" primary market where residential mortgages are originated and serviced. By the late 1990s, mortgage banking companies (which, as noted previously, have no depositors and sell into the secondary market every loan they originate) accounted for 56 percent of all residential mortgage originations, an increase from 35 percent of the market in 1990 (Lereah 1997; Avery et al. 1999). This is a highly competitive business that operates on thin profit margins; it depends heavily on information technology to be able to profit from small, short-term fluctuations in interest rates. This shift and the related consolidation of the banking industry has raised questions about the responsiveness of the conventional mortgage industry to the needs of low-income and minority borrowers and neighborhoods.[12]

In addition, the servicing of residential mortgages—collecting and processing the payments of interest and principal as well as property tax and insurance escrows—has evolved into a separate, specialized and highly concentrated business. As of the end of 1998, 25 so-called mega-servicers held 47 percent of the market. Because their portfolios are national in scope, they lack the firsthand knowledge and flexibility to anticipate and respond sensitively to local economic conditions and individual borrower circumstances. This raises questions about their capacity to handle mortgage delinquency and foreclosure problems at a distance and across the country in the event of a sharp economic downturn (Lereah 1999).

SOME IMPLICATIONS OF THE NEW HOUSING FINANCE SYSTEM

Over the entire postwar period, housing has been the largest single user of credit, but since the late 1970s, it has only been through the new financing instruments and institutions that housing has been able to compete effectively and obtain a large share of available credit. This, in turn, has come about only because the U.S. Treasury has provided direct or implicit backing for so much of the net increase in residential mortgage lending. In the 1980s, almost 56 percent of the net increase in residential mortgage debt was financed through Fannie Mae, Freddie Mac, Ginnie Mae and the Federal Home Loan Banks, and in the 1990s, nearly 72 percent. In terms of potential obligations on the U.S. Treasury, this means that by the end of 2002, federally sponsored housing credit accounted for nearly 50 percent of the federal government's total publicly held liabilities (direct plus sponsored debt) compared with less than 5 percent in 1970, 22 percent in 1980 and 33 percent in 1990 (see Federal Reserve System 2003:Tables L-1, L-126; Stone 1993:Table 5.1).

The changes in mortgage financing that began in the late 1960s had contradictory results. They did give a substantial boost to real growth in the economy before and after the 1973 to 1975, 1980 to 1982 and 1990 to 1992 recessions, but also gave a boost to the unprecedented inflation of the 1970s and the overblown credit bubbles of the past three decades. The new mortgage institutions, especially the federally created and federally backed agencies, have intensified competition for credit, which led to even higher interest rates throughout the system until the 1990s. Therefore, the attempts of mortgage lenders to compete more effectively for funds have been relatively successful but at a real cost. Most directly, for a long time, the higher costs were in the form of higher mortgage interest rates. During the 1990s, nominal mortgage interest rates fell to their lowest levels since the mid-1960s—because of what was happening with the labor market, government spending and the global economy, as discussed previously—contributing to the boom in mortgage borrowing and lending. Taking into account the low rate of inflation throughout most of the decade, inflation-adjusted mortgage interest rates were actually considerably higher in the 1990s than in the 1970s, but nonetheless, they were well below the rates during most of the 1980s.

In short, residential finance is no longer a relatively separate and insulated component of the credit system. Housing finance has become almost fully integrated with the national and international capital markets (see, for example, Hendershott and Van Order 1989; McIntyre 1991; Weicher 1994). But what difference have these changes made for housing affordability and the willingness and ability of the prevailing institutions to meet the housing needs of all Americans? The following sections examine how several major aspects of housing affordability have been impacted by the evolution of the finance system: First, new construction has moved toward larger and more expensive houses, as widening income inequality and mortgage standardization have shifted more of the housing market to higher-income households. Second, for the same reasons, homeownership declined for a while as moderate- and middle-income families found it harder to afford homes but then turned up again due to new, riskier lending programs and changing demographics. Third, the long-term changes and recent measures to support and expand mortgage lending have created financial stress for households, most especially for borrowers of modest income. And fourth, the enormous growth of profit-motivated, government-sponsored secondary mortgage market enterprises (GSEs) has led to institutional arrogance, with great risks for taxpayers and financial markets as well as for the institutions themselves.

The Trend Toward Bigger, More Costly Houses

The abundance of mortgage credit in recent decades has fueled accelerating turnover of houses and increases in house prices. Until the mid-1970s, about three existing single-family houses were sold for every new one sold; since then, the ratio has risen to more than five to one (U.S. Department of Housing and Urban Development 2003). On average, prices of single-family houses have fluctuated with the economy but over the long term have risen considerably more than inflation. Over the 30 years from the high point of the late 1960s through the end of the 1990s, the median price of new single-family houses rose 32 percent more than the Consumer Price Index (CPI), while the median price of existing single-family houses rose 39 percent more than the CPI. But how much of this consists of speculative increases in the market values of the same or similar houses, and how much represents a shift toward bigger, more costly houses?

During the 1970s, there were ups and downs in real (i.e., inflation-adjusted) average construction costs for single-family houses but only a slight upward trend toward larger houses. By contrast, during the 1980s, there was a dramatic rising trend in the inflation-adjusted construction cost of new single-family housing—indicating a historical shift over the decade toward more extravagant new houses that corresponds to and exacerbates the affordability implications of growing income inequality. From 1990 to 1991, the recession brought a dip of 5 percent in average real construction costs, followed by a climb back to the previous level by mid-decade and then a surge to new heights of about $150,000 a unit in 1997 and 1998.[13] The average real construction cost of a new single-family house in 1998 was about 50 percent higher than it would have been if houses similar to those from the late 1960s through the late 1970s had been built. Since middle-income households have seen little increase in their real incomes, it has not been as profitable for developers to build housing for them. High-income households have experienced substantial increases in their real incomes, so more luxurious and costly housing for them has been a growing share of new single-family housing.

For new multifamily housing, changes in average real per unit construction cost have been more complex. In the recession of the early 1970s, multifamily construction dropped precipitously, and with it, the average construction cost of a new unit fell to about $50,000 (in 1998 dollars), where it remained until the late 1970s. Thereafter, through two cycles of the economy, the inflation-adjusted cost rose over 70 percent, to a peak of nearly $86,000 (1998 dollars) in the early 1990s, before dipping and settling at about $74,000 from the mid-1990s on. As with single-family housing, this trend is indicative of the shift to construction for high-income households—in the form of condominiums and luxury rentals.

The affordability implications of this analysis are fairly apparent. Development of new housing is responding to and reinforcing widening income inequality. As a larger proportion of new housing is produced for higher-income households, people with more modest incomes compete for the available supply of less luxurious older housing. This drives the prices and rents of older houses higher than they likely would be if a broader spectrum of new housing were being produced. The result is that in some locales even relatively modest housing is becoming less affordable and hence is moving up the income distribution in terms of who can buy and rent it.

While these patterns are, to a considerable extent, explained by widening income inequality, the restructuring of mortgage markets is also an important part of the story. In order to minimize risks and transaction costs, secondary mortgage market institutions would buy only highly standardized mortgages free of complexity or potential problems—at least until the 1990s, when some special lending programs were created (discussed below). As MacDonald has put it (1996:1184): "Underwriting guidelines established at the national rather than the local level were aimed at filtering out borrowers and properties that posed higher (or unidentifiable) default risks, in order to support the price MBSs would attract in the capital markets." These policies had impacts on lending for multifamily rental housing as well as single-family owner-occupied houses (MacDonald 1996:1185–1190). Thus, the shift to higher-end housing production is not only due to developers directly pursuing housing consumers with the most money. It also reflects the kinds of projects for which developers could most readily obtain financing from primary lenders who wanted to be able place the mortgages expeditiously and profitably in the secondary mortgage markets.

Housing Finance and Homeownership Trends

The U.S. homeownership rate climbed steadily from the late 1940s until 1980, when it reached a record level of 65.8 percent. Then, in the first half of the 1980s, it declined steadily to 63.8 percent in 1986, the lowest level since the mid-1960s, and for the next decade, through 1994, remained almost unchanged at about 64 percent (U.S. Department of Housing and Urban Development 1999:Table 29). Given the continued ideological and economic bias toward homeownership (see Dean 1945; Rakoff 1977; Weicher 1994; Hughes 1996; Berson and Neely 1997), this was a remarkable historical shift. To a considerable extent, the decline in homeownership certainly was due to widening income inequality, the shift in housing construction to the higher-income/higher-cost market and high interest rates. It was also due, though, to the changes in the housing finance system. As noted earlier, the standardization required for mortgages to be marketable in the secondary mortgage markets, especially as imposed by the "duopoly" of Fannie Mae and Freddie Mac (Weicher 1994; see also McIntyre 1991), means that local mortgage originators no longer have had flexibility to make allowances for prospective borrowers whose incomes, assets, debts and/or credit histories are less than sterling (see also Chapter 12).

Then, beginning in 1995, after a decade and a half of decline and stagnation, the homeownership rate began climbing again, reaching a new record rate of 68 percent in 2002 (U.S. Department of HUD 2003:Table 27). What happened? Was it just the fruits of low inflation and low unemployment eventually ripening? Not entirely. In large measure, the expansion of homeownership in the 1990s was the result of deliberate reactive and pre-emptive public and private initiatives. First, advocacy groups, using data produced pursuant to the Home Mortgage Disclosure Act (HMDA) and lending requirements of the Community Reinvestment Act (CRA), became increasingly skilled and successful at getting primary lenders to increase mortgage lending to communities and households of color and/or low income (see, for example, Squires 1992; Schwartz 1998; Avery, Bostic and Canner 2000). Second, in the wake of the S&L debacle of the 1980s, as well as in response to community advocacy, the Federal Housing Enterprises Financial Safety and Soundness Act of 1992 directed HUD to establish and monitor annual goals for Fannie Mae and Freddie Mac to purchase low- to moderate-income mortgages (Canner and Passmore 1995; MacDonald 1995, 1996; Eggers and Burke 1996). Third, mortgage activity by lenders providing subprime and manufactured home financing has accounted for a growing share of all home purchase lending, but most especially to low-income and minority borrowers and neighborhoods (see Canner, Passmore and Laderman 1999).[14] Finally, ideological support for expanding

homeownership, especially among people of color, and more generally those of lower income, was provided by the Clinton Administration beginning in 1995 (Berson and Neely 1997) and was continued by the administration of George W. Bush, in keeping with both presidents' records of rhetorical declarations of expanding opportunity despite substantive actions in housing and other areas that deepened inequality.

With the conjuncture of these initiatives and favorable macroeconomic conditions, the major demographic components of the increase in the overall homeownership rate since the mid-1990s can be examined in relation to the decreases in the 1980s and early 1990s. Among Black non-Hispanics, the homeownership rate first decreased from 46 percent in the early 1980s to 42 percent in 1989, changed little through 1993 and then increased to 48 percent by 2002. Among other non-Hispanic households of color (mostly Asians, although the data do not separate Asians and Native Americans), the homeownership rate dropped from 53 percent in the early 1980s to under 49 percent in 1987 and remained at around 50 percent through the mid-1990s before rising to 55 percent by 2002. Among Latinos, homeownership declined from a little over 41 percent in the early 1980s to 39 percent in 1991. Thereafter, it rose fairly steadily to 48 percent by 2002. Among white non-Hispanics, homeownership dipped slightly from 69 percent in 1983 to a bit over 68 percent in 1986 and has climbed ever since, even during the early 1990s recession, to 74.5 percent in 2002 (U.S. Department of Housing and Urban Development 2003:Table 29). Clearly, the decline in homeownership was overwhelmingly borne by people of color, not by whites. Yet the more recent increase in homeownership rates has been nearly as great among whites as among people of color. Although the changing homeownership rates for Latinos and Asians include the impacts of high rates of immigration (most recent immigrants being renters), the contrast between Black non-Hispanics and whites is not explicable in this way: The homeownership rate for Blacks had a net increase of little more than two percentage points since the early 1980s, while that of whites rose over five percentage points.

Although lower incomes and discrimination by lenders certainly account for lower rates of homeownership among households of color, these factors do not fully account for the substantial declines in homeownership rates among such households in the 1980s. The standardization of mortgage underwriting imposed by Fannie Mae and Freddie Mac, which eliminated flexibility in dealing with applicants whose income and/or credit histories did not quite meet the standardized criteria, most certainly had the effect of narrowing home-buying opportunities for households of color in that period. By the same token, the increase in homeownership among people of color since the 1990s is disproportionately attributable to the specially targeted mortgage programs and subprime lending of the recent decade, even though lower-income white households have also been among the participants.

The advent of specially targeted lending programs, as a way of offsetting some of the consequences of mortgage standardization, does, however, suggest a disproportionate distribution of risk. These programs generally involve very low down payments, which, studies suggest, is a strong predictor of the likelihood of mortgage default (Weicher 1994:60). Perhaps surprisingly, borrower income is not strongly related to loan performance, although triggering events like job loss certainly are significant (Avery et al. 1996). Some institutions with so-called "affordable" home-lending programs have reported that such programs do involve higher costs of origination and servicing in contrast with conventional lending but not significantly higher default rates if flexible acceptance criteria are applied carefully and if there is counseling and education of borrowers.

On the other hand, early quantitative analyses of "affordable" lending by secondary mortgage market institutions and private mortgage insurers do suggest somewhat higher rates of delinquency and default than those found in conventional lending. For example, a study of delinquency rates where the borrower made a 3 percent down payment and another party paid the remaining 2 percent found rates significantly higher than where the borrower put down the full 5 percent (Avery et al. 1996). The Freddie

Mac experience with special programs that have looser underwriting standards has been that the loans show significantly higher default and foreclosure rates, especially on loans that have only 2 percent down and where the bank often pays even this amount (Schnare 1996). Advocacy groups that have negotiated agreements with large banks to channel mortgage loans through them, such as the Neighborhood Assistance Corporation of America (NACA), have had great success at facilitating homeownership for thousands of moderate-income and minority borrowers but are also being criticized for putting some people into untenable financial situations. While most groups refuse to divulge their default rates, mortgage industry officials estimate that the delinquency rate on NACA mortgages through Fleet Bank exceeds 10 percent compared with about 7 percent for other targeted Fleet mortgages and about 2 to 3 percent for conventional mortgages (Browning 1999). Comparing the current programs with the abuses of FHA homeownership programs in the early 1970s that resulted in widespread foreclosures and neighborhood destruction, Ann Schnare, Freddie Mac vice president for Housing Economics, has declared: "In my opinion, it is bad public policy to put individuals into houses they cannot afford to support" (Schnare 1996:177).

Household Debt Burdens and Mortgage Stress

While a great deal of attention has been focused on the inability of young families to buy their first home, the preceding discussion suggests that the more serious problem of homeowner affordability is with the people who have bought homes but are finding it harder and harder to keep up their mortgage payments. This is a problem exacerbated by home equity borrowing and, to some extent, by refinancing that results in higher debt burdens (see, for example, Cannner, Durkin and Luckett 1999; Brady et al. 2000; Bradford 2002; Canner, Dynan and Passmore 2002).

Aggregate statistics on mortgage and consumer debt in relation to disposable income are suggestive of potential debt stress but do not in themselves reveal the burden of debt *payments,* which depend on interest rates and loan terms, not just amount of debt; and aggregate statistics do not reveal the *distribution* of debt burdens among different households. Estimates of actual debt payments in relation to disposable personal income show a cyclical variation, rising during periods of economic expansion and declining during recessions. In the early 1990s, debt payments rose little, on average, despite rising debt:income ratios, because of falling interest rates (Canner, Kennickell and Luckett 1995:324–325). Behind the cyclical pattern, however, there has been an upward trend in payments as households have increased their debt in relation to income (Edelberg and Fisher 1997).

Disaggregated data from the Surveys of Consumer Finances conducted by the Federal Reserve Board reveal significant differences among income groups in the burdens and risks of debt overload. High-income households owe most of the debt, but such households (those with annual incomes of $100,000 or more) have a median ratio of debt payments to income (for mortgage and home equity debt) far lower than for all other income groups. Through the 1980s, payment:income ratios rose for all income groups, but since the late 1980s (according to Canner, Durkin and Luckett 1999) or early 1990s (according to Edelberg and Fisher 1997), the ratio has declined, on average, for higher-income households but continued to rise for lower- and middle-income households. Also, while households with incomes of $50,000 to $100,000 have had the highest median ratio of housing debt payments to income, the biggest *increases* in the ratios since the late 1980s have been among households with incomes under $25,000. Furthermore, in 1998, about one-fourth of all families with incomes of under $50,000 had total debt payments of more than 40 percent of their incomes compared with just 2 percent of those with incomes of $100,000 or more (Kennickell, Starr-McCluer and Surette 2000:Table 14). In 2001, 13.4 percent of families in the lowest quintile of income had debt payments that were 60 days or more past due compared with 10.2 percent of such families in 1995 (Aizcorbe, Kennickell and Moore 2003:Table 14). Many of these families have taken on and been encouraged to assume high debt loads in order

to achieve the American Dream of homeownership, but at what risk?

Among those expressing concern about the dangers of rising debt burdens for lower-income households has been the chief economist of the Mortgage Bankers Association, amidst his otherwise broadly bullish comments on the mortgage industry (Lereah 1997, 1998, 1999). Some of his comments are worth quoting (1999:5):

> Bringing attention to these potential problems is the fact that the share of loans with loan-to-value ratios greater than 90 percent has risen substantially during the past five years (to about 25 percent). This places greater burden on the quality of loan portfolios in a period of deteriorating economic performance. And if and when the economy turns down, the first group to be hit with lost jobs and unreliable wages will be the lower-income group. According to recent income and debt data, the debt burden of low-income households relative to higher-income households is rising. If the economy falters, clearly many households that are at the margin in terms of their abilities to meet their monthly mortgage obligations now will bring delinquency and foreclosure problems for mortgage servicers. Thus, it is the low-income families that are experiencing heavy debt burdens, leaving them more vulnerable to recession and meeting their mortgage obligations, while the higher-income groups are actually reducing their debt burdens (via refinancings and higher wages) and lowering their mortgage obligations.

Long before the downturn, however, there already was a long upward trend in mortgage foreclosures since the late 1970s. During most of the 1970s, the rate of foreclosures was less than about 0.5 percent of all mortgages, actually declining steadily after 1973 to a historic low of 0.3 percent in 1978 (see Figure 4:1). The severe double recession of the late 1970s and early 1980s brought a surge in foreclosures, to more than 0.8 percent in 1982, where it leveled off for two years. Remarkably, though, the boom years of the late 1980s brought not a decline but a steady increase in foreclosures, to nearly 1.1 percent in 1988. The next recession brought another increase, to above 1.3 percent in 1989 and 1991 (with a slight dip in between). The rest of the 1990s then recapitulated the pattern of the late

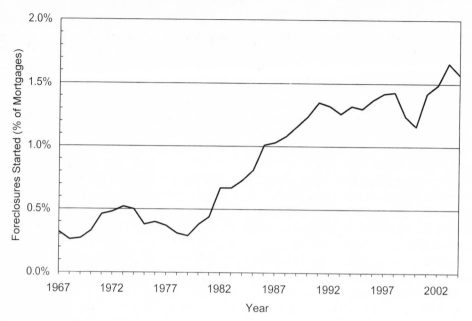

FIGURE 4.1. Residential Mortgage Foreclosure Rate, 1967–2004.
Source: Mortgage Bankers Association.

1980s but at a higher level: Despite steady economic growth and declining unemployment, the rate of foreclosures remained nearly flat at about 1.3 percent from 1992 through 1995 and then began steadily climbing, reaching a new record high of over 1.4 percent in 1998. Over the next two years, as the long boom reached its culmination, there was substantial reduction in the foreclosure rate to less than 1.2 percent. However, the onset of recession brought a sharp reversal, with rate surging to a new high of 1.6 percent in 2003 (Figure 4.1).

The new era of housing finance has ensured a high volume of mortgage money by creating new vehicles and opportunities for profitable investment in housing. But with this abundant supply of capital has come extensive promotion and acceptance of dangerously high levels of debt for buying homes, refinancing existing mortgages and tapping home equity.

Instability in Freddie Mac and Fannie Mae

Freddie Mac and Fannie Mae emerged as the "Pillars of Hercules" in the mortgage system because their private profits are underpinned by public support. On the one hand, as government sponsored enterprises, they have an obligation to provide some mortgage support for lower-income households and underserved geographical areas. On the other hand, and far more significantly, their special status means that their mortgage-backed securities have had the implicit backing of the U.S. Treasury,[15] thus making these securities easy to market and making Freddie and Fannie's stock quite attractive to Wall Street investors. Both entities have thus become Fortune 500 companies, yet they are the only members of this club exempt from regulation by the Securities and Exchange Commission and thus exempt from the disclosure requirements of other corporations with publicly traded stock. As Fred Smith, president of the Competitive Institute in Washington, has put it, Fannie Mae and Freddie Mac are examples of "profit-side capitalism and loss-side socialism" (quoted in Berlau 2003).

Fannie and Freddie's success and special status have led to a certain amount of hubris among their executives. As a result, there was little close scrutiny of their operations until the beginning of 2003, when outside auditors raised issues about some of Freddie Mac's accounting procedures. Then, in June of 2003, Freddie's problems reached the level of scandal: Possible criminal probes were announced as the board of Freddie Mac forced out its three top executives, claiming they had obstructed a probe into the company's accounting. But a growing number of critics say that this is more than a typical corporate scandal: It is a government-policy scandal for which taxpayers could be left holding the bag. And many were wondering if the controversy over accounting issues at Freddie Mac will spill over to its older sister, Fannie Mae (Berlau 2003).

Indeed, in the wake of the Freddie Mac scandal, it was soon revealed that Fannie Mae might have suffered billions of dollars in losses over the preceding two years that were obscured by the complexity of its accounting procedures. Apparently, investors in Fannie Mae securities were unconcerned because they had thought that the federal government would protect them. Nonetheless, Fannie immediately responded that it would take steps to reduce its risks, but some outside analysts still felt that it was taking too much risk and needed to disclose more about its mortgage operations (Berenson 2003).

Congressional hearings were launched in the fall of 2003, and the Bush Administration recommended regulatory changes that would be the most substantial since the S&L crisis confronted the first Bush Administration a decade and half earlier. It was proposed that there be a new regulatory agency within the Treasury Department that would not only provide oversight but also the authority to set one of the two capital reserve requirements of Fannie and Freddie as well as approval authority for new lines of business. It was not proposed to eliminate implicit government backing for their debt and the indirect subsidies associated with this backing and other protections (Labaton 2003a). However, soon thereafter, the Treasury Department raised the possibility of eliminating its special line of credit to the two companies. But the nervous reaction of the capital markets to this trial balloon (Labaton 2003b) revealed how much the capital markets rely on "loss-side socialism" in the mortgage system.

At the end of 2003, Congress had not yet acted on regulatory reform of the mortgage giants, apparently due to resistance of Freddie Mac and Fannie Mae to some of the reforms being con-

sidered (Glater 2003; New York Times Editorial Desk 2003). Adding substance to the debate about the implications of Fannie and Freddie's special status, just before Christmas, a Federal Reserve senior economist released the draft of a study of "The GSE Implicit Subsidy and the Value of Government" (Passmore 2003). The study estimated that the federal government's implicit subsidy amounts to between $119 and $164 billion, with only about one-half of that going to borrowers in the form of lower interest rates, the rest going to shareholders. It also estimated that the reduction in mortgage interest rates due to public subsidy amounts to only seven basis points, and, due to this small impact on rates, the "implicit subsidy does not appear to have substantially increased homeownership or homebuilding" over what they would be if the GSEs operated without government support. Fannie Mae immediately disputed the study, while Freddie Mac did not respond (Andrews 2003).

One final point of significance in the saga of Fannie and Freddie is revealed by the response of a leading housing advocate who was directly involved in helping to establish the so-called "affordable housing goals" of Fannie Mae and Freddie Mac (Fishbein 2003). While fully acknowledging the internal problems at the agencies, he notes that their cost of funds could rise if there were to be reduction in market confidence in the agencies and/or transfer of regulation to a Treasury Department insensitive to the special housing purposes of Fannie and Freddie. He is concerned that an increase in the cost of funds in the capital markets could result in higher mortgage rates, thereby closing off homeownership opportunities for some low- and moderate-income households. His stance is a telling illustration of one of the devil's bargains that is entered into by housing advocates because we do not have a truly social system of housing finance.

CONCLUSION

This chapter has examined the contours of housing finance and the economy since the middle of the 20th century, in order to elucidate some of the limitations, weaknesses and problems of a housing finance system based on private capital markets, mortgage debt and speculative ownership of housing. It is a system that, to be sure, has facilitated the production of vast amounts of housing and has provided access to homeownership for over two-thirds of all U.S. households. At the same time, though, in idealizing conventional (debt-encumbered) homeownership, it has exacerbated the social stigma of renting, inhibited the exploration and expansion of forms of tenure other than conventional ownership and renting, and imposed enormous affordability burdens and risks on many who have bought (and indeed many who rent). Furthermore, the existing system of housing finance has been the source of considerable institutional and financial instabilities. Yet the problems manifested and generated by this system have been dealt with not through fundamental reform and new approaches to housing finance but rather through public policies that for the most part ensure private profits while socializing investor risk.

Rather than idealizing the market and providing endless subsidies and bailouts to private capital, public policy must transcend the market and truly serve social purposes. Overcoming the extensive and persistent problem of affordability will require substantial and sustained public commitment to new concepts of housing finance as well as alternative approaches to housing ownership and tenure. The most significant and straightforward mechanism for overcoming permanently the affordability burden of mortgage payments is by using direct public capital grants to finance the production and acquisition of social housing. In a complementary way, though, it is also essential to reform the financial system in order to deflate the overblown credit system, reduce speculative uses of credit and assure an adequate supply of low-cost credit—as a supplement to capital grants—for productive investment in social housing and progressive economic development. This, though, will require the imposition of social criteria on private capital market participants and institutions. Chapter 12 explores various existing and potential models of social financing, demonstrating what has been done, what is possible and what is necessary (see also Stone 1993:Chapter 8).

NOTES

1. In 2001, the median monthly total housing payment for homeowners with mortgages was $1,015, while their median monthly mortgage payment was $676 (U.S. Department of Housing and Urban Development and U.S. Bureau of the Census 2002:Table 3-19). The ratio is 67 percent. No comparable data are available for renters. However, the proportion of rents that goes for mortgage payments is probably greater, on average, because interest rates are higher on the commercial loans used to finance commercial properties, and landlords are more likely to use multiple mortgages to cash out equity.

2. For detailed discussion of the development of the housing finance system prior to the 1960s, including the origins of the Federal Home Loan Bank System and the Federal National Mortgage Association as well as full discussion and citation of sources, see Stone 1993:Chapters 3,4.

3. This section and the following sections through the 1980s are based on Stone 1993:Chapters 5,6.

4. After selling a loan in the secondary market, the primary lender usually continues to service the loan, including collecting mortgage payments (and sending them on to the ultimate holder of the mortgage) and ensuring that property taxes and insurance are paid. The primary lender, or other servicer, receives a fee from the ultimate holder of the mortgage for handling these activities.

5. Freddie Mac issued its first mortgage-backed security in 1975 and by the end of the decade had issued about $10 billion of such securities (Berkman 1979:69).

6. The net growth of residential mortgage debt had accounted for 24 percent of the net increase in total debt from 1979 to 1980 but dropped to 15 percent and then 11 percent in 1981 and 1982, respectively, before returning to 20 percent in 1983 (Federal Reserve System 1999:Table 5.1).

7. With deregulation, a frenzy of takeovers, conversions to stock ownership and a push for quick profits overwhelmed much of the thrift industry. Between 1980 and 1989, the number of thrift institutions further declined by one-third, while the share of industry assets held by the 50 largest institutions grew to 40 percent (from 25 percent in 1980). Stock-owned institutions increased to 45 percent of all thrifts in 1989, from less than 20 percent in 1980, but these 45 percent of institutions held 75 percent of the assets of the entire thrift industry compared with 27 percent of assets held

by stockholder institutions in 1980 (Barth and Wiest 1989:15).

8. Outstanding advances had been $10.8 billion in 1970 (6.3 percent of thrift liabilities), $24.6 billion in 1974 (8.5 percent of liabilities), and $98.2 billion in 1982 (14 percent of liabilities); by 1988, they were nearly $299.2 billion (22.1 percent of liabilities) (U.S. League of Savings Associations 1989:50).

9. Freddie Mac's total mortgage portfolio was $338 billion in 1990, having grown from virtually nothing in 1970 to $20 billion in 1980. Its volume of mortgage-backed securities grew from nothing in 1970 to $15 billion in 1980, $100 billion in 1985 and $316 billion in 1990, an average annual compound rate of growth of 35 percent during the 1980s (FHLMC 1989:9, 24; U.S. League of Savings Associations 1989:65; FHLMC 1991:16). By the end of 2001, its total mortgage portfolio was $1.14 trillion, and its volume of mortgage-backed securities was $948 billion (FHLMC 2001:21, 25).

Fannie Mae's mortgage portfolio grew from $15 billion operation in 1970 to $57 billion in 1980 to $113 billion in 1990. Its mortgage-backed securities operation only began in 1981, growing to $55 billion by 1985 and $300 billion by 1990 (FNMA 1989:3–4; U.S. League of Savings Associations 1989: 66; FNMA 1991:17). By 2002, its mortgage portfolio was $798 billion, and its volume of mortgage-backed securities was $1.54 trillion (FNMA 2002:39, 49).

Ginnie Mae securities grew from nothing in 1970 to $94 billion in 1980 to $400 billion by the end of 1990 (U.S. Bureau of the Census 1990:503; GNMA 1991). Between 1970 and 2002, over $2 trillion of Ginnie Mae mortgage-backed securities were issued; net of repayments and refinancings, the outstanding balance was $568 billion at end of 2002 (GNMA 2002).

10. Mortgage revenue bonds are, in some ways, similar to the MBSs issued by secondary mortgage market agencies, but they tend to be much more closely tied to individual mortgages or small groups of mortgages rather than large pools.

11. For further added costs in the late 1990s, see Labaton 1998.

12. See Avery et al. 1999 on the effects of consolidation. See Canner, Durkin and Luckett 1999 on the growth of subprime lending. See Bradford 2002 on racial disparities in the subprime market.

13. Note that this figure does not include the costs of land acquisition, site preparation, construction financing, fees, and overhead and profit. See Stone 1993:376, notes 2 and 3 to Chapter 6, for explanation of the methods used.

14. Between 1993 and 1998, subprime and manufactured home lenders more than tripled their share of applications for conventional (for instance, not FHA and VA) home purchase mortgage loans to about 34 percent and nearly tripled their share of loans made to about 14 percent (Canner, Durkin and Luckett 1999:710).

15. Fannie Mae has claimed that the "US government does not guarantee directly or indirectly Fannie Mae's debt securities or other obligations" (FNMA 2002:25). Yet the Federal Reserve states that the mortgage-backed securities of Fannie Mae, Freddie Mac and Ginnie Mae, as well as securities issued by Federal Home Loan Banks "are classified as US government securities" (Federal Reserve System 2003:78, notes to Tables L-125, L-126). See Passmore 2003 for the value of this ambiguity to the GSEs.

REFERENCES

Aizcorbe, Ana M., Arthur B. Kennickell and Kevin B. Moore. 2003. Recent changes in family finances: Evidence from the 1998 and 2001 survey of consumer finances. *Federal Reserve Bulletin*, 89:1–32.

Andrews, Edmund L. 2003. Two big mortgage agencies are criticized in fed study. *New York Times*, December 23.

Avery, Robert B., Raphael W. Bostic, Paul S. Calem and Glenn B. Canner. 1996. Credit risk, credit scoring, and the performance of home mortgages. *Federal Reserve Bulletin*, 82:621–648.

———. 1999. Trends in home purchase lending: Consolidation and the Community Reinvestment Act. *Federal Reserve Bulletin*, 85:81–102.

Avery, Robert B., Raphael W. Bostic and Glenn B. Canner. 2000. CRA special lending programs. *Federal Reserve Bulletin*, 86:711–731.

Bailey, Doug. 1990. S&L cost sparks regional battle. *Boston Globe*, August 25.

Barth, James R., and Philip R. Wiest. 1989. *Consolidation and restructuring of the U.S. thrift industry under the Financial Institutions Reform, Recovery, and Enforcement Act*. Washington, DC: U.S. Office of Thrift Supervision, October.

Benson, Jason Dean. 1996. *The rise and subsequent fall of the mortgage-backed securities market*. Departmental Honors Paper. Economics Department. Cedar Rapids, IA: Coe College.

Berenson, Alex. 2003. What's the story between the lines at Fannie Mae? *New York Times*, July 22.

Berkman, Neil G. 1979. Mortgage financing and the housing cycle. *New England Economic Review*. September/October:54–76.

Berlau, John. 2003. Mortgage giants may be in trouble. *Insight on the News*, July 21.

Berson, David W., and Eileen Neely. 1997. Homeownership in the United States: Where we've been; where we're going. *Business Economics*, 32:7–11.

Bradford, Calvin. 2002. *Risk or race? Racial dispari-ties and the subprime refinance market.* Washington, DC: Center for Community Change, May.

Brady, Peter J., Glenn B. Canner and Dean M. Maki. 2000. The effects of recent mortgage refinancing. *Federal Reserve Bulletin,* 86:441–450.

Browning, Lynnley. 1999. The rebel of afford-able housing has done it again. *Boston Globe,* August 11.

Campen, James. 1991. The second S&L crisis: The Feds mismanage the cleanup. *Dollars and Sense,* April 6–9.

Canner, Glenn B., Arthur B. Kennickell and Charles A. Luckett. 1995. Household sector borrowing and the burden of debt. *Federal Reserve Bulletin,* 81:323–338.

Canner, Glenn B., and Wayne Passmore. 1995. Credit risk and the provision of mortgages to lower-income and minority homebuyers. *Federal Reserve Bulletin,* 81:989–1016.

Canner, Glenn B., Thomas A. Durkin and Charles A. Luckett. 1999. Recent developments in home equity lending. *Federal Reserve Bulletin,* 85:241–251.

Canner, Glenn B., Wayne Passmore and Elizabeth Laderman. 1999. The role of specialized lenders in extending mortgages to lower-income and minority homebuyers. *Federal Reserve Bulletin,* 85:709–723.

Canner, Glenn B., Karen Dynan and Wayne Passmore. 2002. Mortgage refinancing in 2001 and early 2002. *Federal Reserve Bulletin,* 88:469–481.

Carron, Andrew. 1982. *The plight of the thrifts.* Wash-ington, DC: The Brookings Institution.

———. 1986. The rescue of the thrift industry. In *Housing and the new financial markets,* ed. Richard L. Florida, 211–233. New Brunswick, NJ: Rutgers Center for Urban Policy Research.

Dean, John P. 1945. *Homeownership: Is it sound?* New York: Harper and Row.

Edelberg, Wendy M., and Jonas D. M. Fisher. 1997. Household debt. *Chicago Fed Letter,* No. 123, November.

Eggers, Frederick J., and Paul E. Burke. 1996. Can the national homeownership rate be significantly im-proved by reaching underserved markets? *Housing Policy Debate,* 7:83–101.

Federal Home Loan Mortgage Corporation [FHLMC; Freddie Mac]. 1989. *1988 Annual Report.* Washing-ton, DC: FHLMC.

———. 1991. *1990 Annual Report.* Washington, DC: FHLMC.

———. 1999. "Primary mortgage market survey. 30-year fixed-rate mortgages since 1971," August.

———. 2001. *2001 Annual Report.* Washington, DC: FHLMC.

Federal National Mortgage Association [FNMA; Fan-nie Mae]. 1972. *Federal National Mortgage Associ-ation Charter Act, as amended through December 1, 1972.* Washington, DC: FNMA.

———. 1989. *1988 Annual Report.* Washington, DC: FNMA.

———. 1991. *1990 Annual Report.* Washington, DC: FNMA.

———. 2002. *2002 Annual Report.* Washington, DC: FNMA.

Federal Reserve System, Board of Governors. 1999. *Flow of funds accounts of the United States. Flows and outstandings, first quarter 1999.* Washington, DC: FRB, June 11.

———. 2003. *Flow of funds accounts of the United States. Flows and outstandings, second quarter 2003.* Washington, DC: FRB, September 9.

Fishbein, Alan. 2003. Freddie and Fannie under fire. *Shelterforce* September/October, 12–14, 28.

Florida, Richard L. 1986. The political economy of financial deregulation and the reorganization of housing finance in the United States. *International Journal of Urban and Regional Research* 10:207–231.

Fraser, Donald R. 1986. DIDMCA and the savings and loan industry: Evidence from a survey. In *Hous-ing and the new financial markets,* ed. Richard L. Florida, 243–252. New Brunswick, NJ: Rutgers Center for Urban Policy Research.

Glater, Jonathan D. 2003. Freddie Mac understated its earnings by $5 billion. *New York Times,* November 22.

Gosselin, Peter G. 1990a. U.S. nearly doubles thrift bailout cost—estimate is $315 billion. *Boston Globe,* May 24.

———. 1990b. Kennedy, Nader target the rich for cleanup. *Boston Globe,* July 20.

Government National Mortgage Association [GNMA]. 1991. Mortgage-backed securities system. Outstanding balances—end of month, 1982–1990. Washington, DC: GNMA, December 10.

———. 2002. *2002 Annual Report.* Washington, DC: GNMA.

Guttentag, Jack M. 1984. Recent changes in the pri-mary home mortgage market. *Housing Finance Re-view* 3:221–255.

Hendershott, Patric H., and Robert Van Order. 1989. Integration of mortgage and capital markets and the accumulation of residential capital. *Regional Science and Urban Economics* 19:189–210.

Henwood, Doug. 1999. Booming, borrowing, and con-suming: The U.S. economy in 1999. *Monthly Review* July/August, 120–133.

Hershey, Robert D. 1989. Bush signs legislation: Re-making industry starts fast. *New York Times,* August 10.

Heskin, Allan David. 1983. *Tenants and the Ameri-can dream: Ideology and the tenant movement.* New York: Praeger.

Hughes, James W. 1996. Economic shifts and the changing homeownership trajectory. *Housing Policy Debate* 7:2, 293–325.

Kane, Edward J. 1986. Change and progress in contemporary mortgage markets. In *Housing and the new financial markets*, ed. Richard L. Florida, 253–280. New Brunswick, NJ: Rutgers Center for Urban Policy Research.

Kennickell, Arthur B., Martha Starr-McCluer and Brian J. Surette. 2000. Recent changes in U.S. family finances: Results from the 1998 survey of consumer finances. *Federal Reserve Bulletin*, 86:1–29.

Labaton, Stephen. 1998. The debacle that buried Washington; long after the S&L crisis, courts are handing taxpayers a new bill. *New York Times*, November 22.

———. 2003a. New agency proposed to oversee Freddie Mac and Fannie Mae. *New York Times*, September 11.

———. 2003b. Official hints US could end its credit line to loan giants. *New York Times*, October 23.

Lea, Michael. 1996. Innovation and the cost of mortgage credit: A historical perspective. *Housing Policy Debate* 7:147–174.

Lereah, David. 1997. Housing finance: A long-term perspective. *Business Economics*, 32:21–27.

———. 1998. Still bullish for 1998. *Mortgage Banking* 58:10–19.

———. 1999. Eyeing prospects for '99. *Mortgage Banking* 59:8–25.

Low Income Housing Information Service. 1989. Special memorandum: Summary of the Financial Institutions Reform, Recovery, and Enforcement Act, HR 1278 (the S&L Bailout Bill). Washington, DC: LIHIS, August.

MacDonald, Heather. 1995. Secondary mortgage markets and federal housing policy. *Journal of Urban Affairs*, 17:53–79.

———. 1996. The rise of mortgage-backed securities: Struggles to reshape access to credit in the USA. *Environment and Planning A*, 28:1179–1198.

McIntyre, Richard. 1991. The banking crises and housing finance: The political economy of financial deregulation. *Law and Policy* 13:327–342.

Meyerson, Ann. 1986. The changing structure of housing finance in the United States. *International Journal of Urban and Regional Research* 10:464–497. Reprinted in *Housing issues of the 1990s*, ed. Sara Rosenberry and Chester Hartman, 1989:155–189. New York: Praeger.

Moseley, Fred. 1999. The U.S. economy in 1999: Goldilocks meets a big bad bear? *Monthly Review* March, 10–21.

New York Times Editorial Desk. 2003. Watching over Freddie and Fannie. *New York Times*, November 21, 2003.

Passmore, Wayne. 2003. *The GSE implicit subsidy and value of government ambiguity*. Preliminary Draft. Washington, DC: Board of Governors of the Federal Reserve System, December 22. http://www.federalreserve.gov/pubs/feds/2003/200364/200364pap.pdf

Perin, Constance. 1977. *Everything in its place: Social order and land use in America*. Princeton, NJ: Princeton University Press.

Rakoff, Robert M. 1977. Ideology and everyday life: The meaning of the house. *Politics and Society*, 7:85–104.

Schnare, Ann. 1996. Income trends and the housing market. *New England Economic Review*, May/June, 176–177.

Schwartz, Alex. 1998. Bank lending to minority and low-income households and neighborhoods: Do community reinvestment agreements make a difference? *Journal of Urban Affairs*, 20:269–301.

Skidmore, David. 1991. U.S. banking failures dip but perils seen in '92. *Boston Globe*, January 2.

Squires, Gregory D., ed. 1992. *From redlining to reinvestment: Community responses to urban disinvestment*. Philadelphia: Temple University Press.

Stone, Michael E. 1993. *Shelter poverty: New ideas on housing affordability*. Philadelphia: Temple University Press.

Tuck, Curtis W. 1979. The secondary mortgage market. In *The story of housing*, ed. Gertrude Fish, 399–419. New York: Macmillan.

U.S. Department of Housing and Urban Development. 1999. *U.S. housing market conditions. 1st quarter 1999*. Washington, DC: HUD.

———. 2003. *U.S. housing market conditions. 3rd quarter 2003*. Washington, DC: HUD.

U.S. Department of Housing and Urban Development, and U.S. Bureau of the Census. 2002. *American housing survey for the U.S.: 2001*. Washington, DC: GPO.

U.S. General Accounting Office. 1988a. *Thrift industry: Trends in thrift industry performance: December 1977 through June 1987*. Washington, DC: GPO, May.

———. 1988b. *Financial services industry issues*. Washington, DC: GPO, November.

U.S. League of Savings Associations. 1979. *Savings and loan fact book: 79*. Chicago: U.S. League.

———. 1981. *'81 savings and loan fact book*. Chicago: U.S. League.

———. 1989. *'89 savings and loan fact book*. Chicago: U.S. League.

U.S. Office of Management and Budget. 1992. Telephone communication, January 30.

U.S. Office of Thrift Supervision. 1989. *1988 savings and home financing sourcebook*. Washington, DC: OTS.

U.S. Savings and Loan League. 1972. *Savings and loan fact book: 72*. Chicago: U.S. League.

Vartanian, Thomas P. 1986. Regulation and deregulation in the savings and loan industry. In *housing and the new financial markets*, ed. Richard L. Florida, 138–157. New Brunswick, NJ: Rutgers Center for Urban Policy Research.

Weicher, John C. 1994. The new structure of the housing finance system. *Review of the Federal Reserve Bank of St. Louis*, 76:47–65.

White House. 1989. "Statement by the president"; "News conference of the president"; "Press briefing"; "Fact sheet." Washington, DC: Office of the Press Secretary, February 6.

Peter Dreier

5 Federal Housing Subsidies: Who Benefits and Why?

A JULY 6, 1990, ARTICLE appeared in the *New York Times* ("Expanding the Choices in Million Dollar Homes") that described the Pinnacle, a cluster of new homes priced from $975,000 to $1.3 million, in Purchase, New York, in the heart of Westchester County's wealth belt.

The *Times* did not describe the Pinnacle as a "subsidized" housing project, but in its glowing description of the project, the paper unwittingly revealed how taxpayers underwrite the cost of luxury housing.

Subsidy #1: "The project is on a 23-acre site," the *Times* noted, "across the street from the 236-acre Silver Lake Preserve, a county-owned nature preserve."

Subsidy #2: Then, gushed the *Times*, "The project is only a few minutes' drive from the White Plains train station, and is within earshot of Interstate 684." (While the noise of the nearby freeway might detract somewhat from the pride of owning a million-dollar home, the convenient access to a major highway makes up for it.)

Subsidy #3: Likewise, the taxpayer-subsidized Metro North commuter rail lines add significantly to the value of the Pinnacle.

The *Times* did not mention another lucrative tax subsidy—one that is available to homeowners. Pinnacle homebuyers would get huge tax breaks on both mortgage interest *and* property taxes. On a million-dollar home—with a 10 percent down payment, a mortgage at 10 percent interest (the prevailing rate at the time) and an estimated $15,000 a year in property taxes—the lucky homeowner could expect an income tax savings (in effect, a federal subsidy) of $35,000 in the first year alone.

Most Americans think that federal housing assistance is a poor people's program. In fact, relatively few low-income Americans receive federal housing subsidies. In contrast, about three-fourths of wealthy Americans—many living in very large homes—get housing subsidies from Washington in the form of tax breaks. These tax breaks subsidize many households who can afford to buy homes without it. Our policymakers and opinion leaders, however, focus more attention on federal aid to the poor. These programs—such as public housing and rent subsidies—are much more visible than the hidden tax subsidies to the affluent. For example, a Lexis/Nexis search of major daily newspapers for 1999 found 4,822 articles that mentioned "public housing"; 164 references to "Section 8"; and a scant 37 stories with a combination of "mortgage interest" and "deduction."

As a result of housing's weak constituency, Congress has not put low-income housing programs high on its priority list. Despite slight increases in the late 1990s, federal funding for low-income housing has declined dramatically since the late 1970s. And during the 1990s, some members of Congress even proposed eliminating the U.S. Department of Housing and Urban Development (HUD) altogether. Meanwhile, few politicians, journalists or other opinionmakers worry about getting wealthy mansiondwellers off government "welfare."

This chapter first examines the magnitude of federal housing subsidies, focusing on the disparity in the size of tax expenditures for homeowners compared with housing subsidies directed toward low-income households. To understand why these major disparities exist, the chapter provides a historical exploration into the many battles over housing assistance for the poor. An apparent paradox is then presented: Why has the Low-Income Housing Tax Credit fared much better, in terms of marshaling support, than virtually any other federal housing program targeted to low-income people? Given the size and inequity of the homeowners' deductions, it is not surprising that there have been a number of attempts over the years to reduce or remove it altogether. The following section presents an overview of these efforts and the ways in which the real estate industry has harnessed its substantial power and effectively organized to protect its "sacred cow."

THE MAGNITUDE OF FEDERAL HOUSING SUBSIDIES

In 2000, the federal government spent some $148.9 billion (in 2001 dollars) for various housing subsidies, as detailed in Table 5.1.[1] Americans typically associate the phrase "housing subsidy" with the poor. They think of public housing projects, homeless shelters or perhaps rent vouchers, most of which are administered by HUD. But the largest housing subsidies are much more invisible. These are subsidies that come through the tax code in the form of tax breaks or tax expenditures.[2]

There are basically two kinds of housing subsidies—direct expenditures (administered by government agencies) and indirect expenditures—"tax expenditures" (which are incorporated in the federal tax code). As Table 5.7 reveals, in combination, various tax expenditures for housing comprise the largest tax expenditures in terms of revenue loss to the federal government. These tax subsidies for housing go either to homeowners or to investors. The table also shows that tax expenditures account for over $118 billion—over three-fourths (79.2 percent) of the federal government's housing subsidies. Put another way, tax expenditures cost almost four times as much as direct housing subsidies. The Treasury Department—not HUD—is the largest government housing subsidy agency. Moreover, as the data in Table 5.2 show, the gap between direct housing subsidies and tax expenditures has been widening since 1976.[3]

These figures do not include the direct housing subsidies provided by the U.S. Department of Defense for military members and their

TABLE 5.1 Federal Housing Subsidies, 2000
(2001 $, in billions)

Direct Housing Subsidies		
U.S. Department of Housing and Urban Development		$30.82
U.S. Department of Agriculture		0.04
	Subtotal	30.86
Indirect Housing Subsidies (Tax Expenditures)		
Homeowner Subsidies		
Deductibility of mortgage interest on owner-occupied residences		61.55
Deductibility of property tax on owner-occupied residences		22.61
Exclusion of capital gains on house sales		18.93
Investor Subsidies		
Exclusion of interest on state and local government bonds for owner-occupied housing		0.80
Exclusion of interest on state and local government bonds for rental housing		0.16
Depreciation of rental housing in excess of alternative depreciation system		4.84
Low income housing tax credits		3.28
Deferral of income from post-1987 installment sales		1.03
Exemption from passive loss rules for $25,000 of rental loss		4.82
	Subtotal	118.02
	TOTAL	148.88

Source: Office of Management and Budget, Budget of the United States.

TABLE 5.2 Federal Housing Subsidies by Program Category, 1976–2000
(2001 $, in millions)

Year	Homeowner Subsidies	Investor Subsidies	LIHTC	HUD	USDA	Total
1976	$27,509	$1,898	—	$18,522	$6,742	$54,671
1977	23,846	1,422	—	13,328	7,870	46,466
1978	32,483	1,170	—	16,237	8,786	58,676
1979	41,548	998	—	17,972	6,672	67,190
1980	48,644	2,936	—	22,629	7,148	81,357
1981	55,894	3,385	—	24,711	7,039	91,029
1982	57,036	2,234	—	24,230	6,788	90,288
1983	49,861	5,981	—	24,261	5,757	85,860
1984	53,097	5,047	—	24,746	5,312	88,202
1985	55,365	4,916	—	41,649	5,932	107,862
1986	61,502	8,759	—	19,955	4,754	94,970
1987	70,300	5,646	$42	21,161	1,202	98,351
1988	68,899	6,491	219	24,923	5,019	105,551
1989	78,279	12,832	375	24,961	4,838	121,285
1990	79,861	14,871	146	24,620	3,903	123,401
1991	82,148	14,015	989	27,066	4,037	128,255
1992	86,257	12,795	1,332	28,432	2,814	131,630
1993	92,548	12,543	1,795	28,640	1,791	137,317
1994	91,875	10,868	2,189	28,771	1,804	135,507
1995	92,058	10,275	2,516	31,699	2,343	138,891
1996	90,652	9,402	2,838	27,016	1,465	131,373
1997	97,107	9,699	2,462	29,055	1,175	139,498
1998	99,033	9,632	3,293	31,464	464	143,886
1999	100,068	11,534	2,935	33,429	330	148,296
2000	103,094	11,663	3,278	30,828	39	148,902
TOTAL	$1,738,964	$191,012	$24,409	$640,305	$104,024	$2,698,714

families who live on and off military bases. In FY2001, the Department of Defense spent more than $10 billion in housing subsidy (U.S. GAO 1996, 2001).[4] These figures also do not include the proportion of social welfare subsidies— such as Temporary Assistance to Needy Families (TANF), cash assistance (formerly Aid to Families with Dependent Children) and the Earned Income Tax Credit—that families spend on housing.[5]

Whether the federal government uses direct expenditures or tax breaks to subsidize housing is not important on its own terms. But the reality is that most of the direct subsidy programs go to low- and moderate-income people, while most of the tax subsidies go to middle- and upper-class people.

Homeowner Tax Expenditures

By far, the largest federal housing subsidies are the tax breaks for homeowners, totaling $103.1 billion in 2000 (in 2001 dollars).[6] These include the deductions on mortgage interest payments ($61.5 billion),[7] deductions on property tax payments ($22.6 billion) and the deferral of capital gains on home sales ($18.9 billion).[8] About 31.8 million homeowners received at least one of these deductions. As Tables 5.3 and 5.4 reveal, these tax breaks are quite regressive. The highest-income taxpayers with the largest houses and biggest mortgages get a disproportionate share of these federal tax expenditures. Over one-half (59 percent) of the mortgage interest deduction subsidy goes to the richest 10.2 percent of taxpayers, those with incomes over $100,000.[9] The 2.2 percent of taxpayers with incomes over $200,000 received 22.4 percent of the entire amount.

Only 22.6 percent of all 140 million taxpayers took the mortgage interest deduction, but this varies significantly with income. For example, 69.8 percent of taxpayers with incomes over $200,000 took the mortgage interest deduction,

TABLE 5.3 Distribution of Tax Benefits for Mortgage Interest Deductions, FY 2000

Income (thousands)	Number of Returns (thousands)	All Returns (%)	Number of Returns Taking Mortgage Interest Tax Deduction (thousands)	All Returns in Income Category (%)	Value of Mortgage Interest Deductions (Millions)	Value of all Mortgage Interest Tax Deductions (%)	Average Value per Return for Those Taking Mortgage Interest Deduction
Under $10	19,818	14.13	12	—	$1	—	$83
$10–20	23,803	16.97	272	1.1	105	—	386
$20–30	19,493	13.90	906	4.6	386	0.63	426
$30–40	16,210	11.56	2,141	13.2	1,194	1.96	557
$40–50	13,054	9.31	3,016	23.1	2,591	4.27	859
$50–75	21,557	15.37	8,071	37.4	8,165	13.47	1,011
$75–100	11,924	8.50	7,130	59.8	12,423	20.49	1,742
$100–200	11,253	8.02	8,097	71.9	22,131	36.51	2,733
Over $200	3,101	2.21	2,164	69.8	13,619	22.46	6,293
TOTAL	140,213		31,809	22.6	$60,615		

Source: Calculated from data provided in "Estimates of federal tax expenditures for fiscal years 2001–2005," Washington, DC: Joint Committee on Taxation, U.S. Congress, April 6, 2001.

TABLE 5.4 Distribution of Tax Benefits for Real Estate Property Tax Deduction, FY2000

Income (thousands)	Number of Returns (thousands)	All Returns (%)	Number of Returns Taking Real Estate Property Tax Deduction (thousands)	All Returns in Income Category (%)	Value of Real Estate Property Tax Deductions (millions)	Value of All Real Estate Property Tax Deductions (%)	Average Value per Return for Those Taking Real Estate Property Tax Deduction
Under $10	19,818	14.13	21	0.1	$1	—	$42
$10–20	23,803	16.97	298	1.2	40	0.19	134
$20–30	19,493	13.90	930	4.8	152	0.75	163
$30–40	16,210	11.56	2,109	13.0	426	2.10	202
$40–50	13,054	9.31	3,107	23.8	819	4.05	263
$50–75	21,557	15.37	8,229	38.2	2,683	13.25	326
$75–100	11,924	8.50	7,332	61.5	3,833	18.94	522
$100–200	11,253	8.02	8,522	75.7	6,980	31.20	819
Over $200	3,101	2.21	2,396	77.3	5,303	26.20	2,213
TOTAL	140,213		32,944	23.5	$20,237		

Source: Calculated from data provided in "Estimates of Federal Tax Expenditures for Fiscal Years 2001–2005," Washington, DC: Joint Committee on Taxation, U.S. Congress, April 6, 2001.

TABLE 5.5 HUD Budget Authority, 1976–2000
(2001 $, in millions)

Fiscal Year	Budget Authority
1976	$76,978
1977	77,065
1978	80,643
1979	60,704
1980	63,707
1981	56,829
1982	33,264
1983	25,407
1984	26,952
1985	45,533
1986	22,480
1987	20,031
1988	19,674
1989	18,197
1990	21,138
1991	32,875
1992	29,009
1993	30,103
1994	29,302
1995	21,610
1996	22,289
1997	16,984
1998	21,882
1999	26,904
2000	24,324

Source: OMB CD-ROM, Budget of the United States Government, Fiscal Year 2002, Historical Tables, Table 5.2—Budget authority by agency: 1976–2006.

with an average benefit of $6,293. In contrast, less than one-fourth (23.1 percent) of those in the $40,000 to $50,000 bracket took the deduction; those who did so saved an average of $859 on their taxes. Among those in the $20,000 to $30,000 income category, only 4.6 percent took the deduction; those who did so received an average benefit of only $426.

Consider that among households with incomes under $20,000, slightly more than half own their homes. Of those who own their homes, only 28.5 percent have mortgages. Of those who have mortgages, only 6.8 percent itemize. Among households in the $60,000 to $100,000 income bracket, more than 80 percent own their homes. Of those who own their homes, about 78 percent have mortgages. Of those who have mortgages, about 66 percent itemize. Among households in the $120,000 to $140,000 income bracket, almost 91 percent own their homes. Of those, about 82 percent have mortgages. Among this group, about 92 percent itemize.[10]

For many low- and middle-income taxpayers, the mortgage interest deduction offers little or no incentive to own rather than rent. For many of these taxpayers—who can only afford a modestly priced house and are in a low tax bracket—the mortgage interest deduction (on its own and in combination with other itemized deductions) is likely to be lower than the standard deduction.

These tax breaks have significant social consequences. The mortgage interest deduction artificially inflates home prices, since both owners and sellers impute the subsidy into their calculations. This is especially the case at the upper end, but it has ripple effects throughout the housing market. Since the mortgage interest deduction is proportional to the cost of housing, it encourages homebuyers to buy larger homes in outlying areas rather than more modest homes in central cities and older suburbs (Gyourko and Voith 1997; Gyourko and Sinai 2001), thus promoting suburbanization and sprawl. Moderate-income homeowners, who cannot take advantage of the deduction, are concentrated in older suburbs and central cities. The tax code provision (eliminated in 1997) that allowed homeowners to defer capital gains taxes if they purchase a more expensive home, but not a smaller one, exacerbated this tendency, encouraging the purchase of larger homes, typically in suburbs farther from the central city (Bier and Meric 1994). And so by encouraging the suburbanization of housing, the tax code contributes to the well-known costs of metropolitan sprawl—transportation gridlock, pollution, costly infrastructure and related dilemmas. In other words, the "cost" of these housing tax breaks exceeds the amount that appears in the federal budget each year. There are related "external" costs to the environment, public health and other factors that do not show up when policymakers itemize the list of tax expenditures.

EXPENDITURES FOR
LOW-INCOME HOUSING

Low-income housing is supported through both direct and indirect subsidy programs. Direct subsidies are provided through the Department

TABLE 5.6 Housing Subsidy Levels of States and HUD, 1978–1996

(2001 $, in millions)

Year	States	HUD
1978	$531	$65,223
1979	598	47,044
1980	667	47,179
1981	629	40,736
1982	555	21,590
1983	384	13,978
1984	361	15,374
1985	326	14,401
1986	440	12,688
1987	618	11,038
1988	981	10,207
1989	1,346	10,120
1990	1,484	11,553
1991	1,308	20,188
1992	1,190	17,211
1993	1,198	18,340
1994	1,206	17,858
1995	1,178	11,194
1996	1,349	12,225

Source: U.S. Bureau of the Census, Government Finances Report, annual reports 1978–1996; *1998 Green Book.*

of Housing and Urban Development (HUD) and the Department of Agriculture.

Department of Housing and Urban Development

HUD spent approximately $30.8 billion in housing subsidies in 2000. HUD-assisted housing goes almost entirely to low-income households.

As Tables 5.5 and 5.6 reveal, HUD's budget outlays (actual spending in each year) have ebbed and flowed since 1976 (in 2001 dollars), while its budget authority (the authorized amount of obligations in each year regardless of when the spending occurs—thus, an indicator of new spending commitments) declined dramatically during the 1980s and crept up again in the 1990s, though still far from the peak in the late 1970s. During the 1970s and early 1980s, HUD outlays were used both to continue previous commitments and to add new housing units to the inventory. Since then, HUD spending has disproportionately gone to extend prior commitments. In other words, in 1976, HUD's budget authority was spent primarily on expanding the inventory of low-income housing through the production of new units, the rehabilitation of substandard units and rental assistance to needy tenants. By 2000, most of HUD's budget authority was spending on maintaining or improving the existing inventory of low-income assisted housing and renewing subsidy contracts on existing subsidized developments rather than adding to the inventory.

Budget authority declined from a peak of $80.6 billion in 1978 to a low of $18.2 billion in 1989 (in 2001 dollars), then up to $32.9 billion in 1991, falling to $17 billion in 1997, then back up to $24.3 billion in 2000. During the 1980s, in terms of budget authority, HUD shouldered the largest cutbacks of any major federal agency. As a result, the number of new low-income housing units subsidized by HUD funds declined from 300,500 in 1978 to 23,800 in 1996 (Dolbeare 1996:79).

Housing assistance for the poor is not an entitlement, like food stamps or Medicaid. The available funds can only serve a small fraction of those who meet eligibility criteria. In the late 1990s, about 15.8 million low-income renter households were eligible for federal housing assistance. However, only about 4 million households received HUD housing assistance. About 1.14 million households lived in units owned by local public housing authorities, 1.7 million households lived in private, government-subsidized developments owned by private or nonprofit entities and 1.2 million households received tenant-based rental certificates or vouchers that allowed them to pay for unsubsidized private rental units.[11] The distribution of HUD-assisted households is uneven across the country in terms of the proportion of poor families who receive any form of housing subsidies (Kingsley 1997).

That leaves almost 12 million poor households who were eligible for federal housing subsidies but did not receive them. They have to fend for themselves in the private marketplace. Among this group, HUD in 1999 identified 4.9 million households with "worst case" housing needs—those who pay more than one-half of their incomes for housing and possibly live in seriously substandard apartments as well (U.S. Dept. of Housing and Urban Development 2001).

Department of Agriculture

For many years, the Department of Agriculture provided housing subsidies in rural areas under a division called the Farmers Home Administration—now called Rural Housing Services (RHS) (see U.S. GAO 1995). In 2000, RHS spent approximately $39 million for various housing subsidies, an all-time low; the previous year, it spent $330 million. The Department of Agriculture's total rural housing budget fell from a peak of $8.7 billion in 1978 (in 2001 dollars).[12] The Department's rural housing programs primarily target low- and moderate-income households. Between 1984 and 1997, the proportion of Department of Agriculture–subsidized housing targeted for low-income households ranged from 27.9 percent to 61.9 percent.[13] The number of new housing units subsidized by the U.S. Department of Agriculture (USDA) dropped from 101,300 in 1978 to 59,900 in 1996 (Dolbeare 1996; U.S. GAO 1995). It has plummeted even further since then.

TAX-EXEMPT HOUSING REVENUE BONDS

The housing assisted by mortgage revenue bonds (MRBs) and rental housing bonds (both of which are exempt from federal taxes) goes to a mix of low-income, moderate-income and middle-income families. The investors in these bonds are primarily affluent individuals who receive federal tax breaks for their investment. In 2000, federal tax expenditures for mortgage revenue bonds and rental housing revenue bonds cost the federal government $790 million and $160 million, respectively—about $950 million altogether (in 2001 dollars). This is a significant decline from the peak of $4.79 billion in 1987 and even from the $2.74 billion in 1997 (in 2001 dollars). MRBs can be used to purchase new or existing homes.[14]

Congress restricts MRB use to first-time homebuyers who meet income limits and home price limits. Borrowers can earn no more than the greater of their statewide or area median income. (Families of three or more can earn up to 115 percent of this figure.) The cost of an MRB-financed home cannot exceed 90 percent of the average home price in the area. (In a few strictly defined disadvantaged areas, income and home price limits are higher.) Most MRB loans go to families below these program limits. In 1996, 61 percent of MRB-financed homes were in metropolitan areas. Although the breakdown of central cities and suburbs in not available, it is generally recognized that MRBs have primarily benefited suburban homebuyers.

LOW INCOME HOUSING TAX CREDIT

In the Tax Reform Act of 1986, Congress replaced existing tax incentives for construction of low-income housing (such as accelerated depreciation) with the Low Income Housing Tax Credit (LIHTC). The LIHTC provides tax breaks to investors (corporations and individuals) in developments to cover part of the cost of housing construction and rehabilitation.[15] In exchange, rents are set at a level affordable to households with modest incomes. At least 20 percent of the apartments in each development must be rented to households with incomes below 50 percent of the area median; at least 40 percent of the apartments in each development must be rented to households with incomes below 60 percent of the area median income. (In most areas, this is about twice the poverty level.) Under the federal law, rents must be affordable to these target income groups for at least 15 years, after which developers can charge market rents. While the earlier projects adhered to this minimum, by 1995, the average lock-in period was 42 years (E&Y Kenneth Leventhal Real Estate Group 1997; Cummings and DiPasquale 1998).

Since 1987, the LIHTC has been the largest federal program to stimulate housing production for low-income families. From its inception through 1995, it assisted in the production of approximately 900,000 units, with the numbers growing each year as states and developers learned how to utilize the program. (Because many of these units have other federal subsidies, however, there is considerable overlap between LIHTC-assisted, HUD-assisted and USDA-assisted units.) In 2000, it cost the federal government $3.2 billion in 2001 dollars.

The LIHTC program is not administered by any federal agency.[16] Instead, Congress authorizes states (typically, state housing financing agencies) to allocate the tax credits to qualified housing development projects.[17] The size of each state's tax credit allocation is determined by a formula based on population size ($1.75 per state resident).[18]

WHO BENEFITS?

What is the "bottom line" concerning who benefits most from federal housing subsidies? First, federal spending for low-income housing has not kept pace with growing needs. While overall funding has grown, mainly (since the 1980s) to pay for prior commitments, new budget authority—capturing the rate of which new assisted units are added—has fallen dramatically.

Second, tax expenditures for housing, particularly those benefiting higher-income groups, far outweigh direct expenditures for housing. Measured in constant (2001) dollars, tax expenditures for homeowner subsidies and investor subsidies increased almost 300 percent between 1976 and 2000, from $29.4 billion to $117.6 billion. In contrast, federal funds for low-income housing—through HUD, the USDA and the Low Income Housing Tax Credit—increased only 135 percent during that period. More telling, the HUD budget authority for additional housing units declined by 68 percent, from $76.9 billion to $24.3 billion.

In light of the significant increase in low-income families and the widening gap between the supply of affordable rental housing and the need, these trends have exacerbated an already serious problem. Moreover, while states have increased their spending on affordable housing, they have not come close to filling the gap left by federal cutbacks, as Table 5.6 reveals.

THE ONGOING BATTLE OVER HOUSING ASSISTANCE FOR THE POOR

In contrast to federal policies that promote homeownership for the middle and upper classes, programs to help house the poor and near-poor have been continuously vulnerable to political assault. Whereas programs to promote middle-income and upper-income homeownership have essentially been entitlements—available to all those who meet the eligibility standards—housing subsidies for the poor have always been similar to a lottery, available only to a small fraction of eligible households. The weak support for low-income housing assistance is a direct outcome of the historical struggle to promote housing for this group. To understand why these inequities persist, we need to understand the historical role that housing has played in the United States. What emerges is the clear sense that we have always had an ambivalent and sometimes hostile attitude toward providing housing assistance for the poor.

The original vision of government-subsidized housing emerged from the progressive movement in the early 1900s. Until the Great Depression, reformers who advocated a strong federal government role in housing were a lonely voice in the political wilderness. The depression—when at least one-fourth of the workforce was unemployed and many more experienced declining wages and the threat of lay-offs—convinced housing reformers and labor union organizers that the private market and private philanthropy could not solve the economic and housing problems of the poor. Some of the earlier Progressive Era housing reformers like Edith Wood, joined by a younger generation of activists like Catherine Bauer, pushed for a strong government-led response to housing problems. Along with the labor union movement, they lobbied for a public housing program, union-sponsored cooperative housing, and new communities guided by cooperative principles. The early public housing advocates, like their European counterparts, initially envisioned public housing for the middle class as well as the poor, but the real estate industry, warning about the specter of "socialism," successfully lobbied to limit public housing to the poor (Lubove 1962; Oberlander and Newbrun 1999; Wright 1981; Radford 1996; von Hoffman 1996).

The federal public housing program was created in 1937 primarily to stimulate the economy,

TABLE 5.7 Major Tax Expenditures in the Income Tax, Ranked by Revenue Loss, 2000 (*$ millions*)

Rank	Provision	FY
1	Net exclusion of pension contributions and earnings: Employer plans	$84,350
2	Exclusion of employer contributions for medical insurance premiums and medical care	77,670
3	Deductibility of mortgage interest on owner-occupied homes	55,100
4	Capital gains (except agriculture, timber, iron ore and coal) (normal tax method)	40,585
5	Deductibility of nonbusiness state and local taxes other than on owner-occupied homes	37,000
6	Accelerated depreciation of machinery and equipment (normal tax method)	35,465
7	Step-up basis of capital gains at death	27,090
8	Deductibility of charitable contributions, total	25,850
9	Exclusion of interest on public purpose bonds	20,450
10	Deductibility of state and local property tax on owner-occupied homes	19,495
11	Child credit[1]	18,725
12	Capital gains exclusion on home sales	18,540
13	Exclusion of Social Security benefits for retired workers	18,125
14	Exclusion of interest on life insurance savings	14,990
15	Net exclusion of pension contributions and earnings: Individual Retirement Accounts	11,170
16	Deferral of income from controlled foreign corporations (normal tax method)	6,200
17	Exclusion of workers' compensation benefits	5,475
18	Graduated corporation income tax rate (normal tax method)	5,360
19	Earned income tax credit[2]	4,971
20	HOPE tax credit	4,855
21	Exclusion of interest on non-public purpose state and local debt	4,635
22	Workers' compensation insurance premiums	4,585
23	Net exclusion of pension contributions and earnings: Keogh plans	4,255
24	Exception from passive loss rules for $25,000 of rental loss	4,215
25	Tax credit for corporations receiving income from doing business in the United States possessions	4,120

Source: Analytical perspectives: Budget of the United States Government: Fiscal year 2000, 114.

[1] The figures in the table indicate the effect of the child tax credit, on receipts, not outlays. Child tax credits for individuals with three or more children may be refundable and as such are paid by the federal government. This portion of the credit is included in outlays, while the amount that offsets tax liabilities is shown as a tax expenditure.

[2] The figures in the table indicate the effect of the earned income credit on receipts, not outlays. Earned income credits in excess of tax liabilities may be refundable to individuals and as such are paid by the federal government. This portion of the credit is included in outlays, while the amount that offsets tax liabilities is shown as a tax expenditure.

not to address urban slums or housing affordability. From the program's inception, it was aimed at providing housing for the "submerged middle class"—those who could not find suitable housing in the private market—but not the very poor with no means to pay rent. Senator Robert Wagner of New York, principal author of the Housing Act of 1937, declared, "There are some whom we cannot expect to serve . . . those who cannot pay the rent" (Friedman 1968; Freedman 1969; Hays 1995). For years, this arrangement worked. Public housing was often the best housing available to working-class families. By 1942, 175,000 public housing apartments—most in two- to four-story buildings—had been constructed in 290 communities. During World War II, the federal government created the temporary National Housing Agency (NHA) to co-ordinate the government's efforts to provide housing for defense workers. By 1946, another 195,000 units of permanent housing were built, primarily near war industry sites and military bases. After the war, some Democrats sought to make the NHA a permanent agency responsible for housing and urban redevelopment, but in 1946, the Republican-controlled Congress rejected the idea under pressure from the National Association of Real Estate Boards (later renamed the National Association of Realtors), which strongly opposed public housing.[19] Recognizing the pent-up demand for housing and fearing competition from public housing, the real estate industry sabotaged the public housing program by pressuring Congress to limit it to the very poor. That new rule, embodied in the 1949 Housing Act, was the beginning of the decline of public housing's political support, exacerbated by the political climate of the McCarthy era and the Cold War (Davies 1966; Friedman 1968; Radford 1996; Wright 1981; Keith 1973). Several other factors—including changing demographics, costs and design and location—diminished political support for public housing (Vale 1993). As a result, only 1.3 million units have been built in the program's history.

During the 1950s and early 1960s, Democrats in Congress—supported by big-city mayors, along with the liberal National Housing Conference, a coalition of labor unions and public housing advocates—tried unsuccessfully to create a cabinet-level agency to deal with urban problems[20] (Bratt and Keating 1993). After winning a landslide victory in 1964, President Johnson—with the support of civil rights groups, big-city mayors, labor unions and private developers (all key Democratic Party constituencies)—in 1965 created the Department of Housing and Urban Development. Throughout its history, HUD has been controversial, fighting an uphill battle to win political support for its mandate to help house the poor and revitalize cities.

For about a decade following the Civil Rights Movement and the ghetto uprisings of the 1960s, HUD rode the wave of public sentiment to address the problems of poverty and inner cities. Through the late 1960s and early 1970s, HUD was able to gain steady funding from Congress, thanks to the coalition of big-city mayors, sectors of the housing and banking industry, unions, civil rights groups, advocates for the poor and business leaders concerned with revitalizing central business districts through the urban renewal program. Several Presidential reports on urban problems released in 1968—including the National Advisory Commission on Civil Disorders (the Kerner Report)—all cited the condition of ghetto housing as a serious problem and recommended a major new commitment to low-income housing. These forces triggered a new round of federal housing initiatives. Congress sought different approaches than public housing—enticing private developers to build housing for the poor, providing low-income tenants with vouchers and funnel-

ing federal "block grant" funds to cities and community organizations. The Housing Act of 1968 established a housing production goal of 26 million units within ten years, with 6 million for low-income households. Congress turned to the private sector to build low-income housing. Several programs gave private developers low-interest mortgages, tax breaks and, later, rental subsidies. A low-income homeownership program (Section 235) provided low down payment, low-interest mortgages. Eventually, over 2 million units of privately owned subsidized housing were built—almost double the overall number of public housing units. By contrast, between 1968 and 1973, only 375,000 public housing apartments were added.

During his first term (1969–1973), President Nixon and his HUD Secretary (former Michigan governor George Romney), along with a Democratic Congress, promoted a supply-side housing strategy to create a record number of new housing units built by the private sector with federal subsidies. Beginning in the mid-1970s, under President Nixon, a number of urban-oriented programs were folded into the Community Development Block Grant (CDBG) program. Grants under this program were distributed directly to cities, giving control to mayors rather than community organizations. These funds could be used for capital improvements, human services and housing. In 1974, Congress also created the Section 8 program to entice private developers to house the poor with subsidies for new construction, rehabilitation and rent supplements.

New housing starts set records in the 1970s, even if far short of the 26 million goal. Since the late 1960s, about 20,000 privately owned projects with almost 2 million units of privately owned subsidized housing were built under several federal programs.[21] These programs have been criticized as being expensive bribes to lenders and developers. In many cases, construction and operating costs exceeded the per-unit costs of public housing. Moreover, the federal programs gave the owners of many of these developments an option to withdraw after 20 years. As this ticking time bomb began to explode in the late 1980s, Congress passed legislation allowing HUD to entice owners to keep their projects as subsidized housing but at a huge additional cost to taxpayers[22] (see Chapter 7).

During the 1980s, the ideological assault on government activism—by conservative politicians, think tanks and the media—helped to undermine support of programs for the urban poor, including housing (Edsall and Edsall 1991). When President Reagan took office in 1981, the attack on HUD intensified. The Reagan Administration sought to dismantle federal housing programs, claiming that "free and deregulated markets" could address the nation's housing needs. It reduced the budgets for most low-income programs, but low-income housing suffered the largest cuts. As Tables 5.5 and 5.6 reveal, federal support for low-income housing—in terms of additional spending each year—has never recovered from the Reagan-era attack. Although the HUD budget increased during the Bush I and Clinton years, in real terms (adjusting for inflation) it never came close to the pre-Reagan era. In 1980, the year before the Reagan Administration took office, HUD budget authority was $63.7 billion. By 1989, the last budget for which Reagan was responsible, it had declined to $18.1 billion (in 2001 dollars). Although the Republican Party's effort to decimate or dismantle HUD, or to sell off public housing projects, never came to fruition, there was widespread public sentiment that HUD was a wasteful and inefficient agency, a view exacerbated by a HUD scandal, which involved revelations of corruption and political favoritism during the Reagan Administration.

By the time that Clinton took office in 1993, HUD was one of the least popular or respected agencies of the federal government. After the Republicans won control of Congress in 1994, they escalated their attack on HUD as a symbol of the problems of activist government. House Speaker Newt Gingrich told the *Washington Post*, "You could abolish HUD tomorrow morning and improve life in most of America" (Cooper 1994). A year later, the *Post* reported that, "Politically, HUD is about as popular as smallpox" (Gugliotta 1995:A4). That year, Republican Senator Lauch Faircloth of North Carolina, chair of the HUD oversight subcommittee, filed legislation to eliminate HUD, asserting, "I think we need to put this department to rest"

(Adm'n Wins . . . 1995). The 1996 Republican platform called for the elimination of HUD. The Party's presidential candidate that year, Bob Dole, drawing on popular but misleading stereotypes of public housing, called it "one of the last bastions of socialism in the world." Local housing authorities, he said, have become "landlords of misery" (Gugliotta 1996:A5).

Not only conservative Republicans criticized HUD. In 1989, following the HUD scandal, the *New Republic* published an editorial entitled, "Abolish HUD." HUD secretary Henry Cisneros admitted that he had inherited an agency "characterized by slavish loyalty to non-performing programs" (Raspberry 1995). Soon after the 1994 Congressional elections, Clinton, looking for a way to cut federal spending, proposed putting HUD on the chopping block. Cisneros, hoping to save his agency, pledged to "reinvent" it and soon produced a "blueprint" for reform that called for dramatic reduction in HUD's mandate, including the privatization of most federally subsidized housing developments. In 1995 and 1996, Congress cut the HUD budget by more than 20 percent. After the 1996 election, Clinton asked Congress to increase HUD's budget, mostly to fund expiring Section 8 subsidy contracts, but the GOP leadership balked at this request. In October 1996, the *New York Times Magazine* published a cover story by Jason DeParle entitled, "Slamming the Door," claiming that "the Federal Government has essentially conceded defeat in its decades-long drive to make housing affordable to low-income Americans" and that "housing has simply evaporated as a political issue" (DeParle 1996).

How did this happen? One cannot simply blame the country's changing mood toward the poor. After all, low-income programs such as food stamps and Medicaid, while occasionally controversial, have not shared the same fate as federal housing programs. House Speaker Newt Gingrich was candid about the reasons for HUD's vulnerability. Its "weak political constituency," he told the *Washington Post* in December 1994, "makes it a prime candidate for cuts" (Gugliotta 1995). Many Americans now believe that federal low-income housing programs reward a combination of government bureaucrats, politically connected developers and people who engage in antisocial or self-destructive behavior. In particular, stereotypes with regard to public housing and its residents as havens of social pathology have cast a long shadow on all federal housing programs for the poor.

One can identify at least ten major factors that have contributed to the erosion of political support for HUD in general and low-income housing programs in particular.

First, the private housing and financial industries' support for HUD has primarily focused on the Federal Housing Administration (FHA), not its low-income housing programs. The industries have used their political muscle to maintain support for FHA's mortgage insurance program, particularly the segment that promotes home-ownership, but has used little of their influence on behalf of HUD's low-income programs.

Second, the business community's support for HUD was limited to its role in revitalizing central business districts through the urban renewal program. This program was torn by controversy during the 1960s, especially among residents of low-income neighborhoods opposed to bulldozer-style renewal. The controversy over urban renewal led to its demise in the early 1970s, eliminating the backing of local urban growth coalitions (Mollenkopf 1983) from the HUD constituency.

Third, the political influence of big-city mayors (and urban voters) has waned as the nation has become (thanks in part to federal highway and housing policies) increasingly suburbanized. In 1992, for the first time, suburbanites represented an absolute majority of voters in a presidential election. The gap between the growing number of suburban Congressional districts and the declining number of central city Congressional districts has widened (Wolman and Marckini 1998; Sauerzopf and Swanstrom 1999; Dreier, Mollenkopf and Swanstrom 2005). With the exception of the FHA, HUD-funding formulas (such as the CDBG program) have little to offer suburbanites, including blue-collar inner-ring suburbs.[23]

Fourth, HUD has typically been viewed as primarily serving the very poor, with few benefits for the struggling working class. HUD programs have increasingly been targeted to the poorest of the poor. This is reflected in eligibility standards for public and assisted housing. It is reflected in the visibility of HUD efforts to house the homeless. Nevertheless, HUD provides significant support for middle-class families through its FHA homeownership program. Perhaps few Americans identify the well-known FHA with HUD. Also, since HUD programs are neither an entitlement for the poor nor are available to many working- and lower-middle-class people, many families who are not well served by the private housing market still fall between the cracks of HUD's programs—a recipe for resentment and weak political support.

Fifth, as American cities have declined, especially when they erupt in riots, HUD is often blamed for failing to solve the "urban crisis," even though it has never had the resources or authority to address the vast array of urban problems. In fact, other agencies, especially the Department of Transportation (in terms of the emphasis on highways over public transit) and the Department of Defense (in terms of the location of defense facilities and contracts; see Markusen et al. 1991; Anderson and Dreier 1993), play a much greater role in determining the fate of urban areas. Even during the height of the 1960s' War on Poverty, as illustrated by the short-lived Model Cities program, HUD has lacked the power to coordinate the various agencies involved in antipoverty efforts, such as the Office of Economic Opportunity, the Labor Department and the Commerce Department. Since then, HUD's efforts to trigger economic development in cities have been hampered by its lack of control over agencies with key programs, such as the Small Business Administration within the Department of Commerce. Even within its narrow mandate to address housing problems, HUD was not given authority over such agencies as the Federal Home Loan Bank, the Veterans Administration housing programs and the Farmers Home Administration (Bratt and Keating 1993; Mitchell 1985; Scruggs 1995). At the same time, HUD is given little or no credit for the nation's housing successes, including the improvement, in terms of size, amenities and the dramatic decline of physically substandard housing, of the quality of American housing since the 1960s.

Sixth, many Americans identify HUD with public housing and consider HUD-subsidized developments as having contributed to urban misery by warehousing the poor in high-rise "projects." Newspaper stories consistently identify HUD-subsidized housing developments with crime, welfare and social pathology, compounding the media's general misleading stereotypes with regard to the poor (Gilens 1999; Gilliam et al. 1995; Entman and Rojecki 2000).

Seventh, HUD has become increasingly identified as serving the interests of racial minorities. Ironically, one criticism of HUD is that its programs segregate racial minorities and concentrate the poor in urban ghettoes (Massey and Denton 1993; Schill and Wachter 1995a, 1995b; Goering, Kamely and Richardson 1994; Fischer n.d.; Hughes 1997; Jargowsky 1997). A more recent criticism is that HUD seeks to deconcentrate the minority poor into white and more affluent areas. When the Clinton Administration sought to deconcentrate the poor through "Moving to Opportunity"—a small pilot program to help the ghetto poor find apartments in better neighborhoods—Republicans and conservative pundits attacked it as "social engineering" (Dreier and Moberg 1996; Rockwell 1994; Goering and Feins 2003; Rubinowitz and Rosenbaum 2000; Turner 1998).[24]

Since the 1968 Fair Housing Act, one of HUD's responsibilities has been to monitor racial discrimination by landlords, real estate agents, local governments and banks, and to punish violators. In recent years, HUD has also been involved in uncovering redlining by banks. Although HUD has often been lax in carrying out these responsibilities, this mandate has not endeared HUD to the real estate industry.

Eighth, HUD's low-income housing programs have continuously been torn by corruption and mismanagement scandals. Already identified with the poor, ghettoes and minorities, HUD also became identified with mismanagement and corruption. Since HUD began, politically connected developers have fed at its trough of lucrative subsidies and mortgage insurance. Beginning in the 1960s, HUD shifted its emphasis away from public housing toward reliance on the private sector to provide low-income federally-assisted housing. This led to abuses and rip-offs, exacerbated by HUD's inability or unwillingness to effectively monitor its programs. No sooner had these programs started than members of Congress and the media exposed numerous problems, including excessive profits, poor construction, razing stable neighborhoods as part of "slum clearance" and using HUD grants as political payoffs to campaign contributors (Gans 1962; Fried 1972; Boyer 1973; Liston 1974). The first major scandal, which emerged in the early 1970s, involved the abuse of HUD's Sections 223(e) and 235 homeownership programs by realtors and lenders as well as the Section 236 rental program by developers. "This scandal contributed to the quick demise of these programs following the 1973 Nixon moratorium on the construction of federally-subsidized low-income housing" (Bratt and Keating 1993:13). The elimination of these programs further weakened political support for HUD, not only by the public, but also by those private sector constituencies who had profited from them.

And in 1989, as noted previously, soon after Reagan left office, the nation's media uncovered another HUD scandal, revealing that upper-level Reagan Administration officials had used political favoritism to allocate HUD low-income housing production funds, activities which later led to the conviction of several top officials (Howlett 1993). General Accounting Office reports to Congress consistently highlighted HUD's terrible track record of monitoring its programs, contributing to its image as an out-of-control bureaucracy. For more than a decade, the taint of these scandals eroded public and Congressional support for HUD.

Ninth, the consumers of HUD's low-income programs have become increasingly fragmented and politically isolated. HUD's current constituency is composed primarily of those who have a direct stake in housing the poor: big-city mayors and local government housing bureaucrats; private housing developers, landlords and speculators; and poor people and their advocacy organizations. These groups are politically weak, fragmented and generally viewed unfavorably. The various segments of the housing constituency often work at cross-purposes, lobbying for their own specific piece of the HUD pie, weakening the overall impact of their efforts and undermining the likelihood of building broad support for federal housing programs (Dreier 2000). The mayors and housing bureaucrats depend on HUD funding and programs. This "urban lobby" (such as the U.S. Conference of Mayors and the National Association of Housing and Redevelopment Officials) has been steadily losing clout for years, as cities come to represent a smaller portion of the overall electorate and national PACs replace city-based political machines as the keys to winning urban seats in Congress (Nardulli, Dalager and Greco 1996; Paget 1998). HUD's private-sector constituency consists of landlords, developers and real estate lawyers. Advocacy groups—including organizations like the National Coalition for the Homeless, the National Low Income Housing Coalition, Association of Community Organizations for Reform Now (ACORN), the National Community Reinvestment Coalition and the National Congress for Community Economic Development—are often referred to as the "housing movement" (Dreier 1984, 1996). Funded primarily by liberal foundations, these public interest organizations occasionally activate their loose networks of local housing activists (tenants groups, homeless shelters, community and church organizations, nonprofit developers) to protect or expand federal housing programs for the poor. These advocacy groups have had some success in protecting and even improving HUD programs, but they mostly put their fingers in the dike.

Tenth, HUD's programs have increasingly resembled a crazy quilt, with no overall coherence. They have been less ambitious and have become increasingly narrow and balkanized. Since the 1960s, HUD has added a patchwork of programs to accommodate its various narrow constituencies. This makes it a cumbersome and confusing bureaucracy that is ripe for mismanagement and corruption. HUD has many different pockets of money to help public housing agencies and an almost equal number of distinct programs for private owners of HUD-subsidized developments. HUD also has two programs allocated by formulas to municipal governments—the Community Development Block Grant and HOME, both of which have various strings attached.

There are distinct programs for new housing construction, for moderate rehabilitation and for major rehabilitation. There are separate programs to house the elderly, Native Americans, rural populations, people with AIDS and homeless people as well as various subpopulations of the homeless (e.g., veterans, people with AIDS, the elderly, and women and children).

One byproduct of the gradual but steady shift away from production programs toward vouchers is the further weakening of HUD's constituency. Today, about one-third of the households with HUD subsidies are renters with vouchers. This proportion is likely to steadily increase. Tenants who live in a building or complex, or residents who live in a geographic neighborhood, can be mobilized to defend their interests. But tenants with vouchers, scattered across many buildings and neighborhoods, cannot easily be identified, much less organized, to protect these subsidies from elimination by Congress.

The Paradox of the Low-Income Housing Tax Credit

In terms of political support for low-income housing, the federal Low-Income Housing Tax Credit represents an interesting contrast to the programs sponsored by HUD. Since its creation in 1986, the LIHTC has received growing support, not only among low-income housing advocates but also among business leaders as well as the private housing industry. In contrast to the HUD budget, LIHTC funding has increased, reaching approximately $3.2 billion in 2000. It is the largest federal subsidy for new construction and substantial rehabilitation of low-income housing (Newman and Schnare 1997).

What explains the LIHTC's success? There are at least five factors that make the LIHTC politically attractive to a broad coalition of supporters.

First, it is relatively invisible. Like other tax expenditures, it is a subsidy allocated through the tax code rather than through a federal government agency. In theory, it requires no bureaucracy, such as HUD or the Department of Agriculture. Thus, it is not subject to the same political conflicts as programs tied to agencies. In fact, there are administrative costs, primarily borne by state housing finance agencies, but also borne by the Internal Revenue Service (IRS) in monitoring the tax credits.[25] And although the transaction costs are substantial, such costs do not show up in the federal budget, thus masking the LIHTC's inefficiencies.

Second, per unit LIHTC subsidies are quite low ($27,300) compared with other federal housing programs, making the LIHTC appear to be an attractive program. But this figure hides the real subsidy costs. Many LIHTC projects require additional subsidies, including federal subsidies like Section 8 vouchers and certificates. The General Accounting Office estimates that "almost three-fourths of the households in these projects benefitted either directly or indirectly from other housing assistance, such as rental assistance to residents or loan subsidies to project owners" (U.S. GAO 1997:4).[26] Indeed, the patchwork of subsidies necessary to "make the numbers work" is one of the major inefficiencies of the LIHTC program. Some have argued that the structure of the LIHTC is highly inefficient in terms of delivering scarce dollars to the poor because the investors receive so much of the subsidy (Stegman 1990; Stanfield 1994). The LIHTC has become more efficient over the years as state housing agencies and developers become more sophisticated in getting investors and syndicators to put more dollars back into the housing developments. Even so, one housing expert likened the LIHTC to "feeding the sparrows by feeding the horses" (Hartman 1992)—an inefficient and indirect way to accomplish the goal of housing the poor.

Third, corporate investors earn substantial profits through the tax credit—typically a 15 percent return on equity, and they, in turn, have become part of a powerful lobbying group. The LIHTC is not a form of corporate philanthropy, but many corporations nevertheless also earn positive publicity for investing in low-income housing and inner-city neighborhoods. LIHTC investors are recruited by syndicators, state housing finance agencies and other intermediaries. This has spawned an entire industry around the LIHTC: syndicators, intermediaries, lawyers, accountants, development consultants and others. Thus, in addition to some major corporations that act as investors, this "LIHTC industry" has a vested interest in protecting the program when it comes up for renewal in Congress. In addition, the LIHTC industry is able to marshal support from the more influential corporate investors, who represent Fortune 500 and comparable firms. Further, the tax credit constituency is also supported by two of the major intermediaries that support housing production using the tax code—the Enterprise Foundation (founded by developer James Rouse) and the Local Initiatives Support Corporation, which both provide technical assistance and channel private and public resources to community development corporations (CDCs).

Fourth, the banking industry has played a significant role in lobbying on behalf of the LIHTC in Congress. Banks that utilize the LIHTC as investors not only earn substantial profits, they also get credit under the federal Community Reinvestment Act for addressing the credit needs of low-income communities and consumers. As a result, banks are the corporate sector most engaged in LIHTC investment.

Fifth, many of the developers of housing projects utilizing the LIHTC are nonprofit organizations, typically community development corporations, giving the program a positive public image of addressing community needs.[27] CDCs have become the "public face" of the LIHTC and provide legitimacy and positive public relations. They are built by "the community," through partnerships with the private sector. The LIHTC is thus not identified with the same stigmatizing factors—government bureaucracy, large-scale "projects"—as are HUD-subsidized housing developments. CDC projects tend to be smaller in size (see Chapter 16). Also, because the LIHTC does not provide sufficient subsidies to cover the operating costs for 100 percent low-income projects, a significant number of LIHTC developments are mixed-income (U.S. GAO 1997).

In combination, these factors help to explain why Congress has acted favorably in renewing and expanding the LIHTC at the same time it has attacked HUD.

Challenging the Housing Industry's Sacred Cow—The Mortgage Interest Deduction

How do we account for the huge gap between federal housing subsidies for the affluent and

TABLE 5.8 Newspaper Citations for Mortgage Interest Deduction, 1985–1999

Year	All	New York Times	Los Angeles Times	Washington Post
1999	37	4	1	4
1998	58	2	5	6
1997	43	4	1	7
1996	129	7	2	15
1995	109	2	8	11
1994	77	2	5	6
1993	50	6	5	4
1992	83	6	6	4
1991	44	2	5	4
1990	58	7	8	7
1989	62	2	6	11
1988	56	4	11	17
1987	61	10	9	12
1986	49	14	6	14
1985	54	10	12	11

Source: Lexis/Nexis.

those for the poor? Political power and ideology are key factors in answering this question. The disparity in federal housing subsidies for the well-off and the poor is due primarily to the relative political influence of the constituencies who benefit from these different subsidies. The real estate industry's ability to protect the mortgage interest deduction illustrates how the allocation of housing subsidies reflects inequalities of political power rather than the provision of social needs. For example, the industry is among the largest contributors to Congressional campaigns, as Tables 5.9 and 5.10 reveal.

Although homeownership has long been a cornerstone of the American belief system (Heskin 1981; Dreier 1982; Carliner 1998), tax breaks for homeowners initially were not viewed as a key component of federal policy to encourage homeownership.[28] The original income tax applied only to the wealthiest 1 or 2 percent of the population, so the deduction was clearly not intended to broaden homeownership. But as the taxpaying population broadened, particularly after World War II, the deduction grew almost by accident, at first small and little noticed. By the time Brookings Institution, Urban Institute and other economists began suggesting in the 1960s and 1970s (Aaron 1972; Surrey 1973; Andreassi and MacRae 1981; Aaron and Galper 1985; Surrey and McDaniel 1985) that the homeowner deduction was inequitable and unnecessary, the real estate industry was already declaring it sacrosanct (e.g., "Elimination of Mortgage Deduction" 1989).

There is no evidence that when the income tax on individuals was introduced in 1913, its framers viewed it as a vehicle to promote homeownership. The initial bill made a distinction between total income and taxable income; individuals were permitted to deduct from their total income specific sources of income (e.g., gifts and inheritances and interests on state and local bonds) and specific expenses in order to generate a lower level of taxable income. Included in these expenses were interest paid of all indebtedness, including but not limited to home mortgages. At a time when personal and business debt were highly comingled, in part because so many Americans were engaged in agriculture, allowing individuals to deduct all consumer debt was administratively simpler than trying to

TABLE 5.9 Largest Business Contributors to Federal Candidates and Parties, 2000, by Industry ($ millions)

Category	2000	Democrats (%)	Republicans (%)
Finance/Insurance/Real estate	$303.2	41	59
Communications/Electronics	133.3	53	46
Lawyers and lobbyists	128.1	67	33
Health	96.4	39	60
Energy/Natural resources	67.0	25	74
Agriculture	59.2	26	74
Transportation	57.2	28	72
Construction	55.8	32	68
Defense	14.1	35	64
Miscellaneous business	173.7	38	60

Source: Center for Responsive Politics, http://www.crp.org.
Note: Totals include PAC, soft and individual contributions over $200 to federal candidates and parties.

TABLE 5.10 Contributions to Federal Candidates and Parties by Finance, Insurance, Real Estate, and Construction Industry Sectors, 2000
(*$ millions*)

Category	Total	Democrats (%)	Republicans (%)
Commercial banks	$26.0	37	63
Savings & loans	2.5	43	56
Credit unions	2.4	47	52
Finance/credit companies	9.7	31	69
Securities & investment	91.8	44	55
Insurance	41.8	34	65
Real estate	79.8	45	55
Accountants	15.3	38	61
General contractors	20.1	30	69
Home builders	7.3	32	68
Special trade contractors	7.2	30	70
Construction services	11.8	45	54
Building materials/equipment	9.3	19	80
TOTAL	$356.7	39.5	60.5

Source: Center for Responsive Politics, http://www.crp.org.
Note: Totals include PAC, soft and individual contributions over $200 to federal candidates and parties.

figure out what was personal debt and what was business debt (Howard 1997:53–54).

The major tax break for homeowners—the mortgage interest deduction—did not affect a large proportion of the population until after World War II. Before that time, it was a tiny item in the overall federal budget.[29] But changes in tax policy and an expansion of homeownership gave a growing number of Americans a stake in the mortgage interest deduction. Thanks to a strong economy, rising incomes and federal policies to promote homeownership and sub-urbanization, homeownership increased significantly after World War II. The homeownership rate increased steadily from 43.6 percent in 1940 to 55 percent in 1950 to 62 percent in 1960. It then grew more slowly to 65.6 percent in 1980.

During this three-decade period, the federal government lowered the personal income tax exemption and raised tax rates. In 1941, it lowered the personal exemption (which added 5 million additional taxpayers) and increased the tax rate on the lowest brackets from 4.4 percent to 10 percent. A year later, Washington lowered the personal exemption again and raised the tax rate on the lowest bracket to 19 percent. These policy changes meant that millions of middle-class and even working-class families who had previously been exempt from the federal income tax were now paying taxes. In 1939, only 6 percent of all employees paid income taxes; by 1945, the figure had grown to 70 percent (Howard 1997).

In 1944, Congress enacted the standard deduction, which simplified the tax system and lowered taxes for most families. Many homeowners used the standard deduction rather than itemized their deductions because their interest payments were relatively small. By the 1950s, however, the standard deduction did not keep pace with increases in income and the size of mortgages; so as incomes rose, and homebuying and homebuilding grew, more Americans took advantage of the homeowner deduction. They viewed this deduction as part of their calculation when deciding whether to buy a home and how big a home to buy.

At several points during the latter half of the 20th century, whenever there was a suggestion to cut back on the mortgage interest deduction, there was a strong wave of protest, led by the private real estate industry. The visibility of this issue was increased when the concept of "tax expenditures" reached the mainstream in the 1970s. In January 1969, Joseph Barr, the outgoing secretary of the Treasury under President Johnson, testified before Congress, criticizing tax loopholes for the wealthy. He unveiled the nation's first "tax expenditure budget," which exposed the size of the many tax loopholes and even noted how many millionaires had paid no income taxes because of various tax breaks. One of his examples was the mortgage interest deduction, which, he said, cost the government $1.9 billion a year and which disproportionately helped affluent taxpayers. A few years later, Congress required that the list of tax expenditures be published annually. As a result, economists such as Henry Aaron (1972) and Joseph Pechman, echoed by others (Manvel 1991; Poterba 1992; Follain and Ling 1991), began to question the efficiency of the homeowner deductions. Starting in the 1980s, Cushing Dolbeare, founder of the National Low Income Housing Coalition, persistently issued reports identifying the widening gap between housing subsidies for the poor and tax expenditures for the well-off (Dolbeare 1983), and a number of journalists began paying attention to the issue (Downey 1989; Garner 1991; Goodgame 1993; Harney 1990, 1992; "Housing Subsidies for the Well-Off" 1992; Marino 1998; Passell 1993; Salmon 1992). In the late 1980s, Anthony Downs, a prominent Brookings Institution economist and housing expert, drafted a paper for a Senate task force on housing policy that pointedly noted the disparities in federal housing assistance. Downs wrote:

> [H]omeownership tax benefits provide enormously disproportionate aid to high-income taxpayers, even though they need such aid least. Reducing only partly the amount of assistance they receive would make substantially more funds available for housing assistance to low-income taxpayers without increasing federal deficits. It would also increase the equity of housing assistance considered as a whole. By reducing homeownership tax benefits less than 20 percent and taking almost all of that reduction from high-income households the United States government could probably pay for a housing voucher entitlement program serving all eligible very-low-income renter households who applied. (Downs 1990:76)

In 1991, the Twentieth Century Fund issued a report, *More Housing, More Fairly*, that recommended "shifting federal (housing) commitments to make current allocations fair," in particular the tax expenditures for housing.[30]

These reports helped to lay the groundwork for elected officials and their advisers to inject the issue of homeowner deductions into the political arena.

For example, Stanley Surrey, who coined the term "tax expenditures" and became Assistant Secretary of the Treasury for Tax Policy under President Kennedy (Surrey 1973), helped to draft JFK's April 1961 special message to Congress on taxation, which called for limiting the number of tax preferences while reducing overall tax rates, which he claimed would stimulate economic growth and also be fairer. These ideas were embodied in the Revenue Act of 1964, which Kennedy submitted to Congress. One provision permitted taxpayers to deduct only those itemized expenses that exceeded 5 percent of their income. This would lead more taxpayers to take the standard deduction and reduce the value of itemized deductions for many well-off taxpayers. Kennedy's proposal ran into a political buzz saw. For the first time, the major real estate industry organizations—homebuilders, bankers and realtors—lobbied to protect the tax breaks for mortgage interest and property taxes. These combined political forces killed the proposal in Congress. The lobbying effort over Kennedy's proposed tax reform served as a warning that they needed to protect tax benefits for homeownership, which they had previously taken for granted (Howard 1997).[31]

In his 1984 State of the Union speech, President Reagan announced that he had asked the Treasury Department to conduct a comprehensive review of the tax system, with the goal of lowering tax rates, simplifying the system and reducing government. Some Treasury staff were ready to propose sweeping changes, ending or reducing many tax breaks for business and wealthy individuals, including elimination of the mortgage interest deduction.[32] The real estate industry learned what Treasury officials were thinking and launched a political offensive. They lobbied Reagan heavily. In May 1984, an election year, Reagan spoke before the National Association of Realtors in Washington and was asked whether or not the mortgage interest deduction was in jeopardy. Reagan stated: "In case there's still any doubt, I want you to know we will preserve the part of the American dream which the home mortgage deduction symbolizes" (McClure 1986:57).

After the 1984 election, Reagan unveiled his tax reform plan, which called for eliminating some key tax breaks, including charitable contributions and state and local taxes. It also limited the mortgage interest deduction to one home, and it eliminated the deduction for property taxes altogether. This proposal galvanized the real estate industry in an unprecedented lobbying effort.

The various industry lobby groups hired consultants to do studies demonstrating that any tampering with these tax breaks would hurt the economy, undermine the real estate market and reduce homeownership. They argued that vacation states would be hurt by eliminating tax breaks for second homes. They got state and local government officials to join them in claiming that eliminating tax breaks for property taxes would hurt state and local governments. They organized a grassroots lobbying campaign, mobilizing realtors, bankers, builders and others to arrange meetings with members of Congress. They increased their campaign contributions to these officeholders, and they threatened to run candidates for Congress against members who voted to cut real estate tax breaks. Congress bowed to the pressure. Representative Fortney Stark, a key advocate for eliminating some of the tax breaks, observed: "I was just outgunned by a real estate lobby that knows no limits to its greed" (Birnbaum and Murray 1987:140).

Although Congress adopted much of the Reagan tax plan, reducing tax rates and eliminating many tax breaks dear to business groups, it bowed to the real estate industry's pressure by preserving the mortgage interest and property tax deductions for homeowners.[33] By lowering overall tax rates, however, the Reagan plan actually reduced tax expenditures, including the value of the homeowner tax breaks. Also, by increasing the standard deduction and the personal exemption, and indexing both to inflation, it reduced the number of families who would utilize the mortgage interest deduction. The real estate industry could not publicly oppose these provisions to lower income taxes on ordinary families.

The industry got another big scare in 1987, when Congress limited the deduction to mortgage interest on just two homes and capped the subsidy at $1 million of principal eligible for the mortgage interest deduction. These moves frightened the housing industry. The $1 million cap itself affected few taxpayers. But industry lobbyists worried that it might snowball, leading Congress to lower the proposed cap again and again.

Soon after taking office in 1989, President Bush, speaking at a National Association of Realtors convention, vowed to defend the existing homeowner subsidy. Even so, to ensure its support in Congress, the industry's lobby escalated its efforts, highlighting the disastrous consequences of eliminating the deduction (National Association of Home Builders 1989). The industry initiated a nonbinding resolution, sponsored by Representative Marge Roukema (a Republican representing affluent New Jersey suburbs) and Representative Les AuCoin (a Democrat from lumber-intensive Oregon, which provides materials to the housing industry), in support of protecting the existing homeowner tax break.[34] Over one-half of the members of the House of Representatives (including many liberal Democrats) signed on.

An important part of the story concerning the debates about the mortgage interest deduction involves the many proposals to reduce the federal deficit and the need to cut the budget. The Reagan era, by reducing taxes and expanding military spending, left a legacy of a ballooning deficit. By the 1990s, conservatives and liberals alike began looking for ways to reduce the federal deficit and get closer to a balanced budget. Conservatives sought to do it by further slashing domestic social programs. Liberals looked toward raising taxes on the well-off as well as "reinventing government" to be leaner and more efficient. Faced with these dilemmas, both conservatives and liberals began to look at the list of tax expenditures as possible ways to achieve their goals. Not surprisingly, both political camps noticed that one of the largest items on the list was the mortgage interest deduction. A growing number of public officials, policy experts and media outlets began to identify these homeowner tax breaks as being possible targets for reducing the deficit.

Thus, the 1990s saw a new wave of concern about the mortgage interest deduction, fueled primarily by efforts to reduce the federal deficit.

The mainstreaming of this issue is reflected in a 1989 cover story in *Forbes*, a conservative business magazine, entitled "Is the Mortgage Interest Deduction Sacred?" The article quoted veteran Congressman Sam Gibbons (D-FL), who said: "I have no objections when the deduction goes for houses. When it comes to castles, I do."

A Lexis/Nexis search of major newspapers from 1985 through 1992 (see Table 5.8) revealed that articles referring to the mortgage interest deduction remained at a steady level except for two significant upward bumps—in 1992 (when presidential candidate Ross Perot and a number of policy advocacy organizations introduced the notion of revising the deduction to help reduce the federal budget deficit) and in the period from 1995 to 1996 (when the controversy over the flat tax was injected into the presidential campaign).

During the 1992 presidential campaign, candidates' proposals to reduce the deficit were a serious issue, particularly since Reform Party candidate Ross Perot, a Texas billionaire, made it the focus on his platform. Part of Perot's deficit-reduction plan included limiting the homeowner tax break. During the campaign, two centrist policy organizations—the Democratic Leadership Council's Progressive Policy Institute and the Concord Coalition (headed by former U.S. senators Paul Tsongas, a Democrat, and Warren Rudman, a Republican)—issued reports calling for reform of the mortgage interest tax break to reduce the deficit.

After the 1992 election, with deficit reduction a major concern of key opinion makers, the issue remained on the public agenda. A *New York Times* editorial argued that newly elected President Clinton "could also reduce deductions for mortgage interest" in his plan to reduce the deficit ("The Economy" 1993). The *Washington Post* editorialized that what Congress should do is "trim the interest deduction from the top and use the proceeds to support the poor" ("Upside Down Housing Policy" 1994). Other mainstream media outlets kept the story in the public eye (Starobin 1994; Peirce 1994; Inman 1994; Lehman 1994; "20 Ways to Deflate a Deficit" 1993). There was some speculation that Clinton was eyeing the deduction (particularly lowering the ceiling) as part of his deficit reduction plan, especially since one of his key economic

advisers during the campaign, Robert Reich, had criticized the deduction as a major loophole (Klott 1992; Church 1993; Samuelson 1993). Controversy erupted in February 1994, when a draft of a Clinton Administration plan to reduce homelessness, leaked to the *New York Times*, included a critique of the regressivity of the mortgage interest deduction (DeParle 1994). Secretary Henry Cisneros of HUD quickly responded that the Administration opposed eliminating the deduction ("Mortgage Interest Deduction May be Target" 1994).

After the Republicans took control of Congress in November 1994, the momentum for tax reform and deficit reduction—and the controversy over the mortgage interest deduction—escalated.

Soon after taking over as chairman of the Finance Committee, Senator Bob Packwood (Rep-OR) proposed limiting the mortgage deduction to $250,000 in debt (Mariano 1995). Around the same time, the new House Majority Leader Dick Armey (Rep-TX) proposed a 17 percent flat tax that would do away entirely with all deductions, including the homeowner breaks (Brownstein 1995). And a report by the Congressional Budget Office presented ideas for cutting federal spending, among them several ways to reduce the deficit by limiting deductions for mortgage interest:

> Preferential treatment for home ownership encourages people to become homeowners and to purchase larger homes. Increasing home ownership may contribute to social and political stability by strengthening people's stake in their communities and governments. In addition, such preferential treatment may stabilize neighborhoods by encouraging longer-term residence and home improvement. The amount of preference, however, is probably larger than needed to maintain a high rate of home ownership. For example, Canada, which grants preferential tax treatment to capital gains from home sales but does not allow deductions for mortgage interest, has achieved about the same rate of home ownership as the United States.

The CBO estimated that eliminating the mortgage interest deduction would save the federal government $313.3 billion between 1996 and 2000. It also offered three more modest suggestions to limit this tax break for better-off homeowners.[35]

In response to Senator Packwood's proposal to lower the ceiling on the mortgage interest deduction, *Time* magazine and the Cable News Network (CNN) commissioned a national poll on the subject. This is perhaps the only poll that has specifically asked about change in the mortgage interest deduction. Conducted by Yankelovich Partners in May 1995, it found substantial support for a Packwood-style reform. It asked 800 American adults: "As you may know, the tax code subsidizes mortgage loans, even for the most expensive homes. One proposal would limit the tax deduction to $300,000 in mortgage principal, and would save the Treasury $35 billion over five years, while affecting only 1.2 million of the wealthiest taxpayers. Would you favor or oppose such a limit?" Overall, 68 percent of the respondents said they would favor it. There was almost no difference between Democrats, Republicans and independents.

The 1996 presidential elections brought the issue to the fore again, primarily in reaction to candidate Steve Forbes' proposal for a flat tax (Gravelle 1996). Flat tax proponents produced studies claiming that lower tax rates would make homeowners and would-be homebuyers better off, even without the mortgage interest deduction (Seldon and Boyd 1996). The flat tax debate exacerbated divisions among conservatives. Right-wing think tanks like the Heritage Foundation and the libertarian Cato Institute, along with Citizens for a Sound Economy (CSE), a conservative advocacy group, supported the flat tax, including elimination of the mortgage interest deduction (Rosin 1997).

Seeking to ambush any attempt to tamper with this homeowner tax break, five housing industry lobby groups—the National Association of Homebuilders (NAHB), the National Association of Realtors (NAR), the American Bankers Association, the Mortgage Bankers Association (MBA) and America's Community Bankers— issued a 47-page study in March 1996 examining the impact of changing the mortgage interest deduction (Brinner et al.; *The Impact...* 1995). A month later, the MBA issued its own report, concluding that housing values could decline by as much as 25 percent under the flat tax proposed

by Representative Armey (Isaac and Marigon 1996; Sichelman 1996).

The industry also used its political and financial clout to protect the deduction. Unlike industries dominated by a few large corporations, the real estate industry is composed of tens of thousands of firms—builders, real estate agents, lenders and others. The NAR political action committees have vast local networks and deep pockets. The National Association of Realtors' political action committee (PAC) is the largest in the country in terms of contributions. The real estate/finance/insurance industry (through PACs and individuals) is the most generous contributor to Congress of any business sector. As Tables 5.9 and 5.10 show, the industry divides its contributions between Democrats and Republicans. Few members of Congress want to offend these generous donors or be labeled as being anti-homeownership. According to one account, the NAR spent $750,000 in 1995 defending the deduction (Shear 1995). During the 1996 New Hampshire and Iowa presidential primaries, Fannie Mae and Freddie Mac spent over $100,000 in advertising to attack the flat tax proposals, arguing that it would drive down housing values. One ad put the flat tax in the same category as termites and tornadoes, labeling all three "famous American home wreckers" (Haggerty 1996).

The tone of the industry's response suggests that it was clearly on the defensive and that it sensed the public mood was changing. Stephen Driesler, chief lobbyist for the NAR, told the *National Journal*, "It's fair to say that when it's the chairman of the major tax-writing committee saying these things, it's a lot more serious than in the past, when it was usually just a member of the committee, or an isolated member" (Jacobson 1995). An article in *Mortgage Banking* expressed concern that challenges to the mortgage interest deduction indicated that "the quintessential American dream of owning one's home is under attack" (England 1992)

The NAHB's chief economist admitted that the housing lobby was losing the public debate over the mortgage interest deduction. In the February 1995 issue of the NAHB's magazine, *Builder*, David F. Seiders acknowledged that the "once-sacred" tax break was no longer sacrosanct (Seiders 1995:38). "Questions are being raised about the deduction's cost-effectiveness as a tool to broaden homeowner-ship," Seiders wrote. He admitted that "Frankly, it's possible to find countries with homeown-ership rates comparable to those of the United States without deductions." Seiders also ac-knowledged that "it's also hard to defend the de-duction in terms of equality or fairness." "Some characterize the deduction as 'welfare for the rich,'" Seiders noted, admitting that "If the de-duction were eliminated or capped even lower, it would fit with the Clinton administration's theory of 'progressive restructuring' of the tax system." Seiders warned his readership of home-builders that "[I]t's going to be hard to defend the mortgage-interest deduction using only the old arguments about homeownership and the democratic process." A few months later, NAHB president Jim Irvine warned his fellow home-builders that the deduction is "seriously threat-ened as Congress works to contain the deficit," citing Packwood's proposal (Irvine 1995:48).

But the real estate industry's intense lobbying efforts paid off. Forced to take a position on the issue, the GOP candidates differed on the flat tax, but even those who supported the flat tax (Forbes excepted) came out in support of ex-empting deductions for mortgage interest and charitable contributions (Johnston 1996). Dur-ing the 1996 campaign, both Dole and Clinton came out against the flat tax and in favor of pre-serving the tax break. Speaking to the National Association of Realtors, Dole said:

> When we were taking all the heat . . . on the flat tax, millions and millions of dollars of TV ad-vertising directed right at Bob Dole, I stood my ground and said I don't care what hap-pens, we're going to keep the mortgage interest deduction. . . . (Dole 1996)

The same day, President Clinton addressed the NAR. He noted the increase in homeownership rates under his presidency, touted his plan to ex-pand homeownership further and attacked the flat tax plan while implicitly endorsing the mort-gage interest deduction:

> So we ought to balance the budget, but I don't think we should do it in a way that undermines the ability of people to own their own home. If

we can simplify the tax code, I'm all for it. But I don't think we ought to adopt a flat tax that will raise taxes on everybody making less than $100,000 a year, and put homeownership out of the reach of all the people in those categories. (Clinton 1996)

Since the 1996 election, political interest in revising the mortgage interest deduction has waned, although there have been occasional echoes of concern. A number of policy ex-perts and newspaper reporters and columnists have continued to beat the drum for reform (Johnston 1999; Nelson 2000). Most politicians who favor tax reform, including a flat tax, have with a few exceptions exempted the mortgage interest deduction from their proposals. During the 2000 presidential elections, only GOP candi-date Steve Forbes (who favored a flat tax that did not retain the deduction) and Ralph Nader (who favored lowering the ceiling on the deduction and targeting the savings for low-income hou-sing) raised the issue (Garvey 2000; Brownstein 2000). Neither Al Gore nor George Bush add-ressed the issue.

At the same time, the nation's widening economic disparities generated considerable political and media attention during the mid- and late 1990s. Secretary of Labor Robert Re-ich sparked a public debate in the mid-1990s when he put the issue of "corporate welfare" on the nation's agenda (see, e.g., Hage, Fischer and Black 1995). Public debate over economic "fair-ness" is unlikely to abate in the near future. To the extent that the mortgage interest deduction is viewed as primarily subsidizing the well-off without at least comparable government assis-tance going to the middle class and poor, reform will continue to resonate within public opinion, although whether this translates into political change depends on many other factors.

CONCLUSION

The United States has serious housing prob-lems, not only among the poor but also among middle-income households (Stegman 2000; Lipman 2001; Joint Center for Housing Studies 2001; Harkness, Newman and Lipman

2002). The widening gap between the rich and poor, the proliferation of low-wage jobs and the economic insecurity that even many middle-income families face in the new economy exacerbate our national housing crisis (see Chapter 1).

The federal government's efforts to address this problem have been shaped by the realities of political power. There has been much more federal housing assistance for the well-off than there has been for the poor and near-poor. HUD plays only a small part in the federal government's housing puzzle. Despite its name, the agency has much less impact on the economic and physical conditions of our cities and metropolitan areas than other federal agencies and policies. On its own, HUD, with its limited authority and budget, can do little to address the current plight of our cities—including the concentration of poverty, the suburbanization of people and jobs, suburban sprawl and the economic and racial segregation of our metropolitan areas (Markusen et al. 1991; Jackson 1985; Gyourko and Voith 1997; Gyourko and Sinai 2001).

Clearly, the battle over federal housing subsidies must go beyond the HUD budget to address the disparities between assistance for the poor and assistance for the well-off.

During the 1990s, efforts to revise the mortgage interest deduction emerged from three different directions. First, advocates of deficit reduction saw in the deduction a means to address the nation's budget dilemmas. Second, advocates of tax simplification viewed the mortgage deduction as an example of the complexities of the tax code. But one proffered solution to this—the flat tax—proved extremely controversial, particularly since its consequences would have been to make the tax code even more regressive while simplifying it. The flat tax idea still has its advocates, but it has few strong political forces behind it. Third, advocates for the poor, spearheaded by the National Low Income Housing Coalition (NLIHC) and the National Housing Institute, sought to redress the vertical inequalities reflected in the gap between federal tax expenditures for the well-off and housing assistance for the poor (Lehman 1991; Burns 1998). The chief vehicle for this was a bill, drafted by the Coalition, to create a national housing trust fund targeted for low-income households. In its original version, the bill called for lowering the ceiling on the homeowners deduction in order to fund the trust. The Coalition abandoned that approach, and its current version focuses on other sources of funding (see http://www.nhtf.org). In the early years of the 21st century, the Coalition built by the NLIHC has been more successful in getting a significant number of persons in Congress as well as senators to support a housing trust fund, a result of better grassroots organizing, but strong opposition from the Bush II Administration has stymied its efforts to get Congress to enact it.

In recent years, those who view the deduction in terms of economic unfairness have taken a somewhat different approach, seeking to design a progressive tax break for homeowners that would reach households who do not benefit from the current tax provisions (Dreier and Atlas 1992, 1997; Green and Vandell 1996; Collins, Belsky and Retsinas 1999; Green and Reschovsky 2001). The popularity of the Earned Income Tax Credit, a refundable credit for the working poor, suggests that this approach has considerable support. A homeowner tax credit has the advantage of using the same policy tool—tax expenditures—toward the well-recognized benefit of homeownership. Still controversial is whether revenues for this approach should come from reducing the ceiling on the current deduction (i.e., a revenue-neutral approach) or from another source in the federal budget. Regardless, advocates of this approach recognize that this tool is unlikely to benefit very-low-income households in many markets and that increased direct federal housing subsidies for the poor are still necessary. Nevertheless, it suggests that housing advocates have learned some political and policy lessons from the past half-century's experience of trying to reform this tax provision.

Any effort to address this issue must calculate the political consequences—the winners and losers, the geographic impacts (by state and Congressional districts) and the intensity of support and opposition among households in general and lobby groups in particular. One analysis that explored the consequences of substituting a tax credit for the current deduction found that losers would be concentrated in only a few states and Congressional districts, while the winners would be spread out geographically. It also found that a handful of households would lose big, while a much larger number of households would gain benefits though those benefits would be relatively small. The capacity to mobilize political support for reform would be limited by these political calculations (Green and Reschovsky 2001).

Within the homebuilding industry, if a mortgage tax credit significantly helps builders of starter homes targeted for families earning, say, less than $60,000, but hurts builders of luxury homes and second homes, that could potentially divide the homebuilding industry, depending in part on the internal dynamics of the industry's lobby groups (including the number and location of builders that specialize in starter homes).

In light of these political realities, advocates for reform have focused on adding a mortgage tax credit without eliminating the current deduction (Collins, Belsky and Retsinas 1999; Green and Reschovsky 2001). President Bush proposed a very small homeowner tax credit in 2001 with benefits targeted to developers rather than consumers. The Millennial Housing Commission, a bipartisan blue-ribbon task force appointed by Congress to make recommendations to address the nation's housing problems, also proposed a homeownership tax credit in its 2002 report (Millennial Housing Commission 2002). The report briefly mentioned the disparities in federal housing subsidies but did not recommend reducing tax subsidies for the affluent. There is reason to think that a well-crafted proposal could marshal support to increase homeownership by revising the tax code in order to benefit those left out by current regressive tax deductions.

The global assault on labor standards has transformed the U.S. economy and produced growing economic inequality and deepening poverty. America's persistent economic disparities are mirrored in the nation's housing conditions. America's housing crisis is fundamentally about affordability: the gap between housing costs and household incomes. It requires money to fill the gap. Only the federal government has the resources to address the problem, even though federal policy is implemented at the

state, metropolitan and local levels. Some form of government support is necessary to make housing economically manageable for the poor as well as for growing segments of the troubled middle class. The current disparities in housing assistance for the affluent and the poor exacerbate the nation's inequities.

In earlier periods, radical "housers" proposed bold alternatives to existing policies. Their demands were perhaps brazen, but they managed to walk the political tightrope. In today's terminology, they thought "outside the box." Not only did they think big, they organized well. They did not sit on the sidelines and criticize. They were political activists. They built movements and coalitions. In particular, they hitched their ideas to the one political vehicle that could effectively mobilize the political power to enact progressive housing legislation—organized labor. As Catherine Bauer wrote, "there would never be a real housing movement until workers and consumers organized an effective demand: that housing is a major political issue or it is nothing" (Oberlander and Newbrun 1999:106). Bauer's words remain true.

NOTES

1. This analysis excludes a number of other forms of government-subsidized housing. It excludes housing assistance provided by the U.S. Department of Defense for military families who live on and off military bases in the U.S. and overseas. It also excludes federal antipoverty programs, such as AFDC/TANF and the Earned Income Tax Credit, whose recipients use part of this assistance to help pay their housing costs. It also excludes the housing programs of the Federal Deposit Insurance Corporation, the government agency that insures banks that make mortgage loans and which disposes of the real estate assets of failed banks and S&Ls. Also excluded is the Federal Housing Administration (FHA); many middle-class Americans purchased their homes with mortgages insured by FHA, which is a division of HUD. This insurance, backed by the U.S. government, allows banks to reduce the monthly mortgage payments, which is a form of government subsidy. Also excluded are the Veterans Administration (VA, which guarantees mortgages for veterans), Fannie Mae, the Federal Reserve System and the Federal Home Loan Bank System. In addition to providing various housing subsidies, the federal government (primarily through

the Department of Justice but also through HUD) has sought to monitor and reduce housing discrimination, beginning with the Fair Housing Act of 1968. These costs are also not included in this analysis.

2. Overall, the largest 25 tax expenditures cost the federal government more than $550 billion in 1999, as the data in Table 5.7 reveal. See also Howard 1997.

3. Unless otherwise specified, HUD figures used in this chapter are for HUD's budget outlays, most of which are for low-income housing.

4. In 1996, the Department of Defense spent $5.7 billion to provide housing allowances for 569,000 military families in the United States. This covered 80 percent of the typical family's total housing costs, with the family paying the remaining portion. It also spent about $3.9 billion to operate and maintain government-owned or -leased housing for 284,000 military families, covering 100 percent of their housing costs. These figures were provided by Pete Potochney and Dr. Saul Pleter of the Department of Defense. See also U.S. GAO 1996; U.S. Department of Defense 1998.

5. Until Congress passed a "welfare reform" bill in 1996, federal and state governments combined allocated about $21.6 billion annually for Aid to Families with Dependent Children (AFDC), commonly called "welfare," distributed by the Department of Health and Human Services (HHS). Recipients received monthly checks to cover some of their living expenses. One study (Newman 1999) estimated that about 30 percent of this amount—about $6.5 billion—was used to pay rent. Most AFDC recipients received no housing assistance and had to find accommodations in the private market. Most of this group paid at least one-half of their welfare check for rent—and frequently much more. Since most welfare recipients also receive food stamps, they used most (or all) of their AFDC benefits to pay rent. But the variations in housing costs across the country bore almost no relationship to variations in AFDC benefit levels. AFDC payments covered only 35 percent of average rent levels in Texas but covered 125 percent of average rents in Alaska. Nationwide, the median AFDC payment covered 66 percent of market rents. Even if most AFDC recipients found apartments cheaper than the average market rent, the AFDC payment was insufficient to keep a roof over their heads and have enough left over for other necessities (Newman 1999). It is hardly surprising that many welfare recipients supplemented their AFDC payments with work in the underground or informal economy (Edin and Lein 1997; Jencks 1997). Slightly more than 1 million families (about 23 percent) of AFDC recipients also received HUD subsidies. They lived in public or private government-assisted housing or had a rent certificate. These families paid 30 percent of their welfare income for rent, and HUD paid the rest. These families were better housed than those AFDC families without HUD assistance. Because federal housing assistance is

not an entitlement, the proportion of welfare recipients with housing subsidies varied considerably from state to state, from 12.1 percent in California to 56.8 percent in North Dakota. In seven states, fewer than one-fifth of welfare recipients receive federal housing subsidies. (See Newman and Schnare 1994; Newman 1999.) Benefits levels for AFDC and food stamps combined eroded significantly beginning in the early 1980s. They fell further and further below the official poverty line. In 1995, in every state, AFDC benefits were less than the typical monthly rents (see Dolbeare 1996).

6. Each year, the Joint Committee on Taxation of Congress estimates the distribution of benefits of two of the major tax expenditures—the deduction of mortgage interest payment and the deduction for local property tax payments. Unfortunately, the JTC's estimates of the overall cost of these expenditures differ from other sources, including those of the Office of Management and Budget. When comparing tax expenditures with other housing subsidies, I use the OMB figures in *Analytic perspectives: Budget of the United States* (2000). When examining the distribution of tax benefits for mortgage interest and property taxes, I use the JTC figures.

7. In 32 of 42 states with individual income taxes, mortgage interest is deducted in the calculation of state income tax liabilities, increasing the tax subsidy for many homeowners. These states are Alabama, Arizona, Arkansas, California, Colorado, Delaware, Georgia, Hawaii, Idaho, Iowa, Kansas, Kentucky, Louisiana, Maine, Maryland, Minnesota, Mississippi, Missouri, Montana, Nebraska, New Mexico, New York, North Carolina, North Dakota, Oklahoma, Oregon, Rhode Island, South Carolina, Utah, Vermont, Virginia and Wisconsin.

8. Prior to 1997, only homeowners over age 55 and homeowners who sold their homes and then purchased more expensive homes could exclude from their federal taxes capital gains from the sale of their homes. In 1997, Congress changed the law to allow all homeowners to exclude payment of capital gains taxes (up to $250,000 for singles and $500,000 for couples) when they sell their homes. They can only do so once every three years.

9. The figures used in Table 5.7 for the mortgage interest and property tax deductions are different from the figures used in Tables 5.3 and 5.4. The OMB uses a different method for calculating tax expenditures than the Joint Committee on Taxation, but only the latter disaggregates the benefits by income class.

10. These data come from Green and Reschovsky (1997).

11. Different reports use different estimates of both the total number of households eligible for HUD assistance and the total number of households receiving HUD assistance. A HUD study (Casey 1992) using 1989 data estimated the number of poor renters

eligible for HUD assistance at 13.8 million. A more recent HUD report (McGough 1997) put the figure at 15.8 million eligible households in 1993. A Harvard study (Joint Center for Housing Studies 1995) using 1993 data put the figure at 13.4 million. The Congressional Budget Office (1994) reports that 18.6 million households were eligible for aid in 1994. Regardless of which figures are used, the federal government's allocation of housing (via HUD) and income assistance (via AFDC/TANF) for the poor is unequal and inefficient. Of the 13.4 million low-income renter households in 1993, 7.4 million did not receive income or housing assistance; 1.9 million received both housing and income assistance; the other 4.3 million received either housing or income assistance (Joint Center for Housing Studies 1995; Newman and Schnare 1994; Casey 1992; Congressional Budget Office 1994; Kingsley 1997; McGough 1997; U.S. Department of Housing and Urban Development 1996, 1998).

12. Data provided by the Housing Assistance Council.

13. In 1985, the Department of Agriculture subsidized 88,228 housing units, 29.8 percent of which (24,428) were targeted to low-income households. In 1991, the figures were 45,873 total units, of which 61.9 percent (28,383) were targeted to low-income households. By 1995, the figures were 47,233 total units, of which 45.7 percent (21,569) were low-income. In 1997, the figures were 52,400 total units, 31.4 percent of which (16,456) were targeted for the poor—the lowest number since the figures were first tabulated for 1984. (The Rural Housing Program in Fiscal Year 1997; 1998.)

14. States vary considerably in the extent to which they favor MRBs compared with other bonds and in their capacity and commitment to implement this program. Fourteen state housing finance agencies accounted for more than one-half (53.5 percent) the total number of loans in 1997. This figure was calculated by the author from data provided by the National Council of State Housing Agencies. In descending order of number loans closed, these states are Pennsylvania, California, Virginia, Connecticut, Wisconsin, Nebraska, New York, Idaho, Missouri, Minnesota, Ohio, Michigan, Iowa and Alabama. The fact that many states with large populations are not among this group indicates that many large states prioritize uses other than housing under their bond volume cap, while several small and medium-size states prioritize housing over other uses.

15. The program grants investors a dollar-for-dollar reduction in their federal tax liability in exchange for providing funds for the development of qualified, affordable rental housing. The return to the investors largely comes in the form of tax credits, paid in roughly equal annual allotments over 10 years. Developers may claim the credits, but they typically sell them to investors for up-front cash that is put into the project's development. The developer can sell the credits directly to one or more investors but typically sells them to a syndicator, who acts as broker between the developer and investors; the syndicator then markets the credits to potential investors. A number of national and regional syndicators, both for-profit and nonprofit, now dominate the field. Investor profits on the LIHTC have ranged from 10 percent to 18 percent. The proportion of the tax credit that goes into the housing developments (the "net equity") increased from 42 percent to 65 percent between 1987 and 1996, according to a E&Y Kenneth Leventhal Real Estate Group (1997) report, and to 75 percent, according to Cummings and DiPasquale (1997). (See also Cummings and DiPasquale 1998.)

16. The IRS oversees LIHTC compliance to ensure that states and investors do not use more tax credits than authorized.

17. The District of Columbia, the city of Chicago and two agencies in New York State (including New York City) administer their own allocations.

18. This formula has not changed since the LIHTC was initiated, despite the claims by developers that development costs have risen and that the LIHTC's purchasing power has been reduced.

19. Instead, Congress created a weak second-tier (rather than cabinet-level) agency called the Housing and Home Finance Agency to coordinate the public housing, mortgage insurance and urban renewal programs.

20. During the 1960 elections, the Democratic platform called for replacing HHFA with a new cabinet-level agency. Upon his election, President Kennedy tried to create a federal department of urban affairs and housing but was stymied by Congress. Much of the opposition came from Southern Democrats who feared that Kennedy would appoint Robert Weaver (HHFA administrator and the highest-ranking black in the federal government) to run the new agency (Bratt and Keating 1993:6)—a fear that turned into reality in 1965 when the Department of Housing and Urban Development was created (see text below), headed by Weaver, the first African-American cabinet member in the nation's history.

21. Most HUD-subsidized projects—public and private—are well run, but quite a few have been mismanaged by incompetent public housing agency bureaucrats and private landlords who took the subsidies but failed to maintain their properties. Over the years, HUD has used little leverage to make these inept or unfit landlords (whether public or private) toe the line. In some cases, private landlords milked these properties for their tax breaks and then walked away from the buildings, leaving HUD to foreclose and become the owner of ghetto slum housing. Moreover, most HUD-subsidized projects were sited in

segregated neighborhoods, compounding the image of HUD housing as a major factor in creating isolated ghettos (Goering, Kamely and Richardson 1994; Massey and Denton 1993; Schill and Wachter 1995a, 1995b). Local housing agencies and landlords argue, with some justification, that HUD rules requiring them to house only the very poor are responsible for some of the problems. Many HUD-subsidized projects have, in fact, become ghettos filled with troubled families, some of whom engage in crime, join gangs, participate in the underground drug economy and live on welfare and food stamps (Keyes 1992). These "distressed" projects (as HUD labels them) cast a giant shadow on the entire HUD enterprise, stigmatizing "government housing" as housing of last resort.

22. By the early 1990s, about 13,000 developments, with about 1.5 million units, remained in the inventory, exposing the FHA insurance fund to more than $34 billion in insurance obligations (Pedone 1991; Sternlieb and Hughes 1991; Wallace 1994).

23. Henry Cisneros sought to address this shortcoming by focusing attention on regional and metropolitan problems and on the interdependence between cities and suburbs. But neither the Clinton Administration in general nor HUD in particular was able to translate this political insight into a significant shift in federal programs.

24. Democratic senator Barbara Mikulski of Maryland, fearing a voter backlash from Baltimore's blue-collar suburbs, withdrew her support for the MTO program after Republican politicians claimed it would promote an exodus of public housing tenants into their communities (Mariano 1994).

25. According to GAO, state oversight of the LIHTC varies in terms of project costs, eligibility of residents and other matters. The IRS does not adequately monitor state compliance of LIHTC projects (U.S. GAO 1997).

26. Advocates of the LIHTC turn the program's inefficiencies into a benefit by claiming that the credits "allow nonprofit and for-profit developers to leverage additional money to make the housing affordable" and that "[b]ecause it depends on investor capital rather than just direct government subsidies, the LIHTC has imposed a market discipline that makes these housing investments fundamentally sound for the long term" (Enterprise Foundation 1996).

27. The IRS requires that at least 10 percent of each state's annual tax credit allocation be set aside for projects partially or wholly owned by nonprofit organizations, but many states allocate a much larger share.

28. Being a propertyless tenant has never been part of the American Dream. Housing in the United States is symbolized by the free-standing single-family home. Opinion surveys consistently confirm Americans'

strong preference for homeownership (Fannie Mae 1995; Koretz 1998). From the outset, European settlers sought to establish property relations as the legal and moral underpinning of the new colonies. The earliest settlers came to escape oppressive landlords. The abundance of land created enthusiasm about the possibility of individual ownership and "nourished the first settlers' vision of land as a civil right, a right against the long-standing obligations of a crumbling feudal society" (Warner 1972:16). Support for homeownership has been a key element of our civic religion. James Madison believed that "the freeholders of the country would be the safest depositories of Republican liberty" (quoted in Marcuse 1975:197). Thomas Jefferson, who was unusual in favoring tenant suffrage, nevertheless held that "the small landholders are the precious part of a state" (Jefferson 1956). President Andrew Johnson supported the Homestead Act to offer land ownership on the frontier because "it would create the strongest tie between the citizen and the Government" (Johnson 1850:951). In the six decades from the end of the Civil War to the Great Depression, as immigrants from abroad and from rural areas in the United States flocked to the nation's expanding cities, the nature of property ownership changed from an agrarian to an urban phenomenon, but property ownership continued to be viewed as an indication of one's ability and moral worth. Around the turn of the century, with the first wave of population movement away from the downtown industrial districts of cities, only the affluent middle class (thanks in part to the new trolleys) could afford to move to owner-occupied one- or two-family houses in the "streetcar suburbs" (Warner 1962). But as the economy grew and the middle class expanded, homeownership increasingly became not only a symbol of status and achievement but also a goal that working-class families could strive for. It was not until after World War II that this goal would be widely realized, but as early as the turn of the century, the ideology of homeownership as the "American Dream" took root (Marcuse 1980). Presidents Calvin Coolidge, Herbert Hoover and Franklin Roosevelt all waxed eloquent over the benefits of homeownership (see Dreier 1982 for evidence of this). Making the country a nation of homeowners became a central feature of public policy, since homeownership was seen as a bulwark of social stability. For example, during the depression, the banking system collapsed, and homebuilding, homebuying and homeownership declined dramatically. Starting in the depression, the federal government created several institutions (Fannie Mae, the Federal Deposit Insurance Corporation and the Federal Housing Administration) to stabilize the banking system and make the flow of mortgage funds more dependable. These policies created a national market for mortgages and insured individual depositors' accounts from bank failures. These policies allowed lenders to make long-term (typically 30-year) mortgage loans with a relatively low (3 percent to 10 percent) down payment. After World War II, FHA and VA mortgage insurance and guarantees, along with federal highway programs, increased homeowner-ship and suburbanization, especially among white middle-class families. (For a discussion of this history, see Jackson 1985; Mitchell 1985; Hays 1995; Stone 1993).

29. This discussion of the history of the mortgage interest deduction draws heavily on Howard (1997).

30. One member of the Twentieth Century Fund task force—Austin Fitts, an investment banker who served as Federal Housing Administration Commissioner from 1989 to 1990 under George H. Bush, told the *Washington Post*: "We are providing a lot of money for deductions for very big homes and for second homes. If you drive around McLean [Virginia] and Chevy Chase [Maryland], all of those homes were built with subsidies from the federal government" (Salmon 1992).

31. Previously, the real estate industry had exercised its political muscle to keep interest rates low, to get government insurance for mortgage loans and to limit government subsidies for public housing that competed with private rental housing.

32. In fact, Charles E. McLure, Jr. (1986), an economist who designed the Reagan Administration tax reform policy, later observed that, "[e]ven if one grants the case for substantial tax preferences for owner-occupied housing, it is impossible to justify this distributional pattern of benefits."

33. The same legislation reduced tax breaks for investors in real estate, including apartments, but in its place created the Low Income Housing Tax Credit, a new tax break for investors in low-income housing.

34. The resolution concludes with the following: "Resolved . . . that it is the sense of the Congress that the current Federal income tax deduction for interest paid on debt secured by a first or second home should not be further restricted." Memo from National Association of Home Builders in author's possession.

35. According to the Congressional Budget Office (1997), removing deductions just for second homes would increase federal revenues by $3.5 billion over the five-year period from 1998 to 2002. Limiting deductions to $12,000 per return (for single taxpayers) or $20,000 (for couples filing joint returns) would have added $19 billion to the federal coffers. Reducing are the maximum mortgage debt eligible for interest deductions from the current $1 million to $300,000 would generated $12.7 billion in additional revenue. The CBO noted that only a small fraction of homeowners—about one-half a million taxpayers—would be affected by the last policy recommendation.

REFERENCES

Aaron, Henry. 1972. *Shelter and subsidies: Who benefits from federal housing policies?* Washington, DC: Brookings Institution.

Aaron, Henry, and Harvey Galper. 1985. *Assessing tax reform.* Washington, DC: Brookings Institution.

Adm'n Wins First Round of HUD Fight. 1995. *Housing Affairs Letter,* January 30.

Analytic perspectives: Budget of the United States government: Fiscal year 2000. 2000. Washington, DC: Government Printing Office.

Anderson Marian, and Peter Dreier. 1993. How the Pentagon redlines America's cities. *Planners Network Newsletter,* May.

Andreassi, Michael, and C. Duncan MacRae. 1981. *Homeowner income tax provisions and metropolitan housing markets: A simulation study.* Washington, DC: Urban Institute Press.

Bier, Thomas, and Ivan Meric. 1994. IRS homeseller provision and urban decline. *Journal of Urban Affairs,* Vol. 16, No. 2, 141–154.

Birnbaum, Jeffrey, and Alan S. Murray. 1987. *Showdown at Gucci Gulch.* New York: Random House.

Boyer, Brian D. 1973. *Cities destroyed for cash.* Chicago: Follet Books.

Bratt, Rachel G., and W. Dennis Keating. 1993. Federal housing policy and HUD: Past problems and future prospects of a beleaguered bureaucracy. *Urban Affairs Review,* Vol. 29, No. 1, 3–27.

Brinner, Roger E., David Wyss and Mark Lasky. 1995. Residential real estate impacts of flat tax legislation. Prepared for the National Association of Realtors by DRI/McGraw-Hill, May.

Brownstein, Ron. 1995. Republicans wary of land mines surrounding proposal for flat tax. *Los Angeles Times,* December 18.

———. 2000. Slow to define his candidacy, Gore attacked from right and left alike. *Los Angeles Times,* October 30.

Burns, Scott. 1998. Home mortgage tax break helps wealthy borrowers most. *Houston Chronicle,* March 23.

Carliner, Michael S. 1998. Development of federal homeownership "policy." *Housing Policy Debate,* Vol. 9, Issue 2, 299–321.

Casey, Connie. 1992. Characteristics of HUD-assisted renters and their units in 1989. Washington, DC: U.S. Department of Housing and Urban Development, Office of Policy Development and Research, March.

Church, George J. 1993. A call to arms. *Time,* February 22.

Clinton, Bill. 1996. Transcript of remarks by President Clinton to the National Association of Realtors. Washington, DC, April 29.

Collins, J. Michael, Eric Belsky and Nicolas Retsinas. 1999. *Towards a targeted homeownership tax credit.* Cambridge, MA, and Washington, DC: Joint Center for Housing Studies of Harvard University and Brookings Institution Center on Urban and Metropolitan Policy, January.

Congressional Budget Office. 1994. The challenges facing federal rental assistance programs. Washington, DC, December.

———. 1997. Reducing the deficit: Spending and revenue options. Washington, DC, C30.

Cooper, Kenneth J. 1994. Gingrich pledges a major package of spending cuts early next year. *Washington Post,* December 13, A1.

Cummings, Jean L., and Denise DiPasquale. 1998. *Building affordable rental housing: An analysis of the low-income housing tax credit.* Boston: City Research.

Davies, Richard O. 1966. *Housing reform during the Truman Administration.* Columbia, MO: University of Missouri Press.

DeParle, Jason. 1994. Report to Clinton sees vast extent of homelessness. *New York Times,* February 17.

———. 1996. Slamming the door. *New York Times Magazine.* October 20, 52ff.

Dolbeare, Cushing. 1983. The low-income housing crisis. In *America's housing crisis: What is to be done?,* ed. Chester Hartman. Boston: Routledge & Kegan Paul.

———. 1996. *Housing at a snail's pace.* Washington, DC: National Low Income Housing Coalition, August.

Dole, Robert. 1996. Remarks by Senate Majority Leader Robert Dole at National Association of Realtors Conference. Washington, DC, April 29.

Downey, Kirstin. 1989. New Rockefeller mortgage no garden-variety loan. *Washington Post,* February 25.

Downs, Anthony. 1990. A Strategy for designing a fully comprehensive national homing policy for the federal government to the United States. In *Building foundations,* eds. Denise DiPasquale and Langley Keyes. Philadelphia: University of Pennsylvania Press.

Dreier, Peter. 1982. The status of tenants in the United States. *Social Problems,* Vol. 30, No. 2, December.

———. 1984. The tenants movement in the United States. *International Journal of Urban and Regional Research,* 8:2. Reprinted in *Critical perspectives on housing,* eds. Rachel Bratt, Chester Hartman and Ann Meyerson. Philadelphia: Temple University Press, 1986.

———. 1996. Community empowerment strategies: The limits and potential of community organizing in urban neighborhoods. *Cityscape* Vol. 2, No. 2, 121–159.

———. 2000. Labor's love lost: Rebuilding unions' involvement in federal housing policy. *Housing Policy Debate,* Vol. 11, No. 2, 327–392.

Dreier, Peter, and John Atlas. 1992. How to expand homeownership for Americans," *Challenge: The Magazine of Economic Affairs,* Vol. 35, No. 2, 42–47.

———. 1997. The mansion subsidy. *The New Democrat,* Vol. 9, No. 1, January/February.

Dreier, Peter, and David Moberg. 1996. Moving from the hood: The mixed success of integrating suburbia. *American Prospect,* 75–79, Winter.

Dreier, Peter, John Mollenkopf and Todd Swanstrom. 2005. *Place matters: Metropolitics for the 21st century.* Lawrence: University Press of Kansas.

E &Y Kenneth Leventhal Real Estate Group. 1997. The low income housing tax credit: The first decade. Prepared for the National Council of State Housing Agencies, Boston, May.

Edin, Kathryn, and Laura Lein. 1997. *Making ends meet: How single mothers survive welfare and low-wage work.* New York: Russell Sage Foundation.

Edsall, Thomas, and Mary Edsall. 1991. *Chain reaction.* New York: W. W. Norton.

"Elimination of mortgage deduction would raise homeownership costs, studies show," 1989. Press release, National Association of Home Builders, March 22.

England, Robert. 1992. A crack in the foundation. *Mortgage Banking,* March.

Enterprise Foundation. 1996. *Partnerships that perform: The low-income housing tax credit,* www.enterprisefoundation/policy/pubpoll.htm

Entman, Robert, and Andrew Rojecki. 2000. *The black image in the white mind: Media and race in America.* Chicago: University of Chicago Press.

Fannie Mae. 1995. Fannie Mae national housing survey: 1995. Washington, DC: Fannie Mae.

Fischer, Paul B. n.d., *A racial perspective on subsidized housing in the Chicago suburb.* Homewood, IL: South Suburban Housing Center.

Follain, James, and David C. Ling. 1991. The federal tax subsidy to housing and the reduced value of the mortgage interest deduction. *National Tax Journal,* Vol. 44, No. 2.

Freedman, Leonard. 1969. *Public housing: The politics of poverty.* New York: Holt, Rinehart and Winston.

Fried, Joseph P. 1972. *Housing crisis U.S.A.* Baltimore: Penguin Books.

Friedman, Lawrence M. 1968. *Government and slum housing: A century of frustration.* Chicago: Rand McNally & Company.

Gans, Herbert. 1962. *The urban villagers.* New York: Free Press.

Garner, Michael. 1991. Tax breaks for brains, not beach houses. *USA Today,* December 26.

Garvey, Megan. 2000. Nader's different, he says, and he's happy to explain just how. *Los Angeles Times*, November 3.

Gephardt, Rep. Richard A. 1995. A Democratic plan for America's economy: Toward a fairer, simpler tax code. Washington, DC: Center for National Policy, July 6.

Gilens, Martin. 1999. *Why Americans hate welfare: Race, media and the politics of antipoverty policy.* Chicago: University of Chicago Press.

Gilliam Jr., Franklin D., Santo Iyengar, Adam Simon and Oliver Wright. 1995. Crime in black and white: The violent, scary world of local news. Los Angeles: UCLA Center for American Politics and Public Policy, Occasional Paper No. 95-1, September.

Goering, John, and Judith D. Feins, eds. 2003. *Choosing a better life: Evaluating the moving to opportunity experiment.* New York: Russell Sage Foundation.

Goering, John, Ali Kamely and Todd Richardson. 1994. *The location and racial occupancy of public housing in the United States.* Washington, DC: U.S. Department of Housing and Urban Development, Office of Policy Development and Research.

Goodgame, Dan. 1993. Welfare for the well off. *Time*, February 22.

Gravelle, Jane G. 1996. Effects of flat taxes and other proposals on housing: An overview (Report 96-552). Washington, DC: Congressional Research Service, June 17.

Green, Richard, and Kerry Vandell. 1996. *Giving households credit: How changes in the tax code could promote homeownership.* Madison, WI: Center for Urban Land Economics Research, August 6.

Green, Richard, and Andrew Reschovsky. 1997. *The design of a mortgage interest tax credit: Final report submitted to the National Housing Institute.* Orange, NJ: National Housing Institute.

———, eds. 2001. *Using tax policy to increase homeownership among low and moderate income households: Final report submitted to the Ford Foundation.* Madison, WI: Institute for Research on Poverty, November.

Gugliotta, Guy. 1995. Saving HUD. *Washington Post*, February 6, A4.

———. 1996. Dole urges abolition of public housing. *Washington Post*, April 30, A5.

Gyourko, Joseph, and Richard Voith. 1997. *Does the U.S. tax treatment of housing promote suburbanization and central city decline?* Philadelphia: University of Pennsylvania, Wharton School, Real Estate and Finance Departments, September.

Gyourko, Joseph, and Todd Sinai. 2001. *The spatial distribution of housing-related tax benefits in the United States.* Washington, DC: Brookings Institution Center on Urban and Metropolitan Policy, July.

Hage, David, David Fischer, and Robert Black. 1995. America's other welfare state. *U.S. News & World Report*, April 10.

Haggerty, Maryann. 1996. A battle over mortgage interest deduction; realty agents, builders and lenders rise to defense of tax break for homeowners. *Washington Post*, February 17, p. E1.

Harkness, Joseph M., Sandra J. Newman and Barbara J. Lipman. 2002. *Housing America's working families: A further exploration.* Washington, DC: Center for Housing Policy, March.

Harney, Kenneth. Housing subsidies poor excuse for grumbling: Home owners aided most by programs. *Boston Herald*, February 16, 1990.

Harney, Kenneth. Taxes favor higher income groups. *Boston Herald*, May 15, 1992.

Hartman, Chester. 1992. Debating the low-income housing tax credit: Feeding the sparrows by feeding the horses. *Shelterforce*, January/February.

Hays, R. Allen. 1995. *The federal government and urban housing*, 2nd edition. Albany: SUNY Press.

Heskin, Allan David. 1981. The history of tenants in the United States: Struggle and ideology. *International Journal of Urban and Regional Research*, Vol. 5, 178–203.

"Housing subsidies for the well-off." 1992. *Boston Globe*, April 27 [editorial].

Howard, Christopher. 1997. *The hidden welfare state: Tax expenditures and social policy in the United States.* Princeton, NJ: Princeton University Press.

Howlett, Debbie. 1993. Reagan-era scandal revisits courtroom today. *USA Today*, September 7, 3A.

Hughes, Mark Alan. 1997. The administrative geography of devolving social welfare programs. Joint Occasional Paper 97-1. Washington, DC: Center for Public Management and Center on Urban and Metropolitan Policy, The Brookings Institution. www.brook.edu/ES/Urban/admgeo.htm.

Inman, Bradley. 1994. Report claims tax breaks uneven. *Los Angeles Times*, May 22.

Irvine, Jim. 1995. Save the interest deduction. *The Builder*, July, 48.

Is the Mortgage Interest Deduction Sacred? 1989. *Forbes*, March 20.

Isaac, William M., and James A. Marigon (The Secura Group). 1996. The flat tax: implications for homeowners. Washington, DC: Mortgage Bankers Association of America, April 9.

Jackson, Kenneth. 1985. *Crabgrass frontier: The suburbanization of the United States.* New York: Oxford University Press.

Jacobson, Louis. 1995. Hitting taxpayers where they live? *National Journal*, April 15.

Jargowsky, Paul. 1997. *Poverty and Place: Ghettos, Barrios, and the American City.* New York: Russell Sage Foundation.

Jefferson, Thomas. 1956. *A Jefferson profile as revealed in his letters* (selected and arranged by Saul Padova). New York: John Day Co., 37.

Jencks, Christopher. 1997.The hidden paradox of welfare reform: Why single mothers may earn more but do worse. *American Prospect*, May/June.

Johnson, Andrew. 1850. The homestead. *Congressional Globe* (Appendix, July 25), 31st Cong., lst Sess., Vol. 22, Part 2, 950–952.

Johnston, David Cay. 1996. How a flat tax would work, for you and for them, *New York Times*, January 21.

———. 1999. Mortgage tax break: who gets what? *New York Times*, January 10.

Joint Center for Housing Studies. 1995. *The state of the nation's housing: 1995.* Cambridge, MA: Harvard University.

———. 2001. *The state of the nation's housing: 2001.* Cambridge, MA: Harvard University.

Keith, Nathaniel. 1973. *Politics and the housing crisis since 1930.* New York: Universe.

Keyes, Langley. 1992. *Strategies and saints.* Washington, DC: Urban Institute Press.

Kingsley, G. Thomas. 1997. *Federal housing assistance and welfare reform: Uncharted territory.* Washington, DC: Urban Institute.

Klott, Gary. 1992. Clinton could tighten mortgage writeoff limit. *Boston Globe*, December 3.

Koretz, Gene. 1998. The rewards of homeownership. *Business Week*, June 15.

Lehman, H. Jane. 1991. Low-income housing group asks tax shift. *Washington Post*, May 25.

———. 1994. House makes progress in realty issues: Debate still ahead on mortgage loan deduction. *Washington Post*, April 15.

Lipman, Barbara J. 2001. *Paycheck to paycheck: Working families and the cost of housing in America.* Washington, DC: Center for Housing Policy, June.

Liston, Robert. 1974. *The ugly palaces.* New York: Franklin Watts, Inc.

Lubove, Roy. 1962. *The progressives and the slums: Tenement house reform in New York City, 1890–1917.* Pittsburgh: University of Pittsburgh Press.

McGough, Duane T. 1997. Characteristics of HUD-assisted renters and their units in 1993. Washington, DC: U.S. Department of Housing and Urban Development, Office of Policy Development and Research, May.

McLure Jr., Charles E. 1986. Tax treatment of owner-occupied housing: The Achilles' heel of tax reform? In *Tax Reform and Real Estate*, ed. James R. Follain. Washington, DC: Urban Institute Press.

Manvel, Allen D. 1991. Upside-down housing "Aid"? *Tax Notes*, Vol. 53, No. 6, November 11.

Marcuse, Peter. 1975. Residential alienation: Home ownership and the limits of shelter policy. *Journal of Sociology and Social Welfare*, Vol. 3, 182–203.

———. 1980. Ideology of ownership and property rights. In *Housing Form and Public Policy in the United States*, ed. Richard Plunz, 39–50. New York: Praeger.

Mariano, Ann. 1988. Is it a mortgage deduction, or a housing subsidy for the wealthy? *Washington Post National Weekly Edition*, October 24–30.

———. 1994. Hill panel halts plan to move poor families. *Washington Post*, September 3.

———. 1995. Lawmakers take aim at tax deduction for mortgage loans; some lawmakers target tax deduction for mortgage loans. *Washington Post*, March 4.

Markusen, Ann, Peter Hall, Scott Campbell and Sabina Deitrick. 1991. *The rise of the gunbelt: The military remapping of industrial America.* New York: Oxford University Press.

Massey, Douglas S., and Nancy M. Denton. 1993. *American apartheid: Segregation and the making of the underclass.* Cambridge, MA: Harvard University Press.

Millennial Housing Commission. 2002. *Meeting our nation's housing challenges: Report of the bipartisan millennial housing commission appointed by the Congress of the United States.* Washington, DC: U.S. Government Printing Office, May 30.

Mitchell, J. Paul, ed. 1985. *Federal housing policy & programs.* New Brunswick, NJ: Rutgers University Center for Urban Policy Research.

Mollenkopf, John. 1983. *The contested city.* Princeton, NJ: Princeton University Press.

"Mortgage interest deduction may be target." 1994. *Housing Affairs Letter*, February 25.

Nardulli, Peter, Jon Dalager and Donald Greco. 1996. Voter turnout in U.S. presidential elections: An historical view and some speculation. *Political Science* 29(3):480–490.

National Association of Home Builders. 1989. "Elimination of the mortgage deduction would raise homeownership costs, studies show," March 22 [press release].

Nelson, Lars-Erik. 2000. Bush's words tax his credibility. *New York Daily News*, October 25.

Newman, Sandra. 1999. *The home front: Implications of welfare reform for housing policy.* Washington, DC: Urban Institute Press.

Newman, Sandra, and Ann Schnare. 1994. *Back to the future: Housing assistance policy for the next century.* Paper prepared for the Center for Housing Policy, Washington, DC.

———. 1997. "…And a suitable living environment": The failure of housing programs to deliver on neighborhood quality. *Housing Policy Debate* 8(4):703, B41.

Oberlander, H. Peter, and Eva Newbrun. 1999. *Houser: The life and work of Catherine Bauer.* Vancouver, Canada: University of British Columbia Press.

Paget, Karen. 1998. Can cities escape political isolation? *American Prospect*, January/February, 54–62.

Passell, Peter. 1993. Economic scene: To raise federal revenue, reduce those sacred tax preferences. *New York Times*, February 11.

Pedone, Carla. 1991. Estimating mortgage prepayments and defaults in older federally assisted rental housing and possible costs of preventing them. *Housing Policy Debate*, Vol. 2, No. 2.

Peirce, Neal. 1994. Opening the door to homeownership. *National Journal*, March 12.

Poterba, James. 1992. Taxation and housing: Old questions, new answers. *AEA Papers and Proceedings*, Vol. 82, No. 2, May.

Radford, Gail. 1996. *Modern housing for America: Policy struggles in the New Deal era*. Chicago: University of Chicago Press.

Raspberry, William. 1995. At HUD, reinvention by necessity. *Washington Post*, January 4.

Rockwell, Jr., Llewellyn. 1994. The ghost of Gautreaux. *National Review*, March 7.

Rosin, Hanna. 1997. Shades of gray. *New Republic*, April 14, 21–23.

Rubinowitz, Leonard, and James Rosenbaum. 2000. *Crossing the class and color lines: From public housing to white suburbia*. Chicago: University of Chicago Press.

Salmon, Jacqueline. 1992. Mortgage tax break: Time to pare it down? *Washington Post*, May 17.

Samuelson, Robert. 1993. Gutting tax reform. *Washington Post National Weekly Edition*, February 22–28.

Sauerzopf, Richard, and Todd Swanstrom. 1999. The urban electorate in presidential elections, 1920–1992. *Urban Affairs Review*, 35(1):72–91.

Schill, Michael H., and Susan M. Wachter. 1995a. Housing market constraints and spatial stratification by income and race. *Housing Policy Debate*, 6(1):141–167.

———. 1995b. The spatial bias of federal housing law and policy: Concentrated poverty in urban America. *University of Pennsylvania Law Review*, 143(5):1285–1349.

Scruggs, Yvonne. 1995. HUD's stewardship of national urban policy: A retrospective view. *Cityscape*, Vol. 1, No. 3, September, 33–68.

Seiders, David. 1995. Budget ax falls. *The Builder*, February, 38.

Seldon, Barry J., and Roy G. Boyd. 1996. *The economic effects of a flat tax*. Dallas: National Center for Policy Analysis, May.

Shear, Jeff. 1995. From the K Street corridor. *National Journal*, October 28.

Sichelman, Lew. 1996. Flat tax could cause value dip. *National Mortgage News*, April 22.

Stanfield, Rochelle. 1994. Big money in low rents. *National Journal*, May 7.

———. 1997. Give HUD a hand. *National Journal*, February 22.

Starobin, Paul. 1994. There's no deduction like home. *National Journal*, February 5.

Stegman, Michael. 1990. The excessive costs of creative finance: Growing inefficiencies in the production of low-income housing. *Housing Policy Debate*, 2(2):357–373.

———. 2000. *Housing America's working families*. Washington, DC: The Center for Housing Policy, June.

Sternlieb, George, and James Hughes. 1991. Private market provision of low-income housing: Historical perspective and future prospects. *Housing Policy Debate*, 2(2):123–156.

Stone, Michael. 1993. *Shelter poverty*. Philadelphia: Temple University Press.

Surrey, Stanley. 1973. *Pathways to tax reform: The concept of tax expenditures*, Cambridge, MA: Harvard University Press.

Surrey, Stanley, and Paul McDaniel, 1985. *Tax expenditures*. Cambridge, MA: Harvard University Press.

The impact of potential policy changes affecting the mortgage interest deduction on the housing and financial sectors. 1995. Washington, DC: America's Community Bankers, American Banking Association, Mortgage Bankers Association, National Association of Home Builders, National Association of Realtors, March.

The Economy: Pain and candor. 1993. *New York Times*, February 14 [editorial].

The rural housing program in fiscal year 1997. Washington, DC: Housing Assistance Council.

The rural housing program in fiscal year 1998. Washington, DC: Housing Assistance Council.

Turner, Margery Austin. 1998. Moving out of poverty: Expanding mobility and choice through tenant-based housing assistance. *Housing Policy Debate*, 9(2):373–394.

Twentieth Century Fund. 1991. *More housing, more fairly: Report of the Twentieth Century Fund Task Force on affordable housing*. New York: The Fund.

Twenty Ways to Deflate a Deficit. 1993. *Los Angeles Times*, February 14 [editorial].

U.S. Department of Defense. 1998. *Department of Defense budget estimates for FY 1997 (The Green Book)*. Washington, DC.

U.S. Department of Housing and Urban Development (HUD). 1996. *Rental housing assistance at a crossroads: A report to Congress on worst case housing needs*. Washington, DC: Office of Policy Development and Research, March.

———. 1998. *Rental housing assistance—The crisis continues*. Washington, DC: Office of Policy Development and Research.

———. 2001. *A report on worst case housing needs in 1999: New opportunity amid continuing challenges*.

Washington, DC: Office of Policy Development and Research.

U.S. General Accounting Office. 1995. *Rural housing programs.* Washington, DC.

———. 1996. *Military family housing.* Washington, DC.

———. 1997. *Tax credits: Opportunities to improve oversight of the low-income housing program.* Washington, DC, March 28.

———. 2001. *Military personnel: Higher allowances should increase use of civilian housing, but not retention.* Washington, DC, May.

Upside Down Housing Policy. 1994. *Washington Post,* January 10 [editorial].

Vale, Lawrence J. 1993. Beyond the problem projects paradigm: Defining and revitalizing "severely distressed" public housing. *Housing Policy Debate,* 4(2):147–174.

von Hoffman, Alexander. 1996. Vision limited: The political movement for a U.S. Public Housing Program, 1919–1950. Working Paper Series. Harvard University, Joint Center for Housing Studies.

Wallace, James. 1994. The dilemma of disposition of troubled PHA-insured multifamily rental property. *Housing Policy Debate,* 1(5):1–34.

Warner, Sam Bass. 1962. *Streetcar suburbs.* New York: Athenaeum Press.

———. 1972. *The urban wilderness: A history of the American city.* New York: Harper and Row.

Wolman, Harold, and Lisa Marckini. 1998. Changes in central city representation and influence in Congress since the 1960s. *Urban Affairs Review,* 34(2):291–312.

Wright, Gwendolyn. 1981. *Building the dream: A social history of housing in America,* Cambridge, MA: MIT Press.

Peter Marcuse and W. Dennis Keating

6   The Permanent Housing Crisis: The Failures of Conservatism and the Limitations of Liberalism

HOUSING IS BOTH a necessity of life and, in our society, a commodity, provided for profit (see Achtenberg and Marcuse 1983). The tension between the two underlies the vagaries of housing policy in the United States. Liberals and conservatives agree that the market should be the expected provider of housing for all, with the government acting only where the for-profit market "fails." The only disagreement is on how serious that "failure" is and just what government should do about it. The closeness of the two positions can be seen if they are contrasted with a Right to Housing position in which government's first obligation is to see that all are decently housed, and the for-profit market must be managed so as to be subservient to that goal (see Chapter 8). Thus, for liberals and conservatives alike, the for-profit market is the default position, with public action limited to its failures; for those adopting a Right to Housing position, government support for decent housing for all who need it is the default position, with the for-profit market functioning where it does not interfere with that provision. The Right to Housing position is simple (if complex in implementation): The first task is to guarantee the provision of housing to those who need it; the disposition of housing as a commodity must be subordinate to that priority.

Housing policy in the United States has only at one or two times (in 1937 and 1949; see below) come to close to a Right to Housing position. Overwhelmingly, it has alternated between "liberal" and "conservative" approaches. But differences between the two are at the margin, with conservative policies often aggravating housing problems and liberal policies rather tending to ameliorate them. Neither has succeeded in achieving the fundamental official National Housing Goal established in the Housing Act of 1949: the provision of "a decent home and a suitable living environment for every American family."[1] Thus, the housing problem appears to be a permanent feature of the housing scene in the United States. However, liberal and conservative policies do not exhaust the range of what a progressive housing policy could in fact accomplish toward that goal; both draw back from confronting the fundamental problems that need to be solved, and both neglect feasible alternatives that could more directly address those problems. Both draw back from a Right to Housing approach.

We begin with a brief formulation of the principles of the classic conservative and liberal approaches to housing. The bulk of the chapter is then devoted to a historical review of key housing policy developments over time, beginning with World War I and ending with the second Bush Administration, highlighting differences between conservative and liberal policies as well as the issues that neither of them address, which a Right to Housing approach might confront. We consider key characteristics, testing the history against each of them to see how significant the differences really were. We then return to review the similarities and differences in the two approaches and conclude with a summary of the evidence as to the failures, successes and limitations of these policies.

One generally accepted set of conservative principles might be those embodied in the 1982

Report of the President's Commission on Housing, a body appointed under one of the most ideologically conservative of recent American presidents, Ronald Reagan, whose appointees primarily reflected the major elements of the real estate industry (Report of the President's Commission on Housing 1982; Hartman 1983a). Reformulated somewhat, those principles state the following:

- Encourage free and deregulated housing markets
- Minimize government intervention, using it only to establish a safety net for the deserving poor
- Rely on the private sector and its profit incentives as the primary provider of housing
- Practice enlightened federalism, with maximum decentralization to local levels of government
- Permit subsidies to be used through the market—for instance, on the demand side
- Assure maximum freedom of housing choice
- Achieve fiscal responsibility and monetary stability in the economy
- Promote homeownership as a major goal
- Stimulate private accumulation of wealth as a stimulus to economic growth
- Encourage individual responsibility to provide and improve housing

We might add as further characteristics of conservative policies:

- They rely on the Republican Party for implementation in the political arena
- They have the support of the for-profit housing and real estate industry

The liberal approach to housing policy and programs has never been authoritatively articulated, but there might be consensus around the following principles connected with that philosophy:

- Rely on the private housing market as the primary provider of housing but with limited intervention to achieve public goals
- Provide for an important but supplementary role for government and nonprofit agencies as direct providers of housing, assuming both will act with benevolent motives

- Use central government power to achieve the purposes of public policy
- Give priority in social policy to meeting the needs of the poor, assuming that circumstances and not individual failure produce poverty
- Limit excess profits and price-gouging through use of governmental regulation
- Influence the location and form of housing in order to achieve public objectives
- Consider housing as a long-term investment suitable for financing through borrowing
- Promote homeownership as a major goal
- Consider the excessive concentration of wealth and power beyond a certain point a danger to democracy, and acknowledge the fairness of a certain degree of redistribution in order to avoid gross inequalities

We might add as further characteristic of liberal policies:

- They rely on the Democratic Party[2] for implementation in the political arena
- They have the support of tenants, labor unions and advocates for social housing

While there seem to be clear differences between the two approaches that might be reflected during various national administrations and Congresses in dealing with housing issues, both are at sharp variance from what might be considered essential principles of a Right to Housing approach. We do not put forth an outline of the full content of that approach here but merely suggest how far from such a position are both the conservative and the liberal approaches:

- Provide housing as an entitlement to all in need of it rather than specifying in advance the number of units to be provided
- Allow decisions as to the quantity and quality of housing provided, and its location, to be made democratically through the political process rather than through the market
- Recognize the desirability of motivations other than profit for supplying housing
- Allocate housing that is publicly provided on the basis of need, as a right, not on the basis of "worthiness"

We might add as further characteristics of Right to Housing policies:

- They are outside the mainstream of housing policies considered tenable by most in political leadership positions
- They are supported, except under conditions of crisis (depression, civil turmoil), only by a small fraction of housing advocates and then primarily in an ideological, rather than practical political, context

A review of key programs over the past half-century leads us to conclude that there are remarkable similarities and continuities among the policies implemented throughout this history, whether in presumptively liberal or conservative regimes, but that the policies of neither resemble a Right to Housing approach nor have they have been anywhere near adequate to meet the nation's housing needs.

A review of major historical periods in U.S. housing policy supports these general conclusions. We focus on national policy, for reasons of space.

PRE-DEPRESSION (REPUBLICAN PRESIDENT, REPUBLICAN CONGRESS)

The first action by the United States government directly to provide housing was to meet the housing needs of the war effort during World War I. Thus, the Emergency Fleet Corporation was established to house the shipbuilding industry's workers, and the United States Housing Corporation was established to meet the needs of workers essential to the national defense. Only positions for or against involvement in the war effort divided proponents from opponents, and there was general agreement that both programs should be of limited duration. The relevant legislation explicitly required sale of the constructed units immediately following the end of the emergency. The programs were of limited scope: Only 15,183 family units were built under the two programs combined (Colean 1940). After the war, there was a significant difference as to disposition of what was acknowledged to be high-quality housing (Schuman and

Sclar 1996). Liberals sought to have it sold to nonprofit groups, conservatives (who had their way) to private buyers without restrictions. No one argued for continuation of public ownership or further public construction, let alone expanding the program, despite the clear national housing shortage, as a Right to Housing approach might have suggested (Radford 1997:37–45).

Homeownership was the key theme of Republican President Herbert Hoover's housing policy, as it has been consistently for conservative approaches. The President's Conference on Home Building and Homeownership that he convened in Washington, DC, in December 1931 was the beginning of a series of federal moves in support of homeownership, which included the Federal Home Loan Bank Act of 1932, establishing a reserve banking institution for home mortgage lending. The thrust of the effort continued seamlessly with passage of the Home Owners' Loan Act of 1933, designed to refinance home mortgage loans in default, passed with Hoover's support in the first year of the following liberal Roosevelt Administration. The favored status accorded homeownership was then further enhanced with bipartisan passage of the National Housing Act of 1934, creating the Federal Housing Administration (FHA) to provide federal insurance of home mortgages. These developments enshrined a preference for a particular form of individualistic, private tenure in housing whose thrust has never been questioned by either liberals or conservatives to this day.[3]

Those who adopt a Right to Housing position tend be skeptical of the strong priority given to homeownership and to see it more as attractive because of the sense that it provides security of occupancy. They worry about its ambiguous consequences in mixing expanded assumed security and control with commodification, making occupancy dependent on attendant market conditions and market fluctuations, with all the risks (Dean 1945; Kemeny 1981). Those risks are seen as especially sharp for households of low income (Marcuse 1974), and alternative forms of tenure, providing the security without the risk, have been proposed (Institute for Policy Studies 1989).

THE 1930s: THE NEW DEAL
(DEMOCRATIC PRESIDENT,
DEMOCRATIC CONGRESS)

The National Industrial Recovery Act of 1933, adopted as an emergency measure at the height of the Great Depression and rushed through Congress by President Franklin Delano Roosevelt in his first 100 days in office, included a vaguely worded provision for a housing program. Under it, a Housing Division was established within the Public Works Administration (PWA), which directly built some 21,121 units of housing (Fisher 1959), initially available to anyone interested, although in 1936, income limits were placed on admission. But in 1936, a federal court ruled PWA's power to condemn land for housing construction unconstitutional (*United States v. Certain Lands in the City of Louisville* 1935). That ruling essentially ended direct construction by the Housing Division, but not because it was more difficult to build desirable housing only on land voluntarily sold to the division—in fact, progressive housing advocates like Catherine Bauer consistently argued for construction on "green fields," empty land further from the a city's center, as faster and cheaper than building on inner-city land that had to be condemned. Rather, it ended the program of new construction because the power of condemnation was often used in conjunction with slum clearance (28 of 51 project sites were on slum land), which in turn earned it the support of significant sections of the real estate industry, for whom slum clearance was an economic blessing in the Great Depression. Without that support, Harold Ickes, Roosevelt's presumptively liberal head of the PWA, killed the program. Conservatives had consistently opposed public construction of housing and without even the lure of slum clearance were pleased with the result of the litigation (Radford 1997:Chapter 4).

The labor and housing reform lobbies instead pushed for what became the Housing Act of 1937, adopted under President Roosevelt's Democratic Administration during the New Deal, the most clearly liberal period in U.S. history. For the first time, it established publicly owned and operated housing as a permanent part of the U.S. housing scene. It ranks as perhaps the most liberal of any piece of currently effective federal housing legislation.[4] But Congress supported it reluctantly, and only after great if belated pressure by Roosevelt. It was drafted and vigorously lobbied for by the organized labor movement, which saw it both as a way of creating jobs (thus backed in particular by the construction trades) and providing housing for union members. The 1937 act relied on direct public construction by local housing authorities, which built, owned and managed the housing under federal government oversight. The Louisville decision had held that the federal government could not use condemnation powers for housing, but there was little question that state governments could use it and could in turn delegate the power to local authorities. Construction was subject to the Davis-Bacon Act, adopted in 1935, so that workers would be paid prevailing wages in order not to undercut union rates. Eminent domain (with compensation) was used by local housing authorities to assemble building sites, thus exercising the government's legal powers to compel private property owners to sell their property for a public purpose. Conservatives vigorously fought the program tooth and nail, and it was not pushed by the Democratic president, effectively preventing it from becoming law until a year after the beginning of Roosevelt's second term in office.[5]

If public housing was, at its inception, the prototype of a liberal housing program, was it the "opposite" of a conservative program? In key respects, no. Roosevelt's initial lack of interest in pressing for passage of the program was only in part attributable to expected conservative opposition; his stance also reflected a substantive hesitation about the program—at least as to its most progressive or "radical" features. Thus, the bill as finally adopted contained a number of conservative features. Most conspicuous was the program's relation to the housing market. While it provided for direct government involvement in the provision of housing, it severely limited that involvement—in fact, limited it explicitly to groups who were not in the market anyway. The upper limit placed on who could benefit from the housing provided under the program was initially set at 20 percent below the income level at which private housing was affordable so as clearly to avoid any competition with the private housing market. Thus, a large buffer zone was established between the public and the private in order to make sure the former would in no way compete with the latter. If a family crossed that line, they were required to move out and had to re-enter the private market. As Senator Robert Wagner, the prominent liberal sponsor of the bill, told Congress in urging its adoption: "The most important consideration [behind the bill] is, that public housing projects should not be brought into competition with private industry" (U.S. Senate 1936, quoted in Mitchell 1985:247).

Real property owners not only were not hurt by the program, they benefited from it. One of the most contested issues was whether housing projects should be built on slum land or open land. As noted previously, owners of slum buildings saw the potential for being bailed out of properties which, given depression conditions, were not producing profit and so cooperated actively in tying slum clearance to public housing, while advocates for the ill-housed, including the legislation's leading proponents, pressed for use of sites outside of slum areas. Proponents pointed to cost savings in using vacant land and also argued that allowing market forces to depress the value of slum buildings, which could possibly lead to their abandonment, would produce far lower acquisition prices at a later date. This was one of the key issues in the debates between the progressive Langdon Post and the liberal Republican Mayor Fiorello LaGuardia in New York City on where to locate that city's public housing projects in the mid-1930s. Post took the same position that the progressive Catherine Bauer had taken with regard to the earlier PWA Housing Division programs.[6]

Perhaps the most important feature limiting the program's competition with the private sector was that, from the outset, the level of funding was so meager compared with the need that the potential for interfering with the market was minuscule: From 1938 to 1940, the three years after the program was fully under way until the onset of World War II, the dollar value of new public construction was just $300 million compared with $6.8 billion in private construction, only 4.2 percent of housing construction (U.S.

Department of Commerce 1975:Tables N-4, N-20). Thus, public housing was hardly a major interference with the private market. All indications point to the fact that the amount of public construction would have virtually stopped after that had housing for World War II war workers not become of concern for national defense purposes. Today, federal public housing accounts for only 1.3 million units, just over 1 percent of the nation's housing stock. And the effective decentralization of the program to local authorities, appointed by local political leaders, meant that in most communities, no aggressive competition with local real estate interests was likely to occur (Hartman and Carr 1969).

Policies substantially challenging this approach were not seriously considered during this period. In reality, while public housing scores reasonably well as a liberal program, it is hardly at the opposite end of the spectrum from conservative principles. On each of the points described above—income eligibility, slum sites, program scale—liberal proponents of the legislation were forced to compromise. With respect to income limits, for instance, the legislation's proponents agreed with conservatives that public housing should not be allowed to enter where the private market was functioning (even if it was demonstrably functioning poorly). A progressive position might easily have criticized the performance and record of the private sector, showing how the workings of the private market in land and buildings were producing speculative pricing, monopolistic practices and slum conditions, all in the context of profit-making because of private ownership of a basic resource in limited supply. Proponents might have argued for a public housing program analogous to the Tennessee Valley Authority, which brought low-cost electricity to rural areas of the South, producing housing that was directly competitive with the private market and was operating as a yardstick for private market activities, making the cost of housing fairer and more affordable for middle-income families as well. But that was not the liberal program. By the same token, while advocates of public housing wanted a larger program than the one they got, the idea that it might be a substantial element of the nation's housing supply, large enough to have a real impact on the total housing market, was not part of the liberal agenda. One does find in the writings of some of the more radical housing reformers of the period indications of an aggressive agenda (Bauer 1934; Wood 1931; Birch 1976; Oberlander and Newbrun 1999), even approaching a Right to Housing, which may have come about as close as it ever has been in U.S. policy to inclusion in the mainstream of housing policy. That approach, however, was not reflected in the liberals' political practice.

Conservatives notably did support New Deal housing programs that were designed to rescue the bankrupt private housing system. Agencies and programs with this goal—the Federal Home Loan Bank Board, the Home Owners' Loan Corporation, the Federal Housing Administration (FHA), the Federal National Mortgage Association (later to become the essentially private Fannie Mae)—all were eagerly embraced as means to bail out the savings and loan system, reform the home mortgage finance system to benefit housing producers and middle-income homebuyers and create a government-backed secondary mortgage market (Keith 1973). These new federal agencies were administered on the principles and practices of the private market, as best exemplified by the FHA, which adopted the racist "ethics" of the National Association of Real Estate Boards, denying minorities eligibility for participation in its mortgage insurance programs via "redlining" practices (Abrams 1955; Jackson 1985). In the 1930s, liberals and conservatives alike supported these programs; if their incentives to do so varied slightly, their mutual commitment to support homeownership was always identical. Indeed, unanimity on the desirability of the expansion of homeownership has been a hallmark of U.S. policy under every administration since Herbert Hoover (if not indeed since Thomas Jefferson, albeit in the quite different political and economic setting of a more rural society), up to and including the current Bush Administration. That the appeal of homeownership might have the hope of financial speculative profit as its basis rather than housing preference; that it can have severely negative economic consequences for many, particularly those of lower income; that it can lead to massive unplanned suburban

sprawl and environmental pollution and undercuts otherwise desirable policies such as mass transit, is not recognized in either the liberal or the conservative worldview (Kemeny 1981; Marcuse 1972).

THE 1949 HOUSING ACT (DEMOCRATIC PRESIDENT, DEMOCRATIC CONGRESS)

The 1949 Housing Act—the major piece of postwar housing and urban legislation— was of mixed parentage. Liberal prohousing forces—lower-income housing advocates, civil rights groups, ideologically liberal members of Congress, labor unions—wanted to revive the public housing program, in limbo after its defunding following a conservative upsurge in 1939 (Woodyatt 1968:193–229; Freedman 1969) and its conversion to a war housing program after 1940. Conservatives wanted a mechanism to aid the private market in reclaiming downtown real estate in urban centers, where business expansion was made difficult and more expensive by the presence of "incompatible" land uses, often working-class housing and older industrial and warehousing activities. The compromise, acceptable to liberals, was the 1949 legislation, in which Title I established the urban renewal program and Title III re-established the public housing program authorizing long-term (six-year) funding for a total of 810,000 additional units. Public housing as an entitlement was never even marginally considered in the discussions, as a Right to Housing approach might have suggested, even with staged implementation. Key support for the actual compromise came from Senator Robert Taft of Ohio ("Mr. Republican," as he was known—see Gelfand 1975; Freedman 1969). Only a few lone progressives voiced their doubts with regard to the impact of urban renewal on housing for low-income families.[7]

In later years, extensive debate arose about that compromise, when it became obvious that Title I and the liberal purposes of Title III were contradictory. Under Title I, land on which low-income people lived was acquired with public funds, the residents were forced to move, the land was resold to developers at write-down prices, and generally new higher-income residential or business uses replaced their former homes. The hopes of some that redevelopment and urban renewal would be used to expand the supply of low-rent housing were disappointed. In practice, under both Democratic and Republican Administrations, Title I was more often used to advance commercial and downtown business interests than to provide public housing.[8] As a result, by 1967, approximately 400,000 residential units had been destroyed under Title I and only 10,760 public housing units built on their sites (National Commission on Urban Problems 1968; Hirsch 2000). After public protest—some of it militantly in the streets as well as at the ballot boxes—requirements to provide replacement housing for those displaced were added to the legislation. Ironically perhaps, Title III was put to that use, becoming the new homes for those displaced by Title I, who were given priority for admission to public housing by federal law. Therefore, no significant expansion of decent housing available to those with low incomes was accomplished by the 1949 Housing Act. There was more likely a net reduction (National Commission on Urban Problems 1968:163; Hirsch 2000:158–189). The benefits redounded rather to the real estate, development and downtown business interests that profited from Title I's subsidies and local government powers (in particular, eminent domain takings to assemble parcels for redevelopment and their sale at written-down below-market prices).

A position substantially challenging the postwar conservative push around urban redevelopment would have looked for a quite different result. As with the 1930s, it may be argued that what actually happened was forced on liberals as a matter of political necessity. But that is not really true. Liberals did not oppose the basic principles of urban redevelopment embodied in the 1949 act. Under the legislation, private property was fully protected and private profit assured. Although eminent domain (taking) powers were central, for the most part, the land was bought from small property owners and resold at a considerably marked-down price to large real estate developers. Planning for reuse of the assembled sites was in effect left to

the private sector: Local public redevelopment agencies (whose commissioners most frequently represented business interests [Hartman 2002a; Mollenkopf 1983]) had to find private developers to take over the rebuilding/investment process. Land sold to such developers then produced projects constructed, owned and managed by profit-making entities. Liberals did not oppose this use of public powers and funds to facilitate private market development, and the progressive position of some 1930s public housing advocates referred to above favoring undeveloped sites over slum sites was not pushed.

THE CIVIL RIGHTS ERA (DEMOCRATIC PRESIDENT, DEMOCRATIC CONGRESS)

The legislation of the Kennedy-Johnson years, from 1961 to 1969, culminating in passage of the 1968 Housing Act—the first major piece of housing legislation since the immediate postwar period—came in a political climate that was encouraging for liberal policies. The Civil Rights Movement; the urban riots/revolts in major cities across the country, which the report of the President's Commission on Civil Disturbances (the Kerner Commission) spoke of as raising the specter of "two societies, one black, one white—separate and unequal" and a solidly Democratic Congress and President all augured well for liberal housing legislation. It brought to the fore the issues on which liberals distinguished themselves from conservatives,[9] issues of civil rights and race relations and the extent (but not the nature) of government action in the housing field.

Both electoral politics and the turmoil of the civil rights and black liberation movements pushed the Kennedy Administration—elected in 1960 by a slim margin with substantial backing from the African-American vote—to take an affirmative posture toward housing issues. This was first evidenced in the civil rights arena. In 1962, President John F. Kennedy issued Executive Order #11063, banning racial discrimination in federally assisted housing. Legislation followed, first the Civil Rights Act of 1964, then the Voting Rights Act of 1965, followed by Title VIII of the Civil Rights Act of 1968, incorporating into legislation prohibitions on discrimination in much of private as well as publicly assisted housing. Conservatives agreed in principle with liberals on the undesirability of racial discrimination, and both political parties were divided (largely along North-South lines) on how far the federal government should act in the area. In broad summary, both sides agreed that direct discrimination by government based on race should be prohibited and that government should encourage nondiscrimination in private housing. Liberals were much more concerned to push for enforcement of antidiscrimination measures in private housing and differed from conservatives on the means of enforcement (testing and affirmative enforcement vs. responding to complaints) and as to the budgets and powers available to the enforcing arms of government. Conservatives saw federal action limited to prohibiting discrimination; liberals vacillated in going beyond that position and pressing for integration as an affirmative policy goal. Neither camp, since the high point of concern in this period, has made dealing with the race issue a priority for attention in a country whose housing is more segregated than almost any other country in the world, barring South Africa.[10]

The 1968 Housing and Urban Development Act similarly was strongly influenced by the turmoil of the period. Two national commissions fed directly into its drafting: the President's Committee on Urban Housing (the Kaiser Committee) and the National Commission on Urban Problems (the Douglas Commission). What resulted was legislation about which liberals were uniformly proud. The centerpiece of the act was formulation and promulgation, for the first time, of a quantitative housing production goal for the nation, with specific targets for lower-income housing and specific governmental measures to achieve these targets: 26 million new units over ten years, 6 million of them for low- and moderate-income households. The package sought by liberals included expansion of public housing (not included in the final legislation) plus a new program of interest subsidies for rental housing, targeting moderate-income households (Section 236). A

majority of Republican members of Congress supported the legislation, including a program of low-interest loans for homeownership, also addressed to moderate-income families (Section 235—see below regarding scandals under this program). Conservatives and liberals came together on a coherent set of policies; the only issue that set them apart was disagreement on the role of public housing. Even on the issue of discrimination in housing, broad fair housing legislation was separately adopted, although hardly going as far as many wanted (see Chapter 3).

The substance of this seemingly remarkable consensus bears closer examination, however. The Kaiser Committee, which advanced the 26 million unit goal for new housing production, was a heavily business-dominated group, led by industrialist Henry J. Kaiser, and included representatives of every major sector of the industry: builders, financial institutions, building trade unions, architects, materials suppliers. A high numerical housing production goal of course suited them well. The reliance on private construction was unchallenged in the act and fit well with conservative ideology. Indeed, the bulk of federal government involvement was through a writedown of the interest rate on privately originated loans (from market rate to as low as 1 percent)—that is to say, government payment of interest to banks and other lending institutions to finance private construction and purchase of housing. The Kaiser Committee had further recommended on an experimental basis what would later be called a housing allowance program, under which support would be provided to owners of existing private rental housing in order to make it profitable for them to lease their units to low-income tenants. Those approaches, not contested by liberals, later became the centerpiece of President Richard Nixon's conservative housing policies.

The 1968 Housing Act's production goals for subsidized housing lumped together moderate- and low-income households, and through the structure of the programs established in the act strongly favored those of moderate income and provided little for those of low income. Implementation of the programs was left almost entirely with private initiative: Private developers under Sections 235 and 236 applied for financing for developments that they proposed, which then were reviewed locally and funded if they met federal guidelines and fell within HUD's available budgetary allocations.

Thus, the 1968 act, often seen as a highlight of liberal success in housing policy, did not significantly challenge any of the key precepts of conservative housing policy. Despite some general calls for the adoption of a substantive rights approach by leaders such as Martin Luther King, Jr., a Right to Housing was nowhere near the mainstream agenda. No major investment in publicly owned, nonmarket housing was proposed; private profit-motivated developers were relied on to implement the program, and the entitlement approach of a Right to Housing was not discussed; direct government involvement was severely limited and benefits were targeted to those with moderate incomes, rather than to the poor, unemployed or those out of the workforce. The provision setting production goals, modest as they were, had no teeth, and the goals for low-income housing were never even approached. No conflict with conservative ideology was involved, and the resulting package earned the ideological and political support of Republicans and the housing industry. With the change to an ideologically rigid conservative Republican Administration, the earlier liberal Democratic sponsorship of the 1968 act nevertheless was a major factor leading President Nixon in 1973 to proclaim a moratorium on all housing programs, retroactively justified by a review of all federal housing programs that indicted them for high costs, inefficiency and inequity (Bell 1985; Hartman and Keating 1973; HUD 1974). The end result was a full-scale shift to a demand-side policy of subsidies to tenants, to be used in the private rental market.

THE 1974 HOUSING AND COMMUNITY DEVELOPMENT ACT (REPUBLICAN PRESIDENT, DEMOCRATIC CONGRESS)

Community Development Block Grants (CDBGs), embracing the conservatives' desire to extricate the federal government from direct involvement in urban issues, and the Section 8 program, the formal adoption of housing allowances as the chief new form of subsidizing low-income households, were the two main features of the 1974 housing legislation. The CDBG approach followed the consistent conservative preference for reduction of federal involvement in social welfare and was acceptable to liberals in part because it seemed to be consistent with their ideological espousal of grassroots democracy. In practice, it gave greater freedom to local political and business interests to use federal funds with more flexibility than explicit federal involvement would have provided.

The allowance approach, which has a long and checkered history, is ideologically the prototypical conservative concept of how subsidies should be handled, if indeed they are to be paid at all (Friedman 1962). Experience suggested it was neither an efficient nor an equitable method of subsidy (Struyk and Bendick 1981), but it was the method that maximized the role of market forces and minimized the need for direct government action. Liberals did not oppose housing allowances or protest against the substitution of allowances for direct government provision of housing, and only a few progressive voices questioned the approach overall (Hartman 1983b, 1983c). The major criticisms were that they would be ineffective in tight housing markets and/or would inflate the price of housing primarily to benefit landlords. A Right to Housing approach would have further questioned the net result even of an expanded allowance program: that the allocation, location and price of housing would be left for determination by the private market.

But the notion that drawing on existing housing was cheaper than new construction appealed to both sides. And indeed on the face of it, it was a simple and logical approach. But as the history of Section 8 has demonstrated, where inadequate supply is a major cause of housing problems (as is true in most metropolitan housing markets), vouchers and certificates have proven to be an inadequate substitute for construction programs, particularly for minorities (HUD 1999). High rates of returned vouchers from searchers unable to find a suitable unit, landlord resistance to accepting subsidized tenants, substandard conditions of Section 8–subsidized units and other market realities as well as the vagaries of Congressional budgetary politics all are factors undermining this approach.

The more liberal Congress, pressed by housing advocates and representatives of the housing industry, negotiated a modification to the pure housing allowance approach, one that permitted commitments for future Section 8 subsidies to be assigned to a developer (or owner, for rehab), who thus could use them to assure steady rental payments and thereby obtain financing for construction of new housing: the so-called Section 8 new construction program. In the more conservative Congress of 1983 that adaptation of Section 8 was ended.

But a logical progressive alternative to housing allowances for lower-income families could have been implemented. In situations where supply was adequate but effective demand was inadequate, the market could have been allowed to depreciate the price of existing housing and then buy it and retain it in public or other non-profit ownership. Where supply was inadequate, construction of public housing would have been a logical answer. That was the same logic originally advocated by public housing proponents as the best and least expensive way to clear slums: Rather than acquire them immediately via eminent domain, let the market, with new public housing as competition, drive their price down and then acquire them for clearance and rebuilding. In 1974 as well, using an expanded supply of public housing to lower the market price of private housing could have been tried, but no voices were raised from the liberal community for such an approach. It would not have bailed out private landlords and would have interfered with making profit in the private housing market. No liberals pushed for such a progressive alternative to the conservative approach.

THE CARTER INTERREGNUM
(DEMOCRATIC PRESIDENT,
DEMOCRATIC CONGRESS)

The Home Mortgage Disclosure Act of 1975, pushed through in the weakened Republican Administration of Gerald Ford, followed by the Community Reinvestment Act of 1977, passed under the Democratic Administration of President Jimmy Carter, represented victories by liberals in Congress, enacted after a number of years of strong agitation by National People's Action and civil rights groups. It was a high point in a struggle around the issue of redlining, the discriminatory provision of housing credit by lending institutions and the FHA based on race, pursuant to which housing in whole neighborhoods was written off as being ineligible for consideration for loans. By first requiring disclosure of where and to whom housing loans were made and then setting standards for institutions to give loans in all places where they did business, the freedom of private lending institutions to use their own discretion in giving loans was significantly limited. Lenders and conservatives opposed legislation along these lines, arguing instead for voluntary compliance and education, and denying that discrimination was intentional. Conservatives and liberals consistently fought over the provisions of legislation in this area.

Yet the differences remained limited: The obligation of private lending institutions was to not discriminate on the basis of race or a geographical surrogate for race; but both sides agreed that if the rejection of a loan had sound business basis, it was permitted. By preserving the defense of sound business reasons for refusals to lend, lending practices were perhaps rationalized a bit but no serious interference with market considerations was involved. Ironically, as far as is known, lenders who have provided loans in inner-city neighborhoods through Community Reinvestment Act (CRA) agreements have found it to be profitable (Squires 2000.)

An approach differing radically from both the conservative and liberal approaches, such as a Right to Housing might encompass, might have looked at the provision of mortgage financing as a matter of right, an entitlement much as, say, food stamps are provided. Indeed, FHA mortgage insurance is in effect a right, an entitlement, extended to anyone who qualifies. The direct provision of mortgage financing by government (as in other programs, such as those administered by the Small Business Administration) might have moved toward a Right to Housing approach. Even the possibility of a more progressive approach, under which lending institutions might in fact play a redistributive role by using profits from mortgages in higher-income neighborhoods to subsidize mortgages with more risk in lower-income neighborhoods, was never seriously considered (Marcuse 1979).

The most significant contribution of the Carter Administration, despite the fact that he had a Democratic Congress during all four years, was promotion of the neighborhood self-help approach, including creation of a formal division within the U.S. Department of Housing and Urban Development supporting that approach and the direct funding of a limited number of nonprofit organizations. Funding was slight and did not survive the Carter presidency. The theme of a role for nonprofit organizations in housing is, however, one in which the conservative and liberal approaches come together but from very different directions. For conservatives, nonprofit housing is a replacement for government action, a step toward privatization. For liberals, nonprofit action is a replacement for profit-motivated action, a step away from privatization. Conservatives look toward nonprofits ultimately as being entirely emancipated from reliance on government. Liberals, when they are realistic, realize that a significant role for nonprofits depends on government support. Neither side is willing to acknowledge—as nonprofit providers too well know—that they are dependent on government subsidies for their significant contribution, and cannot touch the bulk of the housing problems of low-income households.[11] For conservatives, nonprofits are better than government, and for liberals, nonprofits are better than the market—for neither is there an essential desire to expand the scope of nonmarket housing, and neither side acknowledges the importance of the link between affordable nonprofit housing and government subsidy. As well, neither differentiates between charitable nonprofits, on the one hand, and community and resident-based nonprofits, on the other. A Right to Housing approach, by contrast, would see nonprofit organization as a way of achieving residents' control over their own housing and excluding the speculative profit motive from housing relationships.

THE REAGAN AND GEORGE H. W. BUSH ERAS (REPUBLICAN PRESIDENT, DIVIDED OR DEMOCRATIC CONGRESS)

The professed aim of the Reagan Administration was to reverse New Deal social programs. In the housing area, this meant cutting back drastically and in some cases eliminating federal income-targeted housing subsidy programs, leaving the private market to serve most lower-income Americans. This formulation of course overlooks the contradiction that the so-called private housing market depends heavily on government support, from the massive tax breaks to homeowners (see Chapter 5) and landlords to support given to lenders through the Treasury, the Federal National Mortgage Association (FNMA) and the Federal Reserve System.

Ronald Reagan's 1982 President's Commission on Housing, a major source for the statement of the conservative position on housing, as outlined in the opening section of this chapter, was the major jumping-off point for the accelerated and intensified version of the Nixon Administration's approach. Criticism and rejection of supply-side strategies were central points, underscored by moves to privatize existing public housing. A virulent anti-HUD mood prevailed (House Republicans had opposed creation of the department in 1965), taking the form of heavy budget cuts and, via David Stockman's Office of Management and Budget, ending authority for future construction of low-income housing as well as rescissions of HUD's existing appropriations (Hartman 1986). Reagan's proposals for HUD sought to end all federally subsidized construction programs (which require long-term financial commitments) in favor of short-term housing vouchers. Opposition by low-income housing advocates and their Congressional and state and local government allies created a stalemate. The result was some new construction under the Section 202 program for the elderly and a modest new moderate-income construction program forced on HUD—the Housing Development Action Grant (HoDAG) program. Section 8 became the primary low-income federal housing assistance program (Hays 1995). A further Reagan Administration blow to low-income households was raising the portion of income that tenants had to pay while living in subsidized housing from 25 percent to 30 percent, a savings to the government estimated over five years to total $6 billion—that much taken out of the inadequate family budgets of the low-income beneficiaries of the federal housing programs (Hartman 1986). While the worst of the proposed budget cuts were blunted by a Democratic Congress, the fights were about amounts rather than about programs; liberals even ultimately tacitly accepted the 25 percent to 30 percent increase, and at the turn of the century, a "liberal" HUD Secretary in the Democratic Clinton Administration raised the threshold even higher by considering as the economic threshold for "worst case" housing expenditures paying over 50 percent of income (HUD 2000a).

Tax "reform" was a major part of the conservative agenda. For low-income housing programs, it meant repeal of certain tax benefits earlier accorded to producers of eligible housing to be replaced in 1986 by the Low Income Housing Tax Credit (LIHTC), which provides a credit against federal income taxes in connection with the private development of housing for low- and moderate-income households, the amount of the credit dependent on the proportion of units in a development allocated to such groups. The credit may then be sold by the developer, and since it is most useful to taxpayers in top income brackets, it has maximum appeal to upper tax bracket taxpayers and corporations. The LIHTC is clearly vulnerable to a number of criticisms: It is inordinately complicated, providing a bonanza for specialized intermediaries, lawyers and accountants, who reap a significant part of its benefits; it is regressive, in that its subsidies are channeled through benefits for upper-income taxpayers; and it does not provide deep enough subsidies to provide housing for very-low-income households (Schwartz et al. 1988; Stegman 1992). Yet liberals accepted it, despite their criticisms, and soon saw it as their best hope for financing new construction, as did nonprofit housing sponsors. Fundamental progressive criticism of the very concept was all but forgotten. Raising issues of a Right to Housing would have seemed to be "pure pie in the sky" under the circumstances.

Conservatives and liberals have tread very softly on the tax provision needing the greatest reform of all, the massive collective deduction that homeowners receive for their payment of real estate taxes and mortgage interest, and nontaxation of the imputed income from their ownership—what Peter Dreier has strikingly labeled as the "mansion subsidy." It has been the progressives who have pointed out the gross disparity between the subsidy to upper-income households and that for lower-income households. In 2000 (using 2001 dollars), the total of direct HUD and Department of Agriculture housing subsidies of approximately $31 billion amounted to about one-fourth of the indirect housing subsidies of $118 billion to homeowners and investors. Serious challenges to this regressive subsidy came only from progressives (see Chapter 5), without resonance from liberals or conservatives.

During this period, the only significantly new legislation[12] proposed and pushed through by a Democratic Congress over the objections of the Reagan Administration was the 1987 McKinney Homeless Assistance Act (named after its chief Republican sponsor, who died from complications of AIDS—Foscarinis 1996; Hays 1995). During the 1980s, homelessness had emerged as a major national phenomenon for the first time since the Great Depression. A combination of the reduced supply of available low-rent housing, growth in poverty rates, structural changes in the economy and the deinstitutionalization movement (unaccompanied by provision of adequate community mental health services) greatly increased the need for homeless shelters, social services and low-income housing (Baumohl 1996). In the face of such a dramatically observable need for housing for the poor, the conservative response was based on the ideological conviction that conditions such as homelessness were an individual's *own* problem, for which the individual should be responsible. Conservatives denied that homelessness was a major social problem and rejected the notion of federal responsibility to address it. Consistent with their principled position against federal involvement in social issues, they held this was a problem to be dealt with by local governments and private charities as well as religious organizations. Thus, the Reagan Administration sought to minimize its magnitude and resisted calls for new federal programs to construct emergency shelters. But the public moral shock at homelessness, increasingly visible in almost all major cities, forced even that Administration to approve ameliorative legislation, agreeing with liberals on its terms. That even (or particularly) the homeless had a right to decent, permanent, secure housing in suitable neighborhoods, and that the need could only be met by a large-scale program for the construction of additional housing, was not part of either party's consideration (Marcuse 1988).

The ideological conservative opposition to a federal role on homelessness was part of a general principled opposition, not only to federal affirmative actions on housing issues but to any form of governmental regulation in which progressive social purposes interfered with private housing market profits. The attempt during this period to nullify local rent regulations by tying receipt of various forms of federal assistance to states and localities to the absence of rent regulation illustrates this, ironically putting the two principles in contradiction to each other. But pressures from housing industry interests were enough to have the Reagan Administration attempt to use federal powers to override local decisions to control rents. Ultimately, tenant action (more than liberal political opposition) averted the Administration's proposal to tie federal assistance for other housing and community development programs to elimination of rent controls, but conservatives at local levels, led by well-financed landlord groups, succeeded in limiting or repealing almost all rent regulations, certainly the stronger ones (Keating 1998). The ideological justification relied on the conservative argument that the private, unregulated market will solve the housing affordability problem by increasing the housing supply at the upper ends, leaving it to the filtering-down process to take care of those with lower incomes (Salins and Mildner 1992). Yet, again ironically, certain forms of rent regulation are not so repugnant to conservatives that they cannot endorse them when pragmatically as briefly necessary. Thus, Calvin Coolidge in 1925 could be found endorsing the District of Columbia Rent Act (granted

under pressure; see Havlik 1930, cited in Radford 1997:47, 223), and Richard Nixon in 1971 to 1973 included rents in his price-control measures. Examining the substance of the various forms of rent regulation, however, it becomes clear that both liberals and conservatives considered it appropriate for rent regulation to guarantee a "reasonable return" to landlords. The idea that priority to landlord returns might have to give way to larger social needs, the understanding of the logic of rent regulation (Marcuse 1981, 1986b) that might accompany a Right to Housing, was advanced by neither side.

Both Democrats and Republicans encountered issues of corruption in the administration of their housing programs, and for largely the same reasons. Both relied overwhelmingly on the private sector to build, finance and manage housing within an overwhelmingly private housing market. The private sector is, necessarily, concerned primarily with profit, not with social purpose. It will inevitably tailor its use of public programs so as to maximize profits, and if persuading public officials to bend the rules in its favor is feasible, it will do so. Since conservative administrations favor private sector involvement even more than do liberal administrations, corruption and mismanagement scandals are marginally more likely to occur under Republican than under Democratic administrations. The first major scandal of the postwar period occurred during the Eisenhower Administration, involving the postwar Section 608 program under which the FHA allowed developers to build essentially risk-free rental projects without any real equity investment on their part. Rising FHA foreclosures led to Congressional investigations, which revealed that lax oversight had given developers free rein to profit and then walk away from these financially troubled projects (Welfeld 1988:68–69). Richard Nixon found his Administration mired in a similar housing scandal in the early 1970s. Congressional investigations revealed widespread abuses in the newly created Sections 223 and 235 (homeownership) and Section 236 (rental housing) subsidy programs created by the 1968 Housing Act, both of which involved private construction with significant profit potential. Widespread lax FHA oversight and occasional corruption in the approval process led to extremely high foreclosure rates that cost the Treasury heavy sums in guaranteed bank bailouts and ruined the prospects for lower-income occupants of these subsidized units to obtain better housing (Hays 1995:113–130). The problems in the private use of these programs then, ironically, were used to justify President Nixon's 1973 moratorium on all governmental housing subsidy programs and contributed to the demise of federal subsidies for permanent new low-income housing. The irony is increased by the fact that the one housing program with the greatest direct federal involvement, public housing, has had virtually no widespread scandals in its administration over its more than 60 years of existence. The answer to corruption in the administration of federal housing programs would thus logically be, consistent with the principles of a Right to Housing, to minimize the role of private profit in the implementation of public programs and go in the direction of direct governmental construction, ownership and management; but that progressive approach to corruption has not found favor with either liberals or conservatives.

The direct links between conservative housing policies and the real estate industry are strikingly illustrated by the revolving door between the private sector and top federal policy-making positions. Republican administrations have routinely recruited federal policymakers from the housing industry, even when they opposed the very programs that they are to administer. For example, Albert Cole, Administrator of the Housing and Home Finance Agency (predecessor to the cabinet-level Department of Housing and Urban Development) was a former Congressman who had voted against the public housing program (Keith 1973:110–111). The first Bush Administration's HUD Secretary, Jack Kemp, was ideologically opposed to public housing, which he attempted to privatize.

THE 1990 AFFORDABLE HOUSING ACT (REPUBLICAN PRESIDENT, DEMOCRATIC CONGRESS)

The 1990 Affordable Housing Act was the first in a series of more recent continuing major legislative and administrative moves to reduce and perhaps entirely dismantle the federal public housing program. Three initiatives were involved: the "vouchering-out" of public housing; permitting public housing tenants to buy their own public housing units on apparently very favorable terms; and the programs to deal with "severely distressed" projects, ending in the current HOPE VI program (see below). The remarkable thing about all three initiatives was that they were introduced in a quite conservative Republican Administration but expanded and pressed forward in a presumptively liberal Democratic Administration. At the same time, the Republican legislation also contained provisions for supportive services in subsidized housing, a continuing liberal approach.

"Vouchering-out" gives public housing residents the cash equivalent of the government's public housing subsidy and lets them spend it in the private market, much as they would use a Section 8 voucher, with the added wrinkle that it can be used for home purchase as well as renting. It represents both marketization and subsidy for expanded homeownership, both conservative staples not much different from liberal goals. Vouchering-out puts public housing squarely into the housing market: Public housing managers must compete with the private market for tenants, without the private market having any of the public sector's obligations to provide housing for those most in need, using an existing, often parsimoniously built housing stock that is frequently troubled for social, physical and management reasons. It is not competition between good public, nonprofit and socially oriented housing and private, profit-oriented housing; rather, it simply lowers public housing into the functional equivalent of private housing, with no increase in the housing supply that might drive private sector prices down.

Labeling "homeownership" as turning over title from public housing units to individual tenants fits well into conservative ideology. It was a key element in the conservative program of former HUD Secretary Jack Kemp that ended up as the Homeownership Opportunities for People Everywhere (HOPE) provisions of the 1990 act. There was early and soon justified skepticism (Rohe and Stegman 1992; Peterman 1993) as to how many public housing tenants could or would benefit from the program, but the program is ambiguous with regard to liberal tenets. On the one hand, the economic impact on tenants is of dubious benefit to them. For individuals coming into "ownership," there continue to be restrictions on their ability to make decisions about their units, whether due to the multiple-unit characteristics of most public housing developments or because of legal restrictions on profiting from government subsidies as a result of resale. Tenants get ownership only in a quite restrictive meaning of the term. For low-income households as a class, the total number of units available in the subsidized housing stock is reduced under this approach, since units converted to individual ownership are permanently eliminated from the stock available to future income-eligible claimants. Therefore, liberals have reason to oppose the program. On the other hand, homeownership is a means of empowerment, which has always been a concept appealing to liberals. Thus, opposition to this 1990 program has focused more on details than on principle. But a significant alternative has been neglected: homeownership implemented in collective form, such as a cooperative association in which all tenants/shareholders would be participants, but free of market pressures to sell to the highest bidder on termination of occupancy, thus maintaining the units available to low-income residents and giving them real powers of management. Such an arrangement would also avoid the regressive distributional impact among public housing tenants arising from the program, which gives preference to tenants with resources and initiative over those in greater difficulty. But such an approach, consistent with an effective Right to Housing for all, runs counter to both conservative and liberal ideologies of homeownership as a market-located, asset-building for-profit program.

A further initiative that had both conservative and liberal support has apparently died, largely as a result of its own contradictions: tenant assumption of public housing management responsibilities, presumably as a method of tenant empowerment. Tenants in public housing had for years pressed for a greater role in decision-making over how public housing was run, and

in the militant 1960s achieved some significant successes, ranging from fairer formal leases to rent payments based on a tenant's income up to a ceiling, regardless of the project's varying capital costs and operating expenses. Jack Kemp was a leading force pushing for creation of tenant management corporations in public housing projects, a position consistent with the conservative philosophy that individuals should be responsible for their own condition and that social programs should be decentralized as much as possible. This move also was a way to get government out of the public housing management business. After two widely touted "successes," the federal government was increasingly reluctant to cede real control to tenants and give them the financial support needed to operate a project successfully; tenant management today is more advisory on the smaller details of housing management than a real decentralization of control over the project (Peterman 1998).

THE CLINTON YEARS (DEMOCRATIC PRESIDENT, DEMOCRATIC THEN REPUBLICAN CONGRESS)

HOPE VI is the latest in HUD's programs to deal with the public housing it has inherited. It could be an excellent program, acceptable to both liberals and resident tenants' groups. However, it could raise conservatives' fiscal ire, for it provides funds for improving and modernizing public housing projects that may be in poor physical shape, deserted by tenants or suffering from bad management. There have been some good results with this program.[13] But the dominant paradigm for HOPE VI is demolishing parts or all of "distressed projects," reducing density, introducing mixed-income housing—all perhaps desirable if the reduced number of units available to those in greatest need were replaced (see National Housing Law Project et al. 2002). But there no requirement to do so: An equivalent replacement provision in the original legislation was subsequently deleted (Wexler 2001). Further, the program can serve to introduce or extend gentrification to whole neighborhoods, as the current program in Chicago is accused of doing. It has been tenants at the grassroots level, not liberals in Congress or at HUD, who have fought such uses of the program (see Smith 2000).

The distinction between liberal and conservative positions on housing policy, which we argue has always been a distinction within a limited range of positions—Right to Housing alternatives being excluded from consideration by both—has eroded further in the period since 1968. By the time of the Clinton Administration, the range of differences was increasingly difficult to detect (Meeropol 1998). Not much new happened with housing during the centrist Democratic Administration of President Bill Clinton. Faced in the second half of his first term with a staunchly conservative Republican Congress, it is hard to tell whether what was done should be entered on the liberal or conservative side of the ledger. The Empowerment Zone legislation (Marcuse 1994, 2000), the major urban initiative during Clinton's presidency, specifically excluded subsidies for housing construction or rehabilitation. Indeed, Henry Cisneros, Clinton's first HUD Secretary, put forward a program for "reinventing" his agency that many considered a substantial (if tactical) capitulation to Republican pressures. On the liberal side of the ledger, the dissolution of the Department of Housing and Urban Development was avoided, and the number of demand-side housing vouchers and low-income housing tax credits were increased, both measures quite consistent with the mainstream of conservative as well as liberal housing approaches. On the conservative side, the United States, under liberal leadership, took a position at the United Nations' 1994 Istanbul Habitat II conference, strongly opposing inclusion of a Right to Housing in the conference's final declaration, rejecting inclusion of progressive language supported in principle by a majority of the delegates (see Chapter 8). At no time in the 1990s did housing or urban issues appear as a matter of importance on either the liberal or the conservative agenda. Typically, tax credits, which are a way both of obscuring subsidies for housing and providing major benefits to higher-income taxpayers and corporations, were far greater than direct appropriations for HUD during the entire period, with the former over two-and-a-half times greater than the latter

as of 2001, the end of Clinton's term. The essential harmony between key liberal and conservative housing principles has remained in place to this day; both the Clinton and the Gore 2000 platforms stayed far away from any confrontation with the nation's serious housing problems.

To summarize the net effect of the Clinton period, "the number of households facing worst case housing needs grew, as did the number of homeless; the number of new households assisted per year was the lowest since 1977; there were several years in which no new funding for Section 8 certificates was provided" (Bratt 2003:626).

During the entire period beginning with Richard Nixon's election in 1968 and running through the end of the century with only a slight blip in Jimmy Carter's one term, an essentially conservative approach has dominated the federal government's housing agenda. The liberal posture was more and more defensive, confined not to challenging the key principles of the conservative position but simply trying to squeeze a slightly less penurious level of funding out of the recalcitrant leadership of both major political parties. A serious, challenging alternative was indeed put forward by a few from time to time (Institute for Policy Studies 1989) and eventually even introduced as legislation in Congress by left-leaning Representative Ron Dellums, but it met with no resonance within the liberal housing establishment.

THE SECOND BUSH ADMINISTRATION (REPUBLICAN PRESIDENT, DIVIDED OR REPUBLICAN CONGRESS)

The Administration of George W. Bush took office in 2001 without a housing agenda. Bush's choice as HUD Secretary, Mel Martinez, was an obscure Florida official, presumably chosen in large part because of his Hispanic background (like Clinton's first HUD Secretary, Henry Cisneros, who, however, was known nationally as mayor of San Antonio).

Under the Bush Administration, little attention has been paid to housing. The single major HUD initiative under Bush and Martinez was the announcement in June 2002 of a goal to increase minority homeownership by 5.5 million, with an emphasis on expanded homeownership for minorities (Washington 2004). Promoting homeownership is a traditional conservative position. However, the liberal Congressional Black Caucus also supports this goal, and one of the Clinton Administration's highest housing policy goals and cited achievements had been to increase the rate of homeownership, including that of minorities (HUD 2000b). It is hard to distinguish any significant difference between the two viewpoints on this policy.

The report of the Congressionally formed Millennial Housing Commission in 2002 did little to make housing a national policy priority. The Commission, "appointed by the chairs and ranking minority members of several House and Senate committees and subcommittees, was heavily weighted toward the housing industry, developers, real estate investors, and bankers"; it offered no numerical goals or targets, virtually ignored race issues as well as other key problem areas (rural housing, Native American reservations, migrant workers, homelessness and the needs of those with physical and mental disabilities). Its report was justly ignored by Congress, policymakers and most of the public (Hartman 2002b). "The State of the Nation's Housing 2002," from the Joint Center for Housing Studies of Harvard University, reported that 8.6 million renters and 6.4 million homeowners among the lowest-income Americans were spending more than 30 percent of their income on housing. The Bush Administration has not only ignored this housing affordability problem, but its 2003 HUD budget proposed numerous cuts in programs intended to make housing more affordable. Among these were reductions in operating support for public housing, reductions in Section 8 assistance to poor renters, conversion of the housing voucher program into a block grant to states and elimination of the HOPE VI program. The Administration of self-described compassionate conservative George W. Bush did not support creation of a National Housing Trust Fund, which is the major liberal proposal to begin to address the housing affordability problem. Instead, it proposed a $50 mandatory minimum monthly payment of all public housing tenants and Section 8 recipients rather than retaining the 30 percent income standard, which, for many families, yielded a lower rent for recipients of most federal low-income housing programs. If adopted, all of these proposals will make life more miserable for millions of poor Americans (*Housing Law Bulletin* 2003).

CONCLUSION

Two significant points can be drawn from the history we have recounted. First, despite significant differences between liberal and conservative approaches to housing policy, those differences remain within a narrow spectrum. Both approaches share certain basic and flawed assumptions, thereby excluding major alternatives that deserve serious consideration. Second, neither liberal nor conservative approaches to housing policy have come close to solving the housing problems facing the American people, even though liberal policies have been more ameliorative than the conservative ones. Both leave a situation of permanent housing crisis for a substantial minority and a fluctuating level of difficulty and insecurity for many others.

On the issue of protecting low-income and minority homeowners against predatory lending, there is some distinction in the extent to which regulation was supported. Republicans in Congress tried to preempt state and local laws that were enacted to regulate these practices in favor of much weaker federal oversight. Liberals and consumer advocates opposed the Republican approach and argued for greater protection for those who are most vulnerable and could lose their homes. The idea, consistent with a Right to Housing, that government should step in to provide financing or control of profits in the situations exploited by predatory lenders was raised by none of the major players.

Budget issues involve disagreements about how much, not what: Sharp as they may be, such disagreements take place within limited areas of substantive policy. Thus, the Bush Administration HUD budget for FY2004 proposed significant cuts in funding of the Section 8 program that could, for the first time in its history, mean a loss for existing beneficiaries. Liberals objected. While compromise is likely, no basic issues of principle or approach are involved. Some liberals, following an initiative of the National Low Income Housing Coalition, have proposed a National Housing Trust Fund, one similar to the many state and local housing trust funds in order to build or preserve 1.5 million rental units over a decade—150,000 a year, not an extravagant goal recalling the 600,000 annual additional units proposed in the Housing Act of 1968. The Coalition advocated use of the surplus in the FHA Mutual Mortgage Insurance Fund to finance the trust fund. Bush's HUD opposes use of these funds for this purpose but has not proposed any alternate funding. Thus, in a conservative period, arguments between liberals and conservatives center on budget numbers; programs such as might be expected from a Right to Housing approach have simply been swept off the table by both.

Throughout this decades-long history, both approaches were found to share a number of assumptions and in common mold their different policy stands around them. They include:

1. *The primacy of the profit-driven market as both the instrument for the provision of housing and the mechanism for its allocation.* In both approaches, government action has always been seen as being supplementary to what the private market accomplishes: a safety net to catch those not well served by the market. Both approaches fail to the recognize that the market relies on the profit motive for supplying housing, and thus neither approach will ever provide an adequate supply for those not in a position to produce profit in the market. Both approaches fail to recognize the undesirable social consequences of permitting the market to allocate housing—its location, quality and type—by the income and therefore by the profit-producing status of its users; both will always tend to produce segregation, ugliness and deterioration in large parts of the market and an unconscionable gap between the housing conditions of the rich and the poor. Both approaches refuse to acknowledge the defects of the housing market even in those areas where it does supply adequate housing, including the limitations on competition under circumstances of housing shortage and the inherently monopolistic commodity that is land, so

neither will ever consistently provide housing at appropriate prices generally affordable to most users.

2. *A preference for demand-side as opposed to supply-side policies in those limited areas where government does act on housing issues.* This flows from the primacy accorded the market by both. In both approaches, the direct provision of housing by government, at whatever level—whether in planning, construction, financing or management—is held to the minimum possible. Thus, both approaches surrender precisely those tools that would best enable them to overcome the weaknesses of profit-driven market domination of the housing supply, and both exclude even market-compatible steering mechanisms such as a yardstick function or a limitation on excess profits or speculation that might render the market more "social" in its results.

3. *Subservience to the private real estate and housing industry in the formulation of policy.* This is partial cause and partial consequence of the two approaches described, but in both approaches, it narrows the discussion of possible alternatives in dealing with housing to those acceptable to politically powerful interest groups. Neither can rationally examine the pros and cons of alternatives or logically draw conclusions from the experience of prior policies in shaping new ones. Only in times of severe stress—when opposing political and economic forces clash, whether from tenants and homeowners facing extreme hardship (as in the early New Deal) or from exigencies of a war (as in both world wars)—is the range of the possible expanded and open to consideration by either approach.

4. *Homeownership as a cardinal goal of housing policy.* In both approaches, it is taken as a matter of faith that homeownership is the preferable form of tenure over any other. Both approaches consider increasing the number of homeowners to be a major indicator of the success of housing policy, and both devote substantial policy attention to spreading that particular form of tenure to the broadest possible strata of the population. Both distribute considerable subsidies via tax policies, infrastructure and highway provision and financial aids in a highly regressive fashion among users

of housing, and both support environmentally damaging and inefficient patterns of land use. Neither supports serious consideration of alternative forms of tenure as being positive goals of public policy, whether tenant-owned nonprofit cooperatives, mutual housing associations or social housing such as is common in many other countries.

5. *Ideological rigidities, prominently including opposition to government action as such and limitation of moral concern to the "worthy" poor.* In both approaches, and increasingly since the end of World War II, government action in the social sphere is seen as something "undesirable." On ideological grounds, both approaches favor reduction of government expenditures, reduction of taxes, decentralization of federal government and reduction of regulation. Neither approach is willing to concede that it is an appropriate function of government permanently to act to secure the provision of housing for any underserved group, and neither is willing to confront the fact of a permanent housing crisis in the absence of adequate and sustained government action.

As a result of these shared assumptions, the following continuing failures are clear:[14]

1. *Permanent exclusion at the bottom.* There has never been a time in the United States in which a substantial minority did not face a serious housing crisis. Whether we look at the one-third of a nation that President Roosevelt in 1937 acknowledged to be without adequate shelter; the 6.2 million households paying more than 50 percent of their incomes for rent or the 5.4 million households that the Department of Housing and Urban Development identified in 2000, in a period of unprecedented prosperity, as having "worst case housing needs" (including 10.9 million people, among them 3.6 million children, 1.4 million elderly and some 1.3 million disabled adults—HUD 2000a), the bottom rungs of the economic ladder in the United States have always been excluded from the benefits of adequate housing. While both liberal and conservative approaches claim concern for those who "through no fault of their own" (in the phrase accepted by both) are unable to obtain adequate housing, and liberals tend to be more generous in their response than conservatives, both cling to the importance of "self-help" (as in welfare-to-work programs) and bypass confrontation with the social causes of housing problems, thus leaving homelessness, for example, a permanent part of the housing scene.

2. *Insecurity in housing occupancy.* Housing policy in the United States has never been able to avoid sharp fluctuations in the housing circumstances of the majority of the population. In periods of economic depression or high unemployment, evictions have always grown in number, mortgage foreclosures have increased, affordability has dwindled, overcrowding has increased and quality (especially neighborhood quality) has deteriorated. Improvement has been sharpest in the periods of liberal Democratic government—for instance, the Roosevelt New Deal, the Truman postwar Administration and the Kennedy-Johnson years—but the improvement has been more through having to confront increasingly visible problems and efforts at their amelioration rather than through steps to achieve long-term solutions. In conservative periods, the tendency has been to deny the existence of problems and deal with them in partial, specialized segments (Marcuse 1989), never recognizing any systemic difficulties.

3. *Segregation and discrimination based on race.* The problem of segregation and discrimination in housing has been ongoing in United States history since the founding of the Republic. Liberal Democrats have been more forthright in confronting the issue than have conservatives. There have been advances, but the high level of segregation and continued discrimination in housing sales, rentals and financing is demonstrable. Neither liberal nor conservative approaches have given hope for a real solution to either problem, and to many in the field, levels of segregation and inequality based on race seem to be unalterable (see the debate in *Poverty & Race* 1997, 1998; Massey and Denton 1993; Marcuse 2002).

4. *Environmental degradation.* Sprawl is not merely an issue of declining green spaces and natural habitat; it is wasteful of energy resources both in home heating and cooling and

in transportation, increases air pollution from commuting and uses land and building resources inefficiently. Under both liberal and conservative administrations, sprawl has been encouraged through highway construction, tax policies and financing subsidies (Jackson 1985; Baxandall and Ewen 2000); neither has made a serious attempt to limit sprawl or provide for effective environmentally oriented national land use regulation.

5. *Increasing problems of affordability.* Much is made of the increasing quantity and quality of housing in the United States, for which each administration, whether Democratic or Republican, takes credit. However, primarily the progress has been made among those who have been in a position to obtain their housing through the private market. As a consequence and inevitably, problems of housing affordability have grown as problems of housing quality have declined. Housing affordability problems may be at the highest point today since the Great Depression.

Have liberal and conservative housing policies, then, both been net failures in meeting housing policy goals, if to different degrees? The answer depends on how those goals are defined. Conservative policies have certainly promoted their particular goals and efficient and profitable functioning of the private housing market and the production of large amounts of high-quality housing. Liberal housing policies, by their particular goals, have had some successes. Some of the poor have obtained better housing than they would have had in the private market, there has been some limited redistribution accomplished within the housing sector and benevolence has been displayed toward some of the homeless and the most needy. But if the goal is providing decent, affordable and socially oriented housing for all, both have clearly failed. If one judges liberal housing policies by that standard—attaining decent, affordable and socially distributed housing—the verdict similarly is failure. Judged by the possible implementation of a full-fledged Right to Housing (see Chapter 8), the conclusion on both sets of policies is negative indeed.

As R. Allen Hays (1995:23) has noted:

> ....these two terms [liberal and conservative] symbolize distinct interpretations of a common ideology, democratic capitalism...these two outlooks are firmly rooted in a common capitalist world view. They both support the central economic institutional arrangements of capitalism, but they differ as to how these institutions, and the social order which supports them, can best be stabilized and perpetuated.

That is not to say that there is no difference between liberal and conservative positions on housing—the history shows many such differences. It is only to say that in the full spectrum of approaches to providing adequate housing for all, those that are liberal and conservative seem to be almost equally far from an approach that would guarantee a right to such housing for all.

Even within democratic capitalism, there is a range of alternative policies for housing that is not exhausted by policies advocated and implemented under the two rubrics, "conservative" and "liberal." While liberal remains preferable to conservative, a much broader range of possibilities exists and still remains to be explored both in theory and certainly in practice. Decent, affordable housing has never been available to everyone living the United States. Conservative housing policies have left the permanent housing crisis virtually intact, and liberal policies have only ameliorated it. Alternatives along the lines of a Right to Housing must be sought if the crisis is not indeed to be permanent.

NOTES

1. The Quality Housing and Work Responsibility Act of 1998 amended this statement. It is arguable as to whether the new language constitutes a major or a modest retreat from the original National Housing Goal, which was to be realized "as soon as feasible." In addition, while the original declaration of policy acknowledged the need for participation by the private sector and local public bodies, the new legislation went further in explicitly stating (Section 505) that the federal government alone could not solve the nation's housing problems (Bratt 2003). For citations to the housing crisis before the postwar period, see the appendix to Marcuse (forthcoming).

2. In the years before the mid-1960s, a significant portion of the southern Democratic Party could, for purposes of the liberal/conservative distinction made here, be considered squarely within the conservative ranks.

3. For a succinct account of the encouragement provided by federal policy for homeownership over the years, see Mitchell 1985:247. A more recent treatment is Retsinas and Belsky 2002.

4. It is debatable as to whether the public housing program of today is still the same as that of the 1937 act; see Marcuse 1995.

5. For a blow-by-blow account, see McDonnell 1957; Freedman 1969.

6. In fact, the main conservative opposition to New York City's pioneering, locally initiated public housing program was related to its use of WPA labor in the construction of First Houses rather than to its housing aspects. See Marcuse 1986a. First Houses bailed out Vincent Astor, heir to the Astor fortune and one of New York's largest tenement landlords (Day 1999), from ownership of the unprofitable slum housing that had existed on its site.

7. Catherine Bauer, for instance, called the compromise a "sell-out" (see Weiss 1980:78).

8. In a detailed examination, Marc Weiss (1980) concludes that policy vis-à-vis Title I and its application was essentially the same under both Republican and Democratic Administrations in its encouragement of commercial use rather than low-income housing uses.

9. Civil rights issues did not always separate the two approaches. In the 1930s and 1940s, the FHA redlined, and public housing was segregated—both policies initiated under the liberal Roosevelt Administration—and no serious dissent was raised about either until after the war.

10. For a detailed discussion of this and related variations in the direction and scope of federal action dealing with race in housing and a trenchant critique of its limitations, see Goering 1986:Section IV; Massey and Denton 1993:Chapter 7.

11. For a discussion of Section 202, supporting private nonprofit provision of housing for the low-income elderly and introduced as part of the Housing Act of 1959, see Chapter 13.

12. The Reagan Administration also sponsored legislation partially dealing with the expiring subsidies of existing programs; see Chapter 7.

13. "Transforming Public Housing: The Social and Physical Redevelopment of Boston's West Broadway Development." *Journal of Architectural and Planning Research*, 12(3): 278–305 (Autumn 1995).

14. For detailed figures on the dimensions of the housing crisis almost a century after the federal government began dealing directly with housing issues, see Joint Center for Housing Studies 2003; U.S. Department of Housing and Urban Development 1996, 1999; Center for Housing Policy 2000; National Low Income Housing Coalition 2000. Several of these reports are updated annually.

REFERENCES

Abrams, Charles. 1955. *Forbidden neighbors.* New York: Harper.

Achtenberg, Emily, and Peter Marcuse. 1983. Towards the decommodification of housing: A political analysis and a progressive program. In *America's housing crisis: What is to be done?*, ed. Chester Hartman. Boston: Routledge & Kegan Paul; reprinted in *Critical perspectives on housing*, eds. Rachel Bratt, Chester Hartman and Ann Meyerson. 1986. Philadelphia: Temple University Press.

Bauer, Catherine. 1934. *Modern housing.* Boston: Houghton Mifflin.

Baumohl, Jim. 1996. *Homelessness in America.* Phoenix: Oryx Press.

Baxandall, Rosalyn, and Elizabeth Ewen. 2000. *Picture windows: How the suburbs happened.* New York: Basic Books.

Bell, Robert. 1985. *The culture of policy deliberations.* New Brunswick, NJ: Rutgers University Press.

Birch, Eugenie. 1976. Edith Elmer Wood and the genesis of liberal housing thought, 1910–1942. Unpublished doctoral dissertation, Columbia University.

Bratt, Rachel G. 2003. Housing for very low-income households: The record of President Clinton, 1993–2000. *Housing Studies*, 18(4), July.

Center for Housing Policy. 2000. *Housing America's working families.* Washington, DC, June.

Colean, Miles L. 1940. *Housing for defense: A review of the role of housing in relation to America's defense and a program for action.* New York: Twentieth Century Fund.

Day, Jared N. 1999. *Urban castles: Tenement housing and landlord activism in New York City, 1890–1943.* New York: Columbia University Press.

Dean, James P. 1945. *Home Ownership: Is it Sound?* New York: Harper & Row.

Fisher, Robert Moore. 1959. *20 Years of public housing: Economic aspects of the federal program.* New York: Harper and Brothers.

Foscarinis, Maria. 1996. The federal response: The Stewart B. McKinney Homeless Assistance Act. In *Homelessness in America*, ed. Jim Baumohl. Phoenix: Oryx.

Freedman, Leonard. 1969. *Public housing: The politics of poverty.* New York: Holt, Rinehart and Winston.

Friedman, Milton. 1962. *Capitalism and freedom.* Chicago: University of Chicago Press.

Gelfand, Mark. 1975. *A nation of cities: The federal government and urban America, 1933–1965.* New York: Oxford University Press.

Goering, John M. 1986. *Housing desegregation and federal policy.* Chapel Hill: University of North Carolina Press.

Hartman, Chester. 1983a. Review of "The Report of the President's Commission on Housing." *Journal of American Planning Association,* 92–94, January.

———. 1983b. Housing allowances: A critical look. *Journal of Urban Affairs,* 5(1):41–55, Winter.

———. 1983c. Rejoinder to "Another look at housing allowances," ed. Philip Abrams. *Journal of Urban Affairs,* 5(2):159–170, Spring.

———. 1986. Housing policies under the Reagan Administration. In *Critical perspectives on housing,* eds. Rachel Bratt, Chester Hartman and Ann Meyerson, 362–376. Philadelphia: Temple University Press.

———. 2002a. *City for sale: The transformation of San Francisco.* Berkeley: University of California Press.

———. 2002b. Millenial misfire. A review of the Millenial Housing Commission Report. *Shelterforce,* July/August, 16–18.

Hartman, Chester, and W. Dennis Keating. 1973. Housing: A poor man's home is his business. In *What Nixon is doing to us,* eds. Alan Gartner, Colin Greer and Frank Riessman, 42–57. New York: Harper and Row.

Hartman, Chester, with Gregg Carr. 1969. Housing authorities reconsidered. *Journal of the American Institute of Planners,* January, 10–21.

Havlik, Herbert F. 1930. Recent history of the control of house rents. *Journal of Land and Public Utility Economics,* February, 95.

Hays, R. Allen. 1995. *The federal government and urban housing: Ideology and change in public policy.* Second Edition. Albany: State University of New York Press.

———, ed. 1993. *Ownership, control and the future of housing policy.* Westport, CT: Greenwood Press.

Hirsch, Arnold R. 2000. "Containment" on the home front: Race and federal housing policy from the New Deal to the cold war. *Journal of Urban History,* 26(2):158–189, January.

Housing Law Bulletin. 2003. Administration's FY 2004 budget poses major risks for federal housing programs, Vol. 33, March.

Institute for Policy Studies Working Group on Housing, with Dick Cluster. 1989. *The Right to housing: A blueprint for housing the nation.* Oakland, CA: Community Economics, Inc.

Jackson, Kenneth. 1985. *Crabgrass frontier: The suburbanization of the United States.* New York: Oxford University Press.

Joint Center for Housing Studies of Harvard University. 2003. *The state of the nation's housing,* June.

Keating, W. Dennis. 1998. Rent control: Its origins, history and consequences. In *Rent control: Regulation and the rental housing market,* eds. W. Dennis Keating, Michael B. Teitz and Andrejs Skaburkis. New Brunswick, NJ: Rutgers University Center for Urban Policy Research.

Keith, Nathaniel. 1973. *Politics and the housing crisis since 1930.* New York: Universe Books.

Kemeny, Jim. 1981. *The myth of home ownership.* London: Routledge and Kegan Paul.

Marcuse, Peter. 1972. Homeownership for low income families: Financial implications. *Land Economics,* May.

———. 1974. Home ownership for low income families. *Land Economics,* 48(2):134–143, May.

———. 1979. The deceptive consensus on redlining. *Journal of the American Planning Association,* 45(4), October.

———. 1981. The strategic potential of rent control. In *Rent control: A source book,* ed. John I. Gilderbloom. San Francisco: Foundation for National Progress.

———. 1986a. The beginnings of public housing in New York. *Journal of Urban History,* 12(4):353–390, August.

———. 1986b. The uses and limits of rent control: A report with recommendations. State of New York: Division of Housing and Community Renewal, December.

———. 1988. Neutralizing homelessness. *Socialist Review,* 88:1. Reprinted in part in Lisa Orr. 1990. *The homeless: Opposing viewpoints.* San Diego: Greenhaven Press.

———. 1989. The pitfalls of specialism: Special groups and the general problem of housing. In *Housing issues of the 1990s,* eds. Sara Rosenberry and Chester Hartman, 67–82. Westport, CT: Praeger.

———. 1994. What's wrong with empowerment zones. *City Limits,* May.

———. 1995. Interpreting "public housing" history. *Journal of Architectural and Planning Research,* 12(3):240–258, Autumn.

———. 2000. Federal urban programs as multicultural planning: The empowerment zone approach. In *Urban Planning in a Multicultural Society,* ed. Michael Burayidi, 225–234. Westport, CT: Praeger.

———. 2002. The shifting meaning of the black ghetto in the United States. In *Of states and cities,* eds. Peter Marcuse and Ronald van Kempen, 109–142. New York: Oxford University Press.

———. forthcoming. *The permanent housing crisis.* New York: Columbia University Press.

Massey, Douglas S., and Nancy A. Denton. 1993. *American apartheid: Segregation and the making of the underclass.* Cambridge: Harvard University Press.

McDonnell, Timothy L. 1957. *The Wagner Housing Act.* Chicago: Loyola University Press.

Meeropol, Michael. 1998. *Surrender: How the Clinton Administration completed the Reagan revolution.* Ann Arbor: University of Michigan Press.

Mitchell, J. Paul, ed. 1985. *Federal housing policy & programs: Past and present.* New Brunswick, NJ: Center for Urban Policy Research, 247.

Mollenkopf, John. 1983. *The contested city.* Princeton: Princeton University Press.

National Commission on Urban Problems (the Douglas Commission). 1968. *Building the American city.* Washington, DC: GPO.

National Housing Law Project, Poverty & Race Research Action Council, Sherwood Research Associates, Everywhere and Now Public Housing Residents Organizing Nationally Together (ENPHRONT). 2002. *False HOPE: A critical assessment of the HOPE VI public housing redevelopment program,* June. Oakland, CA: The Project.

National Low Income Housing Coalition. 2000. *Out of reach* 2000. Washington, DC: The Coalition.

Oberlander, H. Peter, and Eva Newbrun. 1999. *Houser: The life and work of Catherine Bauer.* Vancouver: UBC Press.

Peterman, William. 1993. Resident management and other approaches to tenant control of public housing. In *Ownership, control and the future of housing policy,* ed. R. Allen Hays. Westport, CT: Greenwood Press.

———. 1998. The meanings of resident empowerment: Why just about everybody thinks it's a good idea and what it has to do with resident management. In *New directions in urban public housing,* eds. David P. Varady, Wolfgang F. E. Preiser and Francis P. Russell. New Brunswick, NJ: Center for Urban Policy Research, 47–60.

Poverty & Race. 1997. Race initiative symposium. Washington, DC: Poverty & Race Research Action Council, November/December.

———. 1998. The president's initiative on race. Washington, DC: Poverty & Race Research Action Council, January/February.

President's Committee on Urban Housing (the Kaiser Committee). 1968. *A decent home: Report of the president's committee on urban housing.* Washington, DC: GPO.

Radford, Gail. 1997. *Modern housing for America: Policy struggles in the New Deal era.* Chicago: University of Chicago Press.

Report of the President's Commission on Housing. 1982. Washington DC: GPO.

Retsinas, Nicolas P., and Eric S. Belsky, eds. 2002. *Low-income homeownership: Examining the unexamined goal.* Cambridge, MA, and Washington, DC: Joint Center for Housing Studies and Brookings Institution Press.

Rohe, William M., and Michael A. Stegman. 1992. Public housing homeownership: Will it work and for whom? *Journal of the American Planning Association,* 144ff, Spring.

Salins, Peter D., and Gerard C. S. Mildner. 1992. *Scarcity by design: The legacy of New York City's housing policies.* Cambridge, MA: Harvard University Press.

Schuman, Tony, and Elliott Sclar. 1996. The impact of ideology on American town planning: From the Garden City to Battery Park City. In *Planning the twentieth-century American city,* eds. Mary Corbin Sies and Christopher Silver. Baltimore: Johns Hopkins University Press, Chapter 18, 428–448.

Schwartz, David C., Richard C. Ferlauto and Daniel N. Hoffman. 1988. *A new housing policy for America.* Philadelphia: Temple University Press.

Smith, Janet. 2000. The space of local control in US public housing. *Geografiska Annaler B,* 83(4):221–233.

Squires, Gregory D. 2000. *Capital and communities in black and white.* Albany: State University of New York Press.

Stegman, Michael A. 1992. The excessive costs of creative finance: Growing inefficiencies in the production of low-income housing. *Housing Policy Debate,* 2(2):357–373.

Struyk, Raymond J., and Marc Bendick, Jr., eds. *Housing vouchers for the poor: Lessons from a national experiment.* Washington, DC: Urban Institute Press.

U.S. Department of Commerce, Bureau of the Census. 1975. *Historical statistics of the United States.* Washington, DC: GPO.

U.S. Department of Housing and Urban Development. 1974. *Housing in the seventies: The national housing policy review.* Washington, DC: GPO.

———. 1996. *Rental housing assistance at a crossroads: A report to Congress on worst case housing needs,* March.

———. 1999. *The widening gap: New findings on housing affordability in America.* Washington, DC: GPO, September.

———. 2000a. *Rental housing assistance—The worsening crisis.* Washington, DC: GPO, March.

———. 2000b. *A vision for change.* Washington, DC: HUD, November.

United States vs. Certain Lands in the City of Louisville, 9 Fed Supp. 137, Western District, 1935.

U.S. Senate, Committee on Education and Labor. 1936. Legislative hearings for the Housing Act of 1936.

Vale, Lawrence J. 1993. Beyond the problem projects paradigm: Defining and revitalizing "severely distressed" public housing. *Housing Policy Debate,* 4(2):147–174.

———. 2002. *Reclaiming public housing: A half century struggle in three public neighborhoods.* Cambridge, MA: Harvard University Press.

Washington, Wayne. 2004. Bush pushes home ownership opportunities for minorities. *Boston Globe*, March 27.

Weiss Marc, 1980. The origins and legacy of urban renewal. In *Urban and regional planning in an age of austerity*, eds. Pierre Clavel, John Forester and William W. Goldsmith. New York: Pergamon Press.

Welfeld, Irving. 1988. *Where we live*. New York: Simon and Schuster.

Wexler, Harry. 2001. HOPE VI: Market means—Public ends, and midterm lessons of Department of Housing and Urban Development's Urban Revitalization Demonstration Program. Housing Research Foundation, at www.housingresearch.org.

Wood, Edith Elmer. 1931. *Recent trends in American housing*. New York: The Macmillan Company.

Woodyatt, Lyle John. 1968. The origins and evolution of the New Deal Public Housing Program. Ph.D. dissertation, Washington University.

Emily Paradise Achtenberg

7 Federally-Assisted Housing in Conflict: Privatization or Preservation?

UNTIL 1996, the attractive townhouses known as Manassas Park Village in suburban Virginia—20 minutes by commuter rail from Washington, DC—were home to 167 low- and moderate-income families. Today, the "Glen at White Pines" boasts new dishwashers and dryers and a computer room instead of a laundry, at double the rent (Foong 1996:30).

In 1999, 110 low-income elderly and disabled residents of three Iowa housing complexes learned that their rents would be going up by 67 percent (*Housing and Development Reporter* 1999:661 and HUD 1999a:vii). With few other affordable apartments in the vicinity, tenants faced the grim choice of sacrificing food, medicine and other necessities or leaving their friends, family and communities of 20 years.

Scenarios like these have been repeated all across the country, as private owners of government-assisted projects exercise the right to prepay their subsidized mortgages or opt out of their expiring rent subsidy contracts and convert to market-rate housing. They are the latest manifestations of a protracted struggle that has been waged for decades in the federal policy arena between private property rights and social housing needs in subsidized rental housing.

PREPAYMENT OF SUBSIDIZED MORTGAGES

The Problem

The subsidized-mortgage prepayment problem is the legacy of the federal government's first attempt to stimulate private-sector production of low- and moderate-income housing, under Section 221(d)(3) and Section 236 of the National Housing Act. Conceived as an alternative to public housing, these programs produced some 560,000 units during the late 1960s and early 1970s.

In exchange for federally insured loans at subsidized interest rates, tax incentives and virtually no cash investment, developers were required to restrict occupancy to low- and moderate-income families at regulated rents. As an added inducement, most owners were permitted to prepay their 40-year subsidized mortgages after just 20 years, terminate affordability restrictions, and convert the property to its "highest and best" use.[1]

Twenty years later, a typical project built for $20,000 per unit had a market value of $40,000 and an outstanding mortgage debt of just $15,000, leaving a residual equity value of $25,000 per unit. The same project had become a tax liability for its owner, as depleted depreciation and mortgage interest deductions no longer offset taxable income. This created a substantial incentive for owners to prepay, refinance and convert to market housing.

The Federal Preservation Program

In the late 1980s, the first wave of prepayments galvanized tenants and sparked a heated national policy debate over the future of this at-risk housing stock. Owners claimed that prepayment restrictions would constitute a breach of contract and an unconstitutional taking of private property by the federal government. Preservation advocates argued that the original social purpose of the housing should take precedence over paying windfall profits to owners that reflected unanticipated changes in market circumstances.

Faced with the prospect of massive tenant displacement, Congress passed emergency legislation in 1987,[2] followed by a "permanent" statute in 1990,[3] to address the prepayment problem. The new program embraced the view that "preservation . . . is, by far, the most cost-effective strategy available to the government and . . . can be accomplished in a way that protects the interests of the owners, the tenants and the communities in which the housing is located" (U.S. Congress 1990:107).

While effectively prohibiting mortgage prepayment, the preservation program guaranteed owners fair market value incentives to keep the housing affordable to lower-income households for at least another 50 years, at the federal government's expense. The U.S. Department of Housing and Urban Development (HUD) provided additional mortgage insurance, supported by project-based rental subsidies, to finance the owner's "equity takeout" ($25,000 per unit in the previous illustration). Owners could either retain ownership or sell the property on a priority basis to a tenant- or community-based non-profit purchaser who agreed to the same restrictions.

Privatization and Prepayment

By 1991, the political consensus around this "permanent" preservation policy had begun to unravel. Not surprisingly, most owners preferred to secure the incentives for themselves rather than sell their properties to nonprofits, and reports of lucrative equity takeouts with little or no funds reinvested in the property created the appearance of yet another boondoggle for the subsidized housing industry (Grunwald 1994). The HUD Inspector General called the program "an emerging scandal" that could cost taxpayers more than $74 billion over 40 years (HUD 1994:2).

After the 1994 Republican sweep of Congress, bipartisan efforts to discredit preservation

began in earnest. Indeed, the Democratic Administration was desperately seeking to abandon the now dysfunctional props (rental subsidies and mortgage guarantees) created earlier to manage the conflict between private profit and social housing needs, which threatened to cause a budgetary and fiscal crisis of massive proportions. A new federal consensus was emerging around the notion of deregulating the assisted housing stock, "vouchering out" existing tenants, and eliminating any ongoing federal involvement with the real estate. The preservation program, with its focus on protecting the existing subsidized housing stock, was completely at odds with this approach.

Accordingly, in November 1994, the White House's Office of Management and Budget (OMB) proposed to repeal the preservation program, restore owners' prepayment rights and provide affected tenants with vouchers (mobile tenant-based subsidies—OMB 1994:30). OMB also sought to rescind funds that were previously appropriated for preservation. These efforts were supported in varying degrees by the U.S. General Accounting Office (GAO), the Congressional Budget Office and HUD (see, for example, HUD 1995).

Preservation and Social Ownership

During the summer of 1995, tenant organizations, nonprofit groups and housing advocates across the country mounted an unprecedented grassroots campaign to save the preservation program. Using nationally coordinated tactics, such as letter-writing campaigns, press advocacy and lobbying directed at key legislative targets, advocates sought to "put a human face" on the preservation program and demonstrate the economic, social and political costs of prepayment.

Against formidable odds, these efforts achieved remarkable success. While the prepayment right was restored in March 1996, making preservation purely voluntary, the preservation program was extended with an additional $624 million in funding. This represented a 250 percent increase over the prior year appropriation, while the overall HUD budget was slashed by 25 percent (and funding for new housing vouchers was eliminated).

Additionally, the revised program effectively targeted preservation funds for sales to resident and community-based nonprofits and replaced HUD mortgage guarantees with direct capital grants—a far more cost-effective approach conducive to long-term preservation.

Between 1996 and 1998, some 25,000 prepayment-eligible units in more than 30 states were converted to virtually debt-free social ownership with permanent affordability guarantees[4]—a transfer unprecedented in the history of U.S. housing. The average cost of preservation sales with capital grants (including both equity takeout and rehabilitation costs) was approximately $36,000 per unit (GAO 1997:60)—less than one-half the cost of building new subsidized housing in most markets at that time.

Nevertheless, the GAO and OMB resumed their attacks with new vigor, charging the capital grant program with excessive rehabilitation costs and inadequate oversight (GAO 1997:60). The subsidized housing industry, which no longer derived significant benefits from preservation, lent tacit support to this critique. HUD, threatened with extinction by the Republican Congress and abandoned by the Democratic Administration, was unwilling and unable to mount an adequate defense. In October 1997, all preservation funding was terminated. Some 50,000 units awaiting capital grants and loans were left in the approved but unfunded HUD preservation "queue" (HUD 1996b).

Post-Preservation Trends

In total, some 100,000 units were preserved under the various federal programs, including 33,000 units transferred to new owners who were primarily nonprofit purchasers using capital grants (National Housing Trust n.d.). Since the demise of the preservation program, another 110,000 subsidized units have been lost to mortgage prepayment (National Housing Trust 2002a). For prepayments occurring before 1999, the average rent increase was 57 percent (National Housing Trust 2001). While low-income tenants who choose to remain after prepayment can receive "enhanced" preservation vouchers (subject to annual appropriations) at the prevailing market rent, these units are permanently lost as housing affordable to lower-income households once the original tenants move.

EXPIRING SECTION 8 CONTRACTS

The Problem

Starting in 1974, the federal government provided a new incentive to private developers and owners under Section 8 of the National Housing Act, in the form of a direct contract to subsidize the market rents of low- and moderate-income tenants. These contracts were either "project-based" (tied to the unit) or "tenant-based" (mobile certificates or vouchers).

The Section 8 project-based housing stock—now larger than the inventory of traditional public housing units—consists of 1.5 million units and encompasses many different programs. Sixty percent (900,000) of the units are also covered by HUD-insured mortgages. Some of the properties originally were developed under Section 236 and Section 221(d)(3), with Section 8 subsidies added later to make a portion of the units more affordable to lower-income households. These projects typically have below-market rents due to their subsidized mortgages and HUD rent regulation. Historically, these Section 8 contracts have been short-term (five-year renewable).

In other projects originally built or substantially rehabilitated with Section 8, HUD underwrote the initial development by establishing rents high enough to cover market interest rates and construction costs in difficult-to-develop areas. In these projects, HUD also permitted automatic annual rent adjustments, with the result that rents often were above-market. These projects typically have long-term (20+ years) Section 8 contracts.

In the mid-1990s, the combination of long-term and short-term Section 8 contracts expiring simultaneously in the face of new budget constraints catapulted HUD into the spotlight of a looming fiscal crisis. Between FY1996 and FY1998, the cost of renewing all existing Section 8 contracts was projected to grow from about $5 billion to almost $14 billion, with an estimated 1.8 million units expiring—enough to consume the entire HUD budget (Dunlap 1995:12).[5] At the same time, failure to renew contracts with above-market rents could trigger widespread defaults and foreclosures of HUD-insured mortgages, resulting in massive claims on the HUD mortgage insurance fund.

Mark to Market

Struggling for survival, HUD developed a response to the Section 8 crisis that was to become the cornerstone of its 1995 "reinvention" blueprint. HUD concluded that not only was the long-term cost of continuing to provide Section 8 project-based assistance unsustainable, but the subsidy system itself was "deeply flawed" because it eschewed market principles. While above-market units were oversubsidized, below-market units were undersubsidized and undercapitalized, providing perverse incentives for owners. Tenants without market choices were trapped. The federal government, as both subsidy provider and mortgage insurer, was essentially shooting itself in the foot, forced to keep paying for "bad housing" in order to avoid mortgage insurance claims (Retsinas 1995).

Accordingly, HUD proposed that these contracts, upon expiration, would no longer be renewed. Instead, the projects would be "vouchered out" with rents "marked to market" (up or down) and completely deregulated, while residents received tenant-based subsidies. HUD would auction off its mortgages to the highest private bidder (with a partial writedown claim against the insurance fund, if necessary), who would restructure project finances, operations, occupancy and, in some cases, ownership. In this way, HUD hoped to restore market discipline to a substantial portion of the federally-assisted housing stock while ending the government's long-standing involvement with, and responsibility for, the real estate (Retsinas 1995).

In response, preservation advocates charged that HUD's proposal would trigger massive tenant displacement and loss of housing that was affordable to lower-income households through mortgage defaults and rent increases. Alternatively, they noted, any savings from "marking down" rents in the above-market stock would be outweighed by the cost of protecting tenants in "below-market" units with new vouchers at the marked-up rents (Bodaken 1995). Joining the groundswell of opposition was a growing alliance of subsidized housing developers and investors concerned about the adverse tax consequences of debt writedowns, the potential loss of control over their investments, and the generally increased risk of requiring projects long reliant on HUD guarantees to compete in the open market (Grunwald 1995).

In 1997, Congress finally enacted mark-to-market legislation with a decidedly more preservation-oriented flavor.[6] Under this program, HUD was generally mandated to reduce rents and restructure debt in above-market properties with expiring Section 8 contracts while renewing their project-based subsidies. HUD would retain a deferred second mortgage in the amount of the debt writedown—a device not dissimilar to the preservation capital grant, which would minimize adverse tax consequences to owners while facilitating continued public control over the housing. Debt restructuring was required to be carried out by state and local public entities (such as housing finance agencies) on a priority basis.

In exchange for debt restructuring, owners were required to extend low-income affordability restrictions and renew their Section 8 contracts, subject to availability of appropriations, for 30 years. Tenants, nonprofits, and state and local governments were given the right to comment on the restructuring plans.

Once launched, the program encountered substantial owner resistance. And with the general tightening of rental markets during the late 1990s, fewer properties than HUD had originally anticipated appeared to be eligible for or in need of debt restructuring. The majority of owners who did participate elected to absorb voluntary rent decreases without actually restructuring their mortgages, thereby avoiding any long-term affordability or tenant/community participation requirements.

At the same time, the responsibility for administering mark to market shifted increasingly from the public to the private sector. With alternative investment opportunities in the improving economy, many of the original housing finance agency participants balked at HUD's restrictive compensation structure and defected from the program (*Housing and Development Reporter* 2000:549). The new private entities replacing them lent tacit, if not explicit, support to mark to market's drift toward private sector accommodation.

Frustrated by these tendencies, preservation advocates sought to restore some of the program's original social purpose by launching a campaign to facilitate the sale of mark-to-market properties to nonprofit purchasers (National Association for Housing Partnerships and Recapitalization Advisors, Inc. 1999). Many hoped that mark to market—like the earlier federal preservation programs—would provide an "exit strategy" for private owners to transition the housing to nonprofit ownership, supported by federal debt writedowns and long-term affordability restrictions.

In September 2000, HUD announced a new package of incentives to make mark to market more profitable for private owners and encourage their participation in the program (HUD 2000). At the same time, HUD agreed to forgive the deferred second mortgage debt for qualified nonprofits that purchased within three years of debt restructuring and to cover a significant portion of their transaction costs.

In recent years, this "owner-friendly" posture, combined with the general softening of the real estate market, has generated an increased volume of mark-to-market activity. Many owners now perceive mark to market as a beneficial opportunity to put their projects on firmer economic footing, with HUD continuing to absorb the risk through mortgage insurance and subsidies. Private lenders as well are now comfortable with mark to market, which enables them to earn fees—and Community Reinvestment Act (CRA) credits—for refinancing and servicing their existing loans (*Housing and Development Reporter* 2003:115).

As of October 2003, 2,030 properties have completed the mark-to-market process, with another 679 in the active pipeline (HUD 2003a). While the inventory is heavily concentrated in the heartland (e.g., Ohio, Pennsylvania, Kentucky), virtually every state has some

mark-to-market projects (HUD 2003b). In contrast to early program trends, 63 percent of the completed properties have undergone full debt restructuring, and 95 percent of the pipeline projects have initially elected this option (HUD 2003a).

While some nonprofit groups have succeeded in buying mark-to-market properties using the new purchaser initiatives, the program as currently administered has not been conducive to this outcome. A primary factor is the failure of the private administrative entities to adequately reflect property rehabilitation and operating requirements in the debt restructuring process, resulting in the need for nonprofits to raise additional funds to ensure long-term project viability.

Section 8 Opt-Outs

While the 1997 statute focused primarily on "above-market" Section 8 properties, it also permitted HUD to renew project-based contracts in "below-market" properties—but only at the owner's option. Additionally, to facilitate budgetary management and Congressional scrutiny, all expiring Section 8 contracts were renewed only on a year-to-year basis.

With rents escalating rapidly in most markets nationwide, an increasing number of owners found themselves with both motive and opportunity to "opt-out" of their subsidy contracts at the point of expiration. Between October 1996 and April 1999, more than 30,000 units in 500 subsidized properties were lost as housing affordable to lower-income households when owners quit the Section 8 program in search of higher market-rate rents (HUD 1999a).[7]

Once again, preservation advocates focused national attention on the problem through targeted media campaigns in key legislative districts. After the notorious and well-publicized Iowa opt-outs in early 1999, HUD acknowledged that the record-level "worst-case" housing needs documented by its own studies were attributable, in part, to federal policies that facilitated the loss of subsidized units (HUD 1999b). HUD noted that while Section 8 opt-outs had occurred in 47 states, regular replacement vouchers at the local housing authority's "payment standard" often did not protect tenants from displacement. Additionally, HUD found that opt-outs were threatening the best housing in the country affordable to lower-income households and located in good neighborhoods with good schools and economic opportunities.

In the spring of 1999, HUD developed an emergency initiative, subsequently enacted into law,[8] to stem the tide of Section 8 opt-outs. In most cases, HUD will now renew below-market Section 8 contracts at rents "marked up" to prevailing market levels for at least a five-year term (subject to annual appropriations). Where owners choose to opt out instead, tenants will receive enhanced vouchers at prevailing market rents for the property, similar to the prepayment program. Subject to appropriations, all enhanced vouchers, whether for prepayments or opt-outs, are now required to be renewed at market levels in future years.

Preliminary indications suggest that opt-outs have slowed since the advent of the mark-up-to-market program. As of July 2001, owners had opted out of contracts covering some 47,000 assisted units (National Housing Trust 2002b), reflecting an opt-out rate of 600 units per month since April 1999 (down from 1,000 units per month previously). However, it is too soon to tell whether owners who participate in "mark up to market" view the program as a long-term commitment or as a convenient way to transition to market at the government's expense. Additionally, while some nonprofit purchasers have utilized mark-up-to-market to purchase Section 8 properties, without additional resources to support market-rate acquisition in strong market areas, the utility of this program as a tool for social ownership conversion is limited.

CONCLUSION

In a sense, with mark-up-to-market, federal preservation efforts have come full circle. The current cost of preserving a single subsidized unit with market-determined subsidies (whether project-based or tenant-based) is approximately $6,400 per year (U.S. Department of Housing and Urban Development 2003c: N-4).

Over five-and-a-half years, this is roughly the same as the average cost of the upfront capital grants provided to nonprofits under the federal preservation programs ($35,000). Over eleven years, market-based subsidies cost twice as much as preservation capital grants, without considering the additional cost of annual rent escalation. And while preservation capital grants provided permanently affordable housing through social ownership, units marked up to market remain at risk every five years, despite the continued public investment in the housing. In effect, the current market-based strategy retains all of the costs of socially oriented preservation with none of the benefits.

Increasingly, preservation advocates have turned to state and local governments for more permanent, cost-effective preservation solutions with some success (Achtenberg 2002; Galle 1999). For example, many states now earmark a portion of their federal low-income housing tax credits, and, in some cases, tax-exempt bond allocations as well, for subsidized housing preservation. Some states and cities have issued preservation bonds backed by special appropriations or other non-federal revenue sources. These resources generally are targeted to nonprofit purchasers in exchange for long-term use restrictions, sometimes in conjunction with "rights of first refusal" or purchase options if a federally subsidized property is sold. With these additional funds and tools, federal programs such as mark to market, mark up to market and even enhanced vouchers can be used to facilitate a more permanent preservation solution through social ownership conversion.

To be sure, in the context of state and local resource constraints these preservation initiatives will have limited impact and will succeed only at the expense of much-needed new construction. In recent years, preservation advocates have forged new alliances with city, state and grassroots groups to press for a federal matching grant program that would reward state and local preservation funding with federal dollars. These proposals have gained bi-partisan support and are now merged with an even broader campaign to create a federal housing trust fund for both production and preservation of housing affordable to lower-income families.

Yet, with renewed Republican efforts to diminish even further the federal government's role in subsidized housing, emerging alliances between preservation advocates and state and local governments will surely be put to the test. In early 2003, the Bush Administration proposed to convert the entire Section 8 voucher program, including enhanced vouchers that protect tenants when owners prepay or opt out, to a state-administered block grant with few federal standards and no guaranteed funding levels. This is widely viewed as a strategy to reduce Section 8 funding while devolving political accountability to the states (Sard and Fischer 2003). Since funding shortfalls will encourage states to reduce existing voucher subsidy levels, market-based enhanced vouchers could be especially vulnerable to attack.

With 30-year hindsight, the failure of federal efforts to provide and preserve housing for low- and moderate-income families through the private sector is readily apparent. The conflict between private property rights and social housing needs, inherent in the original structure of the federally-assisted housing programs, has never been resolved but only managed in ways that have ultimately served to exacerbate the conflict. Preservation has been possible only when private interests are served as well; when this is not expedient or becomes too costly, social needs are sacrificed.

At the same time, the history of these federal programs shows how organized grassroots constituencies can sometimes fundamentally alter political processes and program outcomes to create meaningful opportunities for social housing ownership and finance, facilitating long-term preservation even under the most adverse of circumstances—an equally important lesson for the future.

NOTES

1. Some categories of owners, including nonprofits and for-profit developers who received special benefits such as direct federal rehabilitation loans ("flexible subsidy") were prohibited from prepaying their mortgages without HUD consent.

2. The Emergency Low Income Housing Preservation Act (ELIHPA), Title II of the Housing and Community Development Act of 1987, P.L. 100–242, February 5, 1988, as amended.

3. The Low Income Housing Preservation and Resident Homeownership Act (LIHPRHA), Title II of the Cranston-Gonzalez National Affordable Housing Act, P.L. 101–625, November 28, 1990, as amended.

4. Extrapolated by the author from HUD 1996a, 1997.

5. This estimate includes both project-based and tenant-based Section 8 subsidies.

6. The Multifamily Assisted Housing Reform and Affordability Act of 1997 (MAHRA), Title V of the FY98 VA, HUD, and Independent Agencies Appropriations Act, P.L. 105–65.

7. This estimate does not include Section 8 units lost in conjunction with subsidized housing mortgage prepayments.

8. "The Preserving Affordable Housing for Senior Citizens and Families into the 21st Century Act of 1999," Section 501 of the FY00 Departments of Veterans Affairs, HUD, and Independent Agencies Appropriations Act, P.L. 106–74.

REFERENCES

Achtenberg, Emily P. 2002. *Stemming the tide: A handbook on preserving subsidized multifamily housing.* New York: Local Initiatives Support Corporation.

Bodaken, Michael. 1995. We must preserve the nation's supply of affordable housing. *Shelterforce,* July/August.

Dunlap, Helen M. 1995. Mark to market: A strategy to recapitalize HUD's assisted housing inventory. *Shelterforce,* July/August.

Foong, L. Keat. 1996. Market-rate bandwagon. *Multihousing news,* October/November.

Galle, Brian. 1999. Preserving federally-assisted housing at the state and local level: A legislative tool kit. *Housing Law Bulletin ,* 29:183.

Grunwald, Michael. 1994. More HUD money flows to Boston landlords. *Boston Globe,* December 19.

———. 1995. Investors wary of HUD plan. *Boston Globe,* July 5.

Housing and Development Reporter. 1999. Decision of Iowa owners to terminate contracts raises concern for tenants. *Current Developments,* Vol. 26, No. 42, February 22.

———. 2000. California, New York City opt out of mark-to-market program. *Current Developments,* Vol. 27, No. 30, January 10.

———. 2003. Mark-to-market program has made progress, OMHAR director says. *Current Developments,* Vol. 31, No. CD-4, February 17.

National Association for Housing Partnerships and Recapitalization Advisors, Inc. 1999. *Mark to market and non-profits: Results from the demonstration and implications for the permanent program.* Boston: The Association.

National Housing Trust. n.d. Funded Title II and VI projects. Washington, DC: The Trust.

———. 2001. Prepayment summary as of 12/31/98. May 7. Washington, DC: The Trust.

———. 2002a. All mortgage prepayments by state as of 12/31/01. June 27. Washington, DC: The Trust.

———. 2002b. All Section 8 optouts by state as of 7/31/01. June 27. Washington, DC: The Trust.

Office of Management and Budget. 1994. FY1996 Passback: Department of Housing and Urban Development, November 21.

Retsinas, Nicholas, P. 1995. Statement before the Housing, Banking, and Financial Services Subcommittee on Housing and Community Opportunity, June 13.

Sard, Barbara, and Will Fischer. 2003. Housing voucher block grant bills would jeopardize an effective program and likely lead to cuts in assistance for low-income families. Washington, DC: Center on Budget and Policy Priorities, May 14.

U.S. Congress. 1990. Managers' Report (Joint Explanatory Statement)—H. REP. No. 922, 101st Cong. 2nd Sess., October 22.

U.S. Department of Housing and Urban Development. 1994. Office of Inspector General, review of multifamily preservation programs. Office of Audit—Region X. Washington, DC, April 20.

———. 1995. Office of Inspector General, HUD's Multifamily Preservation Program. Office of Audit—New England. Washington, DC, July 14.

———. 1996a. Office of Housing, projects funded in FY96. Washington, DC, July 24.

———. 1996b. Office of Housing, preservation funding queue. Washington, DC, November 12.

———. 1997. 1997 preservation funding queue database. Washington, DC, December 10.

———. 1999a. Opting in: Renewing America's commitment to affordable housing. Washington, DC.

———. 1999b. Waiting in vain: An update on America's rental housing crisis. Washington, DC.

———. 2000. Office of Multifamily Housing Assistance Restructuring. Initiatives for M2M owners and purchasers. Washington, DC, September 11.

———. 2003a. Office of Multifamily Housing Assistance Restructuring. Mark-to-market pipeline summary report. Washington, DC, October 30.

———. 2003b. Office of Multifamily Housing Assistance Restructuring. PAE and assigned property status report. Washington, DC, October 31.

———. 2003c. Fiscal year 2004 budget: Congressional justifications for estimates. Washington, DC.

U.S. General Accounting Office (GAO). 1997. Housing preservation: Policies and administrative problems increase costs and hinder program operations. GAO/RCED 97-169, Appendix VIII, July.

Robert Wiener

Privatizing Rural Rental Housing

WHILE NATIONAL attention has focused on losses of HUD-subsidized rental housing through mortgage prepayment, no rental housing produced with federal support has been more vulnerable to prepayment than the housing produced by the U.S. Department of Agriculture's Rural Housing Service (RHS—formerly known as Farmers Home Administration). From 1972 to 1986, in hundreds of small communities, over 1,000 RHS Section 515 rural rental housing loans made prior to 1980 were quietly paid off by the private owners of this housing.[1] Units originally built and subsidized to serve elderly and low-income tenants were wholly privatized—freed of all government controls on rents and occupancy and converted to market-rate buildings, accompanied by increased tenant rents and hardship. By the time Congress placed a moratorium on further prepayments at the end of 1986, more than 7,600 units affordable to low-income households were permanently lost to the low-income housing stock (Collings 1987). Despite subsequent interventions by Congress, these properties continue to prepay to this day.

Prepayment is the logical conclusion of a private sector strategy that has informed U.S. housing policy since the early 1960s, a strategy within which the Section 515 program is firmly embedded. Created by the Senior Citizens Housing Act of 1962, it was intended to stimulate the production of rental housing within markets and for populations not served by conventional lenders. Financing under this program was restricted to rural farm and nonfarm areas, initially only for seniors and later (in 1966) for any low-income household. To meet the need for capital in rural areas, financing was in the form of direct government-subsidized loans, with interest rates as low as 1 percent and maturities up to 50 years. Only nonprofit and public agency sponsors could receive these loans. For-profit sponsors could also participate in the program, but they received insured loans at the government lending rate, to produce housing targeted to a somewhat higher income group.

Congress had always intended that RHS act as a lender of last resort. Thus, by statute, borrowers had to agree to a "graduation" provision, which required that they acquire, or graduate to, non-RHS credit at the earliest opportunity, whenever such credit could be secured on reasonable terms and conditions. The practical effect was that loans could be prepaid at any time. When prepayment occurred, not only was the RHS financing retired, but the borrower was released from enforceable agreements in the note that enabled RHS to control the use of the housing. For tenants, this meant the immediate cessation of all government regulation of admissions and rents and withdrawal of all government subsidies—the "shallow" subsidy provided through the low-interest loan and, in some cases, additional "deep" subsidies provided through RHS's rental assistance program.

Not until the early 1970s, however, did the graduation provision emerge as a real threat to the housing and its residents. During the program's first ten years, there was little possibility of prepayment, since non-profit borrowers were unlikely to change the low-income character of the housing or qualify for private financing. For-profit borrowers held virtual market-rate loans that could be prepaid but with little impact on rents. Two administrative decisions by RHS in 1971 and 1972, however, upset this scheme. First, the agency decided to forcibly reassert its graduation policy because of unacceptably low rates of graduation. Second, it adopted rule changes permitting limited-profit sponsors—typically, syndicated limited partnerships—to receive subsidized loans. In exchange for favorable financing, they had to agree to methods of operation, income controls for tenant admissions and rents that would ensure occupancy by low- and moderate-income households. They also had to accept a limited return on their initial investment.

This second decision substantially altered the character of the program. Production skyrocketed, as intended. But the inclusion of limited-profit sponsors also resulted in a peculiar contradiction. While seeking to expand the supply of units, RHS was still mandated to accept, encourage and compel prepayment but without consideration of the tragic consequences for the very-low-income occupants whom the subsidized loans were intended to help. Unlike before, prepayment by limited-profit borrowers was not only economically feasible but desirable once the main investment incentive—the tax-sheltered depreciation benefits—had expired, usually after ten years. Moreover, some properties had appreciated in value and were worth more as conventional, as opposed to subsidized, properties. In essence, RHS opened the front door to limited profits without closing the back door. No other federal housing program offered borrowers both the advantages of subsidized financing and quick egress from the obligations imposed by that financing.

By the end of the 1970s, loan prepayments were on the rise, and Congress began to pay attention. RHS data indicated that about 500 loans had been prepaid, most from 1977 to 1979. The growing number of limited-profit sponsors expected to reach their tax shelter "burn-outs" augured an even larger wave of prepayments in the 1980s. With this in mind, the first-ever restrictive prepayment legislation was passed in 1979, after a highly ideological debate kept Congressional negotiators at "swords' points"[2] for more than four months. In 1980, however, opponents led by the homebuilding industry were able to repeal the legislation, arguing that retroactivity was unduly harsh, unconstitutional and an overblown reaction to a minor problem. Instead, a 20-year prepayment restriction was placed on all loans approved after December 21, 1979, but earlier projects were still allowed to prepay unilaterally.

Not surprisingly to tenant advocates, prepayments of pre-1979 projects accelerated during the 1980s. By 1987, prepayments had occurred or were pending on 1,329 loans; 37 percent (486) of these loans covering 5,377 units were prepaid from 1983 to 1986.

A California study of some 450 tenants who occupied five projects that prepaid in this period demonstrated the disruptions and harsh economic choices that often awaited tenants (Wiener 1993). Three-fourths of the households were involuntarily displaced prior to or upon prepayment because they could not afford the higher rents; one-half of the displacees moved to nonassisted market-rate housing, including many who moved in with a family member or friend; the average shelter costs of displacees increased by 50 percent, causing huge rent burdens; and most displacees were less satisfied with their new housing. Moreover, two years after prepayment, the study found only marginal improvement. Most shocking was the high number of households indicating that they had experienced a profound sense of loss—loss of economic independence, loss of family and community and, especially among the elderly, loss of physical and mental health—a phenomenon found in urban neighborhoods as well (Fried 1963).

Growing concern about tenant displacement forced Congress to revisit the prepayment issue in 1986, which resulted in a 12-month moratorium. This moratorium remained in effect, with a few small gaps, until adoption of a "permanent" preservation scheme in the Emergency Low-Income Housing Preservation Act (ELIHPA) of 1987.

ELIHPA directs RHS to approve prepayments only after first offering owners incentives to retain ownership and maintain affordability of the housing: equity loans, increased rates of return, access to project reserves and RHS rental assistance. In the event that owners refuse these incentives, RHS is required to force a sale to a qualified nonprofit or public agency through provision of an acquisition loan. Prepayment approval can be granted only under certain limited exceptions: where owners agree to operate the units with restricted rents until 20 years from the date the loan was made and then transfer the property to a nonprofit purchaser; or where there is no likelihood of tenant displacement or adverse impact on housing opportunities for minorities and local supplies of housing affordable to low-income households.

Following the precedent set in ELIHPA, preservation of post-1979 projects was further addressed in subsequent legislation (Anders 1993:79–89). The HUD Reform Act of 1989 prohibited prepayment of any projects with loans approved after December 15, 1989, for the full term of the 50-year Section 515 mortgage. Legislation adopted in 1992 extended the preservation scheme in ELIHPA to all projects with 20-year use restrictions approved after December 21, 1979, and before December 15, 1989. Projects may be prepaid at any time prior to the end of the restrictive-use period, provided the owner agrees to comply with the ELIHPA prepayment exceptions.

The 1992 legislation also directed RHS to establish the Office of Rental Housing Preservation to serve as a national clearinghouse for prepayment approval and data tracking. However, in violation of Congressional intent, the agency waited until the end of 1998 to staff the office, making it difficult initially for external assessment of the successes and shortcomings of the law and RHS implementation.

A comprehensive performance evaluation of the preservation program was undertaken in 1992 by the National Task Force on Rural Housing Preservation. At the time of the Task Force's evaluation, 110,383 pre-1979 and 256,211 post-1979 and pre-1989 units were still at risk of prepayment—a total of 366,594 at-risk units (National Task Force on Rural Housing Preservation 1992:36, 38). RHS had received notices of intent to prepay from owners of more than 300 projects and offered incentives to at least 136 projects, nearly all of which involved owners staying with their properties.

Among other conclusions, the Task Force found that ELIHPA was achieving the goal of preventing the wholesale prepayment and loss of pre-1979 housing. Using a simulation model of owner choices, it predicted that in the absence of the law, the majority of owners would prepay, since they held properties that could support conversion to conventional market rents. However, in many cases, RHS was offering the maximum incentives to properties that appeared to have little market justification for conversion or only marginally more profitable conventional uses. And in exchange for these incentives, RHS was leveraging only the bare minimum 20 years of additional restrictive use, although it had discretion to negotiate much longer commitments for units to stay affordable to low-income tenants.

Since that time, the number of pre-1989 at-risk properties has decreased. According to a report by the Housing Assistance Council, there were 11,114 pre-1989 projects with 290,400 units still at risk of prepayment in 2002, representing 63 percent of all projects and 62 percent of all units remaining in the Section 515 portfolio (Housing Assistance Council 2002:1). The total number of units was 76,000 less than the number identified in 1992. It is unknown how many of these were preserved, allowed to prepay or the result of miscounts.

As of the mid-2000s, owners of Section 515 properties are still subject to the ELIHPA preservation scheme, but ominous signs are on the horizon. Deep cuts in appropriations for the overall Section 515 program and lack of RHS enforcement have effectively crippled the program, with only a small number of the total eligible projects receiving incentive payments. RHS has admitted that it does not have adequate funds to make equity loans to owners with agreements dating back to 1996 (Anders 2003a). Instead, it has attempted to find alternative funding mechanisms to limit the budget impacts of preservation while continuing to approve prepayments, especially in the foreclosure process, without extending use restrictions.

Based on a comprehensive assessment of the Section 515 inventory commissioned by USDA in late 2004, RHS has also taken the position that the most expensive, highest-risk projects should be triaged—allowed to prepay and offered rental assistance. The assessment concluded that 10.4 percent of prepayment-eligible properties (1,648 properties) would be economically viable to prepay (ICF 2004).[3] It recommended debt restructuring, recapitalization and rehabilitation of properties not imminently at risk of prepayment, while allowing prepayment in some properties where tenants were protected against rent increases by rent vouchers. As of Fall 2005, the Administration is considering legislation to repeal ELIHPA altogether; repeal efforts failed in Congress in 2000 and 2002.

Several court decisions have the potential to further weaken ELIHPA. In *Kimberly Associates v. United States*, the United States Court of Appeals for the 9th Circuit reversed an Idaho District Court decision that initially barred an owner's "quiet title" action on procedural grounds. In its opinion, the 9th Circuit suggested that the owner may be entitled to relief under Idaho state quiet title law. The Circuit Court also affirmed the lower court's denial of the affected tenants' right to intervene in the case, finding that because the prepayment had been allowed to proceed, the case was moot. On remand

to the Idaho District Court, the court granted the owner's request for quiet title, effectively abrogating the ELIHPA prepayment restrictions and allowing the owner to prepay (Anders 2002a, 2002b, 2003a, 2003b, 2005). Since then, District Courts in Idaho and Oregon, both in the jurisdiction of the 9th Circuit, have granted quiet title to owners related to those in *Kimberly*. The 9th Circuit trend notwithstanding, in 2005, the United States Court of Appeals for the 8th Circuit staked out a contrary position in *Owens v. Charleston Housing Authority*, agreeing with a Missouri District Court decision that the Charleston Housing Authority's plan to vacate, prepay and demolish a 50-unit project violated ELIHPA and fair housing laws.

Owners have also looked to the courts for money damages, arguing that the ELIHPA prepayment restrictions impaired their contractual rights. In 2004, the U.S. Court of Claims, in *Franconia v. United States*, agreed with the owners' claims. It required the government to pay lost profits averaging about $400,000 per project to the owners of 32 projects. USDA decided not to appeal that decision. Similar lawsuits by hundreds of other owners are pending, as of Fall 2005. If successful, they are likely to encourage the Administration and Congress to repeal ELIHPA in order to avoid additional damage claims.

Although the legislative, regulatory and administrative decisions explaining the incidence of prepayment in the RHS Section 515 program are unique, the ideological origins of the problem and its human consequences are not. The RHS and HUD multifamily programs were premised on the correct assumption that private, profit-motivated owners could be enticed to build, own and operate low-income rental housing in volume. In both instances, however, there was little if any consideration of the consequences for tenants and the long-term preservation of the housing when investor incentives to remain in the programs run out. The fact that owners were allowed to prepay with impunity is consistent with the logic of privatization. Prepayment is the final link in the privatization chain.

The flawed liberal policies of the 1960s reached their fullest expression within the HUD inventory in the mid-1990s as the result of actions taken by Congress that exposed hundreds of thousands of units to risk of conversion. In March 1996, the 104th Congress removed the prepayment restrictions first imposed on HUD rental housing by ELIHPA and later in the Low-Income Housing Preservation and Resident Homeowners Act (LIHPRHA), which succeeded ELIHPA (see main body of this chapter). In 1997, Congress ended the sales program in LIHPRHA that enabled tenant groups and tenant-endorsed nonprofits to acquire the housing as an alternative to prepayment. The same economic rationales that first motivated RHS owners to prepay properties in the 1970s and 1980s are driving HUD owners to prepay in large numbers.

Does the same fate await the Section 515 preservation program? Regrettably, rather than recognize the enormous public investment in this housing, not to mention current and future needs, we seem to be on a course that will permanently and irrevocably dismantle this vital national asset as well. The focus is on "tenant protections", e.g., rental vouchers, not housing preservation.

The experience of prepayment to date should give pause to those who would assume all too casually that the old system of long-term, project-based subsidy can be transformed seamlessly to a tenant-based system reliant on short-term subsidy. The hardships for tenants caused by owners' unwillingness to accept or continue tenancies with Section 8 vouchers, plus other uncertainties inherent in the tenant-based system, belie that. The experience should also clarify the futility of policies that still place the future affordability and disposition of low-income housing in the hands of for-profit owners.

NOTES

1. Approximately 110,000 Section 515 units, out of 400,000 Section 515 units nationwide, were financed between 1963 and 1979 and had no prepayment restrictions until subsequent legislation. See National Task Force on Rural Housing Preservation 1992:5.

2. Statement by Congressman Les AuCoin on House floor, reprinted in Cong. Rec., 96th Congress, 1st Sess. (December 19, 1979), Vol. 125, Part 28, U.S. Government Printing Office, Washington, DC, 1979, 36913.

3. A 2002 assessment by the U.S. General Accounting Office, employing a different methodology, estimated that 24% of properties might have a viable prepayment option.

REFERENCES

Anders, Gideon. 1993. Preservation of FmHA housing projects. *Housing Law Bulletin* (September/October). Oakland, CA: National Housing Law Project, 79–89.

———. 2002a. ELIHPA's prepayment restrictions may subject RHS to damages. *Housing Law Bulletin* (February). Oakland, CA: National Housing Law Project.

———. 2002b. RHS owners allowed to quiet title their property in derogation of ELIHPA. *Housing Law Bulletin* (November/December). Oakland, CA: National Housing Law Project.

———. 2003a. 9th Circuit stays order allowing Section 515 landlord to prepay loan. *Housing Law Bulletin* (March). Oakland, CA: National Housing Law Project.

———. 2003b. NHLP testifies on rural rental housing preservation issues. *Housing Law Bulletin* (August). Oakland, CA: National Housing Law Project.

———. 2005. Phone conversation with Gideon Anders, September 27, 2005.

Collings, Art. 1987. Displacement of tenants through prepayment of FmHA Section 515 loans. Washington, DC: Housing Assistance Council.

Fried, Marc. 1963. Grieving for a lost home. In *The urban condition*, ed. Leonard J. Duhl, 151–172. New York: Basic Books.

Housing Assistance Council. 2002. Rural rental housing preservation and nonprofit capacity to purchase and preserve Section 515 projects. Washington, DC: The Council.

National Task Force on Rural Housing Preservation. 1992. Preserving rural housing: Final report of the National Task Force on Rural Housing Preservation. Washington, DC: Housing

Assistance Council, California Coalition for Rural Housing Project and National Housing Law Project.

ICF Kaiser. 2004. Rural Rental Housing—Comprehensive Property Assessment and Portfolio Analysis: Final Study Report: Appendix. 8–17. Fairfax, VA.

Rural Housing Service. 1997. Year-end reports for FY 1995–1997. Washington, DC: Multifamily Housing Processing Division.

———. 1999. Summary: Preservation of the RHS multi-family housing program: Fiscal Year October 1998–September 1999. Washington, DC: Office of Rental Housing Preservation.

Wiener, Robert. 1993. Crisis in U.S. housing policy: The prepayment problem in FmHA's Rural Rental Housing Program. Unpublished dissertation, Graduate School of Architecture and Urban Planning, University of California, Los Angeles.

Chester Hartman

8   The Case for a Right to Housing

ALTHOUGH ESTABLISHING a right to housing in the United States does not appear to be immediately feasible, that political reality in no way detracts from the argument that our society ought to embrace it. I proceed from a normative, philosophical stance that asserts the wisdom and justice of such a right as well as our society's clear ability to achieve it.

After all, what have "rights" been historically in the United States if not an evolving societal sense of justice and entitlement, won always in political struggle (frequently undergirded by various intellectual efforts)? The right of slaves to be free of bondage was won in that way via armed struggle and political action that produced amendments to our Constitution. The right of women to vote has a similar (albeit less violent) history. Workers won the right to organize, and federal legislation with such guarantees was passed to codify that right. Ending child labor, winning an eight-hour workday and securing unemployment benefits represent other labor victories. The Civil Rights Movement of the 1960s produced a set of legal rights that did not previously exist and changed profoundly at least the public culture and practices with regard to race. In all these instances, the appeal was to a higher sense of justice, to fundamental principles of a democracy and to foundational documents embodied in the creation of our country.

The content of rights is thus a constantly evolving drama, as those lacking what they perceive as fundamental entitlements, together with their intellectual and political supporters, raise new issues, make new demands and organize politically to assert and bring into being new elements to society's understanding and acceptance of what everyone should have.

There are practical, cost-benefit reasons to advocate for a right to decent, affordable housing. For those living in inadequate housing conditions, they include, at a minimum, the multiple health and safety problems that arise from lead poisoning, rat bites, fires, asphyxiation (from poorly ventilated heating systems), communicable diseases, asthma (Rosenstreich et al. 1997), other forms of sickness and electric shock as well as the occasional dramatic event, such as the collapse of an entire building.[1] Overcrowding (apart from the physical condition of the space) can produce or exacerbate stress and family tensions as well as disease (Nossiter 1995). Poor neighborhood conditions are often associated with crime and a lack of personal safety. Housing affordability problems clearly have an impact on diet[2] and, as a *New York Times* headline put it, for poor Americans, there is "A Growing Choice: Housing or Food" (DeParle 1991).[3] Excessive housing costs also affect one's ability to secure other of life's basics as well as various amenities that most of society takes for granted. Segregation, discrimination and isolation based on race and ethnicity and also on class deprive residents of access to employment, economic development opportunities and public facilities, and may result in less good opportunities and services—a phenomenon that

Reprinted with changes from "The case for a right to housing," *Housing Policy Debate* 1998, 9(2), 233–246.

Massey and Denton (1993) label "hypersegregation." Imperfect as the data may be, there are ways of measuring these impacts, however roughly.

A second issue in need of quantification is how these various costs suffered by residents of inadequate housing translate into costs borne by the rest of the community and society. The health problems of poor people caused and exacerbated by poor housing conditions require massive subsidies through Medicaid and other public sources. Emergency fire and police costs, paid for largely via local taxes, are disproportionately high for slum neighborhoods.

The human and financial costs of crime affect everyone, directly or indirectly, as victims and potential victims. Homelessness is accompanied by disproportionate violence of various types (Hombs 1994). The productivity lost as a result of the multiple impacts of poor housing conditions negatively affects the standard of living for others. Educational deficits attributable to inadequate housing harm the entire society.[4] The dominant way in which we now deal with those suffering the most extreme housing problem, homelessness—overnight shelter and emergency services—requires public expenditures that far exceed the costs of a more rational and humane housing approach.[5]

The costs of poor housing and neighborhood conditions—to those directly experiencing them as well as to the broader community—have never been fully assessed or taken seriously as a matter of public policy. Tracing the immediate and long-range impacts of these housing and neighborhood defects—on health, family life (Bratt 2002), crime, education, incomes and employment as well as more subtle issues such as self-concept—is a huge and complex task. Likely, there are limitations on what can be reliably and accurately quantified, but an important step toward building more widespread support for a right to decent, affordable housing would be to carry out whatever studies can be done in describing and attaching dollar amounts to these costs, as a way of recognizing the direct and indirect costs of not fulfilling this right, and identifying what financial offsets should be made against the significant costs of providing

for such a right. That at least will provide a starting point for some hard-nosed thinking about housing policy and programs.

Beyond these mostly tangible, and in theory measurable, practical impacts lies the notion that political participation and political rights, particularly in a democratic society, are closely dependent on satisfaction of basic economic rights.[6] As Michael Stone (1993:314) writes, a right to decent, affordable housing "builds as well upon recognition that the political and civil rights for which we have struggled and continue to struggle have little practical meaning or utility for those among us whose material existence is precarious." The issue here is dignity as well, in the sense of asserting and receiving full respect for membership in one's community and in the society at large (Miller 1993; Miller and Savoie 2002; Sennett 2003). Suffrage in the United States has had a history of property ownership prerequisites—a situation not unrelated to the disenfranchisement of homeless persons for lack of a "real" address, an issue that has recently been successfully fought in the courts.[7]

SUPPORTIVE DOCUMENTS

It is significant that some of the most powerful statements supporting a Right to Housing have come from religious bodies (the same sources that provided leadership in the abolitionism and civil rights movements), highlighting the deep moral connections noted above. A 1975 statement from the U.S. Catholic Bishops asserts, "We begin with the recognition that decent housing is a right" and quotes the Second Vatican Council: "There must be made available to all men everything necessary to live a life truly human, such as food, clothing and shelter" (U.S. Catholic Conference 1975). A 1985 document from the U.S. Catholic Bishops asserts, "[T]he rights to life, food, clothing, shelter, rest and medical care ... are absolutely basic to the protection of human dignity.... These economic rights are as essential to human dignity as are the political and civil freedoms granted pride of place in the Bill of Rights of the U.S. Constitution."

Likewise, the Massachusetts Episcopal Diocese's Episcopal City Mission (1986) issued the following statement:

> Shelter in decent, affordable housing is not a luxury. It is a necessity upon which access to other necessities and the development of healthy, productive families and communities most often depend. Nothing is more essential to the welfare of men, women and children. Nothing is tied more directly to the recognition of the dignity, worth and values of persons. Because housing is so closely related to the welfare of persons and to recognition of their value as persons, nothing is a more basic right than the opportunity, regardless of income or class, to live in that kind of housing which supports the welfare of the family and community.... Whether persons of limited income have access to adequate shelter is thus for us at its heart both a question of justice, and a religious and theological question of central importance.

A December 1987 resolution from the General Board of the American Baptist Churches states, "We proclaim that each person being created in the image and likeness of God possesses an inherent dignity from which stems a basic human right to shelter." Pope John II, in his 1997 Lenten message, asserted, "The family, as the basic cell of society, has a full Right to Housing adequate to its needs, so that it can develop a genuine domestic communion. The Church recognizes this fundamental right and is aware of her obligation to work together with others in order to ensure that it is recognized in practice."

The relevant professions also have issued similar statements. For example, this from the National Association of Social Workers: "All individuals and families have the right to housing that meets their basic needs for a shelter at an affordable level and provides for a rewarding community life" (National Association of Social Workers 2000). And politicians are adding their voice as well: Representative Jesse Jackson, Jr., "would amend the Constitution to guarantee healthcare, education, affordable housing, employment security, equal rights for women and minorities, and a clean environment" (Nichols 2000).

There is wide assertion or recognition of a Right to Housing in a plethora of international documents[8] as well as in the laws of a great many other countries, often embodied in constitutional or statutory language (see Leckie 2003), although the legal, economic, social and political conditions in each country are so different as to render this dimension of interest and utility only as a general context, not for any detailed application to the situation in the United States. However, it should be noted that Canada several years ago considered amending its Bill of Rights to include "the right of the individual to proper housing, at a reasonable cost and free of unreasonable barriers" (1st Session, 36th Parl., 46–47, Elizabeth II, 1997–98). And the limitations of simply expressing such a right rhetorically, even in official documents and pronouncements, are obvious. A recent review of the international housing rights situation notes the following:

> The right to adequate housing finds legal substance within more than a dozen international human rights texts ... and has been reaffirmed in numerous international declaratory and policy-oriented instruments. More than fifty national constitutions enshrine various formulations of housing rights and other housing related state responsibilities ... and a plethora of domestic laws in nearly all countries have a bearing upon one or more of the core elements of housing rights .... Though on the surface a favourable situation, such legal recognition at the international level has rarely been transformed into effective domestic legislative and policy measures seeking to apply and implement—in good faith—international obligations relevant to housing rights .... No government could realistically proclaim that housing rights exist as much in fact as they do in law. (Leckie 1994:14–15; see also Herman 1994)

In short, because housing is so central to one's life, it merits attaining the status of a right. It is at the core of one's social and personal life, determining the kinds of influences and relationships one has and access to key opportunities and services (education, employment, healthcare). Housing also is an outward sign of status and affects the health and well-being of the surrounding community. Probably only those who have experienced how hard it is to create and maintain personal and family stability or land a job without a home, how hard it is to keep up with schoolwork in an overcrowded apartment, how much the sheer pressure to make the rent can overwhelm the rest of one's life—experiences largely foreign to the housing policy analysts, academics and bureaucrats who read and write scholarly articles such as this—can fully comprehend just how central decent, affordable housing is, or might be, and how limiting and burdensome is its absence.

WHY JUST HOUSING?

The question may be raised: Why housing? Why not a right to decent, affordable food? To health care? Why not guarantee people enough income so that, like the majority of Americans, they can purchase the housing, health care and other basics they need in the market? I would answer as follows.

We certainly should have a right to decent, affordable food[9] and health care (in the latter case, the costs, it should be noted, would be somewhat lower were housing-related detriments to good health eliminated); our failure to pass single-payer health reform legislation or otherwise provide these guarantees is a tragedy of massive proportions. It is not an either/or proposition, and movements for basic rights must coalesce into a more potent political force.

Housing has a special character, not only because it consumes so large a portion of the household budget, especially for lower-income families, but because it is, as noted above, the central setting for so much of one's personal and family life as well as the locus of mobility opportunities, access to community resources and societal status (Hartman 1975).

It would make things far easier if everyone in the United States had enough income to satisfy his or her needs in the market, but that goal is even less likely to be achieved than is the goal of decent housing for all. The structure of the job market and the shredding of the social safety net make it hard to imagine how everyone could have enough income to pay for housing and other necessities. In fact, an increasingly large number of Americans are unable to attain a decent standard of living as prices outstrip incomes (see Chapter 2). Moreover, that approach misreads the nature of the housing market. The

profit-maximizing behavior of all actors in that market—landowners, developers, builders, materials suppliers, real estate brokers, landlords, even homeowners—at all points works against assuring that everyone has decent, affordable housing, absent a legally enforceable Right to Housing and explicit commitment of resources to its realization.

AMERICA'S PROGRESS ON HOUSING

To state the obvious, with respect to housing, we have never even come close to providing all Americans with decent, affordable housing. A recitation of statistics on how far we are from this goal is unnecessary here.[10] We certainly will not move toward this goal in the current (2005) political era, turning our back on past approaches. The anti-safety net political climate in Congress and the Administration can only make matters worse. While it would be foolish to maintain that we can or will move toward establishing a right to decent, affordable housing in the immediate future, there is need and wisdom in keeping alive the assertion of and advocacy for such a right. We must not lose sight of what a society needs and can provide as basic standards of decency simply because achieving these goals does not seem possible at the moment. This might be regarded as a preparation period: engaging in the systematic thinking, research and scoping out of details as to how such a right might be defined and implemented—issues that will be itemized below—during a "dark" period. As framed by Margery Turner of the Urban Institute, "If you're going to advocate for a right to housing, . . . I'd urge you to take the broadest approach to that concept that you possibly can . . . . [L]et's think about it in an ambitious way, and maybe whatever headway is made will be more ambitious headway" (Turner 1991:132).

As all U.S. housing policy experts and many nonexperts well know, Congress in its preamble to the 1949 Housing Act promulgated the National Housing Goal of "the implementation as soon as feasible of a decent home and a suitable living environment for every American family." That goal was reiterated in the 1968 Housing Act and, in slightly different versions, in the 1974 and 1990 Housing Acts.[11] The word *affordable* is not mentioned in this formulation, but the postwar context was "slum clearance": The dominant and most widely recognized housing problems were substandard conditions and the lack of enough decent housing. However, affordability now is the nation's dominant housing problem, and it is self-evident that unless decent housing is affordable, it either is unobtainable by lower-income persons or can be secured only at the cost of slighting other basic necessities. Yet a goal is not a right. Although Congress promulgated this goal, it never followed up with the programs or resources to attain it. Nor do the statutory declarations provide the basis for litigation to compel allocation of the needed resources. The 1968 Housing Act took the brave step of setting forth a 10-year numerical target: 26 million units, 6 million of which were to be for low- and moderate-income households, and year-by-year progress reports were mandated. But it failed by a considerable margin, and never again was Congress foolish enough to risk such embarrassment.

By contrast, in the health and education areas, the nation has set specific goals and timetables. A U.S. Department of Health and Human Services publication (1993; McGinnis 1995) laid out specific objectives in 22 areas of health and health promotion to be achieved by the end of the century for the population as a whole as well as for different age groups, racial and ethnic minorities, and low-income persons. A follow-up report (U.S. Department of Health and Human Services 2000) updates and reports progress on these goals, putting forward 467 specific objectives in 28 focus areas. And, maintaining the momentum, Healthy People 2010 goals were launched (Healthy People 2010 goals launched 2000). In April 1994, Congress enacted the "Goals 2000: Educate America Act," which identified eight national educational goals pertaining to the following: school readiness; school completion; student achievement and citizenship; teacher education and professional development; mathematics and science; adult literacy and lifelong learning; safe, disciplined, and alcohol- and drug-free schools; and parental participation. Among other features, the act called for the high school graduation rate to increase to at least 90 percent by the year 2000, a dramatic reduction in the drop-out rate and elimination of the gap in high school graduation rates between students from minority backgrounds and their nonminority counterparts (Goals 2000 1994).[12]

EXISTING ENTITLEMENTS

As of 2005, we still have a number of entitlements in our economic and social system: the Earned Income Tax Credit, food stamps, Medicaid, Medicare, school breakfasts and lunches, Social Security and supplementary security income (SSI).[13] And of course, free K–12 public education has long-standing status as a basic right in the United States.

Thus, our nation has a history of providing a series of rights that prepare and assist individuals to participate in its economic and social order. Throughout the 19th century, educational and land reforms provided citizens with an expanding horizon of social and economic opportunities. For example, the 1862 Homestead Act, under which any settler could receive 160 acres of surveyed land after five years' residence and payment of a $26 to $34 registration fee, exemplifies America's willingness to directly transfer material resources to ordinary people (Robbins 1976; Warner 1972). As the 21st century begins, we need to consider to what equivalent economic and material rights an individual is entitled.

In the meantime, there remains no entitlement to any of the direct government housing programs: public housing,[14] Section 8, Section 202 and so on. (This is true for civilians. The military's family housing program does incorporate, as part of the benefits structure and only for those eligible by terms of pay grade and length of service, an entitlement to either free housing or a housing allowance [Hartman and Drayer 1990].) Something approaching a Right to Housing exists in other government programs, albeit hidden and largely unexplored in the literature. The temporary housing assistance offered under the disaster aid programs of the Federal Emergency Management Administration (FEMA) is in effect an entitlement,[15] although not that much money is involved and much of it is reimbursed by insurance proceeds. Federal aid for foster care—in effect a houser of last resort for children from troubled families[16]—may also be legitimately described as an entitlement; almost 80 percent of the federal government's $4.7 billion child welfare expenditures go to foster care (Russakoff 1998). Finally, and perhaps most important, the significant portion of the Medicaid (an entitlement) expenditure set aside for nursing home care constitutes a quasi-Right to Housing based on age (Redfoot 1993).

Our housing system does, at various levels of government, incorporate some rights (or quasi-rights) with respect to housing—for the most part, rights *against* certain things, negative rights not affirmative ones.[17] A partial list of these includes the following:

1. Local housing codes (which vary enormously with respect to coverage and standards) provide something of a right to decent conditions—although in practice, enforcement is problematic, and attempting to enforce these quality standards may result in loss of the unit, eviction or a rent increase (Hartman, Kessler and LeGates 1973).
2. In many jurisdictions, there are, by statute or case law, "warranty of habitability" and rent-withholding provisions—but these, too, fall short of being a guarantee of decent housing conditions[18] and do not consider at all the issue of affordability.
3. In those few localities that still have rent control ordinances, rent increases are limited, under certain circumstances—although this is no guarantee of affordability.
4. Rights to quiet enjoyment of residential premises exist via nuisance statutes, case law and other legal documents.
5. The right not to be discriminated against in the purchase or rental of housing on the basis of race and other personal characteristics is embodied in a large number of decades-old federal, state and local laws; additional rights based on disability were contained in 1988 Fair Housing Act Amendments (Mental Health Law Project 1989).
6. Due process must be followed in eviction and foreclosure procedures. Beyond this, a "right to stay put" (Hartman 1984) exists in various local condominium conversion ordinances and in "just (or good) cause"

eviction laws, which stipulate legitimate reasons for eviction rather than allowing eviction for virtually any (or no stated) reason; the existence of many loopholes in even the most tightly drawn ordinances substantially weakens this right. Residents of public and many other forms of government-assisted housing have due process rights with respect to eviction. (Military personnel receive special consideration. In an effort to deal with housing problems when people are suddenly yanked out of civilian life and called up for military service, the Soldiers and Sailors Relief Act of 1940 originally provided that any person serving in World War II could not be evicted from an apartment renting for less than $150 a month. During the Gulf War, that act was amended to increase the level of protection to apartments costing $1,200 a month or less and also to offer some protection against mortgage foreclosure [Raskin 1991].)
7. Tenants receiving public housing and Section 8 assistance have the right to be charged no more than 30 percent of their (adjusted) income for rent (a figure the government has revised upward in the past [Hartman 1986] and may again raise, but that, whatever the extant figure, embodies in principle a similar right).
8. If they meet eligibility criteria, veterans purchasing housing are entitled to U.S. Department of Veterans Affairs (VA) loans, in the form of government guarantee of private loans or, in some cases, direct government loans (a feature introduced at the end of World War II).
9. The Community Reinvestment Act, which essentially forbids "redlining" (denial of loans) of minority and low-income neighborhoods, provides what in essence are certain rights (geographically, not individually, oriented) to housing finance.
10. Various federal, state and local laws give existing occupants of rental housing the rights of first refusal regarding purchase of their units.
11. The various homeowners' income tax deductions provide the federal government's only true (civilian) housing entitlement "program": All homeowners are entitled to

deduct from their taxable income base virtually all mortgage interest and all property tax payments and can in most cases avoid capital gains taxes altogether.[19] While not all homeowners actually use this feature, it is available to all. When this "right" is challenged, the howls from the (largely upper-income) beneficiaries[20] and their advocates in the real estate world are deafening—and politically potent.[21]

Other legal steps that move in the direction of a Right to Housing concern the issue of homelessness—although here the issue has been "shelter," not in its generic meaning of housing, but temporary, overnight accommodations. In Washington, DC, voters in 1984 passed by a 72-to-28-percent margin an initiative (placed on the ballot by the Community for Creative Non-Violence [CCNV], headed by the late Mitch Snyder), which stated, "All persons in the District of Columbia shall have the right to adequate shelter. Adequate shelter is that which to a reasonable degree maintains, protects, and supports human health, is accessible, safe, and sanitary, and has an atmosphere of reasonable dignity." While on the surface a clearly established right, in fact, it had a sad history.[22]

In New York City, a similar right to decent temporary shelter for the homeless was won, but in this instance, the route was litigation: A suit was brought under the state constitution to compel the city to guarantee decent shelter for any homeless man; the case never went to trial but achieved its goal via a consent decree. A later step in the litigation expanded this right to homeless women.

As in Washington, DC, however, New York City has been dragging its feet for well over 20 years (the case was brought in October 1979). Advocates for the homeless have been back to court many times seeking to require the City to meet its obligations. Exemplifying this dereliction, a judge in 1996 held Mayor Rudolph Giuliani and two city agencies in contempt of court and levied more than $1 million in fines against the city after she made an unannounced visit to the city's homeless processing center and discovered 254 people sleeping on chairs and desks, even though "for more than a decade, the courts have barred the city from housing homeless people overnight in the offices to which they go seeking shelter" (Swarns 1996).

In Massachusetts, a 1995 Superior Court ruling in a class action case reaffirmed that state law gives homeless families a "right to shelter," striking down a rule by Governor William Weld's administration that denied shelter to families evicted from public or subsidized housing for falling behind in rent (Lakshmanan 1995). But the Weld administration appealed and obtained from the Supreme Judicial Court a reversal of the Superior Court decision (*Dowell v. McIntire*, 424 Mass. 610 [1997]).

In several cities, what might be labeled a "right not to freeze to death" has been enacted in the form of ordinances requiring public buildings to be opened to homeless persons when the temperature goes below a certain level.

In short, the concept of some housing rights is by no means foreign to our legal system or to prevailing standards of justice. To this existing bundle, meaningful elements must be added.

HOW WOULD A RIGHT TO HOUSING WORK?

Some Preliminary Thoughts

Beyond the analytical issue of whether there should be a right to decent, affordable housing, a great variety of concrete questions must be answered with respect to how such a right should be defined and implemented.[23] What are the components of this right? I would include affordability, physical quality of the unit, the social and physical characteristics of the neighborhood environment, and secure tenure.

What should the affordability standard be? Some version of Michael Stone's "shelter poverty" standard (see Chapter 2) is best, taking into account household size, household income and the cost of nonshelter basics, as opposed to a fixed percentage of income.[24] What standards should be used for housing and neighborhood conditions? Local housing codes vary enormously in coverage, detail and standards. The best of these might form the basis for a national code, or the U.S. Department of Housing and Urban Development's (HUD) Housing

Quality Standards might be used. There are few usable neighborhood quality standards at present, and serious work must be undertaken to develop these. Overcrowding standards must guard, on the one hand, against cultural bias (Myers, Baer and Choi 1996; Pader 1994) and, on the other hand, against accepting dramatically lower standards for the poor. Provision must be made for changing or rising standards. Anti-discrimination requirements should permit choice of neighborhoods: the option of in-place as well as dispersion remedies for badly impacted inner-city neighborhoods.

Secure tenure should also be a key element. Provision should be made, however, for legitimate changes in land use that require removal of residents. Defined behavioral infractions can constitute grounds for eviction. Willful non-payment would be grounds for eviction or foreclosure, but systems should be established to provide needed emergency and longer-term subsidies if incomes are inadequate to pay contracted housing costs, in order to avoid loss of one's home.

CAN WE AFFORD A RIGHT TO HOUSING?

To begin with, the costs of providing everyone with decent, affordable housing are greatly affected by the ways in which such a program would be carried out. Relying on the profit-motivated system that currently dominates the U.S. housing scene is by far the most expensive way to go. A vastly expanded social sector, with radically different financing, development, ownership and management arrangements—as put forward in the Institute for Policy Studies (1989) and Stone (1993)—would make the task far less costly.[25]

Beyond that, the question must be partly answered in terms of the costs—to those directly affected as well as to society as a whole—of maintaining the existing inadequate housing system. In other words, can we afford not to have a right to decent, affordable housing?

But given that government budgetary outlays must be far higher than current levels if the National Housing Goal (in its original incarnation) is to become a reality, is the money there? That, I submit, is not a fiscal question but a political one. We do not have any wholly reliable estimates of what realizing a right to decent, affordable housing would cost, but there are approaches that can offer an order-of-magnitude estimate. For example, the detailed 10-year program put forth by the Institute for Policy Studies' Working Group on Housing (1989) has a first-year price tag of between $29 and $88 billion (in 1989 dollars), depending on what mixture of its differently priced elements is chosen; over its life, required outlays are reduced annually.

While the figure sounds high, such expenditures represent a tiny percentage of the current federal budget. The above figure is in line with the amount of subsidy that the government grants under the mortgage interest deduction. According to the U.S. Congress (1997) Joint Committee on Taxation estimates, the mortgage interest deduction alone will amount to $232.6 billion over the period between fiscal years 1998 and 2002. For the same five-year period, the deduction of property taxes on owner-occupied residences is estimated to cost $89.9 billion, and exclusion of capital gains on the sale of principal residences is estimated at $29.6 billion. In sum, it is not that there is no available money to fund a Right to Housing; rather, it is how we choose to spend it. In the housing area, hundreds of billions of dollars were appropriated in the 1990s to bail out the savings and loan industry (see Chapter 4). And while the basic needs of our people go unmet, nearly one-half of the country's FY2005 federal funds outlay of $1,926 billion is devoted to past and current military expenditures (War Resisters League n.d.).

STRATEGIC APPROACHES

Laying out a detailed plan to establish a right to decent, affordable housing is a later step. The initial step is to set forth the rationale for establishing such a right and to challenge those who disagree to assert their arguments and counterarguments. Some preliminary thoughts along these lines are, however, appropriate.

Community and housing organizing and its political activism component is one major tool. There clearly is a need for more housing organizers to work with and bring together tenant groups, homeless advocacy organizations, community-based nonprofit developers, church-based institutions, neighborhood associations and civil rights and minority groups. "There are probably more housing lawyers for the poor than there are organizers," observed John Atlas, president of the National Housing Institute (Atlas 1991). Useful thoughts on the strengths, weaknesses and potential of the country's housing movement are offered by Stone (1993), Dreier (1997), Marcuse (1999), in Chapter 10 and in Chapter 5.

It is likely that a right to decent, affordable housing can be advanced only if coalitions are established that involve organic connections with other groups fighting for progressive reform and advancement of rights in health, food, education and income support programs. Alliances also must be made across class and race lines, revealing the housing system's inability to provide for the basic needs of an ever-growing portion of the population, connecting the problems of the poor with the problems of the middle class and the problems of homeowners with the problems of renters.

The housing question touches deeply on issues of race and racism. A full right to decent, affordable housing inevitably will involve a far greater degree of residential integration than now is the case. Major resistance to dealing with the fundamental flaws in the nation's housing system may stem from society's resistance to dealing with race issues.

There needs to be a recognition, and public education to bring about that recognition, that attaining a right to decent, affordable housing requires major changes in the current housing system with regard to ownership, financing and production. Merely throwing more money at the problem under the existing system—as with the Section 8 voucher/certificate program—can have only limited results. The existing system of production, ownership and finance has shown itself incapable of meeting the needs of an ever-growing portion of the population. We must ask honestly whether the for-profit system of production, management and finance that overwhelmingly dominates the way housing is provided in the United States is consistent with a right to decent, affordable housing; or whether, alternatively, this goal can be reached only through conscious and large-scale development of public and other nonprofit (non-market), permanently affordable units—both new and units transferred from the existing stock to this system. Part of this public education process involves stressing the ways in which and the extent to which virtually all housing in the United States currently benefits from some kind of indirect or direct government subsidy. Op-eds, study groups, year-long education projects such as those done by the League of Women Voters and many other creative ways of teaching the American public about good and bad housing policy are a necessary foundation for basic change of the type advocated in this article.

Selective litigation can be of assistance, although the courts (in particular, the federal courts, following the recent conservative judicial appointments by Republican presidents) are not presently as amenable to advancing economic and social rights as they were in the 1960s and 1970s. Major rights advances have been made this way, from ending legally sanctioned racial segregation in public schools, to abolishing the poll tax, to facilitating receipt of welfare support by eliminating bars based on interstate movement, and requiring due process hearings before aid is terminated. Housing attorney Florence Roisman has put forward a series of imaginative approaches to housing rights, using then-existing public benefit, child welfare and mental health laws (Roisman 1990).

A CHALLENGE

Those who reject a right to decent, affordable housing must ask themselves what future there is for owners and renters—middle-, moderate- and low-income—if existing trends continue, as they surely must, absent serious and radical intervention.

It has been argued (Carr 1998) that advocating a Right to Housing is flawed in that "it implicitly accepts the economic status quo of households trapped at the bottom of America's economic ladder and simply proposes to make that position in life a little more bearable. . . . [A] better solution would be one that not only benefits households at the bottom of the economic ladder but also improves society as a whole." In other words, "declaring a 'Right to Housing' and pursuing that right as the primary goal for a branch of social policy ignores the underlying causes behind concentrations of shelter poverty among certain among certain populations and residents of certain geographic areas."

But those of us advocating a Right to Housing do not ignore those underlying causes. Eradicating the systematic forces that cause concentration of poverty is of course a more desirable goal, but one that is even more elusive and difficult to achieve politically than a Right to Housing. The basic nature of housing gives it a special place as a social goal. And because, as noted above, housing is such a central financial burden for low-income people, serious assistance in that area can have important spillover effects in other areas of one's life: access to good schools, employment opportunities, transportation, for example—particularly if adequate attention is paid to issues of location in implementing this right so as to avoid concentrations by poverty or race. There is no reason, moreover, that organizers and other activists cannot, and will not, pursue several social justice goals simultaneously. A focus on housing need not distract attention and energy from other and deeper goals. Rights, as also noted above, also have a cumulative character: Rights tend to beget rights, both in terms of societal acceptance and the lessons of movement-building and political struggle.

Yet another criticism of the Right to Housing approach advocated in this article (again, Carr 1998) is that "when housing is affordable due only to government subsidy, residents of that housing grow dependent." But such criticism stems in part from an unwarranted distrust of government (as opposed to the market) and ignores as well the "dependency" that virtually everyone has, and should have, on government services and protections, not only in the housing area but throughout our system. With respect to housing in particular, few seem to call the tax system's enormous and enormously regressive homeowner deduction "dependence." There is no way a Right to Housing will be achieved without extensive government subsidies and programs. Local, democratically participatory control of these programs will ensure they are carried out without unnecessary bureaucracy, corruption or rigidity. There is plenty of room for consumer choice and sovereignty within the context of broad government policies. Pretending that "the market" alone can provide these benefits ignores the real history of the housing market in the United States and how it has disadvantaged and oppressed, and continues to disadvantage and oppress, the vast number of Americans without the financial means to function satisfactorily in that market.

And so, I end with a challenge. Let those who do not believe that decent, affordable housing should be a right in American society put forward their views and on what they are based. Let them also play out the scenario of current conditions and trends: What happens to our society if present levels of inequality, discrimination and deprivation are allowed to continue and intensify?

Let them answer why it is better to have tax breaks for the rich rather than a society where fundamental economic and living standards, and also political and civil rights, are guaranteed to all. Responses to some of the detailed considerations as to what this right should and would mean in practice, as well as how we might move in this direction, also are welcome. But the dialogue at the first level should be about the concept itself.

Let it begin.

NOTES

Acknowledgments: The author thanks Rachel Bratt, Mary Ellen Hombs, Steven Hornburg, Robert Lang, Peter Marcuse, Daniel Pearlman and Michael Stone for helpful comments on a draft of this updated article. This discussion owes a great deal to several efforts I have participated in over the past few years: the Working Group on Housing of the Institute for Policy Studies (which produced the document cited in the references); the Right to Housing Working Group convened by the National Housing Law Project and the Legal Services Homelessness Task Force (NHLP 1995); and the Housing Trust Fund Committee of the National Low Income

Housing Coalition, which produced the legislation cited in note 21.

1. See Kennedy (1995) for an account of a building collapse in New York's Harlem, which killed three tenants and injured seven others. Accidents of this sort are even more prevalent and disastrous in other countries. In mid-2000, the collapse of a massive garbage hill in Manila buried a shantytown, killing hundreds of people: Some two hundred bodies were recovered, but "residents estimate that up to four times that number may have died, though a complete toll will probably never be known" (Mydans 2000).

2. A study by Meyers et al. (1995) comparing nutrition status of children living in subsidized housing with those living in unsubsidized housing—and whose families thus pay a far higher proportion of their income for rent—concluded as follows: "Receiving a housing subsidy is associated with increased growth in children from low-income families, an effect that is consistent with a protective effect of housing subsidies against childhood undernutrition."

3. An intriguing and instructive twist on this dilemma was featured in a front-page New York Times story about one Gangaram Mahes, a homeless New Yorker whose modus operandi—a real life, albeit more successful version of the gentleman portrayed in O. Henry's delightful short story "The Cop and the Anthem"—is to slip on his best donated clothes as winter arrives, eat a good meal at a nice restaurant and then allow himself to be arrested after he announces his penniless state upon arrival of the check. He has done this at least 31 times, so as to spend the next 90 days with a guaranteed three meals a day and a clean bed. Legal aid lawyers, according to the account, report a growing number of people who commit petty crimes with the intent of going to prison. While possibly a rational strategy from the individual point of view, "it costs taxpayers $162 a day to feed, clothe and house Mr. Mahes at Rikers Island. His 90-day sentence will cost them $14,580 to punish him for refusing to pay a $51.31 check. In five years, he has cost them more than $250,000" (Bragg 1994). However, some localities now are proposing to charge jail inmates for food (Pan 1998; Clines 2000; "Mass. County" 2002).

4. Homelessness has proven to be a barrier to adequate education for children. See Dohrn (1991) and National Law Center on Homelessness and Poverty (1997b) for reports, respectively, on the failure to meet federal McKinney Act requirements that homeless children in shelters receive an "adequate education" and barriers to preschool education for homeless children. See also National Law Center on Homelessness and Poverty (1990a, 1990b, 1991). For housed and homeless children in low-income households, frequent school changes (as often as three, four, and five times a year) due to housing instability clearly are detrimental to learning (Hartman 2002).

5. An advertisement headed "Which Would You Invest In?" placed in the May 28, 1995, New York Times by the New York City advocacy group Almost Home and signed by several dozen senior executives of corporations and financial institutions, such as Lehman Brothers, Lazard Freres, Merrill Lynch, Goldman Sachs and Bankers Trust, and well-known individuals (including Cyrus Vance, Vernon Jordan and Felix Rohatyn), cited the comparative annual costs in New York City of a psychiatric hospital bed ($113,000), a prison cell ($60,000), a shelter cot ($20,000) and a permanent home with supportive services ($12,500). Holloway (1996) reports annual shelter bed costs as between $18,000 and $23,000 in New York City; by comparison, per-unit HUD subsidies for public housing and Section 8 certificates/vouchers are in the $6,000 to $8,000 range. A similar, more recent full-page ad in the New York Times (January 24, 2001), by the National Alliance to End Homelessness, opposing the increasing trend to criminalize homelessness (thus headed, "At $112 a night, the homeless aren't the only ones paying a high price"), compared the $34 per night cost to provide permanent supportive housing with built-in services such as job training and mental health treatment with the per night cost of putting a person in jail. Annualized, the difference is $12,410 versus $40,800. See also note 3.

6. In recent years, a growing number of human rights organizations have expressed interest in initiating work on economic, social and cultural rights, expanding their legal theories and activism efforts more broadly and creating theoretical, legal and advocacy links between the two areas of concern. See International Human Rights Internship Program (1997).

7. See National Law Center on Homelessness and Poverty (1996) and case citations therein. A bill to codify these rights (the Voting Rights of Homeless Citizens Act of 1997 [H.R. 74, Senate version S. 1503]) has been introduced several times, most recently in 1997, but has gone nowhere, mainly out of Republican opposition, since it is assumed that most homeless persons would vote Democratic.

8. Among the important international documents wherein the right to adequate housing is explicitly recognized are the Universal Declaration on Human Rights (1948); the International Covenant on Economic, Social and Cultural Rights (1966); the Convention on the Elimination of All Forms of Racial Discrimination (1965); the International Convention on the Rights of the Child (1989); the International Convention on the Elimination of All Forms of Discrimination Against Women (1979) and the International Labor Organization Recommendation No. 115 on Workers Housing. For example, the International Covenant on Economic, Social and Cultural Rights, to which 145 states are bound as parties, states in Article 11(1), "The State parties to the present Covenant

recognize the right of everyone to an adequate standard of living for himself and his family, including adequate food, clothing and housing, and to the continuous improvement of living conditions." (See, generally, Centre on Housing Rights and Evictions [1994]). The June 1996 UN Conference on Human Settlements (Habitat II) in Istanbul produced little progress and featured the depressing, embarrassing spectacle of the United States delegation at first giving in to State Department instructions that it "must make clear for the record that the U.S. does not recognize the international human right to housing" (Habitat II Brings Victories 1996). Then, under great pressure from nongovernmental organizations and other governments, it acceded to a weak assertion of the "full and progressive [as opposed to prompt] realization of that right in the context of other international documents." The various UN-sponsored mega-conferences on related issues—the United Nations Conference on Environment and Development (Rio de Janeiro, 1992), the World Conference on Human Rights (Vienna, 1993), the Population Summit (Cairo, 1994), the Social Development Summit (Copenhagen, 1995), and the Women's Summit (Beijing, 1995)—may provide some fuel for movement in the direction of housing rights.

9. The basic necessity of food, as well as clothing, is easier to come by than is housing, via various free or very inexpensive official, nonprofit and informal surplus and giveaway systems (food banks, second-hand clothing stores, hand-me-downs, yard sales and the like.). See Trebay (2000) as well as Mittal (2001).

10. See, for example, Joint Center for Housing Studies (2002); HUD (1998); Lazere (1995); National Low Income Housing Coalition (2001); DeParle (1996). In his second Inaugural Address (1937), President Franklin Roosevelt offered his famous lament that "one-third of the nation is ill-housed, ill-fed, and ill-clothed." While enormous progress has unquestionably been made with respect to clothing and food, it can easily be shown that one-third of American households still are ill-housed, when physical condition, overcrowding and affordability are totaled up. And likely the trajectory is toward even larger numbers and proportions. Although there are no data comparing the depression-era homeless with the current situation, we are gradually realizing the full dimensions of that problem. Link et al. (1994) reported that over the five-year period from 1985 to 1990, 5.7 million people were literally homeless at one time or another (sleeping in shelters, bus and train stations, abandoned buildings, etc.), while 8.5 million people reported some type of homelessness (staying with friends or relatives). Lifetime homeless figures were 13.5 million people (literal homelessness) and 26 million people (all types of homelessness). (See also Marcuse 1989.)

11. Congress, in a subtle and little noticed provision of the Quality Housing and Work Responsibil-

ity Act of 1998 amended this statement, ludicrously maintaining that the government lacked the resources to address the nation's housing needs so fully. (See Bratt 2003.)

12. Overseeing this now-dissolved project was an intergovernmental National Education Goals Panel, with eight governors, four members of Congress, four state legislators and two members appointed by the president. See the Web site: www.negp.gov. However, in 2002, President George W. Bush signed the Education and Secondary School Act, which closed down the Education Goals Panel. (See Hoff 2002 for a useful history and evaluation of the effort.)

13. A general discussion of the entitlement concept is found in Edelman (1991).

14. For an argument that there should be a right to public housing, see Roisman (1971).

15. The Robert T. Stafford Disaster Relief and Emergency Assistance Act (P.L. 93–288), as amended, provides for residents of areas where the president declares a major disaster, among other benefits, temporary relocation housing for up to 18 months; funding for emergency repairs to damaged homes; long-term (up to 30 years), low-interest Small Business Administration (SBA) loans (up to $240,000) for home repair and repair/replacement of furniture and personal possessions; and cash grants of up to $13,400 (a ceiling that is periodically increased via inflation indexing) for those who do not qualify for a loan (see FEMA n.d.; Suchocki 1998; U.S. General Accounting Office 1997; SBA n.d.). While not explicitly labeled an entitlement program, in fact, if proper application procedures are followed and eligibility criteria are met, such aid is given to all who apply.

16. "Through foster care, the government [by the late 1990s] was mother of last resort to a record 502,000 children nationally, almost double the number in 1980" (Russakoff 1998, Part 1, A1).

17. It has been ironically, and not entirely facetiously, suggested that the new emphasis on prison-building and such punitive measures as "three strikes and you're out" laws have created a "right" to affordable shelter with total security of tenure. See also note 3.

18. In a 1972 case, *Lindsay v. Normet* (405 U.S. 56), the Supreme Court ruled that there is no constitutional right to shelter—but see the discussion below of temporary shelter for the homeless. For an earlier, general discussion of a Right to Housing, see Michelman (1970).

19. The 1997 tax reform legislation sweetened the capital gains feature for homeowners enormously, providing a windfall predicted to benefit mostly affluent homeowners to the tune of some $6 billion over the next nine years. See Harney (1997).

20. Seventy percent of the mortgage interest deduction and 65 percent of the homeowners'

property tax deduction went to taxpayers in the $75,000-and-above income class in 1997 (U.S. Congress [1997], Joint Committee on Taxation).

21. A Housing Trust Fund bill—H.R. 1016, crafted by the National Low Income Housing Coalition, was introduced in Congress in 1994, but never garnered Congressional support. The bill would have financed the trust fund by reducing the mortgage interest tax deduction for well-to-do homeowners, which many analysts said doomed it from the start.

In 2000, the National Low Income Housing Coalition embarked on a campaign to establish a National Housing Trust Fund, based on legislation introduced by John Kerry (D-MA) in the Senate and Bernie Sanders (I-VT) in the House. These bills would have used surplus revenue from the FHA mortgage insurance program as the dedicated revenue source for the trust fund and called for production, preservation and rehabilitation of 1.5 million units of rental housing affordable to the lowest-income families. The National Housing Trust Fund Campaign has been endorsed by over 5,400 organizations (www.nhtf.org).

The House bill, H.R. 1102, had 214 co-sponsors at the close of the 108th Congress in 2004. Opposition from Republican leadership in the House prevented the bill from coming up for consideration.

In 2005, in the 109th Congress, the NHTF campaign is pushing legislation to create a new fund from profits from Fannie Mae and Freddie Mac to be used for the same purposes as a the National Housing Trust Fund.

22. The city government never took it seriously. Proponents had to take the city to court in order to get action, with severe sanctions and fines imposed on the city to get a response. In June 1990, the city council "amended" the initiative law to remove its effectiveness. In response, CCNV took the issue to voters again in 1990, this time losing, 49 to 51 percent, partly the result of what has been labeled "compassion fatigue." An attempt to secure a constitutionally grounded right to shelter in Washington, DC, yielded a positive ruling at the trial court level but was subsequently overturned by the U.S. Court of Appeals for the D.C. Circuit (Locy 1997). Recent years have seen a backlash against the homeless, which possibly bodes poorly for support of a right to decent housing. Throughout the country, a range of ordinances and police practices aimed at homeless persons are being enacted and carried out as a general trend toward the criminalization of homelessness. See National Law Center on Homelessness and Poverty (1994, 1997a).

23. This list of issues is drawn from discussions and background papers of the National Housing Law Project/Legal Services Homelessness Task Force Working Group (see the author's acknowledgments under Notes).

24. "Shelter poverty" is a term and concept originated by Michael Stone, referring to the relationship between the cost of nonshelter basics and the cost of housing. In brief, Stone argues that since housing tends to make the first claim on a household's disposable income, the most a household should be required to pay for housing is that which leaves it able to meet nonshelter basics at a minimum level of adequacy. The larger the family, the more it has to pay for nonshelter basics and thus the less it can afford for housing; similarly, the lower the family's income, the less it can afford to pay for housing, since nonshelter basics take up a higher percentage of household income. Using this concept, updated Bureau of Labor Statistics model budgets and actual data on household incomes and expenditures, Stone calculates that some 15 million U.S. households cannot afford one penny for housing and still have enough funds remaining for nonshelter basics. (See Chapter 2).

25. For an argument on the wisdom of using capital grants as opposed to credit, see Chapter 4; Institute for Policy Studies (1989); Marcuse (1986).

REFERENCES

Atlas, John. 1991. Strategies to achieve a right to housing: Public education, litigation, legislation. In *The Right to Housing*, Final Report by Jean R. McRae and Michael U. Mbanaso. Spring 1991 Fannie Mae University Colloquium Series on Domestic Housing Policy, February/April 1991, Housing and Community Studies Development Center, Institute for Urban Affairs and Research, Howard University.

Bragg, Rick. 1994. A thief dines out, hoping later to eat in. *New York Times*, May 19.

Bratt, Rachel B. 2002. Housing and family well-being. *Housing Studies*, Vol. 17, No. 1.

———. 2003. Housing for very low-income households: The record of President Clinton, 1993–2000. *Housing Studies*, Vol. 18, No. 4.

Carr, James. 1998. Comment on Chester Hartman's "The case for a right to housing": The right to "poverty with a roof"—a response to Hartman. *Housing Policy Debate*, 9:247–257.

Centre on Housing Rights and Evictions. 1994. *Legal provisions on housing rights: International and national approaches*. Utrecht, Netherlands.

Clines, Francis X. 2000. Rooms available in gated community: $20 a day. *New York Times*, July 10.

DeParle, Jason. 1991. A growing choice: Housing or food. *New York Times*, December 12.

———. 1996. Slamming the door. *New York Times Magazine*, October 20.

Dohrn, Bernardine. 1991. A long way from home: Chicago's homeless children and the schools. Chicago: Legal Assistance Foundation of Chicago.

Dreier, Peter. 1997. The new politics of housing: How to rebuild the constituency for a progressive federal housing policy. *Journal of the American Planning Association*, 63:5–27, Winter.

Edelman, Peter. 1991. An historical and legal review of the concept of rights and entitlements. In *The Right to Housing*, Final Report by Jean R. McRae and Michael U. Mbanaso. Spring 1991 Fannie Mae University Colloquium Series on Domestic Housing Policy, February/April 1991, Housing and Community Studies Development Center, Institute for Urban Affairs and Research, Howard University.

Episcopal City Mission. 1986. Housing: *A basic human right*. Boston.

Federal Emergency Management Agency. n.d. FEMAFAX Document No. 91101.

Goals 2000: Educate America Act promises new academic standards and opportunities for all students to learn. 1994. *Newsnotes*, Publication of the Center for Law and Education, No. 51, Summer.

Habitat II Brings Victories, Opportunities. 1996. *In Just Times*, newsletter of the National Law Center on Homelessness and Poverty, August.

Harney, Kenneth. 1997. Home tax break comes at a big cost for U.S., states. *Washington Post*, October 4.

Hartman, Chester. 1975. *Housing and social policy*. Englewood Cliffs, NJ: Prentice Hall.

———. 1984. The right to stay put. In *Land reform, American style*, eds. Charles C. Geisler and Frank J. Popper, 302–318. Totowa, NJ: Rowman and Allanheld.

———. 1986. Housing policies under the Reagan Administration. In *Critical Perspectives on Housing*, eds. Rachel G. Bratt, Chester Hartman and Ann Meyerson, 362–376. Philadelphia: Temple University Press.

———. 2002. High classroom turnover: How children get left behind. In *Rights at risk: Equality in an age of terrorism*, eds. Dianne M. Piché, William L. Taylor and Robin A. Reed, 227–244. Washington, DC; Citizens Commission on Civil Rights.

Hartman, Chester, and Robin Drayer. 1990. Military-family housing: The other public housing program. *Housing and society*, 17:67–78, reprinted in Hartman, *Between eminence and notoriety: Four decades of radical urban planning*. New Brunswick, NJ: Center for Urban Policy Research, 2002, 233–245.

Hartman, Chester, Robert Kessler and Richard LeGates. 1973. Municipal housing code enforcement and low-income tenants. *Journal of the American Institute of Planners*, 40:90–104.

Healthy People 2010 goals launched. 2000. *The Nation's Health* (American Public Health Association), March.

Herman, Marc-Oliver. 1994. Fighting homelessness: Can international human rights law make a difference? *Georgetown Journal on Fighting Poverty*, 2:59–82.

Hoff, David J. 2002. Mission imponderable: Goals panel to disband. *Education Week*, January 9.

Holloway, Lynette. 1996. A new debate arises as city leaves the shelter business. *New York Times*, November 12.

Hombs, Mary Ellen. 1994. Continuum of violence: Rethinking advocacy priorities in homelessness. *Clearinghouse Review* Special Issue, 407–415.

Institute for Policy Studies Working Group on Housing. 1989. *The Right to Housing: A blueprint for housing the nation*. Washington, DC.

International Human Rights Internship Program. 1997. *Ripple in still water: Reflections by activists on local- and national-level work on economic, social, and cultural rights*. Washington, DC.

Joint Center for Housing Studies, Harvard University. 2002. *The state of the nation's housing: 2002*. Cambridge, MA.

Kennedy, Shawn. 1995. Collapsed building's owners face crime inquiry. *New York Times*, March 28.

Lakshmanan, Indira. 1995. Court voids a Weld rule on shelters. *Boston Globe*, November 1.

Lazere, Edward. 1995. *In short supply: The growing affordable housing gap*. Washington, DC: Center on Budget and Policy Priorities.

Leckie, Scott. 1994. *Towards an international convention on housing rights: Options at Habitat II*. Issue Papers on World Conferences Number 4. Washington, DC: American Society of International Law.

———. ed. 2003. *National perspectives on housing rights*. The Hague: Martinus Nijhoff Publishers.

Link, Bruce, Ezra Susser, Ann Steuve, Jo Phelan, Robert Moore and Elmer Struening. 1994. Lifetime and five-year prevalence of homelessness in the United States. *American Journal of Public Health*, 1907–1912, December.

Locy, Toni. 1997. Court says D.C. homeless have no right to shelter. *Washington Post*, March 5.

Marcuse, Peter. 1986. A useful installment of socialist work: Red Vienna in the 1920s. In *Critical Perspectives on Housing*, eds. Rachel G. Bratt, Chester Hartman and Ann Meyerson. Philadelphia: Temple University Press.

———. 1989. Homelessness and housing policy. In *Homeless in America*, ed. Carol Laton. New York: Oxford University Press.

———. 1999 Housing Movements in the USA. *Housing, theory and society*, Vol. 16.

Mass. County [Bristol] jail to charge inmates for room and board. 2002. *Washington Post*, March 10.

Massey, Douglas, and Nancy Denton. 1993. *American apartheid: Segregation and the making of the underclass*. Cambridge, MA: Harvard University Press.

McGinnis, J. Michael. 1995. Healthy People 2000 at mid-decade. *Journal of the American Medical Association*, 1123–1129, April 12.

Mental Health Law Project. 1989. *Rights of tenants with*

disabilities under the Fair Housing Amendments Act of 1988. Washington, DC.

Meyers, Alan, Nicole Roos, Deborah A. Frank, Vaira L. Harik, Karen E. Peterson and Virginia Casey. 1995. Housing subsidies and pediatric undernutrition. *Archives of Pediatrics and Adolescent Medicine*, 149:1079–1084, October.

Michelman, Frank I. 1970. The advent of a Right to Housing. *Harvard Civil Rights–Civil Liberties Law Review*, 5:207–212.

Miller, S. M. 1993. The politics of respect. *Social Policy*, 44–51, Spring.

Miller. S. M., and Anthony J. Savoie. 2002. *Respect and rights: Class, race and gender today.* Lanham, MD: Rowman and Littlefield.

Mittal, Anuradha. 2001. Food is a human right, not a charity. http://www.alternet.org/story.html? StoryID=10944.

Mydans, Seth. 2000. Before Manila's garbage hill collapsed: Living off scavenging. *New York Times*, July 18.

Myers, Dowell, William C. Baer and Seong-Youn Choi. 1996. The changing problem of overcrowded housing. *Journal of the American Planning Association*, 66–84, Winter.

National Association of Social Workers. 2000. Social work speaks: National Association of Social Workers policy statements, 2000–2003. Washington: NASW Press.

National Housing Law Project/Legal Services Homelessness Task Force Working Group. 1995. *Housing for all: Keeping the promise.* Oakland, CA.

National Law Center on Homelessness and Poverty. 1990a. *Stuck at the shelter: Homeless children and the D.C. school system.* Washington, DC.

———. 1990b. *Shut out: Denial of education to homeless children.* Washington, DC.

———. 1991. *Small steps: An update on the Education of Homeless Children and Youth Program.* Washington, DC.

———. 1994. *No homeless people allowed: A report on anti-homeless laws, litigation, and alternatives in U.S. cities.* Washington, DC.

———. 1996. Voter registration: The legal rights of homeless people. [Memorandum].

———. 1997a. *Mean sweeps.* Washington, DC.

———. 1997b. *Blocks to their future: A report on the barriers to preschool education for homeless children.* Washington, DC.

National Low Income Housing Coalition. 2001. *Out of reach: America's growing wage-rent disparity.* Washington, DC.

Nichols, John. 2000. Jesse Jackson Jr.: A different vision. *The Nation*, September.

Nossiter, Adam. 1995. Asthma common and on rise in the crowded South Bronx. *New York Times*, September 5.

Pader, Ellen J. 1994. Spatial relations and housing policy: Regulations that discriminate against Mexican-origin households. *Journal of Planning Education and Research*, 13:119–135.

Pan, Philip. 1998. Pr. George's Considers fee for jail food. *Washington Post*, June 1.

Raskin, Marcus. 1991. What we owe to vets. *New York Times*, March 5.

Redfoot, Donald A. 1993. Long-term care reform and the role of housing finance. *Housing Policy Debate*, 4(4):497–537.

Robbins, Roy. 1976. *Our landed heritage, the public domain, 1776–1970.* Lincoln: University of Nebraska Press.

Roisman, Florence. 1971. The right to public housing. *George Washington Law Review* 39:691–733.

———. 1990. Establishing a Right to Housing: An advocate's guide. Parts 1–3. *Housing Law Bulletin*, 39–47, May/June; 65–80, July/August; 107–119, September/October.

Rosenstreich, David, Peyton Eggleston, Meyer Kattan, Dean Baker, Raymond Slavin, Peter Gergen, Herman Mitchell, Kathleen McNiff-Mortimer, Henry Lynn, Dennis Ownby and Floyd Malveaux. 1997. The role of cockroach allergy and exposure to cockroach allergen in causing morbidity among inner-city children with asthma. *New England Journal of Medicine*, 336.

Russakoff, Dale. 1998. When the bough breaks: Who will catch the children? Parts 1–3. *Washington Post*, January 18–20.

Sennett, Richard. 2003. *Respect in a world of inequality.* New York: W. W. Norton.

Small Business Administration. n.d. Disaster Assistance Program. Information sheet.

Stone, Michael E. 1993. *Shelter poverty: New ideas on housing affordability.* Philadelphia: Temple University Press.

Suchocki, Carl. 1998. Telephone interview with the author, January 27. Office of Public Affairs, Federal Emergency Management Agency.

Swarns, Rachel. 1996. Court rulings give homeless little comfort. *New York Times*, May 16.

Trebay, Guy. 2000. Old clothing never dies, it just fades far, far away. *New York Times*, December 5.

Turner, Margery. 1991. Presentation at Panel Session, April 3, 1991. In *The Right to Housing*, Final Report by Jean R. McRae and Michael U. Mbanaso. Spring 1991 Fannie Mae University Colloquium Series on Domestic Housing Policy, February/April 1991, Housing and Community Studies Development Center, Institute for Urban Affairs and Research, Howard University.

U.S. Catholic Conference. 1975. *The right to a decent home—a pastoral response to the crisis in housing: A statement of the Catholic Bishops of the United States.* Washington, DC.

U.S. Congress. 1997. Joint Committee on Taxation. *Estimates of federal tax expenditures for fiscal years 1998–2002.* Doc. JCS 22–97.

U.S. Department of Health and Human Services, Public Health Service. 1993. *Healthy People 2000: National health promotion and disease objectives.* Washington, DC: U.S. Government Printing Office.

———. 2000. Healthy People 2010: *Understanding and improving health.* Washington, DC.

U.S. Department of Housing and Urban Development, Office of Policy Development and Research. 1998. *Rental housing assistance—the crisis continues: The 1997 report to Congress on worst-case housing needs.* Washington, DC.

U.S. General Accounting Office. 1997. *Disaster assistance: Guidance needed for FEMA's "fast track" housing assistance process.* Washington, DC.

Warner, Samuel Bass, Jr. 1972. *The urban wilderness: A history of the American city.* New York: Harper and Row.

War Resisters League. n.d. Where your income tax money really goes. New York: The League.

David B. Bryson[*]

9   The Role of the Courts and a Right to Housing

COURTS PLAY a central role in defining, declaring and enforcing legal rights, and courts in the United States already have made significant contributions toward developing and enforcing various aspects of a Right to Housing. The chapter begins with consideration of the nature of a Right to Housing and, in particular, the components of such a right. It then explores what courts can do to develop and enforce rights. With that background, the chapter explains what courts have done with regard to housing rights, especially in the late 20th and early 21st centuries. Finally, it suggests what courts can and should do in the future to contribute to the development and enforcement of housing rights.

THE ATTRIBUTES OF A RIGHT TO HOUSING

Chapter 8 explained in detail the nature of a Right to Housing that could serve as the foundation for a new social agenda. However, to understand the role of courts, this discussion involves more than just one undifferentiated right. A home has many aspects, including its physical condition, its location, its cost, and the duration of and conditions attached to the residents' right to live in it. A Right to Housing is composed of a series of entitlements related to each of these aspects.

Various individuals and entities, both private and public, may be connected in one way

*David Brady Bryson, author of this chapter and one of the persons to whom this book has been dedicated, died on December 25, 1999, mourned by his family, friends and colleagues in the legal services and housing advocacy worlds. In his chapter, he acknowledged with gratitude the research assistance of Hallie Ness, Esq., his beloved daughter.

At the request of the editors of this book, I have undertaken to bring David's chapter up to date and to perform the revising and editorial functions that fall to any author prior to publication. In doing so, I encountered several points about which I disagreed with David, sometimes with respect to form, sometimes emphasis and sometimes substance. Since David and I often had worked together on briefs and articles, I had what I thought was a good sense of what I could have persuaded him to change and what he would have persuaded me to leave alone. In editing this chapter,

my standard was that I would not change anything I thought I could not have persuaded David to change: this is, after all, his essay, not mine. Using this standard, I have retained some points with which I disagree, notably David's skepticism about the desegregation cases.

Several other colleagues of David's were very helpful in the editing process. I am particularly grateful to Julie Levin, who wrote the section on receivership; to Gideon Anders, Julie Becker, Catherine Bishop, Sylvia M. Brennan, Lynn Cunningham, Michael M. Daniel, Fred Fuchs, George Gould, James Grow, Tom Kelley, Jack McCullough, Barbara Sard, Philip Tegeler, Richard Tenenbaum and William P. Wilen, all of whom provided needed information; to Katie Orton and Andrea Bonds for excellent research assistance; and to the editors of this book.

—*Florence Wagman Roisman*

or another to any home. There may be a landlord, a seller, a lender, neighbors, homeowner associations, utility companies, a local government with regulatory power and responsibility for neighborhood conditions (including security from crime) and one or more other government agencies providing housing assistance. For each of the resident's rights with respect to any aspect of her or his home, there will be correlative obligations imposed on one or more of these individuals or entities.

To achieve the goal of a Right to Housing, everyone must be assured of a home that has the following fundamental attributes:

- It must be in decent physical condition: structurally sound; weather-tight; served by adequate electrical, heating, water and sewage systems; free from dangerous conditions (including lead and environmental hazards), rodents and pests; secure from criminal intrusion and adequately sized for the occupants.
- The residents must have security of tenure so that they will not be forced to move from their homes by arbitrary evictions, mortgage foreclosure for reasons beyond their control or the unreasonable exercise of the government's power of eminent domain.
- Because of this country's history of slavery and conquest, and our society's bias against people from parts of the world other than Europe, residential segregation and discriminatory housing practices based on race and ethnicity are major ills in our nation. A Right to Housing must guarantee people that they will not be excluded from neighborhoods or treated differently with regard to their housing choices because of their race, ethnicity or heritage.
- Because having a place to live is vital for everyone and decent housing is in short supply, there is enormous potential for landlords, managers, lenders and government officials to abuse the power they have over tenants and homebuyers. A Right to Housing must, therefore, include protections for residents against such abuses and guarantees of fair treatment in matters that relate to their homes, including freedom from discrimination on grounds of religion, age, disability, sexual orientation, source of income or the presence of chil-

dren in the family. Tenants must be free from oppressive management practices, including unwarranted invasions of privacy.

- A complete Right to Housing will recognize the importance of location of the housing and guarantee the residents that the neighborhood will be adequately secure from crime, adequately provided with municipal services, insulated from environmental hazards and other negative conditions, and accessible to adequate commercial and professional facilities.
- Finally, housing with the preceding attributes must be within the residents' financial means. They must be assured that they will not have to forego any of these essential characteristics of a decent home, or be left without a home at all, because of lack of income. Nor must they be compelled to spend so much of their income on housing that they are unable to secure other necessities of life.

A review of these attributes of decent housing will provide examples of the roles that the courts have played and can play in creating and enforcing a Right to Housing. The review reveals, also, that the courts' roles will vary from attribute to attribute and situation to situation. First, however, it is necessary to explain more generally the various roles our courts play in developing and enforcing rights.

The Roles of the Courts in Our Society

Contributions made by the courts can be divided into two parts. The first might be called "definitional," in which the courts, along with other governmental institutions, define who has a right to what and who has the obligation to provide whatever it is to which people have a right. The second part is enforcement of the right, in which courts have a primary, but hardly exclusive, role.

In the definitional stage, the courts perform a variety of functions. At times, the courts themselves define particular attributes of the right. In effect, and sometimes very openly, they create the rights. That is particularly true with respect to rights that are part of the common law, which comprises much of the law of real property in most states. An example would be a tenant's right to habitable housing, which is guaranteed by the judicially created implied warranty of habitability (*Javins*).

At other times, the courts define rights by deciding the meaning of laws created by other institutions—for instance, by interpreting constitutional provisions, statutes and regulations. Although the courts do not write the original laws, their role in interpreting laws is far from a mechanical application of dictionary definitions to words written by others. That is particularly true with the interpretation of federal or state constitutions. The federal Constitution was written and amended in the most general terms, for the most part one to two centuries ago. The same is true, although to a lesser extent, of the relevant state constitutional provisions. It is up to the courts to decide what these words mean in a variety of situations and how those meanings evolve over time as society changes. Under our system, the courts have the last word, in the absence of an amendment to the Constitution, as to what each constitutional provision means. The courts, in making those interpretations, are creating rights and duties or, at least, refining the rights and duties created by others. In the housing area, the right not to be evicted from public housing without the opportunity for a prior hearing was produced from the courts' interpretation of the due process clause of the Constitution (*Escalera*).

The courts' creative definitional role does not end with constitutional interpretation. Statutes enacted by Congress and the state legislatures, as well as regulations promulgated by state and federal administrative agencies, present interpretative questions similar to those raised by constitutional provisions. Because statutory language itself often is general and because every question cannot be anticipated before a statute is enacted, it is not always clear what a tenant's or homeowner's rights are in a particular situation. Sometimes the courts decide from facts as well as a prevailing sense of justice what the parties' rights and duties should be and then attribute to the legislature an intent to create those rights. An example of this is the courts' interpretation of the federal housing statutes as implicitly creating a right not to be evicted

from federally subsidized housing without good cause (*McQueen*). At other times, the courts' role is more confined—for instance, determining from the statutory language and legislative history who has what rights in a specific situation, which may or may not have been anticipated during the legislative process. Another way in which courts influence the development of rights in general and rights to housing in particular is to bring a certain injustice to the forefront and place other governmental institutions in a position to develop a solution that confers new rights. At times, the courts' role is merely to acknowledge that something is wrong and then assert that only the legislature, not the court, has the authority to resolve the problem. Several federal court decisions involving limitations on tenants' rights under the Uniform Relocation Act illustrate such a judicial role as well as the Congress' responsive role; these decisions eventually produced more expansive Congressional amendments to the statute. At other times, a court may act more affirmatively, either ordering a party to refrain from action that the court considers unlawful until the legislature or the executive develops a just set of rules, or contriving an initial solution on its own that either encourages or forces the legislature or the administration to develop a resolution. An example of this judicial role is provided by the New Jersey Supreme Court's various decisions in the *Mount Laurel* litigation, dealing with zoning laws that precluded development of low- and moderate-income housing (*Southern Burlington County N.A.A.C.P.* [1983]).

Beyond participating in the creation and development of housing rights, the courts also are crucial players in the process of ensuring that those rights have reality in people's lives. Enforcement of the law is universally recognized as within the province of the courts. They have the responsibility to be sure that laws are complied with; that violations are punished; that private individuals and entities as well as public officials and agencies are ordered to do what the law requires of them; and that people injured by a breach of the law are compensated for the damages they suffer.

Of course, one has to recognize that the courts alone do not have the capacity to guarantee that everyone's housing rights will be respected and that any denial of those rights will be redressed. The courts can act only when cases are brought to them. Even when matters are raised in the courts, judicial resources pale in comparison to the number of situations in which people's rights are infringed. The years that it takes to litigate a major housing case and the infinitesimal time that judges spend hearing each eviction case (Hartman and Robinson 2003) both testify to the courts' limited capacity to ensure that everyone's housing rights are realized.

Thus, full implementation of people's rights to housing obviously cannot depend on enforcement in court alone. In the vast majority of situations, there must be voluntary compliance by public officials and agencies, acting out of a sense of duty. There also must be voluntary compliance in most cases by private individuals and entities, either out of respect for other people's rights or from the deterrent effect of judicial enforcement and large damage awards in those cases the courts have the capacity to handle. Beyond voluntary compliance, there must be additional enforcement by nonjudicial institutions, such as housing code inspection agencies and administrative agencies that provide relief for Fair Housing Act violations. Finally, tenant organizations and neighborhood organizations have some power, through rent withholding, media attention and political pressure, to hold landlords, others in the housing industry and governmental officials accountable for meeting their responsibilities to provide decent housing in suitable neighborhoods. In conjunction with these efforts, courts carrying out their law enforcement function can and will play a significant role in making real a Right to Housing that they and other governmental institutions develop.

THE COURTS' ROLES REGARDING DIFFERENT ATTRIBUTES OF A RIGHT TO HOUSING

Having considered the various attributes of a Right to Housing, we now can consider what courts have done and can do with respect to each of those attributes.

Decent Physical Condition

Development of the implied warranty of habitability doctrine in the late 1960s and early 1970s is a good example of the courts' role in creating housing rights. Under the original common law rules, which were themselves created by the courts, absent a statute or agreement to the contrary, a landlord had no duty to provide or maintain property in habitable condition. Moreover, even if the landlord promised to do so and broke his promise, the tenant's obligation to pay rent would not be affected by the landlord's dereliction. The landlord's promise was considered independent of the tenant's promise to pay rent. The tenant could not withhold rent in response to the landlord's failure to maintain the premises; rather, the tenant would have to bring an independent action to enforce any promise made by the landlord.

Those original common law rules were based upon the social context in which they were developed—namely, an agrarian society in which the land that was the subject of a lease was the essential part of the transaction and any habitation on the land was incidental. In addition, the houses were simple, single-family structures that the tenants were capable of maintaining and repairing. The tenants lived on the land for long periods of time, often for their entire lives, and thus it made some sense for them to take responsibility for the residential structures on the land.

As society changed and most residential tenants came to live in urban areas, the land became an insignificant part of the transaction, and the dwelling structure became the essence of residential tenancies. In addition, the structures were transformed from simple, single-family dwellings with few amenities into modern, often multistoried, apartments with complicated electrical, plumbing and heating systems. As modern life became more specialized, fewer tenants had the skills necessary to accomplish even the repairs routinely performed by their agrarian ancestors; maintaining the housing was beyond the competence and financial capacity of most tenants. Furthermore, people came to recognize that bad housing conditions affected not only the residents of the housing but also neighbors and others. In these changed circumstances, a law that allowed landlords to lease housing that was in bad condition seemed undesirable.

In response to these societal changes, some legislatures imposed on landlords the obligation to place and maintain rental properties in decent condition. For many years, however, most courts interpreted such legislation as being enforceable only by government authorities, not by tenants. But when it became clear that government enforcement was not effective, courts created new legal rules that allowed tenants to enforce a duty on the landlord to provide habitable property and excused the tenant from the obligation to pay full rent when the landlord breached this duty. Many courts did this on their own, expressly acknowledging that they were performing their common law function of creating new legal rules to fit a new context, not merely leaving it to the legislature to create new rights and duties to fit changed circumstances (*Javins*; *Green*).

The courts did not create the implied warranty of habitability in every state. In some, the legislatures took the lead, enacting the tenants' right to habitable housing as well as the tenants' right to enforce that entitlement. Even in those states, however, development of the implied warranty of habitability by the courts in other jurisdictions as a matter of common law created a climate in which legislatures were more receptive to taking the same step by statutory changes.

It is important to recognize that this doctrine does not go further and oblige the government to warrant that everyone will have habitable housing. Indeed, the courts have not even agreed that when a government is a landlord it would be subject to an implied warranty of habitability that tenants could enforce (*Alexander*; *Conille*). This judicially created right to habitable housing works for people who have the money to rent. It does nothing, however, for people who are so poor that they cannot get a landlord to rent to them. It does not necessarily help people who rent from government agencies. And, in practice, it does little for poor people who are unable to afford the minimum amount of rent necessary to cover their landlords' costs of owning and maintaining housing in habitable condition. When such persons cannot pay that minimum rent level, the warranty of habitability leaves them with the choice of either no housing at all or settling for housing in undesirable condition. Only if the government were made subject to a duty to provide habitable housing for all who need it would people who cannot afford decent housing on their own have a true Right to Housing.

Beginning in the 1960s, the courts also developed a similar set of rules granting homeowners rights to well-constructed houses, judicially changing the previous common law that gave them no such rights. Indeed, this change with respect to homeownership was one basis for the decisions with respect to tenancies. Originally, the common law did not hold manufacturers of products liable for defects in their manufacture, and builders of houses enjoyed such immunity for a much longer time than did sellers of goods. However, the courts eventually recognized that the old laws did not make sense in the context of the modern construction and sale of houses. In doing so, they created for homebuyers a Right to Housing that is free of significant construction defects and a right to recover damages from the builders of defective housing (*Schipper*).[1] At least one court extended that right to allow recovery from a party other than the builder, such as the lender that provided the financing that made the development possible (*Connor*). In doing so, the Supreme Court of California rejected an argument that it should wait for the legislature to decide what the law should be and concluded that the court would have to determine the lender's duties in terms of common law, but the California legislature later specified that such lender liability should not be imposed in the future (*Aas*, n.12).

Here, again, the courts have created rights that work only for people who have sufficient income to purchase homes, not for everyone. The parties with duties corresponding to these housing rights are the builders and sometimes others, including lenders who finance the sales. But any person who does not have enough income to buy a house does not have these warranty rights. The courts have redefined the rights that homebuyers can expect from sellers, builders, developers and lenders. By limiting their focus to those parties and not looking at government's obligations toward other people, the courts have failed to create a right to decent housing that extends to people who are not homebuyers.

The courts have tackled issues concerning the obligations of the government to homebuyers when the government is involved in the sales transaction. In a 1961 case, a person who used a Federal Housing Administration (FHA)-insured mortgage to purchase a defectively constructed house sued the United States, alleging that the FHA inspector had been negligent when inspecting the property during construction. The U.S. Supreme Court decided that the homebuyer had no right to collect compensation from the government because the government was inspecting the construction to protect itself, not the homebuyer (*United States v. Neustadt*). Twenty years later, however, a person who purchased a home with a Farmers Home Administration (FmHA)[2] loan was able to secure compensation from the federal government because the home was carelessly inspected during the construction. In this case, the Court found a right to compensation because it concluded that Congress had intended that FmHA would protect the buyer's interest when inspecting the property (*Block*). In the intervening years, other courts had concluded that purchasers of homes with FHA mortgage insurance could secure injunctive relief when FHA had not met its obligation to ensure that the homes were in compliance with local codes (*Davis v. Romney*). In addition, when the U.S. Department of Housing and Urban Development (HUD) has sold defective houses that were acquired through foreclosure, courts have granted the buyers a right to collect damages from HUD (*City of Philadelphia*), holding that the implied warranty of habitability is breached by the sale of a house with hazardous lead-based paint.

In these cases, the courts are interpreting the federal housing statutes in a fashion that increases the homebuyers' rights to homes that are in decent condition. But the courts are not yet taking the next major step of saying that the government has a responsibility to ensure that everyone has a right to decent housing, even if he or she is not buying a home from the government or a government-inspected home. More-over, court decisions from the 1960s and 1970s will not necessarily be followed by the generally more conservative judges sitting in the early 21st century; even when decisions are from the U.S. Supreme Court, judges often will find ways to distinguish and therefore not follow the earlier holdings.

Even within the confines of the liability doctrines that courts have created, there are major limits on what the courts can accomplish. Many of the cases involving unsatisfactory conditions arise in the eviction context, either because the tenant has withheld rent in response to poor conditions or because the landlord is evicting in retaliation for the tenant's having complained to code enforcement authorities. Each eviction case, however, generally is decided by a court in a matter of minutes, not hours or days (Hartman and Robinson 2003). That leaves little time for assertion of the tenant's right to housing that is in decent condition, much less strict enforcement of that right. Furthermore, since tenants are not guaranteed legal representation and usually do not have any, poor tenants are even less able to enforce their rights in court (Community Training and Resource Center & City-Wide Task Force 1993; Scherer 1998). Moreover, if strict enforcement leads landlords to withdraw from the market because providing well-maintained housing to low-income people is not financially feasible, little has been achieved (Hartman, Kessler and LeGates 1974). New methods of enforcement must be devised and new theories of liability developed to impose responsibility on governmental entities capable of bearing the financial costs.

Newer theories have been used in the context of creating judicial oversight over public housing authorities (PHAs) that have violated their obligations to provide safe, decent, sanitary housing for low-income people. Courts have placed PHAs in receivership, thereby mandating the preservation of assets (housing developments and units) operated by the agencies (U.S. General Accounting Office 2003).

The receiver replaces the current management of the local PHA in order to facilitate improvements and to operate its programs. In the late 20th century, the courts ordered four judicial receiverships (*Velez, Perez, Tinsley, Pearson*). These receiverships resulted from lawsuits filed by public housing residents who were concerned with the poor condition of their housing. The PHAs placed in judicial receivership had allowed the housing to deteriorate, resulting in multiple vacancies and crime-ridden buildings.

There are no set guidelines for the duration of a receivership. Of the four judicial receiverships ordered by the courts, only two have been terminated (*Perez*; *Pearson*). The lack of defined standards has resulted in extended receivership periods. If the receivership has produced favorable results, residents are unlikely to ask the court to terminate the receivership.

Judicial receiverships have resulted in significant improvements in public housing units. Performance scores released by the General Accounting Office and HUD show that judicial receiverships averaged an 84 percent improvement over prior PHA performance from the entry into receivership to the last performance evaluation taken in 2002 (General Accounting Office 2003). For example, a decade after the inception of the receivership at the Housing Authority of Kansas City, Missouri, in 1993, most of its public housing units had been modernized or newly constructed, crime rates had dropped, and occupancy rates had increased significantly (General Accounting Office 2003:31; Luedtke 2002). When the Kansas City case initially was filed, the Housing Authority had a vacancy rate of 40 percent (*Tinsley*:1004). A decade later, its vacancy rate was 3 percent (Housing Authority of Kansas City, MO 2004).

Security of Tenure

The courts have played a major role in developing tenants' and homeowners' rights not to lose their homes for reasons beyond their control—that is, by encouraging security of tenure. Historically, landlords have had the power to evict tenants at the end of their leases or on 30 days' notice for month-to-month tenancies, without providing a reason. Under the common law, tenants had no guarantee that they would be able to keep their homes even if they kept their end of the bargain, by paying the stipulated rent on time and complying with all other provisions of the lease. The law gave the landlord the power to take the home back once the term of the ten-ancy expired or to terminate a periodic tenancy simply by giving proper notice.

The courts have developed three inroads into the doctrine that landlords can evict tenants without cause: protection against discriminatory eviction, protection against retaliatory eviction and protection for tenants who live in subsidized housing.

First, beginning in the early 1960s, courts developed a doctrine that prohibited evictions for various discriminatory reasons. In deciding those cases, courts concluded that even though the law did not require a landlord to have a good reason to evict a person, the law did prohibit eviction for a bad reason, such as registering to vote or racial discrimination (*United States v. Bruce*; *Abstract Inv. Co.*). (With some frequency, White landlords evicted Black tenants who attempted to register to vote and White tenants who had Black visitors.) Given the growing number of types of discrimination being made unlawful by local, state and federal legislatures, this exception to the landlord's common law power to evict without cause significantly increases the tenant's security of tenure.

Second, in the late 1960s and early 1970s, courts developed the retaliatory eviction defense, which prohibited a landlord from evicting a tenant if the reason for doing so was that the tenant had complained to housing code authorities about housing code violations (*Edwards*; *Schweiger*). Over time, courts expanded that defense to protect tenants against evictions and other prejudicial conduct, such as rent increases, imposed in retaliation for reporting housing code violations or other activities, such as organizing tenants or exercising rights protected by other laws, such as the federal Farm Labor Contracting Act (*Hosey*; *S. P. Growers*).

This defense creates two benefits for tenants. First, it assures them that they can engage in the protected activity—complaining about code violations or organizing other tenants—without being punished. Second, it strengthens their security that they will not lose their homes for arbitrary reasons.

When creating this defense, the courts looked at the housing code legislation and decided that tenants who complained should have the right not to be evicted for the complaint, as a matter of public policy and legislative interpretation, even though the legislation did not explicitly so provide. The following passage from one of the opinions is illustrative of the view that some courts took of their role:

> In trying to effect the will of Congress and as a court of equity, we have the responsibility to consider the social context in which our decisions will have operational effect. In light of the appalling conditions and shortage of housing in Washington DC, the expense of moving, the inequality of bargaining power between tenant and landlord, and the social and economic importance of assuring at least minimum standards in housing conditions, we do not hesitate to declare that retaliatory eviction cannot be tolerated. (*Edwards*:701)

After a number of courts had recognized the retaliation defense, many legislatures enacted the defense as well. Having recognized some exceptions to the general rule, the next step is for courts (and legislatures) to establish a new general rule—that landlords must have good cause for eviction, a doctrine that they could develop in the same way that they developed the implied warranty of habitability.[3]

Third, for tenants who live in federally subsidized housing, courts have provided a stronger guarantee of security of tenure than is available for others. Unlike tenants in unsubsidized housing, tenants in federally subsidized housing cannot be evicted from their homes unless they have breached their leases or their landlords have other good cause for eviction. This right to security of tenure was developed by the courts in the 1970s, virtually on their own, and not by Congress or the administrative agencies. In states with state or local subsidized housing programs, some state courts developed similar rights.

The case that started the doctrine was *Mc-Queen v. Druker*, decided in 1970. In that case, the landlord sought to evict a tenant in a federally subsidized building when the tenant's one-year lease expired; the landlord claimed that he did not have to offer any reason for doing so. The court rejected the landlord's claim, holding that the tenant had a right not to be evicted without good cause. The court reached this con-clusion after reviewing the National Housing Goal, declared by Congress in 1949, of "a decent home and a suitable living environment for every American family"; the purposes of the federal housing programs; the difficulty that an evicted tenant would have in securing alternative housing; the financial burdens and emotional injury of being forced to move; the injustice of a capricious eviction and the lack of any legitimate grounds for the subsidized landlord to expect that he could evict the tenants arbitrarily (*McQueen*; U.S. Congress 1949). Nothing in the statute at that time stated that tenants had a right to be protected from eviction except for good cause.

Four years later, another court went through a similar reasoning process and reached the same conclusion, stating that "[t]he federal government... hardly expected that a tenant could be evicted at the end of his term simply at the landlord's whim, when substitute housing could be obtained, if at all, only with delay, disruption in living habits and expense" (*Lopez*:948).

In defining this right of subsidized tenants not to be evicted without good cause, the courts looked to the purposes of the housing programs created by Congress and mentioned general statutory language that lent support to their conclusions. Ultimately, however, the courts granted tenants this right because of the courts' own appraisal of the facts and their own sense of justice. Later, in the late 1970s and the 1980s, the executive branch and eventually Congress followed the lead of the courts and enacted regulations (Code of Federal Regulations 2003, 24:247) and statutes (12 U.S.C. § 1715z-1b(b)(3); 42 U.S.C. § 1437f(d)(1)(B)(ii)) that similarly provided subsidized tenants with the right not to be evicted without cause. Without the courts' lead, however, it is unlikely, or at least uncertain, that such statutory rights ever would have been enacted.[4]

The courts have played a similar leading role for homeowners who have federally assisted mortgage loans by creating for them a right not to lose their homes when they default on their mortgages for reasons beyond their control. Both the FHA and the FmHA long have had statutory authority to protect homebuyers against foreclosure, but neither agency had exercised that authority before the courts intervened. For the FHA, the process began in 1973 with a case that came to be titled *Ferrell v. United States Dept. of Housing & Urban Dev.* In that case, the court was strongly affected by the injustice suffered by families who had temporarily fallen on hard times through no fault of their own and lost their homes through foreclosure by callous lenders. Those borrowers had received no assistance from HUD, despite HUD guidelines suggesting foreclosure avoidance in such cases. The court refused to dismiss the homeowners' claim that the 1949 Housing Act's National Housing Goal required HUD to create a system that would protect those homeowners against foreclosure when the defaults were for reasons beyond their control and there was a prospect for bringing the mortgages current. As with the good-cause-for-eviction cases, the court was willing to recognize such a right for the homeowners, not because Congress had expressly created it in a statute, but because the court's perception of justice warranted that result in light of the facts presented. A similar mortgage foreclosure avoidance system, called the moratorium program, was created for the Farmers Home Administration, again as a result of judicial prodding (*United States v. White*).[5]

State courts also have played a role in preventing mortgage foreclosures against persons undergoing financial hardship during difficult economic times. In *In Re: Order of Court Staying Sheriff Sales of Owner-Occupied Properties* (1983), a Pennsylvania state court, acting during a severe economic recession, stayed all sheriff sales involving mortgage foreclosures on owner-occupied properties in Philadelphia for almost a year until state legislative assistance was provided. With regard to these homeowners' rights to avoid arbitrary foreclosure, the courts have played an ongoing enforcement and redefinition role. Numerous times, the *Ferrell* court and other courts forced the FHA to live up to its responsibilities when it began to backslide. In addition, through a series of cases, the courts refined the definition of circumstances in which the owner has a right to avoid foreclosure. The result of this 30-year body of litigation has been that more than 140,000 families have kept their homes despite mortgage defaults.

Both the good-cause-for-eviction and foreclosure avoidance cases also demonstrate the fragility of some court-made law that creates housing rights. In 1996, Congress eliminated the good-cause-for-eviction requirement for decisions not to renew the leases of Section 8 certificate and voucher holders.[6] In that same year, HUD finally succeeded in securing legislation that overturned the mortgage assignment program created by the *Ferrell* litigation[7] (U.S. Congress 1996a; *Ferrell v. U.S. Dept. of Housing & Urban Dev.*). When courts create rights by determining what they deem Congress to have intended, Congress is free to come back later and revise the statutes to eliminate those rights.

The Right to Fair Treatment

Historically, courts have recognized the importance of people's homes, the sanctity of the privacy a home creates and the disastrous consequences of being deprived of one's home. As a result, courts have created rights designed to protect against the abuse of governmental or private power over people's homes.

Because of the judicially developed right to privacy, the Supreme Court has restrained the government's power to regulate what people do in their homes (*Lawrence; Stanley*).[8] It also has placed significant restrictions on the government's power to seize a home or to enter a home to search for evidence of a crime or to arrest its occupants (*Soldal; Payton*).[9] When the government seeks to exercise its power to seize homes that allegedly have been used for illegal purposes, the government must grant the residents prior notice and an opportunity to be heard (*United States v. James Daniel Good Real Property; Richmond Tenants Organization*).

In developing these rights connected to people's homes, the courts have been exercising their responsibility to give meaning to the Constitution. In doing so, they have accorded special significance to property that serves as a home, interpreting the Constitution to provide extra protections against governmental exercise of power when a home is involved.

For subsidized tenants, the courts developed the requirement that a governmental landlord could not take adverse action against a tenant without first providing the tenant notice of the proposed action and a chance to present her or his side of the story. Those rights were developed by the courts in different contexts, including evictions (*Escalera*); mortgage foreclosures (*United States v. White*); the imposition of extra charges for damages (*Chavez*); termination or reduction of subsidies (*Davis v. Mansfield Metropolitan Hous. Auth.*) and rent increases (*Geneva Towers Tenants Org.*). In each case, from the 1960s through the 1980s, time after time, the courts had to act first, interpreting the Constitution as guaranteeing tenants or homeowners a right to be heard in these situations. Only after the courts took the first steps did the responsible governmental agencies begin following the constitutional requirements.

Because being evicted from one's home may be the most devastating deprivation of property rights, since the early decades of the 20th century, the courts of many states have outlawed self-help evictions—that is, have determined that landlords have no right to evict a tenant without first going to court (*Jordan*; Hartman and Robinson 2003). In doing this, the courts were in part interpreting state statutes that created the judicial eviction processes. But, again, that interpretative process was not so much reading what the legislatures had literally written as appraising the relevant facts and applying the court's sense of justice, informed by experience, reason, the decisions of other courts and scholarship. Out of that process arose a right not to be evicted from one's home before being granted an opportunity to present one's side of the case to a court or other impartial decision-maker. With such a right, the landlord's power over the tenant was lessened and the chances for abuse reduced.

Freedom from Racial and Ethnic Discrimination

Discrimination against people because of their racial or ethnic background, including the slavery and conquest with which the discrimination began, is the one of the greatest ills of this country's history. That discrimination continues to operate throughout the housing market. It has involved landlords' refusal to rent to people because of their race or ethnicity; homeowners'

and brokers' refusal to sell; neighbors' violence designed to keep people of color out of white neighborhoods; city ordinances and restrictive covenants segregating neighborhoods by race; policies of lenders, FHA, FmHA, and the Veterans Administration (VA) not to lend or insure loans to people of color or in racially mixed neighborhoods; racial discrimination by private insurance companies; local governments' use of zoning and other powers to concentrate public and other governmentally assisted housing in nonwhite neighborhoods and the federal government's support of such actions; exclusion of people of color from any such housing located in white neighborhoods; preventing individuals with portable housing assistance from moving into white neighborhoods; and the provision of less adequate services in neighborhoods to which people of color are confined.

These discriminatory practices, and the residential segregation and unequal housing and neighborhood conditions they create, have by no means been eradicated from our society. In some aspects of American life—for example, use of commercial facilities, public services and transportation systems—racial discrimination has virtually been eliminated. Housing, however, is at the other end of the spectrum. We still have highly segregated neighborhoods (Massey and Denton 1993). People of color still encounter greater difficulties in renting and buying homes and in securing loans and homeowners' insurance (Turner et al. 2002). We still have concentrations of public and subsidized housing in minority neighborhoods, and it still is more difficult to develop assisted housing in white, middle-income neighborhoods. Individuals and families with housing assistance encounter neighborhood and local governmental opposition when they seek to use their subsidies in those same neighborhoods (Meyer 2000; Rubinowitz and Perry 2002). The neighborhoods where low-income people of color live have a greater incidence of substandard housing and generally are viewed as less desirable in terms of public and commercial services and security from crime.

In the development and enforcement of people's right to be free from discrimination in housing, courts have at best a mixed record. In the early part of the 20th century, the Supreme Court outlawed local ordinances that required residential segregation (*Buchanan*), and in the late 1940s, the Court outlawed judicial enforcement of racially restrictive covenants that often replaced the local ordinances (*Shelley*). As we have seen, lower courts sometimes prohibited hurtful conduct based on race (*Abstract Inv. Co.*). In 1968, the Supreme Court decided that the 1866 Civil Rights Act prohibited private owners from discriminating on racial grounds in the sale of real property, including homes, correcting earlier readings of that statute (*Jones*). But by the time of that decision, the Congress, having just passed the 1968 Fair Housing Act (U.S. Congress 1968), was also actively prohibiting such discrimination.

In the late 1960s and early 1970s, the lower federal courts, straightforwardly enforcing the Constitution and somewhat creatively interpreting a series of federal statutes, determined that discriminating in tenant assignment on the basis of race and concentrating public and assisted housing projects in racially segregated neighborhoods were unlawful activities (*Gautreaux*; see also *Shannon*). Those decisions led the other branches of the federal government to establish systems purportedly designed to avoid such concentrations in the future (Code of Federal Regulations 2003, 24:941.202; Tegeler 1994). However, given the sharp reduction in the development of subsidized housing soon thereafter, it is hardly clear whether the cases materially improved housing opportunities for people of color. To the extent that the cases or other initiatives did direct new development into areas not predominantly African-American, they also had the effect of reducing the chances that people of color could secure newly constructed or rehabilitated subsidized housing in the neighborhoods in which they were living, by choice or otherwise.

Another series of lower federal court decisions found local government efforts to exclude subsidized housing from white, middle-income neighborhoods to be both unconstitutional and unlawful under the Fair Housing Act (*Kennedy*; *Resident Advisory Board*). But, again, the decline in federal funding for production of assisted housing after 1973 reduced the effectiveness of these court cases in creating opportunities for people of color to live in subsidized housing in white, middle-income neighborhoods. The reduced effectiveness of the courts also was exacerbated by Supreme Court decisions confining constitutional challenges to intentional discrimination (as contrasted to claims that the Constitution prohibits governmental action that has the effect of treating groups differently, regardless of the government officials' intent) and limiting the standing of people to challenge housing discrimination (*Village of Arlington Heights*; *Washington*; *Warth*).

The courts have done little to create or enforce poor people's rights to live in a decent neighborhood, and the little they have done has been in the context of racial discrimination. In general, the litigation dealing with location has focused upon the rights of people to move into neighborhoods that are in decent condition, neighborhoods from which they have been excluded because of their race.

In the early 1970s, the Fifth Circuit decided a case challenging the failure of a Mississippi town to provide equal municipal services—streets, sidewalks and water and sewer systems—to the African-American part of the town (*Hawkins*). The court held that the failure violated the equal protection clause of the Constitution. This opened up the possibility of litigation to secure improved services and physical conditions in the long-neglected neighborhoods in which people of color were living. However, the Supreme Court soon thereafter established the principle that plaintiffs complaining about equal protection violations must prove that the government officials intended to deny them equal protection. In the process, the Court criticized the Fifth Circuit's *Hawkins* decision, along with others, for relying upon the effects of the officials' actions without determining whether those actions evidenced intentional racial discrimination (*Washington*:244 n.12). That put a damper on equalization of municipal services litigation.

Beginning in the 1980s, a second wave of cases was filed in many places, attacking the segregated and discriminatory fashion in which federal and local governments have operated public and assisted housing programs (*Young*; *Walker v. City of Mesquite*; *Comer*; *Hollman*;

Thompson; Sanders; Davis v. New York City Hous. Auth.; Langlois). The cases have challenged both the concentration of subsidized housing in minority neighborhoods and the exclusion from white jurisdictions of subsidized housing and people of color with housing assistance. The remedies include demolition of some assisted housing in minority neighborhoods, improvement of other developments in those neighborhoods and opening of opportunities for people of color with tenant-based assistance to move into white, middle-income neighborhoods (Roisman 1999).

In a Dallas case challenging the maintenance of a segregated subsidized housing system, part of the remedy sought and secured was a plan and funding to fix up a West Dallas neighborhood in which racially segregated public housing was concentrated (*Walker v. HUD* 1989, 1990; DHA Developments). The legal theory is that the remedy for the unlawful segregation must include the opportunity not only to live in a predominantly white or racially integrated neighborhood but also to have the neighborhood in which one lives brought up to a condition comparable to the neighborhoods from which one had been excluded.

At this point, it is not possible to determine whether this use of the courts will improve the overall opportunities of people of color to secure decent housing. In most of the cases, one result has been the demolition of some minority neighborhood housing that had served people of color, albeit poorly. In addition, the litigation certainly has contributed, along with other factors, to the federal government's decision to demolish 100,000 units of public housing located in minority neighborhoods, allegedly because the units are too deteriorated to salvage. On the other hand, these cases have committed the federal government and some local governments to much more aggressive use of the Section 8 voucher program to gain access to white, middle-income neighborhoods for low-income people of color, and some of the cases have required one-for-one replacement of the units that were demolished. Nonetheless, these cases sometimes have fueled hostility to the voucher program among elected officials, or at least to its use outside low-income neighborhoods.[10]

The significance of these litigation victories began to diminish as Congress reduced appropriations for HUD, shifted HUD's emphasis from new development to vouchers and transferred federal funding for subsidized housing development from HUD to the Treasury Department's Low Income Housing Tax Credit program. Several new forms of litigation have responded to those shifts.

First, in those states that have laws prohibiting landlords from discriminating against applicants with housing subsidies, there has been some litigation, generally successful, compelling landlords to accept voucher holders (*Commission on Human Rights & Opportunities; Franklin Tower One; Attorney General v. Brown;* but see *Knapp*).

Second, litigation has been aimed at creating a right for families subsidized with vouchers to live in any neighborhoods they choose (*Comer; Langlois; Wallace*). From 1974 through 1987, certificate holders had no portability rights, that is no right to take their certificates outside the municipalities served by the local housing authorities that issued them. Some litigation was brought against public housing agencies that refused to provide subsidies to applicants who were not already residents of their jurisdictions (*Comer; Langlois*). Although no litigation was brought challenging HUD's decision to allow PHAs to confine their subsidy holders to the PHAs' jurisdictions and to allow towns that did not wish to have subsidy holders to exclude them, Congress made the subsidies portable; thus, those structural barriers have been eliminated, but not because of court action.

Third, with respect to the Low Income Housing Tax Credit, litigation brought at the turn of the 21st century has invited the courts to prohibit racial discrimination in the operation of that program (*In Re: Adoption of the 2003 Low Income Housing Tax Credit Qualified Allocation Plan; Asylum Hill Problem Solving Assn.*).

Freedom from Discrimination on Bases Other than Race and Ethnicity

Regarding housing discrimination on grounds other than race, the courts have a mixed record with respect to the generosity with which they have interpreted the relevant statutes. The Supreme Court ruled favorably on challenges to local governments' efforts to keep out homes for people with disabilities and recovering alcoholics and addicts (*City of Cleburne; City of Edmonds*). The Court has, however, defined disability narrowly (*Sutton; Toyota Motor Mfg., Ky.*), and lower courts have divided about the breadth of the requirement of "reasonable accommodation" for persons with disabilities (*Salute; Giebeler*). The prohibition against discrimination on the basis of sex has been interpreted to include sexual harassment (*Beliveau*), but some courts have interpreted narrowly both that provision (*DiCenso*) and the prohibition against discrimination on the basis of familial status (*Mountain Side Mobile Home Estates P'ship*). With respect to all of these issues, the legislation leaves the courts flexibility of interpretation; how individual judges decide depends upon the facts of each case; the quality of the advocacy; and the intellectual, social, psychological and emotional background of the judges (Cardozo 1921).

The most crucial attribute of a Right to Housing, of course, is that the housing be within the person's financial means. Unfortunately, it is with respect to this attribute that the courts have contributed the least. In the 1970s, some people thought the courts might develop a Right to Housing as a matter of federal constitutional law (Michelman 1970; Black 1986). But a series of decisions, some involving housing and others of a more general nature, soon made it clear that, at least for the time being, the Supreme Court is not going to read the federal Constitution as guaranteeing poor people a right to governmental assistance that will bring decent housing within their financial means (*James* [housing]; *Lindsey* [housing]; *Dandridge* [welfare]; *Jefferson* [welfare]; *San Antonio Ind. School Dist.* [education]).

The courts generally have been willing to allow local governments to use their police powers, primarily zoning powers, to create and maintain middle- and upper-income neighborhoods that are well endowed with municipal services and facilities, in good physical condition, secure from crime and, most significantly, exclusive. Early in the 20th century,

the Supreme Court sustained local governments' zoning powers (*Village of Euclid*). In the 1970s, the Court upheld a locality's power to exclude unrelated individuals from neighborhoods zoned for single-family homes (*Village of Belle Terre*). The Supreme Court has been fairly hostile to cases challenging local governments' exclusion of subsidized housing from their borders or neighborhoods within them (*James; Warth; Village of Arlington Heights*), although greater success has been achieved in the lower courts (for example, *Metro. Hous. Dev. Corp.*).

A slightly less ambitious effort involved litigation filed in numerous states to have courts nullify local zoning laws that made the development of housing more expensive and thus within the financial means of fewer people (*Associated Home Builders; Appeal of Girsh*). There were sporadic successes in these efforts, the most well known of which is the *Mount Laurel* litigation in New Jersey (*Mount Laurel* Housing Symposium 1997). The *Mount Laurel* suit involved a challenge to zoning laws that effectively excluded housing for lower-income people, even those who already lived in the town. The challenge succeeded on the theory that the state's constitution required all zoning to be undertaken for the general welfare. That, in turn, obliged each municipality to afford a realistic opportunity for the construction of its fair share of housing for people with all levels of income within the region, including people of low and moderate incomes.

As the New Jersey Supreme Court explained subsequently, the *Mount Laurel* doctrine rests on the principle that the state and its municipalities cannot favor the rich over the poor. It cannot relegate the poor to dilapidated homes in the urban ghettoes and allow everyone else to secure decent housing elsewhere (*Southern Burlington County NAACP* [1983]:209). The court explained why it was taking responsibility for establishing this doctrine:

> We act first and foremost because the Constitution of our State requires protection of the interests involved and because the Legislature has not protected them. We recognize the social and economic controversy (and its political consequences) that has resulted in relatively little legislative action in this field. We understand the enormous difficulty achieving a political

consensus that might lead to significant legislation enforcing the constitutional mandate better than we can, legislation that might completely remove this Court from these controversies. But enforcement of constitutional rights cannot await political consensus. So while we have always preferred legislative to judicial action in the field, we shall continue—until the Legislature acts—to do our best to uphold the constitutional obligation that underlies the *Mount Laurel* doctrine. That is our duty. We may not build houses, but we do enforce the Constitution (*Southern Burlington County NAACP* [1983]:417)

The court's judgment required extensive ongoing enforcement. The court clarified that the localities' obligations reach beyond eliminating zoning restrictions that preclude the development of low-income housing, to include the obligation to facilitate developers' securing housing subsidies from other levels of government (*Southern Burlington County NAACP* [1983]:262–265). The court did not, however, create a duty on the local governments to provide the necessary subsidies.

The New Jersey Supreme Court's ruling subsequently was codified by the New Jersey legislature, and the resulting New Jersey Fair Housing Act has itself been subject to ongoing interpretation and enforcement in the courts (*Bi-County Dev. of Clinton, Inc.*; *Toll Bros., Inc.*).

A principle analogous to that of *Mount Laurel* has been adopted by the New Hampshire Supreme Court (*Britton*) and by a number of state and local legislatures (Roisman 2001:71; Symposium 2001). Court interpretation of the state and local legislation has been essential to securing broad application and effective implementation of the legislation (*Zoning Bd. of Appeals of Wellesley*; *Board of Appeals [Hanover]*).

In other litigation involving economic discrimination, beginning in the late 1980s, a series of cases was brought by homeless people asking the state courts to interpret a variety of state laws, as well as some federal welfare legislation, as imposing a duty on state governments to ensure that everyone, no matter how indigent, has a place to live so that there would in effect be a Right to Housing in this country (Roisman 1990, 1991; Harris 2004). The laws in question include state statutory and constitutional provisions for general assistance for the

poor, protections for people who are homeless, statutes regarding care of foster children and the federal and state statutes governing the former Aid to Families with Dependent Children and emergency assistance programs. Several favorable decisions were secured, including one that required the state to set the shelter component of welfare grants at a level that would make decent housing affordable (*Jiggetts v. Grinker*; see also *McCain*; *Hanson*; *Massachusetts Coalition for the Homeless*). Although Congress eliminated the federal entitlement to aid for families with dependent children, state cases can and sometimes do continue to provide relief (*Jiggetts v. Dowling*).

When Congress has enacted statutes that bring decent housing within the means of poor people, the courts have been fairly effective in ensuring that the rights created by those statutes are enforced. When governmental landlords have sought to limit poor people's access to housing subsidies, the courts have kept them from doing so (*Fletcher*; *Gholston*). When public and private subsidized landlords have tried to charge more for rent than is allowable, the courts again have stepped in with protection (*Wright*; *Barber*). When the federal government refused to implement subsidy programs that would make housing more affordable to poor people, the courts again ordered the government to meet its obligations (*Abrams*). In this supportive role, courts can and do ensure that at least some people have a Right to Housing within their means.

The Courts' Role in the Future

As the preceding review has shown, the courts have played an important role in laying the groundwork for elements of a Right to Housing. The right has been recognized by international bodies (United Nations 1948, 1976; Craven 2003; Leckie 2003), and Congress in 1949 declared the National Housing Goal to be "the realization as soon as feasible…of a decent home and a suitable living environment for every American family" (U.S. Congress 1949). Given this background, it is not unreasonable to anticipate that eventually the United States will make the judgment that everyone is entitled to a decent home and that the societal judgment will become embodied in a constitutional amendment or a statutory enactment. If that happens, the courts will have a significant role to play in the further development, implementation and realization of that Right to Housing.

The courts will have extensive responsibility to work out the details of what such a right means. Part of that responsibility will focus upon the obligations of the providers of housing—the landlords, the developers and the financiers. In developing the common law of real property (a quintessential function of the judiciary), the courts, relying upon the constitutional or statutory Right to Housing, are likely to adjust the rights of landlords and tenants so as to require good cause for all evictions, not only evictions from some subsidized housing, and thus create greater security of tenure. It also is likely that the courts would further develop the right to habitable conditions in both rental and sales housing, as a matter of common law and interpretation of the new Right to Housing.

Another part of the development and implementation of a Right to Housing will concern the obligations of governments, local, state and federal. For example, litigation might eventually establish municipal liability for poor housing conditions. In cases where a city has cut back on code enforcement, which has happened in many cities with the shrinkage of municipal resources, one could ask courts to intervene to make code enforcement effective. The first step would be to ask the court to order the code enforcement agency to perform its statutory duties. If necessary, one could ask that the agencies be placed into receivership, as has been done with housing authorities, school districts and jails.

Because strict code enforcement can drive up the costs of housing beyond the reach of poor people (Hartman, Kessler and LeGates 1974), it would be valuable to use the government's past failure to enforce the codes so as to establish municipal responsibility to fund needed repairs. If it becomes impossible to secure funding from the local government in that fashion, one would have to be careful to combine the litigation strategy with a plan to secure funds in other ways, possibly from the city's Community Development Block Grant program or from the state. That would lessen the risk that strict code enforcement would displace poor people from

their homes. Coordinating the litigation with the efforts of community-based nonprofits to acquire deteriorated buildings and repair them would also guard against displacement. Relying upon a constitutional or statutory declaration of a Right to Housing could help lead to the imposition of financial liability upon local, state or federal governments.

From a constitutional Right to Housing, the courts also may develop local governmental responsibility to ensure security from crime. The provider of housing may have certain responsibilities regarding security—for example, installing and maintaining adequate locks and lighting—but landlords' and developers' ability to protect residents from criminal activities is limited. Courts interpreting a constitutional Right to Housing would eventually have to decide what obligations a local government must assume in that regard.

A similar analytical process would be undertaken with respect to other neighborhood conditions. As attributes of a Right to Housing that relate to location work their way through the judicial system, there will be details regarding local governments' obligations to ensure adequate municipal services, insulation from environmental hazards and accessibility to commercial and professional facilities. New life may be breathed into the original equalization of municipal services cases.

More work also will be done on the remedies for those local governments and public housing authorities that have operated racially segregated housing systems since the 1930s. Strategies need to be developed, now that the federal government is putting so much effort into tearing down large components of those systems, to impose liability upon the government agencies involved to replace the demolished units with decent, affordable housing that is made available to the individuals and groups that have suffered the discrimination in the past.

It also may be possible to expand the bases for governmental liability beyond their having operated segregated public and assisted housing programs. Many other governmental actions have contributed to racial segregation in housing and the unequal neighborhood conditions that people of color have suffered and are still suffering. One example is stimulation of the development of virtually all-white suburban neighborhoods of single-family homes with racially restricted FHA and VA mortgage insurance and guarantees, the funding of highways and other commuter transportation systems and the maintenance of the federal and state mortgage interest deductions and other tax deductions that made homeownership affordable to the white middle class. Another is government choice to locate highways, industry, waste disposal facilities and other uses with deleterious consequences in or near neighborhoods where people of color live, while withholding from such neighborhoods the services and funding that they need to be equally decent places to live (see *South Camden Citizens in Action*). A third is the use of state governmental power to establish separate local governments with their own taxing and spending powers that enable the more wealthy, predominantly white communities to achieve residential environments that are in better physical condition, more secure from crime, better served by governmental agencies, more endowed with commercial facilities and, of course, served by better schools. Litigation based upon these theories would be ambitious to say the least, but achieving a Right to Housing that includes freedom from discrimination will add strength to the litigation theories.

Perhaps the most important attribute of a Right to Housing will be the provision of financial assistance to low-income people by the government. Important, and likely necessary, steps can be taken to restrain housing costs and to make the provision of housing more efficient and thus less expensive. Ultimately, however, a government will have to step in to fill the gap between what poor people can afford and what decent housing costs. The major role with regard to those financial responsibilities will be that of the legislatures—that is, appropriating the funds and designing effective housing assistance programs. But, as the experience with current housing programs demonstrates, the courts also will have to become actively involved. They will have the responsibility to hold the legislature accountable for performance of its constitutional and statutory duties and to interpret the resulting legislative guarantees of affordability in particular situations. The courts also will have

the responsibility of deciding whether legislative determinations are consistent with constitutional provisions, particularly the due process and takings clauses, which protect against deprivation of property without due process of law and against takings save for public use and with just compensation (Smizik and Stone 1988; Budlender 2003).

Interpreting either the federal or state constitutions early in the 21st century, the courts also may establish that tenants cannot be evicted by state courts unless they are represented by counsel, including appointed counsel for indigent tenants. In doing so, the courts would be building on the 20th century doctrine they established that tenants cannot be evicted without court proceedings. The strongest cases would be those in which governmental landlords, such as public housing authorities, are seeking evictions. Then a favorable ruling could eventually be carried over to other landlords, on the grounds that use of the state courts for eviction constitutes sufficient governmental action to bring the due process clause into play. Eventually, the doctrine might be extended to low-income homeowners facing foreclosure of their mortgages.

If such rights were established, tenants and homeowners would be much better able to enforce their housing rights. They would be better able to defend against unlawful evictions, whether these were retaliatory, discriminatory or otherwise unlawful. If a right not to be evicted without cause were to be established, it could be enforced much more effectively if the tenants were guaranteed legal representation. Tenants could more effectively enforce the warranty of habitability if counsel were available to raise breach of the warranty as a defense to evictions for nonpayment of rent. Homeowners could more effectively resist foreclosure in cases where the defaults are beyond their control and alternatives to foreclosure are available. Judicial establishment of a right to counsel in housing cases would be crucial to full realization of any constitutional or statutory Right to Housing.

Until society reaches the judgment that there is a Right to Housing, the courts will have many steps to take regarding people's housing rights. If nothing else, the courts will be called upon to preserve various aspects of a Right to Housing in the near future, especially if Congress continues to step back from its previous activism in developing housing rights (*Ferrell*). Once the other branches of government declare a Right to Housing, the courts will have a major, if not the primary, responsibility to make that declaration a reality.

NOTES

1. Some state legislatures now have codified warranty benefits for homebuyers, often following judicial creation of such warranties (e.g., Indiana Code 32-27-2).

2. The Farmers Home Administration, an agency within the U.S. Department of Agriculture, has been renamed the Rural Housing Service.

3. A few local and state legislatures have imposed a requirement of good cause for evictions, usually in connection with rent control legislation (e.g., N.J. Stat. Ann. 2A:18-61.1; see *447 Associates*; *Bullard*). It is likely that the court decisions played a role in helping legislators feel comfortable about enacting such protections.

4. For a recent illustration of a court's playing this role with respect to newer programs, see *Carter*.

5. Unfortunately, however, the courts have rejected efforts to impose a similar foreclosure-avoidance program on the Department of Veterans Affairs (*Rank*).

6. The requirement of good cause at the expiration of a voucher lease was first suspended in 1996 (U.S. Congress 1996b). The suspension continued for two more years, until Congress eliminated the requirement in 1998 (U.S. Congress 1998).

7. The federal legislation did authorize a substitute "loss mitigation" program (*Ferrell v. U.S. Dept. of Hous. & Urban Dev.*). In Pennsylvania, the Homeowner's Emergency Mortgage Assistance Program (HEMAP), 35 P.S. Sec. 1680.401c, continues to assist homeowners faced with mortgage foreclosure. The program, created in 1983, was modeled after the HUD Mortgage Assignment Program and has broad-based support in Pennsylvania.

8. While *Lawrence v. Texas*, decided by the U.S. Supreme Court in 2003, restricted the ability of government to regulate sexual conduct in the home, a 2002 Supreme Court decision extended the government's power of regulation over allegedly criminal conduct even of guests of public housing residents (*Dept. of Hous. & Urban Dev. v. Rucker*).

9. The Supreme Court has, however, allowed what it considers "reasonable" home visits for public assistance purposes (*Wyman*).

10. [Ed.: When David was alive, he and I very much disagreed about the wisdom and utility of the housing desegregation cases, and I have had particular difficulty speculating about what I might have persuaded him to change in this and the previous sentence. Unable to resolve the difficulty, I have left these two sentences just as David wrote them and will make my points in this footnote. I do not think anyone knows whether or to what extent the desegregation cases contributed to the decision to demolish hundreds of thousands of public housing units. With respect to replacement of demolished units, it is the fact that litigation that contemplated demolition often also required one-for-replacement, even when there was no statutory requirement for such replacement. See, for example, *Walker v .HUD* (1990). It is also the fact that the one-for-one replacement requirement that Congress created in 1990 was eliminated by Congress in 1995 and 1996 (*Henry Horner Mothers Guild*; *Reese*; National Housing Law Project et al. 2002)].

REFERENCES

Aas v. The Superior Court of San Diego County, 24 Cal. 4th 627, 12 P.3d 1125 (2000).

Abrams v. Hills, 547 F.2d 1062 (9th Cir. 1976), *vacated and remanded after settlement*, 455 U.S. 1010 (1982).

Abstract Inv. Co. v. Hutchinson, 204 Cal. App. 2d 242, 22 Cal. Rptr. 309 (Cal. Ct. App. 1962).

Alexander v. U.S. Dept. of Housing & Urban Dev., 555 F.2d 166 (7th Cir. 1977), *aff'd on other grounds*, 441 U.S. 39 (1979).

Appeal of Girsh, 437 Pa. 237, 263 A.2d 395 (1970).

Associated Home Builders v. City of Livermore, 18 Cal. 3d 582, 557 P.2d 473 (1976).

Asylum Hill Problem Solving Revitalization Assn. v. King, 2004 Conn. Super. LEXIS 27 (Conn. Super. Ct. 2004).

Attorney General v. Brown, 400 Mass. 826, 511 N.E.2d 1103 (1987).

Barber v. White, 351 F. Supp. 1091 (D. Conn. 1972).

Beliveau v. Caras, 873 F. Supp. 1393 (C.D. Cal. 1995).

Bi-County Dev. of Clinton, Inc. v. Borough of High Bridge, 174 N.J. 301, 805 A.2d 433 (2002).

Black, Charles L., Jr. 1986. Further reflections on the constitutional justice of livelihood. *Columbia Law Rev.*, 86:1103.

Block v. Neal, 460 U.S. 289 (1983).

Board of Appeals (Hanover) v. Hous. Appeals Comm., 363 Mass. 339, 294 N.E.2d 393 (1973).

Britton v. Town of Chester, 134 N.H. 434, 595 A.2d 492 (1991).

Buchanan v. Warley, 245 U.S. 60 (1917).

Budlender, Geoff. 2003. Justiciability of the right to housing—the South African experience. In

National Perspectives on Housing Rights, ed. Scott Leckie, 207–219. The Hague: Martinus Nijhoff Publishers.

Bullard v. San Francisco Residential Rent Stabilization Bd., 106 Cal. App. 4th 488, 130 Cal. Rptr. 2d 819 (Cal. Ct. App. 2003).

Cardozo, Benjamin N. 1921. *The Nature of the Judicial Process.* New Haven: Yale University Press.

Carter v. Maryland Management Co., 377 Md. 596, 835 A.2d 158 (MD 2003).

Chavez v. Santa Fe Hous. Auth., 606 F.2d 282 (10th Cir. 1979).

City of Cleburne v. Cleburne Living Center, 473 U.S. 432 (1985).

City of Edmonds v. Oxford House, Inc., 514 U.S. 725 (1995).

City of Philadelphia v. Page, 363 F. Supp. 148 (E.D. Pa. 1973), *subsequent opinion*, 373 F. Supp. 453 (E.D. Pa. 1974).

Code of Federal Regulations, Title 24, Section 247 (2003).

Code of Federal Regulations, Title 24, Section 941.202 (2003).

Comer v. Cisneros, 37 F.3d 775 (2d Cir. 1994).

Commission on Human Rights & Opportunities v. Sullivan Assoc., 250 Conn. 763, 739 A.2d 238 (1999).

Community Training and Resource Center & City-Wide Task Force on Housing Court, Inc. 1993. *Housing court, evictions and homelessness: The costs and benefits of establishing a right to counsel.* New York: CTRC & CWTFHC.

Conille v. Secretary of Hous. & Urban Dev., 840 F.2d 105 (1st Cir. 1988).

Connor v. Great Western Savings and Loan Ass'n, 69 Cal.2d 850, 447 P.2d 609 (1968).

Craven, Matthew. 2003. History, pre-history and the right to housing in international law. In *National Perspectives on Housing Rights*, ed. Scott Leckie, 43–61. The Hague: Martinus Nijhoff Publishers.

Dandridge v. Williams, 397 U.S. 471 (1970).

Davis v. Mansfield Metropolitan Hous. Auth., 751 F.2d 180 (6th Cir. 1984).

Davis v. New York City Hous. Auth., 278 F.3d 64 (2d Cir. 2002), *cert. denied*, 536 U.S. 904 (2002).

Davis v. Romney, 490 F.2d 1360 (3d Cir. 1974).

Dept. of Hous. and Urban Dev. v. Rucker, 535 U.S. 125 (2002).

DHA [Dallas Housing Auth.] Developments, (10/29/03). http://www.dallashousing.org/Develop ments.htm

DiCenso v. Cisneros, 96 F.3d 1004 (7th Cir. 1996).

Edwards v. Habib, 397 F.2d 687 (D.C. Cir. 1968), *cert. denied*, 393 U.S. 1016 (1969).

Escalera v. New York City Hous. Auth., 425 F.2d 853 (2d Cir. 1970), *cert. denied*, 400 U.S. 853 (1970).

Ferrell v. Pierce, 560 F. Supp. 1344 (N.D. Ill. 1983), *aff'd*, 743 F.2d 454 (7th Cir. 1984).

Ferrell v. U.S. Dept. of Hous. & Urban Dev., 2002 U.S. Dist. LEXIS 16156 (N.D. Ill. 2002). Original opinion sub nom. *Brown v. Lynn*, 385 F. Supp. 986 (N.D. Ill. 1974).

Fletcher v. Hous. Auth. of Louisville, 491 F.2d 793 (6th Cir. 1974).

447 Associates v. Miranda, 115 N.J. 522, 559 A.2d 1362 (1989).

Franklin Tower One v. N.M., 157 N.J. 602, 725 A.2d 1104 (1999).

Gautreaux v. Chicago Hous. Auth., 296 F.Supp. 907 (N.D. Ill. 1969), *subsequent opinion*, *Hills v. Gautreaux*, 425 U.S. 285 (1976).

Geneva Towers Tenants Org. v. Federated Mortgage Investors, 504 F.2d 483 (9th Cir. 1974).

Gholston v. Hous. Auth. of Montgomery, 818 F.2d 776 (11th Cir. 1987).

Giebeler v. M&B Associates, 343 F.3d 1143 (9th Cir. 2002).

Green v. Superior Court of San Francisco, 10 Cal. 3d 616, 517 P.2d 1168 (1974).

Hanson v. Dept. of Social Services, 193 Cal. App. 3d 283, 238 Cal. Rptr. 232 (Cal. Ct. App. 1987).

Harris, Beth. 2004. *Defending the Right to a Home: The Power of Anti-poverty Lawyers.* Altershot, U.K.: Dartmouth Publishing Co., Ashgate Publishing Ltd.

Hartman, Chester, Robert Kessler and Richard LeGates. 1974. Municipal housing code enforcement and low-income tenants. *Journal of the American Institute of Planners*, 40:90–104.

Hartman, Chester, and David Robinson. 2003. Evictions: The hidden housing problem. *Housing Policy Debate*, 14(1): 461–501.

Hawkins v. Town of Shaw, 437 F.2d 1286 (5th Cir. 1971), *aff'd on rehearing en banc*, 461 F.2d 1171 (5th Cir. 1972).

Henry Horner Mothers Guild v. Chicago Hous. Auth., 1998 U.S. Dist. LEXIS 2688 (N.D. Ill. 1998).

Hollman v. Martinez, 2002 U.S. Dist. LEXIS 16106 (D. Minn. 2002).

Hosey v. Club Van Courtland, 299 F. Supp. 501 (S.D.N.Y. 1969).

Housing Authority of Kansas City, MO, Authority Operation Depart. 2004, March.

Indiana Code § 32-27-2. Chapter 2. (New Home Construction Warranties.)

In Re: Order of Court Staying Sheriff Sales of Owner-Occupied Properties (PA Court of Common Pleas, Jan. Term, 1983, No. 3414).

In Re: Adoption of the 2003 Low Income Housing Tax Credit Qualified Allocation Plan, 182 N.J. 141, 861 A.d 846 (2004).

James v. Valtierra, 402 U.S. 137 (1971).

Javins v. First National Realty Corp., 428 F.2d 1071 (D.C. Cir. 1970), *cert. denied*, 400 U.S. 925 (1970).

Jefferson v. Hackney, 406 U.S. 535 (1972).

Jiggetts v. Dowling, 196 Misc.2d 678, 765 N.Y.S.2d 731(N.Y. Sup. Ct. 2003).

Jiggetts v. Grinker, 75 N.Y.2d 411, 554 N.Y.S.2d 92, 553 N.E.2d 570 (1990).

Jones v. Mayer, 392 U.S. 409 (1968).

Jordan v. Talbot, 55 Cal.2d 597, 361 P.2d 20 (1961).

Kennedy v. City of Lackawanna, 436 F.2d 108 (2d Cir. 1970).

Knapp v. Eagle Property Mgmt. Corp., 54 F.3d 1272 (7th Cir. 1995).

Langlois v. Abington Hous. Auth., 207 F.3d 43 (1st Cir. 2000) *on remand*, 234 F.Supp.2d 33 (D. Mass. 2002).

Lawrence v. Texas, 539 U.S. 558 (2003).

Leckie, Scott. 2003. Where it matters most: Making international housing rights meaningful at the national level. In *National Perspectives on Housing Rights*, ed. Scott Leckie, 3–41. The Hague: Martinus Nijhoff Publishers.

Lindsey v. Normet, 405 U.S. 56 (1972).

Lopez v. Henry Phipps Plaza South, Inc., 498 F.2d 937 (2d Cir. 1974).

Luedtke, Carolyn Hoecker. 2002. Innovation or illegitimacy: Remedial receivership in *Tinsley v. Kemp* public housing litigation. *Missouri Law Review*, 65:655–706.

Massachusetts Coalition for the Homeless v. Sec'y of Human Serv., 400 Mass. 806, 511 N.E.2d 603 (1987).

Massey, Douglas S., and Nancy A. Denton. 1993. *American Apartheid: Segregation and the Making of the Underclass*. Cambridge, MA: Harvard University Press.

McCain v. Koch, 117 A.D.2d 198, 502 N.Y.S.2d 720, *aff'd on other grounds*, 70 N.Y.2d 109, 511 N.E.2d 62, 517 N.Y.S.2d 918 (1987).

McQueen v. Druker, 317 F. Supp. 1122 (D. Mass. 1970), *aff'd*, 438 F.2d 781 (1st Cir. 1971).

Metro. Hous. Dev. Corp. v. Village of Arlington Heights, 558 F.2d 1283 (7th Cir. 1977), *cert. denied*, 434 U.S. 1025 (1978).

Meyer, Stephen Grant. 2000. *As Long as They Don't Move Next Door: Segregation and Racial Conflict in American Neighborhoods*. Lanham, MD: Rowman & Littlefield.

Michelman, Frank I. 1970. The advent of a right to housing: A current appraisal. *Harvard Civil Rights–Civil Liberties Law Review*, 5:207–226.

Mountain Side Mobile Home Estates P'ship v. HUD, 56 F.3d 1243 (10th Cir. 1995).

Mount Laurel Housing Symposium. 1997. *Seton Hall L. Rev.*, 27:1268–1496.

National Housing Law Project, Poverty & Race Research Action Council, Sherwood Research Associates & Everywhere and Now Public Housing

Residents Organizing Nationally Together (EN-PHRONT). 2002. *False HOPE: A critical assessment of the HOPE VI public housing redevelopment program*. Oakland, CA: National Housing Law Project.

N. J. Stat. Ann. § 2A:18-61.1 (2004) (Anti-Eviction Act).

Payton v. United States, 445 U.S. 573 (1980).

Pearson v. Kelly, No. 94-CA-14030 (D.C. Super. Ct. 1994).

Perez v. Boston Hous. Auth., 379 Mass. 703, 400 N.E.2d 1231 (1980).

Rank v. Nimmo, 677 F.2d 692 (9th Cir. 1982), *cert. denied*, 459 U.S. 907 (1982).

Reese v. Miami-Dade County, 242 F. Supp. 2d 1292 (S.D. Fla. 2002).

Resident Advisory Board v. Rizzo, 564 F.2d 126 (3d Cir. 1977), *cert. denied*, 435 U.S. 908 (1978).

Richmond Tenants Organization v. Kemp, 956 F.2d 1300 (4th Cir. 1992).

Roisman, Florence Wagman. 1990. Establishing a Right to Housing: An advocate's guide. *Housing Law Bulletin*, 20:39–48, 65–78, 107–119.

———. Establishing a Right to Housing: A general guide. *Clearinghouse Review*, 25:203–226.

———. 1999. Long overdue: Desegregation litigation and next steps to end discrimination and segregation in the public housing and Section 8 existing housing programs. *Cityscape*, 4:171–196.

———. 2001. Opening the suburbs to racial integration: Lessons for the 21st century. *Western New England Law Review*, 23:65–113.

Rubinowitz, Leonard S., and Imani Perry. 2002. Crimes without punishment: White neighbors' resistance to black entry. *Journal of Criminal Law and Criminology*, 92:335–428.

Salute v. Stratford Greens Garden Apartments, 136 F.3d 293 (2d Cir. 1998).

San Antonio Ind. School Dist. v. Rodriguez, 411 U.S. 1 (1973).

Sanders v. HUD, 872 F. Supp. 216 (W. D. Penn. 1994); *subsequent proceedings, Township of South Fayette v. Allegheny County Hous. Auth.*, 27 F. Supp. 2d 582 (W. D. Penn. 1998).

Scherer, Andrew. 1988. Gideon's shelter: The need to recognize a right to counsel for indigent defendants in eviction proceedings. *Harvard Civil Rights–Civil Liberties Law Review*, 23:557–592.

Schipper v. Levitt & Sons, Inc., 44 N.J. 70, 207 A.2d 314 (1965).

Schweiger v. Superior Court of Alameda County, 3 Cal. 3d 507, 476 P.2d 97 (1970).

Shannon v. Romney, 436 F.2d 809 (3d Cir. 1970).

Shelley v. Kraemer, 334 U.S. 1 (1947).

Smizik, Frank I., and Michael E. Stone. 1988. Single-parent families and a right to housing. In *Women as Single Parents: Confronting Institutional Barriers in the Courts, the Workplace, and the Housing Market,* ed. Elizabeth A. Mulroy, 227–270. Westport, CT: Auburn House.

Soldal v. Cook County, 506 U.S. 56 (1992).

South Camden Citizens in Action v. New Jersey Dep't. of Envtl. Prot., 2003 U.S. Dist. LEXIS 6320 (D. N.J. 2003).

Southern Burlington County NAACP v. Mount Laurel, 67 N.J. 151, 336 A.2d 713 (1975); *subsequent opinion,* 92 N.J. 158, 456 A.2d 390 (1983).

S. P. Growers v. Rodriguez, 17 Cal. 3d 719, 552 P.2d 721 (1976).

Stanley v. Georgia, 394 U.S. 557 (1969).

Sutton v. United Airlines, 527 U.S. 471 (1999).

Symposium. 2001. *Western New England Law Review,* 1–307.

Tegeler, Philip D. 1994. Housing segregation and local discretion. *Journal of Law and Policy,* 3:209–236.

Thompson v. HUD, 220 F.3d 241 (4th Cir. 2000); *subsequent opinion,* 404 F.3d 821 (4th Cir. 2005).

Tinsley v. Kemp, 750 F. Supp. 1001 (W.D. Mo. 1990).

Toll Bros., Inc. v. Township of West Windsor, 173 N.J. 502, 803 A.2d 53 (2002).

Township of South Fayette v. Allegheny County Hous. Auth., 27 F. Supp.2d 582 (W.D. Penn. 1998).

Toyota Motor Mfg., Ky. v. Williams, 534 U.S. 184 (2002).

Turner, Marjorie, Stephan L. Ross, George Galster, John Yinger. 2002. Discrimination in metropolitan housing markets: National results from Phase I HDS 2000: Final report. Washington, DC: The Urban Institute.

United Nations Universal Declaration of Human Rights, G.A. Res. 71, U.N. GABOR, 3d Sess., U.N. Doc. A/810, art. 25 (1948).

———. 1976. International Covenant on Economic, Social and Cultural Rights, U.N. G.A. Res. 2200(A), 21 U.N. GABOR Supp. (No. 16) at 49, U.N. Doc. A/6316 (1966), 993 U.N.T.S. 3; *entered into force* Jan. 3, 1976.

U.S. Congress 1949. Housing Act of 1949, Pub. L. No. 81-717, § 2, 63 Stat. 413, codified as amended at 42 U.S.C. § 1441 (2000); Housing Act of 1968, Pub.L. No. 90-448, § 1601, 82 Stat. 601, codified as amended at 42 U.S.C. § 1441a (2000).

———. 1968. Fair Housing Act, Pub. L. No. 90-284, Title VIII, 82 Stat. 81, codified as amended at 42 U.S.C. § 3601 et seq.

———. 1978. Act of Oct. 31, 1978, Pub. L. No. 95-557, § 202(b)(3), 92 Stat. 2088, codified as amended at 12 U.S.C. § 1715z-1(b) (2000).

———. 1981. Omnibus Budget Reconciliation Act of 1981, Pub. L. No. 97-35, § 326(e)(1)(B)(ii), 95 Stat. 407, codified as amended at 42 U.S.C. § 1437f(d)(1)(B) (2000)..

———. 1996a. Balanced Budget Downpayment Act, Pub. L. No. 104-99, § 407, 110 Stat. 26, codified as amended at 12 U.S.C. § 1715u (2000).

———. 1996b. Omnibus Consolidated Rescissions and Appropriations Act of 1996, Pub. L. No. 104-134, § 281, 110 Stat. 1321, codified as amended at 42 U.S.C. § 1437p (2000).

———. 1998. Act of Oct. 21, 1998, Pub. L. No. 105-276, § 549(a)(2)(A), 112 Stat. 2607, codified as amended at 42 U.S.C. § 1437f(d)(1)(B)(ii) (2000).

U.S. General Accounting Office. 2003. *Public housing: Information on receiverships at public housing authorities.* GAO-03-363, February.

United States v. Bruce, 353 F.2d 474 (5th Cir. 1965).

United States v. James Daniel Good Real Property, 510 U.S. 43 (1993).

United States v. Neustadt, 366 U.S. 696 (1961).

United States v. White, 429 F. Supp. 1245 (N.D. Miss. 1977); *on remand from* 543 F.2d 1139 (5th Cir. 1976).

Velez v. Cisneros, 850 F. Supp. 1257 (E.D. Pa. 1994).

Village of Arlington Heights v. Metro. Hous. Dev. Corp., 429 U.S. 252 (1977).

Village of Belle Terre v. Boraas, 416 U.S. 1 (1974).

Village of Euclid v. Ambler Realty, 272 U.S. 365 (1926).

Walker v. HUD, 734 F. Supp. 1289 (N.D. Tex. 1989); *subsequent opinion at* 912 F.2d 819 (5th Cir. 1990); *Walker v. City of Mesquite,* 169 F.3d 973 (5th Cir. 1999), *cert. denied,* 528 U.S. 1131 (2000).

Wallace v. Chicago Hous. Auth. 298 F.Supp.2d 710 (N.D. Ill. 2003); *subsequent opinion at* 321 F.2d 968 (N.D. Ill. 2004).

Warth v. Seldin, 422 U.S. 490 (1975).

Washington v. Davis, 426 U.S. 229 (1976).

Wright v. City of Roanoke Redev. and Hous. Auth., 479 U.S. 418 (1987).

Wyman v. James, 400 U.S. 309 (1971).

Young v. Pierce, 685 F. Supp. 975 (E.D. Tex. 1988).

Zoning Bd. of Appeals of Wellesley v. Ardemore Apts. Ltd., 436 Mass. 811, 767 N.E.2d 584 (2002).

10 Housing Organizing for the Long Haul: Building on Experience

THE STORY OF HOUSING organizing in the nation's lower-income communities is mainly a story of local community struggles—rent strikes, fights against encroaching highways, hospitals and universities, campaigns to build tenant organizations and many other battles—that are hardly known except to those directly involved. There has been no Joe Hill to spread songs of housing struggle across the nation, no Taylor Branch or Rachel Carson to summarize housing organizing's grand themes in a best-selling book, no glossy magazine like *Ms.* or *Ebony* to validate the grassroots experiences of housing organizers.

Housing organizing has been the arena for the hopes and desperate needs of millions of people acting in their communities. These people have acted with ingenuity, courage and sophistication, and have made significant changes in their communities. Still, their efforts, largely because of their isolation and lack of a broad national context, rarely have explicitly confronted the underlying financial, political and institutional structure of housing, as embodied in the interlocking powers of real estate, government and finance. Thus, most housing organizing involves fighting much the same battles over and over in different places. Even the victories with lasting value across the nation have mostly been known only to those belonging to one or another of the national networks discussed in this chapter that have linked activists together.

The people fighting these fights, from the neighborhood level to the national level, need and deserve a more effective and far-reaching strategic approach to housing organizing. Such an overview must be rooted in an understanding of the larger political dynamic of this society. As Michael Stone wrote in *Shelter Poverty*:

> For housing organizing to begin to realize its strategic potential, activists need a framework for analysis, a developed vision of an alternative model of housing provision, and the willingness and ability to connect people's direct experiences in an effective way to a broader world view that is different from that so forcefully propounded by the dominant cultural institutions. (Stone 1993:278)

This chapter focuses on a method of action that can enable housing organizing to effectively change fundamental conditions around housing and realize a Right to Housing. This method in many ways complements the analytical framework that other contributors to this volume have developed and the housing development practice of community land trusts and limited-equity cooperatives. It owes even more to community leaders and organizers, especially those who built the National Alliance of HUD Tenants, the National Tenants Organization and the National Unemployed Councils. Finally, it is consistent with the exciting revival of organizing exemplified by activists connected to groups like the National Organizers Alliance, the Center for Third World Organizing, the Southern Empowerment Project and the activists who are working hard to renew the U.S. labor movement.

For those already committed to an organizing approach, this chapter will provide not only support and comfort but also analytical tools and historical background to support their practice.

For those who seek to meet housing needs solely by improving the techniques of housing agencies and organizations, while curtailing or avoiding organizing and mobilization, some hard questions will be raised. Above all, this chapter will put housing issues in the context of this nation's history of community and political struggles in a practical and useful way.

Some 70 years ago, the intensity and breadth of housing struggle during the Great Depression made possible a brilliantly clear vision of the landscape of housing organizing. One housing organizer, writing under the name of Sidney Hill (1935), in that historical moment outlined a strategic organizing approach to housing issues. Drawing on that analysis, the chapter proposes a set of benchmarks for housing organizers to assess the impact of their work—national and local—on the structural issues of housing injustice.

These benchmarks are not organizing tips or guidelines intended to ensure that a particular community or tenant organization wins its current fight. There are already many publications that provide such advice[1] as well as numerous training centers and organizing networks.[2] Nor do these benchmarks offer answers for all the questions that serious housing organizing will face. The fact that national housing–related movement organizations like the National Tenants Organization and the National Unemployed Councils, which clearly met these benchmarks, did not become viable permanent organizations, or that powerful local housing movements like those built in New York City in the 1930s and 1940s suffered serious setbacks in later days, points to the complexity of building a lasting housing movement. A critical point is that the success of housing organizing is inextricably linked to overall progressive activism and that the history and examples cited here can only be understood as part of the larger history of power, privilege and poverty of the last 70 years.

Local victories, no matter how bravely or brilliantly fought, will always need to be won over again. The fruits of dedicated volunteer and professional careers will be corrupted or obliterated in a political climate of disrespect for low-income communities and communities of color. Yet local successes with strategic direction, like the Muskegon City rent strike of 1968, discussed below as a bellwether for the National Tenants Organization, or the work of the Boston HUD Tenants Alliance, one model for members of the National Alliance of HUD Tenants, have had lasting movement-building impact far beyond their immediate communities.

The Sidney Hill benchmarks, adapted to a more contemporary vocabulary, and with the issue of race added, are as follows:

1. *Resident Self-Defense:* Housing organizing must focus on mobilizing residents to fight for their own housing needs.
2. *Technical Assistance:* Housing organizing must benefit from the most current and accurate technical information and advice.
3. *Progressive Agenda:* Housing organizing agendas must be included in, and must connect to, the demands and political work of the larger progressive movements of the day.
4. *Right to Housing:* Housing organizing must explicitly include the fight for a Right to Housing and for a large-scale and long-term social commitment to housing.
5. *Anti-racism:* Housing organizing must aggressively attack institutional racism as a central element of housing injustice, especially racism against African Americans, who have been most harshly denied housing opportunities.

These benchmarks can serve as a guide through a chronological overview of the history of housing organizing from the New Deal to today. Seven postwar distinct periods may be identified:

   I. 1933–1948: The New Deal and immediate postwar period—Mass left organizing around labor, relief and other issues made housing a significant national policy issue for the first time in U.S. history.
  II. 1949–1965: The modern structure of housing policy was developed with little organized opposition.
III. 1966–1970: Broad-based progressive coalition efforts, especially those led by Dr. Martin Luther King, Jr., and by the Black Panther Party, made housing one significant issue among many.

I. 1933–1948: UNDENIABLE NEED—AND ORGANIZING—PUT HOUSING ON THE NATIONAL POLICY AGENDA

Housing organizing was a key focus of the Communist Party and other progressive groups throughout the Great Depression and New Deal period. The National Unemployed Councils, formed in 1930 at the call of the Communist Party, took on "the organization of resistance to evictions. Squads of neighbors were organized to bar the way to the dispossessing officers. Whole neighborhoods were frequently mobilized to take part in this mutual assistance" (Winter 1969:61). In New York City alone, "hundreds, possibly thousands, of such incidents occurred during the early depression years" (Lawson 1986:101), and the tactic was also widely used throughout the urban Midwest.

Another housing tactic, with greater long-term impact, was the rent strike. Even before the depression, Party cadres tried to organize a rent strike in Harlem in 1929. In 1932 and 1933, the two tactics came together in New York City, as evictions of rent strike leaders brought as many as 4,000 people into the streets in pitched battles with the police (Lawson 1986:104–105). In the Deep South, Communist Party organizers sought to organize the Sharecroppers Union and reported from rural Alabama in 1933 that the Union had successfully blocked evictions and forced plantation owners to cancel the debts of sharecroppers (Winter 1969:75).

Such direct action led to a real but limited federal commitment to housing those most in need. A contemporary commentator described President Roosevelt as "having no enthusiasm for any bona fide housing program" because

it would require "a lavish outlay of federal funds" and bring "severe damage to the private real-estate-mortgage structure of the country" (Ward 1936:635). Nevertheless, the New Deal and war years saw the creation of new housing agencies. Until the New Deal, low-income people in the United States had no federal housing assistance. The Farm Security Agency and the United States Housing Authority (both established in 1937) laid the groundwork for today's rural and urban housing programs, and local public housing authorities were established across the nation.

How does the housing organizing of this period fare when assessed by the contemporary Sidney Hill benchmarks?

New York City's depression-era resident self-defense was so strong that it was institutionalized in the city's political life. The depression years created "a new form of citywide tenant federation that employed a uniquely effective 'mix' of tactics: expert legal representation . . . reinforced by rent withholding and picketing; careful research on housing issues, which led to legislation projecting a 'tenant perspective'; and aggressive lobbying for tenant interests in cooperation with liberal and left wing organizations" (Lawson 1986:95)—a progressive framework that has survived, and continues to be effective, into the 21st century. At its core, one writer found, have been "working-class Jewish women associated with the Communist Party who kept landlords on the defensive for three generations" (Lawson 1986:7) and who continue to do so today. During the Great Depression, resident self-defense like this was common in many communities, but in most communities, it did not last into the postwar period.

The New Deal created a cadre of professionals in local and national housing agencies who founded professional organizations still active today, including the National Housing Conference (founded as the National Public Housing Conference), whose modern core membership consists of for-profit developers of subsidized housing.[3] The National Association of Housing Officials was the ancestor of today's National Association of Housing and Redevelopment Officials (Fish 1979:212). Not then (or now) accountable to grassroots communities, these groups work with opinion leaders to get and keep housing programs. During this period, technical housing expertise grew but diverged from grassroots organizing.

New Deal housing activism was carried on by a broad informal liberal and progressive alliance, including liberal officials. In 1937, Tenement House Commissioner Langdon Post told New York City's City-Wide Tenants Council that "Nothing was ever gotten in this country except when the people forced it" (Lawson 1986:95). As much as in any other period, housing organizers of this period succeeded in integrating housing organizing into a larger political agenda. As the New Deal continued, activists increasingly focused on their local battles, paralleling the labor movement, the major social justice movement of the New Deal period. Both continued to grow after World War II but became more focused on consolidating its gains and creating an institutional structure. Mobilization for a national Right to Housing, never a major force, decreased.

The New Deal emerged during a period of heightened racism. The decade after World War I saw tremendous setbacks for racial justice, including unchecked mob attacks and lynchings directed against African Americans, the heyday of the Ku Klux Klan and of nativist activism that led to Asian immigration restrictions and other repressive laws. Jim Crow had ruled the South for 60 years, and housing segregation was increasing across the nation, reinforced by the professionalization of real estate.

A "Black and White Unite and Fight" anti-racism, though based on a superficial analysis of race, was key to moving the labor movement forward. However, few white organizers saw antiracist action as strategically central to their organizing. African Americans and other people of color saw little if any improvement in their position relative to whites during this period but did gain experience critical to their next steps toward justice. As the modern housing policy framework was created, racial segregation was an essentially unquestioned part of it. This fact, effectively unchallenged by New Deal housing organizing, had enormous consequences.

The Great Depression brought housing need to the forefront of political decision-making in a way that engaged hundreds of thousands of people, at least briefly, in major struggles around housing issues. While most of these struggles were at best defensive, the inclusion of housing demands in a larger progressive agenda led to a fundamental step forward in how the U.S. government dealt with housing. However, the emergence of a body of housing experts with no accountability to communities, and the lack of a sophisticated anti-racist perspective, set the stage for future setbacks, especially for low-income people and those in communities of color.

II. 1949–1965: THE MODERN HOUSING POLICY FRAMEWORK IS CREATED

By 1949, organized housing activism outside of a few urban centers of tenant organizing was pretty much limited to a few liberal and labor leaders—and to professionals employed by housing organizations. This period was the low point for all aspects of housing organizing. We can quickly review it in terms of the Sidney Hill benchmarks.

With no national organizing networks or political formations to support them, collective self-defense actions by housing residents become invisible in the postwar period. Neighborhoods faced new threats that they had few tools to fight—highways that isolated communities of color, public housing that concentrated poverty and suburbs that gained their cachet from their distances from the poor and people of color. Caught off guard, resident self-defense efforts were less effective and more poorly organized than either before or since.

More and more, the public housing advocates during this period were administrators of existing housing programs. There was no systematic technical assistance to housing organizing. In fact, in New York City, and probably in other less-studied cities, conflicts emerged between nonprofit housing professionals and organized tenants. Columbia University and other local nonprofit institutions formed Morningside Heights, Incorporated, which planned with city government to develop middle-income housing. Tenants in the site area, working with the city-wide United Community to Save Our Homes and the left-wing American Labor Party, fought those plans, packing meetings with angry tenants and providing tenant counseling. Ultimately, the project was built, and the Save Our Homes forces were "discounted as Communist-tainted by liberal housing reformers" (Lawson 1986:158–160). Locally, as with the American Labor Party, housing issues were key to left agendas, but such local efforts were not interconnected nationally.

This period did represent a high point of labor union participation in housing development, including "a blossoming of labor involvement in housing cooperatives in the post–World War II period, especially of housing co-ops for seniors" and the work of "the United Housing Foundation, a co-op sponsor that worked closely with labor unions in New York City to create many thousands of units of cooperative housing" (Yates 1996). However, labor's housing efforts were increasingly focused on benefits for current members and retirees, not on building an inclusive progressive movement.

There were no significant national initiatives for progressive housing organizing. In this period, liberals pressed for more housing and deplored the abuse of housing programs; but they did not question federal housing policy's basic assumptions, as radicals had during the depression. There was no nationally organized effort that sought a Right to Housing.

As *de jure* segregation began to be weakened by the Civil Rights Movement, racism in housing became the bulwark of institutional racism. The lack of an aggressive and effective anti-racist housing organizing agenda in grassroots communities during this period was a determining factor in this nation's history.

The period's federal "slum clearance" provisions, Title I of the 1949 Act, made African-American and Latino communities vulnerable to a new and unprecedented level of attack. Title I gave local authorities "power of a new immensity. Title I of the Housing Act of 1949 extended the power of eminent domain, traditionally used in America only for government-built projects, so drastically that governments could now condemn land and turn it over to individuals" (Caro 1974:777).

Eventually, in every major city, those displaced by this process crowded into existing or newly created slums, some of them high-rise public housing ghettos to which they had admission priority.

At the same time, people of color who could afford to buy homes outside of their "assigned" neighborhoods gained support from the courts. However, the key legal victories invalidating racial covenants in real estate were won by the National Association for the Advancement of Colored People (NAACP) and by Mexican-American civil rights groups. (Henry B. Gonzalez, at the time a San Antonio activist and later chair of the U.S. House Banking Committee, was involved in one case—Quiñones 1990:57). But the Federal Housing Administration (FHA), which underwrote the financing for the suburban development surge, had overtly segregationist policies until 1950 and "accepted unwritten agreements and existing 'traditions' of segregation until 1968" (Wright 1981: 248).

The fight against housing discrimination usually focused on individual solutions, not collective problems. For example, while New York's pioneer State Commission Against Discrimination (SCAD) identified the Title I relocation process as "one of the city's most serious minority housing problems," it chose to respond only behind the scenes and not to take on "any great responsibilities" on this issue (Lawson 1986: 158–159).

The housing activism of the 1950s and 1960s did go further than the left activism of the 1930s on race, reflecting the increasing organized push for civil rights. However, without any connection to grassroots organizing, successful legal assaults on housing discrimination did not protect the vast majority of people of color from increasing segregation.

The modern framework of housing policy was created during this period, but without the active participation of a grassroots movement—and without the suppressed voices of low-income communities of color. The long deferred promise of Reconstruction-era civil rights principles began to be fulfilled, an early effect of the emerging Civil Rights Movement. But for most of those excluded from the suburban boom, this era stifled dissent, grossly limited opportunity and created ominous new restrictions.

III. THE "SIXTIES"—HOUSING ISSUES KEY TO EMPOWERMENT OF URBAN COMMUNITIES OF COLOR

The urban rebellions of the 1960s were a major grassroots response to housing injustice. Though often characterized as irrational outbursts of violence, Platt's *The Politics of Riot Commissions* (1971) and other sources show that these were conscious political efforts, with broad community support. Though illegal and semi-spontaneous, these rebellions clearly were organized acts of resident self-defense. While the usual trigger for these rebellions was an act of violence against African Americans, the relationship between the rebellions and increased attention to housing and other conditions by those in power was clear and public. For example, the New York Urban Coalition, which put "millions of dollars donated by the nation's largest corporations into poor communities," over 27 years, "was a direct response to the riots that had left many of the country's inner cities in cinders" (Kischenbaum 1994:16).

This period saw a heightened and more self-conscious level of resident self-defense. During this period, today's structure of technical assistance to communities was first created. Community Action Agencies and Legal Aid received federal funding to assist communities on a variety of issues, including housing. These organizations took bold, sometimes unsophisticated, steps to assist communities, such as providing legal assistance to tenants, helping them to organize against landlords, often at first with little sense of the inherent political strings attached to federal funds.

When the Civil Rights Movement among southern African Americans, the central progressive effort of this era, emerged as a nationally visible force, housing issues were not central to it. However, the Civil Rights Movement "altered and expanded American politics by providing other oppressed groups with organizational and tactical models" (Morris 1984:286–287). The movement revitalized the broad progressive agenda that was stifled in the previous period.

Among the first to benefit from this revitalization were northern urban African-American communities. For these communities, housing segregation was central to their fight. When southern civil rights leaders, including Dr. Martin Luther King, Jr., joined with existing Chicago organizations to bring the movement north, housing was central from the beginning. Dr. King led marches in the summer of 1966 into "hostile" and "hate-filled" white suburbs of Chicago to protest housing discrimination (Schulke and McPhee 1986:234) The Southern Christian Leadership Conference, which Dr. King led, also participated in tenant organizing drives in Chicago and Cleveland, which contributed directly to the emergence in 1969 of the National Tenants Organization, described in greater detail below (Marcuse 1980).

As Manning Marable has written, Dr. King had "come closest to bringing together a biracial coalition demanding peace, civil rights, and basic structural changes within the capitalist order," and his murder "meant any linkages between these vital reform movements would be much more difficult to achieve" (Marable 1984:117). However, a wide range of movements, including tenant and housing movements, were linked and revitalized during this period and continued to move forward.

Dr. King's murder ended that period's best chance for a broad unified social justice movement. However, another such attempt was made by the Black Panther Party, which sought a united front against capitalism and racism. The fourth point of the Black Panther Party's 1966 Ten Point Program was: "We want decent housing, fit for the shelter of human beings. We believe that if the white landlords will not give decent housing to our black community, then the housing and the land should be made into cooperatives so that our community, with government aid, can build and make decent housing for its people" (Goodman 1970:211).

Allies of the Black Panthers, including the Brown Berets in Chicano communities in the West and the Young Lords Organization in Puerto Rican communities in the East and Midwest, took parallel positions on housing.

At the Poor Peoples' March, which went on after Dr. King was killed, the Brown Berets demanded "housing that would meet Chicano cultural needs" (Quiñones 1990:114). Housing was key to fights for community power and self-definition waged by communities of color in the late 1960s. While the Black Panther Party did not conduct a national mobilization for a Right to Housing, it clearly took such a position. Its positions and those of Latino and other progressive organizations set the stage for the housing nonprofits that have since been a key expression of community activism.

In a period in which African-American leadership set the tone for all progressive movements, anti-racism moved to the forefront of housing organizing efforts. This was a major and crucial change in housing organizing. For better or worse, low-income housing, like "welfare," had become identified with the aspirations of communities of color.

During the 1960s, a number of groups took a head-on organizing approach to fighting housing discrimination. In 1966, in Washington's northern Virginia suburbs, the Action Coordinating Committee to End Segregation in the Suburbs (ACCESS) regularly faced arrest at a segregated apartment complex and other sites, and called for the denial of federal funds to Arlington County, Virginia, because of housing segregation. In Baltimore, in 1969, the Activists, "a coalition of African American and white civil rights advocates," demonstrated and were arrested at the office of a large real estate firm that their research implicated "in the process of changing the racial composition of neighborhoods" (Orser 1994:133–136).

Eventually, such small cadres were worn down and defeated or diverted. Facing high legal costs, the Activists withdrew their civil suit against the real estate firm they targeted. ACCESS, after several months of relatively balanced reporting and peaceful marches, saw increased police harassment and press attacks, while Arlington County's highest elected official stated he was "not unsympathetic" but was "powerless" to end housing segregation.[4] Perhaps most important, these groups acted without mobilizing a strong community base of people impacted by housing segregation.

During this period, the government response was reactive and can only be understood in contrast to the period's radical activism, which questioned all of society, including the whole system of suburbs and ghettos.

While cruel repression of all kinds of progressive activism was one major response, various reforms also went forward, many of them housing-related. HUD was created in 1965, institutionalizing its "programs concerned with the Nation's housing needs, fair housing opportunities and improvement and development of the Nation's communities" (Office of the Federal Register 1995:333). Between 1966 and 1974, major new federal housing and community development programs included the Model Cities program, the Community Development Block Grant program and several programs for funding and financing multifamily housing development by private developers. In general, these programs moved away from widespread slum clearance efforts and toward at least a formal resident participation process.

The programs clearly were responses to the rebellions and activist challenges of the day. President Johnson wrote in his memoirs of "a new approach . . . based on the proposition that a slum is not merely decaying brick and mortar but also a breeding ground of human failure and despair" (Johnson 1971:330). The search for a new approach that went beyond slum clearance, as well as the financial investment that was made, signaled that activism had made an impact on those in power, once again bringing low-income housing needs into the light after 15 years of virtual invisibility. Whether or not they "bred" despair, the slums had bred activism that could not be ignored.

Civil rights legislation, especially the Fair Housing Act of 1968, put the issues of race and housing into federal law for the first time since Reconstruction. While the Fair Housing Act was also a response to rebellion and protest, and a direct reaction to the murder of Dr. Martin Luther King, Jr., this law did not initially speak to the critical needs of communities of color with the greatest housing needs.

To summarize, the "Sixties" period, specifically the last five years of that decade, saw housing organizing regain old strengths and gain new ones. In Malcolm X's famous phrase, "chickens came home to roost" in the 1960s as far as housing was concerned. The ghetto had been sharply defined by the postwar development process, and formal and informal resistance to its exploitative and isolating character erupted. While segregated and deficient housing was only sometimes the mobilizing issue, the ghetto thus created was the key arena of struggle. As in the New Deal era, government responded with a number of housing programs. Organized housing activists lacked the power to win the programs they knew were needed, but the overall activism of the day did win genuine resources and opportunities for some low-income households and communities. However, bridging the enormous gap that had been created between the mostly white suburbs and the largely African-American inner city would clearly be a generational task, which at least some of the emerging generation were willing to take on.

IV. 1971–1988: GRASSROOTS HOUSING WORK GROWS

The activist response of this period was in part a creative response to harsh repression. Two years after the murder of Dr. King, facing brutal secret police tactics, the Black Panther Party splintered and essentially ceased to operate in 1970. In that year, the then-governor of California, Ronald Reagan, answered a press question about "young dissenters" with the words, "If it takes a blood bath, let's get it over with" (Goodman 1970:502). Within a month, student activists were shot dead by authorities on the Jackson State and Kent State campuses.

Rather than respond in kind to the challenge of Reagan and his ilk, with results tantamount to a civil war, most activists narrowed their focus, either to one community or to one issue. Radical author and teacher Carl Boggs described the result as "new movements [that] uphold, in different ways, the ideal of transforming daily life that was only implicit in the sixties" and, that, though typically "more 'moderate' and less disruptive," are "a mature elaboration—not a reversal—of important sixties themes" (Bogg n.d.). Housing justice was one of these themes.

Among the "new movements" that emerged or grew substantially in this period, there are four for which housing is central: the community organizing movement, the community development corporation network, national tenant organizing and fair housing work.

Probably the most powerful of the four housing-related "new movements," and one of the older ones, is the community organizing movement, which is often traced back to organizing work in the 1940s in Chicago by the Industrial Areas Foundation. This movement consists of multi-issue groups in lower-income neighborhoods in every part of the nation as well as regional and national networks of these groups. Their growth in numbers has meant that many more low-income neighborhoods have had the techniques and support needed for effective resident self-defense. To mobilize people in their communities, these groups must choose issues that lead to tangible victories at the neighborhood level but often not to substantial changes in the institutional framework around housing. The one major exception, the Community Reinvestment Act (CRA), is a powerful anti-racist tool, and is described in that context below.

National community organizing networks like ACORN and National People's Action have included tenant organizing in their work and have taken strong housing positions. In 1972, National People's Action adopted a position that "decent housing is the right of all Americans" and that their constituents "need not accept poor housing and the abuse of a large and unresponsive industrial-financial-political housing complex" (NTIC 1995). Community organizing networks tend to work in isolation, not only from each other but also from groups not taking a community organizing approach. This means that most local housing organizers benefit only from the limited cumulative experience and technical expertise of one network.

Housing organizing, however, found its highest national strategic development in two free-standing tenant networks—the National Tenants Union and the National Tenants Organization—which shared membership and methods with the multi-issue networks.

Tenant organizing in the private market housing brought together the groups that formed the National Tenants Union (NTU) in 1979 in discussions of national rent controls. The NTU was active until 1985. Woody Widrow, then a housing organizer at the National Housing Institute, who describes himself as "the closest to paid staff that NTU had," remembers that NTU members developed common policies "on key issues, such as rent control, eviction protections and security issues." However, national rent control never moved forward, and state laws, which govern private tenancies, varied widely, in Widrow's words, "from okay to feudal." This made it difficult to find common ground. For example, rent control was a key issue in New York, New Jersey, Massachusetts and some localities in other states but was a utopian dream in the South.

Widrow sees "a lot of the growth of the CDC [community development corporations, discussed below] movement . . . in reaction to squatters, rents strikes and rent control efforts."[5] Rent control activists also played a major role in cities like Santa Monica and West Hollywood in California and state-wide in New Jersey in building a progressive movement that also takes on non-housing issues. This process was described for Santa Monica as "build[ing] bridges between various disenfranchised groups and bind[ing] them into an organized body, demanding even greater economic and political change in other spheres of life." However, by the late 1980s, rent regulation organizers and activists were "waging an increasingly defensive campaign simply to keep [rent control] alive where it already exists," and many tenant groups had re-focused their work on solutions like "large-scale cooperative housing programs for low- and moderate-income persons" (Gilderbloom and Appelbaum 1988:148).

The National Tenants Organization (NTO), in contrast to the NTU, organized almost entirely in public housing. Unlike most rentals, where landlords are "small operators of limited resources, unorganized, unsophisticated . . . and not susceptible to public pressure," public housing is "built with federal funds [and] controlled by federal regulations." For organizers, "the resources, the political sensitivity, the number of

tenants, the visibility, were all there" (Marcuse 1980:53). For these reasons, NTO was more successful than NTU at developing a national strategy and has had a much longer organizational life. However, NTO faced the problem of any national network of low-income people—functioning with minimal resources. In addition, housing authority staff often seek to control or compromise public housing resident organizations. In some cases, "rival organizations were organized and dealt with" by housing authorities in response to the emergence of local NTO affiliates (Marcuse 1980:53).

NTO was formed in 1969 with assistance from the American Friends Service Committee. It grew out of local organizing, including the Southern Christian Leadership Conference (SCLC)-initiated effort in Chicago as well as the work of Jesse Gray, a long-time progressive activist in Harlem (Lawson 1986:174–176). A key event for NTO was a public housing rent strike in Muskegon City, Michigan, as a result of which a well-organized tenant association won the replacement of housing authority commissioners with commissioners whom they approved, including the association's president (Neagu 1972:41). Thanks to these local actions and national advocacy with HUD, NTO "was able in early 1971 to establish grievance procedures and a 'model lease' in all federally-funded public housing projects" (Burghardt 1972a:15). Through the 1970s and 1980s, NTO continued to be a national resource for public housing residents but mostly as an unstaffed organization. Still, public housing residents, thanks largely to the work of NTO, have more rights and protections than most private market tenants around the nation.

Overall, housing organizing during this period more effectively supported resident self-defense and re-legitimized resident self-defense nationally. The community organizing networks, though not focused on housing, created the conditions that made this possible.

At the local level, housing organizing made a substantial difference. Both NTU and NTO provided technical assistance and models of successful organizing to local tenant groups and helped them to win battles that they otherwise might not even have taken on. Both groups, especially

NTO, also made some difference in national policy. However, the resident self-defense that both groups mobilized did not become a consistently powerful national force.

During this period, national community organizing networks like ACORN and National People's Action, as well as the Center for Community Change, a support center for low-income communities, began to provide specialized assistance to housing organizing efforts. The National Housing Law Project also became a key resource for organized tenants, especially for its information on and advocacy for the rights of federally-subsidized tenants, though the Project was not directly involved in organizing.

This period also saw the flowering of the community development corporation, a manifestation of expertise at the local level, often as one outcome of local organizing. While community development corporations, in theory, work on all aspects of developing a community, housing has been their major focus. Born almost literally from the ashes of urban rebellions of the 1960s, community development corporations have been rediscovered by successive waves of funders and government leaders as a solution to inner-city poverty. Thousands of units of below-market housing, many of them with some degree of community control, have been built by CDCs in projects in every metropolitan area and in many rural areas. According to the National Congress for Community Economic Development, a trade association for CDCs, there are about 2,200 CDCs around the nation. (See Chapter 16.)

A complex relationship exists between community organizing and CDCs. In a 1995 interview, Bob Brehm, the outgoing long-time executive director of a Chicago CDC, noted that early in his CDC career "many of the people who got involved in local community housing organizations were ... doing so as part of their activism, of their part in a larger movement for social change and social justice." However, over time, CDCs had come to show "some of the provider mentality, too little of the activist mentality, and far too much of a 'doing deals' mentality" (Chicago Rehab Network 1995).

This debate is not new. In 1978, the newsletter of the still-new Chicago Rehab Network responded to criticism of CDCs in *Keep Strong*, the magazine of the Intercommunal Survival Collective, with an article entitled "Who's Got the Grassroots?" According to the Rehab Network, *Keep Strong* had accused "neighborhood development corporations" of "play-acting as a surrogate grassroots leadership, while not producing enough housing units or jobs to make a difference." The Network defended the efforts of its members to "develop participatory development organizations that are responsive to community needs" (Chicago Rehab Network 1997).

CDC professionals have been found to "[tend] to look with disdain at community organizing's adversarial tactics" and to see organizing as "outmoded," and perhaps less professional or even less mature (Delgado 1994:25), and to "argue that the community organizing model—a more confrontational, conflict-oriented political approach to addressing poverty—is no longer appropriate" (Stoecker 1996).

To Brehm, on the contrary, "organizing should not be a big part of housing development" so much as "housing development should be a big part of organizing" (Chicago Rehab Network 1995). Brehm's view, however, is hardly typical. Most CDCs, and the networks that serve them, such as the Local Initiatives Support Corporation and the Enterprise Foundation, focus on the contribution of their work to the housing supply and see themselves as technicians in the housing "industry," rather than seeing their work mainly as an adjunct to institutional change and organizing. Brehm critiqued the idea that with "a few hundred or a few thousand units of housing, we can improve our community" as "absurd," stating that "with the limited subsidies, the resources that are available today, we can never build more than a tiny percentage of what is needed" (Chicago Rehab Network 1995).

Of course, there is no objective measure as to whether housing development or job creation is enough "to make a difference." To the person benefiting, even a single affordable housing unit is immensely valuable. Still, nonprofit housing groups do not have the capacity to even to come close to meeting the housing needs in this nation by developing and managing housing. They do, however, have the capacity to support institutional change by working with and for organized communities. Alternatively, they have the capacity to undermine organizing, whether by "compet[ing] for public attention with organizing groups;" or even by "delegitimiz[ing] the organizing group by making it appear more militant" (Stoecker 1996).

Urgency of need and limitation of resources is another issue often raised by CDC advocates and other service providers, such as shelter operators, who argue that they have no time for organizing, or even advocacy, because so much assistance is needed right now from organizations with minimal resources. But sometimes organizing for change can be not only more direct, but just as fast, as the service provider model in meeting people's needs. Randy Stoecker, another CDC critic, answers the "objection that people need housing now,...jobs now,...services now" by arguing that we can as easily "help people occupy vacant housing now,...help them march now on wealthy corporations laying off workers,...help them protest now to politicians attempting to destroy government at every level" (Stoecker 1996).

By the early 1990s, the Chicago Rehab Network had moved from defending its members' roles to touting its organizing effort, the Chicago Affordable Housing and Community Jobs Campaign, which won millions of dollars in commitments from the City of Chicago. The Campaign's success in taking on Chicago's entrenched power structure has not diminished the ability of the Network or its members to develop housing or carry out technical assistance. In fact, the Network's newsletter noted in 1997, "shortly after the success of the Chicago Affordable Housing and Community Jobs Campaign HUD showed its faith in the Network with a new technical assistance contract" (Chicago Rehab Network 1997:33). This occurred despite the fact that the brother of Chicago's mayor, the Campaign's main target, was a member of President Clinton's cabinet. This is no surprise to those who believe that good organizing causes opponents to have more respect for you and to be more, not less, likely to do business with you.

Stoecker, in a 1996 paper, cites a number of examples where organizing has led and nourished community development work:

In Boston, the Dudley Street Neighborhood Initiative (DSNI) focused on organizing as the means to development, while partnering to do actual physical redevelopment. In Minneapolis, the Cedar-Riverside neighborhood residents placed neighborhood organizing and planning in the hands of the Project Area Committee, limiting their CDC to only implementing plans produced through the organizing process. In San Antonio, Communities Organized for Public Service (COPS) resisted pressure to become a CDC (in the words of their lead organizer, Ernesto Cortes, "for the obvious reasons") after they achieved control of much of San Antonio's CDBG budget. (Stoecker 1996)

CDCs can bridge the contradiction between their identities as professional housing provider and as part of communities' struggle for justice, but only by being realistic about the overall needs of their community. When they exaggerate their own impact, CDCs are in effect belittling the urgent and unmet needs for institutional change in the communities in which they claim to serve. Those needs will not be met by "business as usual" but by changes won by mobilized communities.

During this period, there was generally little common progressive ground on housing. In particular, the connection to the labor movement that Sidney Hill had considered crucial became only a formality at best for most housing activists. The traditional New Deal connection between construction unions and housing programs degenerated into frequent antagonism, since many building trades unions were racially segregated, while many housing agencies avoided paying union wages whenever possible. Nor were any clear connections forged between housing issues and the issues of the increasingly powerful feminist and environmental movements.

Beginning in the late 1970s, national housing advocacy organizations emerged, especially the National Low Income Housing Coalition and the National Rural Housing Coalition. While labor and religious groups were key initiators of these organizations, over time, their day-to-day policy came to be dominated by CDCs. CDCs had an increasing need to influence national policy for their own benefit and had increasingly concrete and urgent needs, such as the preservation of the Low Income Housing Tax Credit (a complex tax incentive to channel investment into low-cost housing that became the main means of producing housing for many CDCs).

In principle, these national organizations supported a broad Right to Housing. In 1984, the National Low Income Housing Coalition organized a National Low Income Housing Conference at Howard University, co-sponsored by 45 organizations, from the National League of Cities to the Planners Network, and including ten national faith organizations, the AFL-CIO and constituency-based groups from the American Association of Retired Persons to the National Council of La Raza. (ACORN and National People's Action were not sponsors.) This broad-based meeting affirmed a program that included:

- "Make housing assistance an entitlement for all who need it,"
- "Provide resident control of housing through a strong role for tenant organizations, limited-equity cooperatives, community-based housing groups, and homeownership," and
- "End displacement of low-income people." (NLIHC 1984)

A variety of other national housing and community development advocacy groups subsequently emerged, from the National Coalition for the Homeless to the Local Initiatives Support Corporation. Some groups represented specific constituencies, like the National Council of La Raza, while others, like the Enterprise Foundation or the Institute for Community Economics, built new networks. Meanwhile, state housing coalitions, also mainly rooted in CDCs, emerged during the 1980s in a majority of states across the nation, primarily to fight for state housing funding to partially replace that being lost at the federal level.

During this period, however, none of the national housing advocacy organizations conducted a national political mobilization around a Right to Housing or tried to move forward federal legislation to this effect. Instead, they focused on the supposedly pragmatic path of advocating for specific programs of benefit to their constituents. Most of these programs, of course, lost ground during the period.

Community organizing groups and networks have extensively used the Community Reinvestment Act of 1977, itself a result of organizing by National People's Action and other groups, as a tool to negotiate community reinvestment agreements with lenders. The trigger for this organizing has generally been research showing lenders engaged in race-based denial of resources to low-income communities. Often, media coverage has followed, such as the "Color of Money" series in the *Atlanta Constitution* (Dedman 1988), raising the usually invisible issue of institutional patterns of racism with a directness rarely seen in this society. While disinvestment by lenders is not solely a racial issue, communities of color have been in the forefront of fighting it, and institutional racism is the central factor in its persistence. Community reinvestment data provide "the smoking gun on lending discrimination" (Oliver and Shapiro 1997:141). To refute the evidence of CRA data, a recent conservative critique of CRA found it necessary to slur inner-city communities, blaming disinvestment on the defects of "single-parent household[s]," whose members don't have "time to do simple home improvement or maintenance projects" and of communities "in which roving gangs paint graffiti on the sides of houses and buildings, and otherwise abuse the property of others" (Center for New Black Leadership n.d.).

The National Community Reinvestment Coalition reported that by 1998, more than 250 CRA agreements had resulted in commitments of over $400 billion, mostly for housing lending (Silver n.d.). National People's Action celebrates CRA organizing at its annual meetings with a rally-like display of the millions of dollars in agreements that its members have made. ACORN, CCC and the National Community Reinvestment Coalition also offer support to community groups for community reinvestment work.

Community reinvestment work has been a centerpiece of community organizing, and for good reason. Even though the full $400 billion committed is unlikely to reach the intended communities, this still represents a scale of resources otherwise far beyond the reach of grassroots communities. Community reinvestment organizing enables neighborhood groups to sit down and negotiate for real resources with some of the most powerful people in our nation—the leaders of major banks. Although CRA research has focused mainly on single-family home mortgages, CRA organizing has also produced multifamily rental housing and other financial opportunities for low-income communities and communities of color.

While CDCs and bankers constantly anticipate a day when communities and lenders will work together without the threat of confrontation in the background, everyone involved knows that good community organizing and the federal laws that grew out of it are what makes the relationship work. However, except for CRA organizing, explicitly anti-racist housing activism during this period was almost completely unrelated to the other "new social movements" with housing agendas.

After the passage of federal civil rights legislation, a number of national organizations focused on litigation and lobbying as tools to maintain and broaden civil rights protections. Some of these organizations, like the NAACP, also had a mass base and were involved in local battles, and sometimes militant organizing efforts, but were not involved in national housing policy issues.

Fair housing laws resulted in less confrontational and more professionalized fair housing work focused on discrimination against individual households. Increasing federal funding for fair housing, while a sign of growing concern on this issue, promoted a model of housing discrimination as due to insufficiently educated real estate professionals rather than institutional racism. In addition, litigation has become a source of substantial funds for many fair housing groups, further validating efforts to seek legal redress for individuals rather than redress in the streets for communities. The beneficiaries of fair housing work, like those of CRA activism, are generally more likely to be those who would be eligible to buy homes and get loans but for their race, though increasingly more low-income households, such as those headed by women, have made individual gains through fair housing work.

Modern fair housing nonprofits are typically very aggressive in their pursuit of justice for individuals. However, as Massey and Denton wrote in *American Apartheid* (1993:15), "as long as the Fair Housing Act is enforced individually rather than systemically, it is unlikely to be effective in overcoming the structural arrangements that support segregation and sustain the ghetto." Most fair housing nonprofits had little contact during this period with either nonprofit housing producers or housing organizers and were engaged in entirely separate fields of national policy work. This functional division has meant that community development corporations, and most community organizers, have defined housing issues in generally non-racial terms, while fair housing organizations, with the responsibility and the analytical tools to identify continuing housing segregation, have been isolated from the development of housing and from the development of overall housing policy.

Ultimately, then, while communities of color gained substantial resources for local fights during this period, including the powerful CRA tool, these resources did not coalesce into a strategically effective anti-racist component in national housing organizing efforts.

During this era, new movements emerged as legacies of the 1960s upsurges. Several of them had housing at the center of their agendas but had profoundly different approaches to the issue. They also had some serious work to do, as the housing situation got worse for millions of Americans. At the community level, some real accomplishments were won, and housing networks began to emerge to take on national and state-level issues.

V. 1988–1993: MOMENT OF OPPORTUNITY FOR THE HOUSING MOVEMENT

During these years, rival national public housing organizations to NTO were formed, in line with the approach of George W. Bush's

HUD Secretary, Jack Kemp, who undertook an idiosyncratic and unrealistic crusade to make public housing tenants into owners of their units. This further weakened NTO, since the rival organizations had well-known resident leaders and were much better funded than NTO. While public housing residents still provide some of the most effective local leaders on housing and other issues, NTO has not regained its strength of the early 1980s.

Many of the national groups that had emerged in the 1980s, such as the National Low Income Housing Coalition, had member groups that had fought effective local battles for resident self-defense. But staff and leaders tended to develop policy without much input from these grassroots groups—and to be ineffective at mobilizing grassroots action on issues. As the visibility of resident self-defense efforts grew, some national groups began to seriously try to connect local work to national issues.

One key step was the establishment by the Center for Community Change (CCC) of the CDBG Monitoring Project. The CDBG (Community Development Block Grant) program, created in 1974 for the benefit of low-income people, in many communities became a slush fund for downtown development and other politically popular uses. Such abuses led to grassroots activism, such as the successful organizing by COPS in San Antonio, cited above. ACORN in 1979 took a national position to "ban the use of [CDBG] funds for downtown commercial projects until the basic needs of low- and moderate-income neighborhoods are met" and to "give democratically elected neighborhoods the power to make decisions on how CDBG funds are spent within the neighborhood" (ACORN 1979).

CCC involved grassroots organizations in a network that not only assisted local organizing on the issue but also fed the results of that organizing back into the national policy process. In 1986, local and national groups involved in the Project formed the Coalition for Low-Income Community Development, which has fought for changes in the CDBG program but also urges neighborhood groups to "get involved and organize around getting more CDBG dollars for their communities," noting that "public officials tend

to be far more interested in using CDBG funds to cover government's administrative expenses, basic public services, downtown development projects and public works than in using them for low-income housing and other low-income neighborhood priorities" (Nilsson 1993). CCC's CDBG Monitoring Project provided a model for national organizing-related activities of other organizations, especially those of the Low Income Housing Information Service (then the sister organization to the National Low Income Housing Coalition).

As the 1980s began, few states spent any revenues on low-income housing and shelter for the homeless. By the end of the decade, the majority of states did so because, for the first time in this nation's history, in almost every state there was an organization of housing professionals committed to housing advocacy, if not housing organizing.

The growing network of CDCs and other local housing nonprofits began to form state housing coalitions in the 1980s. (A 1995 National Low Income Housing Coalition survey of state housing coalitions found only six that had existed before 1981.) Most of these state coalitions were dominated by CDCs and were focused on gaining funding streams for them—and state budgets had become a likely source for such funding. The coalitions used the technical expertise—and community credibility—of CDCs to become a political force for housing. In some states, such as New York, New Jersey and Indiana, the state coalitions came to include a significant base of grassroots activists—usually tenant leaders or grassroots homelessness activists.

The National Low Income Housing Coalition, in order to engage the state housing coalitions that had accomplished this change in national and more effective state advocacy, kicked off its National Housing Policy Initiative in 1993. The Initiative strengthened networking among state coalitions, coordinated national activities for coalitions to participate in and provided funding to strategically selected coalitions.

By 1988, a network of experts, some associated with Legal Services, were working to head off or mitigate the conversion of privately owned subsidized housing to upscale uses, as discussed above. The NLIHC supplemented this work by reaching out to grassroots organizers and tenant leaders, pulling together a network that constituted itself in 1992 as the National Alliance of HUD Tenants (NAHT). At its core were tenant organizing efforts in Chicago, Boston, Dallas, Los Angeles and other cities.

NAHT has had a substantial impact on housing policy, working with other national housing groups, often in "good cop, bad cop" cooperative efforts. A 1996 academic report found that NAHT "achieved three major victories," namely:

- "the creation of a Residents' Rights and Responsibilities brochure, co-written with HUD" and distributed to tenants all over the nation;
- "a new chapter for tenants in the HUD Management handbook, spelling out tenants' rights clearly while making them a part of the process"; and
- "a $3 million training program funded by HUD" to inform tenants of their rights, since expanded to include a multiyear commitment of VISTA positions to the network (Nyden 1996:33).

In addition, the Low-Income Housing Preservation and Resident Homeownership Act, a compromise among owners, tenants and Jack Kemp's approach, included major tenant gains, won by the groups that formed NAHT and the professionals working with them. These provisions assisted residents to purchase their buildings on their own or with nonprofits and created notice requirements that have enabled tenants to prepare for threatened conversions. NAHT has its own technically skilled staff and has also worked with a network of technical experts organized as the National Preservation Working Group.

The 1989 Housing Now! march, discussed below, mobilized groups from across the progressive landscape to support the housing issue. Whether this merely meant that housing was the "flavor of the month" or implied more solid connections was never fully explored by national housing activists. Also, housing concerns began to more frequently overlap with other concerns, such as AIDS, mental illness and domestic violence. In the process, activists on such issues gained housing program knowledge.

Some of the most militant groups opposing assaults on the poor, especially welfare repeal, included housing justice as an element of their struggle. Tent cities, like the Hoovervilles of the 1930s, again became a means of dramatizing issues—and of meeting peoples' needs. In Boston, a tent city protest of a major downtown project ultimately won a large affordable housing complex, appropriately named Tent City. The Kensington Welfare Rights Union has "established Tent Cities in North Philadelphia since 1991 to meet immediate housing needs" and, as important to them, to politically "educate families turned away by the shelter system."[6]

"Housing Is a Human Right" had been the slogan of the National Low Income Housing Coalition since the 1970s. In *Shelter Poverty*, Stone noted a mid-1980s campaign to add this right to the Massachusetts state constitution and saw the issue "percolat[ing] into the realm of organizing and political action" (Stone 1993:317). In 1989, Congressman Ronald Dellums had introduced legislation to establish a universal social housing program, based on ideas developed by a working group sponsored by the Institute for Policy Studies (1989a, 1989b).

In 1988, the National Low Income Housing Coalition's sister organization, the Low Income Housing Information Service (LIHIS), committed itself to "build a definable low-income constituency base for housing production and advocacy" and to "involve the constituency in development of proposals for policy change," and stated as a goal "make housing recognized as a human right" (LIHIS 1988). LIHIS had established projects to support local antidisplacement efforts as well as support statewide housing coalitions—both aiming to build a national grassroots-based housing constituency.

As these efforts began, however, a new force for housing justice emerged. New nonprofit agencies had emerged in response to homelessness—many of them informal, egalitarian and with leaders driven by a deep moral calling. A significant few of these leaders displayed eloquent prophetic anger against homelessness. Foremost among them, because of his personal gifts and his location in the nation's capital, was Mitch Snyder. Snyder, following some local political victories, began to share a vision of a national housing march, which got such a positive reaction that it became an inevitability. In October 1989, the Housing Now! march brought tens of thousands of people to the nation's capital.

Like all such marches, this one required a massive logistical effort costing hundreds of thousands of dollars. But the march also required grassroots mobilization, which was largely done by the new breed of homelessness nonprofits. A list of contacts from the organizing effort for the march shows that of 80 contacts around the nation whose affiliations can be identified, 35 were working with homelessness-focused organizations, mainly shelters, 17 with other non-housing social service agencies, and only 13 with housing nonprofits.[7] Yet CDCs had generally been around longer, had more resources and were more numerous than homelessness groups.

The National Low Income Housing Coalition, which played an important logistical role in the march, used the occasion to launch its first national mass campaign—Two Cents for Housing. This campaign called for the federal government to increase its funding commitment to housing to two cents—2 percent—of the overall federal spending dollar. Some communities sent in hundreds of postcards with two pennies attached to them, adding up to tens of thousands of postcards sent to Congress, and some national advocates felt the campaign helped to bring about the National Affordable Housing Act (see below). However, after the campaign, the NLIHC did not follow up immediately with another mobilization effort.

Because fair housing was, for the most part, treated as a separate issue and advocacy effort, the various new mobilization and organizing efforts during this period did not fundamentally attack the institutional racism in housing. However, people of color did gain new positions of leadership at the national level in and through organizations like the National Low Income Housing Coalition and the Center for Community Change as well as in local organizations, from CDCs to organizations of homeless people.

Housing went back on the national agenda, with a charismatic cabinet member (Jack Kemp), a national march on Washington and widespread concern about homelessness. However, there was no national organizing effort that had the tools or the strategy to seize this opportunity. Local and state organizing on housing issues continued to grow.

VI. MIXED SIGNALS IN THE MID-1990s

Following the failure to seize the national opportunity of the early 1990s, there have been many more local or limited efforts that exemplify the Sidney Hill benchmarks. Homeless activism, while not as visible as in 1989, has never stopped. The National Coalition for the Homeless has continued to provide a connecting point for this work. A major focus of this work has been the increasing pressure by urban governments to "criminalize the homeless." In late 1997, the Coalition announced the National Homeless Civil Rights Organizing Project to work on this issue, a clear form of resident self-defense (Safety Network 1997).

In the latter part of the 1990s, the earlier media emphasis on white homeless families and the "new poor" was overwhelmed by the reality of persistent poverty in communities of color. More and more, homeless activism, though disorganized and sporadic, has elements of resident self-defense as well as charitable benevolence. Homeless activism is also a place where connections between movements are made, since many young activists in colleges and elsewhere spend time working on homeless issues.

In Seattle, homeless and formerly homeless people and their allies led direct action against development-driven downtown demolition of low-cost housing. In 1991, "Operation Homestead, a loosely organized group of anarchists, independent leftists, homeless people and housing activists," carried out a four-and-a-half-day occupation of the abandoned Arion Court apartments in downtown Seattle. Working closely with more mainstream housing nonprofits, the occupiers got a commitment from the owner to donate the building for self-managed housing (Oldham1992:32).

Seattle's downtown, with its long tradition of low-cost housing, has been an arena for policy struggles, due to rapid speculative development continuing over several decades. Although many housing units have been lost (the Seattle Displacement Coalition estimated that 1,500 downtown units were lost in three years in the mid-1980s), activists have succeeded in gaining condominium conversion and housing preservation laws, and a short-lived moratorium on downtown demolition.[8]

Battles like these, with homeless people and their allies fighting for their survival in an atmosphere of speculation, returned the fight for housing as a human right to the public policy arena. All of the Sidney Hill benchmarks are evident in this kind of organizing.

During this period, local activists have gained some technical tools not controlled by housing professionals outside of the community. The Consolidated Plan required by HUD, based on the requirements of the 1990 National Affordable Housing Act, gave local activists detailed information on local housing needs. Several successful organizing efforts in this arena are detailed in the NLIHC report *Slicing the Pie*, including an effort in Rock Island, Illinois, that "used the city's planning process to save 225 units of public housing slated for demolition" and funds that were targeted more effectively to low-income communities in Oakland, Akron and other cities (Wise 1995:20–21). HUD has also provided more and more such information on the World Wide Web and through other electronic means.[9]

NAHT, described above, continued to fight to prevent conversion of HUD-assisted housing to market-rate housing; to provide protections when conversion became inevitable; and to enable resident groups, and nonprofits working with them, to purchase this housing in order to prevent its conversion. NAHT, local and national nonprofit developers (especially the National Housing Trust), and local and state governments have accomplished the long-term preservation, in resident or nonprofit ownership, of almost 85,000 units of housing in 736 housing communities around the nation (Organizing Times 1998a). The fight to save the hundreds of thousands of units still at risk continued. The

Pennsylvania Housing Coalition's Resident Education and Action Project is typical—working with Pittsburgh community leaders to ensure that residents "play an important role in saying what happens to these properties," even though federal protections are no longer in place (Moses and Russell 1998).

NAHT's annual conferences in recent years brought together about 300 activists and supporters from NAHT's "130 to 140" tenant association members, located from coast to coast (Basey 1997). A key NAHT focus was on the right to organize. At its 1998 conference, NAHT raised issues that included the arrests of HUD tenant organizers in Los Angeles and got HUD support for "regulations confirming the right of tenants to leaflet and door-knock their neighbors" and "the right of organizers to leaflet and door-knock" (Organizing Times 1998b). While NAHT's work is dependent on organizers and housing professionals, its approach to the issues in HUD-assisted properties has always been that "the people who call these buildings home are the ones whose voices need to be heard" (Minnesota Housing Partnership 1998)

NAHT's record fits the Sidney Hill benchmarks. Resident self-defense is at its core. It has organized one of the few national groups working on any issue whose board consists entirely of low-income people, the majority of them people of color. It effectively uses technical assistance, both from its own staff and leading members and from outside groups.

In the 1990s, the Institute for Community Economics (ICE), a national organization that provides financing and technical assistance to community land trusts, proposed a conscious alliance of housing networks around a set of defined principles. ICE's leadership included peace and justice activists as well as inner-city leaders of communities of color.

Community land trusts, along with mutual housing associations and limited-equity housing cooperatives, represented a "second wave" of housing nonprofits. Community land trusts hold land in trust in order to reduce housing costs and increase community control. Like mutual housing associations and limited-equity housing cooperatives, community land trusts go beyond assisted housing efforts of the past in several ways, especially in resident participation and in removing properties from the speculative real estate market. For these groups, the proposal of the Black Panther Party and its allies that "the housing and the land should be made into co-operatives so that our community, with government aid, can build and make decent housing for its people" was still relevant.

In 1995, ICE began a self-conscious effort to bring together these efforts as Permanently Affordable Resident and Community Controlled (PARCC) housing. The model challenged this nation's basic paradigm of real estate ownership. But it also spoke to many of the public's known concerns about low-income housing programs, which are seen, sometimes correctly, as wasteful, bureaucratic in structure and not based on local initiative. Among the groups that ICE reached out to in this effort was the National Association of Housing Cooperatives, which includes labor-initiated cooperatives from as long ago as the 1920s. The PARCC effort, though not fully followed up on, was a building block in the long-term process of forging a broader progressive movement for change.

In February 1994, the National Low Income Housing Coalition approved a Housing Justice Campaign with three main policy components:

- to re-direct the home mortgage deduction tax subsidy for higher-income homeowners toward "providing housing benefits to every low and moderate income family";
- to "substantially strengthen the community-based nonprofit sector involved . . . on behalf of greater housing opportunity," especially by directing resources to "frontline organizations responsive to people of color, women, disabled persons, low-income people, and others subject to discrimination"; and
- to seek "full funding at authorized levels for all current low-income housing programs."[10]

As part of that campaign, Housing Justice Day brought housing activists to Springfield to lobby Illinois legislators in May 1994. That November, the Washington State Housing Justice Campaign was kicked off by a formerly abused and formerly homeless woman living in subsidized housing, the Director of the Tahoma Indian Center and the Speaker of the State House. Similar activities occurred in Texas, Louisiana, Connecticut and elsewhere.

Legislation reflecting a detailed program worked out by NLIHC members and leaders was introduced in Congress in February 1995 by Congressman Major Owens, a leading progressive from New York. At NLIHC's annual conference, Owens called for a broad progressive movement to march on Washington on housing and other issues. In the same month, hundreds of militant Philadelphia public housing tenants and supporters, working with the Pennsylvania Low Income Housing Coalition, rallied in Washington.

The election of a conservative Republican Congress in 1994 led many housing advocates to feel that the Housing Justice Campaign was no longer appropriate. In mid-1995, partly due to lack of funding, NLIHC's field organizing staff was laid off or left, and most of the Housing Justice Campaign's media and organizing activities came to a halt.

Since at least the time of the Brown Berets, whose 1968 demands were noted above, oppressed ethnic and cultural groups in the United States have fought for culturally appropriate housing. In the Twin Cities, urban Indian groups gained low-income housing designed in cooperation with the community. In Albuquerque, the long-established Hispanic neighborhood of Sawmill has established a community land trust in a process that has used culture and history, especially mural art, as a tool. In Stockton, California, a low-income housing development has enabled a Cambodian immigrant community to express its solidarity and maintain some of its culture (Yates 1996). The Tenants' and Workers' Support Committee in Alexandria, Virginia, after succeeding in its twelve-year fight to establish a cooperative housing community owned largely by Salvadoran immigrants, has expanded its housing-based work to "those problems that most affect the Latino community," including living wage and health issues. (VOP 1998).

Ethnic groups are not alone in fighting for appropriate housing. Contradictions among non-profit housing groups surfaced when ADAPT (Americans Disabled for Attendant Programs Today) of Philadelphia, part of a national network of persons with disabilities, crashed a fundraising event for Habitat for Humanity, with demands for Habitat houses to be more accessible (ADAPT 1998:24). ADAPT's key fight since the 1990s has been for their MiCASA proposal, "a national program of home and community services so we are not forced into nursing homes" (ADAPT 1998:1).

Such struggles will be key to future fair housing fights. Fair housing must go beyond the right of people from different ethnic groups to obtain their share of the American Dream—such as suburban homeownership. Many Americans, including the majority of African Americans, are not likely to be included in that dream in their lifetimes. Other communities, like the Cambodians in Stockton, may have a dream different from that of the majority.

While national awareness of housing as an issue diminished during this period, the fight for housing justice continued at the local and state level, and took more creative forms, benefiting at the community level from an uninterrupted 30-year tradition of housing organizing. Nationally, however, the agendas of CDCs and their intermediaries are the only voices consistently heard nationally, and those voices are but whispers in the national policy conversation.

VII. ORGANIZING NETWORKS TAKE UP THE BURDEN: 1997–2004

The turn of the century, and the intensified conservative dominance that has accompanied it, have not been kind to housing programs. But these conditions have moved housing organizing networks, including a new network of public housing residents, to the fore.

In the area of resident self-defense, two developments stand out. One is the continued operation of the National Alliance of HUD Tenants, formed in 1991 and still meeting annually, connecting tenants nationwide 13 years later. Such longevity is rare in housing organizing. NAHT continues to aggressively engage with HUD. For example, in September 2003, high-level HUD officials turned down a request for a meeting of the kind that NAHT consistently was granted over the last decade. In response, NAHT passed out a leaflet "blasting" then–HUD Secretary Mel Martinez to HUD employees coming to work. NAHT reported on its website that "The letter appeared to strike a positive chord with many HUD employees . . . equally frustrated with . . . Bush Administration political appointees." As has been the case in the past, NAHT did get a meeting with HUD officials after once again taking a strong stand.

The second important development is that NAHT has been joined by a parallel national network—ENPHRONT—Everywhere and Now Public Housing Residents Organizing Nationally Together. Much as NAHT grew from a network brought together by the National Low Income Housing Coalition, ENPHRONT came out of an advisory committee brought together by the Center for Community Change. In 1997, that advisory committee of public housing residents came together as the Public Housing Residents National Organizing Campaign. That Campaign focused on opposing devastating legislative changes to public housing programs and won some fights around rent increases and tenant tenure. In November 2001, ENPHRONT was formed at a meeting of public housing residents from around the nation. In the words of Ed Williams, founding president of ENPHRONT, its purpose is create "a national infrastructure of residents throughout the nation to achieve what we need to achieve in this era where we are losing our housing, standing in lines waiting for a place to live and being 'relocated' to parts unknown."

For the first time, there are parallel networks of the two largest populations of low-income tenants—those in public housing and those in subsidized housing. Ed Williams spoke to the 2003 NAHT Annual Convention, and his message of cooperation on common issues was welcomed by NAHT membership and leadership. In addition, both NAHT and ENPHRONT have working relationships with the Center for Community Change, which has moved in recent years to take on national policy issues more aggressively. This development, along with the relative longevity of the current tenant movement, is bringing tenant organizing more into the mainstream of the broader community organizing movement.

At the same time that homelessness grows and threats to subsidized housing increase, homeownership continues to grow. It appears that the influx of immigrants committed to investing in homes and the continued low interest rates are contributing factors. A lot of technical assistance has focused on this area, given the minimal resources available to provide rental housing for very-low-income people. In addition, there have been no major innovations or technical changes in housing development programs, and so no basis for experts to devise new methods of providing housing based on such changes. There were three main housing initiatives listed on the website of the Local Initiatives Support Corporation in May 2004— the Center for Home-Ownership, the Housing Authority Resource Center and the Affordable Housing Preservation Initiative. While all three have worthy goals, none of them is aimed at increasing the stock of newly affordable rental housing. Similarly, another major technical assistance network, NeighborWorks, listed five items on the home page of its website during that same month, four of which dealt with homeownership. While these technical assistance networks continue to be active and to meet real needs, they do not appear to offer innovations in meeting the most serious needs.

The progressive agenda of this period, on the other hand, is active and changing but has largely been defensive. After all, even the business media are a bit awed and concerned by the rise of corporate power in this period, as in this quote from the cover story for the September 11, 2000 issue of *Business Week:*

> [N]o one's reining in business anymore. Most of the institutions that historically served as a counterweight to corporate power—Big Government and strong unions—have lost clout since Ronald Reagan came to town crusading for deregulation and local control. The conservative ascendancy that followed discredited much of the New Deal social structure, leaving corporations to fill the vacuum.

The necessity of responding to oil wars, civil liberties violations, environmental rollback and other retrogressive moves by those in power has made defense a full-time job for progressives. However, housing groups frequently appear in the coalitions formed for these purposes. For example, the membership of the national coalition United for Peace and Justice, organizer of several major national anti-war events, includes such groups as [NYC] City Council District 7 Housing Taskforce, the Tenants' and Workers' Support Committee and the Center for Community Change. The coalition's rallies regularly include the message that "money spent on the military action has meant less money was available for health care, education and housing," as the *New York Times* reported in March 2004.

The Poor People's Economic Human Rights Campaign, a nationally active network with its base in the Kensington Welfare Rights Union in Philadelphia, announced plans for a March for Our Lives: Stop the War at Home at the August 2004 Republican Convention, with an emphasis on the issues of health care, housing, education and living wage jobs. These plans included a Bushville shantytown in New York City.

Of course, housing policy groups continue to be active and in fact have joined together in a broad campaign for a National Housing Trust Fund. This campaign, united behind specific federal legislation, is supported by a wide range of organizations. However, the two central groups are the National Low Income Housing Coalition and the National Coalition for the Homeless (NCH), which now share office space in Washington and coordinate closely. In 2001, Donald Whitehead became the Executive Director of NCH, the first formerly homeless person and the first African American to serve in that position. (Whitehead was living on the street in 1996.) Since he took on the job, NCH has begun to build deeper and stronger links to civil rights organizations around their common issues. For example, in 2003 the Leadership Conference on Civil Rights joined in NCH's call for study by the General Accounting Office of hate crimes against the homeless. Well-known activist figures like Jim Wallis of Sojourners and Martin Luther King III are building relationships with NCH; Wallis was the keynote speaker at the October 2003 annual meeting of NCH. Another significant change at NCH was the unionization of the staff in 2000; perhaps as a result, the American Federation of Labor–Congress of Industrial Organization's (AFL-CIO) Director of Organizing also spoke to the October 2003 meeting.

The National Housing Trust Fund legislation is not intended to establish a Right to Housing but has an ambitious goal of funding 1.5 million units of housing by 2010. For NCH, though, the Trust Fund legislation is part of its Bringing America Home campaign. The centerpiece of that campaign, the Bringing America Home Act (HR 2897), would establish a Right to Housing as well as universal health care and a living wage or income. Taking a widely comprehensive approach, NCH also includes reauthorization of Head Start and the Individuals with Disabilities Education Act in this campaign, emphasizing the interrelatedness of poverty, unemployment and housing needs. Whitehead, like Ed Williams, spoke to the 2003 NAHT Conference, and NAHT is an active participant in the Bringing America Home campaign. (In stating its support on its website, NAHT emphasizes the fact that the campaign "references Housing as a human right.")

Each of the key organizations described above—NAHT, ENPHRONT and NCH—has people of color in leadership, either in staff or on the board, or both. This has put the issue of racism at the forefront as it perhaps never has been before in the housing movement, and has brought anti-racist figures like Martin Luther King III and Jim Wallis as well as others like Congressman John Conyers, to support their efforts. For the first time, people of color are the face of leadership, not just the face of the "victim." The language of universal human rights, which has been key to the African-American community since the time of Malcolm X and is also critical to the struggle of indigenous people, is also becoming the language of the most dynamic elements of the housing movement.

To summarize, on the one hand, relatively little progress has been made on housing issues since the late 1990s, given the conservative and corporate grip on power in all branches of the U.S. government. On the other hand, the core organizing components of the housing movement have clearly grown in strategic position, in their focus on broader and deeper issues, and in their links to larger movements.

As it has been since the Great Depression, the fate of housing policy is linked to the overall state of the progressive movement. There is unlikely to be any significant change in housing policy, especially in the resources devoted to housing, without a larger progressive upsurge. However, if a reaction to the current conservative dominance does take place in the near future,

the organizing-oriented elements of the housing movement appear to be positioned to be benefit from it, and to move housing issues forward in a way that has not been seen for many years.

SUMMARY AND ANALYSIS

The history recounted in this chapter shows that since 1949 the multiplicity of community-based housing organizations and housing organizing efforts in this country have not given rise to a continuing and well-focused effort to organize strategically around housing as a human right. What are the reasons for this disappointing reality? The Hill benchmarks can help us understand it.

Resident Self-Defense

National and most state-wide housing organizations have never put this activity at the center of their work, preferring instead to act as brokers between community development corporations and policymakers. There have been some exceptions. The Housing Now! march, as we have seen, was largely based in groups organizing with homeless people and those who work directly with them, and was intended to strengthen local organizing. Going further back, the National Unemployed Councils and the Black Panther Party depended on and sought to reinforce the activism of poor people mobilized for self-defense.

The experience of the National Alliance of HUD Tenants and the National Tenants Organization is especially instructive here. Though each of these two organizations reached at best a few thousand of the hundreds of thousands of tenants eligible to join them, they both chose an organizing approach. By using their resources to build leadership and to focus on issues that made immediate sense to low-income tenants, NTO and NAHT each substantially changed the debate in a major housing policy area while opening up new arenas for resident self-defense. Housing advocacy campaigns that mobilize one-time appeals to policymakers sometimes win a single victory but do not build movements rooted in the communities where housing need is greatest.

Housing activists are a relatively small group with a lot to do, and organizing is labor-intensive. But housing activists would find support from other organizations if they focused on supporting and mobilizing resident self-defense. Community organizing networks played a key role in building local components of NAHT and NTO and can be expected to be part of any good fight in the future. If housing issues offer such opportunities again, networks like ACORN and National People's Action will be there. It is not unlikely that the labor movement will be an ally in future organizing efforts; currently, labor activists are looking for community issues around which to build alliances at the same time that they are reaching out to communities of color, women and immigrant populations who have serious housing needs.

Putting Hill's first point in modern terms: *National housing policy efforts must be much more based in grassroots resident organizations, especially in communities of color.*

Technical Assistance

How can grassroots activists gain control of technical resources? As shown above, by organizing based on Consolidated Plan information, we are close to the point where communities can rapidly call up government-provided information for the organizing needs of the immediate moment. But this is only a small fraction of what is possible. The real estate, lending and insurance sectors have by far the greatest amounts of information on housing. The Home Mortgage Disclosure Act has made a large body of information on financing practices accessible. In *American Apartheid*, Massey and Denton (1993:233) propose that "realtors serving black clients must be given complete access to multiple listing services." Activists opposing housing segregation should build on these partial steps and insist that information that is now proprietary to major housing-related private institutions in fact has profound social significance. Insurance companies, lenders and developers, all to some extent regulated and all with fair housing responsibilities under the law, possess massive amounts of data that could illuminate for community leaders and residents how our hous-

ing system works. Hard evidence on how insurance companies, developers and other real estate businesspeople make their decisions would provide concrete details of the institutional racism and other unjust practices in the housing sector. Facts, no matter how shocking, do not substitute for struggle, but they make for more effective strategies and for more effective public education.

Communities will continue to need housing professionals whose groups develop housing, working within the limitations of the current housing system, as "niche organizations most useful for bridging the gap between activists, service providers, and resource holders" (Stoecker 1996). But the greatest need grassroots organizations have was named by NTO activists in 1972—professionals working on research and planning "under the firm direction of a tenant union" (Burghardt 1972b:200). Such experts already are employed to provide technical support to communities—where there has already been a political fight to make technical information accessible, as with the Home Mortgage Disclosure Act or environmental Right-to-Know legislation. The reality is that progressive activists working on all issues need "damn good research" tied to "organizing expertise" (Pintado-Vertner 1998).

Restating Hill's second point for today: *National and local organizations should build powerful technical assistance systems to support organizing and should press for accurate, current and detailed information from government and from the private sector on housing needs at all levels in forms that can easily be used for local organizing.*

Including Housing in Progressive Politics

Hill's pamphlet also suggested that "housing demands" be in "the programs of local labor candidates for political office." Not only today's nascent Labor Party but also other progressive forces and alliances should be called on to include housing demands in their programs, whether electoral or not. The Progressive Challenge, the Independent Progressive Political Network and the Third Parties '96 effort, all three of which brought together a number of parties and groups on the left, have already done so. The Progressive Challenge agenda includes "increasing funds for low-income housing assistance by roughly half the cost of the entitlement to housing assistance enjoyed by upper income home owners" as one of its demands for "Adequate Social Investment"[11]—a demand that echoes the NLIHC's Housing Justice Campaign.

Community development corporations, in particular, are often loath to identify themselves with progressive political directions, casting themselves as technicians who would endanger their work by getting involved with advocacy. Yet, as Bob Brehm noted, housing nonprofits have never come close to providing enough housing in any community in this nation. This is not because CDCs are deficient but because of political conditions that will only change as a result of the organizing and activism that CDCs eschew and sometimes even block.

Nonprofit developers often justify political inaction by asking for patience, claiming they are on the verge of a "new age" of housing development, in which the old methods have been put behind, and the right partners, the right resources and the right programs are finally going to lead to the right solutions to our housing problems. Of course, the demands of funders for innovative projects and politicians' need to distinguish themselves from their predecessors motivate many of these claims. The reality is that the "new age" always turns out to be basically a recycling of the same old relationships and partnerships of government, for-profits and nonprofits, with no lasting benefit for the communities in need. Thus, for example, *City Limits*, a housing magazine, reported that as the New York Urban Coalition was failing in the 1980s, the New York City Partnership was emerging, and drawing "corporate backers who were once likely prospects" for the older group, no doubt with much of the same rhetoric (Kischenbaum 1994:17).

The incremental and insider-oriented approach, though well-intentioned, has allowed housing and other resources for the poor to steadily diminish for 20 years, while only prisons and shelters grew substantially as low-income housing providers. No major expansion of housing subsidies and of programs that have

genuinely served low-income people's housing needs has ever come from such insider efforts alone, no matter how profoundly thought out. Significant increases in resources to meet real housing needs have always been a response to an upsurge of mass organizing and action around a broad range of progressive issues, like those that forced the New Deal and the Great Society programs into existence.

In today's national-level progressive world, dominated by single-issue organizations, housing advocates may legitimately fear having their issue submerged. Yet there is not, and never has been, any other reliable source of support for housing programs but a strong, broad-based and well-mobilized progressive movement. Hopeful signs, such as the existence of multi-issue organizations like the Black Radical Congress and the National Organizers Alliance, are beginning to emerge, while cross-cutting issues like environmental justice and corporate welfare are raising community issues that intersect with the concerns of communities organized around housing. And, at least at this moment, the labor movement is moving, erratically perhaps, toward a vision that, in the words of one activist, "would embrace the economics of sustainable development that serves the entire community, rather than only those fortunate enough to hold union jobs" and "with strong ties to communities and to the various struggles against oppression of others" (Eisenscher 1998:47).

Hill's third point, then, can be read today like this: *The housing movement must put its main hope in organizing and activism, and, as a small movement that is most effective when larger social movements are successful, it must make alliances with other progressive movements.*

Housing as a Right

Hill suggested that "a campaign...be waged to establish housing as a part of state and federal social insurance, so that tenure will be secure in the event of unemployment, illness or old age." In modern jargon, this means the establishment of housing as a federal entitlement.

Many housing professionals—and perhaps most observers of contemporary politics—will be quick to describe this as an "unrealistic" demand. Recently, national housing advocates have learned, using focus group research, that there is deep public cynicism about government and developer housing programs, and even about the poor who need housing. This is important information. It is vital that we recognize the power of the doubts, prejudices and fears that sustain the current system. Perhaps it is even true that "housing as a human right is not an effective message any more," one advocate's reaction to that focus group research (Saasta 1998:43).

Focus groups in 1932 would have shown a far uglier picture, in a nation where the Klan paraded openly and the majority of African Americans and Mexican Americans were denied the right to vote. Franklin Roosevelt was elected on a platform that reflected the "realism" of his Democratic Party before mass movements forced changes. It called for "an immediate and drastic reduction of governmental expenditures . . . to accomplish a savings of not less than twenty-five percent in the cost of federal government" (Commager 1963:237), a level of austerity of which contemporary budget cutters could only dream. Yet in Roosevelt's first administration, the radically innovative foundations of all current housing programs and of the welfare system, labor law and many other reforms were laid down.

The struggle for decent housing is a harsh and difficult one, perhaps decades away from resolution. But the only strategy that has ever been effective on a large scale is the organizing-based approach outlined here. It must not be discarded to concentrate on deals and programs whose benefits are washed away with each wave of conservatism. Activists seeking only what today's decision-makers consider realistic will gain nothing worth having. *Housing organizers should be part of a conscious and long-term national grassroots-based campaign for a housing entitlement.*

Anti-racism

This brings us to the issue that even Hill's audacity did not allow him to fully face—race, which is central to the way housing is provided in this nation.

The real estate system has become a major institution for hoarding the gains of centuries of white privilege—and its role in perpetuating institutional racism is not limited to storing up the gains of the past. Its central dynamic, the definition of "good" and "bad" neighborhoods, continues to distribute wealth along a racial continuum. The syndrome of "not in my back yard" and of resistance to placement of low-income housing in middle-class neighborhoods, like housing discrimination itself, are not mere civil rights "problems." They are key means of organizing people in this country so that class, caste and other divisions are maintained. As *American Apartheid* states, "residential segregation is the institutional apparatus that supports other racially discriminatory processes and binds them together into a coherent and uniquely effective system of racial subordination" (Massey and Denton 1993:8).

Racial segregation is also the source of much of the enormous asset base that real estate represents. This economic reality is not reflected in the rhetoric of the currently existing fair housing groups, which is typified by statements like "it's good business to promote equal professional service and to ensure objectivity in underwriting to African Americans and all consumers" (Berenbaum 1998). The reality is that most businesses involved in real estate and related finance still find it profitable and customary to discriminate, and to exploit the weaknesses of lower-income communities and communities of color, if sometimes in more subtle ways than in the past. Discrimination may not be "good business" from a moral point of view, but until society decisively changes, apparently it is still "good" financially.

The existing fair housing groups, aggressive and sophisticated as they are, will not change this situation on their own. After all, in the words of the National Fair Housing Alliance, the national association of these groups, "thirty years after the passage of the federal Fair Housing Act, equal access to apartments, homes, mortgage loans and homeowners' insurance is not a reality for the vast majority of people the law was designed to protect against discriminatory practices" (NLIHC 1998). The Alliance goes on to appeal for more and better targeted resources for fair housing complaints and decries current attacks on the fair housing law in Congress. But how likely is it that "more of the same" will make a fundamental difference or, for that matter, that there will be significantly more resources for fair housing without a broad mobilized political movement against housing discrimination?

Groups like NAHT and the neighborhood organizations that have fought the expansion of hospitals and universities, bank redlining and gentrification must be recognized as the leading forces in fighting discrimination. Those who seek to oppose housing discrimination should look to such groups for leadership and offer them genuine support. If liberal housing advocates and housing professionals had supported the New York City tenants who fought Title I relocation schemes 50 years ago, and that fight had spread nationwide, we might be looking at quite different nation today—a nation without the racially concentrated communities that nourish both fearful conservative suburban majorities and the feared and maltreated underclass. *Opposition to discrimination in housing, especially against African Americans and other people of color, must be central to housing organizing and activism—and organizing must be central to opposition to discrimination.*

CLOSING THOUGHTS

In 1949, our nation's leaders stopped far short of their stated National Housing Goal of "a decent home and a suitable living environment for every American family." They provided a public housing program that they knew could not meet the nation's full need for low-cost housing. The structure they created has not been able and will never be able to meet the needs of "every American family," although it provided unprecedented housing wealth to many families. Like the generation that won this nation's independence and the generation that saved the Union in our great Civil War, the generation that fought the war against fascism faltered when it came to providing "justice for all."

This chapter offers some benchmarks to the housing organizers of the future, based on experience. The central lesson it offers is that the fundamental issues of housing will not be re-solved by housing technique, narrow changes in policy or new programs. These issues are rooted in racism, in lack of democracy and in maldistribution of wealth.

When these fundamental problems are attacked with some success by organized action, successful housing programs are one result. When these problems are neglected, the process of meeting housing needs also stagnates. Housing activism gets bogged down in saving existing housing programs. Only by working in partnership with organizing can housing experts and professionals truly contribute to meeting housing needs on a large scale.

Sidney Hill's vision came to him in a terrible moment of our history and was part of a fierce and often simplistic left-wing analysis of what needed to be done. Millions paid in pain and thousands in heroic effort for the clarity that brought about the New Deal and improved the lives of their children and grandchildren. We should, of course, all do what we can to reduce the prospects of violence and social disruption. But there is functional truth in the slogan, "No justice, no peace."

Most people who care about housing needs are not organizers. But all of us can contribute to housing organizing that is resident-centered, technically informed, politically conscious, focused on a Right to Housing and seriously anti-racist. Some of us can provide information; some of us can provide resources; some of us can help build coalitions. Some of us can create or run housing projects and programs that include resident power in their design and that do not compromise on questions of race and wealth.

Above all, we can all respect and support the efforts of tenants, of homeless people and of lower-income homeowners to defend themselves from a callous and often predatory system. We can all ask, whenever decisions are made, that those who have been excluded from the six-decade-old promise of a decent home finally have an active part in every decision that affects them. We can understand that the most responsible, and even the most kind, step we can take is to always remember the quintessential democratic truth that is in the words that close *Housing Under Capitalism*: "Better housing will be achieved in the same manner that workers have made other gains, and that is by organizing and fighting for them" (Hill 1935:39).

NOTES

1. Bobo, Kendall, and Max (1991) is one of the best.

2. The National Organizers Alliance, located in Washington, DC, is a beginning point for learning about them.

3. Information from the National Housing Conference World Wide Web site at http://www.nhc.org.

4. *Northern Virginia Sun*, various articles, July and August 1966.

5. Interview of Woody Widrow by the author, December 1997.

6. "MARCH FOR OUR LIVES: Homeless march from Philadelphia to NYC," Kensington Welfare Rights Union, kwru@libertynet.org. Press Release: May 26, 1997; received by the author from an Internet email list.

7. The author's analysis, using the document "List of housing now staff and regional contacts," undated, but from internal indications prepared by the national office of Housing Now! in the summer of 1989.

8. Letter from Seattle Displacement Coalition, April 23, 1990.

9. An example is the HUD Communities Information World Wide Web site. http://www.hud.gov/states.html.

10. "Housing justice campaign to fight for trust fund," the Low Income Housing Information Service. *Roundup*, March 1994, No. 165.

11. "The progressive challenge continues—A fairness agenda for America" n.d.

REFERENCES

ACORN. 1979. *The people's platform*, ratified at ACORN's 1979 St. Louis Convention.

ADAPT. 1998. *Incitement*, newsletter of ADAPT, Fall.

Basey, Alice. 1997. National Alliance of HUD Tenants. *Shelterforce*, July/August.

Berenbaum, David. 1988. Insurance industry neglects to market to diversity. *The Fair Housing Report*, newsletter of the Fair Housing Council of Greater Washington, Winter.

Bobo, Kim, J. Kendall, and J. Max. 1991. *Organizing for social change: A manual for activists in the 1990s.* Santa Ana, CA: Seven Locks Press.

Boggs, Carl. n.d. From New Left to social movements. *Radical America*, Vol. 21, No. 6.

Burghardt, Stephen. 1972a. The development of the movement. In *Tenants and the urban housing crisis*, ed. Stephen Burghardt. Dexter, MI: The New Press.

———. 1972b. Rent strike or tenant union? The building of a permanent organization. In *Tenants and the urban housing crisis*, ed. Stephen Burghardt. Dexter, MI: The New Press.

Caro, Robert. 1974. *The power broker.* New York: Knopf.

Center for New Black Leadership. n.d. http://www.cnbl.org/index.html.

Chicago Rehab Network. 1995. Changing of the guard: Interview with Bob Brehm. *The Network Builder*, Winter.

———. 1997. Who's got the grassroots? From *The Network Newsletter*, Vol. 1, No. 3, April/May, 1978. Reprinted in *The Network Builder*, Fall/Winter.

Commager, Henry, ed. 1963. *Documents of American history.* New York: Appleton-Century-Crofts.

Dedman, Bill. 1988. The color of money. *The Atlanta Journal and Constitution*, May 1–16.

Delgado, Gary. 1994. *Beyond the politics of place: New directions in community organizing in the 1990s.* Oakland, CA: Applied Research Center.

Eisenscher, Michael. 1998. Beyond mobilization: How labor can transform itself. *Working USA*, March/April.

Fish, Gertrude, ed. 1979. *The story of housing.* New York: Macmillan, sponsored by the Federal National Mortgage Association.

Gilderbloom, John I., and Richard P. Appelbaum. 1988. Rent control and the tenants' movement. In *Rethinking rental housing*, Chapter 7. Philadelphia: Temple University Press.

Goodman, Mitchell. 1970. *The movement toward a new America.* Philadelphia: The Pilgrim Press.

Hill, Sidney. 1935. *Housing under capitalism.* New York: International Pamphlets.

Institute for Policy Studies. 1989a. [Richard P. Appelbaum]. "A progressive housing program for America." In *Housing issues of the 1990s*, eds. Sara Rosenberry and Chester Hartman, 313–331. New York: Praeger.

———. 1989b. [Dick Cluster]. *The Right to Housing: A blueprint for housing the nation.* Washington, DC: IPS.

Johnson, Lyndon B. 1971. *The vantage point: Perspectives of the presidency, 1963–1969.* New York: Holt Rinehart and Winston.

Kischenbaum, Jill. 1994. Requiem for a sixties dream. *City Limits*, August/September.

Lawson, Ronald, with assistance of Mark Naison. 1986. *The tenant movement in New York City, 1904–1984.* New Brunswick, NJ: Rutgers University Press.

LIHIS. 1988. Overview of proposed priorities for LIHIS/NLIHC for next three years. Developed by the Board of the Low Income Housing Information Service at its July 1988 meeting.

Local Initiatives Support Corporation. What we do: National programs. http://www.lisc.org/whatwedo/programs/#housing.

Marable, Manning. 1984. *Race, reform and rebellion: The second Reconstruction in black America, 1945–1982*. Jackson: University Press of Mississippi.

Marcuse, Peter. 1980. The rise of tenant organizations. In *Housing urban America*, eds. Jon Pynoos, Robert Schafer and Chester Hartman, 2nd Ed. Chicago: Aldine Publishing Company.

Massey, Douglas, and Nancy Denton. 1993. *American apartheid: Segregation and the making of the underclass*. Cambridge, MA: Harvard University Press.

Minnesota Housing Partnership. 1998. Update on tenant organizing activities. *Bullet*, newsletter of the Minnesota Housing Partnership, Fall.

Morris, Aldon. 1984. *The origins of the Civil Rights Movement: Black communities organizing for change*. New York: Free Press.

Moses, George, and Cherrié Russell. 1998. Resident education and action project. *Housing News*, newsletter of the Pennsylvania Low Income Housing Coalition, Summer.

National Alliance of HUD Tenants. "NAHT board sends rebuke to former HUD secretary." www. saveourhomes.org

National Coalition for the Homeless. n.d. Bringing America home: The campaign.

NLIHC. 1984. Background information for participants in the Second National Low-Income Housing Conference, June 24–28. Washington, DC: National Low Income Housing Coalition.

———. 1998. Housing discrimination continues unabated throughout the U.S., by the National Fair Housing Alliance. *Round-Up*, quarterly publication of the National Low Income Housing Coalition, August.

NTIC. 1995. *Disclosure, the national newspaper of neighborhoods*. Published by the National Training and Information Center, sister organization to National People's Action, Chicago, July/August.

Neagu, George. 1972. Tenant power in public housing—The East Park Manor rent strike. In *Tenants and the urban housing crisis*, ed. Stephen Burghardt. Dexter, MI: The New Press.

NeighborWorks. Strengthening communities and transforming lives. http://www.nw.org/network/home.asp.

Nilsson, Warren. 1993. *CDBG Primer*. Baltimore: Coalition for Low-Income Community Development.

Nyden, Philip (principal author). 1996. *Saving our homes: The lessons of community struggles to preserve affordable housing in Uptown*, a joint activity of Loyola University and the Organization of the North East.

Office of the Federal Register. 1995. *The United States Government Manual*.

Oldham, David. 1992. Direct action in Seattle. *Z Magazine*, October.

Oliver, Melvin, and Thomas Shapiro. 1997. *Black wealth, white wealth*. New York: Routledge.

Organizing Times. 1998a. HUD tenants face loss of homes. *Organizing Times*, newsletter of Coalition for Economic Survival, Los Angeles, Spring.

———. 1998b. *Organizing Times*, Summer/Fall.

Orser, W. Edward. 1994. *Blockbusting in Baltimore*. Lexington: University Press of Kentucky.

Pintado-Vertner, Ryan. 1998. Research: Power tool for organizers. *The Ark*, magazine of the National Organizers Alliance, Fall.

Platt, Anthony. 1971. *The politics of riot commissions*. New York: Macmillan.

Quiñones, Juan Gómez. 1990. *Chicano politics: Reality and promise, 1940–1990*. Albuquerque: University of New Mexico Press.

Saasta, Timothy. 1998. *How to tell and sell your story, Part 2*. Washington, DC: Center for Community Change.

Safety Network. 1997. *Safety Network*, the newsletter of the National Coalition for the Homeless, October/November.

Schulke, Flip, and Penelope McPhee. 1986. *King remembered*. New York: Pocket Books.

Silver, Joshua. n.d. *NCRC catalog and directory of community reinvestment agreements*. Washington, DC: National Community Reinvestment Coalition.

Stoecker, Randy. 1996. The community development corporation model of urban redevelopment: A political economy critique and an alternative. http://131.183.70.50/docs/comm-org/papers96/cdc.html. Email: randy@uac.rdp.utoledo.edu.

Stone, Michael E. 1993. *Shelter poverty: New ideas on housing affordability*. Philadelphia: Temple University Press.

United for Peace and Justice. Member groups of United for Peace and Justice. http://www.unitedforpeace.org/article.php?id=1879.

VOP. 1998. Building a healthy community. *Virginia Organizing*, newsletter of the Virginia Organizing Project, July.

Ward, Paul. 1936. Planning future slums. *The Nation*, May 20.

Williams, Ed. 2002. Message from the president. *Housing Matters*, February.

Winter, Carl. 1969. Unemployment struggles of the thirties. *Political Affairs*, September. Reprinted in *Highlights of a fighting history: 60 Years of the Communist Party USA*, chief ed. Philip Bart. New York: International Publishers, 1979.

Wise, Dana. 1995. *Slicing the pie: A report on state and local housing strategies*. Washington, DC: Low Income Housing Information Service.

Wright, Gwendolyn. 1981. *Building the dream: A social history of housing*. New York: Pantheon.

Yates, Larry, ed. 1996. *Community Economics*, magazine of the Institute for Community Economics, Springfield, MA, Fall.

Michael E. Stone

11 Social Ownership

IN ORDER TO REALIZE a Right to Housing, a large and increasing share of housing must be treated as a social resource rather than as a commodity yielding private windfalls. Indeed, all housing contains both social and individual rights and interests, differing only in the nature and extent of their social characteristics. It is thus appropriate and useful to conceptualize a continuum of housing ownership forms. As discussed in this chapter, "social ownership" encompasses that portion of the spectrum where the overriding social interest is to ensure security of tenure and permanent affordability.

Social ownership of housing and land may be traced back to neolithic villages and Native American cultures. Within the capitalist era, various alternatives to the commodification of material life were put forth during the 19th century, ranging from socialist revolution to utopian models of shared property and including a spectrum of working-class demands for cooperative and social housing. Many European countries accepted the notions of social ownership earlier and have gone much further toward their realization than has the United States (see Donnison 1967; Wynn 1984; Gilderbloom and Appelbaum 1988: Chapter 8; Harloe 1995; Fuerst 2000; Stone 2003). Even in the United States, significant strands of nonspeculative and social ownership have emerged, despite the ideological domination and political force of the purveyors of unfettered private ownership. They amount to a little over 4 million housing units, about 4 percent of all housing in this country.[1] Their accomplishments and potential provide encouragement and hope, while their limitations and contradictions provide valuable lessons on the dilemmas of partial and piecemeal reform.

The chapter begins with an overview of the social dimensions of all housing. This is followed by a definition of the more particular concept of social ownership and explanation of how the housing tenure available to residents of socially owned housing differs from both conventional renting and conventional homeownership. The bulk of the chapter then examines the nature and scope of existing models of social ownership, grouped into two major categories: socially owned rental housing, consisting of public housing, nonprofit rental housing and mutual housing associations; and nonspeculative homeownership, consisting of limited-equity cooperatives, ownership with community land trusts and some resale-restricted individual ownership. The models are evaluated in terms of differences in the degree of social control. The chapter concludes with identification of various routes through which the amount of social housing can be increased.[2]

THE SOCIAL COMPONENTS OF HOUSING OWNERSHIP

While "property" is usually understood to mean material things such as houses, land, cars and furniture (as well as nonmaterial forms of wealth such as "intellectual property"), in more precise legal terms, property consists of socially created and enforced rights and obligations regarding the acquisition, use and disposition of such wealth. That is, even in an ostensibly "private free-market" economy, the terms under which someone can obtain and dispose of a house (and other property) is not by individual (private) whim but instead by procedures established by constitutions, statutes, common law, case law and administrative regulation. The relationships between private parties regarding property ownership are socially governed.[3]

Furthermore, even where there are extensive private rights within these social procedures of ownership, the government, as the legal representative of the social interest, retains for itself rights vis-à-vis private owners of houses, land and other so-called real property. In the U.S. legal system, these are the powers of taxation, eminent domain and police power.

The power to tax real property has long been the prerogative of and principal means of revenue-raising for local governments, implicitly if not explicitly based on the premise that real property has economic value, not merely because of the activities and investment of an individual owner but because of the activities of other owners ("neighborhood effects") and the provision of public services that benefit private property owners, such as roads, public safety, schools and so forth. Furthermore, the obligation on an otherwise "private" property owner to pay assessed property taxes creates a potential lien on the property—a form of property right that is "owned" by the government and is legally superior to the rights of the nominal owner and any other private parties with rights to the property (e.g., mortgage holders). Such tax liens constitute an old and well-established form of "resale restriction" on private property.

Eminent domain is the power of governments to take property for public purposes. While governments must exercise due process and provide compensation for seizing and extinguishing private property rights, the social power of eminent domain transcends all private rights and interests.

The police power enables government to regulate private property to protect the "health, safety and morals" of the society and to "promote the general welfare." The society holds an array of such rights that owners of housing, land and other real estate are expected to accept and abide by, with civil penalties—sometimes including forfeiture of the property—and sometimes criminal penalties for violations. These rights include not only building and health codes, zoning and subdivision regulations, fair housing laws, landlord-tenant laws and environmental standards but also use restrictions and resale restrictions accompanying receipt of public benefits. Such powers constitute an enforceable social interest in all housing and other real estate.

In addition to these legal and governmental manifestations of social control of housing, there are material and experiential ways in which housing is inherently social. Because housing is so durable and long-lived (if reasonably well built and maintained), over the course of its useful life, a house accommodates the needs of many different households. Few houses are built in response to the unique needs and requirements of a particular household. Even those that are so built typically undergo adaptations and modifications as different people live in and use the housing over the course of generations and even centuries, giving each dwelling a rich and complex social history and identity. Indeed, no other major item of personal and family consumption is passed on in this way from user to user to user. That is, housing is not only inherently social but uniquely social.

THE CONCEPT OF SOCIAL OWNERSHIP

Beyond the universal social elements possessed of all housing, housing is defined here as socially *owned* if it meets all of the following criteria:

- it is not owned and operated for profit;
- it cannot be sold for speculative gain; and
- it provides security of tenure for residents.

Social ownership embraces the notion that housing should be permanently removed from the possibility of resale in the speculative private market. This means that once the original cost of producing or acquiring the housing is paid off, the only costs would be for operations and any additions, alterations and capital improvements. Even if nothing else were to change, the substantial expansion of such a "social sector" of housing would, over time, mean a sizable reduction in the housing costs for a growing proportion of the population. It would also mean slowing and eventually reducing the growth of mortgage debt as the mortgages on existing housing are paid off once and for all.

There are many different forms that "social housing" can take, including:

- ownership by public agencies, such as local and regional housing authorities;
- ownership by private nonprofit organizations; and
- ownership by residents themselves, individually or collectively, with resale restrictions that permit, at most, a "limited-equity" return on investment.

The unifying concept is not the particular type of entity owning the housing but the existence of enforceable provisions preventing the housing from being sold in the speculative private market. Indeed, for housing to be fully social, these provisions should apply "permanently," "forever," or "in perpetuity" (the phrases most often used).

Social housing clearly is not equivalent to government ownership because the concept includes not only public housing but also so-called third-sector housing (Gilderbloom and Appelbaum 1988; Davis 1994), which is housing outside of both the private profit-driven market and public ownership. Social housing also encompasses but is broader than "permanently affordable resident or community controlled" or PARRC housing (Institute for Community Economics 1995), a definition that excludes both public housing and private nonprofit housing not controlled by residents or the local community. Nonetheless, it might be argued that social ownership should embrace the principle of substantial resident control of housing, including that owned by public housing agencies and private nonprofits.

Social housing could be produced and acquired with mortgages, and most of the existing social housing in this country other than public housing is mortgaged. However, this means that even though such housing is not sold and hence may eventually be free of its original mortgages,

there is still a 20- to 40-year period during which time the housing is saddled by mortgage payments that have to be borne by the residents and as well may or may not be subsidized in some way. In order to address this affordability burden directly, ideally the production and acquisition of social housing should be through direct public capital grants rather than debt (see Chapter 12; see also Stone 1993:218–224, 258–261; Stone 2003:19–21, 56–58).[4]

AN ALTERNATIVE FORM OF TENURE

Creation of a large social housing sector would provide housing choices and benefits that are not now available through the current alternatives of private rental, subsidized rental and conventional homeownership. A new form of tenure would be established, providing people with security, autonomy, control and affordability. For the large majority of renters who have no realistic prospects of achieving conventional homeownership (and for those renters who might some day afford but do not necessarily aspire to ownership), the advantages are substantial. Yet, even in relation to conventional homeownership, the social and economic benefits of this alternative tenure form would, on average and over the long term, be at least comparable and in several ways superior.

All occupants of social housing should have the right of permanent occupancy and control over their living space. As long as they wish to remain, they should not be required to move, except for those few situations of otherwise unresolvable conflicts with neighbors or eminent domain for legitimate public purposes. Indeed, with no mortgage payments and no possibility of resale into the private speculative market, residents would have security against eviction or displacement far exceeding that enjoyed even by homeowners under the existing system, since there would be no risk of mortgage default and foreclosure. Also, a household should have the right to pass their unit on to members of their family as long as the heirs meet general eligibility requirements and occupy the unit. In addition, secure tenure undoubtedly would increase the kind of informal voluntary care-taking and improvement that for the most part is associated with homeownership—including the freedom to modify one's dwelling, make repairs and renovations oneself and use the house in ways that personalize it, give it meaning and adapt it to changing household needs and circumstances.

Security of tenure in social housing might also substantially reduce and possibly eliminate some of the negative social attitudes and behaviors caused by the existing ownership system. Concern about the protection of property values is a frequent explanation given for the exclusionary behavior that homeowners currently manifest against people of color, low-income households and so-called incompatible developments and land uses. Absence of anxiety about protecting one's investment (anxiety that often is based on misperception or on agitation by realtors and others) may reduce resistance to increased neighborhood diversity and socially beneficial new development. Reduction of the locked-in feeling that homeownership now tends to produce—again out of concern for protecting one's investment or reluctance to incur high turnover costs such as brokers' commissions and other closing costs on selling and buying—may provide people with a greater sense of freedom to take advantage of employment opportunities in other locales or otherwise pursue changes they might like to make in their living situations.

In addition to security of tenure, control over one's living space and the sense of social status, conventional homeownership also offers significant economic advantages over renting. To be a viable alternative to homeownership, social tenure has to confront the strength of this appeal. Under the existing housing system, homeownership provides three economic advantages over renting. First, for an identical house bought at the same time and the same price, a homeowner will have somewhat lower monthly outlays than a renter because there is no payment for the landlord's cash flow profit and overhead costs. Yet a resident of social housing would have much lower housing costs even than a homeowner—as much as two-thirds lower (see Chapter 4)—if the housing is financed with capital grants rather than mortgage loans.

The second economic advantage of homeownership consists of the income tax benefits generated from being able to deduct mortgage interest and property tax payments from taxable income (if one itemizes deductions rather than uses the standard deduction). The cost savings available in social housing with no mortgage payments would much more than offset these benefits received by owners of conventionally-owned and -financed housing, especially for lower-middle-income households who have seen homeownership slip out of reach and for whom the tax benefits have been quite limited at best (see Chapter 5).

The third and most significant economic advantage of conventional homeownership is the ability to build up wealth through ownership. A homeowner's equity is established initially with the downpayment and is then increased through mortgage principal payments and rising property values. As long as the choice is between renting in its present form and homeownership in its present form, equity build-up is a real economic advantage of homeownership, although the advantage is often less than commonly believed. Social tenure, by contrast, offers a way of accumulating wealth that would be competitive with homeownership in most parts of the United States and over the long term. Suppose a moderate-income, prospective first-time homebuyer had the choice between conventional homeownership, on the one hand, and, on the other, occupancy of a comparable house with little or no downpayment and no mortgage payments, with security of tenure and control but no opportunity to re-sell the housing on the private market. It turns out that, in general and on average, the money saved by choosing the social housing option more than compensates for giving up the right to re-sell and reap a potential speculative profit in the private market (see Stone 1993:196–198). And if the limited income-tax benefits that the current system provides to moderate-income homeowners were also eliminated or equalized for renters, the advantages of this alternative tenure form would be even greater. A household choosing this form of tenure may be termed a "resident-saver," since a valid comparison with the equity-accumulation benefits of conventional homeownership involves the assumption that such a household would place the money that otherwise would have gone for a downpayment and monthly mortgage payments into savings.

If our society were to establish a large social sector of housing, this alternative tenure could be available not only to shelter-poor households but would be an option for moderate-income households closed out of conventional homeownership or able to achieve such homeownership only with substantial personal sacrifice and risk. The existing homeownership market would still be available for those who can afford it and who, for whatever reason—whether it be the hopes of speculative gain or ideological attachment—prefer to obtain housing in that way. Those eligible for and choosing to enter the social housing sector would have all the benefits of homeownership but would not have to possess the personal savings needed for a downpayment, and what savings they might possess could accumulate at a faster and more stable rate than if invested in buying a house, paying off a mortgage and worrying about property values. In addition, their savings would be available when and as needed—not only for investment, but for consumption, college education for their children, travel and the like—without having to mortgage or sell their home.

Also, with the creation of a large social sector, the allocation of social housing could be through a "social market" that would provide resident choice, eliminate bureaucratic procedures and achieve a degree of efficiency never realized in the existing housing market, rather than through current practices of waiting lists, priority categories and lotteries (see Stone 1993:214–217 for discussion of how such a social market might work).

SOCIAL RENTAL HOUSING

Public Housing

Public housing is by far the most extensive and most maligned form of social ownership in this country. As of 2001, local housing authorities owned 2 million housing units (U.S. Census Bureau and HUD 2002:Table 1A-7), about 2 percent of all housing: 1.3 million of these under the federal program (U.S. Department of Housing and Urban Development 2000)—a reduction of about 100,000 from the early 1990s (Dolbeare 1991)—the remaining 700,000 under various state and local programs. In addition, the Department of Defense owns and operates about 400,000 family housing units, the "other public housing program" (Hartman and Drayer 1990; Twiss and Martin 1999).

The origins of public housing are well known, as are the ways in which the real estate industry from the outset attacked public housing ideologically and constrained it operationally through restrictions on design, location and management as well as funding, making virtually inevitable the well-publicized problems with some public housing (Bratt 1986). Yet despite these problems and the too-successful attempts to discredit the concept of public housing (and social enterprise generally), more complete and balanced examinations reveal that for the most part public housing has had a remarkable record of success in providing physically decent, nonspeculative, mortgage-free and cost-effective housing to poor people (Bratt 1986, 1989:Chapter 3; Council of Large Public Housing Authorities 1986). "Public housing serves more tenants with extremely low incomes, more tenants who are nonwhite and more households headed by a single parent than any other housing program" (National Housing Law Project 1990:15). In addition, for several decades starting in the late 1960s, a combination of tenant organizing, lawsuits, regulatory reforms and some (though inadequate) funding for modernization and operating subsidies brought about physical improvements in some older developments; more competent and responsible management of a number of local housing authorities; a measure of tenant protection in terms of leases, grievance procedures and collective bargaining rights; and in a few cities and individual developments, tenant membership on housing authority boards and even tenant management.

Public housing remains a vital resource despite its checkered history and reputation (Fuerst 2000). Many housing authorities have more people on their waiting lists than are currently living in their developments. Some have closed their waiting lists because the wait is as long as 20 years. In some cities, the turnover is so low that until deregulation policies were put into effect in the mid-1990s, federal preferences successively established over the decades had limited new occupancy to those who were victims of fire or other disaster, were able to demonstrate past denial of admission due to racial discrimination, or were homeless or paying over 50 percent of their incomes for housing (Vale 1999:14). As a result, by 1997, the median annual income of public housing households was under $7,000, less than 20 percent of the national median income (CLPHA 2000).

While giving priority for public housing to the most needy households is quite appropriate in a society where low-cost housing is scarce and housing is not a right, the deepening concentration of the poorest households in public housing added fuel to attacks on the very idea of public housing, blaming public ownership and management (and/or the residents themselves) for the poverty of the residents (see, for example, Husock 1997; Evans 1998; Hickman 1998 and the debate between Timothy Ross [1997, 1998] and Tom Angotti [1997]). Furthermore, in some cities, large public housing developments are situated in areas where, in recent decades, urban redevelopment and gentrification have raised land values, making the sites ostensibly too valuable for poor people. Thus, since the 1980s, there have been increasingly strong forces working to reduce the amount of public housing, through density reduction in existing projects, wholesale demolition, sale to private developers and conversion to mixed-income (including market-rate) housing—without requiring (since 1995) one-for-one replacement of lost units, let alone increasing the number of low-income units. In addition, behavioral requirements for residents, similar to those under welfare "reform," and greater autonomy for local housing authorities under the Quality Housing and Work Responsibility Act of 1998, increase the likelihood of many residents losing their homes even if their units are not physically lost (see, for example, Ranghelli 1999; Keating 2000).

During the 1980s, some public housing underwent renovation and revitalization, which,

while reducing the number of units, did retain public ownership of the housing for low-income people. Other cases, though, involved replacement of public housing—wholesale physical and social transformation into privately owned mixed-income housing, with the loss of units for low-income families far exceeding the physical reduction (Vale 1999:19). The prevailing public housing policy of the 1990s and into the new millennium—known as HOPE VI—largely embodies the principles of public housing replacement, with substantial displacement and loss of units even where local housing authorities retain ownership (Pitcoff 1999; Vale 1999; Keating 2000; National Housing Law Project et al., 2002).

As of the late 1990s, it was projected that HOPE VI would result in the demolition of about 100,000 units, with a net loss of as many as 60,000 low-income units (Keating 2000:385). This process has proceeded apace, despite evidence that in many cases public housing demolished or slated for demolition was not physically unsound and that, contrary to prevailing beliefs, resident satisfaction was often remarkably high prior to redevelopment (Keating 2000; see also Varady and Preiser 1998 on resident satisfaction). Indeed, despite being promoted as a vehicle for redeveloping "severely distressed" public housing, a federal audit in the mid-1990s concluded that HOPE VI was increasingly targeting public housing in locations where there is a market for profitable higher-income housing rather than solid evidence of "severe distress" (National Housing Law Project et al., 2002:ii).

In the introduction to their scathing critique of the HOPE VI program, the National Housing Law Project and its co-authors state (2002:ii):

HOPE VI plays upon the public housing program's unfairly negative reputation and an exaggerated sense of crisis about the state of public housing in general to justify a drastic model of large-scale family displacement and housing redevelopment that increasingly appears to do more harm than good.

Their report provides extensive evidence regarding a whole host of problems with HOPE VI, including the loose definition of "severe distress"; reduction in the amount of housing affordable the lowest-income households; few meaningful opportunities for resident participation; worsened housing situations for displaced residents and inadequate record-keeping and monitoring by the U.S. Department of Housing and Urban Development (HUD). Also, a field report of residents' experiences under HOPE VI, conducted by the Center for Community Change for the national organization of public housing tenants (ENPHRONT 2003), poignantly documents the human costs in residents' own words. Even the Urban Institute's research has acknowledged that while some public housing residents have been helped by HOPE VI, "vulnerable families face significant barriers" (2002; also, Popkin 2002).

While prevailing current sentiment gives little encouragement, public housing is an essential ingredient in addressing the housing crisis and realizing a Right to Housing, in part because it is unequivocally outside the speculative market and also because it includes an established, operational infrastructure for producing, financing and managing housing, including the power of eminent domain.

The amount of public housing should be increased not only through new construction but even more expeditiously and cost-effectively through acquisition of some existing housing. Several housing authorities have acquired and substantially rehabilitated older buildings or purchased rehabilitated buildings under "turnkey" contracts with private developers. Some authorities have purchased existing housing units not in need of rehabilitation. For example, the Houston Housing Authority bought some Federal Housing Administration (FHA)–foreclosed homes during the mid-1980s' downturn in the economy of the region. Some Massachusetts housing authorities purchased condominium units in multifamily buildings that had been converted during that state's 1980s real estate boom. More recently, the Watertown, Massachusetts, housing authority purchased several two- and three-family houses as scattered-site public housing for large families (Stone, Werby and Friedman 2000:20).

In some instances, the possibility of non-speculative resident ownership of some public housing (as mutual housing or limited-equity co-ops—see below) should be considered, under certain conditions: (1) physical modernization and tenant capacity development have taken place; (2) there are enforceable guarantees of deep affordability subsidies and future modernization funding in perpetuity; (3) residents are given full opportunity to choose whether to take title on the basis of full independent evaluation of the trade-offs and risk; and (4) resident ownership is nonspeculative forever. If these conditions were required by law, then tenant ownership of public housing might contribute to the goal of resident empowerment while simultaneously retaining it as social housing and enhancing it physically and economically.[5]

As an alternative to selling public housing to residents, greatly increased resident power offers the potential for improving conditions in the housing and developing a sense of dignity, self-esteem and solidarity among some of the poorest and most oppressed members of society. If strong tenant organizations are created, if there are sufficient technical and financial resources, and if an adequate legal and regulatory framework for collective bargaining and shared decision-making with the housing authority is in place, public housing tenants can achieve these benefits while holding management and the government operationally and financially accountable. Moving into tenant management while the housing still is under public ownership may offer residents certain further advantages in terms of day-to-day operational authority, skills development and collective responsibility but also certain pitfalls, in terms of resource uncertainty and lack of control over the larger context—economic and physical—that shapes the lives of the poor. Tenants may be left administering their own dependency, with the leadership becoming the focus of blame for problems beyond their control. But as long as there is public ownership, there is also some legal and political leverage over government resources and responsibility (Peterman 1987).

With real tenant power, adequate public resources for modernization, adequate affordability subsidies and a gradual expansion of the economic mix of residents as the amount of social housing increases, public housing can be revitalized physically and socially. These changes will not be easy to achieve, as trends have been in the opposite direction, but the accomplishments and potential of public housing are still worth recognizing and fighting for.

Nonprofit Rental Housing

Unfortunately, there are few precise figures on how many housing units are under ownership by private nonprofits, due to the ambiguity of definitions, overlap of categories and lack of any entity (public or private) that has been given or assumed responsibility for compiling and disseminating such information. Nonetheless, I estimate that as of the early 21st century, there are about 1.3 to 1.7 million rental units in nonprofit ownership. This consists of about 1.1 to 1.3 million subsidized rental units, plus roughly 200,000 to 400,000 other rental units in nonprofit ownership that have received no government subsidies or possibly just capital assistance from nonfederal public or private sources.[6] This is a significant number, but it is just slightly over one-half the number of units owned by local public housing authorities, and about $1\frac{1}{2}$ percent of all housing units in the United States.

While ideological factors kept public housing from our nation until the 1930s, in the late 19th century, moral righteousness and enlightened self-interest on the part of some capitalists stimulated a modest move toward "philanthropic housing." Nonprofit projects were developed in a number of cities in the early part of the 20th century, totaling several thousand units (Abrams 1946:170ff). By eliminating development and rental profits, the housing was slightly less expensive initially than speculative new housing. But with construction costs to be paid off from rents, the units were still more expensive than the tenements occupied by poor and working-class people, so the residents were mostly of middle-income. Had these developments remained out of the speculative market, by today, they might be debt-free social housing and hence much less expensive than speculatively owned apartments of the same vintage or newer. However, most were eventually sold. As Charles Abrams aptly put it (1946:175), "Philanthropy could no more solve the problem of housing than it could solve the problem of poverty."

In the modern era, private nonprofit housing has evolved and expanded through several phases, in which the lessons of this historical experiment have been learned gradually and unevenly but sufficiently to hold the promise of an increasingly important role in the growth of the social sector of housing.

The most clearly identifiable and longest-lived component of modern nonprofit ownership consists of federally financed and subsidized Section 202 housing for the elderly and handicapped, a program created in 1959 as the first of a series of subsidized housing production programs for private development and ownership. Unlike all subsequent programs, though, 202 has from the outset been restricted to development and ownership by nonprofit (and public) entities. The result has been the emergence over the past four decades of a set of organizations specializing in such housing, although some regional and community-based nonprofits have included 202s among their broader housing repertoire.

Section 202 housing was financed through below-market direct federal loans until changed to capital grant financing by the Housing Act of 1990. Projects built since 1974 also receive Section 8 rental subsidies. In addition, an owner may not sell the housing into the speculative market, at least during the 40-year term of federal financing and regulation. And even in the rare instances of foreclosure, Section 202 projects have been transferred to other nonprofit owners. These features, together with the capital grant financing and supportive services provided by the 1990 Housing Act, make the 202 program a premier model of privately owned nonspeculative housing (see also Bratt 1989:184–185). As of the late 1990s, there were about 200,000 units of Section 202 housing (HUD 2000).

Unfortunately, there does not exist a well-established model of nonelderly housing that embodies all of the attractive features of 202 housing. During the 1960s and early 1970s, socially motivated nonprofit developers did produce nearly 200,000 housing units under the FHA Section 221(d)(3) and 236 interest-reduction programs that had been created primarily for profit-making developers. (Nonprofit production comprised over a one-fourth of the total under these programs—[Clay 1987:9].) However, many ended up defaulting on their mortgages (as did many profit-motivated owners but at a somewhat lower rate). The housing was taken over or resold by HUD, in some cases to speculative owners, so this experience does not offer the encouragement of provided by the Section 202 program. Also, apart from weaknesses in the federal programs themselves, nonprofit owners had to contend with inadequate resources, lack of experience, an unsympathetic HUD and the challenges of trying to serve and empower some of the neediest populations and communities (Bratt, 1989:185–191). Nonetheless, approximately three-fourths of these units remain in some form of nonprofit ownership.[7]

Beginning in the late 1960s, another type of nonprofit housing model was emerging, one that has proven much more successful at producing and operating housing under the government subsidy programs. However, in order to be successful, these housing providers have had to buy into many of the rules of profit-making development and stretched the meaning of nonprofit ownership. Community development corporations, regional housing development corporations and "intermediaries" providing technical assistance have been set up, with staffs that attempt to combine training and experience in business and finance with social concern. While these entities are themselves nonprofit corporations, and their housing commitment almost always is to permanent nonspeculative ownership, in order to benefit from the financial incentives provided through the Internal Revenue Code (notably the Low Income Housing Tax Credit), they have to enter into partnerships with profit-motivated investors. (See Chapter 16.)

When a nonprofit organization needs to market its housing plans to potential investors and also meet the underwriting criteria of mortgage lenders to obtain financing, the needs of prospective residents may at times have to be compromised. Once the housing is occupied, in order to maintain investor confidence in the

development and the organization, the housing may need to be managed quite conservatively in terms of tenants' rights and rent levels. Even though these tensions may be mitigated with deep, income-determined subsidies, a nonprofit owner can face disturbing role conflicts between its obligations to the residents and the investors. Furthermore, because the tax benefits are of finite duration (typically 15 to 20 years, depending upon the type of tax benefit), down the road the investors will want to bail out when they no longer have any financial incentives. Unless the deal has been structured so that they can fully recover their initial investments as well as their profits from the tax shelters, the investors will expect to be bought out at this point—necessitating sale of the housing to owners who might turn it into market-rate housing, unless financing is available for the nonprofit or the residents themselves to buy out the investors.

In sum, the current prevailing model of nonprofit development and ownership might more properly be understood to be "quasi-nonprofit" or even "compromised nonprofit" ownership. Only if social financing replaces dependence on profit-motivated investors can the growing number of these community-based and regional nonprofit housing providers have a viable alternative to partnerships with profit-motivated investors and thus be able to achieve true social ownership.

Mutual Housing Associations

There is one other, more fully social model of nonprofit ownership—the mutual housing association (MHA)—that began in Europe over a century ago but has only emerged in the United States over the past two decades (Goetze 1987; Bratt 1990). One version, the federated MHA, consists of a group of resident-controlled limited-equity co-ops (see below) or nonprofit developments (Krinsky and Hovde 1996:10). The other version, referred to as an integrated MHA, has been promoted since the late 1970s by the Neighborhood Reinvestment Corporation (NRC) and differs from other models of social ownership in several significant respects.

First, the NRC mutual housing approach has deliberately eschewed outside profit-seeking investors in order to avoid role conflict and possible pressure to sell the housing when the tax shelters run out. Second, NRC MHAs try to finance nearly all acquisition and development costs through upfront capital grants, although often they have had to use some debt due to limited availability of grant resources. Third, residents are expected to make a modest initial capital contribution (often waived for low-income people), which is recoverable with interest upon moving out but cannot otherwise grow and is not a marketable property interest; the goal is for residents to put up 5 percent of the total cost, with capital grants covering the rest. Fourth, a portion of each resident's monthly charges is supposed to go into a fund that will provide part of the capital grants for additional units, although generally only middle- to high-income residents pay high enough monthly charges to contribute to the capital fund. Fifth, the membership of each NRC mutual housing association consists of residents, prospective residents and local public and community officials. A majority of the governing board consists of residents and prospective residents, so the housing is largely owned and controlled collectively by residents. Sixth, organizational development is emphasized as much as the physical development of the housing, with residents required to participate and expected to take care of minor maintenance of their units, even though professional management is an integral part of the model. Finally, residents have lifetime security of tenure, as long as they meet their financial and other membership obligations and do not violate the rights of others. They may designate a family or household member as the successor to their unit but may not sublet; this ensures that every resident is an association member who is expected to participate in the organization.

Because of the experimental nature of this mutual housing model and because it has attempted to operate outside prevailing government programs and financing mechanisms, it has grown slowly and remains limited in scale despite early interest and enthusiasm. As of late 2002, there were only eleven NRC mutual housing associations that together owned about 8,300 occupied units (NeighborWorks Network 2005). Nonetheless, an encouraging analysis found that mutual housing associations would be more cost-effective to the federal government than nearly any other approach in assisting very-low-income households on a long-term basis (Bratt 1990). Thus, despite its extremely small scale so far, there are compelling economic as well as social advantages to the mutual housing model. It is an emerging approach that comes quite close to realizing many of the goals set out here for true social housing.

Resident Security, Power and Control in Socially Owned Rental Housing

People who reside in housing owned by public agencies, nonprofit organizations and integrated mutual housing associations are legally tenants. Some people regard this as a fundamental weakness of these forms of ownership, as residents ostensibly have no opportunity to realize any of the psychological, social and economic benefits of homeownership. It is important, though, to challenge the notion of a sharp binary polarity, a great divide, between rental and ownership.

Even in the private housing market, neither tenancy nor homeownership is a unitary concept. And previously suggested, an alternative form of tenure under social ownership, in combination with no debt costs, can yield resident benefits that are competitive with conventional homeownership. Of greater subtlety and more immediate relevance, though, concepts of residential property have been undergoing considerable evolution so that the diverse forms of ownership, as well as their combinations and modifications in practice, have produced virtually a continuum on the dimensions of security of tenure, resident control and economic benefits.

For example, even in private rental housing the history of tenant organizing, legislation and litigation reveals that there are significant objective differences among tenancy-at-will, lease tenancy, tenancy with formal resident organization and collective bargaining, and tenancy with statutory and regulatory controls on conditions, evictions and rents.

Within existing subsidized rental housing, the history of public housing certainly demonstrates how low-income residents can be disenfranchised, abused and degraded almost as much by public as by private landlords. Yet in public housing, as discussed earlier, organizing and advocacy led to legislative and administrative redefinition of the scope of residents' power and rights and the meaning of public ownership, even if some of these rights have been undermined since the late 1980s. Public owners have enforceable (though not always enforced, to be sure) legal, constitutional and financial obligations to residents greater than can be imposed on private owners. Thus, resident ownership is not necessarily the only or best route to greater power, security and control.

For tenants in private nonprofit housing and mutual housing associations, the legal leverage and claims on public resources are, of course, less than for public housing residents. However, the organizational circumstances are usually quite different as well. Certainly, some of the socially oriented nonprofits that developed subsidized housing in the 1960s and 1970s lacked the financial capacity and organizational ability to sustain their social commitment to their tenants. When HUD foreclosed on the federally insured mortgages, the housing came into the public domain, where the outcome for the residents has depended upon their political strength and skill. In the best of circumstances, such as Boston's Methunion Manor, with sophisticated organizing and technical assistance the residents were able to force HUD to absorb the outstanding mortgage debt and agree to provide financing for rehabilitation and guarantee rental subsidies for at least 20 years. After winning this agreement, they took title as a limited-equity co-op, at which point they were no longer tenants (Stone 1986).

In contrast with many of the early nonprofits, some community development corporations and all mutual housing associations have explicitly involved residents in decision-making and, in some cases, management and operation of the housing as an integral part of the philosophy of the organizations. In such situations, there is not only objective resident power and security of tenure but also a considerable sense of "ownership" in the psychological sense even if in formal legal terms the residents are tenants.

In addition, while residents do not build up any wealth through their housing, resident-savers can on average do as well financially as conventional owners, as explained above, depending upon the financing and cost structure of the housing.

Furthermore, residents of participatory nonprofit rental housing can in principle have as much autonomy to fix up and change their units as do residents of physically equivalent limited-equity co-ops or condominiums. Finally, what must be weighed against some formal differences in legal status between participatory social rental and nonspeculative homeownership are differences in financial risk. In the contemporary situation of ownership by a community development corporation, mutual housing association or regional nonprofit housing corporation, the ownership entity transcends not only the individual unit but also the particular building or development and usually is connected to an infrastructure of intermediaries that have provided financial and technical assistance. This means that the residents, most of whom are low-income people, do not have to carry fully by themselves the cost burdens of unanticipated housing problems or changes in their own economic circumstances or of their fellow residents, in contrast with individual private ownership.

Along most dimensions, being a tenant in socially owned rental housing is not necessarily inferior to being a nonspeculative homeowner—or speculative owner. It may have real advantages and attractions not only for those of low or moderate income but for many of those with higher income as well.

NONSPECULATIVE HOMEOWNERSHIP

Limited-Equity Cooperatives

As of 2003, there were approximately 1.2 million housing units under cooperative ownership in the United States. About 425,000 of these are limited-equity or zero-equity co-ops, of which over one-half are in New York. The remaining 765,000 are market-rate cooperatives (National Association of Housing Cooperatives 2003). The latter group includes 550,000 conversions from rental housing, mostly in New York City, similar to condo conversions in other parts of the country. The other 215,000 market-rate co-ops are mostly middle-income developments that originally had resale restrictions but in most cases now permit members to sell their shares at the market price.

During the 19th century, programs for cooperative ownership of workplaces and residences were integral parts of the utopian and revolutionary critiques of capitalism in the United States as well as in Europe. In this country, as early as 1869, Melusina Fay Peirce advocated cooperative residential neighborhoods as part of a vision she shared with many feminists and some socialists who saw a seamless connection between the public and private and the productive and reproductive realms in a radically transformed industrial society (Hayden 1984:29, 72–74). However, the earliest U.S. co-ops (in New York between 1876 and 1885) did not embody this radical vision but were instead a form of homeownership for high-income urbanites, presaging modern luxury co-ops and condos (Siegler and Levy 1987:14).

It was not until the 20th century that the first nonspeculative, socially oriented co-op housing was developed. Most of these were in New York City and under union auspices. In the early part of the century, several workers' housing cooperatives were developed (Abrams 1946:181; Siegler and Levy 1987:14), but most did not last. In the late 1920s, New York State passed a limited-dividend housing law that, among other things, facilitated co-ops for moderate- to middle-income people (Siegler and Levy 1987:14). One of the first was the Workers Cooperative Colony in the Bronx developed by the Amalgamated Clothing Workers. With the first units completed in 1928, it grew eventually to 1,400 units and still remains a co-op (Wright 1981:198–199; Hayden 1984:91; Siegler and Levy 1987:14; Krinsky and Hovde 1996:18). However, despite state tax exemptions, the co-ops developed by labor groups in New York were affordable only to higher-paid workers. Furthermore, subletting and turnover tended to undermine the socially oriented philosophical foundations (Abrams 1946:181–182). During the 1930s, depression conditions led to increased

national interest in co-ops, but postwar era ideological and economic conditions shunted co-ops to the margin of housing policy (Leavitt 1995).

While these early housing cooperatives were structured to assure continued affordability to members of the affinity group, there is nothing intrinsically nonspeculative about cooperative ownership. In any co-op, the housing is owned by a corporation made up of "cooperators," with each share in the corporation corresponding to either a particular dwelling unit or a proportion of the square footage of the entire building. Unless explicitly defined otherwise, a share is a marketable commodity that may be sold for whatever the owner can get. Furthermore, although ownership of co-op shares is not legally equivalent to ownership of the dwelling unit, for income-tax purposes the Internal Revenue Service (IRS) allows each share owner to deduct the pro-rata share of mortgage interest and property taxes attributable to that unit. In addition, unless the co-op agreement requires the owner of shares to be a resident of the unit, an owner may sublet the unit and charge whatever the market will bear.

Within this framework, the distinctly limited-equity form of co-op emerged as a housing strategy for helping to maintain long-term affordability and resident control for people of moderate if not low income. In a limited-equity co-op, the share price is set by formula, not by the market, in order to restrict or eliminate any speculative gain. The co-op corporation retains a first-option right to purchase a departing member's share at the formula price. In addition, occupancy and share ownership are generally coterminous—apart perhaps from approved temporary subletting—in order to prevent "landlordism" and to ensure that residents are people who have a legal and financial stake in the housing.

Interestingly, the growth of interest in the limited-equity co-op model over the past two decades does not simply hark back to the early co-ops. It also rests upon a substantial but little known historical foundation of several hundred thousand co-op units developed in the three decades prior to 1980. The great majority of these were unsubsidized, middle-income cooperatives, with federal or state government mortgage insurance or financing. In addition, an entire infrastructure evolved to undertake development and provide technical assistance, services and training for co-op housing (Siegler and Levy 1987:16–19; National Association of Housing Cooperatives 1990). Indeed, after World War II, some progressive housers advocated a large-scale co-op program as part of urban redevelopment, to complement public housing for households who could not qualify for the latter and as a model for eventual conversion of public housing to resident control (Abrams 1946:179–187). However, as indicated above, from the mid-1950s until the mid-1960s, interest in co-ops by middle-income households waned in the face of "anti-collectivist" ideology and the suburban triumph.

In the late 1960s and the 1970s, several factors led to renewed interest in nonspeculative housing cooperatives, within a rather different political and economic context. The emphasis on community control and resident empowerment in the federal antipoverty program (and in response to the urban riots) contributed to the eligibility of co-ops for federal housing subsidies. About 60,000 co-op units were created under the HUD Section 221 and 236 programs between the mid-1960s and mid-1970s (National Association of Housing Cooperatives 1990). Also, the emergence of the modern women's movement rekindled interest in co-ops—integrally connected with supportive services, as in the 19th century feminist notions—as a residential model especially well suited to the needs of single women (young and elderly) and women as single parents (Hayden 1984; Novac and Wekerle 1995).

In addition, wholesale disinvestment and abandonment of vast amounts of housing in major cities across the country led to some spontaneous, grassroots building takeovers of unoccupied buildings and resident operation of occupied buildings. Especially in New York City, where effective title of many thousands of buildings passed to the city, the movement demanded not only rehabilitation but also title to the buildings as limited-equity co-ops (Kolodny 1973, 1986; Schuman 1986; Lawson and Johnson 1986; Leavitt and Saegert 1990). However, since the late 1970s, the limited-equity co-op movement has been impelled rather less by the housing needs of the very poor than by declining opportunities for conventional (or even condominium) homeownership among moderate- to middle-income people. Over this period, about 150,000 additional limited-equity co-op units have been developed, with more than one-half of these being in New York City (National Association of Housing Cooperatives 2003).

Ironically, the ideal of resident control in a limited-equity co-op includes the risk that the residents may at some point reorganize as a market co-op. Because cooperatives are legally autonomous corporations, this possibility is real and has been occurring (Levy 1997). Only if the co-op incorporation documents preclude such dissolution, or if there is an entity that has some legal leverage and a broader public interest, can this risk be avoided. Where there is public involvement—through, say, mortgage insurance, publicly donated land or public grants, loans or subsidies—then contractual requirements or deed restrictions can protect the limited-equity requirement indefinitely. The strongest legal protection of permanency, though, is through ownership of the land by a government agency or broadly based community land trust (described in the next section). Under such an arrangement, the co-op corporation owns the structures but leases the land, with the ground lease stipulating retention of the co-op's limited-equity character.

Nonspeculative co-op units have been created through both new construction and building conversions. Most have involved multifamily structures, but some, such as the Route 2 Co-op in Los Angeles (Heskin 1991), include one-family houses. While income mixes vary, including some low-income and some higher-income people, the middle range prevails. Although some public programs and public funds in the form of land, loans and grants have often assisted, financing has generally come from quasi-public mortgage lenders (such as state housing finance agencies and the National Cooperative Bank) that offer terms slightly below market. Each co-op has tended to be unique, not only in the circumstances that led to its creation but also in the resident mix, the financing sources and terms, and the limited-equity formula (Heskin and Leavitt 1995). While this uniqueness reflects an encouraging creativity and resourcefulness, it also makes more difficult policies that could facilitate more rapid expansion of the model.

Limited-equity and zero-equity co-op housing constitutes one of the three main pillars of social housing in the United States, the other two being public housing and nonprofit housing. The cooperative model can make a significant contribution to a Right to Housing—and realize the vision of cooperation not only in legality but in living—but only when it achieves strict equity limitation, permanence in nonspeculative ownership and transcendence of debt and tax-syndication financing.

Ownership with Community Land Trusts

While the origins of most of the other models of nonspeculative ownership are primarily urban, the community land trust (CLT) has rural roots. These traditions include Native American concepts as well as several 19th century movements, most notably utopian socialist experiments in common ownership of land and other productive resources; Henry George's notions of land as the principal locus of unearned wealth and social exploitation; and aristocratic support for nongovernmental nature preserves and parks (e.g., the Audubon Society, the Massachusetts Trustees of Reservations).

Yet, despite its roots, the land trust movement that began in the 1960s and has been growing at an accelerating rate since the late 1970s does not seek to restore a vanished past or opt out of modern society. It operates within, while seeking to transform, contemporary real estate law. It is concerned with the active productive uses of land, including but not limited to residential use, in opposition to speculative holding and use of land. It is, in this sense, concerned with issues of responsible and active land use and planning, rather than preservation per se and resistance to development. And it seeks to use land tenure as the organizing locus for the expansion and realization of democratic decision-making (Institute for Community Economics 1982:Chapter 1; Davis 1984; White and Matthei 1987; Krinsky and Hovde 1996).

The model vests title to the land itself in a nonprofit community organization—the land trust—to be held in nonspeculative ownership in perpetuity. Individuals are granted the right to use the land for their own benefit and with considerable individual autonomy. The formal legal link between the trust that owns the land and the people or organizations who use it is the ground lease, which grants lifetime or 99-year tenure (inheritable and renewable), subject to certain conditions. Thus, as it relates to housing, the form of ownership of the buildings may be anywhere on the ownership spectrum depending upon the terms of the ground lease under which the housing owners are allowed to use the land. In principle, the house owner could be a landlord renting the dwelling for whatever the market rent might be or a homeowner free to sell the house at the market price (exclusive of land). In practice, the land trust movement has been committed primarily to "permanently affordable homeownership" (Davis and Demetrowitz 2003), using the ground lease terms to enhance affordability, security of tenure, resident ownership and nonspeculative transfer of houses in perpetuity. The actual form and conditions of ownership of the dwellings depend on the local context and individual circumstances.

Community land trusts acquire land by donation if possible, but often by purchase. Therefore, their immediate impact on the cost of housing depends upon their ability to obtain land at less than market prices, gain access to below-market financing for land acquisition that may include development as well and subsidize residents through resources the CLT receives as a charitable organization. Over the long term, housing costs are reduced primarily by preventing resale of the land and controlling the price at which the residential structures may be resold. As with other forms of nonspeculative ownership, deep affordability remains constrained by continued dependence on debt financing and by residents' incomes.

The ways in which the community land trust approach distinguishes itself are, first, the dual ownership structure, which explicitly accepts individual property rights while establishing and protecting social or community rights. On one side, the private ownership of one's dwelling, opportunity to accumulate some wealth through homeownership and unrestricted right to pass the home to one's heirs enhance the appeal of the model by building on deeply rooted ideological traditions. On the other side, broad-based land trusteeship is intended to provide a legal and social framework for maintaining nonspeculative ownership forever. The goal is to strengthen established—though weaker—traditions of community, in ways that skirt popular skepticism about government. The second distinctive feature is the broader community development and land reform agenda, which, it is argued, can facilitate economic development and community empowerment and hence begin to address the income side of the affordability issue and aspects of the quality of life beyond just housing itself (Institute for Community Economics 1982:Chapter 2; Davis 1984:219–222; White and Matthei 1987:47–64; Krinsky and Hovde 1996).

However, just as each of the other social housing models faces certain fairly distinctive constraints, so does the CLT approach. First, because a CLT allows a leaseholder to own the buildings on the land, imposing a limited-equity and first-option resale restriction on building owners may lead to legal challenges as "restraints on alienation" (Davis 1984:223), although apparently this concern has been overcome (Institute for Community Economics 2001).

Second, because the supply of land that can be acquired through donation or below-market purchase will always be small, and the ability of CLTs to purchase substantial amounts of private land at market prices will always be limited, only a broader and more radical land reform agenda will enable the CLT movement to alter significantly the effects of land speculation on housing costs.

Finally, while the CLT model departs significantly from Henry George's 19th century proposals, the emphasis on land as the decisive element of wealth and power reflects some of the "Georgist" neglect of financial, industrial and commercial wealth and associated power in the modern world. Those people who do not own great wealth but have considerable economic security as members of the "upper middle class"

have not achieved their relative power and status because they own land, but through their occupational position. Their class, race, gender and associated educational opportunity have given them access to employment income that in turn has enabled them to accumulate equity in their residences (including the underlying land), not vice versa. There are compelling reasons for trying to remove land from speculative ownership, but real redistribution of power will require much broader redistribution of wealth, with land as only one and not necessarily the most decisive element.

Given the grandness of the vision, the recent emergence of the model and the lack of public programs and resources specifically for land acquisition, it is not surprising that the land trust movement is still modest in scale. Between the late 1960s and the mid-1980s, the number of community land trusts grew slowly, with some losses along the way; in 1985, there were fewer than 20. Since 1985, though, the growth has been substantial, reaching almost 50 in 1991 and 133 in operation or development by 2001 (Institute for Community Economics 2002). This upsurge has emerged directly out of the housing affordability crisis, as land trusts increasingly have been created in cities and towns, with "forever" housing as their primary focus. Although CLTs have been established in all parts of the United States, about one-half are in New England, which has experienced some of the most severe affordability problems and where grassroots organizing—both rural and urban—has long been a way of life.

In the entire country, there were only about 6,000 housing units on CLT-owned land as of the end of 2001 (Institute for Community Economics 2002). Nonspeculative housing under the CLT model is thus comparable in scale to mutual housing associations and orders of magnitude less than public, nonprofit rental and limited-equity co-op housing. Nonetheless, again analogous to mutual housing associations, the land trust emphasis on organizational development, participation and personal growth, along with the creation of permanently affordable homeownership housing, will undoubtedly make the model increasingly popular.

Resale-Restricted Individual Ownership

Since the 1980s, the principal response to declining opportunities for conventional homeownership has not, in fact, been promotion of social ownership programs but those public (and some private) programs to assist first-time homebuyers with mortgage financing at interest rates somewhat below market, "soft" second mortgages (i.e., deferred repayment), reduced or waived closing costs and proposals for tax-exempt or tax-deferred saving for downpayments. In addition, many localities have provided publicly owned land at little or no cost and offered below-market construction financing and even some partial capital grants to stimulate construction of below-market housing for homeownership. Because the participating homebuyer is able to obtain a house with below-market financing, possibly at a below-market price, most programs impose some resale restrictions in order to lessen the potential for owners to reap windfalls when they sell in the speculative market.

In most instances, however, the provisions are so weak that the housing may not be characterized as nonspeculative even for the initial owner, and generally the housing is fully in the speculative market with the second and subsequent owners. The weakest restrictions permit the owner to sell freely in the speculative market but then repay the subsidies out of the sales proceeds.[8] While this supposedly enables the funds to be recycled to other buyers, repayment typically is interest-free (and inflation-free), and often the amount that must be repaid declines with time, so eventually no recapture occurs. Another approach places limits on the price for which the house may be sold, usually allowing an annual increment above the original purchase price equal to the overall rate of inflation or some fixed rate, such as 5 percent. The public agency then has a first option to purchase at this price or may require sale at this price to another qualified buyer. While this might appear to prevent speculative windfalls, it does not, because of the financial leverage involved in low downpayment residential purchases, even assuming modest market appreciation.[9]

Although rarely done in practice, there is no reason why the formula for resale-restricted individual ownership could not be a limited-equity formula comparable to those used in limited-equity co-ops. Under such circumstances, it would be possible to achieve nonspeculative individual ownership. There are, however, some legal and practical problems with the enforcement of most resale restrictions, whether mild or strong. Recapture provisions pose the least difficulty because they are easily secured through property liens, which pose no legal or enforcement difficulties, since the owner would not be able to sell without discharging the lien. Price, equity and first-option limitations are more problematical because they generally involve deed covenants, which in most states are legally limited in duration and enforceability.[10] The best approach is thus to allow the buyer to own the house but not the land—to have the land owned by a land trust or public agency.[11]

Some might wonder why a low-income family should be forced to accept a resale restriction, and especially a permanent limited-equity restriction, in order to achieve homeownership. Why shouldn't such households be permitted to accumulate whatever wealth the real estate market provides, just as higher-income households have been able to achieve? Are not resale restrictions a form of discrimination, against low-income homebuyers in general and homebuyers of color in particular, as the latter have for so long been denied homeownership through discriminatory sales and lending practices?

Certainly, any household who wishes to have unrestricted homeownership should be able to do so through conventional purchase and financing terms, without discrimination—but also without public or community financial assistance. If, however, a household receives downpayment grants, below-market loans and possibly deferred payment loans, that household is in effect entering into shared ownership with the community—the community thus legitimately having certain rights to the property. What does the homebuyer get from such an arrangement? First, access to homeownership, with the associated status and security of tenure that presumably would not otherwise be affordable. Second, exclusive use and control of the living space—for instance, it is not necessary to share the space with the community "co-owner" nor be constrained by a landlord. Third, potential income tax benefits from the deductibility of mortgage interest and property taxes. Fourth, no rent payments on the community's share of the property. Fifth, the opportunity to build wealth on the homebuyer's share of the property. What does the homebuyer *not* get? The right to sell the community's share and thereby appropriate for private gain the wealth that rightly belongs to the community. Nonspeculative homeownership, with permanent limited-equity resale restrictions, is thus not only not discriminatory but is more than fair to those who participate in it.[12]

INCREASING THE AMOUNT OF SOCIALLY OWNED HOUSING

How could the amount of social housing in our nation be expanded? There are a variety of routes, including:

- production of new housing, by nonprofit or public developers, or by for-profit developers for transfer upon completion to social ownership (see Chapters 16 and 17);
- preservation of existing subsidized rental housing, with transfer from for-profit owners to social owners (see Chapter 7);
- conversion of private rental housing, where owners are irresponsible or are otherwise willing to sell, through the use of receivership, eminent domain and tenant buy-out rights and assistance (see Stone 1993:228–231, 248–249);
- foreclosure protection and equity conversion as an option for low-income and elderly homeowners in return for their agreeing to current or future transfer to social ownership (see Stone 1993:226–228, 238–239; Stone 2002);
- permanent limited-equity resale restrictions with subsidized first-time homebuyer programs (see Stone 2002).

Historically, most of the social housing in the United States has been provided through publicly subsidized new construction and substantial rehabilitation, even though this is the most capital-intensive, costly, time-consuming and complex of the available routes. Recently, however, considerable attention has been focused on strategies to preserve subsidized housing that was built by private developers in the 1960s and 1970s and convert it to true social ownership (see Chapter 7). However, to date, relatively little effort has gone into the other routes, which are surely the most cost-effective ways of achieving substantial increases in stock of social housing.

CONCLUSION

The notion that housing can be situated outside the speculative market has a long and established albeit constrained and little-recognized history in the United States. Various forms of nonspeculative ownership exist in practice, and real estate law continues to evolve to encompass new ideas and new economic and political realities. Each form of ownership has its trade-offs, its partisans and its critics. They differ in the degree to which they are truly and permanently nonspeculative and should be evaluated along these dimensions. Nonetheless, the various forms of socially owned rental and nonspeculative homeownership have a number of common components that distinguish them from both conventional rental and speculative homeownership and point toward true resident-controlled social ownership. The notion that housing should not and need not be a speculative commodity clearly is growing in legitimacy. As a practical matter, achievement of a Right to Housing will require that social housing not only become more acceptable in concept but will be greatly expanded in quantity and become the attractive alternative to conventional homeownership.

NOTES

1. The sources and methods used to arrive at the components of this estimate are included in the sections below on various types of socially owned housing.

Fewer than 3 million of this total consist of federally subsidized public and nonprofit housing units. The balance are nonspeculative units that either receive subsidies from state and local governments or no government subsidies.

2. This chapter is in part adapted and updated from portions of Stone (1993:Chapter 7, Chapter 9).

3. For a thoughtful philosophical analysis of the nature of property, critique of conventional notions of private property and proposal for an egalitarian alternative, see Christman (1994).

4. For social housing owned by public agencies or nonprofit organizations, grants could cover 100 percent of the acquisition or development costs. For limited-equity resident-owned housing, residents might make a small downpayment, with the rest of the cost covered by upfront grants. See the discussion below of the mutual housing association model, which uses this financing approach.

5. Approximately 20,000 units of public housing in the United States have actually been converted into zero equity or limited equity cooperatives (National Association of Housing Cooperatives 2003).

6. First, as indicated in the text, there were about 200,000 occupied 202 units in 1998 (U.S. Department of Housing and Urban Development 2000).

Second, under the Section 221(d)(3) BMIR, Section 236 and Rent Supplement programs, 192,000 units were originally under nonprofit ownership (Clay 1987:9). However, due to financial difficulties in both for-profit and nonprofit developments, HUD took over about one-fourth of all the units. While there are differing figures on how many remain in direct nonprofit ownership, how many are still held by HUD and how many have been resold to nonprofits (Clay 1987:9; U.S. General Accounting Office 1986:23; Achtenberg 1989:228–229), I estimate conservatively that at least 150,000 units originally produced under the programs are still owned by nonprofits.

Third, about 180,000 units owned by nonprofits were developed under various early unsubsidized FHA mortgage-insurance programs but subsequently received Section 8 subsidies, or, in a very few cases, other subsidies (U.S. General Accounting Office 1986:23). No hard data are available on how many are still part of the subsidized nonprofit inventory, but I am assuming at least 150,000.

Fourth, while there is virtually no official information on nonprofit ownership of units produced under the HUD Section 8 and HOME production programs, the best estimates come from studies of community-based developers. A 1998 census of such developers revealed that they have produced about 550,000 below-market units (National Congress for Community Economic Development 2000). Given the history of these organizations, most of these units have been rental housing. However, as Rachel Bratt points out

in Chapter 16, to some extent they have been producing units for homeownership. Without hard data, there is no way of knowing how many of the 550,000 CDC units are in the latter category, but it is probably less than 100,000. So, I am conservatively including 450,000 CDC units in the total of nonprofit rentals.

Fifth, the latter group of organizations does not include city-wide and regional nonprofits that do not fit the "community-based" definition. Such regional nonprofits have produced or preserved over 300,000 below market rental units (Housing Partnership Network 2002). It is likely that some of the at-risk subsidized housing such entities have preserved from going to market-rate rents includes some of the older nonprofit housing in the third category above. So to be conservative, I have assumed their net addition to the total below market "social" rental housing stock to be 250,000 units.

Combining the estimates for the five groups yields an aggregate estimate of 1,200,000 subsidized units in nonprofit ownership. Allowing for a margin of error of 100,000 units yields the text estimate of 1.1 to 1.3 million units.

Not included in this total are nonprofit rental units without subsidies developed under the various early federal mortgage-insurance programs. No estimates are available for the number of units in this category. Also not explicitly included in the estimate are Farmers Home Administration Section 515 subsidized rental units. There are about 300,000 units under this program (National Low Income Housing Preservation Commission 1988:17). It is not known how many are under nonprofit ownership, but it is possible that some if not most of these are included in the categories above. Note, finally, that the text estimate does not include nonprofit housing produced or acquired without federal involvement, either under state or local programs or with no government assistance at all. Again, no estimates are available for this category. It is thus likely that the actual total figure for nonprofit rental units is somewhat higher.

7. This is a very rough estimate based on anecdotal evidence, since no systematic accounting is available.

8. Consider, for example, the purchase of a $100,000 house, involving the Massachusetts Housing Partnership "Soft Second Loan Program" (MHPF 2003). There is a requirement of a 5 percent down payment, but only 3 percent must be out-of-pocket; the rest may be a gift or grant. So suppose the household puts down $3,000, with the rest as a grant. The remaining $95,000 is financed through a conventional mortgage for $75,000 and a below-market second mortgage for $20,000, with payments on the second mortgage limited to interest only until the property is sold as well as a public subsidy of up to 75 percent of such interest

with partial repayment on sale. There is no restriction on resale price. To facilitate comparison, suppose conservatively that the price appreciated by 5 percent per year (in fact, Massachusetts prices have appreciated at a far greater rate). If sold after six years, the net appreciation would be $33,000. Since 20 percent of this would have to be repaid, the household would be left with a net gain of $26,400 as well as recovering their initial $3,000—a compound rate of return of over 40 percent.

9. For example, suppose a moderate-income household is able to buy a house for $100,000 with an out-of-pocket downpayment of $2,000 and a resale restriction on price increases of 5 percent a year. Suppose they sell after six years: The price is $134,000. Because this is a nonmarket sale, there will be no brokerage fee, but there will be other closing costs of no more than $1,000. So they have recovered their original $2,000 investment plus a gain of $33,000 (and a modest additional amount for accumulated mortgage principal payments over the six years). This is a compound rate of return of 60 percent per year on their original cash investment!

10. However, Massachusetts has a statute (Mass. General Laws Chapter 184, Section 31), which defines an "affordable housing restriction" as "a right, either in perpetuity or for a specified number of years,. . . (a) limiting the use of all or part of the land to occupancy by persons, or families of low or moderate income in either rental housing or other housing or (b) restricting the resale price of all or part of the property in order to ensure its affordability by future low and moderate income purchasers or (c) in any way limiting or restricting the use of enjoyment of all or any portion of the land for the purpose of encouraging or assuring creation or retention of rental and other housing for occupancy by low income persons and families." I do not know whether any other states have also explicitly created such a legal framework.

11. The first systematic evaluation of resale-restricted homeownership using the land trust model has yielded encouraging results (Davis and Demetrowitz 2003). The study of 97 resales of homes and condominiums of the Burlington (VT) Community Land Trust found, on the one hand, that the annualized rate of return on initial investment averaged 17 percent, yet on the other hand, affordability not only was preserved on resale, it was actually deepened: On average, at initial sale, the BCLT homes were affordable to households with 62 percent of area median income (AMI), while on resale, they were affordable to households at 57 percent of AMI.

12. There are no figures available for the number of non-CLT individual homeownership units (including condos) with long-term or permanent resale restrictions. It is unlikely, though, that it is more than a few tens of thousands.

REFERENCES

Abrams, Charles. 1946. *The future of housing*. New York: Harper and Brothers.

Achtenberg, Emily Paradise. 1989. Subsidized housing at risk: The social costs of private ownership. In *Housing issues of the 1990s*, eds. Sara Rosenberry and Chester Hartman, 227–267. New York: Praeger.

Angotti, Tom. 1997. It's not the housing, it's the people. *Planners Network*, No. 126, November/December.

Bratt, Rachel G. 1986. Public housing: The controversy and the contribution. In *Critical perspectives on housing*, eds. Rachel Bratt, Chester Hartman and Ann Meyerson, 335–361. Philadelphia: Temple University Press.

———. 1989. *Rebuilding a low-income housing policy*. Philadelphia: Temple University Press.

———. 1990. *Neighborhood reinvestment corporation-sponsored mutual housing associations: Experiences in Baltimore and New York*. Washington, DC: Neighborhood Reinvestment Corporation.

Christman, John. 1994. *The myth of property: Toward an egalitarian theory of ownership*. New York and Oxford: Oxford University Press.

Clay, Phillip L. 1987. *At risk of loss: The endangered future of low-income rental housing resources*. Washington, DC: Neighborhood Reinvestment Corporation, May.

Council of Large Public Housing Authorities (CLPHA). 1986. *Public Housing Today*. Washington, DC: CLPHA.

———. 2000. November 13. www.clpha.org

Davis, John Emmeus. 1984. Reallocating equity: A land trust model of land reform. In *Land reform, American style*, eds. Charles C. Geisler and Frank J. Popper, 209–232. Totowa, NJ: Rowman and Allanheld.

———, ed. 1994. *The affordable city: Toward a third sector housing policy*. Philadelphia: Temple University Press.

Davis, John Emmeus, and Amy Demetrowitz. 2003. *Permanently affordable homeownership. Does the community land trust deliver on its promises? A performance evaluation of the CLT model using resale data from the Burlington community land trust*. Burlington, VT: Burlington Community Land Trust.

Dolbeare, Cushing N. 1991. Unpublished tables prepared for Low Income Housing Information Service.

Donnison, D. V. 1967. *The government of housing*. Baltimore: Penguin.

Evans, Marlwyn. 1998. Privatization of public housing. *Journal of Property Management*, March/April, 25–30.

Everywhere and Now Public Housing Residents Organizing Nationally Together (ENPHRONT). 2003. *A*

HOPE unseen: Voices from the other side of HOPE VI. Washington, DC: Center for Community Change.

Fuerst, James S. 2000. Public housing in Europe: Lessons from abroad. *Journal of Housing and Community Development*, January/February, 25–30.

Gilderbloom John I., and Richard P. Appelbaum. 1988. *Rethinking rental housing.* Philadelphia: Temple University Press.

Goetze, Rolf. 1987. *The Mutual Housing Association: An American demonstration of a proven European concept.* Washington, DC: Neighborhood Reinvestment Corporation.

Harloe, Michael. 1995. *The people's home? Social rented housing in Europe and America.* Oxford: Blackwell.

Hartman, Chester, and Robin Drayer. 1990. Military-family housing: The other public housing program. *Housing and Society*, 17:67–78.

Hayden, Dolores. 1984. *Redesigning the American Dream: The future of housing, work and family life.* New York: Norton.

Heskin, Allan D. 1991. *The struggle for community.* Boulder, CO: Westview.

Heskin, Allan, and Jacqueline Leavitt, eds. 1995. *The hidden history of housing cooperatives.* Davis: Center for Cooperatives, University of California.

Hickman, Philip A. 1998. Privatizing today's public housing. *Real Estate Issues*, 23:27–32.

Housing Partnership Network. 2002. *Corporate report 2001–2002.* Boston: The Housing Partnership Network.

Husock, Howard. 1997. Policy analysis: The inherent flaws of HUD. Cato Policy Analysis No. 292, December 22. www.cato.org/pubs/pas/pa-292.html

Institute for Community Economics (ICE). 1982. *The community land trust handbook.* Emmaus, PA: Rodale Press.

———. 1995. PARCC housing initiative. *Community Economics*, No. 32.

———. 2001. *The community land trust legal manual.* Springfield, MA: ICE.

———. 2002. *Community land trust (CLT) activity in the United States.* Springfield, MA: ICE.

Keating, Larry. 2000. Redeveloping public housing: Relearning urban renewal's immutable lessons. *Journal of the American Planning Association*, 66:384–397.

Kolodny, Robert. 1973. *Self-help in the inner city: A study of lower income cooperative housing conversion in New York.* New York: United Neighborhood Houses.

———. 1986. The emergence of self help as a housing strategy for the urban poor. In *Critical perspectives on housing*, eds. Rachel Bratt, Chester Hartman and Ann Meyerson, 447–462. Philadelphia: Temple University Press.

Krinsky, John, and Sarah Hovde. 1996. *Balancing acts: The experience of mutual housing associations and community land trusts in urban neighborhoods.* New York: Community Service Society of New York.

Lawson, Ronald, with Reuben B. Johnson III. 1986. Tenant responses to the urban housing crisis, 1970–1984. In *The tenant movement in New York City, 1904–1984*, ed. Ronald Lawson with Mark Naison, 209–276. New Brunswick, NJ: Rutgers University Press.

Leavitt, Jacqueline. 1995. The interrelated history of cooperatives and public housing from the thirties to the fifties. In *The hidden history of housing cooperatives*, eds. Allan Heskin and Jacqueline Leavitt, 79–104. Davis: Center for Cooperatives, University of California.

Leavitt, Jacqueline, and Susan Saegert. 1990. *From abandonment to hope: Community households in Harlem.* New York: Columbia University Press.

Levy, Herb Cooper [Executive Director of the National Association of Housing Cooperatives]. 1997. Telephone conversation, January 7.

Massachusetts Housing Partnership Fund (MHPF). 2003. The soft second loan program. http://www.mhpfund.com.

National Association of Housing Cooperatives (NAHC). 1990. Summary of housing cooperative units in the United States. Alexandria, VA: NAHC, March.

———. 2003. Summary of housing cooperative units in the United States. Washington, DC: NAHC, January.

National Congress for Community Economic Development. 2000. November 14. http://www.ncced.org

National Housing Law Project. 1990. *Public housing in peril: A report on the demolition and sale of public housing projects.* Berkeley, CA: National Housing Law Project.

National Housing Law Project, Poverty & Race Research Action Council, Sherwood Research Associates, Everywhere and Now Public Housing Residents Organizing Nationally Together. 2002. *False HOPE: A critical assessment of the HOPE VI public housing redevelopment program.* Oakland, CA: National Housing Law Project.

National Low Income Housing Preservation Commission. 1988. *Preventing the disappearance of low income housing.* Report of the Commission. Washington, DC: The Commission.

NeighborWorks Network. 2005. Summary Report. Neighborworks Main Production Indicators. http://www.nw.org/network/nwdata/documents/summary.pdf.

Novac, Sylvia, and Gerda Wekerle. 1995. Women, community, and housing policy. In *The hidden history of housing cooperatives*, eds. Allan Heskin and

Jacqueline Leavitt, 281–293. Davis: Center for Co-operatives, University of California.

Peterman, Bill. 1987. New options for resident control. *Shelterforce*, January/February, 14–15.

Pitcoff, Winton. 1999. New hope for public housing. *Shelterforce*, March/April, 18–21, 28.

Popkin, Susan J. 2002. *The HOPE VI program: What about the residents?* Washington, DC: The Urban Institute, December.

Ranghelli, Lisa. 1999. 1,000,000 homes at risk. *Shelterforce*, March/April, 26–27.

Ross, Timothy. 1997. It's housing, not public housing. *Planners Network*, No. 126, November/December.

———. 1998. Two corners of the same tent: A response to Tom Angotti. *Planners Network*, No. 127, January/February.

Schuman, Tony. 1986. The agony and the equity: A critique of self-help housing. In *Critical perspectives on housing*, eds. Rachel Bratt, Chester Hartman and Ann Meyerson, 463–473. Philadelphia: Temple University Press.

Siegler, Richard, and Herbert J. Levy. 1987. Brief history of cooperative housing. *1986 Cooperative Housing Journal*. Washington, DC.: National Association of Housing Cooperatives, 12, 14–19.

Stone, Michael E. 1986. Homeownership without speculation. *Shelterforce*, November/December, 12–14.

———. 1993. *Shelter poverty: New ideas on housing affordability*. Philadelphia: Temple University Press.

———. 2002. *The ECHO program: Equity Conversion and Homeownership Opportunity*, May. http://www.cpcs.umb.edu/users/mstone/Stone-ECHO_Program_May02.pdf.

———. 2003. *Social housing in the UK and US: Evolution, issues and prospects*. London: British Foreign and Commonwealth Office, Atlantic Fellowships in Public Policy. http://www.cpcs.umb.edu/users/mstone/Stone-UK_Soc_Housing_Oct03.pdf.

Stone, Michael E., Elaine Werby and Donna Haig Friedman. 2000. *Situation [critical]: Report 2000.*

Meeting the needs of lower-income Massachusetts residents. Boston: Center for Social Policy, McCormack Institute, University of Massachusetts Boston, September. http://www.mccormack.umb.edu/csp/publications/mccormack%20institute%20report%202000.pdf.

Twiss, Pamela, and James A. Martin. 1999. Conventional and military housing for families. *Social Science Review*, 7:240–260.

U.S. Census Bureau and U.S. Department of Housing and Urban Development (HUD). 2002. *Current housing reports. American housing survey for the United States in 2001.* Report H150/01. Washington, DC: GPO, October.

U.S. Department of Housing and Urban Development (HUD). 2000. A picture of subsidized households. Summary of the United States. July 11. www.huduser.org/datasets/assthsg/statedata98/us.html

U.S. General Accounting Office. 1986. *Rental housing: Potential reduction in the privately owned and federally assisted inventory.* Washington, DC: GPO, June.

Urban Institute. 2002. *HOPE VI helps many in America's worst public housing, but vulnerable families face significant barriers*, December 10. www.urban.org/urlprint.cfm?ID=8048.

Vale, Lawrence J. 1999. The future of planned poverty: Redeveloping America's most distressed public housing projects. *Netherlands Journal of Housing and the Built Environment*, 14:13–31.

Varady, David P., and Wolfgang F. E. Preiser. 1998. Scattered-site public housing and housing satisfaction. *Journal of the American Planning Association*, 64:189–207.

White, Kirby, and Charles Matthei. 1987. Community land trusts. In *Beyond the market and the state*, eds. Severyn T. Bruyn and James Meehan, 41–64. Philadelphia: Temple University Press.

Wright, Gwendolyn. 1981. *Building the dream: A social history of housing in America*. New York: Pantheon.

Wynn, Martin, ed. 1984. *Housing in Europe*. London: Croom Helm.

Michael Swack

12   Social Financing

AS DISCUSSED IN Chapter 4, housing has been extremely dependent on debt financing through private capital markets. High amounts of debt contribute to high housing costs and are a major factor affecting the affordability of housing, thus as well contributing significantly to housing access problems. Social financing can reduce debt costs and make housing more affordable for low- and moderate-income people. This chapter examines the specific goals of social financing, then briefly reviews the structure of the U.S. mortgage system and the practice of underwriting housing loans. It then reviews models and examples of social financing institutions and mechanisms, ranging from public financing to community development financial institutions (CDFIs) to programs developed by conventional lenders. The chapter concludes by making recommendations about the most effective ways to structure social financing so as to overcome some of the problems in the nation's predominant system of housing finance. The chapter addresses issues related both to single-family homeownership and the production of multifamily housing under a variety of ownership structures. Although single-family and multifamily housing share many financing issues and problems, there are some important differences, which will be noted as appropriate.

WHAT IS SOCIAL FINANCING?

Social financing is financing that is not motivated exclusively, primarily or even at all on the basis of earning market rates of return. Social investors, both institutional and individual, may vary in their need or desire for rates of return, but all expect to see social benefits emerge from their investments. Although the chapter focuses primarily on the suppliers of capital, it is important to note that financial capital is not the only factor needed to create stable communities. Nurturing the demand for credit by providing technical assistance to low-income borrowers and nonprofit organizations is also an important task of the many institutions that promote social financing.

In the housing field, social financing has four goals:

1. To make housing more affordable by reducing or eliminating the cost of debt service;
2. To provide financing for housing and related community development needs that the private financial market does not meet due to factors such as prejudice, high costs related to learning about and transacting loans to certain individual and organizational borrowers, and lack of knowledge about how to underwrite certain types of housing, such as cooperatives and land trusts;
3. To reduce the dependence of housing on the vagaries of the global capital markets, which are becoming increasingly centralized and standardized in their approach to housing lending; and,
4. To provide opportunities for private financial institutions and investors to be more socially accountable.

These goals provide a framework to evaluate the effectiveness of the social financing institutions and mechanisms detailed below.

BASIC ELEMENTS OF THE MORTGAGE SYSTEM

The mortgage market has traditionally been a distinct segment of the capital markets because mortgages differ from other debt instruments. A mortgage is a pledge of property as security for a loan to an individual or other legal entity to buy a house or units of housing or other real property. The lender is willing to lend money based on the value of the property. The borrower promises to repay the loan over time. If the borrower fails to do so, the lender can foreclose, take title to the property and sell it. The default risk of the loan depends on the change in the value of property and on the circumstances of the owner, such as job loss or bankruptcy. Real estate markets were traditionally seen as local markets, so evaluating a piece of real estate required local expertise. Most loans were held in the portfolios of the local lenders. Thus, mortgages were typically illiquid, and other investors were willing to buy loans from local lenders only if they had the knowledge required to evaluate them.

This system began to change dramatically in the 1970s and 1980s. The 1970s saw enormous growth in the federally supported secondary mortgage markets, and the 1980s saw a tremendous growth in the mortgage bond and other mortgage-backed securities markets. Prior to the 1980s, many of the mortgage securities commonplace today did not exist. However, with the creation of new financial instruments, the underwriting criteria for mortgages changed. Locally based criteria that took into account the economic realities of a community or region gave way to uniform criteria designed to satisfy the needs of the investors who would ultimately purchase these mortgage-backed securities. Local lending institutions could no longer rely upon their knowledge of local community conditions or even the character of the borrower but instead relied on the criteria of mortgage brokers pooling mortgages for sale to investors. Any local lender resisting this trend found itself without sufficient capital to make new loans or increase its returns. Thus, questions concerning social criteria or "what's best for a community" quickly faded from the mortgage business.

Primary and Secondary Markets

The residential mortgage system in the United States is composed of a primary market and a secondary market. The primary mortgage market provides funds directly to the borrower. Mortgage loans are provided by depository institutions, such as commercial banks or savings and loan institutions as well as by nondepository institutions, such as mortgage companies. The secondary mortgage market is the market in which existing loans are bought and sold by investors. The two largest secondary market institutions in the United States are the Federal National Mortgage Association, known as Fannie Mae, and the Federal Home Loan Mortgage Corporation, known as Freddie Mac. Secondary market institutions such as Fannie Mae and Freddie Mac aggregate single- and multifamily housing loans into pools and then—with the pools of mortgages, and ultimately the real estate, serving as collateral—create mortgage-backed securities (MBSs). The securitization process attracts institutional investors who provide the capital for home mortgage loans. Fannie Mae and Freddie Mac standardize the underwriting and servicing components related to the mortgage process, aggregate the loans into pools, maintain the credit risk of these loans on their books and sell the mortgage-backed securities to investors at a fixed rate of return.

The idea underlying creation of the secondary market is that while housing markets are local, the system of finance need not be local: National capital markets can provide the funds for local housing markets. With the proceeds from the sale of mortgages, primary lenders replenish their money supply and use it to make more loans. If primary lenders cannot sell their loans, they must keep them in their portfolios. It is important for primary lenders to sell most of the loans they originate in order to maintain liquidity, or they will be unable to serve the needs of new borrowers.

For a number of reasons, primary lenders shy away from loans aimed at creating housing affordable for low-income people:

1. The relatively small size of many below-market multifamily housing projects means that the lender may not earn enough income to cover staff costs. If the loan package is complicated (which is often characteristic of multifamily low-income housing), the costs of collecting information and understanding the financial structure of the project will exceed the lender's income (Lappin 1993);

2. Complex government subsidies for multi-family housing, such as those provided by the Low Income Housing Tax Credit and the HOME Investments Partnership Program, add to information costs by requiring the lender's staff to become familiar with the workings of the range of federal and state programs;

3. Many primary lenders perceive risks of lending in particular neighborhoods to be too high; and,

4. Primary lenders may have trouble selling many financial packages for below-market housing because secondary markets for low-income, multifamily housing debt are small and often defined narrowly (Lappin 1993). For example, a small multifamily housing unit with a commercial unit on the ground floor would be excluded from sale to the secondary market.

As noted above, in order for a national secondary mortgage market to operate efficiently, mortgage loans must be standardized to a large extent, regardless of the local market in which they are originated. In order to be priced, mortgages must have similar structures and terms, with similar borrower qualification requirements (DiPasquale and Wheaton 1996). But standardization is a big problem for low-income borrowers and the organizations serving them. Much low-income housing takes nonstandard forms (cooperatives, land trusts, single room occupancy buildings, etc.), and these individual and organizational borrowers do not necessarily meet the standard underwriting guidelines. For example, individual borrowers generally cannot

qualify for a mortgage if annual housing expenses for that mortgage, plus taxes and insurance, exceed 28 percent of annual household income. Additionally, much low-income housing has various kinds of subsidies and unique financing structures that conflict with the standardized features of the secondary market institutions.

Underwriting

A brief description of several elements of the underwriting process will illustrate how financial markets view the issue of risk in mortgage-lending. The question of underwriting is important to the field of social finance because institutions involved in social finance often modify standard underwriting procedures in order to finance low- and moderate-income housing.

Underwriting is the process of collecting and analyzing data on a borrower, a property and a community to determine the degree of risk presented by a loan or investment. Underwriting guidelines provide a basis for understanding how lenders view the risks associated with lending for both single-family and multifamily mortgages. The guidelines used by most primary lenders are dictated to a large extent by the guidelines used by the two major secondary market players, Fannie Mae and Freddie Mac. Their guidelines are neither legislatively mandated nor regulated by any government institution—they simply are created by these institutions to make their operations as efficient as possible and maximize the marketability of their mortgage-backed securities.

A review of three of Fannie Mae's guidelines—employment/income, creditworthiness and savings/assets—illustrates some of the issues primary lenders face when underwriting loans. These guidelines apply to Fannie Mae's nonstandard, so-called community lending and neighborhood loans, which have somewhat more flexible terms than their conventional loans. Eligible borrowers under the community lending and neighborhood programs include individuals and approved nonprofit organizations and public agencies. Fannie Mae's community lending mortgages generally must be secured by single-family residences and thus do not cover multifamily projects. Guidelines for underwriting multifamily mortgages are similar to underwriting standards on commercial property, which are considered higher-risk investments and thus are subject to more stringent underwriting standards (e.g., in the appraisal method).

1. *Employment/Income* Documenting and verifying employment stability can be somewhat tricky. Fannie Mae requires two consecutive years in the same job as meeting its satisfactory employment standard for a mortgage applicant. Fannie Mae will consider less time in a job if the reason for a job change is to increase opportunity. Fannie Mae also allows primary lenders to consider borrowers with secondary sources of income or seasonal jobs, if the income is consistent. However, a great many low- to moderate-income people have several jobs of variable duration and income from a variety of formal and informal activities. Many low- to moderate-income families have relatively stable income but not stable employment. Many rely on a range of part-time and seasonal jobs. They would prefer to have one stable, full-time job with benefits, but this is not always possible. Often, the cost of documenting employment for people of low- and moderate-income is more expensive to the lender because of the varying sources of income. Documenting income of residents may also be a problem in multifamily housing developments. For example, a nonprofit organization assisting a group of tenants who wish to organize a cooperative must often verify the income of each tenant in order to secure financing.

2. *Creditworthiness* Fannie Mae allows primary lenders to develop nontraditional credit histories for those borrowers who have either no credit record (not atypical for low- and moderate-income borrowers) or a derogatory credit rating. Fannie Mae allows lenders to consider a borrower's record of payment of rent or utility bills. Some primary lenders are willing to look at this type of information and develop a nontraditional credit history, others are not. Developing a history is often more expensive than simply relying on a standard credit report issued by a credit bureau.

3. *Savings/Assets* For most of their "community loans," Fannie Mae requires the borrower to make a 3 percent downpayment on the property with funds from his or her own assets. Assets generally include bank accounts, proceeds from the sale of assets, government bonds or a previous home (Fannie Mae 1993). But sweat equity, cash-on-hand and alternative savings plans (e.g., group savings systems practiced by some ethnic groups) generally do not count toward the downpayment. Again, the cost of documenting and verifying funds for downpayment and closing costs can be quite expensive for a conventional primary lender. Although Fannie Mae allows some flexibility, many banks and private mortgage insurance (PMI) companies hesitate to use this flexibility (Valentine 1991). This last point is important because Fannie Mae requires all mortgages originated under its community lending products to carry mortgage insurance coverage. If PMI is unavailable, then the borrower cannot get the commitment of a primary lender who wants to sell the mortgage to Fannie Mae.

The process of primary lenders underwriting loans to sell to Fannie Mae involves much more than the above, but these examples begin to illustrate why conventional primary lenders may not be interested in making loans to low- and moderate-income borrowers even when Fannie Mae guidelines offer flexibility. It is important to note that Fannie Mae, as well as a number of other lenders, is increasingly relying on credit scoring to make loan decisions. Credit scoring is a method used to make loan decisions based on a statistical assessment of a person's creditworthiness. A credit scoring model considers a range of variables, including credit history, income, outstanding debt and a variety of other factors and assigns a score to the applicant. The rising importance of credit scoring has begun to change the way Fannie Mae and other lenders use any particular underwriting factor.

In sum, the costs and the perception of risk may be high. Thus, a clear financing gap exists for low-income borrowers, since they often do not meet the various underwriting guidelines. Insufficient downpayments, high debt ratios, unstable employment histories (but not necessarily unstable income) and complicated or insufficient credit histories impede the ability of primary lenders to sell to the secondary market.

CONCEPTS, MODELS, AND EXAMPLES OF SOCIAL FINANCING

In order to overcome the financing problems presented so far, there needs to be a system of social financing substantial in scope, not driven by profit-maximizing market criteria or current secondary market restrictions, making less use of debt than does the current system and requiring a major public role. This section examines various social financing institutions, models and mechanisms. A wide range of social financing models and vehicles exist, from direct public intervention to community development financial institutions to initiatives developed by conventional lenders. It is important to note that the range of models and mechanisms described do not constitute a true *system* of social finance. Each embodies the goals of social financing to some extent and provides information and lessons on how to promote the social financing of housing. For each model or institutional type, the goals cited above will be applied as an evaluative framework. The final section offers a set of recommendations that would promote development of a system of social financing and better integrate the various components described below.

Public Intervention

Three basic types of public sector intervention affect housing finance: direct intervention through provision of grants and loans; financial incentives to promote provision of equity and credit from the private sector; and use of regulation to promote private sector financing.

Direct Intervention: Grants. Housing that has some degree of social ownership (i.e., housing that is not completely market-oriented, such as land trust housing, limited-equity cooperatives, public housing and nonprofit housing (see Chapter 11) should be financed, as much as possible, with direct public grants. Not only does grant financing have a directly beneficial effect

on affordability, it is technically less complicated and involves less bureaucracy and administrative overhead than the various recurring subsidy programs and tax schemes aimed at producing affordable housing (Stone 1993).

Most important, direct grants are "more cost-effective than debt financing over the long term, even though in the short term they must either produce less housing impact for a given level of public spending or require greater public appropriations to achieve a given amount of social housing" (Stone 1993:221). The federal government allows Community Development Block Grant (CDBG) funds as well as HOME Investment Partnership funds to be used as capital grants for the development and rehabilitation of low- and moderate-income housing. Public housing development and housing for the elderly under the U.S. Department of Housing and Urban Development's (HUD) Section 202 program are also financed with direct federal grants. Both CDBG and HOME funds may also be used for low-interest loans and other types of subsidies and credit enhancements.

HOME funds are highly targeted: They cannot be used to assist families with incomes greater than 80 percent of the area median. In fact, nearly one in three homebuyers, seven in ten homeowners and about nine in ten renters whom HOME assists earn 50 percent or less of area median income. Many states and localities report that they cannot meet demand for HOME funds. States receive 40 percent of HOME funds, localities 60 percent. In 2002, Congress funded the HOME program at $1.85 billion (National Council of State Housing Agencies 2003).

Clearly, grants contribute equity that serves to lower the overall debt burden and therefore allows low-income people greater access to housing opportunities. However, in the current funding environments at both the federal and state levels, prospects for additional grant funding are slim. The current political environment presents the greatest barrier to financing improvements that would have a positive effect on the creation of low-income housing. Indeed, government contributions towards equity in low-income housing increasingly emphasize use of tax credits rather than grants (see below).

One source of grant or equity money for low-income housing that may be available at the state or local level is housing trust funds. These are mechanisms created by state or local governments that commit an ongoing source of revenue to a special fund, used to provide equity or debt to finance low-and moderate-income housing. Nationwide, more than 280 housing trust funds exist (Center for Community Change 2003). Housing trust funds can receive their revenue from a wide variety of sources, including taxes on real estate sales, interest on real estate escrow accounts, fees paid by developers of office buildings or repayments of government loans. Overall, housing trust funds commit over $750 million to housing projects each year through dedicated revenue streams, along with additional money through appropriations and other designated funds (Center for Community Change 2003). Housing trust funds typically provide grants, loans or both to nonprofit housing development organizations, private developers, local governments and individuals.

One of the key characteristics of housing trust funds is that they often support the types of housing that conventional capital markets do not. In addition to focusing on low- and moderate-income housing, many trust funds require housing financed by the fund to remain affordable for long periods of time. The Vermont Housing and Conservation Board (VHCB) gives priority to projects with perpetual affordability clauses. This type of clause gives priority to housing such as land trust housing, limited-equity cooperatives and nonprofit housing. Between 1987 and 2002, the VHCB invested in the construction and rehabilitation of 6,700 units of housing and the conservation of more than 95,000 acres of agricultural land (Center for Community Change 2003).

There have also been efforts to create a National Housing Trust Fund, most recently in 2003 (National Housing Trust Fund Campaign 2003). The National Affordable Housing Trust Fund would be capitalized initially with excess revenues of Federal Housing Administration (FHA) and the Government National Mortgage Association (Ginnie Mae). It would allocate funds to states and localities and would fund a variety of programs to promote homeownership for low-income families and enable the development of low-income rental housing. The campaign aims to generate sufficient funds for 1.5 million new, rehabbed and preserved low-income units over a ten-year period.

Direct public intervention through the use of grants meets the identified goals of social financing: It makes housing more affordable by reducing debt service, and it provides financing not available from private financial markets. It also provides opportunities for private financial institutions to participate in financing affordable housing through creating stronger individual and institutional borrowers. That is, the provision of public equity leverages private debt markets. The major drawback to this approach is the initial cost to the public treasury, although over the long term, the costs are lower because there are no interest payments and debt administration costs. Currently (2004), grants to promote housing affordable for low- and moderate-income people are not high on the political agenda.

Direct Intervention: Loans. The public sector provides debt financing for both single-family and multifamily housing, typically at a subsidized rate of interest. The difference between a market rate of interest and the rate charged represents a subsidy to the project or individual. One of the most common mechanisms for providing public sector debt to housing is through state housing finance agencies (HFAs). HFAs typically target a share of their resources to low- and moderate-income people through mixed-income projects that combine below-market with market-rate units.

HFAs are able to provide relatively low-cost, long-term, fixed-rate financing with money raised by issuing tax-exempt bonds. The power to issue tax-exempt mortgage revenue bonds (MRBs) is granted by Congress. Housing bonds are lumped under a cap along with bonds for manufacturing, environmental projects, redevelopment and student loans, limited in each state to $75 times its population (or $228 million total, if greater). Between 1974 and 2002, state HFAs issued more than $145 billion in MRBs for nearly 2.2 million mortgage loans (National

Council of State Housing Agencies 2003). Recent limitations on the issuance of MRBs have led some HFAs to issue 501(c)(3) bonds, issued by an HFA on behalf of a nonprofit, tax-exempt 501(c)(3) organization. These bonds are outside the caps imposed by Congress on tax-exempt MRBs but are still exempt from federal taxation.

HFAs are often responsible for administering housing trust fund money and can mix and match trust fund money with bond money, thus allowing them to provide both equity and debt for a given project. HFAs are often one of the few sources of long-term, fixed-rate financing for nonprofit housing development and special forms of below-market housing, such as cooperatives, land trusts and special needs housing.

Direct provision of public sector debt financing also meets the goals of social financing, but in a more limited way than equity financing. Public sector debt financing makes housing more affordable by reducing the cost of debt service. However, public sector debt financing is dependent on private capital markets to buy the bonds issued; thus, the public sector must underwrite its debt somewhat conservatively. Without the assistance of public sector equity financing, housing financed by public lending tends to serve moderate-income people, not low-income people. Additionally, public debt often does not leverage private debt. Although conventional financial institutions may service loans originated by HFAs, they typically do not invest in the same projects (Shabecoff 1994).

Public Sector: Incentives. The public sector can induce private institutions and individuals to finance housing through the use of economic incentives. The major form of incentive used by government is tax credits. A major source of equity for housing is provided through the federal government's Low Income Housing Tax Credit (LIHTC). The LIHTC allows corporations to lower their federal tax liability by extending tax credits for investments in the construction or rehabilitation of low-income rental housing. LIHTCs are allocated to states on the basis of $1.75 per capita. Under the LIHTC, investors in low-income rental housing receive a credit of 9 percent of the total construction costs for new construction or rehabilitation. The credit decreases to 4 percent if the project receives any other federal subsidies or any tax-exempt financing. The LIHTC program has been used in the development of nearly 1 million rental housing units from 1986 through 2002. Over $10 billion in private funds were invested in LIHTC projects between 1986 and 2000; more than $2 billion has been invested into nonprofit-developed housing during this same period (http://lihtc.huduser.org/).

The LIHTC is widely used, due to lack of alternate forms of equity, and it can be quite costly. It requires substantial amounts of organizational time to put together, and a significant portion of funds raised goes to pay the expenses of lawyers and accountants. Stegman (1991) points out that the two greatest sources of inefficiency of the LIHTC are (1) the difference between the cost of the tax credit to the federal government in terms of foregone revenues and the amount of equity raised from the tax credit; and (2) the large amount of gross equity raised from the sale of the tax credit that pays for the legal and accounting costs and thus is not invested in housing. The deals are often quite good investments for the investor. In 1990, institutional investors expected an 18 percent aggregate after-tax internal rate of return, although by 1999, that yield had fallen to approximately 8 percent (Roberts and Harvey 1999). As noted previously, tax credits are typically more costly than if the government simply gave the money in the form of a capital grant. Another disadvantage to the nonprofit developer is that control of the property for the 15-year syndication period is not with the developer. Typically, there are no guarantees that the nonprofit sponsor or the tenants will be able to maintain ownership of the property at the end of the syndication period, although LIHTC-financed apartments must remain affordable to low-income people for 30 years. Finally, although a large number of the units financed using the LIHTC are available to low-income people, they are not affordable to truly poor families. Fewer than 40 percent of tax credit units are rented by tenants with incomes at or below 30 percent of median income, which is roughly equivalent to the poverty line. Most of the poor renters who do live in these units receive a rental subsidy, such as a Section 8 voucher, to help them pay the rent (Daskal 1998).

Supporters of the LIHTC point out that the involvement of private partners builds rigor into the development and management of the housing; that the formation of partnerships creates linkages and mutual interests among nonprofit corporations and for-profit investors; and that the program is no more complex than other federal programs (see Grogan and Roberts 1992; Committee for Economic Development 1995; Roberts and Harvey 1999). The program has become significantly more efficient over the years 1986 to 2000. Investor demand for the credit drove up equity prices (the amount an investor is willing to pay up front for $1 of tax credit, spread over 15 years) from 42 cents to close to 80 cents per dollar. Higher equity prices mean that the credit is buying more private resources and costing the federal government less than in the past. Competition for the credit has also forced the private sector to accept longer affordability lock-in periods, beyond the 30-year standard (Roberts and Harvey 1999).

An alternative approach to the LIHTC is utilized by the New Hampshire Community Development Finance Authority (CDFA). The CDFA underwrites various community economic development projects and ventures, including low-income housing. It then awards tax credits to businesses that donate property for the housing or cash to develop the housing. The business may then claim a tax credit of 75 percent of the value of the donation. The nonprofit gains access to equity financing, and the state foregoes revenue. However, the private donor is contributing 25 percent of the cost of the donation, the process is simple to administer and almost all of the money ends up in the project. This tax credit raised over $35 million of equity for housing and economic development projects between 1994 and 2002 (New Hampshire CDFA 2002).

This form of tax credit has the advantage of requiring community organizations to participate in the housing project. It also encourages banks to make direct loans for low-income housing by improving the overall capital structure of the project. With more equity in the project, banks have shown greater willingness to provide the debt component of the project. The projects also have lower debt service costs, thus enabling them to serve people with lower incomes.

Incentives such as tax credits can meet some of the goals of social financing. Incentives can help raise equity, provide financing that the private market would not otherwise provide and offer opportunities for conventional lenders to participate in financing affordable housing. However, incentives may be inefficient, are not well targeted and affect the structure of ownership of the housing itself. (The LIHTC, the primary source of equity financing for housing, can only be used to create rental housing.)

Regulation. The government can use its power of regulation to steer private money into the housing sector. The best known regulatory approach for steering money into low- and moderate-income housing is the Community Reinvestment Act (CRA). Passed by Congress in 1977, the CRA requires banks and thrifts to meet the credit needs of low- and moderate-income communities. Bank regulators conduct CRA examinations as part of the regular examinations all banks must undergo. Under the law, bank regulators assign one of four ratings: outstanding, satisfactory, needs to improve or substantial noncompliance. A rating of "needs to improve" or "substantial noncompliance" does not necessarily result in any penalties to the bank. Rather, if a bank applies to merge with or acquire another bank, individuals and organizations can challenge that application based on the bank's poor lending record in low- and moderate-income communities. Although merger applications are rarely denied, banks dislike the bad publicity that accompanies poor CRA ratings and do not want to risk denial or delay of a merger application because of CRA noncompliance. Thus, the CRA regulation encourages banks to develop programs that lend specific amounts of money for specific types of projects.

From 1977 to 2005, banks and community organizations have entered into more than 428 agreements worth more than $4.2 trillion in reinvestment dollars for traditionally underserved populations. As part of a Treasury Department study, Harvard University researchers documented that lenders made more loans to low- and moderate-income borrowers in geographical areas in which they have negotiated CRA agreements with community groups (NCRC 2005). Examples of CRA agreements include New Jersey Citizen Action, which negotiated a comprehensive agreement with NatWest Bank in which the bank agreed to provide over $151 million in below-market rate mortgages for low- and moderate-income families; discounted home improvement loans; loans for construction and permanent financing for nonprofit housing developers and loans to minority and women-owned businesses (Bohner 1995:13). In 1999, Washington Mutual Bank made a ten-year commitment of $120 billion targeted to underserved communities, including $81.6 billion in affordable housing loans (California Reinvestment Committee 2003).

Although CRA regulations have encouraged some lenders to increase their lending to low- and moderate-income people and communities, the loans are typically made at market interest rates. Changes in the CRA instituted in 1995 have made financial institutions more receptive to loan applications from projects in low-income communities, but this has not meant that lenders have relaxed their standards for reviewing applications or their criteria and conditions for approving loans. As noted earlier, bank lending for housing is often tied to Fannie Mae underwriting standards.

Banks also receive CRA credit by lending to low-income housing projects through lending consortia and bank-owned community development corporations (CDCs). Bank consortia are often able to provide permanent fixed-rate financing in situations where individual banks will not. The California Community Reinvestment Corporation, a pooled fund of several banks, provides fixed, market-rate mortgage financing with terms of 25 years. In 2002, JP-Morgan Chase, in partnership with Fannie Mae, and using its subsidiary, the Chase Community Development Corporation, committed $35 billion for low- and moderate-income housing and other community development projects.

In 2005 the federal banking agencies eased CRA exam regulations for banks with assets between $250 and $1 billion. Under the new regulations, these mid-size banks will no longer need to collect and report CRA loan data on small business, small farm, and community development lending. Without access to annual data, it will become more difficult to monitor the lending performance of financial institutions in traditionally underserved areas.

In addition, mid-sized banks will be evaluated under a dual test system: the small bank lending test and a new community development test. The regulators claim that the community development test will offer more flexibility; but it is unclear how communities, especially those in remote rural areas, will benefit form this new framework. By lowering the banks' accountability, community groups are concerned that branches in low- and moderate-income areas may provide fewer investments, services, and community development loans to the neighborhoods they serve. (National Community Reinvestment Coalition 2005).

Another example of government regulation that has provided both debt and equity for low- and moderate-income housing development is the Financial Institutions Reform, Recovery and Enforcement Act (FIRREA) of 1989. The twelve regional Federal Home Loan Banks administer a program for affordable housing mandated by Congress in FIRREA. The FHLB system was created by Congress in 1932 to promote home finance by providing financial services to banking institutions that commit a significant portion of their assets to home mortgage loans. Institutions eligible for membership include thrifts, commercial banks and credit unions. Members are the sole customers and stockholders of this private corporation. FIRREA includes provisions that create two community lending programs, the Affordable Housing Program (AHP) and the Community Investment Program. Under FIRREA, 10 percent of each regional bank's net income is set aside each year to support subsidized advances and direct subsidies. Between 1990 and 2001, FHLB's Affordable Housing Program awarded $1.4 billion in subsidies to affordable housing initiatives (FHLB 2003).

Affordable Housing Program subsidies are channeled through member banks, usually to nonprofit organizations. The member bank works with the nonprofit to prepare the application and then applies to the FHLB regional bank in a competition for the funds. The member bank awards funding to the project, often in the form of a grant—thus contributing equity to the project. AHP is an effective method for financing low-income housing. It provides equity and low-cost, long-term debt financing at fixed rates. The FHLB provides technical assistance and training as well as markets the program aggressively both to banks and nonprofit entities. The major problem with the program is its modest size. Demand for funds far outweighs availability.

Regulation meets some of the goals of social financing, and certain types of regulation are more effective than others. Regulations that encourage equity financing (e.g., FIRREA), target funds effectively to low- and moderate-income individuals and allow flexibility (e.g., using funds for equity and lower-cost debt) can greatly assist the financing of low- and moderate-housing. CRA financing tends to be most useful in meeting the housing needs of low- and moderate-income individuals when it is combined with some other form of public or private subsidy that helps to lower the overall financing cost. AHP financing does make housing more affordable, provides capital not available in the private financial markets and promotes flexibility in financing that encourages private financial institutions to participate in financing affordable housing. However, the overall lack of sufficient amounts of flexible capital through various public sector mechanisms, such as regulation, financial incentives and direct financing, has given rise to a new set of private sector intermediaries.

COMMUNITY DEVELOPMENT FINANCIAL INSTITUTIONS

Increasingly, new intermediaries called community development financial institutions (CDFIs) are entering the financial market. CDFIs are committed to meeting the credit needs for low-income housing and serving community-based development organizations. CDFIs are typically community-based nonprofit organizations or national intermediaries with local offices. They are sensitive to local needs, market-wise and able to develop loan and investment products that

differ from conventional loan products. CDFIs are also sophisticated in their approach to meeting credit needs and providing assistance to borrowers, both organizational and individual. CDFIs that serve housing needs include community development loan funds, community development credit unions, community development corporation loan funds and community development banks. All except community development banks are structured as private, nonprofit corporations.

CDFIs such as the Self-Help Credit Union of Durham, North Carolina; the Reinvestment Fund of Philadelphia; Coastal Enterprises of Wiscasset, Maine; and the Local Initiatives Support Corporation are examples of different kinds of CDFIs. They share a commitment to providing credit and technical assistance to nonconventional borrowers (i.e., low-income individuals and community-based development organizations) and filling capital gaps, gaps that conventional lenders do not or cannot fill. Leibsohn (1995:3–4) lists the following types of lending carried out by CDFIs in low-income communities:

1. Predevelopment financing in the early stages of a project that allows it to reach the stage where it is bankable;
2. Cushioning conventional loans with junior financing above certain loan-to-value (LTV) ratios (e.g., loans over 75 percent LTV);
3. Seasoning loans to demonstrate their safety so that conventional institutions can later purchase or refinance them;
4. Demonstrating the effectiveness of new lending approaches, underwriting and loan products (e.g., mobile home cooperatives) so that conventional institutions can become comfortable with the new approaches and products;
5. High transaction cost loans: loans that are too small or complicated and thus cost too much because of the time involved;
6. Loans that allow community development organizations or entrepreneurs to gain experience and a track record so that they can use conventional lenders in the future; and,
7. High-risk loans, in general, for reasons such as lack of organizational financial strength,

lack of take-out financing, difficult neighborhood, scattered sites or nontraditional income stream.

There does appear to be a difference between the default experience of conventional lenders and those lenders that focus on lending for low- and moderate-income housing, at least for multifamily housing, with the specialized lenders, such as CDFIs, reporting much lower default rates (DiPasquale and Cummings 1992). The success of CDFIs may be due to special expertise in underwriting and management, and the fact that CDFIs spend more time on project management and finance fewer projects than is true for conventional lenders (DiPasquale and Cummings 1992:A-27).

Conventional lenders may hesitate to enter the market for lending to low-income housing because they possess insufficient information and insufficient expertise to exploit the opportunities. Lenders are unlikely to voluntarily enter a market until they have some reasonable level of expectation that they will earn a profit (Beshouri and Glennon 1996). If, however, this reluctance is based upon prejudice rather than real economic reasons, then advocates should pressure government to be more forceful with conventional lenders.

National CDFIs

CDFIs may be local organizations, meaning that they serve a specific city or region, or they may be national intermediaries with local affiliates. The three most prominent national CDFIs in the field of low- and moderate-income housing are the Enterprise Foundation, the Local Initiatives Support Corporation (LISC) and the Neighborhood Reinvestment Corporation (NRC). The national organizations help form partnerships to raise loan and grant money for their local affiliates from foundations, corporations and private individuals. The national organizations also provide technical assistance and training for their local affiliates. All three intermediaries have succeeded in attracting investment from major corporations, and all have developed small secondary market mechanisms that purchase loans originated by their local affiliates,

other nonprofit developers and intermediaries such as CDFIs.

The Enterprise Foundation has a national network of more than 2,400 organizations in 860 locations across the country. Enterprise borrows money at below-market rates from national commercial banks, foundations and socially minded corporations. From 1982 to 2002, Enterprise and its related organizations raised and invested $4.4 billion in loans, equity (e.g., from the Low Income Housing Tax Credit) and grants to create 144,000 homes for low-income people (www.enterprisefoundation.org).

LISC was established by the Ford Foundation and six community groups in 1980. It operates local programs in 38 cities and rural programs in 37 states. The organization has raised over $4 billion from over 2,200 investors, lenders and donors and, working with local community development corporations, helped to build or rehabilitate 128,000 units of housing from 1980 to 2002 (www.lisc.org).

The Neighborhood Reinvestment Corporation is a Congressionally chartered corporation that works through a network of over 220 local affiliates called NeighborWorks organizations. Local Neighborhood Works organizations lend at flexible rates and terms to neighborhood residents who do not qualify for conventional financing. NRC then provides a secondary market for its local revolving loan funds. They purchase blocks of loans from local programs and sells notes backed by these loans to institutional investors, including insurance companies, savings and loans and pension funds. NRC purchases the loans from its affiliates, accepting low yields, and then seeks social investors to participate in providing funds to the local programs at below-market rates (Widener 1993). Since its inception in 1976 through the end of 2000, NRC affiliates originated over $430 million in loans (Neighborhood Housing Services of America 2001).

Local CDFIs

Local CDFIs come in many forms, including development banks, community development credit unions (CDCUs) and community loan funds. Local CDFIs serve a specific geographical area, such as a city or a state. Some local

CDFIs have a broad lending focus that includes housing, small business and commercial lending. Other local CDFIs specialize in a particular sector, such as housing.

Development banks—for example, the South Shore Bank of Chicago—are government-regulated financial institutions and typically have the highest capitalization of the various CDFI models. The ability to offer federal deposit insurance attracts depositors. Operating within a regulatory environment tends to make development banks somewhat more conservative than unregulated community loan funds.

Community development credit unions are regulated financial institutions, capitalized by member deposits, that mainly serve the consumer banking needs of their members. Although some CDCUs (e.g., Self-Help Credit Union in North Carolina) are able to do mortgage-lending, many are too small to offer mortgage loans to their members.

Community loan funds are typically unregulated financial intermediaries that attract social investment capital from individuals, churches and other socially motivated investors and lend to borrowers, such as community-based housing organizations, at a below-market interest rate. Community loan funds often make the types of loans that banks are unwilling or unable to make (e.g., junior mortgage loans or loans that are subordinated to a senior lender, such as a bank).

The development of CDFIs is still at an early stage. Most of them were created since 1980, and most remain small by conventional standards. However, the CDFI industry has begun to scale up. The CDFI Data Project, a foundation-funded initiative, collects industry-wide data on CDFIs. As of the end of 2001, the CDFI Data Project reported that there were over 800 CDFIs operating in the United States. The Project collected data from 512 CDFIs in 2001. Collectively, they control a lending pool of $8.2 billion and financed over 43,000 units in 2001. The CDFIs' net loan losses were less than 1 percent of their outstanding loans, and they had sufficient reserves and equity bases to cover those losses (National Community Capital Association 2003).

The growth of CDFIs has accelerated since 1995, due in large part to creation of the CDFI Fund, a program within the Treasury Department. The Fund was established in 1994 to support CDFIs and make capital available to CDFIs working with underserved communities and individuals. The CDFI Fund is the largest source of funding for CDFIs, providing over $530 million in awards from 1995 to 2002 to community development financial institutions (CDFI Fund 2003).

CDFIs have met some of the goals of social financing discussed previously. Many CDFIs are able to provide financing for housing that the private financial market does not provide, often at a below-market interest rate. (Community loan funds, in particular, are likely to offer below-market interest rates.) CDFIs are often able to reduce dependency on centralized global markets and are beginning to work effectively with private financial institutions to finance affordable housing. However, many issues need to be addressed in order to strengthen the capacity of CDFIs to provide capital in poor communities and achieve scale in lending and operations. Most CDFIs are limited in the type of investments they can make by their sources of funds. That is, they do not necessarily have the type of capital, such as equity, that is needed to make equity investments or long-term, fixed-rate, low-cost debt. CDFIs have limited capital as an industry, and most individual CDFIs are understaffed. Finally, relationships between CDFIs and conventional lenders and capital markets (both primary and secondary markets) have developed slowly. CDFIs need to increase their own scale and capacity and develop stronger relationships with conventional lenders if they are to have a significant impact on meeting the needs of borrowers. Partnerships between CDFIs and conventional lenders can greatly expand the amount of flexible capital necessary to promote the financing of low- and moderate-income housing on a much larger scale.

CONVENTIONAL LENDERS

Conventional private lenders, particularly banks, have become much more involved in financing low- and moderate-income housing over the past 20 years. Much of this involvement can be traced to government incentives such as the Community Reinvestment Act. However, there are innovative models developed by banks for financing low- and moderate-income housing initiatives. As mentioned previously, banks have increasingly utilized the consortium approach to lending. One of the first bank consortia was created in California in the 1970s, and growth of consortia accelerated through the 1990s. As of 2001, there were loan consortia in 22 states and the District of Columbia. In 2001, the Association of Reinvestment Consortia for Housing (ARCH) was formed by bank consortia in 13 states. Collectively, ARCH represents over 400 commercial banks, thrifts and savings and loans with loan commitments totaling over $1.5 billion and over 60,000 units of housing financed (Mendez 2002).

Some banks have also become more involved in financing low- and moderate-income housing. The Socially Responsible Banking (SRB) Fund of Vermont's Chittenden Bank is the first state-wide commercial bank program in the country that allows customers to specify that their deposits be used only for socially responsible loans. Chittenden Bank is not a CDFI; it is a conventional lender. However, through creation of the SRB Fund, the bank has been able to develop some creative lending approaches. The Fund makes loans in five areas: affordable housing, the environment, agriculture, education and small business. As of 2003, the SRB Fund was managing over 16,000 accounts with over $131 million in deposits and over $105 million in outstanding loans (Chittenden Bank 2003). Loan officers in all of the bank's 31 branches may make SRB Fund loans. The Fund provides technical assistance to the loan officers in the various branches, and Fund loans have consistently had low delinquency rates and have experienced no delinquencies on loans to nonprofit developers.

The SRB Fund differs from most conventional lenders in several key respects:

1. Although the SRB Fund typically lends at market interest rates, it commits time and resources to making low- and moderate-income housing loans that generally exceed the commitment made for conventional lending. The SRB Fund staff recognizes the complex task of low- and moderate-income housing lending, the mix of public and private players, the multiple financing sources and the community input.
2. The Fund is willing to hold a limited number of long-term, fixed-rate affordable housing mortgages in its portfolio.
3. The SRB Fund actively seeks to sell low- and moderate-income multifamily housing loans to socially responsible institutional investors, essentially an alternative secondary market.

Many conventional lenders have begun to develop loan products that are targeted to moderate-income individuals. Relaxed underwriting standards by Fannie Mae have encouraged banks to try to serve moderate-income borrowers. On the whole, conventional lenders have been more effective in providing financing that meets the needs of low- and moderate-income individuals when they are responding to government incentives and regulations, such as the CRA or the Low Income Housing Tax Credit.

A SYSTEM OF SOCIAL FINANCING—RECOMMENDATIONS FOR SCALING-UP

The introduction to this chapter stated the four goals of social financing: to make housing more affordable to low- and moderate-income individuals; to provide financing for needs that the private financial market does not meet; to reduce the dependency of the housing finance system on the vagaries of the global capital markets and to provide opportunities for private financial institutions to invest in social housing. Although each of the goals of social financing is met to some extent through the range of activities carried out by the public, private and nonprofit sectors, the overall effort falls significantly short of meeting the financial need. Government grant and loan programs do not meet the demand for those funds, and conventional lenders and CDFI efforts are either too small or are not structured to meet the need for equity and low-cost, long-term debt. As noted above, the range of models and mechanisms do not constitute a true *system* of social finance. The financing of low- and moderate-income housing involves a patchwork of mechanisms and programs that are inadequate and inefficient (Stegman 1991).

Developing a system of social finance will require commitment and innovation from all participants in the housing finance system: conventional lenders, secondary market institutions, CDFIs and government agencies. In addition, the financial markets must address the issues of access *and* cost of capital in order to fully address the problem of low-income housing finance. There is a need for both equity (including equity in the form of grants) and long-term, low-cost, fixed-rate debt financing. Although this chapter has cited examples of institutions that address these financing problems with some degree of success, the major problem is that the overall financial effort is too modest. The most successful models of social finance are far too small to meet the need. A true system of social finance needs to weave the various sectors together in a way that is more coherent and less ad hoc. Piecing together a system will require some experimentation, but perhaps the roles of the institutional players can be clarified. Both CDFIs and conventional lenders must individually and collectively form the financial delivery system. Government must provide substantial grant money and credit enhancements both to lower housing costs and facilitate the participation of the secondary market. The secondary market must creatively package loans originated by conventional lenders and CDFIs so as to create the appropriate markets for selling low- and moderate-income housing loans. The concluding section examines how these sectors, conventional lenders, the secondary market, CDFIs and the public sector can expand their respective roles and develop a more systematic approach to promoting social financing for low-income housing and begin to reach a scale appropriate to the need.

The Private Sector

CDFIs will never have sufficient capital to meet all the financing needs for low-income housing, nor do they currently have the capacity to replace conventional lenders. Conventional lenders and CDFIs must look for ways to create new partnerships that will provide access to appropriate types and amounts of capital for low-income housing ventures. Possibilities include:

1. Conventional lenders and CDFIs could develop joint programs in which a pool of conventional lenders makes loans, while the CDFI undertakes much of the cost of administration and underwriting, in order to reduce the lenders' costs. The conventional lenders would pool their funds in order to pool risk and increase underwriting oversight. California's Low Income Investment Fund utilizes this approach, working with a pool of 18 lenders in the state (Low Income Investment Fund 2003).
2. Conventional lenders could increase their support of CDFIs through grants, equity investments and long-term, fixed-rate loans. This is discussed in greater detail below.
3. More complete partnerships could be created by expanding participation beyond conventional lenders, CDFIs and the public sector to include nonconventional lenders, such as pension funds, foundations and religious institutions. Broad-based partnerships generate more resources for CDFIs, fill gaps that go beyond the capacity of smaller partnerships and create greater support for a range of community development activities in local communities (Leibsohn 1995).

Secondary Markets

Successful lending and investment in low-income housing must remain rooted in local underwriting and origination. The specialized knowledge, expertise, flexibility and commitment of the best local lenders demonstrates that low-income housing lending, both single-family and multifamily, can be done safely. However, the development of a strong, substantial and flexible secondary market is essential. Typically, secondary markets are synonymous with standardization. It has been mentioned that the danger of a standardized secondary market is that it will exclude the types of housing that often typify low-income housing developed by nonprofits, including cooperatives, land trust housing, special needs housing and single room occupancy (SRO) housing. However, secondary markets could be customized to meet the needs of different types of low-income housing. Separate underwriting standards for specific categories of housing could be developed for the secondary markets. Secondary markets could also move away from examining each loan, and several intermediaries could be organized as conduits from primary lenders to secondary market agencies. The Enterprise Foundation established an initiative to package loans for rental housing and sell them to Fannie Mae. Conventional primary lenders could also provide credit enhancements, such as sharing the risk on a portion of each loan so that the secondary market would buy the loan more willingly.

Fannie Mae and Freddie Mac could customize mortgage-backed securities where they can find a social investor to buy the MBS at a discounted price. The benefit of this type of arrangement is that the investor takes the rate risk but still has principal and interest payments guaranteed by Fannie Mae or Freddie Mac. In this way, Fannie Mae or Freddie Mac could help to create a secondary market for below-market rate loans and be an effective conduit for investors whose main objective is preservation of principal (Kantor 1996). In addressing special types of low-income housing, such as co-ops, land trusts and SROs, it is important to look for ways that Fannie Mae and Freddie Mac could securitize smaller affordable housing projects, as many of these projects are in the $200,000 to $2 million range, and the secondary markets do not like to deal with projects this small.

Community Development Financial Institutions (CDFI)

In order to become serious partners with conventional institutions in providing capital to meet low-income housing needs, CDFIs need to scale up so as to expand their impact, moving beyond impact that is very localized and quite small in volume and scope. In scaling-up, CDFIs enhance their ability to form legitimate, strong partnerships with conventional financial institutions. Scaling-up can occur in four ways: quantitative scaling-up, functional scaling-up, political scaling-up and organizational scaling-up (Uvin 1995).

Quantitative scaling-up refers to expansion, increasing the geographic areas in which CDFIs serve and the number of loans and investments that they are able to originate and manage effectively. Functional scaling-up refers to the number and types of activities undertaken by CDFIs, including the ability to form effective partnerships with conventional lenders and secondary markets and effective coalitions and alliances with other CDFIs and public agencies. Political scaling-up refers to the extent to which CDFIs move beyond the delivery of services toward changing the structural causes of inadequate financial resources for housing and community development. Political scaling-up also involves mobilizing political power so as to influence the flow of funds and resources to CDFIs. This type of activity might focus on extending the provisions of the Community Reinvestment Act to insurance companies, other nonbank lenders and mutual funds as well as influencing the flow of funds from federal, state and local government to CDFIs.

Finally, organizational scaling-up is necessary to increase organizational strength, effectiveness and sustainability of activities. Organizational scaling-up refers to increasing the degree of financial sustainability of CDFIs, creating external links with public and private intermediaries and improving the management capacity of staff. Organizational scaling-up will involve developing a generation of appropriate managers and staff for CDFIs with the specialized knowledge, skills, commitment and ability to innovate and make community development lending successful.

There is no particular order or hierarchy among these four types of scaling-up, but organizational scaling-up is unique. It can occur alone, with CDFIs improving their management structures while keeping their activities stable. However, organizational scaling-up is the corollary for all other types of scaling-up (Uvin 1995). Increasing the scale of CDFIs is a key element for developing a system of social finance. Although there are relatively few CDFIs and they control a relatively small amount of money, subsidizing CDFIs to meet specialized housing needs and target assistance to specific neighborhoods may be more effective than mandating procedural requirements for existing conventional institutions (Calomiris et al. 1994).

The Role of Government

Even with a more substantial CDFI sector and active private participation, government will continue to play an essential role in social finance. Government affects financing in a multitude of ways, both passive and active. It can formulate regulations (such as the Community Reinvestment Act); it can provide various incentives to the private sector (e.g., through the tax system); and it can intervene directly in financial markets by providing both debt and equity to projects. What follows is a range of policies available to various levels of government:

1. Federal, state and local agencies could provide credit enhancements, such as mortgage insurance programs or guarantees that are capitalized by a dedicated revenue stream (as in housing trust funds), to provide insurance for loans issued either by conventional lenders or CDFIs. The nonprofit Community Preservation Corporation in New York City used city and state insurance programs to help direct over $3 billion in lending from banks, insurance companies and pension funds to low-income housing from 1974 to 2002 (Community Preservation Corporation 2002).

2. The federal government could establish a national housing trust fund, as described previously. Such an entity could raise and allocate funds from mandatory payments by all private entities that engage in credit-market borrowing. The most progressive approach for capitalizing such a fund would be a wealth tax on credit-market instruments held by all private financial institutions. A tax of one-quarter of 1 percent would generate over $50 billion a year (Stone 2003). Another approach would be to require all capital market participants to use a minimum percentage of their net new funds to purchase long-term, low-interest bonds issued by the trust and backed by the U.S. Treasury. It has been estimated that such an approach could have raised between $20 and $25 billion a year as of the early 1990s if 10 percent of net new funds raised in the credit markets by private financial sectors and nonfinancial institutions would have been invested in these bonds (Stone 1993); currently, this would be closer to $50 billion a year (Stone 2003). In the short run, these amounts would exceed the capacity of nonprofit developers and CDFIs, but in the long run, the availability of such funds would help to build capacity and aid in the scaling-up process. A national housing trust fund could allocate money to CDFIs and public agencies, for use as either equity or low-cost, long-term debt.

3. The Federal Home Loan Bank could offer a special category of membership to CDFIs, thus giving CDFIs access to long-term, fixed-rate financing at relatively affordable costs. The federal government could also mandate this change, similar to the mandate in FIRREA that established the current affordable housing programs at the FHLB in which a portion of the bank's profits are dedicated to low-income housing.

4. Federal tax laws could be changed to provide for tax-free interest income to individuals and corporations making below-market rate loans to CDFIs. This would help attract funds to CDFIs, but it may not attract the long-term capital that is most needed for low-income housing. Nonetheless, it could be a useful source of capital for CDFIs.

5. The federal government could extend Community Reinvestment Act provisions to cover nonbank financial institutions, such as insurance companies, mortgage companies and mutual funds. Extending CRA would also address bank concerns that the current regulation unfairly discriminates against banks and places them at a competitive disadvantage among financial institutions.

There are a number of appropriate and useful actions that can be taken by conventional financial institutions, the private nonprofit sector and government to enhance the availability of capital for social housing. Many of these recommendations are designed to operate within the present capital market system or to alter it somewhat. Most of them rely upon some government-backed incentives to make capital investment in low-income housing attractive from the standpoint of risk and return. Except for the Community Reinvestment Act, most of them do not rely on the political power of the government to force change. As the role of non-deposit mortgage banks and bankers increases, the effectiveness of the Community Reinvestment Act to challenge behavior comes into question unless it is extended to nonbank financial institutions.

We need a more substantial, effective and generous system for financing the production and rehabilitation of low- and moderate-income housing in the United States. The existing system has insufficient capital; is too reliant on debt financing, particularly market-rate debt financing, and is often inefficient in allocating existing capital. A concentrated and coordinated effort is needed to increase the availability of social finance, both equity and debt. Such an effort must include provision of flexible grant funds by federal, state and local governments; a system of appropriate incentives and regulations for the private sector; increased creativity and participation by the private sector, including not only banks but other nonbank financial intermediaries, such as insurance companies, mortgage companies and mutual funds; and a larger, more sophisticated CDFI sector.

REFERENCES

Beshouri, Chris, and Dennis Glennon. 1996. CRA as market development or tax: An analysis of lending decisions and economic development. Washington, DC: Office of the Comptroller of the Currency.

Bohner, Chris. 1995. CRA and HMDA: Tools for reinvestment. *Shelterforce*, Vol. XVII, No. 3, May/June.

California Reinvestment Committee. 2003. www.calreinvest.org.

Calomiris, Charles W., Charles M. Kahn and Stanley D. Longhofer. 1994. Housing-finance intervention and private incentives: Helping minorities and the poor. *Journal of Money, Credit and Banking*, Vol. 26, No. 3.

CDFI Fund. 2003. www.cdfifund.gov.

Center for Community Change. 2003. www.communitychange.org.

Chittenden Bank. 2003. The good investor. June 30. www.chittenden.com.

Committee for Economic Development. 1995. Rebuilding inner-city communities: A new approach to the nation's urban crisis. New York: Committee for Economic Development.

Community Preservation Corporation. 2002. Annual report. New York: The Corporation.

Daskal, Jennifer. 1998. In search of shelter: The growing shortage of affordable rental housing. Washington, DC: Center on Budget and Policy Priorities.

DiPasquale, Denise, and Jean L. Cummings. 1992. Accessing capital markets for affordable rental housing. In *From the neighborhoods to the capital markets*. Washington, DC: National Task Force on Affordable Housing.

DiPasquale, Denise, and William C. Wheaton. 1996. *Urban economics and real estate markets*. Englewood Cliffs, NJ: Prentice Hall.

Fannie Mae. 1993. *Underwriting low and moderate income borrowers: Building on the basics*. Washington, DC: Fannie Mae.

Federal Home Loan Bank (FHLB) System. 2003. www.fhlbanks.com.

Grogan, Paul S., and Benson F. Roberts. 1992. Debating the low-income housing tax credit: Good policy, good politics. *Shelterforce*, Vol. XIV, No. 1, January/February.

Kantor, Robert. 1996. Unpublished memo. Fannie Mae, Hartford Partnership Office, March 25.

Lappin, Michael D. 1993. The community preservation corporation: A national model for financing affordable housing. In *Housing America*, ed. Jess Lederman. Chicago: Probus Publishing Company.

Leibsohn, Daniel, M. 1995. Meeting capital needs in low income communities. San Francisco: Low Income Housing Fund.

Low Income Investment Fund. 2003. www.lihf.org.

Mendez, Fred. 2002. The association of reinvestment consortia for housing. *Community investments*, June. www.frbsf.org.

National Community Capital Association. 2003. www.communitycapital.org.

National Community Reinvestment Coalition (NCRC). 2005. www.ncrc.org.

National Housing Trust Fund Campaign. 2003. www.nhtf.org.

Neighborhood Housing Services of America, Inc. 2001. www.nhsofamerica.org.

New Hampshire CDFA. 2002. Annual report. Concord, NH: CDFA.

Roberts, Benson, and F. Barton Harvey. 1999. Comment on Jean L. Cummings and Denise DiPasquale's "The low income housing tax credit: An analysis of the first ten years." *Housing Policy Debate*, Vol. 10, No. 2, 309–320.

Shabecoff, Alice. 1994. Deals from hell: How creative nonprofits pull off affordable multifamily housing with only 11 funders. Washington, DC: Community Information Exchange, Spring/Summer.

Stegman, Michael A. 1991. The excessive costs of creative finance: Growing inefficiencies in the production of low-income housing. *Housing Policy Debate* Vol. 2, No. 2.

Stone, Michael E. 1993. *Shelter poverty: New ideas on housing affordability*. Philadelphia: Temple University Press.

———. 2003. Private letter to author, September 1.

Uvin, Peter. 1995. Scaling-up the grassroots and scaling down the summit: The relations between third world nongovernmental organizations and the United Nations. In *The U.N., NGOs and global governance*, eds. Thomas Weiss and Leon Gordenker. Boulder, CO: Lynne Rienner.

Valentine, Charles. 1991. The impact of mortgage industry policies on low-income minority communities: A case study of eastern North Philadelphia. Philadelphia Commission on Human Relations, April.

Widener, Mary. 1993. Neighborhood housing services of America. In *Housing America*, ed. Jess Lederman.Chicago: Probus Publishing Company.

Jon Pynoos and Christy M. Nishita

13 The Elderly and a Right to Housing

ON THE SURFACE, it appears that the housing situation of older persons is a testament to the success of American housing policy. For example, of householders age 55 or older, close to 80 percent own their homes, most having been supported by government-backed financing and tax advantages. Home equity represents about 44 percent of the assets of older households and provides a significant financial resource (HUD 1999a). Housing for older persons is generally in good condition, and few older persons live in overcrowded conditions. Older persons have also been major beneficiaries of direct housing subsidies: Over 1 million elderly[1] households receive housing assistance in the form of such programs as public housing, Section 202 housing, Section 221d3 housing and Section 8 vouchers (HUD 1999a). With these findings in mind, it is understandable that over two-thirds of persons 50 years and older in a national survey reported that they were "very satisfied" with their housing and their neighborhoods (AARP 1996).

These achievements, as impressive as they seem, present an overall picture of older adults that masks the serious housing-related problems of specific subgroups and the difficulties of securing housing and services. First, older persons with low incomes, women, minorities and those living alone warrant special attention because of concerns related to housing affordability. These older adults live on fixed incomes and have limited ability to increase earnings. Second, many older adults express a strong desire for continuity in their living arrangements yet often live in physically unsupportive environments,

disconnected from services. Instead of facilitating older persons' ability to grow old safely, independently and with dignity, many settings have instead become a source of the problem itself. Third, despite their preference to remain in their own homes, many older persons with low or moderate health or behavioral problems must relocate to more institutionalized settings.

The problems of affordability and suitability underscore the need for housing to be an entitlement. The home plays a disproportionately vital role in the lives of older adults. Those older adults who are frail and disabled spend a greater amount of time at home. If older adults' economic and social resources are limited in late life, the home and neighborhood play critical roles in their life chances and identity (Saegert 1985). Moreover, housing is a major determinant of safety, ability to get out into the community, and the ability to afford other basic necessities of life. This chapter examines the current housing situations of older people, then emphasizes the need for affordable and suitable housing. In addressing these needs, promising and innovative residential programs for frail older persons will be discussed. The chapter concludes with several strategies to improve the housing situation of elderly persons in the future.

THE HOUSING SITUATION OF OLDER PERSONS

Homeowners versus Renters

More than eight in ten older adults aged 45 and older own their homes (AARP 2000). Although the rate of homeownership decreases with advanced age, the majority (78 percent) of older adults over age 75 still own their own home (JCHS 2003). Homeownership rates, however, are lower among the most economically disadvantaged subpopulations. In 2002, 80 percent of whites age 75 and older were homeowners compared with 74 percent of blacks, 65 percent of Hispanics and 59 percent of Asians (JCHS 2003). Homeownership is also lower among elderly women (70 percent—HUD 1999b) and seniors with incomes below $20,000 (62 percent—AARP 2003).

In comparison to owners, the approximately 5 million elderly renters are more likely to be poor and comprised of women, minorities and persons who live alone and have had little opportunity for ownership. But this category also includes an estimated 1.57 million elderly renters who owned their previous residence. Some of these elderly were forced into a rental condition because of declining health, depletion of financial resources or substandard housing conditions (HUD 1999a).

About 8 percent of older persons, both renters and owners, live in dwellings and neighborhoods specifically planned for their exclusive occupancy. These range from accommodations that primarily support a post-retirement leisure-oriented lifestyle (active retirement communities) to those that predominately cater to frail persons who need personal assistance and nursing services (Golant 1992; Pynoos and Golant 1996).

A major advantage of homeownership is accumulation of equity. Homeownership has provided many older persons with a valuable asset. The distribution of net worth, however, is bimodal, with 23 percent having a net worth under $25,000 and the same percentage having between $100,000 and $250,000 in net worth (Schafer 1999b). As noted, home equity accounts for 43.6 percent of accumulated assets. Comparing elderly homeowners with elderly renters, the 1995 median net worth for the former was $141,300 but just $6,460 for the latter (HUD 1999a). American Housing Survey data for 1995 indicate that 48 percent of renters have incomes below $10,000 compared with only 19 percent of owners. Homeownership can be potentially advantageous because it provides security of occupancy, residential control, low cash outlays for shelter and a potential source of income for those with little or no mortgage debt.

Housing Costs Remain a Serious Problem for Older Persons

The most prevalent housing problem of the elderly is the burden of excessive housing costs. The conventional concept of affordability is the proportion of a household's income that can be reasonably spent on housing, which the federal government has set at 30 percent. As of 1995, 17 percent of elderly households have moderate housing cost burdens (30 to 49 percent of their income spent on housing), while an additional 14 percent spend more than 50 percent of their income on housing, indicating a severe housing cost burden (HUD 1999b).

Affordability problems are concentrated primarily among renters rather than homeowners. Renters are three times more likely to have severe housing costs. Fifty-seven percent of all renters have moderately to severely high housing costs (HUD 1999a). Although approximately 1.5 million elderly, low-income households live in government-assisted housing, such housing assistance is far from adequate to meet the needs of all elderly, low-income individuals (HUD 1999a).

Fifty percent of homeowners with severe housing costs are still paying off a mortgage (HUD 1999a). The other half own their homes free and clear, but many still report problems such as the cost of utilities, taxes, insurance and maintenance. Overall, however, homeowners tend to have higher incomes with which to address these cost issues.

Certain demographic subpopulations are extremely vulnerable to high housing costs. Approximately two-thirds of senior households with severe housing cost burdens are women, and two-thirds live alone (HUD 1999b). Seventy percent of black and 53 percent of Hispanic elderly households have severe housing cost burdens compared with 25 percent of white elderly households (HUD 1999a).

How do the housing cost problems of older adults compare with those of nonelderly households who have the added burden of child-related expenses? Stone (1993 and Chapter 2) suggests an alternative view of affordability based on whether individuals or families have enough money to pay for other necessities such as child care, food or medical care after paying for housing. Rather than a set percentage, the standard is calculated on a sliding scale based on household size and income. Those who spend more than this amount are considered shelter-poor. Examining the housing affordability issue from this perspective reveals that nonelderly households have higher rates of shelter poverty than elderly households, due to their greater expenses and higher taxes. Nonetheless, in the lowest income bracket (less than $5,000), nearly all elderly and nonelderly are shelter-poor. A significant portion (48 percent) of shelter-poor elders are single women, most of whom live alone. Based on Stone's perspective, fewer older adults are overburdened with housing costs compared with nonelderly households, but these households are in much greater need than indicated by conventional standards.

The Physical Repair Needs of Housing

Excessive housing costs and low incomes can prevent persons from maintaining their place of residence. Older adults tend to live in older homes, usually built prior to 1960. Nearly 1.5 million older households live in dilapidated housing that is in severe need of physical repairs related to such housing systems as plumbing and heat. Among these households, over 1 million are homeowners and 400,000 are renters (HUD 1999a). Although inadequate housing affects more owners than renters, homeowners are more likely to be able to afford repairs and have the authority to make them. Only a small percentage of owners who need to repair their homes are poor. On the other hand, more than one-half of elderly renters who need home repairs have incomes under $10,000 and no assets (HUD 1999a).

Inadequate housing conditions are especially concentrated among older households who are poor, minorities (e.g., African-Americans and Hispanics), widows, very old (85 years or older) and frail (HUD 1999b). Elderly households living in rural areas, and to a lesser extent those living in central cities of metropolitan areas, are also more at risk of occupying housing in poor condition (Golant and La Greca 1994). Elderly persons living in low-priced, furnished rental units of residential hotels, rooming houses or transient hotels located in the inner city, skid row and edges of the urban downtown are especially socially marginalized. Even though most estimates suggest that the elderly are a relatively small proportion of the overall homeless population (Weiss 1992), they represent a particularly difficult population to serve.

Overhousing Has Been Raised as an Issue

Only infrequently are older households overcrowded, defined by the U.S. Census as more than one person per room. In fact, some analysts contend that over 5 million older households are overhoused because they live in dwelling units in which bedrooms outnumber household members by more than one (HUD 1999b). The majority of the overhoused are homeowners, many of whom live in the same home in which they raised their children. It can be argued that better use could be made of this underutilized space by older persons sharing their homes with others or by moving out altogether. However, few such persons desire to move because of their emotional attachment to the home, and most use extra bedrooms for family visitors, storage and accommodations for a person providing services (Pynoos and Golant 1996).

HOUSING NEEDS OF OLDER ADULTS

The most significant housing needs of older adults are affordability and suitability. The statistics on severe housing costs noted above highlight the need for more affordable senior housing. In addition, there is a need for suitable housing, defined as housing that provides a supportive setting and services to older adults. A continuum of housing options is needed so that older adults can find a place that is suitable to their level of need.

Affordability

Federally Subsidized Housing Is in Short Supply. Long waiting lists and low vacancy rates for subsidized housing indicate a shortage of affordable housing. Currently, the Section 202 program, sponsored by nonprofit organizations, houses over 350,000 older persons in over 3,500 facilities (Heumann, Winter-Nelson and Anderson 2001). Residents of Section 202 housing, one of the government's best programs, have their own private apartments, and rents do not exceed 30 percent of tenant incomes. The buildings are generally well maintained, and residents are highly satisfied with their accommodations (Golant 1992). Over 1.2 million rental households of all ages benefit from Section 8 rental subsidies, including 500,000 older households (Kochera, Redfoot and Citro 2001). Federally subsidized housing for the elderly benefits a disproportionate number of low-income, older women who live alone, including a high percentage of minorities; these residents cannot afford other housing options.

Nevertheless, in Section 202, Section 8 and public housing, there is a large gap between the number of wait-listed applicants and the number of available housing units. It is common for applicants to wait over four years for Section 202 housing (Pynoos et al. 1995). Some applicants cope by cutting expenses, moving in with others or asking relatives and friends for assistance, but most have already reduced their expenses as much as possible (Pynoos et al. 1995).

The problems of low-income persons are exacerbated by losses from the current subsidized housing stock. Under HUD's Section 8 program, landlords receive low-interest loans, subsidies and other incentives to house low-income families, the disabled and the elderly. Some developers are paying off their loans early and converting to market rents or are opting not to renew their Section 8 contracts. It is estimated that approximately 300,000 units were lost between 1997 and 1999 (Commission 2002). At the same time, the current production rate of 5,000 to 6,000 Section 202 units per year is far below the

20,000 units per year in the late 1970s (Commission 2002). The 2002 Commission on Affordable Housing and Health Facilities Needs for Seniors in the 21st Century (also known as the Seniors Commission) was created by Congress to review current housing and health needs of older Americans and to make policy and legislation recommendations for increasing the availability of housing and services. It recognized the loss of subsidized housing as a serious problem. The Seniors Commission acknowledged the need not only to preserve the existing housing stock but also to renovate and refinance Section 202 projects. An encouraging step in the right direction was $683 million authorized by HUD for Section 202 housing production in FY2003, an increase of $4 million over the previous year.

Suitability

An Aging Society Needs Suitable Housing Linked with Services. While housing costs and conditions remain serious problems for a large number of older persons, the issue of suitable housing linked with services for frail older persons has risen rapidly on the public agenda. Concern about housing for those persons is driven by the large increase in the old-old population and their needs for supportive housing linked with services.

The rapid growth of the elderly population is by now common knowledge. By 2000, there were 36 million Americans over age 65. That population will expand to almost 70 million persons by the year 2030, at the height of the aging of the baby boom generation. Just as important in terms of housing policy, however, is the growth of the old-old segment of the population. From 1980 to 1990, the number of persons 85 and older increased 37 percent. In 2050, the oldest-old may make up 25 percent of the population aged 60 and older (Rogers 1999). The rates of disability and the need for supportive settings linked with services increase significantly at such advanced old age.

Approximately 29 percent of persons age 70 and older need help with at least one activity of daily living (ADL) (Schafer 1999a). Limitations include the performance of such basic ADLs as walking, bathing, feeding, eating and toileting. The prevalence of such physical disabilities increases with age. For example, nearly 19 percent of persons age 70 to 74 experience difficulties with ADLs, rising to 53 percent of those age 85 to 89 (Schafer 1999a). Rates of cognitive problems also increase with advanced old age: the prevalence of cognitive impairment increases about 10 percent for every 10 years of age after age 65 (Unverzagt et al. 2001).

Despite functional and cognitive difficulties, the majority of older persons express a strong desire for continuity in their living arrangements. For example, in an American Association of Retired Persons (AARP) (2000) survey of persons age 45 and over, over 80 percent of respondents agreed with the statement: "What I'd really like to do is stay in my own home and never move." Such a strong attachment to place is understandable when length of tenure is taken into account; in 1995, nearly one-half of all elderly homeowners had lived in the same home for more than 25 years. For many such residents, their current housing represents a sense of security, proximity to friends and familiar services, and memories of where they raised their families. In another AARP (2003) survey, 54 percent of respondents thought they would be able to stay in their current home for the rest of their life.

A living environment with supportive features can greatly benefit all older adults who prefer to age in place and especially those who are frail or disabled. It can enhance their ability to have meaningful lives, exercise choice, maintain social ties and carry out activities. However, the overwhelming proportion of single-family homes and apartment complexes in which older persons live were developed for independent residents. These dwelling units have been referred to as "Peter Pan" housing, designed for persons who will never grow old. Such housing frequently has barriers, such as stairs, that make getting into the unit and up to a second floor difficult, and bathrooms that are unsafe.

Physically supportive settings provide accessibility inside the dwelling unit as well as to the outside and are adaptable to the limitations of their residents. They include features that are controllable by residents (e.g., individual thermostats at appropriate heights); forgiving (e.g., carpeted floor surfaces that may reduce injuries from falls); easy to use (e.g., places to sit while cooking) and supportive (e.g., grab bars and handrails). Such settings can make it easier for older persons to carry out tasks and enhance safety. Persons with cognitive problems such as Alzheimer's disease may also benefit from living in familiar environments that allow them to exercise whatever capabilities remain for self-direction. They may, however, need special features that allow for safe wandering, devices that compensate for memory problems (shut-off devices for stoves), visual cues that help them find their way around the house and simplified environments (e.g., removal of clutter).

Although the addition of supportive features in homes has been increasing, most of the current housing stock is unsuitable for frail older persons or younger persons with disabilities. Approximately 1.14 million older persons with health and mobility problems have unmet needs for additional supportive features in their dwelling units (HUD 1999a)

In addition to physically supportive environments, older persons may also require personal assistance in tasks such as preparing meals, ambulating, bathing and shopping. Family members continue to furnish approximately 80 percent of such personal care, with 20 percent provided by outsiders, such as homemakers, home health aides, nurses and personal companions (Kane, Kane and Wilson 1998). In either case, caregiving is facilitated by adequate spaces within which to assist in tasks (e.g., bathing) and supportive features (e.g., grab bars, walk-in showers).

At some point, a physically supportive home and personal assistance may not be enough to meet an older adult's needs. If individuals have severe health problems or disability, a threshold may be reached whereby relocation to a more service-enriched setting may be necessary. This threshold can vary, depending on the severity of health or disability, the presence of behavior problems stemming from Alzheimer's disease, the availability of a caregiver or the financial ability to afford nursing home care. For certain older adults, remaining at home may not make sense from a resource allocation perspective, given their high level of need.

Responsibility for providing supportive environments and services has become an especially important issue in government-subsidized housing serving the elderly. However, most government-subsidized housing has a major shortcoming: It was intended for independent older persons. Over time, however, residents have aged in place and new tenants have moved in at an older age. For example, in 1999, managers of Section 202 projects reported that 30 percent of residents were age 80 and older and 22 percent of residents were frail (Heumann, Winter-Nelson and Anderson 2001). Such residents need more physically supportive environments and services than initially are available in most federally assisted housing in order to avoid unnecessary moves to more institutional settings, such as board-and-care or nursing homes. As will be discussed later, until recently, HUD has taken only limited responsibility for assisting residents in aging in place.

Legislation and Programs Present Barriers to Aging in Place. Despite the benefits of linking housing and services to promote aging in place, legislation and programs hamper progress in this direction. Government response to improving the suitability of conventional housing has been slow to evolve. The Fair Housing Amendments Act of 1988, the major piece of federal legislation that requires physically accessible housing settings, applies only to buildings of four or more dwelling units, leaving out entirely single-family houses and smaller housing complexes, including most townhouses. The section of the bill that refers to retrofitting existing multiunit dwellings calls for "reasonable accommodations" for persons with disabilities and allows tenants to make adaptations but is vague on the responsibility of the owner to pay for changes, even in the common areas.

Programs that provide funds enabling elderly people who live in their own homes to make adaptations in the physical environment are few and far between, supported primarily by programs such as Community Development Block Grants, which was created in 1974, and the Older Americans Act of 1965, neither of which provides substantial resources to solve these problems. Medicare pays for what are considered medically necessary devices, such as walkers and wheelchairs, but does not cover features such as walk-in showers, stair lifts or structural changes. Therefore, older persons have at their disposal only a patchwork delivery system of inadequately funded services. Many older persons forego adaptations that could improve the quality of their lives because of the paucity of home modification programs and the difficulty of having to pay out of pocket for many adaptations, especially those that are costly.

Home modification and other supportive services to facilitate aging in place are difficult to achieve because the financing of long-term care is biased toward institutional care. Medicaid, the primary government-subsidized program that pays for long-term care services needed by chronically ill low-income elders, overwhelmingly funds nursing home care. In 2000, Medicaid spent $67 billion on long-term care, 75 percent of which paid for nursing home and institutional care (Wiener, Tilly and Alecxih 2002). While nursing home care has become a form of entitlement, community-based care services are still optional. Medicaid does not pay for the full range of home care services needed by most persons who are functionally dependent. Consequently, it has been easier for older persons in need of long-term care to become eligible for Medicaid payments if they enter a nursing home, and Medicaid has traditionally covered more services in nursing homes than in other settings.

PROMISING HOUSING STRATEGIES

The lack of affordable and suitable housing is a barrier to appropriate care for frail older persons. In order to address these problems, there have been several promising housing strategies that attempt to improve the affordability and suitability of elderly housing: reverse mortgages, home modifications, programs to make federally subsidized housing more supportive, innovative community-based care services, assisted living, small group residential facilities and nontraditional housing options.

Reverse Mortgages as a Source of Income

A reverse mortgage enables older adults to use their home as a potential source of income to make their long-term care, home repair or home modification needs more affordable. It allows older persons to stay in their homes and draw down the cash value through a monthly stipend, a lump sum payment or a line of credit (Scholen 2000). The loan is then repaid, with interest, when the home is vacated. Early proponents of reverse mortgages pointed out that almost one-half of the elderly at risk of needing health and personal care services lived in single-family dwellings. The potential market for such mortgages are persons over 62 years of age who own their homes free and clear or nearly so.

Many analysts have been optimistic about reverse mortgages because of the high rate of homeownership among the elderly. The aggregate amount of equity tied up in homes of the elderly is large (estimates range from $600 billion to $800 billion). Rasmussen, Megbolugbe and Morgan (1997) note that studies have estimated that from 3 to 5 million elderly households are eligible for a reverse mortgage.

In order to promote such mortgages, HUD in 1989 began to insure a specific type of loan referred to as a Home Equity Conversion Mortgage (HECM). The HECM is available for persons 62 years of age and older who own their homes with little to no mortgage debt. The HECM provides either for a monthly payment as long as the borrower resides in the home, monthly payments for a period of time set by the borrower, a line of credit or a combination of these options (HUD 2000a). The average borrower in the HECM program is a 76-year-old widow with a median income below 125 percent of the poverty level; however, recently a greater number of younger retirees are beginning to use the program. A study on the potential impact of reverse mortgages (Kutty 1998) estimated that 564,080 households in 1991 would have been above the official poverty threshold if they had obtained an HECM. The HECM is just one of a diverse offering of reverse mortgages available. The Fannie Mae Home Keeper program and other banks, mortgage companies or private lenders are beginning to offer reverse mortgages to their existing clients.

The uptake on HECMs has been somewhat slow, but the program has expanded over the past few years partly because of lower interest rates and declining retirement income from stocks and savings accounts. According to the Federal Housing Administration (FHA), since the program's first closing in 1989, approximately 75,000 HECMs have been insured and endorsed, two-thirds of which have been endorsed in just the past three years alone. The slow growth of reverse mortgages of all types is related to their complicated nature, the reluctance of many older persons to tamper with a major asset, the high closing costs that often accompany initiation of the mortgage, unwillingness to return to debtor status and the relative newness of the concept. Nevertheless, accessing home equity by the poor elderly with failing health is common, according to HECM loan originators (Rasmussen, Megbolugbe and Morgan 1997). Such use raises a potential problem: States may aggressively attempt to recover their expenditures for care from the equity in the home. As Redfoot (1993) points out, such an outcome would discourage consumers from using reverse mortgages, outweighing their advantages of promoting independence and choice. Another factor that discourages consumers are deceptive practices of lenders who fail to disclose all fees, charge exorbitantly high fees or ask borrowers to sign documents without fully reading or understanding them (Wong and Garcia 1999).

A recent initiative encourages older homeowners to use reverse mortgages to purchase long-term care insurance. Passage of the American Homeownership and Economic Opportunity Act of 2000 is a step in this direction. It waives the upfront fee for the mortgage insurance premium for older Americans who use the money from an HECM for long-term care insurance. This approach would lessen the reliance on Medicaid, a dominant payer of nursing home care. At the same time, older adults would not have to spend down and sell their home in order to qualify for Medicaid. Older adults with long-term care insurance would have more options to remain at home with home health care services or move to an assisted living facility (Scully 2003). This policy initiative represents an emphasis on using one's own resources first to support long-term care before relying on public programs. Nevertheless, the use of reverse mortgages for such purposes can be seen as another form of spending down to receive long-term care. This approach underscores the problem that neither housing nor long-term care are entitlements.

Suitability: Supportive Environments and Services

Home Modification and Repair. Home repair and modifications are physical adaptations to the living environment that improve the suitability of the home and facilitate "aging in place." Repair involves fixing roofs, foundations and equipment to make the home safer and more energy-efficient. Home modifications can range from inexpensive lever door handles, hand-held showers and grab bars to more expensive ramps, stair-glides and fully remodeled bathrooms and kitchens. On a daily basis, these modifications make it easier to carry out tasks such as cooking, using stairs and cleaning. Home modifications can also have long-range benefits, such as increasing independence, preventing accidents, facilitating caregiving and minimizing the need for costly institutional care. Finally, home modifications play a role in multifactorial interventions to prevent falls that include risk assessment, exercise, educational materials and programming, and follow-up (Shekelle et al. 2002).

The majority of publicly funded home modification and repair is funded through HUD's Community Development Block Grants. Nevertheless, there is an absence of federal direction and earmarked funding for home modification and repair. Several states and a large number of localities have stepped into the breach to provide assistance for home modifications. For example, the Minnesota Housing Finance Agency (MHFA) uses housing revenue bonds to support a $20,000,000 Fix-up Fund to assist homeowners in increasing the livability, accessibility and energy efficiency of existing homes. The low-interest loans are made to homeowners by locally participating banks, credit unions and housing agencies. The MHFA also has a deferred payment Accessibility Loan program funded by state appropriations that targets households who have one or more members with a long-term physical disability that substantially affects functioning in the home. The Ohio State Department of Aging provides funds for housing specialists who provide technical assistance and information about a variety of housing options, including home modifications. The Philadelphia Corporation on Aging, an Area Agency on Aging, uses a variety of funds from such sources as Community Development Block Grants and Medicaid waivers to provide a range of modifications for older and younger persons with disabilities.

Despite the existence of such comprehensive programs, problems remain for persons seeking to modify their home. Significant gaps exist in the geographical coverage of programs, with rural areas particularly underserved. In addition, the existence of these programs is constantly threatened by a lack of stable sources of funding. In areas without programs, older adults and their families face a difficult task of coordinating the many different providers that may be needed to play a role in home modification, such as occupational therapists, remodelers, contractors, tradesmen, handymen, medical supply companies and social service agencies. These problems continue to act as barriers to older adults who want to age in place.

Making Government-Subsidized Housing More Supportive. To improve the suitability of housing for aging residents, service providers have begun to test the effectiveness of clustering services at housing sites in order to take advantage of economies of scale in serving multiple clients with fewer workers (Feldman, Latimer and Davidson 1996). The most concentrated efforts to make federally subsidized housing more supportive, however, are found in HUD's Congregate Housing Services (CHSP) and service coordinator programs.

The CHSP began in 1959 as a demonstration serving approximately 3,000 persons in 63 sites. The CHSP model uses a service coordinator to arrange assessments and pays for services such as meals, transportation and homemaking.

The program is targeted toward very frail older persons who are experiencing at least two problems with activities of daily living. Participants receive many benefits by participating in the CHSP: They continue to live in a residential environment, have greater control of discretionary spending than they would in a nursing home and receive emergency and day-to-day assistance. Perhaps the greatest benefit is the ability to postpone or avoid moving into a nursing facility. With passage of the Housing and Community Development Act of 1992, the program expanded operations to almost double the number of original sites. However, instead of HUD paying for most of the basic services, the revised program requires a 50 percent match from other sources as well as 10 percent payment from residents, changes that discouraged some potential projects from applying. Unfortunately, HUD no longer funds new programs, and the first contracts expired in 1998 (HUD 2000b).

Based on the CHSP and a Robert Wood Johnson Foundation Supportive Services in Senior Housing Demonstration, Congress—through the Housing and Community Development Act of 1992—authorized expenditures for a service coordinator program. Service coordination is a less intensive model than the CHSP and relies more on linking residents with services rather than providing them directly. Unlike the CHSP, coordinators in this program do not have budgetary authority for services, but they can serve a somewhat broader group of frail older residents. According to the American Association of Service Coordinators, in 2003, there were approximately 3,000 service coordinators in Section 202, public housing and other programs. An evaluation of the program revealed that service coordinators successfully marshaled a number of new services for residents, who report high levels of satisfaction with the program (KRA Corporation 1996). Services coordinated for residents include meals on wheels, in-home supportive services, hospice care, home health for those who meet Medicare or Medicaid eligibility, transportation services, on-site adult education and monthly blood pressure checks. Although there is also assistance with locating other living arrangements, such as assisted living or a nursing home when it becomes necessary, the primary focus is on assisting residents to continue living in their current apartments.

Despite the apparent success of CHSP and service coordination, both programs have faced a lack of HUD support and difficulties in securing funding. For years, HUD has contended that the provision of services rested with other agencies, such as the Department of Health and Human Services (HHS). However, there are some promising developments. In FY2003, the HUD budget provided an additional $3 million for the service coordinator program, bringing the total to $53 million. This increase is well-aligned with the Seniors Commission's recommendation to appropriately fund service coordination programs in federally subsidized housing. The Seniors Commission also called for increased interdepartmental cooperation between HUD and the HHS to improve the link between housing and services (Commission 2002). However, the Seniors Commission, along with many other groups, has lamented the reduction of public housing units and the expiration of housing contracts that have reduced the overall number of federally assisted units occupied by the elderly.

Suitability: Providing a Greater Range of Housing Options

Assisted Living: Housing for Frail Older Persons. Assisted living (AL) strives to improve the suitability of housing for more frail older adults by providing more intensive supportive and nursing services in a group setting that is residential in character and appearance. It has the capacity to meet unscheduled needs for assistance and is managed in ways that aim to maximize the physical and psychological independence of residents. AL is intended to accommodate physically and mentally frail elderly people without imposing on them the heavily regulated, institutional environment found in many nursing homes (Redfoot 1993; Regnier 1994; Regnier, Hamilton and Yatabe 1995). The typical resident of an AL is female, age 83 or over, widowed and requires help with 2.8 activities of daily living (ALFA 2001).

The private sector played a significant role in developing AL. In the 1990s, the corporate sector aggressively constructed new buildings and converted existing ones into AL. Even traditional nursing home providers have shifted some of their inventory toward AL. For example, Sunrise Senior Living, formerly known as Sunrise Assisted Living, is a publicly traded company that has developed several hundred properties across the nation. The company has recently shifted its focus from property ownership to management. In 2003, the company acquired Marriott Senior Living Services, a move that will increase the number of properties that Sunrise will manage to include nursing homes and independent living centers (Pristin 2003). The private-sector AL industry has catered to middle-income persons who have had a pent-up demand for attractive residential settings with available services and amenities. These companies prefer to operate in unregulated or loosely regulated environments.

Affordability of AL, however, remains a problem because its average monthly cost is $2,159 (MetLife 2002). According to Redfoot (1993:519), "though assisted living is the fastest growing segment of the senior housing industry, the costs associated with this type of service have generally been out of reach for older persons with low or moderate incomes." Blanchette (1997) notes that some policymakers are concerned that if states subsidize the costs of services in AL for low-income persons, state long-term care costs will increase. Consequently, the government would be providing incentives for older persons to leave their homes and enter assisted living, thereby avoiding less attractive options such as board-and-care, foster care or nursing homes.

States have attempted to make AL more affordable and reduce nursing home costs by utilizing Medicaid to reimburse service costs. Coverage may be provided under the Medicaid state plan or under a Home and Community-Based Services (HCBS) waiver. These waivers provide flexibility to states to develop innovative residential alternatives for Medicaid-eligible individuals who would otherwise need institutional care (Mollica and Jenkens 2001). As of 2000, 38 states used Medicaid state plans or waivers to cover services in either AL or board-and-care facilities (Mollica 2000). Medicaid, however, does not cover room and board costs for AL. Medicaid recipients usually pay for room

and board costs through Supplemental Security Income (SSI) benefits and state supplements to SSI. Even here, "double standards for the rich and poor have emerged" as low-income frail elders often have to share their residential units (Golant 1999:42). The Seniors Commission recommended that Congress institute a Medicaid shelter allowance under the Medicaid HCBS waiver programs with incentives for state implementation (Commission 2002).

In 2000, HUD's budget included $50 million for the conversion of entire buildings or floors of Section 202 housing for the elderly into AL facilities, representing another attempt to make AL more affordable. HUD also authorizes the use of housing vouchers in AL. Although these programs will facilitate aging in place, they reduce the number of units for more independent older persons and raise concerns about regulating quality of care. The experience of various states with converting Section 202 into AL suggests that projects increase residents' access to services and maintains a residential environment. However, projects need more stable sources of funding and face difficulty integrating staff from both housing and services backgrounds (Wilden and Redfoot 2002). In addition, complying with building codes and other regulations associated with AL licensure can be difficult (Hilton 2004). If successful, such policies will make AL more available to low- and moderate-income older persons but still fall considerably short of the need.

As states and federal programs attempt to reduce long-term care costs and make AL more affordable, there are concerns about whether AL is a substitute for nursing home care. In an analysis of six studies of AL residents, Golant (2004) found that despite wide variation in impairment level, older residents in assisted living were less physically and cognitively impaired than those in nursing homes. A nationally representative study found that among residents who leave assisted living, most move to a higher level of care; nearly 60 percent end up in nursing homes (Phillips et al. 2003). However, Oregon's affordable AL program has lower rates of residents moving to nursing homes (20 percent) because of the state's liberal skilled nursing care provisions and flexible nurse delegation statutes (Golant 1999). These statistics suggest that even in Oregon, where AL facilities accommodate more physically and cognitively impaired residents, a significant number of residents still relocate to nursing homes.

The closer that AL comes to housing nursing home–eligible residents, the more attention will be paid to regulations that protect residents and ensure quality of care. These regulations could shift AL away from a social model to a "medicalized" approach. In any case, there is not an unlimited demand for AL. Most older people still prefer to age in place in their own homes or apartments. Wahl and Gitlin (2003:293) predict that the "primacy of the private-home environment" will not only persist but become more significant for elders in the future.

Small Group Residential Facilities. Small group residential facilities are a housing option that meets the needs and preferences of certain older adults. When an AARP (1996) survey asked respondents where they would prefer to live if they were forced to move, 69 percent indicated a residential care facility. Among residential care facilities, older persons strongly preferred small homes providing care to a few people or apartment buildings with services. Over the last 20 years, there has been a slow growth in small group homes, which are also known as residential care facilities, board-and-care homes and adult foster care homes (Streib, Folts and Hilker 1984; Hawes, Wildfire and Lux 1993). Golant (1999) suggests that middle-income persons who have lived in board-and-care have gravitated to more high-end AL facilities.

While many small group homes are actually found in existing residential structures, there has been a recent growth of newly built small group homes. These range from shared living arrangements for moderate-income older persons experiencing some limitations in activities of daily living to residences specially designed for persons with Alzheimer's disease. The latter often provide housing for six to eight residents in early to middle-stage dementia, including persons who are nonverbal and incontinent. These small group home facilities provides meals, personal care, laundry and protective oversight for residents. They vary widely in size and ambiance.

Some are attractive and family-like, while others are sparse and institutional. Although most states require the licensing of such homes, many places remain unlicensed. For the most part, even the licensed homes are loosely regulated (Hawes, Wildfire and Lux 1993). Moreover, residential care facilities continue to face zoning barriers.

Nontraditional Housing Approaches. The availability of a continuum of housing options will enable older adults to choose a setting that is suitable to their needs. Over the past decade, a number of nontraditional housing approaches have been tried in the United States, from supporting naturally occurring retirement communities (NORCs) to accessory units and shared housing.

A considerable number of older people live in buildings or communities populated by large concentrations of the elderly. Twenty-seven percent of older people live in a building or neighborhood where more than 50 percent of the residents are over age 60 (AARP 1996). Some of these places are neighborhoods in which a cohort of once younger persons has aged in place. Other settings include small rural towns and urban areas from which there has been a large outmigration of younger persons, leaving a concentration of elders behind. Most of these NORCs were not intentionally planned for older persons, and they usually lack the services, amenities, facilities and housing types to adequately support aging in place. NORCs offer the opportunity to rebuild communities so that they are "elder-friendly" in terms of facilities such as senior centers, available services, appropriate transportation and mutual helping networks. So far, the longest-lived and best-known NORC program is New York City's Penn South Program for Seniors (PSPS). PSPS provides or coordinates social, educational, housekeeping, personal care and health services for approximately 6,000 older residents of a large housing cooperative encompassing several buildings (Lanspery 1998). In 2003, the Administration on Aging awarded $5.6 million in grants to 12 cities in order to establish demonstration programs that improve access to health and supportive services for older adults in NORCs.

Accessory apartments are complete living units, including a private kitchen and bath, created within a larger single-family home. Older adults who rent out these apartments can earn additional income, while the renter may pay lower than market rates in exchange for help with chores and other tasks. Elder cottage housing opportunity units (ECHO), also known as Granny Flats, are small, portable homes installed adjacent to a single-family home. This option enables older adults to be near their family but still provides privacy. Nevertheless, the growth of these two options has been slow, partly due to consumer reluctance, the physical difficulty of placing units in areas such as inner cities and inner suburbs and neighborhood opposition reflected in restrictive zoning codes. In California, a state law passed in 2003 eases restrictions on building these second dwelling units in single-family and multifamily neighborhoods.

Shared housing is an arrangement in which two or more unrelated people share a home or apartment. This option can provide the elderly with additional income, companionship, social support and security. However, the growth of shared living residences and matching programs for older persons has been slow. Most elderly do not want to live with nonspouse relatives or other persons. On the other hand, according to an AARP study (1996), 17 percent of respondents indicated they would contemplate moving in with a family member; 3 percent said they were seriously considering such a move. Nevertheless, with advancing age, especially for women, the prevalence of shared housing with relatives increases. After age 85, one in four women live with a family member other than a spouse, and the frequency is higher among black and Hispanic women (Pynoos and Golant 1996). The elderly person may view this as the best of the limited options available (Pynoos and Golant 1996).

FUTURE DIRECTIONS

Advances in areas such as reverse mortgages, home modifications, linking housing and services, community-based care, assisted living and nontraditional housing options have provided more choices for frail older persons. These choices reflect a greater awareness that older adults have a right to age in place in residential settings that are physically supportive and suitable to their needs. Nevertheless, such changes are incremental and leave the country unprepared to address the housing and service needs of the growing number of very old persons and the baby boom generation that will soon enter retirement. In order to progress more rapidly, several major policy shifts are necessary: changing the continuum of housing paradigm, insuring the affordability of housing and long-term care, providing universally designed housing, creating new models of housing and reducing competition between the elderly and other groups.

THE CONTINUUM OF HOUSING: CHANGING THE PARADIGM

There has been a long-standing assumption that as persons become more frail, they need to move along a housing continuum from one setting to another. Along this continuum are found a range of housing options, such as single-family homes, apartments, congregate living, assisted living and board-and-care homes, with the end point most frequently identified as a nursing home (Kendig and Pynoos 1996).

Although the continuum of housing identifies a range of housing types, there is increasing recognition that frail older persons do not necessarily have to move from one setting to another if they need assistance. Semi-dependent or dependent older persons can live in a variety of settings, including their own homes and apartments if the physical setting is more supportive and accessible. A revised framework has therefore emerged that emphasizes the elasticity of the conventional housing stock in terms of its ability to accommodate a wide spectrum of frail older persons and younger persons with disabilities. At the same time, it stresses the importance of having a wide spectrum of housing alternatives that allow older persons choices in terms of settings that offer different levels of on-site services, supervision, sociability, privacy and amenities.

For over 20 years, researchers and advocates for the elderly have been proposing programs that extend the ability of housing types to support frail older persons and the creation of new alternatives that provide service-rich, supportive environments. Such proposals were main agenda items at the 1981 and 1995 White House conferences on aging. These concepts have finally been addressed in principle by HUD's Housing Security Plan for Older Americans (HUD 1999a), which promotes the concept of communities assembling and coordinating "a comprehensive continuum of care to meet the changing housing and services needs of their elders."

THE AFFORDABILITY OF HOUSING AND SERVICES

Frail older persons are caught in a double bind in relation to living environments: Neither housing nor long-term care are entitlements in our society. Housing itself is a major expense for older persons, especially for those who have low and moderate incomes. When expenditures for needed personal services are added to housing costs, as in the case of assisted living, the total amount escalates beyond the budgets of the great majority of older persons. While 64 percent of older persons have annual incomes under $25,000, the average annual fee for housing and services in assisted living is $32,400 (Schuetz 2003). But in order to allow frail older persons to stay out of institutional settings, both parts of the equation need to be addressed: The right to affordable housing for older persons needs to be accompanied by the right to affordable long-term care. As discussed previously, long-term care policy in the United States has packaged services and housing assistance for older persons primarily through Medicaid, which pays for personal and nursing care as well as costs associated with staying in a licensed nursing home. Also, government support for services that allow someone to stay in other settings is quite limited.

One proposed approach to address the long-term care problem is to unbundle housing and long-term care reimbursement so that housing and services are paid for separately. Housing and service costs could be subsidized using portable payment methods, such as vouchers or cash grants, thereby providing older persons with a broad set of choices of where to live. Consequently, older persons with moderate levels of need would not necessarily have to move to specific service-rich settings such as nursing homes or even assisted living in order to obtain care.

Several countries, such as Denmark and Sweden, have developed a system based on entitlements for both long-term care services and housing (Pynoos and Liebig 1995). They have basically stopped building nursing homes and instead allocate resources to help older persons stay at home or in service houses, which resemble assisted living. Along these lines, the United States has been experimenting with a voucher approach that funds both services and housing but does not tie them to particular settings as well as Medicaid waivers that pay for services in individual homes, small group homes and assisted living.

The federal government, however, remains cautious in terms of funding such programs. Given that families still provide the bulk of personal care for frail older persons living in the community, government budget analysts are concerned that large numbers of families will come to depend solely on the use of community-based services, should they become widely available.

An equally perplexing problem in pursuing a strategy of unbundling housing and services concerns regulations and licensure (Kane and Wilson 1993). Owing to the at-risk nature of their residents and the role of government, nursing homes are subject to a plethora of state and federal regulations concerning the physical facilities, staffing and quality of care. Although the nursing home regulatory process has its problems, it is in place. The potential proliferation of other care settings for frail older persons opens up a Pandora's box in terms of what to regulate, how to do it and who will carry out the regulatory process.

Although limits might still exist concerning the extent to which services could be efficiently delivered to all settings, choice would be based more on older persons' preferences for sociability, privacy, activities, location and other lifestyle features rather than just the need for care. Some frail older persons would choose group living situations, such as assisted living, while others might prefer staying in their own homes or apartments. The unbundling concept would work best if home care, adult day care and transportation were more widely available. In addition, housing would need to be accessible and affordable as well as contain supportive features.

PROVIDING UNIVERSAL HOUSING

Many of the physical problems that existing housing and neighborhoods present for older persons would be eliminated if appropriate supportive and adaptable settings were built in the first place. Toward this end, a worldwide movement has been advocating for adaptable housing and age-sensitive communities that benefit both the elderly and those with disabilities (Christenson 1999). These homes and neighborhoods would be accessible to persons in wheelchairs and persons with sight or hearing impairments as well as other limitations. Universal design emphasizes that the design of all products and environments be usable by all persons to the greatest extent possible without the need for adaptation or specialized design. Although somewhat more costly initially, universal design, as applied to housing, will ultimately reduce later expenditures necessary for remodeling or retrofitting.

In terms of housing, universal design is a broad concept that emphasizes accessibility throughout the home. At a minimum, housing units of all types would include the features enumerated in the Fair Housing Amendments Act of 1988, such as accessible entrances, hallways, bathrooms and kitchens; raised electrical outlets and plywood backing in bathrooms for installing grab bars. In the United States, there has been progress in this direction with the adoption of "visitability" codes in localities such as Atlanta, Austin, Urbana (IL) and Pima County (AZ) and states such as Vermont, Georgia and Texas. Visitability is a narrower concept that requires entrances and the first floor of homes to be accessible. Such advances, however, continue to be resisted by developers, who

argue that mandates will increase the cost of housing and require buyers to purchase features that they do not want. Builders prefer voluntary programs or incentives that waive building permit fees. Progress in this area therefore requires an educated group of consumer advocates who are convinced enough about the benefits of universal design to take on the building industry.

CREATING NEW MODELS OF HOUSING

A broader, multigenerational conceptualization of senior housing is needed that better integrates older adults within the community. While age-specific housing has many benefits associated with security and mutual support among residents, it can be overly insular and isolating. Increased flexibility in the use of funds at the state and local levels would allow the creation of new models of housing that incorporate community spaces and provide services to the adjacent neighborhood. More integrative models of elderly housing (e.g., service houses) in some European countries and a few locations in this country (1) co-locate restaurants, shops, day care, health clinics and senior centers so that housing for the elderly is better connected to the community; (2) provide services to older persons and younger persons with disabilities living in adjacent neighborhoods and (3) create age-integrated housing. Age-integrated housing can foster greater interaction between young and old and increase the vitality of the community.

New models of senior housing also need to address changing living arrangements, such as the growing trend of grandparents raising grandchildren. During the 1990s, the number of grandparent-headed households increased due to drug abuse, AIDS and incarceration. However, much of the nation's government-assisted housing for the elderly has been developed for their exclusive occupancy and does not allow children. In public housing, proof of legal guardianship is needed to prevent eviction, while grandparents living in senior housing can be evicted for taking in their grandchildren. Grandparents without legal custody do not qualify as "family" and therefore do not meet Section 8 eligibility requirements. Policymakers need to re-examine existing requirements within senior housing to accommodate this rising trend.

REDUCING COMPETITION BETWEEN THE ELDERLY AND OTHER GROUPS

Competition among groups representing the elderly, persons with disabilities and families with children will continue in the future as they fight for the limited amount of subsidized housing. Some critics argue that older adults receive more than their fair share of such subsidies. They assert that elderly households are less likely to experience excessive housing costs than nonelderly households (Golant and La Greca 1995) and that families are more likely to have multiple housing problems, often living in inadequate housing, overcrowded conditions or paying over 50 percent of their income for rent (Khadduri and Nelson 1992). Nevertheless, as was pointed out earlier, low-income seniors are at a disadvantage in that they live on fixed incomes. Critics also argue that seniors have had an advantage because it is easier to get communities to approve elderly housing developments as opposed to family housing. However, even senior housing developments have recently faced considerable opposition from neighborhood groups. Despite criticism, senior housing should be more broadly framed as an intergenerational issue that benefits persons of all ages. Senior housing offers a sense of security to families with older relatives. Affordable and suitable housing will lessen the strain on families, especially low-income families, to provide caregiving and economic support for older relatives. Furthermore, creating "elder-friendly" homes and communities will ensure a more secure old age for everyone.

CONCLUSION

Our nation made important strides in improving housing for older persons during the 1990s. Nevertheless, many older persons still pay too much for housing and live in substandard conditions. Just as troublesome are the increasing numbers of frail older persons who need physically supportive housing linked with services. We can build upon our experience to preserve and enhance existing multiunit housing for the elderly, better link housing and services, expand assisted living, increase home modifications and repairs, develop new types of housing and encourage the appropriate use of reverse mortgages. The federal government has taken an important step in this direction by announcing its Housing Security Plan for Older Americans in 1999, emphasizing a continuum of care.

However, government efforts so far have attempted only to remedy the housing and long-term care problems without addressing the needs for more radical change in how the government finances and provides housing and long-term care. Future efforts should emphasize universal design, build on a new housing paradigm, create innovative models of housing and ensure that both housing and long-term care services are affordable and more widely available. Such radical change requires the government to recognize housing as a fundamental right of all persons, including the elderly, alongside health care, long-term care, and retirement income security. Affordable and suitable housing will not only honor the preferences of older adults to age in place but also ensure their health and economic well-being.

NOTES

1. There is some ambiguity concerning the definition of elderly. In this chapter, most of the statistics presented use age 65 years or over. At times, an even younger age (45+) is used, but it is explicitly noted. However, this distinction is somewhat arbitrary. The definition of "elderly" can vary within the U.S. government from agency to agency and even from program to program within a given agency. Also, there is considerable age diversity within the older population itself. Thus, some of the statistics make the distinction between the young-old (those age 65 to 74), the middle-old (those age 75 to 84) and the old-old (those 85+)—categories used to denote groups of elderly in terms of their likely health status and need for personal care services.

REFERENCES

American Association of Retired Persons (AARP). 1996. *Understanding senior housing into the next century: Survey of consumer preferences, concerns, and needs.* Washington, DC: AARP.

———. 2000. *Fixing to stay: A national survey on housing and home modification issues.* Washington, DC: AARP.

———. 2003. *These four walls: Americans 45+ talk about home and community.* Washington, DC: AARP.

Assisted Living Federation of America (ALFA). 2001. *The assisted living industry, 2001: An overview.* Fairfax, VA: The Federation.

Blanchette, Katherine. 1997. *New directions for state long-term care systems, Volume III: Supportive housing.* Washington, DC: American Association of Retired Persons.

Christenson, Margaret A. 1999. Embracing universal design. *OT Practice,* 12–25.

Commission on Affordable Housing and Health Needs for Seniors in the 21st Century. 2002. *A quiet crisis in America.* Washington, DC: The Commission.

Feldman, Penny H., Eric Latimer and Harriet Davidson. 1996. Medicaid-funded home care for the frail elderly and disabled: Evaluating the cost savings and outcomes of a service delivery reform. *Health Services Research,* 31(4):489–508.

Golant, Stephen M. 1992. *Housing America's elderly: Many possibilities, few choices.* Newbury Park, CA: Sage Publications.

———. 1999. The promise of assisted living as a shelter and care alternative for frail American elders: A cautionary essay. In *Aging, autonomy, and architecture: Advances in assisted living,* eds. Benyamin Schwartz and Ruth Brent, 32–59. Baltimore: Johns Hopkins University Press.

———. 2004. Do impaired older persons with health needs occupy U.S. assisted living facilities? An analysis of six national studies. *Journal of Gerontology,* 59B(2):S68–S79.

Golant, Stephen M., and Anthony J. La Greca. 1994. City-suburban, metro-nonmetro, and regional differences in the housing quality of U.S. elderly households. *Research on Aging,* 16:322–346.

———. 1995. The relative deprivation of U.S. elderly households as judged by their housing problems. *Journal of Gerontology,* 50B(1):S13–S23.

Hawes, Catherine, Judith Wildfire and Linda Lux. 1993. *The regulations of board and care homes: Results of a survey in the 50 states and the District of Columbia.* Washington, DC: AARP.

Heumann, Leonard F., Karen Winter-Nelson and James R. Anderson. 2001. *The 1999 survey of Section 202 elderly housing.* Washington, DC: AARP.

Hilton, Lisette. 2004. Making affordable assisted living viable. *Practices,* March/April, 34–37.

Joint Center for Housing Studies. 2003. *The state of the nation's housing.* Cambridge, MA: Joint Center for Housing Studies of Harvard University.

Kane, Rosalie A., Robert L. Kane and Richard C. Wilson. 1998. *The heart of long-term care.* New York: Oxford University Press.

Kane, Rosalie A., and Karen B. Wilson. 1993. *Assisted living in the United States: A new paradigm for residential care for frail older persons?* Washington, DC: AARP.

Kendig, Hal, and Jon Pynoos. 1996. Housing. In *The encyclopedia of gerontology,* ed. James Birren, 703–713. San Diego: Academic Press.

Khadduri, Jill, and Kathryn P. Nelson. 1992. Targeting housing assistance. *Journal of Policy Analysis and Management,* 11(1):21–41.

Kochera, Andrew, Don Redfoot, and Jeremy Citro. 2001. Section 8 project-based rental assistance: The potential loss of affordable federally subsidized housing stock. Washington, DC: AARP.

KRA Corporation. 1996. *Evaluation of the service coordinator program.* Washington, DC: U.S. Department of Housing and Urban Development.

Kutty, Nadinee K. 1998. The scope for poverty alleviation among elderly home owners in the United States through reverse mortgages. *Urban Studies,* 35(1):113–129.

Lanspery, Susan C. 1998. *Linking housing and services, Part II: It's not just for senior housing anymore.* Los Angeles: National Resource and Policy Center on Housing and Long Term Care, University of Southern California.

MetLife Mature Market Institute. 2002. *MetLife survey of assisted living costs 2002.* Westport, CT: The Institute.

Mollica, Robert L. 2000. *State assisted living policy: 2000.* Portland, ME: National Academy for State Health Policy.

Mollica, Robert L., and Robert Jenkens. 2001. *State assisted living practices and options: A guide for state policy makers.* Washington, DC: NCB Development Corporation.

Phillips, Charles D., Yolanda Munoz, Michael Sherman, Miriam Rose, William Spector and Catherine Hawes. 2003. Effects of facility characteristics on departures from assisted living: Results from a national study. *The Gerontologist,* 43:690–696.

Pristin, Terry. 2003. Big assisted living company shifts away from property ownership. *New York Times,* July 30, C5.

Pynoos, Jon, and Stephen M. Golant. 1996. Housing and living arrangements for the elderly. In *Handbook of aging and the social sciences,* eds. Robert H. Binstock and Linda K. George, 303–324. New York: Academic Press.

Pynoos, Jon, and Phoebe Liebig. 1995. *Housing frail elders: International policies, perspectives, and prospects.* Baltimore: Johns Hopkins University Press.

Pynoos, Jon, Sandra Reynolds, Elyse Salend and Anna Rahman. 1995. *Waiting for federally assisted housing: A study of the needs and experiences of older applicants.* Washington, DC: AARP.

Rasmussen, David W., Isaac F. Megbolugbe and Barbara A. Morgan. 1997. The reverse mortgage as an asset management tool. *Housing Policy Debate,* 8(1):173–194.

Redfoot, Donald. 1993. Long-term care reform and the role of housing finance. *Housing Policy Debate,* 4(4):497–537.

Regnier, Victor. 1994. *Assisted living housing for the elderly: Design innovations from the United States and Europe.* New York: Van Nostrand Reinhold.

Regnier, Victor, Jennifer Hamilton and Suzie Yatabe. 1995. *Living for the aged and frail: Innovation in design, management, and finances.* New York: Columbia University Press.

Rogers, Carolyn C. 1999. Growth of the oldest old population and future implications for rural areas. *Rural Development Perspectives,* 14(3):22–26.

Saegert, Susan. 1985. The role of housing in the experience of dwelling. In *Home environments,* eds. Irwin Altman and Carol M. Werner, 287–309. New York: Plenum Press.

Schafer, Robert. 1999a. *America's elderly population and their need for supportive services.* Cambridge, MA: Joint Center for Housing Studies of Harvard University.

———. 1999b. *Housing America's elderly population.* Cambridge, MA: Joint Center for Housing Studies of Harvard University.

Scholen, Ken. 2000. *Home-made money: Consumer's guide to home equity conversion.* Washington, DC: AARP.

Schuetz, Jenny. 2003. Making affordable assisted living a reality. *Housing facts & finding, Fannie Mae Foundation,* 5(3):1, 4–7.

Scully, Thomas A. 2003. *Perspectives from the Centers for Medicare and Medicaid Services.* A paper presented at the Georgetown University Long-term Care Financing Project. The 21st Century Challenge: Providing and Paying for Long-term Care, Washington, DC.

Shekelle, Paul, Margaret Maglione, John Chang, Walter Mojica., Sally C. Morton, Marika J. Suttorp and Laurence Rubenstein. 2002. *Falls prevention interventions in the medicare population.* Baltimore: RAND-HCFA Evidence Report Monograph, HCFA Publication #HCFA-500-98-0281.

Stone, Michael E. 1993. *Shelter poverty.* Philadelphia: Temple University Press.

Streib, Gordon F., W. Edward Folts and Mary-Anne Hilker. 1984. *Old homes—New facilities: Shared living for the elderly.* New York: Columbia University Press.

Unverzagt, Frederick W., Sujuan Gao, Olusegun Baiyewu, Adesola O. Ogunniyi, Oyewusi Gureje, Anthony Perkins, Christine L. Emsley, et al. 2001. Prevalence of cognitive impairment: Data from the Indianapolis Study of Health and Aging. *Neurology,* 57(9):1655–1662.

U.S. Department of Housing and Urban Development. 1999a. *The challenge of housing security: Report to Congress on the housing conditions and needs of older Americans.* Washington, DC: HUD.

———. 1999b. *Housing our elders: A report card on the housing conditions and needs of older Americans.* Washington, DC: HUD.

———. 2000a. *Evaluation report of FHA's home equity conversion mortgage insurance demonstration.* Washington, DC: HUD.

———. 2000b. *Report to Congress: Evaluation of the HOPE for Elderly Independence Demonstration Program and the New Congregate Housing Services Program.* Washington, DC: HUD.

Wahl, Hans-Werner, and Laura N. Gitlin. 2003. Future developments in living environments for older people in the United States and Germany. In *Aging independently: Living arrangements and mobility,* eds. K. Warner Schaie, Hans-Werner Wahl, Heidrum Mollenkopf and Frank Oswald, 281–301. New York: Springer Publishing Co.

Weiss, Lillian M. 1992. *There's no place like ... no place: Confronting the problems of the aging homeless and marginally housed.* Washington, DC: AARP.

Wiener, Joshua M., Jane Tilly and Lisa Maria B. Alecxih. 2002. Home and community-based services in seven states. *Health Care Financing Review,* 23(3):89–114.

Wilden, Robert, and Donald L. Redfoot. 2002. *Adding assisted living to subsidized housing: Serving frail older persons with low incomes.* Washington, DC: AARP.

Wong, Victoria, and Norma P. Garcia. 1999. *There's no place like home: The implications of reverse mortgages on seniors in California.* San Francisco: Consumers Union of U.S., Inc.

Susan Saegert and Heléne Clark

14 Opening Doors: What a Right to Housing Means for Women

GENDER DIFFERENCES in access to money and power as well as gender-specific cultural norms and social roles affect options for stability and achievement as well as in finding housing. Culturally and statistically, women are domestically central to the making of homes and economically marginal compared with men (Franck 2002; Hayden 2002). By domestic centrality, we mean that women bear most of the responsibility for taking care of the home, children, and dependent parents. (Domosh and Seager 2001; Hayden 2002). Women's economic marginality lies in the lower wages they most often receive in the economic marketplace as well as the remnants of their historical role as a reserve labor force (Costello, Wight and Stone 2002; Hayden 2002). The combination of domestic centrality and economic marginality makes them frequently dependent on men or the state to provide housing. In a culture and epoch in which dependency is a very risky situation, women often have to make do with inadequate and unsafe housing or become homeless.

This chapter examines the ways in which women's access to housing is eclipsed by cultural and economic structures that mitigate opportunities to obtain affordable and suitable housing. The deep cultural and historical roots of these barriers to housing mean that access to decent housing for women would require more than a legal status right. It would also require basic changes in the culturally accepted understanding and practices concerning gendered domestic responsibilities. We begin by taking a look at women's current position in the housing market in the United States, a context in which multi-person households maintained by single women increased from 1 in 8 in 1973 to 1 in 4 in 1993 (U.S. Department of Commerce 2000).

First, we review women's domestic roles in providing homes for others and then delineate the many ways in which women are economically disadvantaged in achieving a basic Right to Housing. In order for this chapter to be relevant to public policy, we need to do more than illustrate the layers of disadvantage conveyed by gender in obtaining housing. Therefore, we examine the ways in which public policy both reinforces and institutionalizes disadvantage and the ways in which policy can do the opposite: redress cultural and economic forces and provide opportunities for women to find housing that is appropriate to diverse and changing lifestyles.

We also examine the ways in which the absence of a Right to Housing in the United States particularly undermines women's access to housing because it combines with female economic disadvantage, especially when magnified by racial disadvantage and responsibility for children. To some extent, opposition to a Right to Housing derives from the same cultural assumptions that make women's domestic centrality a disadvantage in the labor and housing markets: Domestic life is a "private" responsibility. The consequences of these assumptions for access to housing and jobs are manifested in public policies related to wages, the structure of paid work, and the provision of public services and housing. Workplace and public service policies affect women's abilities to earn the income necessary to obtain housing. Housing and community development patterns set the time-space matrix within which this difficult balancing act must be accomplished. Data on the housing conditions of single women, especially when their participation in the labor and housing markets is further compromised by membership in disadvantaged ethnic groups and responsibility for children, are presented to illustrate the most extreme gender-related consequences of the absence of a Right to Housing. Finally, we examine ways in which public policy and community planning can redress cultural and economic forces that constrain not only women's access to decent housing but also the development of communities that support the diverse and changing lives that Americans are living.

The conflicts and constraints associated with women's social and economic position are nested within other social categories, especially race and marital status. In general, being married improves women's economic position, leaving unmarried women at a disadvantage in the housing market and unmarried mothers over-demanded at home and under-supported economically. In addition to these practical constraints, lesbians face further stigma and discrimination in both the job and housing markets. However, even for women with male partners, the racial, social and economic status of the men with whom women become involved affects the kind of housing that they attain and the sorts of homes they can make. When women's partners abuse them, their choice is often between physical and psychological danger and homelessness (Rollins, Saris and Johnston-Robledo 2001). Women come to their homes in the process of making their lives from within the specific social, historical, geographical and biographical positions they occupy. The dilemmas faced by women in attempting to obtain and create decent, affordable housing provide a lens through which to view the cultural definitions and the political and economic arrangements within which we all strive to make our homes.

What is general about women's situation with regard to housing is the way in which gender becomes institutionalized in policies relating to income, work, housing, child care and the myriad other intersections of the "private lives" of households and the public regulation of these lives (Garber and Turner 1995). Women's domestic centrality and economic marginality are reinforced by the failure of either the public or private sector to provide support for combining homemaking with work outside the home. Employment and educational policies and practices that facilitate women's entry and advancement in the workplace and child care that nurtures both the child and the woman's employment opportunities remain elusive even for the most privileged women (Goldin 1997). "Good enough" solutions achieved by some women often exploit other women who are also marginalized by their race, immigration and educational status and class (Amott and Matthaei 1996; Domosh and Seager 2001). The strains inherent in individual solutions to institutional shortcomings also take their toll on family life through divorce and stress (Goldin 1997; Spain and Bianchi 1996). For poor households, child care, welfare, employment and housing policies have exacerbated rather than resolved the conflict between working outside the home and the need to make a home for children and men (Edin and Lein 1997; Spain and Bianchi 1996). These institutional practices and policies do not require gender conformity, but they structure the rewards and obstacles for men and women.

A RIGHT TO HOUSING

Given the disproportionate number of women who are homeless, the frequent dependency on men to provide housing, the need to balance child care with work and the poverty of many female-headed households, a Right to Housing would be a giant leap in providing safety from the dangers and instability of homelessness and poverty, as well as providing independence. However, because of women's dual role as homemakers and workers, and the persistence of poverty for many women, we are concerned that a Right to Housing is not enough.

A Right to Housing could relieve women of the burden of staying in abusive or unsatisfying relationships just to have a roof over their heads. Compared with the existing subsidy preferences, a universal Right to Housing could provide housing access for young women and childless women that they now lack. It might also contribute to greater housing security in old age, a benefit that would be important to older women who suffer most from poverty in their late years (Saegert and McCarthy 1998). However, for women to improve the quality of their lives, they need access to housing that contributes to their nurturing, maintenance and income-producing activities.

An approach to a Right to Housing needs to recognize the different forms of housing women need to improve their lives as well as to care for their home and their children. To the extent that public housing has physically reinforced women's social disadvantage, these burdens have been borne disproportionately by women of color, compounding other disadvantages with regard to education, employment and wealth accumulation. To the extent that a Right to Housing fails to challenge and change the racialized and gendered order of education, employment, wealth accumulation and access to services, its contribution to the improvement of women's lives would be limited. Finally, a Right to Housing alone will not correct the many problems women face when public policies are developed around an ethic and discourse based on individual rights and a reliance on the market for basic needs. A Right to Housing would provide a substantial material benefit and a platform for future development of women's lives. It is a necessary, but not complete, step in securing housing that supports personal development for all people.

THE POSITION OF WOMEN IN THE UNITED STATES' HOUSING MARKET

Domestic Centrality

The cultural dictum that "a woman's place is in the home" is lived out in the empirical reality that women spend more time at home, do more housework and in some cultures may not leave the home without a culturally designated male escort (Ardener 1981; Berk 1980; Darke 1994; Domosh and Seager 2001; Robinson and Godbey 1997). In many, perhaps most, cultures,

women literally make a house a home. Mason sums up the public aspect of this process nicely:

> The production of the home for public scrutiny... does not mean simply making the physical environment look nice for visitors, although that is an element of the procedure. Rather, it means producing the home—including its members—for public approval. In other words, producing the home means upholding in some public sense the status of the family household... women in my study were engaged continually and routinely in this kind of process. (Mason 1989:120)

For women, homemaking includes an intensely and ambivalently personal side. Several studies have indicated that women more often invest the home with their personal identity but that identity is often of a relational rather than individual nature (Hunt 1989; Saegert and Winkel 1980). The work of making a home nurtures both the homemaker and her household, as it also uses up her time and energy and restricts her other activities.

Some of the ambivalence and constraint involved in homemaking arise from the social definition of both mothering and homemaking as private activities outside of the economy. Homemaking is a chore for individual households, and within those households, primarily for women. But homemaking depends on having a home. Traditionally, providing for the home has been a man's job. Despite changes in household form that require more women to provide their own homes or contribute to the household income that provides housing and other needs, women are disadvantaged in the housing market. Men, especially white men, are better positioned in the economy to obtain housing in what is in the United States the most economically rewarding, legally secure and socially valued form—owning. When homeownership is not possible, the control over housing that is a necessary precondition of making a home becomes more precarious.

Jarrett's (1995) research on how black single mothers think about their relationships with men contains poignant discussions of the close association between finding a good breadwinning male to marry and having the home of one's dreams. When these single mothers spoke of aspiring to the mainstream ideal of marriage, that ideal included a man who earned a good living and could provide a home for them. But as one of them stated, "It was just a little white girl's dream." The reality they faced was that the men they became involved with were not in a position to provide for either the relationship or the home of their fantasies. Many of the men continued to live with their mothers and hold episodic jobs. Many sojourned in prison for at least some period of time. The women found that they were better able to secure housing on their own, often through the use of welfare housing allowances, other housing subsidies or public housing. Yet the rented housing alternatives they were able to obtain were often seen, if not by them then by the broader society, as "not real homes." And certainly, the current public discourse presents them as "not real homemakers."

Economic Marginality

Expectations that women will marry, stay at home and take care of their children, men and homes provide the foundation, consciously or not, for many aspects of U.S. public policy that marginalize women economically. This assumption, which was never valid for poor and working-class women, has been increasingly at odds with reality for the U.S. population as a whole. Between 1975 and 2000, the proportion of married women in the paid labor force rose from 30 percent to 71 percent (Farley 1996; Costello, Wight and Stone 2002). At the same time, the number of married-couple households has declined, while households of women with children have increased substantially, as have single individual households for both men and women. (The proportion of male-headed households with children has increased dramatically, but the absolute numbers remain small relative to female-headed[1] households.) Female-headed households, with and without children, have grown rapidly and are the most likely to be poor (Farley 1996; McFate, Lawson and Wilson 1995; Costello, Wight and Stone 2002).

Marriage increases the chances that a woman or man will have a higher household income and better housing. While single men and male-headed households are less affluent than married-couple households, the risk of poverty is greatest for women who head their own households. Poverty is of course associated with lower-quality housing. In the 1980s, numerous authors empirically demonstrated the overwhelming preponderance of women living in poverty and in substandard housing. Since then, both the numbers and proportions of female-headed families have increased. Female-headed households are the major users of housing programs of any type, except for low-income homeownership loan programs and the homeownership mortgage deduction. (However, the homeownership program aimed at those with the worst risk profile includes 40 percent female-headed households—Quercia et al. 2002). Therefore, changes in these programs mostly affect women. For example, in 1996, 76 percent of families in public housing in the United States were female-headed households (CLPHA 1996). Thus, the reduction of the public housing supply going on in our nation since that time most affects the lives of female-headed households.

Women who head their own households are most exposed to the negative consequences of domestic centrality combined with economic marginality. In 2000, there were over 31 million households headed by women, an increase of 2.5 million since the 1990 Census and an increase of almost 8 million since 1980 (Simmons 1997; U.S. Department of Commerce 2000). Overall, the percentage of female-headed households has been edging up for decades (Costello, Wight and Stone 2002). Economically, the changes are much more dramatic, reflecting not a trend but a crisis. Twenty-seven percent of female-headed families with children under the age of 18 were living in poverty in 2000 compared with 14 percent of all families with children (U.S. Department of Commerce 2000). According to the Department of Housing and Urban Development (HUD), the number of very-low-income families with worst-case housing needs was 5.3 million in 1997 and 4.86 million in 1999, with crisis-level need increasing by 400,000 households per year through 1995, and remaining constant thereafter. By 1997, 59 percent of households with worst-case needs were female-headed households or women living alone (U.S. Department of Commerce and the U.S. Department of Housing and Urban Development 2001). In 2003, women continued to live in homes with more housing problems, a trend exacerbated for single mothers (Joint Center for Housing Studies 2003).

Homeownership provides the major economic asset for most Americans (Joint Center for Housing Studies 2003). Married couples are far more likely than other types of households to own their housing (Domash and Seager 2001). The 2000 U.S. Census indicated that marriage rather than gender made the biggest difference in homeownership rates. Eighty-three percent of married couples owned their homes compared with 45 percent of single women and 51 percent of single male households. Women living alone more frequently owned their homes than did single men, probably because women often keep the home following a divorce and often outlive their spouses. While overall homeownership rates were lower for blacks and Hispanics, couples in these populations were also much more likely to own homes.

For families with children, the marriage gap in ownership is greater: In 2001, 79 percent of all households with children under age 18 owned their home compared with less than 39 percent of single-parent families with children under age 18. While these figures are averages for all Americans, and available sources do not report data by both gender of household head and the presence of children, it appears that there is a gender gap in housing ownership for single parents.

In 2000, as in earlier years, renters were poorer than owners, with female-headed households that rented by far the most likely to live in poverty (Table 14.1). However, single women living alone who owned their homes were more likely to live in poverty than couples or male-headed households who rented. As Table 14.2 shows, the lower incomes of female-headed households often resulted in their spending 30 percent of their income for housing, whereas their male counterparts paid about 25 percent, and couples averaged only 16 percent.

Taken together, population statistics show that the economic conditions of women

TABLE 14.1 Percent in Poverty for Renters and Owners by Household Composition

	Renters (%)	Owners (%)
Married Households	16	6
Unmarried Multiperson		
* Households*		
Male-Headed	16	8
Female-Headed	36	16
One-Person Households		
Male	20	11
Female	29	20

Source: Calculated from American Housing Survey (2001), U.S. Department of Commerce and U.S. Department of Housing and Urban Development.

continue to lag behind those of men, especially for unmarried women. This economic marginality translates into poorer housing conditions, greater cost burdens and lesser accumulation of wealth through homeownership.

Magnifying Marginality: Minority Female-Headed Households

The burgeoning literature on the urban underclass indicates that minority female-headed households suffer extreme economic marginalization (Jargowsky 1997; Wilson 1987). In fact, it is commonplace to use the presence of large numbers of female-headed households in a community as an indicator of social malaise (Wilson 1987). Racial segregation and discrimination are deeply interwoven with both the higher prevalence of female-headed households in black communities and their spatial concentration (Galster and Hill 1992; Massey and Denton 1993). By 2000, 43 percent of black households were headed by women, while 23 percent of Hispanic and 14 percent of white households were female-headed (Costello et al. 2002).

These studies and others (Oliver and Shapiro 1995) identify institutional practices related to housing that perpetuate racial inequality. Government policies, as well as real estate, financial and insurance industry practices, have restricted access of blacks to homeownership, contributed to the lower economic value of their homes and steadily supported racial segregation. Discrimination in educational institutions and the labor

TABLE 14.2 Housing Cost Burden for Total Population and Minority Populations

	Total population			Hispanic population			Black population		
	Total income (%)	Median monthly rent	Median income	Total median (%)	Median monthly rent	Median income	Total median (%)	Median monthly rent	Median income
Married Households	16	$783	$56,698	22	$742	$40,716	18	$730	$49,252
Multiperson Unmarried Households									
Male-Headed	25	700	33,933	30	683	27,243	28	639	27,294
Female-Headed	30	639	25,167	37	658	21,221	33	572	20,675
One Person Households									
Male	22	531	29,426	26	555	25,660	29	478	19,795
Female	30	455	17,911	44	512	14,007	37	455	14,685

market have contributed to lower incomes. At the same time, programs to assist the poor, such as public housing and welfare, have mirrored and reinforced racial segregation and labor force disadvantage while perpetuating inequality in asset accumulation. All of these institutional forces write the script for gender and race in the United States. The backdrop of patriarchal expectations, plus lower incomes among blacks, has made it harder for black men to play the breadwinner role, making marriage less attractive for both themselves and the women who might marry them. Meanwhile, the economic advantages for adults and for their children of living in a couple household have led to a larger and larger divide in quality of life and expectations for the future in which single household heads, especially women, lose (Angel and Angel 1993; Edin and Lein 1997; Jarrett 1995; Wilson 1987). The association of marriage and race with homeownership contributes to the intergenerational magnification of the gap in wealth in the United States favoring whites (Joint Center for Housing Studies 2003).

While minority male-headed and couple households experience higher rates of poverty and housing disadvantage than white households, minority women who head their households clearly occupy the intersection of disadvantage. Table 14.3 documents the difference in percent of households in poverty as a function of household type and race. In 2001, 35 percent of black female-headed households and 34 percent of Hispanic female-headed households lived below the poverty line. Thirty-six percent of

Hispanic and 31 percent of black single females were poor. If poverty rates for similar types of male- and female-headed households are compared, we see an even larger gender gap for black and Hispanic households.

The double marginality of minority women translates into poorer housing conditions. Table 14.4 shows that while minority households reported more housing problems overall, couples in these populations generally reported fewer housing problems than other minority households. Going back to Table 14.2, we see that housing cost burdens were higher for Hispanic households, following the same pattern of greater burdens for female-headed households and single women. Higher housing costs were also prevalent among black female-headed households and single women.

Gender and ethnicity both contribute to the risk for homelessness. Grimm and Maldonado (1995) estimated that one-half of all homeless people in the mid-1990s were women, compared with one-fourth ten years previously. They also reported that one-half of all homeless persons were black, about one-third were white and the remaining were Latino, Native American and Asian. Interestingly, they found that age and ethnicity intersected for homeless women. In a survey of 27 cities, it was found that 14 percent of the homeless population was comprised of single women, and 67 percent were single-parent families. Fifty percent of homeless persons were African-American and 35 percent were white. The remaining 15 percent were Hispanic, Asian and Native American (National

TABLE 14.3 Distribution of Household Types for Total Population and Minority Populations Broken Down by Percent in Poverty

	Total population		Hispanic population		Black population	
	% of Total	% Poor	% of Total	% Poor	% of Total	% Poor
Married Households	52	5	54	14	32	6
Multiperson Unmarried Households						
Male-Headed	4	12	8	13	6	16
Female-Headed	12	25	18	34	28	35
One-Person Households						
Male	11	17	7	24	12	29
Female	15	24	8	36	16	31

Source: Calculated from American Housing Survey (2001), U.S. Department of Commerce and U.S. Department of Housing and Urban Development.
Note: Percentages do not add to 100% because certain forms of residences such as institutions are not included.

Law Center on Homelessness and Poverty 2001). Younger homeless women were more likely to be black with dependent children; older homeless women were more likely to be white with mental illness and substance abuse problems. For women, pregnancy, recent childbirth and domestic abuse frequently precipitate the loss of a home, illustrating again the risks to housing access related to women's domestic ties (Rollins, Saris and Johnston-Robledo 2001).

When culture is taken into account, in addition to the transgenerational impact of institutional practices, the extreme economic marginalization of minority female-headed households is even more complex than most of the literature on race and gender suggests. The terms "black," "Hispanic" and "white" are really inadequate categories for the U.S. population. In 1991, the number of foreigners who emigrated to the United States was six times as many as

entered in 1950 (Farley 1996). Hispanics make up almost one-half of the 25.3 million immigrants coming to the United States since 1980 (Joint Center for Housing Studies 2003). Even immigration is too simple a term to characterize the international flow of populations. This flow of populations reflects and perpetuates cultural connections of women with domestic (and sexual) service and economic marginality. The "maid trade" has been estimated at approximately 1.7 million women who work as domestic servants outside their home country at any one time (Domash and Seager 2001). They are joined by millions of female refugees and unknown numbers of girls and women in the sex trade (Domash and Seager 2001). Some return home, many are illegal immigrants; many have children in the different countries that they enter and leave. Since household form and the implications of gender are heavily culturally

TABLE 14.4 Percent of Different Household Types with Housing Problems, Total and Minority Populations

	Total population (%)	Hispanic population (%)	Black population (%)
Married Households	4	9	9
Multiperson Unmarried Households			
Male-Headed	7	10	13
Female-Headed	10	14	15
One-Person Households			
Male	10	12	17
Female	7	9	11

Source: Calculated from American Housing Survey (2001), U.S. Department of Commerce and U.S. Department of Housing and Urban Development.

determined, a real understanding of these various intersections requires attention to both the statistics and the lived reality in particular locales.[2]

CURRENT HOUSING POLICIES AND WOMEN

The economic marginality of women makes them less well served by the housing market, and historically their domestic centrality in the form of responsibility for children has made them most often the targets for low-income housing policies. Clearly, national policy and local implementation are moving away from the direct government provision of housing as a safety net for poor or single-parent families. This change of direction reflects the national, and even international, trend against direct provision of government services in favor of greater reliance on the market to meet all human needs. However, many women cannot obtain secure and adequate housing through the market. Policies based on a Right to Housing would look drastically different from current housing policies. The critical examination that follows of major current policies and trends helps to reveal some elements of how a Right to Housing could be implemented in a way that would build on the good ideas embedded in different approaches while eliminating the basic flaws of limited access and insufficient funding.

Public Housing and Vouchers

Changes of historic significance have taken place in public housing, and the impact on women is enormous, based on the overwhelming proportion of women and single mothers in public housing and on women's limited access to other economic resources. While the specifics of these changes have varied from year to year since 1996, the directions have been constant. Public housing policies no longer define success by the number of poor families served but rather by the extent to which problems of crime, isolation and concentrations of poverty associated with existing developments are improved. Public housing,

both in absolute numbers of units and in the proportion of the poor it houses, is being dismantled. The stock that remains in the next ten years as public housing, if current experiments succeed, will be substantially smaller and increasingly mixed-income.

Reduction in the supply of public housing in order to improve what is left means a net loss in units for the many women who are its tenants. Many will be displaced as a direct result of renovation and demolition. Presumably, they will be eligible for rental vouchers, so their housing costs will not become unaffordable, but they may not be able to find adequate housing through vouchers. Those currently not in public housing, but who are in precarious living situations, will not have public housing as an option if they lose their other housing possibilities. Overall, while some women will benefit by improvements to their communities through renovation of public housing, the availability, flexibility, term limits and outcomes of individual vouchers are critical areas for housing policy to monitor and evaluate.

Public housing illustrates some of the dilemmas that must be faced in implementing a Right to Housing, both politically and functionally. Public housing has consistently provided better housing for poor, frequently female-headed and minority households than they could otherwise obtain (Stockard 1998). Yet spatial concentration of housing for those with the most need can lead to locational disadvantages and prevent access to jobs, community resources and integration into communities of opportunity. The long list of distressed public housing in the United States shows that housing for those in most need may lack the political support to assure high-quality, decently maintained buildings. The ways in which these dilemmas are resolved will particularly affect women, who most often head the neediest households with the least chance of moving to other types of housing (Freeman 1998).

The negative effects of concentrations of poverty such as that found in public housing and many neighborhoods is intended to be offset by vouchers. However, vouchers may create other problems for women, even if they are attainable. If women move away from the housing and neighborhoods where their social networks are located, the support of family and friends who provide the real safety net for many poor women and their children may be disrupted.

While vouchers appear more compatible with a market-based approach to a Right to Housing, the cost of such an approach would likely be high, possibly unleashing the same political backlash that undermined the growth of Section 8 vouchers in previous years. Unless coupled with the development of low-cost housing, vouchers alone cannot solve the problem of access to housing in many parts of the country with tight housing markets.

Homeownership Programs

Since 1994, Fannie Mae has committed itself to developing new programs that make home-ownership more widely accessible to Americans (Eggers and Burke 1996). Decreasing the ownership gap between lower- and higher-income groups and between white and minority households has been identified as a particularly important goal. However, analyses of how gender of household head relates to the feasibility and desirability of this strategy are largely absent. The record on homeownership suggests that within racial and income groups, couples would be by far the most likely type of household to increase homeownership rates. It is also likely that the kinds of homeownership different types of households would choose would be influenced by their incomes. Thus, the increase in ownership of mobile homes might be expected to accrue disproportionately to young couples and households headed by women under 45, who in 1995 had the highest rates of mobile home ownership (U.S. Department of Commerce 1996), while couple households with children were more likely to purchase single-family homes. A national policy that disproportionately encourages homeownership also produces a shift in population from central cities to suburbs, creating neighborhood problems for those left behind (Eggers and Burke 1996). There is also evidence that the move to homeownership reinforces racial segregation, even while dispersing ethnic minorities to suburbs (Joint Center for Hous-

ing Studies 2003). Some cities are developing homeownership programs of their own in one- to four-unit buildings in order to encourage people to stay in their communities.

The most likely downside of homeownership strategies for female-headed households, especially in minority populations, is the inability to keep up with mortgage, property tax and repair costs. Two ethnographic studies that examine the constraints on minority homeownership tell the stories of female-headed households as examples of the difficulties encountered but interpret the problem solely in relationship to race (Oliver and Shapiro 1995; Ratner 1996).

The domestic demands experienced by women are also likely to be affected by homeownership. According to Rossi and Weber's (1996) analysis, wives and husbands who owned their homes reported that the wives did more hours of work around the home compared with the reported hours of domestic work for wives who rent. There were no significant differences for men's domestic labor.

The absence of convenient public transportation and public amenities in some suburban environments also burden women more than men when women are left without a car and with responsibility for providing care and amusement for children as well as provisioning the home. Kasarda and Ting (1996) identify similar issues as impediments to the employment of poor women in central cities who find it hard to combine their domestic and care-taking responsibilities with a reverse commute. These ecological factors, combined with affordability problems, may also keep lower-income, especially minority, women out of the suburban housing market. A study of suburban women's housing preferences found that single female heads of households preferred the shared services, amenities and convenience of planned unit developments (Rothblatt, Garr and Sprague 1979). Women historically have been found to prefer denser settlement patterns, older suburbs, closer to work locations, places with better public transportation and a greater supply of services and public amenities (reviewed in Saegert 1982).[3] Promotion of homeownership may thus shift more women into environments that do not well support their double duties. For this reason, programs and policies that support homeownership opportunities in multifamily housing and in inner-city and older, denser suburbs are especially important for women. Aging and shrinking smaller city downtowns and even older, no longer competitive shopping malls provide development opportunities, both for homeownership and housing projects of community development corporations (Hayden 2002).

On the other hand, for women who share in or hold title outright to housing, and who can afford the costs of upkeep and service provision, ownership can be a significant step up economically, giving them both control over housing costs and a valuable, fungible property. Homeless women as well as women with substantial means aspire to homeownership (Darke 1994; Rollins, Saris and Johnston-Robledo 2001). And the economic challenges women face may make housing equity especially important. For example, a large study of the elderly in Florida found that older women living alone needed both economic assets and a job in order to escape poverty (Hardy and Hazelrigg 1993).

However, that study also revealed the high levels of poverty among elderly women living alone and the obvious fact that with advanced age, continued employment is often impossible. While assets plus Social Security allowed most couples and single men to avoid poverty, elderly single women lived on a much thinner edge. For many minority women not in couples, their lower incomes and higher housing costs make entry into homeownership difficult. With the demands of maintenance costs, they face an increased likelihood of having to sell their home to meet other needs compared with couples, men and white women. The feasibility and usefulness of homeownership for women without men might be greatly increased through creative uses of reverse mortgages, not only for the elderly (see Chapter 13) but to support investments in human capital and, in some cases, simply to avoid poverty (Rasmussen, Megbolugbe and Morgan 1997).

In 1996, the White House Office for Women's Initiatives and Outreach partnered with the National Partners in Homeownership to create a joint initiative promoting homeownership for women. Homeownership Opportunities for Women (HOW) includes English and Spanish information hotlines, a mentoring program and training for women on how to navigate credit and loans. The program also uses peer counselors to work with women who are making the transition from welfare to work.

Limited-equity co-ops and mutual housing associations are alternative forms of ownership that seem to provide some of the benefits of ownership without the same level of financial investment and risk (Saegert and Benitez 2003; see also Chapter 11). The Quality Housing and Work Responsibility Act of 1998 allowed the use of Section 8 vouchers for homeownership programs sponsored by the local public housing authority, including lease purchase and purchase of cooperatives. Research in New York City has documented that residents of limited-equity co-ops most often say that the right to remain in their housing is what makes co-op ownership most valuable (Clark et al. 1990; Rae 1997; Saegert 1993, 1995; Saegert and Winkel 1999). Their previous experience with landlord ownership, the long waits for public housing and the prevalence of homelessness in their communities contrast strongly with the sense of security felt by limited-equity residents with regard to their cooperative tenure—feelings that are validated by the much longer lengths of residence common in this ownership form when compared with other types of low-income housing.

Studies of Canadian limited-equity co-ops have demonstrated that they can work well for female-headed households because of the small equity investment and the collective provision of housing and service amenities beyond what they could otherwise afford (Wekerle 1988). Canadian studies also indicate that many younger households benefit from the ability to save money while in relatively inexpensive housing, thus making future homeownership more possible.

The relationship of co-op ownership to wealth varies, depending on the degree of limitations on equity. Restrictions on the use of property for income-generating activities are governed by zoning ordinances and sometimes by co-op rules. However, in our experience, apartments are freely used for home-based businesses. Some co-ops include commercial spaces. While some co-ops have used these properties to anchor needed services in the community and to generate income for building improvement, others located in distressed neighborhoods have not been able to make these spaces work well financially or socially.

The salience of gender in low-income limited-equity co-ops is quite different from what it is in public housing. Not surprisingly, given the low incomes of residents, the majority of households are female-headed when they begin their quest for ownership. The high housing quality, safety, security of tenure and affordability of limited-equity co-ops offers a unique market niche for meeting the needs of female householders. Women, especially elderly minority women, also play key leadership roles in the development and operation of limited-equity co-ops (Saegert 1989). However, over time, limited-equity co-ops tend to have more male-headed households than do buildings owned by community groups (Saegert 1993, 1995). Reasons for the difference include less dependence on governmental subsidies that give preference to female-headed households. Although we do not have specific data on the topic, it may also be that the ownership and self-help aspects of co-op residency appeal more to male-headed households than do other low-income housing options. Case studies of buildings suggest that when tenant organizing for ownership begins before or soon after landlord abandonment, male-headed households are less likely to move out in search of better options (Leavitt and Saegert 1990).

The Not-for-Profit Housing Sector

Locally based community development organizations have filled part of the gap left between the cutbacks to the public housing sector and the private market. Evaluations of the effectiveness of this sector vary (Cowan, Rohe and Baku 1999; Gittell and Wilder 1999; Glickman and Servon 1999). The share of rental housing developed by community development corporations (CDCs) is less significant (Schill 1994) than their rising importance in the federally funded low-income stock (Koshinsky 1998). The role of nonprofit housing has increased since 1970 and generally appeals to conservatives and liberals alike, as it does not require direct government involvement and provides a lot of latitude for local needs and decision-making. However, recent CDC failures, downsizing and mergers may threaten this source of housing (Rohe and Bratt 2003; see also Chapter 16). If this trend continues, women's residential choices would be especially reduced.

Women appear to particularly benefit from CDC housing. While we know of no statistics on the proportion of female-headed households living in housing built by CDCs, experience with CDCs around the country indicates that female-headed households do have access to this form of housing. Most CDCs target families with incomes below the median and at or near the poverty level and often locate in minority communities. Female-headed households with children are prevalent in this segment of the population. Women with children have had better access to Section 8 certificates and other rental subsidies as well as in the past receiving a shelter allowance as part of welfare. This combination of need and rental subsidy allows CDCs to fulfill their social mission while sustaining financial solvency. Since many CDCs provide programs in job-training, employment counseling, job-matching, micro-enterprise and youth employment, they are likely to continue to target female-headed households with children.

A holistic approach to the needs of families especially helps women who must juggle child care, the personal needs of the whole household and work. Gittell and her colleagues (1994, 1999) have found that gender and race play a part in CDCs' decisions to offer various programs. They found that the CDCs providing a range of services beyond housing had more board members and staff who were women and members of racial minorities.

Women-led CDCs have pioneered the integration of housing, schools, child care, adult education and job training and placement. The Boston- and Rhode Island–based Women's Housing and Development Corporation began such an effort in the 1970s. Similar efforts occurred in Canada and England at that time. Since then, new women-led CDCs have sprung up, such as the Women's Housing and Economic Development Corporation in the South Bronx. These groups foreshadowed approaches that have gained increased attention as a result of welfare reform.

In the 1990s, Comprehensive Community Initiatives were launched across the country, mostly by foundations. These initiatives usually seek to address the needs of children and youth, to promote education and employment for adults and to improve the safety of the community at the same time that they promote decent housing at below-market costs and the development of new local businesses (Connell et al. 1995). In the absence of public funding of services and amenities, these initiatives may especially contribute to building communities that support women's caregiving and social obligations while assisting them with housing and income generation.

The increased popularity and impact of CDC housing does not at all ensure its survival or its evolution to more fully meet women's needs. Nonprofits often depend on tax credits, which are currently finite, as well as on the availability of rental vouchers and public assistance for rents, also finite. The shortfall between need for these subsidies and supply leaves CDCs vulnerable to financial failure and complicates the demands on them. The complexity and difficulty of putting together financing for development often distracts from program development in other areas. Changing formulas for financing and rental subsidies can also undermine tenant security and participation in tenant selection and other housing decisions by requiring the CDC to seek out new tenants who fit the requirements (Saegert and Winkel 1999). Welfare reform raises new challenges by forcing CDCs to cope with possibly lower tenant incomes due to loss of welfare benefits in a context of shrinking and restructured federal support for subsidized housing, self-sufficiency programs that demand large-scale and quick results, and complex new relationships as housing programs devolve to states (Bratt and Keyes 1998). Changes in housing markets, management and leadership, the local political and economic context, and even the very successes of the CDC may threaten its continued viability (Rohe and Bratt 2003).

A Right to Housing could potentially fuel a large expansion of the nonprofit housing sector if the mechanisms included both capital and operating subsidies. As we describe below, women stand to benefit from this form of implementation because of the holistic approach to community development that it might support and because of the potential for greater participation in housing decisions, in the absence of traditional homeownership. Since CDCs also provide many types of transitional and service-enriched housing (Koschinsky 1998), this approach could not only increase the volume of housing suitable to the needs of women but also provide continuity between the right to immediate shelter in an emergency and the right to shelter appropriate for long-term habitation. The greatest challenge for CDCs in serving women's needs is most likely in the area of promoting democratic control of housing and strong social networks while providing high-quality services. Much could be learned by CDCs' productively engaging women who have had the job of balancing the needs of their households against a tight budget in planning and decision-making.

Lessons from Current Housing Policies

The successes and failures of existing housing policies provide a number of lessons for implementing a Right to Housing.

1. Female-headed households are disproportionately the beneficiaries of housing policies and programs meant to serve those who are left out of the market. A Right to Housing would undoubtedly serve these women and others who have failed to seek or qualify for public subsidies or subsidized housing. Yet, eligibility requirements that favor female-headed households disrupt family ties and often exclude poor, especially poor minority, men from forming families. Income limits can act as a disincentive for improving income in tight housing markets with many low-wage jobs. Thus, public housing has had the undesirable consequence of concentrating and isolating uniformly poor populations (Goering, Kamely and Richardson 1997), while the financial demands on nonprofit

housing can lead to "churning" the tenant population in pursuit of new, deeper subsidies or families with greater rent-paying ability (Saegert and Winkel 1999).

2. Access to subsidized housing is important in helping poor women enter and stay in the job market (Edin and Lein 1997; Saegert et al. 2000). Further, the proximity to friends and relatives that many public housing developments provide for women residents can help poor women strike a balance among the competing demands of parenting, working, contributing to the well-being of others in the family and community, and attempting to advance educationally and occupationally (Saegert et al. 2000). A Right to Housing would allow greater access and, depending on implementation, greater security of tenure not just for individuals but for more extended networks of family, friends and neighbors.

3. Location of subsidized housing substantially affects the safety, educational opportunities and job opportunities of residents (Leventhal and Brooks-Gunn 2000; Rosenbaum 1991). Implementation of a Right to Housing needs to take context and tenure into account. A Right to Housing that provides the equivalent of shelters for homeless people or victims of domestic violence, which are notoriously hard to site, is not the same as the social provision of a large and non-stigmatized proportion of the housing market (Stone 1993).

4. By most estimates, the quality of housing available to poor households varies by ownership type, but the way in which it varies depends on the history of housing and the state of the housing market in particular locales. Judging from media reports and public opinion, privately owned housing is generally regarded as being superior to public housing. Yet in specific areas, studies of housing quality reveal the opposite (c.f. Schill and Scafidi 1997). Although the evidence is limited, CDC housing and tenant-owned cooperatives appear to provide higher-quality housing than other options available to their residents (Briggs and Mueller 1997; Saegert and Winkel 1999). As Evans, Wells and Moch (2003) document in their extensive literature review, the quality of housing is important for the well-being of women, children and (no

doubt) men, although fewer studies have examined housing quality consequences for men. But the dimensions of housing that Evans, Wells and Moch (2003) found to affect mental health and child development were not the simple inadequacies measured in the Census and most housing surveys. They included the number of stories in the building, floor level, architectural features and general housing quality, such as dampness, reliability of plumbing and other housing services, indoor temperature and the more subtle dimension of resident control over housing. Implementation of a Right to Housing must seriously address decisions about the definition of and standards for housing quality employed.

5. Ownership form has historically been related to the extent to which occupants can control their housing. While private ownership has often been seen as the ultimate form of control of housing, research on poor women suggests that the cost of owning plus maintenance demands may limit this value. In fact, the collective responsibility for housing upkeep has been cited by low-income co-op residents, most often women, as a positive feature of co-op ownership (Rae 1997). However, most residents of public housing and the scholars who studied them would, we believe, conclude that residents' control of their lives and space in public housing has usually been seriously compromised. How ownership of housing is organized presents important implementation challenges for a Right to Housing.

Implementing a Right to Housing

Implementing a Right to Housing by expanding the "social" or nonprofit housing sector (c.f. Dreier 1997; Stone 1993) appears most likely to benefit households in need of improved housing and lower costs while also providing other services these households need. Women could particularly benefit, both because of their lower incomes and their traditional, and by no means extinct, requirements for combining domestic work, caretaking and paid employment. However, larger changes would be required for women to benefit equally from a Right to Housing and to avoid being ghettoized. Women carry much of the burden of providing work considered not economically productive that is undervalued by cultural as well as economic systems. Changing this unequal division of labor and devaluing of the work of caring would be a fundamental cultural and economic challenge. Innovative physical, financial and institutional forms of housing are required to support caregiving, the production of home life, daily maintenance and multiple demands on time and to avoid the potential for cumulative disadvantage inherent in pursuing other than economic goals. Implementation of even a limited Right to Housing would disproportionately benefit individual women. But in a constricted and minimal form, such a right would perpetuate gender-based inequality by shunting women in need into places, financial arrangements and institutional forms that make the caretaking work that they perform harder and their financial marginality greater as well as limiting their control of their lives. Concerns about the perpetuation of gender inequality lead to several principles that would be important to observe in implementing a Right to Housing.

A Large and Flexible Social Housing Market

Exercising a Right to Housing must not restrict the kinds of households that have access to a full range of housing options. This goal will be difficult to achieve because family size and composition help to define the sort of housing that serves the needs of different households; households' needs change over time and the ability of households to pay influences what they can obtain. This criterion implies a large, well-financed social housing sector accommodating needs as diverse as immediate emergency shelter for households of all types, without requiring the households to break up, to homeownership opportunities for households in which the adults devote time to caregiving and the development of human capital, sometimes at the expense of economic productivity. Starting from where we are now, women more often maintain responsibility for children through emergencies and at the expense of economic achievement. If there is a low-rent, barely acceptable form of housing meant to

be temporary, poor women, especially minority women, are likely to be stuck there. A Right to Housing must be defined as a right to permanent and adequate housing, not be used to encourage exacerbating a system of development in which cheap, isolated and stigmatized housing is created for those lowest in the social and economic strata.

Unless the financial benefits of homeownership over generations change, implementation of a Right to Housing that excludes ownership for profit will not only disadvantage specific families headed by women but perpetuate the collective economic disadvantage of blacks and any other group in which female-headed households are common. At the moment, the pressures toward an ever larger reliance on homeownership suggest that it is important to find ways for women to benefit equally from financing and other innovations designed to promote homeownership. At present, this is not the case (Quercia et al. 2002). If a Right to Housing excludes ownership, then alternate and equally productive asset accumulation strategies must be developed and pursued to avoid adding to the cumulative disadvantage of those who benefit from this right.

Housing policies and practices, subsidies and the physical housing itself must be configured so as to promote stability of social ties while providing choice. Knecht (1999) has analyzed the ways in which the physical and institutional forms that not-for-profits have developed to replace single room occupancy housing have created their own dilemmas. On the one hand, they do provide better—although still spatially minimal—housing for those who have been or who are at risk for being homeless. The services, communal kitchens and amenities support a fuller life and often nurture community. On the other hand, these facilities often confine residents and define them as being "different." Unlike the SROs that they replace, they require deep subsidies to build and operate. Knecht proposes applying some of the design and programming techniques that have supported individual and community growth to neighborhood-level design and planning, and looking for small-scale, market-based strategies to obviate the need for high-level subsidies.

Enriched Networks of Support

As long as women continue to rely on and be relied on by their social networks for support of all kinds, access to varied housing forms should be found at the neighborhood or proximal community level. At the same time, helping networks that support child-rearing, care of the sick and assistance for the elderly should be enriched through public and not-for-profit agencies in order to reduce the burden on women. Social housing and service providers must work with the business community and other employers to allow time and space for caregiving activities and to support alternatives, both financially and through the services that they provide.

Housing and programs that support the transition from childhood to adulthood for both men and women are especially lacking for poor households. Young minority men who go to prison, and their female counterparts, risk homelessness or live in unstable doubled-up quarters with extended family members. Middle-class and wealthy households find ways to balance the independence and supervision needs of adolescents through summer camps, school sports, music, and arts programs, class trips and residential colleges. These same needs for poor youth are mostly neglected. Many of the young men and women who now can be found in shelters and transitional facilities for runaway and homeless youth, shelters for mothers with young children and prisons seem to have gotten there because of the same impulses, immature decisions and experiments that wealthier youth safely live through in their college dorms. In the absence of settings for peer support with trained but limited supervision, good health services and counseling, and educational advancement, the residential careers of low-income, especially minority, youth diverge in gender-specific ways that work neither to the advantage of women nor men. A Right to Housing should include group living opportunities that support and enhance youth development and engage parents as well as youth in finding successful and satisfying niches for the next stages of their lives.

Mothers of young children face other, especially daunting challenges as welfare and public housing reform require them to work out-side the home (Newman 1999). Social housing can provide a secure setting for child-rearing. But in order for children to get the attention and engagement they need for healthy development, and for mothers to combine the demands of parenting, employment and advancing their own education, social networks among mothers, their extended families and the larger community need to be nurtured. A study of mothers in New York City public housing found that those who worked on and off, or at part-time jobs, were better able to be involved with children's school progress, advance their own education and obtain jobs with benefits. They also contributed more both to informal helping networks and to more formal voluntary associations that improved the quality of life and civic engagement of their communities (Saegert et al. 2000). This group of women seemed to especially benefit from long-term residence in public housing developments where many kin and friends were also living. This suggests that organizations providing both housing and services should try to find ways to support, legitimate and make economically feasible the social and human capital-creating activities of these mothers and their networks.

Housing and Urban Design for Gender Equality

For at least the last two-and-a-half decades, scholars have explored the landscapes and house forms that better support women in their domestic lives and offer the possibility of greater economic equality (Appleton 1995; Birch 1985; Hayden 1980, 1984; Saegert 1982).

Most existing housing and settlement patterns do not support the combination of domestic life and paid employment for women. Suburban single-family homes and landscapes increase the competing demands of domestic life and work for pay when they isolate women from work opportunities because of location, zoning or transportation; require greater investment in domestic chores and chauffeuring; and culturally support a more traditional definition of gender. Urban environments are associated for women with fear of crime and dissatisfaction with housing and outdoor space for family life and child-rearing, but with greater satisfaction with and access to work and cultural opportunities and less gender stereotyping. Feminist designs for living emphasize community, clustered housing, flexible work spaces in and near the home, nearby nature and play spaces, integration of communal or commercial services with residences and housing that can adapt to changes in family composition and income.

The dominant patterns of development that segregate residences and workplaces and disperse services make housing that supports productive lives for women hard to find even when housing cost is not the major factor. The type of housing, zoning, cost, density and patterns of land use, services and transportation can make it easier or more difficult for women and men to balance domestic life and paid employment (Franck 2002; Hayden 2002; Saegert 1982; Saegert and Winkel 1980; Wright 1983). While electronic communication offers some potential for easing the time/space constraints of multiple duties, those most in need—for example, welfare-to-work mothers in the inner city—are least likely to have the knowledge, access and money to take advantage of the job and service provision from such sources. Even single, childless women face an unlevel playing field in their search for satisfactory housing due to their lower wages compared with similar men. Their disadvantage thus often worsens because of deficits in the safety, social acceptance and satisfying leisure activities as well as access to employment in the residential communities that they can afford. Poor women in many areas face the additional trade-off of low-cost housing versus proximity to jobs that fit their skill levels, a problem compounded by their reliance on inadequate public transportation (c.f. Coulton, Leete and Bania 1999). For minority women, racial discrimination further constrains their ability to live near good work opportunities. While minority men also suffer from these constraints, women may be less likely to work at all when the choice between domestic duties and paid employment is a stark one.

Kasarda and Ting (1996) examined the impact of skills and spatial mismatches as well as welfare dependency separately for men and women and for blacks and whites. They conclude that both factors affect poverty and joblessness. However, both race and gender differentiate their findings. Blacks show a higher association between joblessness and welfare receipt, which Kasarda and Ting relate to continuing prejudicial practices in the job market. Regarding gender, they observed the following:

> The powerful effect of spatial mismatch on female joblessness suggests that gender bias in urban design and transportation services also needs to be considered. The deconcentration of metropolitan jobs, together with restricted transport choice, differentially impacts the least mobile—that is, less-educated inner-city women. These women are most likely to (1) depend entirely on public transportation, (2) travel close to home, (3) seek only jobs with short commute times, (4) avoid work that requires traveling through nearby dangerous areas (especially after dark), and (5) need to balance multiple domestic responsibilities with work schedules. As a result, job options for these women tend to be much more restricted spatially and temporally, often limiting them to low-paying and part-time work closer to home. These constraints no doubt pose strong work disincentives.... Perhaps the greatest policy challenge to facilitating the transition to work is overcoming spatial and temporal constraints that prevent women with children from accommodating their domestic and work responsibilities. (412–413)

As Susana Torre (1999) points out, overcoming the time/space constraints confronted by poor women requires more than design schemes. The racial and economic segregation inherent in the political, institutional and financial processes of housing development must be successfully challenged.

Ownership, Control, Participation

A government-implemented Right to Housing would need to exist along with traditional private homeownership in the United States, but it may also reduce the attractiveness of that alternative and point out its limitations. Homeownership in our country is assumed to provide the greatest amount of control over housing and the greatest freedom to enjoy one's property and to use it for personal gain. However, for women, these benefits not only may be compromised by forms of development at the local or regional scale that impose time/space dilemmas, but the house forms themselves may assume patterns of use and preference deriving from idealized and patriarchal assumptions about a "good" house and what will sell. Friedman's studies (1999) of upper-middle-class and wealthy women who have commissioned their own homes from architects reveal their struggles to achieve less patriarchal house forms. These women clients wanted to mix spaces for their "work": domestic labor and relaxation—including family and servants, inside and outside, in unconventional ways. While they achieved novel housing forms, these forms embodied compromises with convention required by finance and insurance institutions and resale concerns. Feldman's discussion (1999) of a participatory design process with the women leaders and residents of a public housing development reveals both the psychological and social significance of being involved in design decisions. The process also demonstrates the difficulties of finding solutions that break out of stereotypical building forms, suit the residents' image of their hoped-for future and are financially viable.

Implementation of a Right to Housing may open up new forms of ownership, such as limited-equity cooperatives, that increase women's freedom to enjoy their homes, pursue their goals in life and feel secure about their futures. But this will happen only if the bureaucratic and institutional control of housing that has been the norm for public housing and many not-for-profit developments is replaced by successful methods of involving users in design decisions, residents in housing governance and citizens in housing development and allocation processes. All too often, public housing authorities' control over tenants' lives has been demonstrated in acts of unexplained interference with legitimate uses of public housing property, such as shutting tenants out of community spaces, refusing permission for economic development ventures and undermining or ignoring democratically elected leadership (Feldman 1999). Genuinely involving larger numbers of women in the provision and control of housing at every level would probably help. But control usually comes down to financial capacity and economic ownership, whether at the individual or collective level. Social housing has pioneered some promising forms of development, but the dominance of economic concerns remains a challenge. Patriarchal cultural assumptions as well as realistic legal and economic responsibilities need to be redefined. For women to truly benefit from a Right to Housing, women residents must have access to leadership positions as bureaucrats, CDC leaders and staff and public officials. They also must be involved fully in debates and discussions, such as the ones that sparked the creation of this book and those it will presumably generate.

NOTES

1. Most households that designate themselves as being female-headed are headed by single, separated, divorced or widowed women. However, a small but increasing percent of married households choose the designation female-headed (Meyers 1992).

2. One of the major factors in increasing immigration to the United States is the impact of economic restructuring both here and abroad. Economic restructuring also affects the housing options for women. For example, the influx of immigrants in northeastern and western U.S. cities and suburbs has resulted in higher levels of residential crowding and housing costs, both conditions that can especially affect women because of the greater time they spend in the home and their lower incomes. However, the replacement of an industrial economy with a higher-tech economy in Boston and Pittsburgh allowed women to gain higher paid and more professional jobs, improving their position in the housing market as well as their economic standing (Jezierski 1995).

3. Most of the studies of women's preferences for housing and amenities date back to the 1970s and 1980s, when women were entering the labor force in great numbers.

REFERENCES

American Housing Survey (2001), U.S. Department of Commerce and U.S. Department of Housing and Urban Development.

Amott, Teresa, and Julie Matthaei. 1996. *Race, gender and work*, Rev. Ed. Boston: South End Press.

Angel, Ronald J., and Jacqueline L. Angel. 1993. *Painful inheritance: Health and the new generations of fatherless families.* Madison: University of Wisconsin Press.

Appleton, Lynn M. 1995. The gender regime of American cities. In *Gender in urban research*, eds. Judith A. Garber and Robyne S. Turner, 44–59. Thousand Oaks, CA: Sage Publications, Inc.

Ardener, Shirley, ed. 1981. *Women and space: Ground rules and social maps.* London: Croom Helm.

Berk, Sarah F. 1980. The household as workplace: Wives, husbands, and children. In *New Space for Women*, eds. Gerda Wekerle, Rebecca Peterson and David Morley, 65–81. Boulder, CO: Westview Press.

Birch, Eugenie Ladner. 1985. *The unsheltered woman: Women and housing in the 80s.* New Brunswick, NJ: Rutgers University Press.

Bratt, Rachel G., and Langley C. Keyes. 1998. Challenges confronting nonprofit housing organizations' self-sufficiency programs. *Housing Policy Debate*, 9(4):795–824.

Briggs, Xavier de Souza, and Elisabeth Mueller (with Mercer Sullivan). 1997. From Neighborhood to community: Evidence of the social effects of community development. New York: Community Development Research Center, New School for Social Research.

Clark, Heléne, Susan Saegert, Eric K.Glunt and William Roane. 1990. The future of limited equity housing in New York City: Residents struggle for stability. New York: Center for Human Environments.

Connell, James P., Anne C. Kubisch, Lisbeth B. Schorr and Carol H. Weiss. 1995. *New approaches to evaluating community initiatives: Concepts, methods, and contexts.* Washington, DC: The Aspen Institute.

Costello, Cynthia B., Vanessa R.Wight and Anne J. Stone. 2002. *The American woman 2003–2004.* New York: Palgrave Macmillan.

Coulton, Claudia, Laura Leete and Neil Bania. 1999. Housing, transportation, and access to suburban jobs by welfare recipients in the Cleveland area. In *The home front: Implications of welfare reform for housing policy*, ed. Sandra Newman. Washington, DC: The Urban Institute Press.

Council of Large Public Housing Authorities (CLPHA). 1996. *Summary tenant statistics.* Washington, DC: CLPHA.

Cowan, Spencer M., William M. Rohe and Esmail Baku. 1999. Factors influencing the performance of community development corporations. *Journal of Urban Affairs*, 21(3):325–340.

Darke, Jane. 1994. Women and the meaning of home. In *Housing women*, eds. Rose Gilroy and Roberta Woods, 11–30. London: Routledge.

Department of Housing and Urban Development. 1999. *HOPE VI fact sheet.* www.hud.gov/pih/programs/ph/hope6/facts.pdf.

Domash, Mona, and Joni Seager. 2001. *Putting women in place: Feminist geographer make sense of the world.* New York: Guilford Press.

Dreier, Peter. 1997. The new politics of housing: How to rebuild the constituency for a progressive federal housing policy. *Journal of the American Planning Association*, 63(1):5–27.

Edin, Katheryn, and Laura Lein. 1997. *Making ends meet: How single mothers survive welfare and low-wage work.* New York: Russell Sage.

Eggers, Frederick J., and Paul E. Burke. 1996. Can the national homeownership rate be significantly improved by reaching underserved markets? *Housing Policy Debate*, 7(1):83–102.

Evans, Gary W., Nancy M. Wells and Annie Moch. 2003. Housing and mental health: A review of the evidence and a methodological and conceptual critique. *Journal of Social Issues*, 59:475–501.

Farley, Reynolds. 1996. *The new American reality: Who we are, how we got here, where we are going.* New York: Russell Sage.

Feldman, Roberta. 1999. Participatory design at the grass roots. In *Design and feminism: Re-visioning spaces, places, and everyday things*, ed. Joan Rothschild, 135–148. New Brunswick, NJ: Rutgers University Press.

Franck, Karen A. 2002. Women and environments. In *Handbook of environmental psychology*, eds. Robert Bechtel and Arza Churchman, 347–362. New York: Wiley and Sons.

Freeman, Lance. 1998. Interpreting the dynamics of public housing: Cultural and rational choice explanations. *Housing Policy Debate*, 9(2):323–352.

Friedman, Alice T. 1999. Shifting the paradigm: Houses built for women. In *Design and feminism: Re-visioning spaces, places, and everyday things*, ed. Joan Rothschild, 85–98. New Brunswick, NJ: Rutgers University Press.

Galster, George C., and Edward M. Hill. 1992. *The metropolis in black and white.* New Brunswick, NJ: Rutgers Center for Urban Policy Research.

Garber, Judith A., and Robyne S. Turner. 1995. Introduction. In *Gender in urban research, X-XXVI*, eds. Judith A. Garber and Robyne S. Turner. Thousand Oaks, CA: Sage Publications, Inc.

Gittell, Marilyn, Jill Gross and Kathe Newman. 1994. *Race and gender in neighborhood development organizations.* New York: The Howard Samuels State Management and Policy Center, Graduate School and University Center, City University of New York.

Gittell, Marilyn, Sally Covington and Jill Gross. 1994. *The difference gender makes: Women in neighborhood development organizations.* New York: The Howard Samuels State Management and Policy Center, Graduate School and University Center, City University of New York.

Gittell, Marilyn, Isolda Ortega-Bustamante and Tracey Steffy. 1999. *Women creating social capital and social change: A study of women-led community development organizations.* New York: The Howard Samuels State Management and Policy Center, Graduate School and University Center, City University of New York.

Gittell, Ross, and Margeret Wilder. 1999. Community development corporations: Critical factors that influence success. *Journal of Urban Affairs*, 21(3):345–361.

Glickman, Norman J., and Lisa J. Servon. 1999. More than bricks and sticks: Five components of community development corporation capacity. *Housing Policy Debate*, 9(3):497–539.

Goering, John, Ali Kamely and Todd Richardson. 1997. Recent research on racial segregation and poverty concentration in public housing in the United States. *Urban Affairs Review*, 32(5):723–745.

Goldin, Claudia. 1997. Career and family: College women look to the past. In *Gender and family issues in the workplace*, eds. Francine D. Blau and Ronald C. Ehrenberg, 20–58. New York: Russell Sage Foundation.

Grimm, K., and Jaime C. Maldonado. 1995. No home of her own: Gender and homelessness. *Women & Environments*, 14(2):20–22.

Hardy, Melissa. A., and Lawrence D. Hazelrigg. 1993. The gender of poverty in an aging population. *Research on Aging*, 15(3):243–278.

Hayden, Dolores. 1980. What would a non-sexist city be like? Speculations on housing, urban design and human work. *Signs*, 5 (Supp.):167–184.

———. 2002. *Redesigning the American Dream: Gender, housing, and family life* (revised and expanded). New York: Norton.

Hunt, Pauline. 1989. Gender and the construction of home life. In *Home and family: Creating the domestic sphere*, eds. Graham Allan and Graham Crow. Basingstoke: Macmillan.

Jargowsky, Paul A. 1997. *Poverty and place: Ghettos, barrios and the American city.* New York: Russell Sage Foundation.

Jarrett, Robyn. 1995. Growing up poor: The family experiences of socially mobile youth in low-income African American neighborhoods. *Journal of Adolescent Research*, 10:111–135.

Jezierski, Louise. 1995. Women organizing their place in restructuring economies. In *Gender in urban research*, eds. Judith A. Garber and Robyne S. Turner, 60–76. Thousand Oaks, CA: Sage Publications, Inc.

Joint Center for Housing Studies. 2003. State of the nation's housing. Cambridge, MA: Harvard University.

Kasarda, John D., and Kwok-fai Ting. 1996. Joblessness and poverty in America's central cities: Causes and policy prescriptions. *Housing Policy Debate*, 7(2):387–419.

Knecht, Barbara. 1999. Special needs and housing design: Myths/realities/opportunities. In *Design and feminism: Re-visioning spaces, places, and everyday things*, ed. Joan Rothschild, 99–108. New Brunswick, NJ: Rutgers University Press.

Koshinksy, Julia. 1998. Challenging the third sector housing approach: The impact of federal policies (1980–1996). *Journal of Urban Affairs*, 20(2):117–119.

Leavitt, Jacqueline, and Susan Saegert. 1990. *From abandonment to hope: Community households in Harlem.* New York: Columbia University Press.

Leventhal, Tama, and Jeanne Brooks-Gunn. 2000. The neighborhoods they live in: The effects of neighborhood residence upon child and adolescent outcomes. *Psychological Bulletin*, 126 (2):309–337.

Mason, Jennifer. 1989. Reconstructing the public and private: The home and marriage in later life. In *Home and family: Creating the domestic sphere*, eds. Graham Allan & Graham Crow. Basingstoke, UK: Macmillan.

Massey, Douglas S., and Nancy A. Denton. 1993. *American apartheid: Segregation and the making of the underclass.* Cambridge MA: Harvard University Press.

McFate, Katherine, Roger Lawson and William Julius Wilson. 1995. *Poverty, inequality and the future of social policy: Western states and the new world order.* New York: Russell Sage.

Meyers, Dennis. 1992. *Analysis with local census data: Portraits of change.* New York: Academic Press.

National Law Center on Homelessness and Poverty. 2001. Overview. http://www.nlchp.org/FA_HAPIA/.

Newman, Sandra, ed. 1999. *The home front: Implications of welfare reform for housing policy.* Washington, DC: The Urban Institute Press.

Oliver, Melvin L., and Thomas M. Shapiro. 1995. *Black wealth/White wealth: A new perspective on racial inequality.* New York: Routledge.

Quercia, Robert B., Michael A. Stegman, Walter R. Davis and Eric Stein. 2002. Performance of community reinvestment loans: Implications for secondary market purchases. In *Low-income homeownership: Examining the unexamined goal*, eds. Nicolas P. Retsinas and Eric S. Belsky, 348–374. Cambridge, MA: Joint Center for Housing Studies.

Rae, Ruth. 1997. *Ownership and equity: Perceptions of ownership by low-income owners of limited equity cooperative housing.* Doctoral dissertation, The City University of New York Graduate School and University Center.

Rasmussen, David W., Isaac F. Megbolugbe and Barbara A. Morgan. 1997. The reverse mortgage as an asset management tool. *Housing Policy Debate*, 8(1):173–194.

Ratner, Mitchell S. 1996. Many routes to homeownership: A four-site ethnographic study of minority and immigrant experiences. *Housing Policy Debate*, 7(1):103–146.

Robinson, John P., and Geoffrey Godbey. 1997. *Time for life: The surprising ways Americans use their time*. University Park, PA: The Pennsylvania State University Press.

Rohe, William M., and Rachel G. Bratt. 2003. Failures, downsizings and mergers among community development corporations. *Housing Policy Debate* 14(1/2):1–46.

Rollins, Joan H., Renee N. Saris and Ingrid Johnston-Robledo. 2001. Low-income women speak out about housing: A high-stakes game of musical chairs. *Journal of Social Issues*, 57(2):277–298.

Rosenbaum, James E. 1991. Black pioneers—Do their moves to the suburbs increase economic opportunity for mothers and children? *Housing Policy Debate*, 2(4):1179–1213.

Rossi, Peter H., and Eleanor Weber. 1996. The social benefits of homeownership: Empirical evidence from national surveys. *Housing Policy Debate*, 7(1):1–36.

Rothblatt, Donald N., Daniel Garr and Jo Sprague. 1979. *The suburban environment and women*. New York: Praeger.

Saegert, Susan. 1982. Towards the androgynous city. In *Cities in the 21st century*, eds. Gary Gappert and Richard V. Knight. Beverly Hills, CA: Sage.

———. 1989. Unlikely leaders, extreme circumstances: Older Black women building community households. *American Journal of Community Psychology*, 17(3):295–316.

———. 1993. Survey of residents of currently and previously city-owned buildings in the Bronx. In *Housing in the balance: Seeking a comprehensive policy for city-owned housing*, ed. M. Cotton, 17–48. Consumer Farmer Foundation for the Task Force on City Owned Property.

———. 1995. What we have to work with: The lessons of the Task Force surveys. In *No more housing of last resort: The importance of affordability and resident participation in in Rem housing*, ed. Michelle Cotton, 35–63. New York: Parodneck Foundation for the Task Force on City Owned Property.

Saegert, Susan, and Lymari Benitez. 2003. *Limited equity housing cooperatives: A review of the literature*. Report to the Taconic Foundation. New York: Global Foundations Group of JPMorgan Private Bank.

Saegert, Susan, Phillip J. Thompson, Robert Engle and Joselyn Sargent. 2000. *Stretched thin: Employment, parenting, and social capital among mothers in public housing*. New York: Foundation for Child Development, Working Paper.

Saegert, Susan, and Gary Winkel. 1980. The home: A critical problem for changing sex roles. In *New space for women*, eds. Gerda Wekerle,

Rebecca Peterson and David Morley. Boulder, CO: Westview.

———. 1999. CDCs, social capital, and housing quality. *Shelterforce*, March/April, 22–24.

Saegert, Susan, and Delores E. McCarthy. 1998. Gender and housing for the elderly: Sorting through the accumulations of a lifetime. In *Environment and aging theory: A focus on housing*, eds. Richard J. Scheidt and Paul G. Windley. Westport, CT: Greenwood Press.

Schill, Michael. 1994. The role of the nonprofit sector in low-income housing production: A comparative perspective. *Urban Affairs Quarterly*, 30(1):74–101.

Schill, Michael H., and Benjamin P. Scafidi. 1997. *Housing conditions and problems in New York City: An analysis of the 1996 Housing and Vacancy Survey*. New York: Center for Real Estate and Urban Policy, New York University School of Law, Working Paper 97-7.

Simmons, Patrick A. 1997. *Housing statistics of the United States: First edition*. Lanham, MD: Bernan Press.

Spain, Daphne, and Suzanne M. Bianchi. 1996. *Balancing act: Motherhood, marriage, and employment among American women*. New York: Russell Sage.

Stockard, James G., Jr. 1998. Public housing—the next sixty years. In *New directions in urban public housing*, eds. David P. Varady, Wolfgang F. E. Preiser and Francis P. Russell, 237–264. New Brunswick, NJ: Rutgers Center for Urban Policy Research.

Stone, Michael E. 1993. *Shelter poverty: New ideas on housing affordability*. Philadelphia: Temple University Press.

Torre, Susana. 1999. Expanding the urban design agenda: A critique of the new urbanism. In *Design and feminism: Re-visioning spaces, places, and everyday things*, ed. Joan Rothschild, 35–44. New Brunswick, NJ: Rutgers University Press.

U.S. Department of Commerce. 1996. *United States Census, Bureau of the Census*.

———. 2000. *United States Census, Bureau of the Census*.

U.S. Department of Commerce and the U.S. Department of Housing and Urban Development. 2001. *American Housing Survey for the United States in 2001*.

Wekerle, Gerda R. 1988. Canadian women's housing cooperatives: Case studies in physical and social innovation. In *Lifespaces: Gender, household, employment*, eds. Caroline Andrew and Beth Moore Milroy, 102–140. Vancouver: University of British Columbia Press.

Wilson, William Julius. 1987. *The truly disadvantaged: The inner city, the underclass, and public policy*. Chicago: University of Chicago Press.

Wright, Gwendolyn. 1983. *Building the dream: A social history of housing in America*. New York: Pantheon.

Rob Rosenthal and Maria Foscarinis

15 Responses to Homelessness: Past Policies, Future Directions, and a Right to Housing

WHEN HOMELESSNESS reemerged as a significant social issue in the United States in the late 1970s and early 1980s, three questions dominated public debate: how many, who and why? The range of answers to these questions corresponded to a variety of proposed responses to homelessness, from those that stressed changes in the behavior of individual homeless people to those that called for systemic, social solutions. Since that time, a degree of consensus has been reached on those initial key questions, and the need for some form of government response is accepted; with that evolution, debate has shifted to a discussion of the nature of that response. In the early years of the new century, a resurgence of interest in policy responses has begun to come forth at the federal, state and local levels, along with a new focus on policies to end and prevent homelessness.

This chapter begins with a discussion of the initial debates dominating the response to homelessness and their implications for policy. We then briefly discuss the ways in which local, state and federal governments have helped to create large-scale homelessness and then examine responses to the crisis. We consider the extent to which these responses aimed at ameliorating the conditions of homeless life, aiding exit from homelessness or preventing homelessness, and discuss the evolution of government responses to homelessness, noting that the limited amount of funding available has made true prevention strategies relatively rare. In the last half of the chapter, we discuss the strategies that are most promising, building on existing programmatic successes but emphasizing the role of housing to

a far greater extent than government responses to homelessness have done thus far.

THE 1980s: EARLY QUESTIONS, DEBATE AND POLICY RESPONSES

The question of the size of the homeless population generated much controversy in the early 1980s, at times dominating public debate on the issue. As a political matter, the size of the homeless population had important policy implications: If there were only a few homeless people, locally or nationally, then it could be argued that government had little or no obligation to act. But by the late 1980s, even those who had at first minimized the problem could no longer deny that the numbers were quite large in comparison to the preceding 40 years. By most accounts, between half a million and a million Americans were "literally homeless" (meaning in shelters or on the streets) every night—perhaps several millions if the count were expanded to include "hidden homeless" populations as well. A study by Bruce Link and his colleagues (1994) estimated that an astounding 3 percent of the U.S. population had been literally homeless at some time between 1985 and 1990.

Who, then, were these homeless people? Were they hippies, alcoholics and addicts? Mothers with children or unemployed working people? Were they members of the "deserving" or "undeserving" poor? Again, there were policy implications. For instance, if homeless people were "transients," then local government could argue that it had little responsibility to them. If they were alcoholics and addicts whose substance abuse was ostensibly a chosen way of life, then all levels of government could argue that they had little claim to government aid.

This was tied to the third question: Why were these people homeless? Public discourse—framed within the individualistic tradition that generally informs American public debate, based on inherited folk wisdom and reacting to the most visible homeless people—initially attributed homelessness almost entirely to personal characteristics, perhaps involuntary (such as those resulting from mental illness), but often "voluntary" (where homelessness is a chosen lifestyle; or resulting from substance abuse, as a failure of self-control). This emphasis on the individual fit fairly well with the major academic theory inherited from the last wave of concern with homelessness (skid rows in the 1950s and 1960s), "Disaffiliation Theory," which stressed the more or less voluntary withdrawal of people from mainstream society for a variety of reasons—social incompetence, desire to drink, fear of disclosure of homosexuality and so forth.[1]

By the mid- to late 1980s, researchers, advocates and homeless activists had increasingly challenged such individually based explanations of homelessness with another perspective that stressed the *involuntary displacement* of people from housed lives by large social processes over which they had little control—in particular, the scarcity of low-income housing, deindustrialization, deinstitutionalization, increasing holes in the welfare safety net and changes in family structures. Disaffiliation, when it appeared, was described more often as a result of homelessness rather than the cause of it.

The explosion of homelessness in the first half of the 1980s was powerful evidence for this "displacement" perspective. By any measure or definition, it was clear that the number of people who were homeless by 1985 was several times as great as just a decade before, this being after 40 years of relative stability in the size of the homeless population nationally. To accept personal incompetence or irresponsibility as the primary cause of homelessness required believing that hundreds of thousands—probably millions—of people had suddenly caught

incompetence or irresponsibility like the flu. Such an explanation was not convincing.

Displacement theorists generally argued that of all the social causes involved, the crisis of low-income housing was the most significant (Hopper and Hamburg 1986; Wright 1989; Hoch and Slayton 1989). Specifically, the gap between tenants' incomes and rents that grew so rapidly in the 1970s and 1980s was most severe for those on the lowest end of the income spectrum; at the same time, it was at the bottom of the housing market that the number of units declined most severely, particularly in single room occupancy (SRO) hotels (Hartman and Zigas 1991). The result, inevitably, was an explosion of homelessness for a segment of the poorest Americans, caught in a game of musical chairs in which there were simply not enough affordable units to go around.

This is not to say that those who ended up homeless were only random victims of structural problems: Many had other problems as well. But the resources for dealing with such "personal problems"—substance abuse, domestic battering, lack of job training and the like—were also in short supply; in each area, there was a game of musical chairs. As in any such game, personal characteristics—preparation, sobriety, skill as well as luck—play a role in who ends up with and without a chair. But the situation itself mandates that *some* will be caught without a chair—or, in this case, a home. For many displacement theorists and some homelessness activists, the centrality of the connection between homelessness and the dearth of low-income housing raised the question of establishing a Right to Housing (Roisman 1991).

By the late 1980s, this more structural view of homelessness had become increasingly common in public discourse, changing public perceptions of possible solutions. If larger social causes were to blame, homeless people were then to be seen as victims rather than villains responsible for their fallen state. Thus, the first of three major lines of argument against aiding homeless people—the "moral question"—seemed largely overcome. That is, if it could be shown that homeless people had created their problems themselves or maybe had no desire to escape their condition, they had no moral claim on the goodwill of government or the general citizenry. But once homelessness is granted to be at least in part due to social processes beyond the control of those who become homeless, a sense of decency demands governmental response, much as we aid victims of natural disasters. In fact, the agency responsible for initial overview of federal programs in this area was the Federal Emergency Management Agency (FEMA). Ironically, FEMA (now part of the Department of Homeland Security) responded to the massive homelessness caused by Hurricane Katrina yet, as of this writing, is providing housing assistance only to those made homeless by this disaster, not to those who were previously homeless.[2]

THE 1990s: BACKLASH AND PROGRESS

Despite increasing government aid in the 1990s, homelessness did not go away. Public opinion, fluid and malleable, continued to show support in polls for more socially oriented approaches but often supported more punitive approaches when these were advanced by politicians (Link et al. 1995; Guzicki and Toro 2002). At the local level, new ordinances penalizing acts such as begging or sleeping in public were enacted in some places (National Law Center on Homelessness and Poverty [hereafter NLCHP] 1991, 1993, 1994, 1996, 1999). Clearly, the public wanted something done, and the very failure to solve the problem engendered resentment.

In academic and policy circles, the 1990s saw some backlash against the displacement emphasis as well. Some researchers accused displacement theorists of denying the existence of any pathology among homeless people (Baum and Burnes 1993) and stressed the importance of individual disaffiliation (as cause as well as effect). While some continued to stress individuals' lack of "independent living skills" (Institute for Children and Poverty [hereinafter ICP] 1998a; Grunberg 1998), by the mid- to late 1990s, many theorists argued that homelessness could best be explained by some combination of macro and micro factors (Jencks 1994; Main 1998). Recognizing that at least some homeless

people needed more than simply housing and seeking to establish firmer links to a broader anti-poverty platform, advocates developed policy proposals that included the full range of issues that needed to be addressed to truly end homelessness: housing, income and social services (NLCHP 1992).

Yet even when and where homelessness had been accepted as a social issue requiring social solutions, governmental response remained torturously slow at all levels. Though the "moral question" might be muted, two other "practical" arguments were harder to overcome, especially at the local level: the "magnet theory" and the "cost argument."

The magnet (or Mecca) theory argues that providing services will attract more homeless people to a locality, thus worsening the problem locally. There is little evidence that homeless people as a group are significantly more mobile than housed people (Rosenthal 1994:144; Burt 2001),[3] and strong evidence that those who leave the community where they became homeless do so largely because of lack of jobs and affordable housing, not lack of social services; but availability of services may be one of several factors in choosing the community to which they move (Burt 2001). The fear of becoming a magnet for homeless people was—and still is—a regularly cited rationale for cities' limitations on aid and programs for homeless people, including prohibition of efforts by private individuals and organizations to offer aid or establish housing and other programs. This suggests that both prevention strategies and regional approaches to services for those who do become homeless are ultimately likely to make more sense for local governments.

Local governments have also often made the cost argument: Whatever their sympathies or wishes, they simply do not have money to meet existing need (let alone help those who might be attracted by the town's generosity). In fact, local governments were often spending considerably more than they realized, since while they were aware of their manifest costs dealing with homelessness (such as emergency shelters), they may have been unaware of a wide range of hidden costs, from police costs for arrests to medical costs incurred at local emergency rooms (Research Atlanta 1984; Rosenthal 1994). During the 1990s, evidence began to accumulate that progressive social solutions to homelessness (discussed below) would be cost-effective for society at large and, in the long run, for localities as well (Rosenthal 1994; Lindblom 1996). More recently, a 2002 study demonstrated that the cost of providing supportive housing—housing with services, such as mental health care, substance abuse treatment, case management—for even the most troubled homeless people would be nearly offset by savings in crisis responses such as emergency room use and incarceration (Culhane, Metreaux and Hadley 2002:135–140).

These calculations, however, rest also on the question of what level of response is intended. Programs may be aimed at *amelioration*—that is, easing the lives of those already homeless (such as shelters or soup kitchens); they may be designed to facilitate *exit* from homelessness for those already homeless (such as housing); they may be aimed at *prevention* of homelessness (such as creation of additional low-rent housing, rent control and eviction protections). Up through the 1990s, government responses to homelessness focused primarily on amelioration. Yet they did not provide even enough shelter beds, for instance, to meet need, leaving little or nothing for exit and prevention programs.

THE 2000s TO DATE: CURRENT DEBATE AND FOCUS

With the beginning of the current decade, however, there has been a new drive to prevent and end homelessness. A proposal to end homelessness in ten years, advanced by the National Alliance to End Homelessness (NAEH), emphasizes the importance of engaging the mainstream anti-poverty programs as well as building "infrastructure," incorporating the earlier call for housing, income and services. While the NAEH plan outlines a general framework rather than specific proposals, it identifies as a first priority ending homelessness for chronically homeless people through increased sup-

portive housing, citing recent research indicating that a disproportionate amount of services are consumed by this population (NAEH 2002; Culhane 2002). Others argue that policy must aim to end all forms of homelessness and that to do this the much bigger issue of the affordable housing crisis must be addressed (NAACP et al. 2003). Omnibus legislation introduced in Congress in 2003, the Bringing America Home Act, contains a wide range of proposals that explore the need for housing, income and social services—including health and child care—and that calls for a Right to Housing.

GOVERNMENT'S ROLE: CREATING AND RESPONDING TO HOMELESSNESS

Throughout the 1980s, activists and advocates argued that far from helping to resolve homelessness, government at all levels had played an enormous role in helping to *create* large-scale homelessness. Federal housing and fiscal policies, in particular, were crucial. Many of these are discussed in detail elsewhere in this text: tax laws that traditionally rewarded practices that led to escalating housing costs; failure to control interest rates, a key variable in the demise of low-income housing in the 1980s; and most prominently, the slashing of the federal housing budget during the Reagan/Bush I years as the low-income housing market crumbled. Despite the Clinton Administration's early denunciations of these cuts in housing programs, it retreated in the face of the Republican Congressional victory of 1994, and FY1996, FY1997 and FY1998 budgets submitted by the President maintained those cuts; the FY1999 budget reversed this trend somewhat, continuing through the FY2001 budget. The proposed budget for FY2002, the first presented by the new Bush Administration, signaled the start of a new downward trend, with significant cuts in new Section 8 units requested. The most current (mid-2005) proposal, for FY2006, was lower yet, calling for cutting the total HUD budget by over $5 billion, or 11.5 percent, and included a proposal to eliminate the Community Development Block Grant (CDBG) program and move those functions to the Department of Commerce without any assurance that housing would continue to be an eligible activity. (NLIHC 2005). Further, retroactive administrative changes caused low-income people across the country to lose their housing: In April 2004, the Department of Housing and Urban Development (HUD) announced that it would no longer pay for the full cost of existing vouchers.

This is not to say that it has been only federal housing policies that helped to create and exacerbate homelessness on a large scale. Local governments, especially those facing financial disaster as their middle classes fled to surrounding suburbs, have played a significant role, encouraging the wave of gentrification that destroyed so much of the low-rent housing stock in many cities, particularly SROs, without providing for the relocation of those displaced. Social service policies—at all levels of government—have also been involved. In the 1960s and 1970s, the mental health policy of deinstitutionalization, though laudably intended to improve the lives and treatment of mental health patients by greatly expanding their treatment options, foundered on the federal failure to fully fund promised residential treatment facilities, coupled with local resistance to the creation of such facilities. The resulting gaping holes in coordination and services led to a sharp increase in homelessness among mentally ill people. Assistance levels in means-tested entitlement programs not indexed to inflation dropped too low to cover housing costs and other necessities; tightened eligibility and application requirements initiated in the early 1980s prevented many from receiving assistance at all. Discretionary social service programs aided only a small fraction of those eligible. Nor has this changed much: Currently, for example, about three-fourths of those who are eligible do not receive any federal housing assistance (Sard and Fischer 2003). The repeal of the federal welfare entitlement for families, along with the denial of supplemental security income (SSI) benefits to those disabled by drug and alcohol addiction—both the result of the 1996 welfare reform legislation—contributed to increases in homelessness among those who lost these forms of assistance (NAEH 2003; Norris et al. 2003).

THE LOCAL AND STATE RESPONSE

Until the mid-1980s, shelters and soup kitchens—almost always operated by nonprofits, mainly religious groups—were the only direct response to homelessness in most places, as they had been for 40 years at least. But one indicator of the seriousness of the explosion of homelessness in the 1980s—and the success of activists and advocates in pressing demands on government—was that by 1996 (the most recent year for which data are available), government had become the primary conduit for funding and organizing the delivery of most services for homeless people (Burt 2001:260–261).

Initially, the burden fell primarily on local government. Starting in New York City with a suit to establish a "right to shelter," ultimately formalized in a consent decree, lawsuits established some state and local obligations to provide shelter and other immediate assistance to homeless people. Similar suits were filed in other jurisdictions, including Atlantic City (NJ), West Virginia and Los Angeles; in Washington, DC, a ballot initiative led to a right to shelter in that city in 1984. Parallel to the litigation, other advocacy initiatives, coupled with early federal emergency appropriations, resulted in some aid, primarily emergency in nature (U.S. GAO 1985:40–42). In the mid- to late 1980s, local government responses to homelessness increased as the first significant federal dollars for social approaches to homelessness began to reach the local level.

Beginning in the early 1990s, however, some localities began to adopt or reinstitute more punitive approaches to homelessness. Despite the increased funding, shelter space was not sufficient to meet the need, leaving many homeless people living in public spaces. In response, many localities began adopting the "leafblower approach" (as one local official referred to it, cited in Simon 1994:152), attempting to move homeless people away from their streets, neighborhoods or communities. Treating homelessness as a police matter, local governments passed or resurrected laws that criminalized activities such as "public sleeping," "illegal camping" and "aggressive panhandling"; in practice, police officers often used these laws to require homeless people to "move along" or else face arrest. These laws and enforcement practices spurred numerous court challenges to their constitutionality, leading to several court rulings striking them down. At the same time, some of the gains of the 1980s were restricted or reversed. The already inadequate availability of shelter was further diminished with new restrictions and eligibility requirements, including time limits, work requirements and proof that homelessness was not the result of "fault"; in 1994, Washington, DC, repealed its right to shelter law (Foscarinis 2004).

While these punitive approaches continue (NLCHP and NCH 2001; NLCHP 2003), more constructive approaches are also emerging in some localities, at least partly in response to advocacy and litigation. The leading case challenging the "criminalization" of homelessness, *Pottinger v. Miami*, resulted in a favorable court ruling striking down the city's policies as unconstitutional; that ruling led to a consent decree that included a "no bed, no arrest" provision, marking some recognition of shelter as a minimum necessity. Moreover, following the litigation, Miami's Dade County passed a special meal tax to fund aid—both short- and longer-term—for homeless people, raising some $7.5 million annually for shelter, housing, employment service and substance abuse treatment (Rohter 1993; Foscarinis 1996a).

Nonetheless, regardless of the approach, it is unrealistic to expect local efforts alone to meet the crisis adequately. An inevitable diffusion of financial responsibility (since who bears the eventual cost is not necessarily tied to who could prevent the original problem), coupled with the limits on local resources, all too often interferes with a proactive approach that would make sense financially, socially and morally as well. Local governments, operating within fixed time frames and financial constraint, have argued that the costs of homelessness, hidden or manifest—to ameliorate, exit or prevent homelessness—are more than they can bear alone in the immediate present, even with the best of intentions.

By and large, state governments have not filled the gap. Beginning in the mid-1990s, the federal Continuum of Care approach (described below) has greatly encouraged states to design collaborative plans and match federal dollars. These initiatives are important, but states remain generally "middlemen," allocating money from Washington. A few states— including Massachusetts, New Jersey and New York (Watson 1996; Lindblom 1996:191–192; Culhane 2002)—have launched significant initiatives, investing their own resources in preventing and ending homelessness. Following welfare reform, at least some states have used Temporary Assistance for Needy Families funds for homelessness prevention (Culhane 2002).

In the past few years, a number of state and local governments have developed plans to end "chronic" homelessness in their communities. Much of this effort has been spurred by the 2002 White House announcement of a goal to end chronic homelessness in ten years (OMB 2002:171; 2003:164, 169), followed by a call from the Interagency Council on Homelessness to cities and states to develop plans to do so (ICH n.d.). The Council challenged the nation's 100 largest cities to develop plans by January 2003 to end chronic homelessness, and the U.S. Conference of Mayors subsequently adopted a resolution to work with the Bush Administration to meet that goal (U.S. Conference of Mayors 2003b). According to the Council, as of February 2004, over 80 cities had made commitments to develop such plans.

Among the cities that have developed or are currently developing such plans are New York, Atlanta, Washington, DC, San Francisco and Chicago as well as state plans from California, Rhode Island, Minnesota and Georgia, and a variety of counties, such as Maricopa County (Arizona), Montgomery County (Maryland) and Columbus and Franklin Counties (Ohio). While the plans vary significantly in level of detail and approach, many emphasize the importance of preventing homelessness and increasing housing resources. In particular, many include preventing institutionalized persons from being discharged into homelessness and support for the "housing first" model that emphasizes speedy placement in permanent housing, circumventing insofar as possible emergency shelter and transitional housing (Lowe 2004).

Some plans also call for additional state or local resources, both government and private. For example, the Atlanta plan includes proposals for additional city funding, "as resources permit." San Francisco's plan includes a proposal for city incentives to developers to build supportive housing. Nevertheless, while the plans have galvanized state and local efforts and refocused their attention on homelessness and the related issues of housing, income and supportive services, much of the focus of the state and city plans is on strategies to engage the resources of the mainstream—mainly federal—anti-poverty programs. Indeed, homeless initiatives of any magnitude are largely dependent on the federal government for funding.

THE FEDERAL RESPONSE

In the early 1980s, the initial position of the Reagan Administration was that homelessness simply did not exist; in 1982, an Administration official stated publicly that "no one is living on the streets" (Hopper and Hamburg 1986). The federal Interagency Task Force on Food and Shelter for the Homeless, created in 1983, stated in its charter that "[h]omelessness is essentially a local problem" and that "[n]ew federal programs for the homeless are not the answer" (GAO 1985). In 1984, President Reagan expressed the view that homelessness was not a social problem at all but that people were homeless "by choice" (Boston Globe 1984). Nevertheless, in response to the growing crisis, Congress appropriated $140 million for food and shelter for homeless people in 1983; an additional $70 million was appropriated the following year. These funds were to be administered by FEMA, the entity responsible for responding to natural disasters such as floods and earthquakes; no separate program was authorized. But as pressure mounted from advocates, homeless people and local governments, the federal response improved.

The Stewart B. McKinney Homeless Assistance Act of 1987, the watershed event in federal support, authorized a little more than a billion dollars over a two-year period for changes in seven existing programs and creation of fif-

teen new programs providing aid to homeless people. Actual appropriations were $350 million in 1987 and $362 million in 1988 (Foscarinis 1996b). Later named McKinney-Vento,[4] the act provided primarily emergency aid, with most of the funding going to emergency shelter and food. As enacted, the McKinney Act was essentially the first part—titled emergency relief—of an ambitious legislative agenda drafted by advocates; parts two and three, which provided for preventative relief (mainly discharge planning and eviction prevention) and long-term solutions (mainly housing) were not enacted. Given the political context at the time, advocates pressed for the most immediate relief, which also had the greater likelihood of being passed. During the debate on the legislation, Congressional supporters noted that the McKinney Act should be seen as only a first step in the federal response to homelessness (Foscarinis 1993).[5]

Implementation of federal programs in the early years was characterized by the General Accounting Office as "inadequate" (U.S. GAO 1990:2), with federal agencies delaying or refusing to implement them despite statutory timelines and mandates. Key provisions, such as a program to make underutilized properties available to local governments and nonprofit organizations to assist homeless people, were ignored. Implementation, still inadequate, began through a court order that remains in effect and that has been supplemented by additional enforcement orders. Inadequate federal attention also allowed states to overlook new federal obligations that the McKinney Act imposed on states, such as Title VII's guarantee of access to education for homeless children; litigation also was needed to enforce these provisions (Foscarinis 2004). But over the years, while some implementation problems have remained, there has been undeniably significant progress.

In 1993, the incoming Clinton Administration declared homelessness a top priority for HUD. Funding for McKinney Act programs increased significantly, reaching a high of $1.377 billion in FY1995. The Republican Congressional gains in 1994 slowed the growth of some initiatives and reversed the growth of others, with total funding declining to $1.031 billion in FY1996, then beginning to rise again, reaching just over $1.62 billion in FY2003 and just over $1.68 billion in FY2004. The Administration's FY2006 budget request included an increase of just over $200 million from FY2005 to $1.78 billion.

The direction of funding also began to change significantly. In the mid- and late 1980s, the bulk of funding went primarily to emergency aid, such as shelter, food, mobile health care and some transitional housing. The number of shelters and food programs, and their capacities, grew rapidly; a decade later, many communities reported doubled to tripled shelter capacity (Burt 2001:243–245), although across the country need remained greater than resources (U.S. Conference of Mayors 2003a). Activists and advocates were not satisfied with this approach, however, nor did the problem go away. For one thing, despite the great increase in funding, considerably more was needed to cover even sufficient emergency aid. But a more fundamental problem remained: If the game of musical chairs was not to go on forever, the ultimate object had to be to prevent and end homelessness rather than attempt to make it easier to tolerate for those already caught up in its whirlwind.

Beginning in the early 1990s, changes to the McKinney Act shifted the emphasis of some of the programs away from emergency aid and toward exit and prevention. The 1990 McKinney Amendments included a new "Shelter Plus Care" program which provided housing assistance tied to services for homeless people with disabilities; added prevention activities as an eligible use within the Emergency Shelter Grants program; and strengthened the newly renamed Projects for Assistance in Transition from Homelessness (PATH) Program, aimed at mentally ill homeless people. These changes stressed coordination of services and programs, and ending and preventing homelessness, as opposed to amelioration. This trend was continued and expanded with the Clinton Administration's adoption of a "Continuum of Care" (CoC) approach for the McKinney housing and shelter programs, beginning in 1994 (ICH 1994:68–75). As initially formulated, the CoC approach emphasized community-wide coordination and linkages between housing and services (Barnard-Columbia 1996:1). By awarding most funding to programs

that applied as part of a "consolidated" CoC application submitted by a local or state-wide coalition, the federal government drastically altered the way in which local communities were approaching homelessness, effectively requiring communities to come together, minimize duplication and turf wars, and plan how to match local funds to federal dollars (Burt et al. 2002:5–7).

Under CoC, the Emergency Shelter Grants program remained as a formula program, but funding was combined for the three competitive McKinney programs administered by HUD: Supportive Housing (mainly for creation of transitional housing with services for families and disabled people); Shelter Plus Care (mainly aimed at providing permanent housing with services for homeless people with disabilities); and Section 8 Moderate Rehabilitation Single Room Occupancy Program (to increase the supply of SRO units; supportive services are optional). Vastly increased funding was pledged, especially from HUD, much of it for programs that went beyond amelioration. Whereas one-fourth of McKinney HUD allocations in 1990 went to emergency housing and one-half to transitional housing, by 1995, only 16 percent of new allocations were going to emergency housing, 37 percent to transitional housing and almost 50 percent to permanent housing (calculated from data in Barnard-Columbia 1996:22). The National Survey of Homeless Assistance Providers and Clients, the most comprehensive national survey to date, found that while emergency shelter units had grown by 21 percent from 1988 to 1996, the number of transitional and permanent housing units for homeless people created with McKinney funding had "exploded," from "basically none in 1988 to 274,200 by 1996." According to these data, by 1996, permanent housing accounted for almost 19 percent of all HUD McKinney programs (shelter, transitional housing and permanent housing) serving homeless people (Burt 2001:243–244).

Much of the initial emphasis of the CoC strategy was on transitional housing. For example, in 1995, the proposed number of persons to be assisted in transitional housing initiatives was about four times as great as the number to be assisted in permanent housing, only in part a reflection of the greater turnover in transitional programs; growth in the number of people supplied with permanent housing, while very impressive, was only about two-thirds that of growth in transitional housing (Barnard-Columbia 1996:18). Most of the permanent housing created was for those already homeless, rather than for prevention. Of the four major McKinney HUD programs, only the smallest, the Section 8 Moderate Rehabilitation Single Room Occupancy Program, had as at least one part of its mandate creation of permanent housing for people who may not yet be homeless. Through the mid-1990s, the other programs grew three to nine times as quickly; the largest (Supportive Housing) served a hundred times as many people (calculated from data in Barnard-Columbia 1996:29).

The CoC process evolved through the 1990s and beyond. While initially the main goal of CoC was "to assist *homeless* individuals and families to move to self-sufficiency, to the extent possible, and to permanent housing" (Barnard-Columbia 1996:9, emphasis added), as currently formulated, a full CoC ideally also includes prevention.[6] According to a 2002 Urban Institute study of 25 CoCs, most of the systems studied incorporated prevention strategies; some also included efforts to incorporate mainstream services in the CoC (Burt et al. 2002).[7] These changes were driven by new federal policies and incentives: In 2000, Congress required that 30 percent of McKinney shelter and housing funds be used to provide permanent supportive housing for homeless persons and required grantees to coordinate and integrate their programs with "mainstream" programs, again through amendments to the appropriations bill, thus seeking to connect assistance to homeless people to the much greater resources provided by the "mainstream" anti-poverty programs. Congress also added discharge planning activities as an eligible use of emergency shelter grants.

Amendments to the McKinney Education of Homeless Children and Youth program, made as part of its reauthorization in 2001, shifted that program's focus as well. Requirements that homeless children be integrated into the mainstream public school system—rather than segregated in separate schools—were strengthened,

as were requirements that children be allowed to continue in the school they attended before becoming homeless rather than made to transfer to a school in whatever district they were then living. Also strengthened was a requirement that schools coordinate school placement with shelter or other housing placement, laying the groundwork for greater overall coordination of homeless families' needs. Funding for the program was increased substantially as well (Jullianelle and Foscarinis 2003).

Perhaps most dramatically, in 2002, President Bush (in proposing the FY2003 HUD budget) declared "ending chronic homelessness in the next decade a top objective" of his administration (OMB 2002:179). This policy emphasis was accompanied by revitalization of the Interagency Council on the Homeless, which had lost its funding and lain dormant for years, and the appointment of a homeless advocate to direct it. While limited to "chronically" homeless people—those who are homeless over long periods of time and generally have multiple problems, such as mental disability or substance abuse—and thus excluding the vast majority of homeless families and children, these steps are significant.

As publicly stated commitments, at least, these mark a shift in national policy and are a dramatic contrast to the policy of the earlier conservative administration of Ronald Reagan. The new rhetoric helps shift public debate away from merely ameliorating the conditions of homeless life to aiding exit from homelessness and ultimately prevention of homelessness altogether. As such, they present opportunities for advocates to press for new policies and funding to meet these goals.

Nonetheless, these commitments have remained rhetorical. They have not been accompanied by significant new funding; indeed, the Administration has actually proposed cuts in McKinney-Vento programs. To date (mid-2005), the Administration has announced $55 million in funds for its new "Collaborative Initiative to End Chronic Homelessness" to fund additional supportive housing for disabled homeless people, cobbled together from discretionary funds from HUD, the Department of Health and Human Services (HHS) and the

Department of Veterans Affairs[8]; an additional $13.5 million in HUD and Department of Labor funds has been made available for housing and employment programs for persons experiencing chronic homelessness. In FY2005, the Administration requested a $70 million appropriation for its "Samaritan" initiative, which would continue this effort, with $50 million proposed for HUD and $10 million each for HHS and the Department of Veterans Affairs; however, this request was not funded by Congress. As outlined above, proposed FY2006 funding for McKinney-Vento includes an increase of just over $200 million; most of this would go to an expansion of the HUD McKinney-Vento programs.

Further, the revitalized Interagency Council on Homelessness has devoted most of its efforts to pressing state and local governments to respond to homelessness. Following the White House commitment to end chronic homelessness in ten years, the Council challenged cities to develop plans to do so; according to the Council, as of this writing, 200 have committed to develop such plans.[9] Advocates have criticized the Council for this focus, noting that the Council's primary, statutorily mandated mission is to coordinate and lead the federal response to homelessness. In fact, however, despite the Administration's emphasis on plans to end homelessness, there is no such federal plan in place or in process.

At the same time, Administration actions and proposals affecting anti-poverty and social programs threaten increases to the causes of homelessness. The demolition of public housing without one-for-one replacement pushes more low-income people into homelessness. The increases in numbers of relatively higher-income residents admitted to public housing means fewer units available for those most at risk. Changes in Supplementary Security Income (SSI) and Social Security Disability Insurance (SSDI) disability benefits (and therefore access to Medicaid) that disqualify disability based on substance abuse have led to increases in homelessness and other hardship (Norris 2003). The repeal of welfare as an entitlement in 1996 has in some cases led to increases in family homelessness (Chicago Coalition for the Homeless 2000; NAEH 2003). As discussed above, the

Administration's proposed FY2006 budget for low-income housing programs as a whole includes significant cuts in funding. And the most recent tax cuts and defense expenditures—as well as the consequent tremendous increase in the deficit—raise the political hurdles for efforts to increase funding for discretionary anti-poverty programs.

Given this context, simply allocating limited McKinney and other federal homeless dollars to permanent housing creates an untenable conflict between two necessary tasks: aiding those already homeless and preventing those at risk from becoming homeless.[10] Engaging the "mainstream" anti-poverty programs—and insisting that they address the needs of homeless people—would certainly help programmatically; engaging those resources and the communities that care about them would also help to build political support. However, these programs are ultimately themselves inadequate, and those inadequacies—such as benefit levels that are too low to support housing costs—can contribute to causing rather than ending and preventing homelessness. To really end and prevent homelessness, these larger failures must also be addressed.

WHAT IS TO BE DONE?

Some theorists have argued that market economies will inevitably produce some homelessness (Hope and Young 1986:269), just as they will inevitably produce some unemployment. Yet the great variation in the extent of homelessness found in Western industrialized countries (Burt 2001:329; UN Centre for Human Settlements 2000:40–43) suggests that enlightened social policies can make a significant difference. What follows is a proposal for a number of such policies to ameliorate, aid exit from and prevent homelessness. While housing policies are central, other areas—particularly public assistance, employment, education and health care—are also important. Policies for exiting and preventing homelessness must be envisioned in a larger context, which in turn requires the federal government to play a leading role. But crucially, housing policy must be re-thought and, in particular, a Right to Housing must be incorporated.

While homelessness is complex, both as a mass phenomenon and in the life of a family or individual, the key lesson of the displacement school remains true: Housing lies at its crux. At the most simplistic level, if you have housing, whatever else your problems, you are not homeless; if that housing and your tenure in it are relatively stable, you are far less likely to become homeless in the foreseeable future. For instance, Shinn et al. found that "having one's own apartment and having subsidized housing were protective" against homelessness; personal characteristics, such as high school graduation, teen motherhood, work experience and "measures of disorder" made insignificant contributions to their predictive model (1998:1653). As stated by Burt and colleagues, reviewing her own and others' past research: "Every available study indicates that giving homeless people housing, through shelter plus care, vouchers, group homes, or any other mechanism, helps ensure that they will not be homeless any more" (Burt et al. 2001:323).

But housing is also crucial because many of the other problems that may contribute to, exacerbate and prolong homelessness—joblessness, substance abuse, mental illness, physical abuse, family break-up—are both far easier to withstand when housed, and are more likely and more damaging when housing is unstable or lacking and the downward cycles of homelessness have set in. As Shinn et al. note, "Where ties to the housing market are fragile, disruptions may precipitate crises" (1998:1665). Once an individual or family becomes homeless, an extra layer of problems is created on top of whatever led to the homelessness in the first place, including the search for temporary shelter, declining health, depression, threat of loss of children and loss of documents and resources. Exiting homelessness becomes more difficult as the need to simply satisfy daily basic needs, intensified and vastly complicated by homeless status, interferes with job training, education and job or housing searches. Further, dealing with a homeless individual's or family's personal problems, whatever they may be, is almost impossible without the stability provided by reliable housing (Oakley

and Dennis 1996; Fosburg et al. 1997). These downward cycles may explain in part why losing one's housing can begin a generational cycle of homelessness: Childhood homelessness increases the risk of adult homelessness later (Burt 2001:224–232; Better Homes Fund 1999:33). In short, prevention of homelessness is necessary for ending homelessness; and ensuring enough low-cost housing to meet actual (not market) need is the key to preventing homelessness.

Prevention: Housing Strategies

Our goal must be the realization of the human Right to Housing—in essence, the fulfillment of the 1949 Housing Act's goal of "a decent home and a suitable living environment" for all Americans. This requires, first, protection of existing housing and the tenancy of those already in place. On the one hand, this means protecting the units themselves and maintaining them as low-cost housing, whether this requires controlling demolition and conversion of privately owned housing or preventing government destruction of public housing without concomitant one-for-one replacement of comparably sized units. On the other hand, this means protection of tenants living in low-rent units, including protections against unjust evictions, legal assistance and mediation in landlord/tenant disputes, referral to appropriate entitlement programs and, as a final safety net, providing emergency rental and utility assistance when necessary. Inability to pay the rent or being forced to leave by the landlord are among the top four reasons for leaving the last residence prior to becoming homeless (ICH 1999:30–31; Burt 2001:66–68; Hartman and Robinson 2003).

Numerous studies—for example, Shinn et al. (1998), Burt (2001) and those cited therein—have demonstrated the crucial role subsidized housing plays in whether a family avoids or exits homelessness. Section 8 and other "demand" programs augment a tenant household's effective demand for housing by increasing the amount of rent it can pay; in theory, this can lead to new construction as the demand calls forth new supply from the market. But although crucial at this time, support for demand programs must be seen as a stop-gap measure.

Supply programs would be far more efficient. The most famous of these—public housing— has been widely condemned in this country as a total disaster, but this is a wildly inaccurate assessment of its actual effect (Bratt 1986). Preserving decent public housing through providing realistic operating subsidies and modernization funding is absolutely necessary, as is prohibiting the demolition of public housing units without prior or simultaneous one-for-one replacement. But even more promising is the wide array of other models for expanding the supply of housing permanently outside the private market, controlled by those living within it (see Chapter 11).

The component of Section 8 that has led most directly to production—project-based subsidized (but privately owned) housing—has achieved some modest success in spurring production of below-market housing, but much of that housing faces threat of reversion to unregulated status, and thus market-level rents, through expiring use and contracts. Beginning in 2000, housing, anti-homelessness and other anti-poverty advocates launched a campaign for a National Housing Trust Fund, with the goal of producing, rehabilitating and preserving a total of 1.5 million additional units of low-income housing over ten years; a key element of the proposal is creation of a dedicated federal funding stream for low-income housing. While this alone would not close the gap between need for and availability of affordable housing—estimated at 4.7 million units (Joint Center for Housing Studies of Harvard University 2003:28)—it would be a major step forward. Legislation based on the proposal was introduced in Congress in 2002 and 2003 (Bernstein and Saraf 2003) and as of mid-2005 is pending.

Regulatory reforms are required in order to ensure that, once funded, affordable housing can actually be sited. Local exclusionary zoning laws designed to prevent "undesirable" kinds of housing (such as supportive housing, shared housing or low-income housing in general) should be modified at the state or federal level, and existing fair housing protections should be better enforced. Models that emphasize community outreach and education,

with a view toward nonadversarial resolution of Not In My Back Yard (NIMBY) opposition, should be promoted as well. More proactively, inclusionary zoning laws should be enacted to promote the development of affordable housing.

Some policies confront important but mutually contradictory goals. For instance, diversifying the income levels of those in public housing, as mandated in the 1998 Housing Act, is certainly a good idea for many reasons—as it would be in any community. Yet instituting such a policy through lowering the percentage of very-low-income applicants who get priority in a project will undoubtedly expose more vulnerable families to homelessness, while slightly better-off families get available units. When a pie is too small, there will always be such irresolvable dilemmas. This is true of regulations governing who should get priority for scarce units, as it is for competition between the funding needs for forms of housing aimed at amelioration, exit or prevention. Without the realization of the human Right to Housing (see Chapter 8), we will continue to play a game of musical chairs.

Prevention: Nonhousing Strategies

Housing is a necessary condition for ending homelessness but not sufficient for dealing with the many problems that underlie or accompany homelessness and poverty generally. The most promising initiatives to prevent homelessness combine housing with programs aimed at employment, public assistance, social services and health services.

The issues involved are complex and interrelated. This is true not only for those immediately confronting homelessness but also for those a step or two away. Homelessness prevention initiatives necessarily involve measures that deal with poverty and its components generally, policies that affect the far larger pool of people from which the significant but relatively small group of people who actually become homeless is drawn. While the policies for ameliorating and exiting homelessness discussed below have important components tied to the homeless state of the people for whom they are aimed, prevention policies are much more broadly based and apply to far greater numbers within the general population.

Employment. Over the course of a month, 44 percent of homeless people report working full- or part-time, according to the most recent comprehensive national survey on homelessness (ICH 1999:29). Clearly, employment in and of itself may not prevent homelessness. According to an analysis of 2002 Census data, nearly two-thirds of all poor families with children included a worker in that year (Center on Budget and Policy Priorities 2003). In 2004, the average hourly wage a worker needed in order to earn enough income to be able to rent the average two-bedroom apartment available on the open market while spending only 30 percent of that income on housing (the legal maximum in federal housing programs such as Section 8 and public housing as well as the government's suggested limit for others) was $15.37, almost three times the minimum wage. (NLIHC 2004a).

Adequate income is the other side of housing affordability: No housing unit is affordable if a person's income is too low in relation to its cost. To prevent homelessness, the minimum wage should be set at a level that ensures that, when combined with the Earned Income Tax Credit, households can afford adequate housing in their area without paying more than 30 percent of their income on rent. The conservative fear that raising the minimum wage will lead to economic chaos has proven unfounded each time it has been raised (Bernstein and Schmitt 2000:19–20; Harrington 1984:111). In addition, the Earned Income Tax Credit can be further increased to ensure that income is sufficient to pay for housing and prevent homelessness, and expanded outreach is necessary to make poor people aware of the credit and assist them in claiming it when eligible.

Training and education must also be available to ensure that those who are capable of working can actually do so; this not only helps to prevent homelessness, it also makes eminent sense societally. For such efforts to succeed, however, the conditions that make training and education possible must be met: adequate training pay, affordable child care[11] and transportation assistance. Moreover, training must be linked to placement in jobs that pay wages sufficient to afford housing either through hiring incentives or other inducements to the private sector or through government-created jobs.[12]

For employment strategies to effectively prevent homelessness, training and education can only be a first step. Health care, child care, transportation and adequate wages must be assured, as illustrated by studies of the impact of the 1996 welfare reform legislation. For example, an Illinois study reported that of those families who left welfare for work, only 37 percent were employed continuously six to eight months later, 25 percent had difficulty buying food, 31 percent had difficulty paying for child care, 30 percent had no health insurance and 21 percent reported being unable to pay the rent at least one time since exiting Temporary Assistance for Needy Families (TANF) (Lewis et al. 2000). Without such supports, training alone risks creating another game of musical chairs in which a few are able to gain the employment sufficient to prevent homelessness, while others are left behind in low-wage jobs without support—and at risk of homelessness.

Public Assistance and Social Services. For those who are unable to work, safety net programs are essential to preventing homelessness. Economic growth alone cannot provide for those whose ability to work is diminished or precluded by individual or family problems or disabilities. Current safety net programs must be reformed so that they provide true protection against homelessness and so those in need of them are actually able to receive them.

Key programs include SSI and SSDI for disabled people. Despite the high proportion of physically and mentally disabled people among the homeless population, only 14 percent receive these benefits; because Medicaid or Medicare generally follow, this gap is doubly significant. Food stamps and TANF are also important safety net programs, but homeless people often fail to receive these as well. Complicated application processes, lack of information about the programs and address requirements keep eligible homeless people from receiving benefits under these programs (Rosen 2001; U.S. GAO 2000). Reform efforts are under way to make these resources more available to homeless people: For example, in response to advocacy and Congressional directive, the Social Security Administration in 2002 released a plan to remove barriers to SSI and SSDI for homeless people. In 2003, Congress appropriated $8 million to fund demonstration grants for outreach and application assistance (House Report 2003).

Discharge planning for those who are institutionalized is another important prevention strategy, as those being released from hospitals, mental institutions, prisons or jails without resources or housing are at imminent risk of becoming homeless. The dramatic increase in the prison and jail populations in the last decade makes this concern particularly pressing: According to the most recent data, each year some 600,000 prisoners are released from prisons (Beck, Karberg and Harrison 2002:7); millions more are released from jails. (National Commission on Correctional Health Care 2002). Persons in state systems of care, such as youth aging out of foster care, should also be included in discharge planning. This is especially important, since childhood experience of foster care is known to be a risk factor for later homelessness (Burt 2001:332; ICH 1999:52).

A pre-release program established by federal law in 1986 allows eligible institutionalized persons to apply for SSI, SSDI or food stamps prior to release, with the explicit aim of preventing such persons from becoming homeless (Homeless Eligibility Clarification Act 1986; NLCHP 2003). However, the program is voluntary; to implement it, institutions must enter into agreements with social service agencies, and few have done so to date (Rosen et al. 2001). This program should be expanded to include housing in the prerelease process, and it should be publicized and have incentives established so that all institutions participate in it. Planning for youth exiting foster care should also include planning for housing, job training and placement or education and any benefits for which the youth is eligible (Massachusetts Shelter and Housing Alliance 1999).

Mental Illness and Substance Abuse. As with public assistance and social service programs generally, key issues for prevention of homelessness among those with mental illnesses and problems of substance abuse are coordination,

organization and availability of services, levels of aid and outreach. Deinstitutionalization led to a vacuum of responsibility in which there was little overall direction or coordination from the federal to local level.

Deinstitutionalization as a national policy was based on the premise that 2,000 community board-and-care facilities would be built; fewer than 800 actually materialized (Torrey 1995). A crucial component for a coherent policy is the willingness of communities to allow supportive housing to be established locally so that there is an alternative to the streets for those discharged from mental hospitals and other institutions who cannot move back with family. The great success of McKinney Act Supportive Housing and PATH programs in caring for mentally ill homeless people illustrates the necessity of having adequate supportive housing for those at risk of homelessness. Humane and cost-efficient substance abuse policies follow along these same lines: Help should be universally available (as opposed to our present two-tier system in which poorer people have little chance of receiving real help); intervention and outreach should be stressed.

Of course, one of the most important steps toward prevention of homelessness associated with substance abuse and mental health problems—and physical health problems as well—would be establishment of universal health coverage. Inability to work and exorbitant medical costs due to any of these disabilities means disaster, including the possibility of eventual homelessness, for the more than 24 percent of all low-income people without health insurance (Center on Budget and Policy Priorities 2003). In the meantime, access to Medicaid and Medicare must be increased, and the aid provided must be expanded.

Overall, a number of principles regarding supportive services are important for any prevention strategy:

First, early intervention is essential; increased outreach and application assistance, if needed, for all programs can help to ensure this.

Second, at each level of government, simplification and coordination of services should be maximized. Caseworkers should be assigned to clients, not to programs: Having a single caseworker who a client can turn to, whatever the issue or program, greatly increases the likelihood that a client will receive the services to which he or she is entitled, avoiding crisis (Rosenthal 1994:156–157; Chicago Coalition for the Homeless 2000).

Third, benefit levels should be sufficient to allow recipients to afford housing and other basic necessities, and should be indexed to inflation; accumulation of savings should not affect eligibility or assistance levels until they are great enough to assure a family of stability, should unforeseen crises arise.

Fourth, family integrity must be truly supported. Policies that encourage the break-up of families or other mutually supportive households—such as moving children from impoverished but otherwise viable families into foster homes while their parents go to emergency shelters, instead of supplying emergency financial assistance to avoid eviction—should be discontinued.[13]

Finally, to the greatest extent possible, assistance should be delivered through universal programs (with varying benefit levels defined by need). A single income support program, such as a negative income tax, would be a far simpler and more complete way of accomplishing income stability (Ellwood 1988; Tobin 1966). Universal programs would also help to counter the divisiveness and stigma now associated with welfare and other public assistance programs, and emphasize that in contemporary society no one is truly "self-sufficient" (see Chapter 18).

EXITING HOMELESSNESS FOR THOSE CURRENTLY HOMELESS

While prevention strategies by their very nature are aimed at all those who are at risk of homelessness, exit strategies can be aimed at a much smaller group and thus require comparatively modest programs. But homelessness itself so complicates the lives of those it catches that solutions become much more difficult to implement.

Exiting homelessness for those already homeless must begin with finding housing of some sort, from shelter to transitional to long-term.

Housing provides the stability and sense of permanence necessary for gathering the energy and resources needed to make the journey back to independence. Take employment, for example. Studies indicate that the vast majority of homeless people want to work, and that in fact many do (Rosenthal 1994:215nn; ICH 1999:29;). But while the housed poor job-seeker may need training, day care help, transportation and even training pay, each of these is likely to be more critical and harder to meet for the homeless job-seeker. Beyond that, he or she will also need a place to get clean, do laundry, get some rest, perhaps type up a resume and provide a "home" phone and address to put on an application—all to give the appearance of stability and reliability that an employer will demand. Finally, time will need to be devoted to survival needs, such as finding food and shelter. Thus, the most successful job-training and employment programs for homeless people (including programs for those with substance abuse problems or mental illness) are those that also supply housing and other necessary services (NLCHP 1995:23–33; ICP 1998b:19–25; Rog and Holupka 1998; Pew Partnership 2002). Of course, job training without job creation and job placement is insufficient.

Similarly, social services that are linked to housing are much more successful than services offered alone.[14] A growing "housing first" approach by some providers and policy advocates posits that, rather than requiring people to move sequentially from shelter to transitional housing to permanent housing, permanent housing should be provided as quickly as possible and any needed services should be provided at that housing (Beyond Shelter 2003; Pew Partnership 2002). Treatment for ailments, from respiratory disease to mental illness to drug abuse, is difficult, if not impossible, without providing some kind of stability for patients; indeed, it does little good to treat any illnesses if the basic survival needs of people are not met (Garrett 1989; Shipley et al. 1989). Follow-up case management is also essential.

Beyond services, homeless people need money, but they are less likely to be receiving the public assistance they are entitled to than are other poor people (Rosenthal 1994; ICH

1999:29–30; Burt 2001:202). Centralization and coordination of assistance programs is perhaps even more essential to reach homeless people than precariously housed poor people, and having a single entry point, easily accessible and with minimal screening barriers, is extremely valuable. Worker-client ties must supersede worker-program ties. Aggressive outreach, not only to those in shelters but to those on the streets, is necessary, but outreach to doubled-up families and others hiding within more traditional residences needs to be pursued in ways that will not expose them to eviction should their presence come to the attention of private landlords or public housing authorities. Exit through the public assistance system would also be facilitated if all local offices were realistic about the mismatch of some regulations to the conditions of homelessness, in particular relaxing proof-of-residency requirements, regulations regarding documentation (such as birth certificates) that homeless people are unlikely to be able to readily provide and restrictions on savings (NLCHP 2004a).

But most people will not be able to exit homelessness through public assistance alone, given the levels now established. To make this possible, benefits should be set at levels that allow renting of decent housing by spending 30 percent or less of household income. Given that renting a new home often requires paying first and last months' rent and a deposit up front, homeless people in particular should not have entitlements cut due to savings needed to cover three times rent plus a reasonable contingency fund for emergencies. Further, social services and material aid should remain in place for a period of time after permanent housing has been obtained, in order to help prevent relapse into poverty and homelessness. These strategies must seek to support families (however defined); social service policies should always encourage families or other supportive households to stay together and never offer incentives for desertion.

The mentally disabled homeless population is arguably the most difficult to aid. Outreach can be most difficult here but also most crucial. Again, housing (as well as other necessities) is essential, both for its psychic impor-

tance and because it provides the chance for an ongoing patient-doctor relationship. Programs specifically aimed at creating supportive housing for mentally disabled people and those which create or preserve the type of housing traditionally used by mentally ill people (such as SROs) must be protected and expanded; for some, transitioning into independent living is an unrealistic hope, and long-term supportive housing is necessary. In either case, ensuring that homeless people receive the disability and health care benefits to which they are entitled under the Social Security Act is crucial.

Exiting homelessness for those who are dependent on substances requires similar steps: outreach on their home turfs, stable housing as a first step, ensuring receipt of assistance for which they are eligible and combining substance abuse treatment with other necessary social services—all within a coordinated system that ties workers to clients and delegates responsibility from a central agency. The success of substance abuse treatment is severely restricted when those completing a program have no stable housing to return to and therefore no nexus of support services (Wittman 1989; Shipley et al. 1989; Rog and Holupka 1998; Pew Partnership 2002). Therefore, housing linked to post-detoxification services is imperative. At the federal level, a small demonstration program to fund substance abuse treatment specifically for homeless people was created in 2001; expanding these resources to meet the need would advance the health and well-being of both housed and homeless people.

Finally, exiting homelessness may be thought of in the long term. Between 900,000 and 1.4 million children are homeless annually (Burt 2001). Childhood homelessness increases the risk of adult homelessness (Burt 2001). Increasing the stability of these children, and ensuring their education, would help to prevent them from becoming homeless adults. The McKinney-Vento Act, especially after the 2001 amendments, is an important tool for ensuring that homeless children have access to school and school services, such as meals. Federal funding to local schools to provide extraordinary attention to homeless children's school needs, including nutrition, books and transportation, should continue and be expanded, and federal oversight to ensure state and local implementation should be increased.

AMELIORATING HOMELESSNESS

If we are not to play musical chairs forever, our approach to homelessness must emphasize prevention strategies. And yet this involves a dilemma, since the need is so real and immediate for those already homeless. Homelessness is a severely traumatic event for virtually all who experience it. That trauma is easily seen by looking at homeless children—for example, 47 percent manifest problems such as depression, anxiety and withdrawal (Better Homes Fund 1999:13); children who change schools due to unplanned moves, such as those associated with homelessness, score lower on standardized tests and have lower academic achievement (Better Homes Fund 1999:23; Julianelle and Foscarinis 2003:42). Homeless adults show similarly distressed portraits, in some cases the cause of their homelessness but also as a result. Both the moral imperative and the social and fiscal costs of inaction mandate that we help those who are caught now in the downward cycles of homelessness. While exiting homelessness must be the focus for the individual homeless person or family, if immediate placement in housing is not possible, a humane society will, in the meantime, provide a number of baseline guarantees:

First, immediate placement in safe and appropriate shelter, with a minimum of bureaucratic trappings, followed as quickly as possible by placement in permanent housing, with services, if needed and appropriate.

Second, food and clothing.

Third, centralization of local services in a single office to the greatest extent possible.

Fourth, health care, particularly preventative health care. The health profile of homeless populations is truly shocking: The infant mortality rate for children born to homeless mothers in New York City is twice that of the population in general (ICP 1998a:6), while over one-half of homeless children suffer from a chronic health condition (ICP 1998a:60). Homeless peo-

ple in general suffer from very poor health (Burt 2001:80). The greatest preventive health measure we could provide to homeless people would be to assure them of the basic necessities of food, clothing and housing; in the meantime, health care needs to be guided by two (by now familiar) overarching principles: prevention and outreach. Homeless people often avoid treatment until their medical conditions become too serious to ignore, causing distress to themselves and additional costs to taxpayers for eventual treatment. As with public assistance and mental health work, outreach must extend to where homeless people are rather than waiting for them to avail themselves of those services that are in place. Treatment programs must allow easy entry without invasion of privacy or significant monetary costs. Further, health care will never be successful without stable housing for recovering patients which affords protection from the elements as well as the possibility for a stable relationship with a health care professional. Until such time as universal health care becomes a reality, and perhaps even beyond, health care for homeless people will require a great deal of flexibility and outreach, already apparent in many of the projects funded by the McKinney Health Care for the Homeless Program and the related Consolidated Heath Center Programs.

Fifth, opportunities to work. The extra series of barriers that lack of a home base presents to homeless job-seekers can best be overcome by locally created job centers that provide a home base, combining laundry, storage and shower facilities with the "home" address and phone that are so necessary to find work. Informal day labor markets, notorious exploiters of homeless people, need to be regulated.

Sixth, respect for the civil rights of homeless people. As a class, homeless people endure abridgment of their civil rights that would be unthinkable for most other groups: barriers to their children's education, dispersal from downtown areas, and resistance to their right to vote, receive medical care or receive local entitlements. In particular, laws prohibiting "public sleeping" or "public camping" should be removed in any locality that cannot demonstrate an available place in a decent and appropriate shelter for every homeless person seeking one.

Added together and including the crucial component of low-cost housing, the kinds of strategies to ameliorate, facilitate exit from and prevent homelessness sketched here create a comprehensive "continuum" that also delineates basic elements of a Right to Housing. Along with the principles of coordination, prevention, stability and outreach that have been stressed, such a holistic approach should exhibit the following characteristics:

- easy entrance and minimal screening at entry levels;
- encouraging empowerment and a sense of efficacy in clients;[15]
- effective aftercare—services that have helped a family or individual exit or stave off homelessness must be available for some time after the crisis in order to avoid relapse into crisis.

Programs to ameliorate and exit homelessness for small groups of people have been more readily funded (comparatively speaking) than prevention programs, mainly because their price tags are smaller—or appear to be. Providing a shelter meal and a cot intuitively seems less expensive than subsidizing precariously housed people in permanent housing, but available evidence suggests otherwise. A New York City study of supportive housing for homeless people with severe mental illness found that reduced use of acute care services nearly offset the cost of the housing. (Culhane, Metraux and Hadley 2002). The National Law Center on Homelessness & Poverty estimated that incarceration in a jail costs almost twice as much as a bed in a shelter (NLCHP 1998:1, citing U.S. Department of Justice 1995:10). To the extent that prevention requires additional resources, such as construction of new housing, costs will obviously be higher. These too, however, may be seen as being cost-effective, perhaps not in actual financial savings but certainly in the decrease in human suffering and the increase in quality of life for us all.

In addition to potential cost savings, another key to the adoption and success of prevention programs—which necessarily much be aimed at a much broader population—is to present them as universal programs. Of course, level of benefits will vary by income. But the great difference in the way people generally perceive Social Security (and other non–meanstested programs) as an earned right, but "welfare" (and other means-tested programs) as a charity, speaks eloquently to the need to move toward non–means-tested programs generally.

THE ROLE OF THE FEDERAL GOVERNMENT

The past decade has seen important changes in homeless initiatives. Among those have been the increases in total funding and adoption of the Continuum of Care approach by the federal government. More recently, the increased focus on housing as a long-term solution, the commitment to end "chronic homelessness," and the revitalization of the Interagency Council on Homelessness offer at least the possibility of progress. These initiatives must continue and expand, and the commitment must be extended to all homeless people as well as backed up and implemented with the allocation of substantial new funds. Even more important, housing and other anti-poverty programs must not be cut but rather bolstered so that they prevent poor people from becoming homeless.

Moreover, the size of the problem, the limits on local resources, and localities' fears that they will become a magnet for low-income people all point to the importance of a substantial federal role in funding. Further, the kind of coordination, centralization and linking of services advocated here can only be imposed by the highest level of government. The success of the Continuum of Care approach in leveraging local dollars and inducing previously reluctant individual programs to adopt a community-wide approach is powerful evidence of the persuasiveness of federal funding guidelines in encouraging necessary regional thinking.

One of the great problems in mounting meaningful initiatives to deal with homelessness has been the diffusion of responsibility referred to above. Localities know that there is no necessary connection between where a person becomes homeless and where he or she receives help, or between where a homeless person receives help and where he or she resumes life as a contributing taxpayer. Only the national government is able to truly realize the cost efficiency of preventing homelessness in the long run. Only the federal government is able to avoid the diffusion of responsibility, by declaring homelessness a national problem requiring a nationally funded and administered—but locally directed—attack.

Finally, the federal government bears a good deal of responsibility for the explosion of homelessness. It not only failed to control the private market forces that were destroying low-cost housing, it (and local governments) abetted them while largely withdrawing its commitments to public and other low-income housing, a national mental health system and a real safety net.

Within overall federal resources and strategies, local governments, nonprofit groups and other private entities have significant tasks. The first is to implement federal programs locally, since, despite the similarities in roots of homelessness across the nation, local conditions are different in important particulars. Only those familiar with each local situation (including, of course, local homeless people) can steer resources efficiently. The second task is to develop and carry out local policies that do not exclude, but rather promote and include, needed housing and services, and leverage additional local resources to supplement federal aid. But while doing so, local governments and other interested parties must be engaged in the third task: constantly lobbying national policymakers for whatever changes are necessary, as discovered in practice at the local level, and for the truly significant funding that will be necessary to adequately fight homelessness and house the nation. While homelessness is largely created by national policies, it is at the local level that it is most sharply felt.

In the late 1990s, the Clinton Administration hailed the new federal budget surplus, arguing that it would allow a progressive national agenda in regard to both homelessness and housing to emerge (NLIHC 1999b). Since that time, the political and fiscal landscape has shifted dramatically, and advocates now fear that the growing deficit—resulting from tax refunds and military expenditures—will trump claims for social justice. Legal entitlements provide much stronger (though not necessarily permanent) protection amidst the vicissitudes of budgets and politicians.

One of the clearest and most powerful ways to place housing above partisanship would be for the federal government to declare housing a right, as have numerous governmental bodies across the world (NLCHP 2004b; Foscarinis 2000; see also Chapter 8). Step by torturous step, federal policy has recognized how crucial housing stability is—to disabled veterans to battered women to substance abusers to those with mental illnesses and so forth. Viewed through a housing rights lens—and defined and conceptualized as such—this kind of incremental prioritizing of groups can also be seen as movement toward recognition of a Right to Housing. Simply declaring a Right to Housing or a goal of universal access is insufficient, of course: It must be backed up by action and adequate funding.

According to the most recent reliable estimates, some 2.5 to 3.5 million people are now homeless in the United States during the course of each year (Burt 2001:49–50); at a given point in time, some 840,000 are homeless (according to figures obtained in a 1996 survey—Burt 2001:50–51). While emergency shelter and especially transitional and permanent housing programs for homeless people grew dramatically during the 1990s, in 1996, total capacity was not quite 608,000 beds (Burt 2001:243–244). Simply reacting to each new case will not close this gap.

Three out of ten American households now have housing affordability problems (see Chapter 2); of that number, 14.3 million are severely cost-burdened, paying over 50 percent of income for housing (Joint Center for Housing Studies 2003:25). We can continue to have people falling in and out of homelessness, some of them recovering and going on to lead mainstream lives, others sucked into a whirlpool that drags them and others, including their children, down. Or we can decide a civilized nation ensures that every resident is adequately housed.

As a strategy for ending and preventing homelessness, declaring a Right to Housing makes programmatic sense; it may make economic sense as well. Prevention is very likely a cost-effective strategy, given the costs of ameliorating and exiting homelessness once it has already occurred—to say nothing of the costs of the alternatives of crisis response and incarceration—and it additionally promises to return money to the various levels of government through the re-establishment of independent, self-sufficient taxpayers. But further, declaring a Right to Housing has the strength of all universal programs: It's in the interests of the vast majority of Americans. Affordable housing has become an issue for working- and middle-class people as well as those living in poverty.

As a nation, we need to reconsider how we think of housing: Is it a right or a privilege? As with public education, the argument for housing as a guaranteed right is that it is good for both the individual and the society as a whole. As with public education, we can guarantee everyone a decent standard without preventing those who want a superior standard from obtaining it for themselves.

Finally, a declaration of a Right to Housing and its fulfillment would avoid one of the most unfortunate effects of much homelessness legislation: As "special interest" legislation, it creates a backlash from those who feel they too have a just claim on resources (as in local fights between homeless and precariously housed people over priorities for subsidized and public housing).

Despite much talk in the last few years about a "hardening" of public opinion concerning homeless people, the review of public opinion polls by Link and his colleagues indicates that "most Americans would be willing to pay more in taxes to help homeless people, and that an even higher percentage favor increased government spending on the problem....Moreover, most members of the public believe the federal government should do things like build more affordable housing for poor people and give rent subsidies to people who need them" (1995:551). But, as they also argue, such attitudes are not firm: Political leaders can manipulate them in a number of directions. It is therefore necessary to mount a political coalition with enough clout

to convince politicians that social approaches to homelessness and a Right to Housing are popular stances.

Homeless activism was, on one level, quite successful in the 1980s, altering public opinion and successfully pressing the case for a social, rather than police, response to homelessness. But it is unlikely the movement against homelessness can do much more unless and until it makes alliances with other segments of the population on issues of housing, employment, public assistance and social services. A Right to Housing suggests itself as one of the most important struggles for homeless activists and advocates at this time. Prevention is the key to ending homelessness, and housing is the key to prevention.

NOTES

Acknowledgment: Maria Foscarinis is grateful for the assistance of Meagan Leatherbury.

1. Some disaffiliation theorists tied their more individualistic and psychological explanations of homelessness to structural frameworks; see, for example, Bahr (1973). For a recent argument that the Disaffiliation School as a whole was actually structuralist in orientation, see Main (1998).

2. This policy was criticized by advocates, and a new initiative was announced to provide housing assistance to people who were previously homeless or receiving housing assistance. See U.S. Department of Housing and Urban Development, Jackson and Chertoff Announce Comprehensive Transitional Housing Assistance program for Katrina Evacuees. Sept. 23, 2005.

3. For a fine debunking of the related proposition that "welfare magnets" attract poor people in general, see Hanson and Hartman (1994).

4. The change was made in 2000, following the untimely death of Rep. Bruce Vento, an original co-sponsor and author of the legislation and major Congressional champion of aid for homeless people.

5. The Homeless Eligibility Clarification Act (HECA), enacted in 1986, consisted of other small parts of the original advocacy agenda. These were aimed at removing barriers to homeless persons' receipt of "mainstream" benefits—though they did not remove barriers in the application process. HECA also included a "prerelease" program that was intended to keep poor people leaving institutions from becoming homeless upon exit. Federal reports had already sounded the note that "it is more cost-effective and

certainly less disruptive to assist people before they become homeless, than to serve their needs after they become homeless" (GAO 1990:11, cited in NLCHP 1995:5)

6. As indicated by its name, the CoC approach envisions a "continuum" of programs, beginning with outreach and shelter, then moving to "transitional" housing (defined to be include a two-year time limit), and then to permanent housing. Advocates and providers are increasingly promoting a "housing first" approach that seeks to place people as quickly as possible into permanent housing.

7. These numbers are not nationally representative, however, because the study looked specifically at the most developed continuums (Burt et al. 2002).

8. An additional $6.5 million reallocated HOME funds are being targeted toward this effort and $13.5 million in Department of Veterans Affairs and Department of Labor funds for an employment initiative for homeless veterans.

9. In the Cities and Counties: Nation's 200th 10-Year Planning Partnership Launched in Reno, Nevada, Interagency Council on Homelessness website, updated September 28, 2005.

10. In 2003, a survey of large cities found that 30 percent of requests for emergency shelter went unmet (U.S. Conference of Mayors 2003a).

11. ICP notes that one in three unemployed homeless parents interviewed in metropolitan New York shelters cited lack of appropriate and affordable child care as the reason for their current unemployment (ICP 1998a:57–58).

12. As there is an argument to be made for a Right to Housing, so is there for a policy of full employment, with the government as employer of last resort. (See Harrington 1984; Ginsburg 1983; Levison 1980.)

13. In the long run, the United States needs to move toward the kind of integrated family policies found in many European countries, which include family allowances to help cover the costs of child-rearing, quality state-run child care centers, family planning services, and maternity and health benefits. Such a system effectively strengthens family units to prevent crises rather than responding to crises when vulnerable families begin to break apart.

14. This, however, raises a difficult problem: Should housing be contingent on accepting services? Though one is tempted in some situations to agree, respect for all people's right to determine such matters for themselves and the practical fact that requirements of any kind tend to reduce program use suggest offering, but not requiring, service use.

15. This means putting into practice the 1992 amendment to the McKinney Act, which requires the involvement of homeless people "to the maximum extent practicable." Homeless people should help design,

oversee and run programs as well as each individual or family exercising as much initiative as feasible.

REFERENCES

Bahr, Howard. 1973. *Skid road.* New York: Oxford University Press.

Barnard-Columbia Center for Urban Policy. 1996. *The continuum of care.* Washington, DC: U.S. Department of Housing and Urban Development.

Baum, Alice S., and Donald W. Burnes. 1993. *A nation in denial.* Boulder, CO: Westview.

Beck, Allen J., Jennifer C. Karberg and Paige M. Harrison. 2002. Prison and jail inmates at midyear 2001. Washington, DC: U.S. Department of Justice, Bureau of Justice Programs.

Bernstein, Jared, and John Schmitt. 1998. Making work pay. Washington, DC: Economic Policy Institute.

———. 2000. The impact of the minimum wage. Washington DC: Economic Policy Institute.

Bernstein, Nancy, and Irene Basloe Saraf. 2003. New rental production and the National Housing Trust Fund campaign. *Journal of Affordable Housing and Community Development Law,* Vol. 12, No. 4, Summer.

Better Homes Fund. 1999. Homeless children: America's new outcasts. Newton, MA: The Fund.

Beyond Shelter. 2003. Housing First 101, in Workshop Notebook, November 3–4.

Boston Globe. 1984. (February 1). From Mark J. Green and Gail MacColl, *Reagan's reign of error.* 1987. New York: Pantheon Books.

Bratt, Rachel G. 1986. Public housing: The controversy and contribution. In *Critical Perspectives on Housing,* Rachel G. Bratt, Chester Hartman and Ann Meyerson, eds. Philadelphia, PA: Temple University Press.

Burt, Martha R. 2001. What will it take to end homelessness? Washington DC: Urban Institute, October 1.

Burt, Martha R., Dave Pollack, Abby Sosland, Kelly S. Mikelson, Elizabeth Drapa, Kristy Greenwalt and Patrick T. Sharkey. 2002. Evaluation of continuums of care for homeless people: Final report.

Burt, Martha R., Laudan Y. Aron, Edgar Lee and Jesse Valente. 2001. *Helping America's homeless.* Washington, DC: Urban Institute.

Center on Budget and Policy Priorities. 2003. Poverty increases and median income declines for second consecutive year. www.cbpp.org/9-26-03pov.htm

Chicago Coalition for Homeless. 2000. Families hardest hit: The effects of welfare reform on homeless families. Chicago: The Coalition.

Culhane, Dennis P. 2002. New strategies and collaborations target homelessness. *Housing Facts and Findings*, Vol. 4, No. 5.

Culhane, Dennis P., Stephen Metreaux and Trevor Hadley. 2002. Public service reductions associated with placement of homeless persons with severe mental illness in supportive housing. *Housing Policy Debate*, Vol. 13, No. 1.

Ellwood, David T. 1988. *Poor support*. New York: Basic.

Fosburg, Linda B., Gretchen Locke, Laura Peck and Meryl Finkel. 1997. *National evaluation of the Shelter Plus Care Program*. Washington, DC: U.S. Department of Housing and Urban Development.

Foscarinis, Maria. 1993. Beyond homelessness: Ethics, strategy and advocacy. *St. Louis Public Law Review*, Vol. 12, No. 1.

———. 1996a. Downward spiral: Homelessness and its criminalization. *Yale Law and Policy Review*, Vol. 14, No. 1.

———. The Federal Response. 1996b. In *Homelessness in America*, ed. Jim Baumohl. Phoenix: Oryx.

———. 2000. Homeless and human rights: Towards an integrated strategy. *St. Louis Public Law Review*, Vol. 19. No. 2.

———. 2004. Homelessness, litigation and law reform strategies: A U.S. perspective. *Australian Journal of Human Rights*, Vol. 10.

Garrett, Gerald R. 1989. Alcohol problems and homelessness. *Contemporary Drug Problems*, 16:301–332.

Ginsburg, Helen. 1983. *Full employment and public policy*. Lexington, MA: Lexington.

Goffman, Erving. 1986 [1963]. *Stigma*. New York: Touchstone.

Grunberg, Jeffrey. 1998. Homelessness as a lifestyle. *Journal of Social Distress and the Homeless*, 7:241–261, October.

Guzicki, Melissa, and Paul Toro. 2002. Changes in public opinion on homelessness from 1994–2001. Annual Convention of the American Psychological Association, Chicago, IL.

Hanson, Russell L., and John T. Hartman. 1994. Do welfare magnets attract? Discussion paper no. 1028-94, Institute for Research on Poverty, University of Wisconsin–Madison.

Harrington, Michael. 1984. *The new American poverty*. New York: Holt, Rinehart and Winston.

Hartman, Chester, and Barry Zigas. 1991. What's wrong with the housing market. In *Homeless children and youth*, eds. Julee H. Kryder-Coe, Lester M. Salomon and Janice M. Molnar. New Brunswick, NJ: Transaction Publishers.

Hartman, Chester, and David Robinson. 2003. Evictions: The hidden housing problem. *Housing Policy Debate*, Vol. 14, No. 1.

Hoch, Charles, and Robert A. Slayton. 1989. *New homeless and old*. Philadelphia: Temple University Press.

Homeless Eligibility Clarification Act, P.L. No. 99-570 tit. XI, Oct. 27, 1986.

Hope, Marjorie, and James Young. 1986. *The faces of homelessness*. Lexington, MA: Lexington.

Hopper, Kim, and Jill Hamberg. 1986. The making of the new Homeless: From Skid Row to new poor, 1945–1984. In *Critical perspectives on housing*, eds. Rachel G. Bratt, Chester Hartman and Ann Meyerson. Philadelphia: Temple University Press.

House Report 108-010 (Consolidated Appropriations Resolution): PL 108-7, February 20, 2003.

Institute for Children and Poverty [ICP]. 1998a. *The cycle of family homelessness*. New York: The Institute.

———. 1998b. *Ten cities: A snapshot of family homelessness across America, 1997–1998*. New York: The Institute.

Institute for Women's Policy Research. 1995. *Welfare that works*. Washington, DC: The Institute.

Interagency Council on the Homeless (ICH). 1999. Findings of the national survey of homeless assistance providers and clients: Summary.

———. 2005. In the Cities and Counties: Nation's 200th 10-Year Planning Partnership Launched in Reno, Nevada, http://www.ich.gov.

———. n.d . Ten year plans to end chronic homelessness. http://www.ich/gov/slocal/index.html

Jencks, Christopher. 1994. *The homeless*. Cambridge, MA: Harvard University Press.

Joint Center for Housing Studies of Harvard University. 2003. The state of the nation's housing. Cambridge, MA: The Center.

Julianelle, Patricia, and Maria Foscarinis. 2003. Responding to the school mobility of children and youth experiencing homelessness: The McKinney-Vento Act and beyond. *The Journal of Negro Education*, Vol. 72, No. 1.

Levison, Andrew. 1980. *The full employment alternative*. New York: Coward, McCann, Geoghegan.

Lewis, Dan A., Kirsten L. Shook, Amy Bush Stevens, Paul Kleppner, James Lewis and Stephanie Riger. 2000. Work, welfare and well-being: An independent look at welfare reform in Illinois. University Consortium on Welfare Reform. www.jcpr.org/wpfiles/IFStechnicalreport. PDF

Lindblom, Eric. 1996. Preventing homelessness. In *Homelessness in America*, ed. Jim Baumohl. Phoenix: Oryx.

Link, Bruce G., Sharon Schwartz, Robert Moore, Jo Phelan, Elmer Struening, Ann Stueve and Mary Ellen Colten. 1995. Public knowledge, attitudes and beliefs about homeless people. *American Journal of Community Psychology*, 23(4):533–555.

Link, Bruce, Ezra Susser, Ann Stueve, Jo Phelan, Robert E. Moore and Elmer Struening. 1994. Lifetime and five-year prevalence of homelessness in the United States. *American Journal of Public Health*, 84:1907–1912.

Lowe, Eugene T. 2004. Eighty cities commit to ending chronic homelessness. Washington, DC: U.S. Conference of Mayors. www.usmayors.org/uscm/us_mayor_newspaper/documents/02_09_04/homelessness.asp

Main, Thomas. 1998. How to think about homelessness. *Journal of Social Distress and the Homeless*, 7:41–54, January.

National Association for the Advancement of Colored People, . 2003. Letter to Philip Mangano, Executive Director, Interagency Council on the Homeless, July 17. On file with authors.

National Alliance to End Homelessness. 2002. A plan to end homelessness in ten years. Washington DC: The Alliance.

National Commission on Correctional and Health Care. 2002. The Health status of soon-to-be-released inmates.

National Law Center on Homelessness & Poverty [NLCHP]. 1991. *Go directly to jail*. Washington DC: The Center.

———. 1992. *Beyond McKinney*. Washington, DC: The Center.

———. 1993. *The right to remain nowhere*. Washington, DC: The Center.

———. 1994. *No homeless people allowed*. Washington, DC: The Center.

———. 1995. *Smart programs, foolish cuts*. Washington, DC: The Center.

———. 1996. *Mean sweeps*. Washington, DC: The Center.

———. 1998. *Housing options*. Washington, DC: The Center.

———. 1999. *Out of sight, out of mind?* Washington, DC: The Center.

———. 2002. *Illegal to be homeless* (with National Coalition for the Homeless).

———. 2003. *Punishing poverty*. Washington, DC: The Center.

———. 2004a. *Photo identification barriers faced by homeless persons: The impact of September 11*. Washington, DC: The Center.

———. 2004b. *Homelessness in the United States and the human right to housing*. Washington, DC: The Center.

National Low Income Housing Coalition [NLIHC]. 2004a. Out of Reach: 2004. http://www.nlihc.org/oor2004/introduction.htm

———. 2005. 2005 Advocates Guide to Housing and Community Development Policy. http://www.nlihc.org/advocates/hudbudget.htm

Norris, Jean, Richard Scott, Richard Spieglman and Rex Green. 2003. Homelessness, hunger and material hardship among those who lost SSI. In *Contemporary drug problems*.

Oakley, Deidre, and Deborah L. Dennis. 1996. Responding to the needs of homeless people with alcohol, drug, and/or mental disorders. In *Homelessness in America*, ed. Jim Baumohl. Phoenix: Oryx.

Office of Management and Budget. 2002. Proposed FY2003 budget. http://w3.access.gpo.gov/usbudget/fy2003/pdf/bud16.pdf, viewed January 14, 2004.

———. 2003. Proposed FY2004 budget. www.whitehouse.gov/omb/budget/fy2004/hud.html, viewed January 14, 2004.

Pew Partnership. 2002. Beyond Shelter receives national recognition, May 20.

Pottinger v. Miami. 810 F. Supp. 1551, S.D. Fla. 1992.

Research Atlanta. 1984. *The impact of homelessness on Atlanta*. Atlanta: Research Atlanta.

Rog, Debra, and C. Scott Holupka. 1998. Reconnecting homeless individuals and families to the community. http:// aspe. hhs.gov/progsys/homeless/symposium/11-Reconn.htm

Rohter L. 1993. Miami meal tax to aid homeless. *New York Times*, August 3.

Roisman, Florence. 1991. Establishing a Right to Housing. *Clearinghouse Review*, Vol. 25.

Rosen, Jeremy, Rebecca Hoey and Theresa Steed. 2001. Food stamp and SSI benefits: Removing access barriers for homeless people. *Clearinghouse Review*, Vol. 34, Nos. 11–12.

Rosenthal, Rob. 1994. *Homeless in paradise*. Philadelphia: Temple University Press.

Sard, Barbara, and Will Fischer. 2003. President's budget requests insufficient funding for housing vouchers in 2004. Washington DC: Center on Budget and Policy Priorities.

Shinn, Marybeth, Beth C. Weitzman, Daniela Stojanonic, James R. Knickman, Lucila Jimenez, Lisa Duchon, Susan James and David H. Krantz. 1998. Predictors of homelessness among families in New York City. *American Journal of Public Health*, 88(11):1651–1657.

Shipley, Thomas E., Irving W. Shandler and Michael L. Penn. 1989. Treatment and research with homeless alcoholics. *Contemporary Drug Problems*, 16:505–526.

Simon, Harry. 1994. Municipal regulation of the homeless in public spaces. In *Homelessness in America*, ed. Jim Baumohl. Phoenix: Oryx.

Tobin, James. 1966. The case for an income guarantee. *The Public Interest*, Summer, 31–41.

Torrey, E. Fuller. 1995. *Surviving schizophrenia*. New York: HarperCollins.

United Nations Centre for Human Settlements. 2000. *Strategies to combat homelessness.* Nairobi.

United States Department of Justice, Bureau of Justice Statistics. 1995. Jails and jail inmates 1993–94. Washington, DC: Office of Justice Programs.

United States General Accounting Office (GAO). 1985. *Homelessness: A complex problem and the federal response,* GAO-HRD-85-40. Washington, DC: GAO.

———. 1990. *Homelessness: Access to McKinney Act programs improved but better oversight needed,* GAO/RCED-91-29. Washington, DC: GAO.

———. 2000. Homelessness: Barriers to using mainstream programs, GAO/RCED-00-184. Washington DC: GAO.

U.S. Conference of Mayors. 2003a. A status report on hunger and homelessness. Washington, DC: The Conference.

———. 2003b. Resolution endorsing 10-year planning process to end chronic homelessness. www.usmayors.org/uscm/resolutions/71st_conference/cdh_08.asp

Watson, Vicki. 1996. Responses by the states to homelessness. In *Homelessness in America,* ed. Jim Baumohl. Phoenix: Oryx.

Wittman, Friedner D. 1989. Housing models for alcohol programs serving homeless people. *Contemporary Drug Problems,* 16(3):483–504.

Wright, James. 1989. *Address unknown: The homeless in America.* New York: Aldine de Gruyter.

Rachel G. Bratt

16 Community Development Corporations: Challenges in Supporting a Right to Housing

COMMUNITY DEVELOPMENT corporations (CDCs) are important producers of housing for low-income households. They are joined by public housing authorities and a number of other nonprofits as well as private for-profit developers, which have also contributed to the overall stock of housing affordable to this group. But CDCs have a number of unique attributes making them particularly attractive as owners and managers of this housing. At the same time, the work of CDCs, and their position in the local political economy, is hardly simple or straightforward, as they constantly encounter major challenges. In view of the many assets of CDCs and the constraints they face, this chapter examines the potential of CDCs to play a major role in a Right to Housing initiative.

The first section provides an overview of CDCs—their history and production records. The chapter then assesses the strengths and limitations of CDCs and explores how they could position themselves to assume major responsibilities in promoting a Right to Housing. The focus here is on the organizational/programmatic, contextual and structural attributes of CDCs and the challenges CDCs are currently facing and would be likely to face in such a new initiative. The final section presents comments about CDCs and their overall potential to play a significant role in implementing a Right to Housing.

HISTORY AND PRODUCTIVITY OF CDCS

Community development corporations are nonprofit organizations that are characterized by their community-based leadership and their work primarily in housing production and possibly job creation. CDCs are formed by residents, small business owners, congregations and other local stakeholders to revitalize low- and moderate-income communities. CDCs typically produce affordable housing and create jobs for community residents. Jobs are often created through small or micro business lending or commercial development projects. Some CDCs also provide a variety of social services to their target area (National Congress for Community Economic Development 2005).

Thus, the various activities undertaken by CDCs are intended to contribute to the broader goal of improving the physical and social environment of a target neighborhood—often referred to as neighborhood revitalization, community building or, most frequently, community development. As nonprofit organizations, CDCs are exempt from paying taxes under Section 501(c)(3) of the Internal Revenue Code, and donations to these groups qualify as tax deductions for the donor.

There is a long history of nonprofit involvement with housing. Preceding the formation of CDCs in the 1960s, there were at least three types of organizations. These included the efforts of the early 20th century reformers and philanthropists who promoted model tenements; the nonprofits in the federal Section 202 program for the elderly and the nonprofits that were involved in implementing the Section 221(d)(3) and 236 programs in the late 1960s and 1970s (Bratt 1989). But while all these groups were focused on housing production for low- or moderate-income households, it was not until the late 1960s that the nonprofit housing agenda became explicitly identified with a broader set of goals that revolved around the economic and physical redevelopment of severely deteriorated urban areas.

Partly in response to urban unrest and integral to the War on Poverty, the 1966 Special Impact Amendment to the Economic Opportunity Act and Title VII of the Community Services Act of 1974 provided substantial resources to support the fledgling CDCs. According to journalists Neil Peirce and Carol Steinbach:

> The modern CDC movement was launched on the February day in 1966 when Senator Robert F. Kennedy toured the dilapidated streets of Bed-Stuy [Bedford-Stuyvesant, a poor, predominantly African-American section of Brooklyn, NY] and planted the seeds for what would become the federal involvement in CDCs. Kennedy was despondent over urban riots, just begun with Watts in 1965. The idea emerged: rather than federal aid alone, rather than simply opening the doors to political participation of the poor, it was time to create new economic bases in troubled communities. (1987, 20)

But while the idea may have been newly conceptualized from a political standpoint, in reality, the approach was already being pioneered by the Ford Foundation through its Gray Areas program, which provided funding directly to local community groups and served as a prototype for the War on Poverty's community action program. Between 1966 and 1980, over $500 million in federal dollars was provided to CDCs through the programs enacted in 1966 and 1974 (National Center for Economic Alternatives 1981, 25; see also Abt Associates 1973).

This early group of CDCs was focused more on economic development and social service delivery than on housing. Nevertheless, in addition to creating jobs, providing human services and supporting small businesses, several thousand units of housing were built or rehabilitated (National Center for Economic Alternatives 1981). At about the same time, another group of community-based organizations—housing development corporations (HDCs)—were being supported by the Office of Economic Opportunity and the Model Cities program. HDCs,

which were the forerunners of many of the community-based housing groups that still exist, made significant progress in identifying and packaging the technical and financial resources needed to do nonprofit housing development. Even in that era, however, these early efforts revealed the challenges that persist today: "They are saddled with goals and objectives that are far beyond their resources to achieve" (quoted in Keyes 1971, 169).

In addition to local programs that were stimulated, at least in part, by federal funding, most CDCs emerged in response to the serious problems that were beginning to be articulated, such as redlining, arson, inadequate housing conditions and urban renewal (see, for example, Berndt 1977; Zdenek 1987; Keating, Rasey and Krumholz 1990; Vidal 1992). The first major assessment of CDC activities and the factors contributing to their success was presented in a study of a group of neighborhood development organizations (synonymous with CDCs)[1] that had received funding through the federal Neighborhood Self-Help Development Program, launched in 1980 (Mayer 1984). And in 1992, Avis Vidal produced a seminal study on urban CDCs, which presented a comprehensive profile of the origins, size and activities of these organizations.[2]

Since the mid-1970s, CDCs have gained increasing recognition for their contributions to the low-income housing and community development agendas. With about 3,600 such organizations across the country, and more than 550,000 units of housing produced or rehabilitated, CDCs are often viewed as key engines for community renewal (National Congress for Community Economic Development 1999).[3] While the majority of CDCs (52 percent) operate in urban areas, 26 percent serve rural areas; the remainder serves a mixture of urban and rural locales (National Congress for Community Economic Development 1999). (See "Box" by Robert Wiener on Rural Housing Nonprofits.) In 1990, nonprofits produced approximately 17.2 percent of the total number of federally assisted housing units (Walker et al. 1995, 22).

CDC-owned housing is an important component of the social housing sector in the United States, which Stone estimates to comprise a little more than 4 million units (see Chapter 11). While we know that CDCs have produced or rehabilitated over a half million units, we do not know exactly how many of those units continue to be in the social sector, as opposed to owner-occupied units that do not include caps on equity appreciation, for example.

In addition to production by CDCs, there are many other nonprofit producers of housing, including 84 regional nonprofit housing organizations. These groups, which do not confine their work to small geographic areas as do most CDCs, have developed, financed or preserved over 400,000 units of "affordable" rental housing and 220,000 single-family homes (The Housing Partnership Network 2005).

In a large-scale Right to Housing initiative, the number of CDC-produced units in the social housing sector as well as other public and nonprofit socially owned housing would grow dramatically, probably over a period of several decades.

STRENGTHS AND LIMITATIONS OF CDCs

The question of how CDCs could contribute to a Right to Housing involves an understanding of their various attributes, most of which have both positive and negative aspects. These are organized into three categories, encompassing organizational/programmatic, contextual and structural facets of CDC operations.

Organizational/Programmatic Issues

Organizational/programmatic issues include a number of aspects of CDC operations—their role as housing producers, their ability to make inroads on the larger community development agenda, and their ability to represent community interests.

Housing Producers. There are at least two ways of assessing the record of CDCs as housing producers. Looking at the cup half-empty, we observe that the production record of CDCs and other contributors to the social housing stock pales against the need for housing that is afford-

able to low-income households. But this should not diminish the importance of the work of CDCs. To the extent that the cup is half-full, we need to remind ourselves that with public housing authorities producing very few units of new housing, nonprofit organizations in general and CDCs in particular, are major players in whatever housing is being produced for those with the lowest incomes.

Since the housing needs of these groups are so acute, a significant amount of research has been devoted to understanding the obstacles that CDCs face in becoming larger producers. It has often been noted, for example, that for a CDC to produce low-income housing, it must engage in "patchwork financing," the assembling of numerous types of loans, grants and tax credits (Clay 1990; Stegman 1991; Hebert et al. 1993; Walker 1993). This is a complex, costly and time-consuming process, and is far less efficient than a single-source deep subsidy program.

Other researchers have investigated the performance of the developments owned and managed by nonprofit organizations. The first major study on this topic concluded that while CDCs are managing to do a reasonably good job in terms of day-to-day activities, there are a number of danger signs that should be heeded, and additional support and resources for CDCs are needed, which would allow them to continue to provide high-quality housing services (Bratt et al. 1994). In a subsequent study, another team of investigators examined some exemplary nonprofit-sponsored developments, both homeownership and rental, and found that overall, they were performing well. Concerning the rental developments, and similar to the findings by Bratt et al. (1994), researchers found that developments typically had inadequate reserve funds, making them vulnerable to increases in expenses or decreases in revenues (Rohe, Quercia and Levy 2001).

In addition to encountering difficult development and management challenges, CDCs generally face complex staffing issues. Salaries are typically low, hours are long and the obstacles to completing tasks can be significant. It is not uncommon, for example, for staff members at all levels to experience "burnout"—exhaustion after several years that results in a resignation.

This presents serious problems for CDCs as they struggle to develop a competent, stable work force.

In light of this type of work environment, which is almost a "given" in the CDC world, a number of researchers have questioned how the capacity of CDCs can be increased so they can better deal with the constraints that they face. A major philanthropic initiative has involved a number of foundations, financial services corporations, and the Department of Housing and Urban Development (HUD) in an effort aimed at accelerating the growth, scale and impact of CDCs in 23 cities across the country. Known as the National Community Development Initiative, over $253 million was provided over a ten-year period to the Local Initiatives Support Corporation and the Enterprise Foundation (see n. 7), which, in turn, funneled funds to the CDCs.[4] A study of the program reported substantial overall gains between 1991 and 2001 in terms of increased capacity of the CDCs to undertake community development projects, especially housing production. The researchers also highlighted the role of collaborations and networks in assisting and supporting CDC activities and noted that investments in CDCs helped to increase the reputation of this sector and enabled them to launch more sophisticated initiatives in order to attack neighborhood problems (Walker and Weinheimer 1998; Walker 2002; Walker, Gustafson and Snow 2002).

Further research on CDC partnerships and how support systems can be set up to assist CDCs comes from another multiyear study. With funding for 17 partnerships coming from the Ford Foundation, investigators studied the strengths, weaknesses and future prospects for these partnerships. The key issues explored were whether and how CDC capacity to undertake additional activities was increased through the partnership and, ultimately, whether there were positive impacts on the economic and social conditions of the low-income neighborhoods. The researchers point out that it is difficult to assess capacity with precision. For example, creation of more CDCs may be one criterion but, in some cities a goal of the partnership may be to reduce the (too) large number of CDCs. Similarly, if one tries to use production numbers,

it is difficult to know the extent to which they can be attributed to the activities of the partnership in strengthening CDC capacity (Nye and Glickman 1995; 1998). The researchers posited that "capacity" is a multidimensional term, consisting of resource, organizational, networking and programmatic and political elements (Glickman and Servon 1999a). And while they recognized the difficulties of ascribing causality to the partnerships, they concluded that partnerships do indeed make a difference in CDCs' quest to build capacity (Glickman and Servon 1999b).

Despite the continued obstacles CDCs face in terms of enhancing productivity, there is recognition that they are able to accomplish the job of building housing. The growing appreciation for the work of CDCs has been reflected in a number of legislative initiatives. For example, CDCs were given prominent roles in disposing of federally owned properties that were previously owned by failed savings and loan associations and commercial banks; they have key responsibilities in the HOME; Low Income Housing Tax Credit and Empowerment Zones/Enterprise and Renewal Communities programs; and they are prominent in both the Community Development Financial Institutions program (including the New Markets Tax Credit program) and in initiatives to preserve federally subsidized, privately owned housing for low-income tenants.

How can we assess the overall production record of CDCs and their potential to increase capacity so that they could play a significant role in promoting a Right to Housing agenda? Based on the challenges involved in "growing" CDCs, and the millions of dollars expended in trying to achieve this goal, CDCs would not be likely to emerge as the only producers of housing for low-income households. Even if one were to envision a significantly enhanced system to support the work of CDCs, including organizational operating support and deep construction subsidies as well as long-term subsidies to reduce monthly housing costs, it is most likely that CDCs would evolve as only one of the key housing providers. They would be accompanied by the regional nonprofits and other nonprofit organizations with, for example, nonspatial orientations (such as unions, other trade associations, or groups who target their services to particular sub-groups of the population, such as single mothers) in addition to a revitalized public housing sector. Thus, while CDCs would likely emerge as important players, and their production records would likely increase substantially, we should not assume that they would be able to carry out the extensive amount of work involved, unassisted by other key providers. Moreover, any such expectation would be unwise, since it would not fully utilize the capabilities of other important contributors to the social housing sector.

Programs beyond Housing. As noted above, in addition to housing, CDCs are also committed to producing wider-scale community benefits. Because CDCs often adopt a comprehensive approach to community development and work at a local level, they are thought to be in a good position to coordinate effective community improvement efforts (Blakely 1989). Whether a given group's community development agenda involves crime watch programs, preschool and youth programs, meals-on-wheels for the elderly and infirm, park and open space beautification, employment counseling, job training, commercial redevelopment, small business assistance or some combination of those elements, most CDCs are involved with a range of activities beyond housing (Vidal 1992). The particular mix of initiatives that a CDC selects depends on its mission, the community's needs, the CDC's staff capacity, and the availability of funds and other types of assistance (Leiterman and Stillman 1993; Vidal 1997). One of the key ways that CDCs decide on which activities to pursue is through their organizing efforts, which will be addressed later in this chapter.

Since at least the early 1990s, researchers and analysts have been producing numerous case studies and vignettes highlighting the many ways in which CDCs have contributed to community improvements (e.g., Vidal 1992; Leiterman and Stillman 1993; Sullivan 1993; Robinson 1996; Bratt and Keyes 1997; Grogan and Proscio 2000; Von Hoffman 2003).[5] Briggs and Mueller note that theirs was "perhaps the first-ever attempt to analyze rigorously collected data on a wide range of effects of CDC practices on the lives and attitudes of neighborhood resi-

dents" (1997, 1). Among their many findings was that two of the three organizations studied "had measurable effects on the social fabric of their neighborhoods" and that in all cases, "CDC housing is a 'move up,' especially for the most disadvantaged residents. Whether in terms of housing conditions, social-service programming, feelings of safety, and/or other conditions in the neighborhood, residents recognize improvements even as they expect more" (Briggs and Mueller 1997, 7–8).

While housing is the foundation of most CDC activity and is usually viewed as part of a wider-scale community development agenda, many CDCs also, explicitly or implicitly, strive to promote resident "self-sufficiency."[6] Such activities include personal responsibility-building; skill-building for work; service delivery; economic development; community-building through organizing, advocacy and political consciousness-raising; and homeownership (Bratt and Keyes 1997).

As CDCs have gone beyond producing "housing alone" (no small achievement in itself), they have emerged as leaders in providing—or in many cases helping to coordinate—housing plus services. A robust Right to Housing initiative would involve a full array of programs connected to housing that would enable the members of each household to maximize their own capabilities and productivity. To the extent that CDCs have been among the pioneers in this realm, they would be well positioned to further develop and facilitate housing plus services programs.

Representatives of Community Interests. Among the various positive qualities of CDCs is their supposed connections to their local communities: They are alleged to be good representatives of community interests. This view is based, in part, on the origins of many CDCs—a large number grew directly out of local protest and advocacy movements and more than one-half of the members of CDC boards are generally drawn from the local community (Vidal 1992). Herbert J. Rubin provides a number of powerful examples of the ways in which community-based development organizations (which include CDCs) work to empower the poor and to respond to community concerns (1993,

106). He adds that the actions of these organizations open up the decision-making process by showing that it is the right of community members, rather than the business community, to set a neighborhood development agenda. The success of community-based development organizations, organizations that are open to the poor and responsive to the community, to "sit at the table" focuses the attention of the broader society to the importance of social equity when doing community development (1993, 119).

The perception that CDCs are indeed linked closely to community interests was underscored by researchers at the Urban Institute who found compelling evidence of community leadership and strong alliances both inside and outside their neighborhoods (Walker 2002, 35). These attributes are part of what is viewed as unique about CDCs—their ability to understand the needs of their local community and to create programs that explicitly respond to those needs.

It is also clear, however, that the community is not a monolithic entity (Heskin 1991; Bratt 1996). Any given "community" is likely comprised of tenants and homeowners of varying income levels, resident as well as absentee landlords, small businesses and larger commercial outlets. And there is no reason to assume that all these various groups—"the community"—will agree on all issues.

Despite the complexities of trying to understand and represent the "community," there is a widespread view that community-based organizations "are particularly effective at delivering services because of their relationships and standing in the community" (HUD 1996, 22). In a full-scale Right to Housing initiative, CDCs—because of their close connections to their communities, however diverse and complex they may be—would be expected to play a key role in bridging the gap between resident needs and desires and the housing production system. But there is an open question about the extent to which CDCs would be able to mediate the various community interests and to produce housing and services that are optimally aligned with the community's agenda, as discussed below. However imperfectly CDCs would (and do) play this role, it is not clear what types of organiza-tions would be better positioned to carry out this critical function.

Contextual Issues

Contextual issues arise outside the control of CDCs, but they all have a significant impact on CDC productivity. The larger environment in which CDCs operate includes local economic and market trends and the efforts of the national nonprofit intermediaries as well as city, state and national policies and funding priorities. In reflecting on how CDCs could play a significant role in a Right to Housing initiative, it is important to consider which of the contextual issues would continue to present obstacles and which would essentially disappear as other public priorities became realigned.

Local Economic and Market Trends. CDCs typically emerge in areas with some combination of significant poverty, deteriorated housing, weak or nonexistent financial investment by the private sector, limited or poor-quality public amenities such as parks and open space, and inadequate or poorly coordinated social services. Since their creation, CDCs have always been viewed as key vehicles for improving these types of conditions and, overall, promoting community development.

After several decades of CDC activities as well as other types of federal and local community development initiatives, it is clear that there are still many locales that continue to be plagued by the most seemingly intractable problems (see Rusk 1999). At the same time, however, many locales have been experiencing an urban renaissance, where once neglected and severely deteriorated neighborhoods are now "turning around" (Grogan and Proscio 2000; Von Hoffman 2003).

Whether a CDC is attempting to counter market trends and to promote housing and economic development, or whether it is operating in a gentrifying area and attempting to safeguard existing residents against displacement, it is certain to be facing significant challenges. On the one hand, it must struggle to do development in areas that have been abandoned by the private sector and that are often plagued by high crime rates, with the possibility of theft of building materials or vandalism of structures in the midst of rehabilitation or construction. And once the buildings are completed, adverse neighborhood factors make the task of management that much more difficult (Bratt et al. 1994). On the other hand, some CDCs are now operating in areas that have begun to show a resurgence of economic activity, private market investment and interest by a new wave of urban settlers, or gentrifiers. Such groups are challenged by a lack of affordable land and buildings, all of which makes their work as housing developers nearly impossible (Rohe, Bratt, and Biswas 2003). This points to one of the ironies of community development:

> The more CDCs succeed in renovating and reselling or renting dilapidated and derelict properties, the more they contribute to community revitalization. This revitalization, in turn, leads to higher house prices and fewer vacant properties; thus, CDCs are priced out of the market. (Rohe, Bratt, and Biswas 2003, 31)

In addition, some CDCs are finding it increasingly difficult to persuade higher-income residents, particularly homeowners, to permit the construction or rehabilitation of additional housing targeted for low-income people (Goetz and Sidney 1994). In essence, we are seeing NIMBY (not in my back yard) attitudes in the neighborhoods, not just in affluent suburbs (Rohe, Bratt, and Biswas 2003, 69).

It is impossible to predict the extent to which market factors would still present obstacles to CDCs in the context of a broad-based Right to Housing initiative. While such a new program might mean that the role of the market would be significantly dampened, we cannot predict whether CDCs would still encounter the problems associated with strong and weak markets as well as NIMBY-ism. For the present, it is sufficient to note that in any Right to Housing effort, attention would need to be paid to the types of market conditions that would likely prevail and to work to ensure that they are acknowledged as possible factors in the ability of CDCs and other social housing providers to do the work that they are committed to doing. And of course, beyond recognizing these factors, mechanisms to overcome adverse market conditions would need to be devised.

National Nonprofit Intermediaries. CDCs have enjoyed substantial support from state and local government, nonprofit and philanthropic initiatives (Bratt 1989; Goetz 1993; Committee for Economic Development 1995; Yin 1998) as well as from the three national nonprofit intermediaries—the Local Initiatives Support Corporation (LISC), the Enterprise Foundation and the Neighborhood Reinvestment Corporation.[7] A fourth intermediary, the Center for Community Change, was created in 1967, years before the other groups, and is unique in its overriding concern with advocacy and in serving as a link between activist CDCs and technical assistance and in its commitment to grassroots empowerment (Rubin 2000).

The national intermediaries play an important role in influencing and supporting the work of CDCs. Both LISC and the Enterprise Foundation raise funds primarily through private corporate and foundation donations, while the Neighborhood Reinvestment Corporation receives annual Congressional appropriations. These three organizations disseminate funds to local chapters that in turn provide funds directly to affiliate organizations working in urban neighborhoods or rural locations.

In recent years, the role of intermediaries has grown significantly due, in part, to the substantial investments that these organizations have received from major funding efforts such as the National Community Development Initiative. In fact, Walker (2002) has noted that:

> The number one accomplishment of the community development leadership system in the 1990s was the creation or strengthening of strong intermediary institutions—the collaborations, partnerships, coalitions and alliances, and other bodies that help engage leaders from multiple sectors as contributors to community development. (48)

There is a prevailing view that CDCs are better able to deliver services with the assistance of intermediaries than without them. Specifically, intermediaries and local collaborations facilitate multi-year funding for CDC operations, and they tend to increase the level of investment; they establish performance standards and monitor CDC progress; and they shift administrative burdens for grant-making and management away from the grantor to the intermediary (Walker 2002, 40).

However, there is also some question about the extent to which intermediaries interfere with the agendas of CDCs. Von Hoffman (2001) says that they do not, while other researchers have pointed out that the position played by intermediaries in the CDC support system carries some inherent conflict.

The main issue...is when and how the intermediaries and funders should intervene in CDC affairs. CDCs believe they are autonomous organizations that serve locally defined needs and as such should not be dictated to by intermediaries and funders. Yet intermediaries and funders have their own interests to consider, and it is reasonable for them to set conditions for receipt of their funding. The challenge, then, is for intermediaries and funders to find a balance between allowing CDCs autonomy to fulfill their missions as they see fit and imposing conditions for support.... [And more specifically,] how can intermediaries and funders create standards for performance along with sanctions for noncompliance, without appearing too heavy-handed and overwhelming the CDCs' own agendas? When, how, and to what extent should intermediaries and funders intervene in CDC affairs? (Rohe, Bratt, and Biswas 2003, 35, 65)

According to Rubin:

Developmental activists fear that in accepting help they will end up having to comply with the ideologies put forth by the intermediaries or the foundations.... [They] appreciate the difference between an intermediary or foundation mandating that the community-based development organization do it their way, and the constructive interaction that can occur between knowledgeable foundation or intermediary officials and community activists.... Still in many other cases, developmental activists expressed intensely negative feelings that support organizations simply don't understand what community development is about. These activists fear that by pushing for bricks-and-mortar projects, LISC distracts attention from the more radical

social change needed to repair a capitalist economy. (2000, 112–113)

Despite these strong words of caution, Rubin concludes that intermediaries and foundations generally work well and constructively with the staff members of community-based development organizations. Characterizing their disagreements as "family arguments," he contends that participants recognize their shared agenda, that frank discussions do occur and that "while money speaks loudly, [it] does not drown out other conversations" (2000, 132).

If there were a full-scale Right to Housing initiative, it is quite possible that there would be little need for the intermediaries, in their current form. To the extent that federal funds would be available to nonprofits and other housing producers, the key role of the intermediaries in raising and disseminating funds would not be needed. Presumably, adequate federal funding would be available, and an allocation mechanism would be developed. But one of the strengths of the national intermediaries is their role as providers of technical assistance and vehicles for sharing and communicating "best practices." This set of functions would quite possibly still be needed.

Whether or not intermediaries continued to serve as conduits for funds in an era of a Right to Housing, it is likely that many of the questions that have surfaced about their role would present similar challenges for the new funding entity (presumably the federal government). Specifically, there likely would be ongoing questions about the extent to which the funder would participate in determining the agenda of the housing provider and how the nonprofits or public agencies would be held accountable for that funding.

Public Policies and Funding. Much of the literature on CDCs acknowledges the challenges they face in a changing policy environment (Stoecker 1997; Vidal 1997; Bratt et al. 1998; Rohe 1998). As federal dollars available for community development activities declined during the 1980s and 1990s, the number of nonprofit organizations undertaking these kinds of initiatives grew, partly in an effort to fill the void (Goetz 1993;

National Congress for Community Economic Development 1999). At the same time, reductions in federal funding have meant that a large number of organizations are chasing after fewer available resources, making it increasingly difficult for groups to cover their basic operating costs as well as to launch development deals (Rohe, Bratt and Biswas 2003; see box on p. 360).

The extent to which housing in general has been receiving less and less federal assistance is documented in the Introduction to this book. For the purposes of this chapter, it should be noted that, unlike the 1970s and early 1980s, when both nonprofit and for-profit producers of housing could look to a single source of deep subsidy in the Section 8 New Construction and Substantial Rehabilitation Program, this type of funding is no longer available. Since the Reagan years, CDCs and other nonprofits have had to piece together deals using a complex and multi-layered assortment of public and private funding.

By the mid-1990s, the context in which CDCs operate began to be characterized as the devolution of policy-making down to state and local levels (Galster 1996; Ammann and Salsich 1997). But this devolution has not come with nearly as deep pockets as in the pre-1980s federal housing subsidy era. Funding decisions at the local level are far from static, and resources are generally scarce. And either a city's decision to emphasize one type of housing over another (such as homeownership rather than rental) or its own economic constraints can have dramatic implications for the viability of CDCs (Rohe, Bratt and Biswas 2003). Any reduction in administrative, predevelopment and development funds, as well as ongoing subsidies that enable the housing to continue to be provided to low-income households, results in an extremely difficult environment in which groups are forced to operate. However, it has been argued that CDCs are in a good position to organize themselves into a powerful constituency to demand that federal low-income housing policies must be responsive to the needs of the nonprofit sector (Koschinsky 1998). More concretely, we have already seen how the efforts of the national trade and advocacy organization for CDCs—the National Congress for Community Economic

Development—have resulted in increased visibility for CDCs and new designated roles for CDCs in major federal initiatives.

A Right to Housing initiative would address this key problem of resource availability. It is tantalizing to contemplate how CDCs would respond in a system in which funding for competent producers was guaranteed and not subject to either large fluctuations or sudden termination. The infusion of substantial funds through the National Community Development Initiative provides evidence of the extent to which CDC capacity and productivity would increase if funding for CDC activities were widely available and if a larger number of promising groups could avail themselves of financial and technical assistance.

Structural Issues

Beyond the inadequacy of resources available to carry out their broad and sweeping missions, there are a number of deeper weaknesses in the CDC approach as pointed out by a small group of analysts. These weaknesses bring to question whether CDCs should, in fact, exist at all, given the position they are attempting to play within our capitalist political economy. Closely connected to these issues is the question of whether CDCs are structurally able to carry out organizing and advocacy work.

Capital versus Community. Over the past several decades, a number of critics have identified conflicts between the ways in which CDCs operate and their socially oriented objectives. To what extent can CDCs, organizations whose names include the word "corporation" and that are forced to work closely with financial institutions and city governments, really be advocates for their low-income constituents? To what extent do the tasks involved with development and management (like acquiring the necessary permits, assembling financing and collecting rents) conflict with the needs of low-income communities and their residents? Is it really possible to be working with the powerful interests of a community while staying true to the needs of those who live at the margins? To what extent do CDCs deal with the symptoms of poverty as opposed to the root causes? And, if they only address the former, is that sufficient?

A small advocacy organization based in Cambridge, Massachusetts, sponsored one of the earliest critiques of community housing development corporations. Citing poor quality housing, high rents and a small overall impact, the report underscored that:

> [T]he most serious conflict of interest between the community housing sponsor and the community . . . comes when the sponsor assumes the role of landlord . . . . In the community housing development process, the rights and needs of the tenants come last, only after all other parties involved in the development have been satisfied. (The Housing and Community Research Groups 1973, 39, 41)

Researchers at the Urban Institute, in presenting an evaluation of three early CDCs, observed:

> A development institution such as a CDC is inevitably placed in a situation where it must perform simultaneously a dual role, since it is not self-sufficient. On one hand, the CDC's planning, programming, and program allocations must relate to the needs and interests of its community constituents. On the other hand, the CDC's resource mobilization activity must relate to development support institutions. If the contrast between the view of those providing funds and the community's is sharp, the CDC may not be able to generate sufficient funds to become self-sufficient even if most programs are devoted to generating revenue. (Garn, Tevis and Snead 1976, 131)

Berndt (1977) continued this overall analysis by pointing out the problems inherent in the operations of CDCs, including their inability to deal with the structural causes of poverty. Nearly a decade later, Schuman's (1986) reflections on self-help housing had important implications for CDCs. Specifically, he noted that such programs reduce "pressure on government to maintain its legitimacy by alleviating the failures of the private market with social programs" (467). Schuman also offered this note:

> The precarious financial picture of self-help housing has led more than one community group to enter joint venture agreements with private investors through the sale of equity shares. [This] demonstrates the pressures to conform to the private market for housing. Although no neighborhood group can be faulted for seeking critical financial assistance, there is at least an element of irony in the attempt to solve housing problems by reinforcing the tax-shelter and investment mechanisms that maintain a housing system based on profit rather than need. (1986, 469–470)

Schuman concluded his analysis by acknowledging that while self-help may be "a dangerous diversion, shunting attention from the structural aspects of the housing problem into a bottomless pit of small-scale self-exploitation . . . in the absence of a mass movement for decent housing as a public responsibility, the self-help sector can be a valuable starting point (471).

In recent years, Stoecker (1997) has, perhaps, done the most work exploring the built-in contradictions between the work of CDCs and their position within our capitalist system. His argument posits that the fundamental conflict between capital and community introduces a virtually insurmountable obstacle to CDC success.

> Community's tendency is to preserve neighborhood space as a use value for the service of community members, while capital's tendency is to convert neighborhood space in to exchange values that can be speculated on for a profit. This sets up an antagonistic relationship. Capital's conversion of neighborhood space into exchange values drives up rents, destroys green space, eliminates neighborhood-based commerce, and disrupts neighboring patterns. Capital is less willing to invest in neighborhood redevelopment that maintains neighborhood spaces as use values because that would prevent speculation and limit profit accumulation. Either through destructive investment or disinvestment community suffers. (Stoecker 1997, 5)

And, further, Stoecker continues:

> CDCs manage capital like capitalists, but do not invest it for a profit. They manage projects but within the constraints set by the funders. They try to be community oriented while their purse strings are held by outsiders. They are pressured by capital to produce exchange values in the form of capitalist business spaces and rental housing. They are pressured by communities to produce

use value in the form of services, home ownership, and green spaces. This is more than a "double bottom line" (Bratt et al. 1994). It is the internationalization of the capital-community contradiction and it leads to trouble. (1997, 6)

Others disagree. For example, Leiterman and Stillman report that among the 32 organizations in their survey, there was a generally positive feeling that housing was a good basis for enabling tenants to exercise control over their environments. One tenant living in a building owned by a CDC observed that:

This CDC is the only landlord I know that gets personal. The CDC looks at what the tenants go through and what they want. The CDC has helped realize the whole picture—legal issues, management, tenant responsibilities, and so on. At meetings, we discuss how we as a community will come together. (1993, 30–31)

Another team of researchers points out that other types of neighborhood associations are more likely to be dominated by residents with higher incomes than are CDCs and that CDCs have played important roles in assisting low-income residents when neighborhood associations have become dominated by conservative property owners (Goetz and Sidney 1994). Political scientist Tony Robinson further contends that rather than becoming a pawn of capital, CDCs can "be very successful at altering the political balance of development politics in the city, at changing the calculus of capital investors, and at enhancing the social and psychological fabric of a neighborhood" (1996, 1648). And he adds that "increasingly professional CDCs incorporated in relationships with government and private developers, have become *more*, not less, powerful, as outside forces have become co-dependent on the political and economic resources that CDCs can 'bring to the table'" (1996, 1660). Rather than being marginal players, Robinson suggests that CDCs may actually be contributing to systemic change (1996, 1667).

Rubin offers this sweeping assessment of the role that community-based development organizations play in a capitalist economy:

[They] tie together a social mission with capitalist realities.... [They] provide the hope to combat the self-reinforcing cynicism that has led to the abandonment of many neighborhoods. They follow a pragmatic ideology of a humane capitalism for social change that community members, as well as politicians of both conservative and liberal leanings, can accept.... Community-based development organizations are not about leading an in-the-streets revolution, but they are about increasing social equity and demonstrating that a market economy still can have a heart. By reshaping the underlying symbols of a capitalist society to serve a social need, [they] end up renewing hope in neighborhoods of despair. (2000, 273, 274)

If there were a Right to Housing initiative, the built-in contradictions between capital and community would be lessened. With a well-funded program, the needs of communities and individuals would be able to function more independently from traditional sources of capital. This, then, would further weaken the conflict, and CDCs would be in a good position to more unequivocally serve the needs of their constituents. Even in the present era, while tensions may surface, CDCs appear to be doing a good job of mediating the two worlds and, much more often than not, keeping true to their missions to serve low-income people and communities.

Organizing and Advocacy. Although many CDCs arose from an organizing and advocacy agenda, as their work became increasingly focused on the technical aspects of development, many groups began to lose sight of their mission to organize and advocate for community needs. This conflict was identified early in the growth of CDCs, as they were evolving into important players on the community development landscape.

Just to exist, they [CDCs] have to engage in virtually nonstop fund raising. Then they face the administrative nightmare of conceiving and carrying out complex development projects with multiple partners. Each negotiation may present obstacles; foot-dragging by any one partner can imperil a larger project. Another factor: closer association with the private sector and local government may discourage advocacy. Few organizations are anxious to alienate new-found funding partners. (Peirce and Steinbach 1987, 32, 34)

While supportive of the work of CDCs, Rubin acknowledges the inherent tensions in their operations, and he presents a scenario of how a CDC could temporarily lose touch with its community:

> Organizations might begin with an ideological fervor, pushing for empowerment and community participation. As external funds dry up and the only money available is that for efficiently building affordable housing, the mission does change, or else the organizations simply die, as many have. But as some semblance of economic stability returns, the recognition occurs that building homes is not enough, that services are required, as is a more holistic approach to renewal, and once again developmental activists attempt to build, to serve, and to empower. (2000, 66)

Other analysts have also pointed to the potential for CDCs to overemphasize technical concerns and the "nuts and bolts" of housing development, and they voice a skepticism that the scale of CDC activity could ever provide more than the proverbial "drop in a bucket" (Mollenkopf 1983; Traynor 1993; Fisher 1994).

Expanding this analysis, Stoecker (1997) has argued that organizing should be carried out by other neighborhood-based organizations, since CDCs are not able to mediate the contradictions of working within a capitalist development model, while also serving as advocates to low-income communities. He has recommended that CDCs adopt a community-controlled planning process and that they become high-capacity and multi-local. In a critique to Stoecker's argument, I argued that the traditional CDC model, which attempts to combine both development and organizing agendas, is still viable and merits support (Bratt 1997). However, Lenz cautions that while organizing of poor communities may not be the exclusive job of neighborhood development organizations, development-oriented groups should subordinate their plans to the organizing agenda. Citing the experience of a Chicago CDC, he continues:

> As important as the actual housing units is the fact that a whole new group of neighborhood leaders has been educated on housing and the potential of community organizing. The hope and promise of this approach to neighborhood development is that by building the capacities and power of low-income people, they will be

in a position to demand even more far-reaching economic and political changes in the future. (1988, 30)

Rubin recorded a similar sentiment in an interview with the head of a community-based development organization:

> We think of ourselves as catalysts....Over the years we've done over six hundred units of housing. And there...are [probably] at least fifty families in this community that could use it for everyone we've served....But the fact of the matter is, it is a drop in a bucket. So if that drop doesn't...ignite activism and ignite a sense among people about what can be done when people work collectively and struggle for what is needed, then we've done little. (2000, 139)

According to one team of researchers, organizing emerged as a constant theme among those interviewed, and one CDC executive director commented: "Organizing is like breathing—it is part of everything we do" (Leiterman and Stillman 1993, 30). Further, they reported that among the thirty-two CDCs they studied, most are active advocates on behalf of their communities. Most commonly, CDCs advocate for housing funds, increased police protection, supermarket development, day care and other social services. In setting strategy, organizations are less likely to take an adversarial role (like sitting-in in front of City Hall), and more likely to negotiate, work the bureaucratic channels, and develop allies and constituents among targeted supporters (Leiterman and Stillman 1993, 34).

Sara Stoutland, in a major review of research on CDCs, concluded that some CDCs "have become important advocates at city hall for their neighborhoods, and it is not difficult to argue on principle that support for the organizations should continue for this reason alone" (1999, 233). Nevertheless, she also pointed out that "it is difficult to measure or assess the importance of this advocacy, especially when there are other sources of neighborhood leadership in many of the places where the organizations operate" (1999, 233).

It is not easy for groups to merge the two agendas—organizing and development work. For example, in Cleveland, Neighborhood Progress, Inc., a group representing the area's

50 largest corporations and major foundations, originally was interested in assisting CDCs to increase their productive capacity. By the mid-to late 1990s, however, acknowledging that CDCs were losing touch with their local communities, NPI promoted an organizing/advocacy initiative targeted to the city's CDCs and provided funding to help CDCs reconnect with their neighborhoods. In response, Slavic Village Development developed a new organizing arm and was successful in a highly visible effort to keep a neighborhood hospital from closing (Rohe, Bratt and Biswas 2003).

At about the same time, members of the Massachusetts Association of Community Development Corporations, the trade organization representing the state's CDCs, decided

> to renew their emphasis on organizing in order to re-energize their development work. CDC leaders reached this conclusion from experience: some had celebrated the completion of new housing developments only to find themselves faced with problems of crime and drug dealing in that neighborhood; others had suffered when a political change resulted in the withdrawal of support for a project. (Massachusetts Association of Community Development Corporations 2003)

In Massachusetts, the sense that organizing and development could not only co-exist but could also be mutually reinforcing was partially based on the work of some of the state's most noteworthy CDCs. Lowell's Coalition for a Better Acre (CBA), for example, has been credited for its development of over 360 units of housing, as well as creating a program to train low-income Latina and Cambodian women to be home day care providers and helping to establish the city's first Spanish-language cable television station. According to one commentator:

> CBA has won these victories through basic community organizing techniques—knocking on doors; meeting one-to-one to develop relationships; building coalitions with churches and other allies; training resident leaders; holding accountability sessions with public officials; and, when necessary, through direct action. CBA has been successful because it sees its mission not just as building buildings, but as building power. (Winkelman 1998, 4)

But CBA has also faced obstacles from the city and from other stakeholders. Its success appears to be due, in part, to its "relative power and its ability to find ways to get what it wants while the city gets something too . . . . In the end, it is CBA's abilty to mobilize residents—who are also voters—that has allowed it to maintain city funding and influence city practices" (Winkelman 1998, 4, 5).

It appears that, beyond these concrete examples, many CDCs incorporate advocacy and organizing into their work. Based on a sample of 1,057 CDCs, two-thirds reported that they were involved in community organizing (Walker et al. 1995). More recently, in another national study of 163 CDCs in 23 cities, researchers found that 80 percent of the groups indicated they were involved with activities that included "neighborhood planning, community organizing and advocacy work, community safety, neighborhood cleanup, and other programs that require active participation of residents and businesses" (Walker 2002, 13). Further, many CDCs are actively striving to strengthen their organizing capabilities. CDCs in this sample also reported that the area in which they had made the second-most progress was in developing community linkages and community organizing; the area in which the most gains were reported was in building development capacity (Walker 2002, 36). And nearly one-fourth of the groups surveyed indicated that community organizing was one of their priority areas for organizational improvement (Walker 2002, 38).

Compounding the complexity of merging organizing and development is the fact that many of the problems CDCs encounter originate outside the local community. As Lenz notes:

> Until these trends and policy decisions can be affected, community development will be limited in what it can accomplish. The best that can be hoped for at present is that well-organized, activist neighborhood development organizations can contribute to the political process needed to address these extra-neighborhood issues. (1988, 30)

One of the ways that CDCs have contributed to the political process and have advanced progressive agendas is by joining advocacy coalitions—groups of nonprofits as well as other advocates who are committed to a similar set of goals (Goetz 1996; Rubin 2000). Despite the apparent successes, there is still a group of organizers and critics who "fear that CDC efforts deflate and divert social movements" and that "for poor and working people CDC activity has a place, but only if it is part of a larger political activist strategy" (Fisher 1994, 190).

It is neither simple nor easy to effectively combine organizing with development. Involving residents and providing real opportunities for them to define an organization's agenda, as well as allowing them to make real decisions, can be labor-intensive, time-consuming and filled with conflict and may be beyond the reach of any local initiative. Yet, it is also clear that the two types of activities can be undertaken together and that the outcomes, in terms of organizational strength, resident empowerment and concrete development projects, can readily justify what are inherently difficult tasks to carry out simultaneously.

Even the most skeptical analysts, such as Randy Stoecker, appear to have reached a similar conclusion. In a recent contribution to the debate about the compatibility (or lack thereof) between development and organizing, Stoecker concluded that "a CDC can accomplish community organizing when it is structured to manage the potential contradictions involved" (2003, 509). And further, "It is possible for CDCs to use traditional confrontational power tactics in their organizing activities" and that there are a number of initiatives under way that are exploring ways to manage the organizing-development dialectic (2003, 510).

My sense is that the debate is moot. One solution is not appropriate to all organizations. While some groups may be able to merge the two agendas, others may not be. While some groups should be working at a larger geographic scale, others should stay locally focused. We have not yet developed an appropriate set of measures to assess which groups are best suited for which types of approaches. But the argument should be put to rest. Organizing is important. Development is important. And it is important that both be accomplished in the current environment as well as part of a Right to Housing initiative. It is

less important, however, which type of organization does what. Since so many CDCs believe that their work involves combining the two, it makes little sense to undermine this mission by overemphasizing the structural weaknesses of a merged agenda. To produce the needed units of housing, both now and in the future, we will need all kinds of competent organizations, and hopefully, they will be well connected with community needs and visions.

OVERALL ASSESSMENT OF CDCS AND THEIR ROLE IN A RIGHT TO HOUSING

Indicators of CDC success have traditionally been "bricks-and-mortar" measures—number of housing units generated, jobs created, square footage of business or commercial space made available, development dollars leveraged and the like. However, as discussed in this chapter, CDCs usually go beyond physical development to include the delivery of social services, community organizing and other activities related to the somewhat amorphous concept of community development. Thus, the full array of changes for which CDCs may be responsible and which they are attempting to achieve are difficult to measure and, as a consequence, may be overlooked by researchers as indicators of success (Temkin and Rohe 1998).

It is not surprising that various observers offer quite different overall summations of CDC effectiveness. Rohe (1998) has noted that claims of success are often made with little or no supporting evidence and that even examples of successful CDCs fail to provide convincing evidence of the superiority of CDCs over other community development initiatives. In addition, Stoecker (1997) cites numerous analysts who are unable to show that CDC activities are effective enough to reverse neighborhood decline or that the development for which they take responsibility would not have happened without their involvement. And, writing from a conservative perspective, Husock argues that CDCs are bad for cities because they "keep the poor frozen in poverty and cities forever frozen as warehouses for the eternally poor"; that they are nothing more than a decentralized HUD and that they are prone to corruption (2001, 68, 73).

Probably the most scathing attack of CDCs appeared in a *New York Times Magazine* article by Nicholas Lemann. Arguing that community development is a myth, he sees CDCs and other neighborhood-focused efforts as major disappointments. Instead, he suggests that urban policy should focus on people-oriented programs—human service initiatives and efforts to provide inner-city residents opportunities to move to nonpoverty areas (Lemann 1994). One of the numerous rebuttals questioned whether we must "really give up on poor communities in order to help poor people?" And, in answer, "We cannot simply write off poor communities, and we shouldn't when there are reasons for cautious optimism" (Schwartz 1994, 1).

Focusing on the specific contributions of CDCs, a team of researchers concluded: Most of the doubts about CDCs are either dispelled or partly dispelled. The CDCs experienced vigorous growth and change.... Parochialism characterized some CDCs but was countered by the development of extensive networks.... The addition of service delivery and housing development functions, which provided evidence of the narrowing tendencies that concerned many observers, coexisted with vigorous policy advocacy in many cases (Clavel, Pitt and Yin 1997, 451).

In one of the most recent assessment of CDC activities, which focused on the experiences of 163 CDCs in 23 cities:

> Field researchers found widespread agreement among community development practitioners... that some CDC investments have produced improvement in community quality that have been recognized by the market and thus *capitalized* in higher real estate values.... [Furthermore], CDC directors, intermediary staff, city officials, bankers, foundation staff, local academics, and others... identified, neighborhoods with upswings in housing markets *thought to be due*, in some large part, to CDC redevelopment efforts. In about two-thirds of cities, practitioners credited CDCs with successful neighborhood turnaround in at least one neighborhood. (Walker 2002, 9; original emphasis)

Even more convincing evidence comes from an econometric analysis of five neighborhoods. Researchers found that in two of the neighborhoods:

> [E]conometric trend analysis produced solid evidence that the increases [in property values] resulted from CDC activities and the supporting investments made by private and public agencies.... The conclusion: "Policy" interventions of the sort represented by CDCs' community development investments can produce real results that are scientifically measurable. (Walker 2002, 7)

Aside from the various evaluations of CDC performance, a number of practitioners and researchers have begun to explore why some organizations are having difficulty and, in some cases, are being forced to close their operations. One of the first reports to identify this problem focused on the situation in Chicago as of 1995 and noted that:

> Three high-profile CDCs... terminated their development activities and essentially [went] out of business... leaving behind a troubled portfolio of low-income residential projects that they had developed and managed over the years. In addition, several other CDCs were going through unsettling leadership changes. (Futures Committee on Community Development in Chicago 1997, 3)

And, since then, one of the largest and most prestigious CDCs in the country, East Side Community Investments in Indianapolis, has also closed its doors (Reingold and Johnson 2003).

What are the causes of CDC failures? According to Tony Proscio, who recorded the proceedings of a LISC-sponsored conference on six CDCs that had failed or encountered serious difficulties, none of the groups was able to identify a single "trigger" factor—something that altered the situation from that of a problem to a full-scale crisis. "Serious crises, the kind that jeopardize an organization's survival, are cumulative affairs in which individual problems—no one of which is fatal—gradually gain mass and momentum until the available forces for remedy are too little, too late" (Proscio 1998, 5).

This problem was further explored by Rohe, Bratt and Biswas, who similarly concluded that

"It is often not possible to identify a single "fatal" problem. Instead . . . various factors—which are invariably both contextual and organizational—interact, resulting in a serious challenge to organizational viability" (2003, 57). While this team of researchers acknowledges that not all CDCs should be saved (such as where there is organizational incompetence or market forces that create adverse conditions for CDCs), their recommendations are aimed at providing guidance to CDCs and their support communities to make sure that as few CDCs as possible face organizational extinction.

The reason we need to be concerned about CDC survival is simple: As one of the key producers of housing affordable to low-income residents, it is critical that CDCs be supported and helped to thrive. If and when a Right to Housing initiative is created, its smooth and efficient implementation will depend on the existence of an experienced and competent infrastructure. CDCs are well positioned to assume a major role in a wide-scale effort to develop housing and other community services. While they would still encounter some of the same problems that they currently face, a well-funded national program, supplemented by supportive and technically competent local and national intermediaries, would go a long way toward our ability to significantly increase housing production.

In the meantime, as part of an overall commitment to provide increased funding for housing, the public sector should make sure that its investments strengthen CDCs and other nonprofits. In particular, these groups continue to need a steady source of income to cover operating expenses. And they also need a simpler subsidy mechanism that would allow them to package deals and develop projects much more efficiently than the current system that requires the use of multiple subsidies and funding sources.

A number of existing programs, such as the Community Development Block Grant Program, Community Development Financial Institutions, including the New Markets Tax Credit Program, and HOME, are good conduits for funding CDCs. But bringing back a deep, single subsidy such as the Section 8 New Construction and Substantial Rehabilitation Program would be a top priority. Another possible source of funding would come through a new National Housing Trust Fund, which would provide a dedicated source of revenue aimed at producing, rehabilitating and preserving 150,000 units per year within the span of a decade (The National Housing Trust Fund Campaign 2005).

Another proposal would target resources directly to CDCs and create a pool of technical assistance and capacity-building funds to assist CDCs. The Community Economic Development Expertise Enhancement Act (H.R. 2683) would authorize, over a three-year period, $225 million to provide technical assistance and capacity building funds for community-based development corporations, helping to leverage private dollars to create affordable housing and jobs in disinvested communities (National Congress for Community Economic Development 2004).

Alternatively, the federal government could bring back an old initiative, the Neighborhood Self-Help Development program,[8] which provided categorical funding for neighborhood development organizations. Finally, all developments aimed at low-income households should be permanently affordable to this group; subsidies need to be provided over the long term to make sure these restrictions stay in place.

The mechanisms needed to support CDCs and other producers of social housing are well understood. We are not confronted by a lack of knowledge about how to solve our housing problems; the limiting factor is our collective political will.

NOTES

1. Another term used synonymously with CDCs in this chapter is "community-based development organization."

2. A small portion of the literature reviewed in this chapter was first presented in Rohe, Bratt, and Biswas (2003).

3. The National Congress for Community Economic Development tracks the growth of CDCs and presents an image of uninterrupted growth, from some 200 groups in the mid-1970s to about 1,500 to 2,000 groups in 1988 to 3,600 groups in 1999 (National Congress for Community Economic Development 1989, 1999). However, anecdotal evidence, as well as recent research, reveals that CDCs not only are

created, but they also go out of business (Rohe, Bratt, and Biswas 2003).

4. In 2001, funders committed to another ten-year investment; NCDI was incorporated as a non-profit with a new name: Living Cities: The National Community Development Initiative.

5. Since about 1990, a growing movement, known as Comprehensive Community Initiatives (CCIs), has incorporated and expanded upon the community-building mission of CDCs. Funded by a number of foundations, CCIs generally have one or more CDCs as central actors in broad-based, community development initiatives (Eisen 1992; Connell et al. 1995; Roundtable on Comprehensive Community Initiatives for Children and Families 1997; Fulbright-Anderson, Kubisch, and Connell 1998).

6. "Self-sufficiency" is a frequently used term that generally refers to a household's ability to provide for itself without government subsidies. However, it is a problematic term, since virtually no one in society is truly "self-sufficient"; virtually everyone receives one or more forms of direct or indirect public assistance (Bratt and Keyes 1997). Also see Chapter 18.

7. The Neighborhood Reinvestment Corporation's institutional origins can be dated to 1975, when the Federal Home Loan Bank created an office dedicated to neighborhood reinvestment. Three years later, Congress enacted the Neighborhood Reinvestment Corporation Act, which transformed the office into a freestanding federally funded agency. Its mission was to promote "reinvestment in older neighborhoods by local financial institutions in cooperation with community, residents, and local governments" (NeighborWorks 2003, 3). The NeighborWorks network, which was created and supported by the Neighborhood Reinvestment Corporation, consists of more than 240 local nonprofit organizations whose goal is to create affordable housing and to promote community revitalization (NeighborWorks 2005). In FY2004, nearly $152 million in NeighborWorks revolving loan fund and capital investments leveraged more than $2 billion in other direct investments in neighborhoods served by affiliate organizations (NeighborWorks 2004). The Enterprise Foundation was created in 1982 with the assistance of real estate developer James Rouse. Since then, the organization has secured and made close to $6 billion in investments and contributions. Through their network of more than 2,500 organizations, more than 175,000 homes affordable to low-income families have been built or rehabilitated (The Enterprise Foundation 2004). The Local Initiatives Support Corporation (LISC) was created in 1980 and is committed to working with CDCs to rebuild communities. Technical assistance and financial support are provided to local programs operating in 38 cities as well as to 37 statewide rural programs. LISC raises money from private investors, lenders and donors (over

$6 billion) which, in turn, leverages additional public- and private-sector funds. Since its inception, the organization has provided assistance to 2,400 CDCs, which have built or rehabilitated 158,000 affordable homes and created over 22 million square feet of commercial, community and educational space (LISC 2005).

8. The Neighborhood Self-Help Development program provided $15 million in direct federal grants targeted to neighborhood development organizations. There were two rounds of funding, in 1979 and 1980; it was abolished as a freestanding program in 1981 and became an eligible activity under the Community Development Block Grant program.

REFERENCES

Abt Associates, Inc. 1973. *An evaluation of the Special Impact Program final report.* Vol. 1. Summary. Report prepared for the Office of Economic Opportunity, Cambridge, MA.

Ammann, John J., and Peter W. Salsich, Jr. 1997. Non-profit housing providers: Can they survive the "Devolution Revolution"? *St. Louis University Public Law Review,* 16(2):321–353.

Berndt, Harry Edward. 1977. *New rulers in the ghetto: The Community Development Corporation and urban poverty.* Westport, CT: Greenwood Press.

Blakely, Edward J. 1989. *Planning local economic development: Theory and practice.* Beverly Hills, CA: Sage.

Bratt, Rachel G. 1989. *Rebuilding a low-income housing policy.* Philadelphia: Temple University Press.

———. 1996. Community-based housing organizations and the complexity of community responsiveness. In *Revitalizing urban neighborhoods,* eds. W. Dennis Keating, Norman Krumholz and Philip Star, 179–190. Lawrence, KS: University Press of Kansas.

———. 1997. CDCs: Contributions outweigh contradictions, a reply to Randy Stoecker. *Journal of Urban Affairs,* 19(1):23–28.

Bratt, Rachel G., and Langley C. Keyes. 1997. *New perspectives on self-sufficiency: Strategies of nonprofit housing organizations.* Medford, MA: Department of Urban and Environmental Policy, Tufts University. Funded by the Ford Foundation.

Bratt, Rachel G., Avis C. Vidal, Alex Schwartz, Langley C. Keyes and James Stockard. 1998. The status of nonprofit-owned affordable housing: Short-term successes and long-term challenges. *Journal of the American Planning Association,* 64(1):39–51.

Bratt, Rachel G., Langley C. Keyes, Alex Schwartz and Avis C. Vidal. 1994. *Confronting the management challenge: Affordable housing in the nonprofit sector.* New York: New School for Social Research.

Briggs, Xavier DeSouza, and Elizabeth J. Mueller. 1997. *From neighborhood to community: Evidence on the social effects of community development.* New York: Community Development Research Center, Robert J. Milano Graduate School of Management and Urban Policy, New School for Social Research.

Clavel, Pierre, Jessica Pitt, and Robert Yin. 1997. The community option in urban policy. *Urban Affairs Review,* 32(4):435–458.

Clay, Phillip L. 1990. *Mainstreaming the community builders: The challenge of expanding the capacity of nonprofit housing development organizations.* Cambridge, MA: Massachusetts Institute of Technology.

Committee for Economic Development 1995. *Rebuilding inner-city communities: A new approach to the nation's urban crisis.* New York: Committee for Economic Development.

Connell, James P., Anne C. Kubisch, Lizbeth B. Schorr and Carol H. Weiss. 1995. *New approaches to evaluating comprehensive community initiatives: Concepts, methods, and contexts.* Washington, DC: The Aspen Institute.

Eisen, Arlene. 1992. *A report on foundations' support for comprehensive neighborhood-based community empowerment initiatives.* New York: The New York Community Trust.

The Enterprise Foundation. 2004. *Leadership in action: 2004 annual report.* Washington, DC.

Fisher, Robert. 1994. *Let the people decide: Neighborhood organizing in America, Updated Edition.* New York: Twayne Publishers.

Fulbright-Anderson, Karen, Anne C. Kubisch and James P. Connell. 1998. *New approaches to evaluating community initiatives.* Washington, DC: The Aspen Institute.

Futures Committee on Community Development in Chicago. 1997. *Changing the way we do things: Recommendations and findings of the Futures Committee.* Chicago: Local Initiatives Support Corporation.

Galster, George. 1996. *Reality and research: Social science and urban policy since 1960.* Washington, DC: Urban Institute Press.

Garn, Harvey A., Nancy L. Tevis, and Carl E. Snead. 1976. *Evaluating community development corporations—A summary report.* Washington, DC: The Urban Institute.

Glickman, Norman J., and Lisa J. Servon. 1999a. More than bricks and sticks: Five components of community development capacity. *Housing Policy Debate,* 9(3):497–539.

———. 1999b. *By the numbers: Measuring community development capacity.* New Brunswick, NJ: Rutgers University, Center for Urban Policy Research.

Goetz, Edward. 1993. *Shelter burden: Local and progressive housing policy.* Philadelphia: Temple University Press.

———. 1996. The community-based housing movement and progressive local politics. In *revitalizing urban neighborhoods,* eds. W. Dennis Keating, Norman Krumholz and Philip Star, 164–178. Lawrence, KS: University Press of Kansas.

Goetz, Edward, and Mara Sidney. 1994. Revenge of the property owners: Community development and the politics of property. *Journal of Urban Affairs,* 16(4):319–334.

Grogan, Paul S., and Tony Proscio. 2000. *Comeback cities: A blueprint for urban neighborhood revival.* Boulder, CO: Westview Press.

Hebert, Scott, Kathleen Heintz, Chris Baron, Nancy Kay, and James E. Wallace. 1993. *Nonprofit housing: Costs and funding. Final report.* Prepared by Abt Associates, Inc. under contract to U.S. Department of Housing and Urban Development, Washington, DC.

Heskin, Allan David. 1991. *The struggle for community.* Boulder, CO: Westview Press.

The Housing and Community Research Groups. 1973. *Community housing development corporations: The empty promise.* Cambridge, MA: Urban Planning Aid, Inc.

The Housing Partnership Network. 2005. September 26. www.housingpartnership.net

Husock, Howard. 2001. Don't let CDCs fool you. *City Journal,* 68–75, Summer.

Keating, William D., Keith P. Rasey, and Norman Krumholz. 1990. Community development corporations in the United States: Their role in housing and urban redevelopment. In *Government and housing: Developments in seven countries,* eds. Willem van Vliet– and Jan van Weesep, 206–218. Newbury Park, CA: Sage Publications, Inc.

Keyes, Langley C. 1971. The role of nonprofit sponsors in the production of housing. In *Papers submitted to U.S. House Committee on Banking and Currency; Subcommittee on Housing Panels on Housing Production, Housing Demand, and Developing a Suitable Living Environment,* 92nd Cong., 1st Sess, Pt. 1, 159–181.

Koschinsky, Julia. 1998. Challenging the third sector housing approach: The impact of federal policies (1980–1996). *Journal of Urban Affairs,* 20(2):117–135.

Leiterman, Mindy, and Joseph Stillman. 1993. *Building community: A report on social community development initiatives.* New York: Local Initiatives Support Corporation.

Lemann, Nicholas. 1994. The myth of community development. *New York Times Magazine,* January 9.

Lenz, Thomas J. 1988. Neighborhood development: Issues and models. *Social Policy,* 19:24–30, Spring.

Local Initiatives Support Corporation. 2005. LISC facts at a glance. September 26, 2005. www.liscorg/whatwedo/facts/

Massachusetts Association of Community Development Corporations. 2003. "Community organizing." December 6, 2003. www.macdc.org/docs/rhico.html.

Mayer, Neil S. 1984. *Neighborhood organizations and community development: Making revitalization work.* Washington, DC: The Urban Institute Press.

Mollenkopf, John. 1983. *The contested city.* Princeton, NJ: Princeton University Press.

National Center for Economic Alternatives. 1981. *Federal assistance to community development corporations: An evaluation of Title VII of the Community Services Act of 1974.* Report prepared for the U.S. Community Services Administration, Washington, DC.

National Congress for Community Economic Development. 1989. *Against all odds: The achievements of community-based development organizations.* Washington, DC.

———. 1999. *Trends and achievements of community-based development organizations.* Washington, DC.

———. 2004. The Community Economic Development Expertise Enhancement Act. January 6, 2004. www.ncced.org/policy/ceda/cdcexpertise.html

———. 2005. September 26, 2005. http://www.ncced.org/aboutUs/faqs.html#cdc.

The National Housing Trust Fund Campaign. 2005. September 26, 2005. www.nhtf.org.

NeighborWorks. 2002. *Annual report: Programmatic results and independent auditor's report.* Washington, DC: Neighborhood Reinvestment Corporation and the NeighborWorks Network.

———. 2004. Annual report: Transforming lives, strengthening communities. Washington, DC: NeighborWorks America and the NeighborWorks Network.

———. 2005. September 26, 2005. www.nw.org/network.

Nye, Nancy, and Norman J. Glickman 1995. *Expanding local capacity through community development partnerships.* New Brunswick, NJ: Rutgers University, Center for Urban Policy Research.

———. 1998. *Working together: Building capacity for community development.* New Brunswick, NJ: Rutgers University, Center for Urban Policy Research.

Peirce, Neil R., and Carol F. Steinbach. 1987. *Corrective capitalism: The rise of America's community development corporations.* New York, NY: Ford Foundation.

Proscio, Tony. 1998. Building durable CDCs. A summary of the proceedings of a conference organized by the Local Initiatives Support Corporation, Glen Cove, NY.

Reingold, David A., and Craig L. Johnson. 2003. The rise and fall of Eastside Community Investments, Inc.: The life of an extraordinary community development corporation. *Journal of Urban Affairs,* 25(5):527–549.

Robinson, Tony. 1996. Inner-city innovator: The non-profit community development corporation. *Urban Studies,* 33(9):1647–1670.

Rohe, William M. 1998. Do community development corporations live up to their billing? A review and critique of the research findings. In *Shelter and society: Theory, research, and policy for nonprofit housing,* ed. C. Theodore Koebel. Albany, NY: State University of New York Press.

Rohe, William M., Roberto G. Quercia, and Diane Levy. 2001. The performance of non-profit housing developments in the United States. *Housing Studies,* 16(5):595–618.

Rohe, William M., Rachel G. Bratt, and Protip Biswas. 2003. *Evolving challenges for community development corporations: The causes and impacts of failures, downsizings and mergers.* Chapel Hill, NC: The University of North Carolina, Center for Urban and Regional Studies.

Roundtable on Comprehensive Community Initiatives for Children and Families. 1997. *Voices from the field: Learning from the early work of comprehensive community initiatives.* Washington, DC: The Aspen Institute.

Rubin, Herbert J. 1993. Community empowerment within an alternative economy. In *Open institutions: The hope for democracy,* eds. John W. Murphy and Dennis L. Peck, 99–121. Westport, CT: Praeger.

———. 2000. *Renewing hope within neighborhoods of despair: The community-based development model.* Albany, NY: State University of New York Press.

Rusk, David. 1999. *Inside game/Outside game.* Washington, DC: Brookings Institution Press.

Schuman, Tony. 1986. The agony and the equity: Self-help housing. In *Critical perspectives on housing,* eds. Rachel G. Bratt, Chester Hartman and Ann Meyerson, 463–473. Philadelphia: Temple University Press.

Schwartz, Ed. 1994. Reviving community development. *The American prospect,* 5(19):1–6. www.prospect.org/print-friendly/print/V5/19/schwartz-e.html.

Stegman, Michael. 1991. The excessive costs of creative finance: Growing inefficiencies in the production of low-income housing. *Housing Policy Debate,* 2(2):357–376.

Stoecker, Randy. 1997. The CDC model of urban redevelopment: A critique and alternative. *Journal of Urban Affairs,* 19(1):1–22.

———. 2003. Understanding the development-organizing dialectic. *Journal of Urban Affairs,* 25(4):493–512.

Stoutland, Sara E. 1999. Community development corporations: Mission, strategy and accomplishments. In *Urban problems and community development,* eds. Ronald F. Ferguson and William T. Dickens, 193–240. Washington, DC: Brookings Institution Press.

Sullivan, Mercer L. 1993. *More than housing: How community development corporations go about changing lives and neighborhoods.* New York: Community Development Research Center, New School for Social Research.

Temkin, Kenneth, and William M. Rohe. 1998. Social capital and neighborhood stability: An empirical investigation. *Housing Policy Debate,* 9(1):61–88.

Traynor, Bill. 1993. Community development and community organizing. *Shelterforce,* 68, March/April.

U.S. Department of Housing and Urban Development. 1996. *Beyond shelter: Building communities of opportunity.* The United States Report for Habitat II, Washington, DC.

Vidal, Avis C. 1992. *Rebuilding communities: A national study of urban community development corporations.* New York, NY: Community Development Research Center of the Graduate School of Management and Urban Policy, New School for Social Research.

———. 1997. Can community development re-invent itself? The challenges of strengthening neighborhoods in the 21st century. *Journal of the American Planning Association,* 63(4):429–438.

Von Hoffman, Alexander. 2001. *Fuel lines for the urban revival engine: Neighborhoods, community development corporations, and financial intermediaries.* Washington, DC: Fannie Mae Foundation.

———. 2003. *House by house, block by block: The rebirth of America's urban neighborhoods.* New York: Oxford University Press.

Walker, Christopher. 1993. Nonprofit housing development: Status, trends, and prospects. *Housing Policy Debate,* 4(3):361–414.

———. 2002. *Community development corporations and their changing support systems.* Washington, DC: The Urban Institute.

Walker, Christopher, and Mark Weinheimer. 1998. *Community development in the 1990s.* Washington, DC: The Urban Institute.

Walker, Christopher, John Simonson, Thomas Kingsley, Bruce Ferguson, Patrick Boxall, Joshua Silver and Joe Howell. 1995. *Status and prospects of the nonprofit housing sector.* Prepared by the Urban Institute. Washington, DC: U.S. Department of Housing and Urban Development.

Walker, Christopher, Jeremy Gustafson, and Chris Snow. 2002. *National support for local system change: The effect of the national community development initiative on community development systems.* Washington, DC: The Urban Institute.

Winkelman, Lee. 1998. "Organizing renaissance: Twin Cities leads exploration of organizing by Massachusetts CDCs." *Shelterforce Online,* Issue #101, September/October: December 6, 2003. www.nhi.org/online/issues/101/winkelman.html.

Yin, Jordan S. 1998. The community development industry system: A case study of politics and institutions in Cleveland, 1967–1997. *Journal of Urban Affairs,* 20(2):139–157.

Zdenek, Robert. 1987. Community development corporations. In *Beyond the market and the state,* eds. Severyn Bruyn and James Meehan, 112–127. Philadelphia: Temple University Press.

Robert Wiener

Old and New Challenges Facing Rural Housing Nonprofits

NONPROFIT ORGANIZATIONS have played a major role in shelter provision in rural areas for decades. In the 1930s, the American Friends Service Committee attempted to promote self-help housing for the depression-era poor in Appalachia. In the 1960s, the Institute for Community Economics developed the community land trust model to house southern black farmers. Today, rural housing nonprofits across the country build, repair and acquire housing for the elderly, large families, farmworkers and other special-needs populations. One study found that almost 900 local groups were involved in some aspect of rural housing assistance (Housing Assistance Council 1995). Another found nearly 1,400 community development corporations (CDCs) providing assistance to rural communities, 81 percent of them (1,134) involved in some aspect of housing (Rural LISC 2002). As of 1999, CDCs had produced 115,000 units in rural areas, 21 percent of all CDC-produced units nationwide (Steinbach 1999). Over one-half of the rural units (53 percent) were for homeownership, compared with 22 percent of the urban units.

Despite recent growth in the number of housing nonprofits serving rural communities, including urban and suburban CDCs that have expanded their geographic reach, housing improvement in many rural areas is still beset by the traditional limitations and obstacles that have always confounded assistance efforts. These limitations and obstacles include:

Lack of Organizational Capacity—Although some of the oldest and most sophisticated CDCs originated and still operate in rural areas, vast rural parts of the country are either unserved by any nonprofit developer or are greatly underserved. Typically, existing rural nonprofits and local governments lack the expertise and skills to apply for housing assistance and to implement housing development. Outside training and technical support are hard to come by. Capacity needs include generation of administrative funds, development of professional management skills and acquisition of technical proficiency in developing and operating projects as well as using the new information technologies.

Lack of Credit and Capital—Historically, rural communities have been characterized by endemic shortages of funds for residential lending and investment (Strauss 1999). Creation in 1949 of a housing component in the U.S. Department of Agriculture (USDA), the Farmers Home Administration (now renamed the Rural Housing Service [RHS]), with direct lending authority, was based on a recognition of these shortages. Rural communities often lack conventional lenders, such as banks and savings and loans, and rural "redlining" is a fact of life. In addition, secondary mortgage lenders entered rural markets much later than they entered urban areas (Wilson and Carr 1999). Unlike large cities, local governments in rural areas are unable to generate sufficient tax revenues to finance projects and are greatly dependent on nonentitlement funds from highly competitive federal and state funding pools.

Lack of Buildable Sites and Infrastructure— While the common perception is that rural areas are blessed with huge tracts of inexpensive land ripe for development, in practice, housing production for low-income households is more constrained than in many cities. Constraints include the total absence or limited capacity of sewer and water facilities; lack of other supports, such as transportation routes, health and educational facilities, and employment opportunities; growth controls to protect agricultural land, coastal zones and other environmentally sensitive areas; and the existence of large public holdings.

Lack of Local Political Will and Support— Finally, rural housing nonprofits operate in some of the most politically conservative areas of the country, where resistance to most forms of government intervention is powerful. Government-assisted housing development suffers from the images that rural citizens have of inner-city slums. Opposition often takes the form of restrictive zoning, permit denials and NIMBY (not in my back yard) reactions that are, at least in part, driven by strong racial and ethnic stereotypes about the prospective occupants of low-income housing.

A NEW PROBLEM FACING RURAL NONPROFITS: THE CALIFORNIA STORY

In rural parts of the country that are experiencing population growth and urbanization pressures from expanding cities and suburbs, a new problem is emerging—competition from urban and suburban CDCs. California is a good case example and perhaps a harbinger of what is to come in other states. On the one hand, it is characterized by a core group of established and highly sophisticated development organizations that have their roots in rural communities; in fact, they pre-date the emergence of most comparable urban and suburban CDCs. Some of these organizations formed to meet the opportunities for self-help housing development in poor rural and farmworker communities made possible, beginning in the 1960s, by the federal Office of Economic Opportunity and then by the USDA. Later, they and newer organizations expanded into other areas of rural housing provision, funded by the USDA, Department of Housing and Urban Development (HUD), and state and local housing agencies. On the other hand, vast areas of rural California have faced the same limitations and obstacles to housing improvement as in other states because of lack of local capacity and the inability of the established organizations to extend their reach.

However, recent expansion of urban and suburban nonprofit developers into rural communities in search of new development opportunities has created a new dynamic. Until the 1990s, rural housing developers had worked in environments that were considered more collegial than competitive. Many had operated mostly unchallenged in service areas defined by relatively large county and multi-county regions, unlike the areas served by urban groups, which were often limited to smaller neighborhood, city or metropolitan regions. For the most part, the areas served by CDCs—rural and urban—are self-selected and bound only by organizational charters and, in some cases, funder restrictions. In general, organizations are not guaranteed the exclusive right to develop in a specified area, but most have held to informal understandings that respect each organization's territorial boundaries.

Rural nonprofits, as well as many of their urban counterparts, now fear that this pattern of reciprocity and mutuality is in jeopardy. Research on California's nonprofit housing sector, including its rural housing developers, revealed a pervasive sense that competition had increased in recent years and would continue to increase in future years (Wiener 1997).[1] Increased competition was identified as resulting from huge growth in the number of nonprofits and relative decreases in federal, state and local spending for housing. Competition today is a struggle by too many nonprofits—as well as for-profits—for too few financial resources, which in turn threatens to undermine traditional ways of doing business.

In the California study, a majority of organizations reported that the number of developers operating within their service areas had grown in recent years. Indeed, starting in the early 1980s, California saw unparalleled growth in the nonprofit housing sector. This can be attributed to several factors. Federal, state and local programs of the mid-1980s to early 1990s encouraged existing nonprofits to expand and encouraged start-up organizations to enter the field, including a new generation of community-based developers.[2] Growth was also stimulated by major private foundations and lending consortia, which created intermediary lending programs, and by individual lenders offering more attractive financing products in order to meet federal Community Reinvestment Act obligations. The emergence of a strong technical support system in the late 1970s and early 1980s (such as the Local Initiatives Support Corporation, Enterprise Foundation and Rural Community Assistance Corporation) and the development of nonprofit trade organizations helped to train and nourish new housing professionals and increase nonprofit capacity.

The new financing programs and institutional supports have had the unanticipated effect of weakening the strong position that rural nonprofits have held in some localities within the programmatic specialties that they had dominated for years. At the same time, migration of great numbers of people into the interior and rural regions of the state during the 1980s and 1990s, beyond the urban fringe of the expensive and congested coastal cities, has created new pressures and opportunities for housing development for low-income households.

COMPETITORS OF RURAL NONPROFITS

Four new types of competitors are now challenging the primacy of rural nonprofits:

Regional Housing Nonprofits—Large nonprofits from urban areas that have outgrown their original service areas because of limited funding and sites, high development costs, growth controls and other factors are now seeking development and management opportunities in the new growth centers.

Multipurpose Social Service Agencies—Urban-based service providers desiring to meet the shelter needs of their clients have formed housing development arms and, like regional housing nonprofits, are expanding into the new growth centers.

Community-Based Housing Development Organizations (CHDOs)—New nonprofits formed by local governments, existing nonprofit developers, citizens' groups and others are competing in funding programs that favor local development and ownership of housing.

For-Profit-Controlled ("Captive") Nonprofits—New nonprofits have been formed or have been sponsored by profit-motivated entities to gain access to government programs and local entitlements (such as property tax exemptions) that provide a preference for or are restricted to properties developed and owned by nonprofit organizations.

FUTURE PROSPECTS

The vagaries of federal, state and local spending for housing, which is currently in great jeopardy throughout the country, together with the growth in the nonprofit housing sector that occurred when conditions were more favorable, portend hard times for some organizations. Even with infusions of new funding, such as California experienced with passage of Proposition 46 in 2002,[3] it is quite likely that the day of reckoning will only be delayed and that the current number of nonprofits will decline in the future, with only the strongest and most opportunistic surviving.

To survive in this highly competitive era of limited resources, many nonprofits are making operational changes in development activities, staffing patterns, target populations and service areas in order to best respond to the new competitive challenges. In the California study, a significant number of urban nonprofits reported that competition figured in strategic decisions to expand service area boundaries and develop housing in new jurisdictions. The majority of expansions were into a new county or multicounty area—in some cases a jurisdictional leap far from their main business address. Some expansions were into small towns and unincorporated areas served by existing groups. These trends are most troubling to the older, limited-purpose rural housing developers who are highly dependent on vulnerable housing programs and fear challenges to their traditional turf from "service-area creep" by urban-based competitors.

Thus, the challenge in coming years will be twofold: to increase the development capacity in rural and remote rural communities that are currently unserved or underserved and to minimize and mitigate the worst manifestations of competition that threaten the viability of the established rural housing sector, which is uniquely committed to the shelter needs of small cities and rural locales. This becomes especially critical at times of funding scarcity and as we move inexorably toward a "devolved" federal housing system dependent on state and local administration (see Chapter 17). Healthy competition can stimulate greater efficiencies and community responsiveness. But a mad scramble for shrinking funding resources, without respect for traditional community loyalties and services missions, can have the opposite effect and undermine the future health and integrity of the nonprofit housing industry.

NOTES

1. The research, funded by the Aspen Institute, investigated the impacts of growth and competition on seventy-four California nonprofit producers of rural and urban housing that was affordable to low-income households.

2. While overall federal and state government outlays for housing declined during the 1980s and 1990s (see Introduction and Chapter 5), new programs emerged during this time that encouraged community-based, nonprofit development. These include the federal Low Income Housing Tax Credit and the various programs of the McKinney Homeless Assistance Act of 1987 and the National Affordable Housing Act of 1990, including the HOME program, Housing Opportunities for People Everywhere (HOPE), Housing Opportunities for People with AIDS (HOPWA) and Title VI Preservation (see Chapter 7).

3. In November 2002, California voters approved $2.1 billion in bonds to fund a variety of existing and new state housing programs, including programs limited to or providing preferences for nonprofit-developed housing.

REFERENCES

Housing Assistance Council. 1995. Filling the gaps: A study of capacity needs in rural nonprofit housing development. Washington, DC: The Council.

Rural LISC. 2002. Directory of rural community developers, 2002 Edition. Washington, DC.

Steinbach, Carol. 1999. Coming of age. Washington, DC: National Congress for Community Economic Development.

Strauss, Leslie. 1999. Credit and capital needs for affordable rural housing. In *Housing in rural America*, eds. Joe Belden and Robert Wiener. Thousand Oaks, CA: Sage Publications.

Wiener, Robert. 1997. Too much demand, too little money! Competition in California's nonprofit housing sector. Sacramento: California Coalition for Rural Housing Project.

Wilson, Harold L., and James H. Carr. 1999. Impact of federal interventions on private mortgage credit in rural areas. In *Housing in rural America*, eds. Joe Belden and Robert Wiener. Thousand Oaks, CA: Sage Publications.

John Emmeus Davis

17   Between Devolution and the Deep Blue Sea: What's a City or State to Do?

DEVOLUTION IS A political storm, many years in the making, which has finally arrived in full force. At the center of this turbulence is a dubious idea that is simplicity itself. It costs the federal government far more to operate most domestic programs, so the argument goes, than it would cost the less bureaucratically burdened governments of the nation's cities or states to administer the same programs. For every federal dollar spent on subsidized housing, community development or social welfare, anywhere from a dime to a quarter is needlessly "wasted" because Washington is running the show instead of officials who are closer to the problems and closer to the people these programs are meant to serve. To eliminate such waste, say devolution's devotees, responsibility for most domestic programs should be turned over—"devolved"— to a lower level of government. Give states and cities most of the money previously controlled by the Feds, grant them the flexibility to "reinvent" these programs and they will find creative, efficient and effective ways to do more with less. Bureaucracy will be steadily shrunk. Money will be better spent. People will be better served.[1]

Lurking behind all the talk of devolving authority and reinventing government, however, are sinister specters that are deeply disturbing to those who struggle day-by-day to provide housing for lower-income people and to improve conditions in lower-income communities.

Less money for housing and community development. Promises of flexibility, efficiency and democracy resulting from devolution have frequently been used to deflect criticism of proposed cuts in the federal budget and to insulate Congress from the backlash engendered by those cuts. The irony here, especially for governors who have championed devolution, is that many members of Congress have come to believe the overblown rhetoric about saving 25 cents on the dollar. That's a lot of "fat" for committee chairs to capture for their pet projects—or for the tax reduction crowd to remove from the budget altogether. Even when housing dollars remain in the budget, there is seldom any guarantee that a greater proportion of them will reach the streets. Bureaucracy does not disappear simply by chopping it into smaller pieces. Devolution's proponents may or may not be correct in their gloomy assessment of federal inefficiency, but they are certainly wrong in their rosy predictions of the efficiencies to be gained—and the savings to be had—from turning over dozens of programs to 50 states and to hundreds of cities.[2]

Less targeting and less oversight by federal agencies. The whole point of devolution is to "get the Feds off the backs" of cities and states so that a thousand innovations and efficiencies can bloom. The record of earlier attempts to give cities and states more sway over federally funded programs for housing and community development shows, however, that devolution has usually resulted in fewer dollars being directed to the poor (and to the neighborhoods in which they live); fewer dollars going to any tenure of housing other than market-priced homeownership and fewer dollars benefiting persons of color.[3] "If it ain't a federal dollar," as one inner-city resident commented long ago when reflecting on the Model Cities program, "you can hang it up as far as minorities are concerned" (Browning, Marshall and Tabb 1984, 207). True then; true now.

More political clout by private real estate interests and suburban constituencies. "By practically any measure," notes Etzioni (1995), "the typical state government is even less responsive to its citizens than Washington." Most state legislatures, on the other hand, are quite responsive when it comes to protecting the interests of real estate developers, landlords, bankers and landowners, especially when a maverick municipality goes "too far" in challenging the boundaries of housing reform.[4] A few examples: When tenants in Philadelphia succeeded in getting their city council to adopt an 18-month moratorium on the conversion of rental housing to condominiums in 1979, developers, landlords and realtors hustled off to the Pennsylvania legislature and got the moratorium eradicated by a state law preempting local condominium ordinances.[5] When the voters of Burlington, Vermont approved an antispeculation tax on rental housing in 1986, the state legislature blocked its enactment by refusing to allow Burlington to amend its municipal charter to levy such a "confiscatory" tax. In 1995, the California state legislature imposed vacancy decontrol (beginning in 1999) on every city with rent control, preempting the power of local governments to decide for themselves the circumstances under which price-controlled rentals could return to the market (Keating 1998). Also in 1995, a state-wide referendum in Massachusetts eliminated rent control in Boston and two other cities that had enacted municipal rent control (Keating 2003, 25). It is no accident that the real estate industry (among other business interests) has usually preferred regulations and dollars to flow from state government rather than from either the federal or municipal government.[6]

Although this picture may seem devoid of portents or possibilities for housing strategies of a more progressive bent, the future is not totally bleak. Nor was the past. After all, the current enthusiasm for turning over federal programs to lower levels of government is the continuation of a long-term trend in the case of subsidized housing and community development.[7] Public officials at the state and municipal levels have been forced to live with creeping devolution for many years. Unlike their federal counterparts, they have not had the political luxury of simply turning away from the deepening poverty of their citizens, the deteriorating housing of their neighborhoods, and the widening gulf between household incomes and housing costs. Nearly inundated by a sea of need, most cities and states have tried to do *something* to house their lower-income citizens. Some of what they have done has been hastily conceived and deeply flawed. None of what they have done has come close to replacing the billions of housing dollars that have been steadily withdrawn by the federal government. Nevertheless, here and there, cities and states have made a difference. Attempting to do "some" thing for housing, they have occasionally found their way, by accident or design, toward doing the "right" thing.

What they are doing—and, more to the point, what they should do—is the subject of the present chapter. Devolution is not a passing disturbance but a climatic change in the political environment, one likely to be with us for quite a while.[8] There are dangers in this shift of dollars, powers and responsibilities. There are limits in the ability (and will) of cities and states to cope with these changes.[9] Yet there are also opportunities that should not be ignored, offering room to maneuver and reason to hope that some of the innovations being tried by nonfederal units of government may nudge the entire system in a positive direction, moving a little closer toward making a Right to Housing a reality. Cities and states have been pioneers in the past. They may play a similar role in the future.

PROGRESSIVE STRATEGIES FOR CITIES AND STATES

Cities and states that are serious about doing the "right" thing for housing can choose from a menu of strategies, arrayed among four goals: redistributing the benefits of growth; expanding the supply of nonspeculative housing; preserving the lower-cost housing that presently exists; and enabling residential mobility, both social and geographic. I attempt to show what should be done by selecting concrete examples of what cities and states are already doing.

The good news is that there are so many examples from which to choose. Cities and states have displayed a remarkable degree of innovation over the last few decades in attempting to address the housing needs of their populations.[10] The bad news is that so few of these innovations have been adopted widely enough or funded fully enough to allow a complete assessment of their replicability and worth. There are interventions aplenty for each of the strategies that follow, but they generally indicate what might be done to realize a particular strategy. None is proposed as a legislative or programmatic ideal that should be uncritically embraced. They are "works in progress." Some are "failures in progress"—good ideas that were legislatively compromised from the beginning or poorly implemented later on; or good programs that were initially effective but eventually terminated when a more conservative regime took office. Nevertheless, contained within each is a kernel of inspiration for answering the question of "what's a city or state to do?"

Progressive Housing Strategies for Cities and States	
Goals	Strategies
Redistributing the benefits of growth	Tapping into development
	Reinvesting deposits
	Taxing transfers
Expanding nonspeculative housing	Prioritizing project funding
	Subsidizing nonprofit operations
	Delegating assets and powers
	Sanctioning affordability controls
Preserving lower-cost housing	Protecting against loss of units
	Protecting against evictions
	Protecting against rising costs
Enabling residential mobility	Removing barriers
	Penetrating enclaves
	Promoting choice

Two caveats about what is missing from my list of recommended strategies: Except for some mention of rental assistance, there is no discussion of governmental programs for supplementing the income of poverty-level households. The meagerness of such supplements in the past and the shrinkage of such supplements in the present impose major constraints on the ability of any city or state to house its most impoverished citizens or to redevelop its most dilapidated

neighborhoods. A generous and just incomes policy, combined with guarantees of a livable wage for all who find work, would make almost any housing policy more effective. Nevertheless, for reasons of focus and space, I have chosen to omit "supplementing income" from my list of goals and strategies.

Nor is "producing more housing" to be found on my list of progressive goals and practical strategies. The construction of new housing is treated here as a means to an end, not as an end in itself. Cities and states should prioritize the preservation of the lower-cost housing they already have before diverting scarce resources to the construction of new housing. They should promote production as one tool (among many) for pursuing the goals of expanding nonspeculative housing or enabling residential mobility. Creating new units may also be justified as one tool (among many) for rebuilding or revitalizing a distressed locale. Production is not exactly missing from these policy prescriptions, but it is treated as incidental to goals and strategies with a prior claim over public resources.

One final note: Dividing multiple strategies among four different goals is an expository device that tends to obscure the many overlaps that can—and should—occur across these descriptive divides. The most effective interventions tend to advance more than one housing goal at a time, to utilize more than one housing strategy and to blur the line between what Rusk (1999) has deemed the "inside game" and the "outside game"—that is, measures that are targeted internally toward a particular neighborhood, city or town versus measures that are targeted regionally, across numerous jurisdictional boundaries. In practice, there is (or should be) an interdependence among these interventions as well as an intersection of the "inside game" and the "outside game." These interventions are part of the same comprehensive policy, each providing an essential piece of an interlocking puzzle. None should be pursued in isolation.

Redistributing the Benefits of Growth

Davidoff (1978:69) once suggested that the best way to determine whether a planner is engaged in meaningful, moral and effective work is to ask, "Are you a redistributionalist?...Are you for maintaining the distribution of goods, services, opportunities and processes as they are, or do you favor a redistribution so that those who now have the least will receive considerably more and thus the gap will be reduced?" If the planner's work is not aimed at redistribution, he argued, his or her efforts will be counterproductive at best, amoral at worst. Krumholz (1996) reached a similar conclusion in arguing for what has come to be called "equity planning." The goal that he and his planning staff embraced in Cleveland during the 1970s was "more choices for those who have few."

Imbued with a similar impulse toward redistribution, the present chapter assumes that a paramount concern for a planner, policymaker or community activist whose work is focused on housing must always be, *Who gets what*? Will the investment of public resources or the exercise of public powers aimed at providing housing or improving neighborhoods help those who have the least or those who have the most? Will opportunities and conditions for persons of different classes, races, abilities and ethnicities be made more equal—or less? The former is the prize on which the eyes of the progressive planner or the equity planner must always be fixed.

Redistribution as the aim of public policy is put to its stiffest test by the issue of growth, especially at the municipal level. A steady increase in capital investment, real estate values and population—what Logan and Molotch (1987, 32) once called the "unrelenting search... for more and more"—is eagerly sought by political elites in nearly every city, even in those where a more progressive agenda has come to the fore.[11] What distinguishes progressive planners from their more conservative colleagues is not a disregard for growth but a commitment to redistributing its benefits and burdens. When applied to housing and community development, progressives proceed from a recognition that real estate development has traditionally allowed property owners to *internalize*—to claim for themselves—not only the appreciation that they personally create through their own dollars and efforts but appreciation that is socially created by public investment in the neighborhood, by private investment in adjoining

parcels, or by growth in the city (or region) as a whole. Conversely, the owners and developers of real estate are allowed to *externalize* many of the costs of their projects, imposing social, economic and environmental burdens on residents, neighbors and municipal budgets that are usually ill-prepared to shoulder them.

To realign this imbalance, many cities, some states and a few regions have enacted a variety of measures to ensure that the fruits of growth are more equitably shared while preventing the costs of growth (or decline) from falling disproportionately upon those with the least ability to pay. These are not necessarily "progressive" regimes. Even the most pro-growth, pro-business government can, on occasion, find itself forced by political reality or economic necessity into taking a redistributionist stance. What is important, therefore, is not where the sponsors of a measure happen to be on the political spectrum, but whether the *outcome* of that measure redistributes resources, rights or power from groups who have a lot to groups who have less.

Nearly every state or municipal initiative discussed in this chapter serves this redistributionist end. There are some, however, that *depend* on growth; they are possible and effective only in the presence of growth, especially a strong and expanding real estate market. By tapping into profits (and taxes) generated by residential and commercial development, by reinvesting assets deposited in banks and by taxing transfers of real property, cities and states can mobilize new resources for housing lower-income people and revitalizing lower-income neighborhoods.

Tapping into Development. For-profit real estate development is an attempt to reap an economic reward from property values created by others. There is, of course, a stream of income that directly results from the developer's own creation of a useful structure which others are willing to lease or purchase. But the most significant return on a developer's investment typically comes from tapping into the "web of externalities" (Qadeer 1981, 172) that dumps value onto his or her site simply because it is uniquely and opportunistically *there*. What else is implied, after all, by the popular saying that only three things truly matter in real estate: "location, location and location"?

One of the most common ways that cities and counties have found to force residential developers into sharing some of this locational largess is by inclusionary zoning. The developer is required to sell or to rent at an "affordable" price a specified percentage of any housing units produced through new construction or substantial rehabilitation. In New Jersey, where this type of zoning has been a mainstay of municipal and state housing policy since 1983, the "normal" inclusionary set-aside is 20 percent, divided equally between units made affordable for households earning between 50 and 80 percent of a locality's median income and units made affordable for households earning under 50 percent of median (Calavita, Grimes and Mallach 1997; Mallach 1994).[12] Outside of New Jersey, this mandated set-aside has varied greatly. In California, for example, where 107 cities and counties have some form of inclusionary zoning, the percentage of below-market units required ranges from as little as 4 percent in San Clemente to as high as 35 percent in Davis (NPH/CCRH 2003). There is also considerable variation in New Jersey, California and elsewhere in the requirements for how "affordable" the prices of inclusionary homes must be, how long such affordability must last and how large a project must be before being subject to inclusionary zoning. Behind these variations, however, the redistributionist logic is essentially the same: The sellers of buildable land, the developers of market-rate housing and the buyers (or renters) of market-rate units are made to bear most of the cost of providing housing at a below-market price, "sharing the wealth" with households less affluent than themselves.

Linkage is infused with a similar logic. Formally defined as "the mandatory municipal regulation of unsubsidized large commercial development in order to obtain housing exactions as a condition of development approval" (Keating 1989, 211), linkage is really nothing more than a means of redistributing wealth from the downtown to the neighborhoods.[13] The developers of commercial real estate are required either to construct (or rehabilitate) off-site housing themselves or to pay fees in-lieu-of-production into

a housing trust fund, administered by the municipality. All of the housing produced through such exactions is priced to be affordable—and, in many cases, to remain affordable—for persons earning below 80 percent or 50 percent of median income.

Linked downtown-neighborhood development policies mandating exactions for housing have been adopted in San Francisco (1981), Santa Monica (1981), Boston (1983), Jersey City (1985), Berkeley (1986 and 1993), Cambridge (1988) and Sacramento (1989). San Diego adopted a hefty linkage fee in 1990 to capitalize the city's housing trust fund but then reduced it by one-half in 1996. Seattle has had a voluntary linkage program since 1989, allowing commercial developers to purchase extra floor-area ratio for their projects if they provide affordable housing, child care or other amenities (Avault and Lewis 2000). Many other cities, including Miami, Denver, Hartford, New York, Chicago, Portland (OR) and Washington, DC, negotiate agreements on a case-by-case basis, linking commercial development to the development of lower-cost housing.

What may be the most effective and lucrative strategy for tapping into development, however, is one that has rarely been implemented in the United States: regional revenue sharing. Every city in a region contributes to a regional pool a percentage of the growth in its property tax base resulting from new commercial, industrial and residential development. These pooled revenues are then redistributed among the region's cities. High-growth, high-tax-capacity municipalities become net contributors to this pool. Low-growth, low-tax-capacity municipalities become net beneficiaries. Where the percentage of the tax increment captured by this regional pool is significant, fiscal disparities among a region's cities can be gradually reduced, along with the deadly competition for growth. The region surrounding Minnesota's Twin Cities (Minneapolis and St. Paul) has had a mandatory tax base sharing system in place since 1971, where each city in the metropolitan region contributes 40 percent of the growth of its commercial and industrial tax base into a regional pool (Orfield 1997, 87). Dayton, Ohio and 26 out of 30 of its surrounding townships and municipalities adopted a voluntary plan in 1991 for sharing 13 percent of the growth in both their property taxes and payroll taxes (Rusk 1999, 201–221). The impact on existing fiscal disparities has been small in both of these cases. There is, nevertheless, the potential in such multi-jurisdictional revenue sharing for tapping into suburban development, not only to invest in declining communities that need it the most, but to fund lower-cost housing in thriving communities that often resist it the most.

Reinvesting Deposits. Since the 1930s, most federal and state laws regulating commercial banks and savings and loan associations that are in the business of providing credit to the public have contained a provision asserting that these regulated institutions should serve the "convenience and needs of their communities" (FFIEC 1992, 3). There was an assumed reciprocity here: Government gave the financial institution a charter to do business, insurance for its deposits and access to discounted capital; members of the public gave the institution their savings; and, in return for these privileges and trust, the institution helped to meet the credit needs of the entire area from which it drew its deposits. At least that was the way it was supposed to work. In reality, the practice of many banks was to restrict access to credit for people of color and for residents of certain low-income neighborhoods.

The federal Community Reinvestment Act (CRA) of 1977 was aimed at changing that, as were various antiredlining, fair lending and mortgage disclosure laws enacted by many state legislatures.[14] The CRA and its state-level cousins reaffirmed the principle of reciprocity, declaring that a financial institution could not receive privileges from government and collect deposits from the public without meeting an "affirmative obligation" to help meet local credit needs, even in low-income communities. Equally significant, the CRA handed community activists, local officials and the press a new means of monitoring the lending policies and practices of these regulated institutions, along with a means of pressuring them into doing better. These nonfederal actors have frequently proved more effective in uncovering CRA violations than the federal regulators. In Atlanta and

Detroit, for example, it was the press that blew the whistle on discriminatory lending practices (Dedman 1988, 1989; Everett 1992). In Chicago, Pittsburgh, Milwaukee, Cleveland, Cincinnati, Dallas, Denver and Washington, DC, it was community activists who took the lead in exposing and confronting local lenders who failed to meet their CRA obligations (Squires 1994, 76–83). Many of these struggles yielded negotiated settlements with offending financial institutions, making millions of dollars available for mortgages, home improvement loans and small business loans in neighborhoods that were previously overlooked. Even without formal settlements, the CRA has been generally effective in increasing the level of mortgage lending to people and places underserved in the past (Squires 2003, 12; Apgar and Duda 2003).

Municipal officials, including those in Boston, Cleveland and Milwaukee, have occasionally entered the fray on the side of community activists, wielding the "stick" of the CRA. State officials, including those in Connecticut and Pennsylvania, have sometimes personally negotiated CRA agreements (Taylor and Silver 2003). Most cities and states, however, have been more inclined to use the "carrot" of their own deposits to nudge lenders toward community reinvestment. Implemented through either administrative policy or legislative action, these "linked deposit" measures reward financial institutions that exhibit a record of fair lending and a commitment to meeting the credit needs of lower-income neighborhoods. By 1994, at least a dozen cities and 14 states were requiring the depositories of public funds to have a "good community reinvestment record" (Squires 1994, 82). In most cases, this has meant granting "good" institutions favored status in competing to receive and manage public deposits. Chicago has gone further. By municipal ordinance, the City is prohibited from doing business with predatory lenders or their affiliated banks.

Taxing Transfers. Finally, a redistributionist strategy can be pursued by taxing away some of the short-term gains that make the speculative buying and selling of residential real estate so lucrative for some and so damaging for others. Such a strategy can serve either a preservationist or a redistributionist end. If successful in discouraging speculation, it can relieve pressure on the existing stock of lower-cost housing. If unsuccessful as a deterrent to speculation (often because it was never intended as such), taxing transfers can at least capture a portion of the speculative value when properties change hands, using those revenues to subsidize housing for low- and moderate-income people.

Although no city or state has gone very far in actually trying to stop speculation, once dubbed by Hite (1979, 49) "the great American game," a few have enacted taxes that either slow it to a less destructive pace or share its gains more broadly. Washington, DC and the state of Vermont provide two examples. The former adopted a Real Property Transfer Tax in 1978, aimed at the "flipping" of residential rental properties; the latter adopted a Land Gains Tax in 1973, aimed at the speculative turnover of larger parcels of unimproved land. Both make use of graduated taxes pegged to the period that a property is held between purchase and re-sale. The shorter the holding period, the higher the tax on the property's appreciated value. Similar antispeculation taxes have been considered but not adopted by state legislatures in California, Hawaii, Maryland, Massachusetts, Montana, Oregon, Virginia and Washington.[15]

By contrast, the Dade County, Florida Documentary Surcharge Program, created in 1983, was never intended to impede speculation but merely to raise revenues for lower-cost housing. By tapping into the appreciated value of real estate transfers other than those of single-family homes, Dade County captures millions of dollars per year for its housing trust fund.[16] This approach to funding affordable housing went state-wide in 1992, when the state of Florida raised its own real estate transfer tax and directed these new revenues toward the creation of affordable housing.[17] Real estate transfer fees collected by Maine, New Jersey and several other states are used in similar ways, with considerable variation in the types of housing targeted and the mix of populations served.

Although each of these strategies generates significant resources for subsidizing lower-cost housing, it must be admitted that the amount of redistribution that typically results from tapping

into development, reinvesting deposits or taxing transfers is relatively small. As implemented to date, none of these strategies goes very far in closing the gap between those with wealth and those without. More to the point, none of these strategies necessarily results in the kind of housing that is most needed and most affordable, unless they are explicitly designed with this in mind. Many inclusionary zoning and linkage programs, for example, create housing with eligibility thresholds that are set too high or affordability controls that are lost too soon.[18] Many CRA settlements and linked deposit programs create mortgage pools for homebuyers of modest means but provide few benefits for poorer populations or for alternative forms of tenure. Many housing trust funds, including some that are funded by real estate transfer taxes, do little to limit the speculative buying and selling of the housing they assist—inadvertently contributing to the very problem of unaffordable housing that they are trying to address.

Redistributing the benefits of growth, therefore, is only one of several goals that a city or state should pursue when setting out to "do something" to house lower-income populations. It should not be pursued by itself. Strategies of redistribution must be combined with strategies associated with other progressive goals, especially the goal of expanding the supply of residential units that are permanently removed from the speculative market.

Expanding Nonspeculative Housing

Nonspeculative housing goes by many names, including "decommodified housing," "perpetually affordable housing," "social housing" and "social ownership" (see Chapter 11). Such housing can be owned and operated by public housing authorities, by private, nonprofit organizations or by the residents themselves, as in the case of limited-equity housing cooperatives, limited-equity condominiums, community land trusts and single-family houses with resale restrictions incorporated into a deed, mortgage or lease. Regardless of owner, all nonspeculative housing is operated without a profit and is transferred without a speculative gain. Residents are given security of tenure. They are also given an opportunity, in some cases, to realize limited appreciation when reselling the homes that are theirs. Owners may not rent or sell, however, to whomever they want or for whatever the market will bear. The property is permanently removed from the market, priced to remain relatively affordable for lower-income households, one transfer after another.

Of late, the fastest-growing segment of nonspeculative housing has been the private, non-market housing produced or sponsored by private, nonprofit organizations with the direct assistance of cities and states. It is here, in seeding and sustaining new models of nonmarket tenure, often accompanied by new modes of nonprofit production and new methods of nonbank finance, that cities and states have been especially innovative during the last few decades. It is here, in adopting and refining what I have previously called a "third sector" housing policy (Davis 1994, 2000), that cities and states are most likely to show initiative and innovation in the years ahead.[19]

That is not to say that public housing authorities or residents themselves cannot be significant players in expanding the stock of nonspeculative housing. Most of the strategies for meeting this goal can be tailored to support publicly owned housing or resident-controlled housing, with or without the involvement of a nonprofit developer. A number of housing authorities have, in fact, begun to play a more active role in recent years both in developing new housing and in revitalizing housing they already own (cf. Vale 1997, 2002; CHAPA 2001).

On the other hand, present political realities suggest that public-private partnerships with nonprofit organizations are probably the path of least resistance for nonspeculative housing. In a time of privatization, when anything governmental seems suspect and when public housing in particular is often in disrepute, cities and states find it easier to venture into uncharted territory with a nonprofit partner at their side. In a time of retrenchment, when Washington's commitment to declining urban and rural areas is itself in decline, elected officials in cities, counties and states find themselves looking for new models and new partners to help them rebuild distressed communities. A growing number of

these public officials have concluded, along with Barton (1996, 111), that "social ownership is virtually the only way to keep housing viable in neighborhoods undergoing drastic disinvestment and abandonment by the private sector; moreover, social housing organizations typically strengthen the organizational skills of the residents, promoting community self-help and mutual aid as well as advocacy for a more equitable distribution of municipal resources."

Not all nonprofits behave this way. Many do little to strengthen the organizational skills of people residing in the units that they develop or the neighborhoods which they serve. Even more problematic for a progressive housing policy, not all nonprofits believe that the housing they produce should be permanently removed from the market—especially when that housing is owner-occupied. Nonprofit housing and nonspeculative housing are not always the same.

On the other hand, as Bratt has pointed out (1989, 199), when it comes to maintaining the affordability of the housing they produce, "the commitment of most community-based housing developers is more similar to the long-range commitment of public housing authorities and contrasts with the relatively short-lived involvement of private, for-profit developers of subsidized housing." To the extent their commitment to long-term affordability is real, private nonprofits have been—and will probably continue to be—the principal vehicles through which cities and states attempt to expand the supply of nonspeculative housing.

Cities and states that embrace this goal commonly use one or more of four different strategies.[20] They prioritize funding for the construction or rehabilitation of units that are owned and operated as nonspeculative housing; they support the operations of the nonprofit organizations that produce such housing; they delegate assets and powers, previously the purview of the public sector, to private, nonprofit organizations; and they provide legal sanction for permanent affordability.

Prioritizing Project Funding. An explicit policy of governmental support for nonspeculative housing means, first and foremost, that a city or a state's resources for housing are directed predominantly toward forms of private (or public) nonmarket ownership that preserve public subsidies and perpetuate affordability. These housing resources include pass-through funding from various federal programs, the allocation of Low Income Housing Tax Credits and the distribution of various state and municipal revenues.[21] Under a nonspeculative housing policy, priority in awarding such public funds—whether for the construction of nonmarket housing, the acquisition and rehabilitation of units previously owned and operated as market housing or the acquisition and rehabilitation of units previously owned and operated as subsidized housing—goes to projects for which there is a guarantee that any subsidized units will remain affordable for a targeted class of low- or moderate-income residents.

How long affordability must last varies greatly from one locality to another. Ideally, nonspeculative housing is removed permanently from the market; it is perpetually affordable. Some cities and states have, in fact, been quite explicit about pursuing this elusive ideal. Burlington, Vermont has made a commitment to "perpetual affordability" the cornerstone of its housing policy since 1984. Connecticut's "forever housing policy," instituted in the late 1980s but dismantled by a later administration, declared that "state-assisted housing should be permanently removed from the speculative market" and proceeded to prioritize funding for limited-equity housing cooperatives, community land trusts, mutual housing associations and other nonmarket models designed to preserve "the long-term affordability of housing generated by public funds."[22] Affordability requirements lasting anywhere from 40 years to the "useful life" of the assisted property can also be found in selected housing programs of the City of Boston and the Boston Redevelopment Authority (Collins and White 1994); in the housing trust funds of Ann Arbor, Cambridge, Berkeley, San Francisco, San Diego, Los Angeles and Washington, DC; and in the housing trust funds of Ohio, Oregon, Rhode Island and Vermont (Brooks 1994, 2002). The state of California began providing $1 million to $2 million grants to local housing trust funds in 2003, requiring a dollar-for-dollar match from

local sources and requiring all of these funds to be used for the construction of rental housing with affordability restrictions lasting a minimum of 55 years.

Housing projects with continuing affordability are sometimes given a public boost in another way as well. A number of cities and states offer private, nonmarket housing either short-term or long-term reductions in property taxes. Most common are temporary abatements for a limited number of years or for a specified component of a project's total assessment (such as not collecting taxes on the incremental value created by rehabilitating a dilapidated residential building). Less common, but more significant, are the permanent abatements provided in New Jersey, Vermont, Oregon and a handful of other states, where local assessors recognize that privately owned housing with long-term restrictions on rents and re-sales has a lower value. The owners of such "encumbered" property pay lower property taxes than owners who can rent or resell their properties for whatever the market will bear.[23]

Subsidizing Nonprofit Operations. It is no accident that the most stable, sophisticated and accomplished nonprofit housing networks are found in those cities and states that have historically been the most generous in providing operational support for community development corporations, mutual housing associations, community land trusts and other nonprofit producers of below-market housing. Chicago, Cleveland, Minneapolis, St. Paul, Seattle, Boston, Burlington and Portland, Oregon, for example, are cities in which nonprofit developers have come to play a major role—indeed, the starring role—in producing, preserving and operating such housing. Municipal support for bricks-and-mortar residential development, in each of these cities, is regularly supplemented by direct municipal support for the core operations of the nonprofits being asked to undertake such development.

A particularly promising innovation in the area of operating support has been the recent growth of local "partnerships" and "collaboratives" for community development (Nye and Glickman 2000). These are city-wide intermediaries, using funds contributed by municipal agencies, community foundations and private corporations, that provide a reliable, predictable stream of operating grants, training opportunities and technical assistance for nonprofit producers of affordable housing. Examples of such partnerships can be found in Boston, Cleveland, Detroit, Los Angeles, New Orleans, Philadelphia, Washington, DC, and Portland, Oregon.

Although state agencies have tended to be far more reluctant than their municipal counterparts to provide dollars for the ongoing operations of nonprofit developers, there are notable exceptions. Massachusetts, New Hampshire, New York, North Carolina, Oregon and Vermont, for example, are states with a long history of making "capacity grants" available to the nonprofit producers of state-assisted affordable housing.[24]

It should be emphasized again that *nonprofit* housing is not necessarily *nonspeculative* housing. Indeed, there are cities with extensive nonprofit housing development networks, like Cleveland and Pittsburgh, where lasting affordability is barely a part of the policy agenda. Subsidizing the operations of nonprofit producers is a strategy for meeting the goal of expanding nonspeculative housing only where nonprofits are committed to creating—and where cities and states insist on creating—housing that is affordable to low- and moderate-income households both initially and continually.

Delegating Assets and Powers. Accompanying the shift of responsibilities from higher to lower levels of government, there has been a parallel trend over the past 25 years of transferring increased responsibilities, powers and assets from the public sector to nonprofit organizations (cf. Smith and Lipsky 1993). Such a trend may eventually hold as many dangers for low-income people and low-income communities as devolution, but it has also offered a number of unexpected opportunities for nonprofits to expand the supply of nonspeculative housing.

It has become common practice, for instance, for cities and states to give nonprofit organizations responsibility for administering revolving loan funds, capitalized with public funds. Acting as the municipality's (or the state's) agent, the nonprofit loans and re-loans these funds to low-income homeowners, mom-and-pop landlords or small businesses within a targeted area. Although it is rare for these revolving loan programs to impose lasting restrictions on the affordability of assisted projects, nonprofits with a commitment to nonspeculative housing have often used these lending programs (and fees generated by them) to subsidize their own operations, to expand their social base and to stabilize market-rate housing proximate to the social housing they own and operate.

Another delegation of municipal power has been granted to nonprofit developers in several cities that have either enacted ordinances controlling the conversion of rental property to condominiums or mandated the set-aside of "inclusionary" units in newly constructed projects. Required by ordinance or enforced as a policy of the agency administering the ordinance, nonprofits have been given the first right to purchase, at a below-market price, any housing units slated for conversion or any inclusionary units offered for sale. As a quid pro quo, the nonprofit purchaser is expected to guarantee the affordability of these units for low-income tenants or low-income homebuyers for a lengthy period of time.

Even more common is the practice of making nonprofits, limited-equity housing cooperatives or tenant associations the preferred recipients of surplus public property or foreclosed private property seized by a city for nonpayment of taxes.[25] New York City's Tenant Interim Lease Program (TIL) and its Community Management Program (CMP), established in 1978, are among the oldest and largest of these municipal programs for transferring tax-foreclosed property into nonspeculative ownership. Under these programs, the tenants of tax-foreclosed buildings receive training in the organization and management of cooperative housing, funding for repairs and rehabilitation, and, eventually, clear title to their building (Chen 2003; Leavitt and Saegert 1990; White and Saegert 1997). By 2003, according to New York City's Department of Housing Preservation and Development, 795 buildings, containing 16,692 units, had been converted through TIL and CMP into tenant-owned, low-income, limited-equity housing cooperatives.[26]

The most extraordinary delegation of public power, however, occurred in Boston in 1988. The Boston Redevelopment Authority conveyed to the Dudley Street Neighborhood Initiative (DSNI) the power of eminent domain over 30 acres of inner-city land (Medoff and Sklar 1994). While this sovereign power of the state has often been delegated to hospitals, universities and utilities, it had never before been granted to a community-based nonprofit for the purpose of redeveloping its own neighborhood. All of the real estate obtained by DSNI, through eminent domain or otherwise, is conveyed to a community land trust, ensuring long-term community control over the land and lasting affordability for any below-market housing developed on that land.

Sanctioning Affordability Controls. Despite the variation that exists in property law from one state to another, two common law principles apply nearly everywhere. They are known as the "rule against perpetuities" and the "rule against unreasonable restraint on alienation." These rules presume that privately owned real estate, including housing, is a marketable commodity that should be freely transferred at the highest price a willing buyer will pay to a willing seller. Courts tend to frown on any contractual restraints that last too long and interfere "unreasonably" with this market transaction.

Nonspeculative housing, in seeking to place perpetual restraints on rents and resales, is contrary to the spirit of these rules. Proponents have prevailed, however, when able to demonstrate that such restraints are "reasonable," especially insofar as they serve a necessary and worthy public purpose. To buttress the argument that price-restricted housing does indeed serve a public purpose, several states have given statutory sanction either to affordability controls in general or to specific models of housing that incorporate affordability controls into their definition. The "affordable housing covenants" allowed by state law in Maine, the "housing subsidy covenants" allowed in Vermont and the "affordable housing restrictions" allowed in Massachusetts are examples of the first.[27] Cooperative housing statutes

enacted by Minnesota, Massachusetts, California and Vermont are examples of the second.[28]

Preserving Lower-Cost Housing

A preservationist policy with a progressive bent is one that discourages the removal of low-cost housing and the displacement of low-income people. Although exceptions to this rule may occasionally be justified, these exceptions should be narrowly defined and strictly regulated. Any persons displaced should be fully compensated. Under most circumstances, what Hartman (1984) once called the "right to stay put" should take precedence over the "right to displace."

It is lower-cost housing that is the principal concern of progressive preservation. Priority in the application of public powers and the investment of public dollars is given to preventing the loss of housing units that rent or sell for prices that are relatively affordable for persons of modest means. This is not to belittle various historic or aesthetic aspects of the existing stock, which may also be worth saving, even at public expense. Preserving the affordability of that housing, however, while maintaining and improving its condition as a source of safe and decent shelter, should exert a prior claim over public resources. Whatever housing is most affordable, moreover, serving people with the least ability to obtain and retain decent housing on their own, should command the most attention from public officials.[29]

Progressive preservation is focused, therefore, not only on maintaining the physical stock of lower-cost housing but also on enhancing the residential security of the lower-income people who occupy that housing. Residents need protection against the loss of units. They need protection against unjust eviction. They need protection against housing costs that rise beyond their ability to pay. A comprehensive—and progressive—preservationist policy requires all three.

Protecting Against the Loss of Units. The existing inventory of lower-cost housing in most cities and states includes: (1) publicly subsidized rental housing, either publicly owned by a housing authority or privately owned by a for-profit or nonprofit corporation; (2) unsubsidized, privately owned rental housing; and (3) unsubsidized, owner-occupied housing.

SUBSIDIZED RENTAL HOUSING. Federal rules that once governed the operation of 1.3 million units of public housing are relaxing. Federal contracts that once protected the affordability of 1.9 million units of privately owned, publicly subsidized housing are expiring. The condition of both types of assisted housing is deteriorating. Much of this stock of affordable housing is at risk of being lost (see Chapter 7 text and box). Making matters even worse, affordability controls on the first 23,000 units of more than a million built since 1986, using Low Income Housing Tax Credits, started expiring in 2002, with another 180,000 units set to follow during the next ten years (Bodaken 2002, 6).

UNSUBSIDIZED RENTAL HOUSING. "Public attention," as Apgar (1991, 206) noted long ago, "tends to focus on maintaining the current stock of subsidized housing, but curbing the loss of privately owned, unsubsidized units is also essential." Between 1974 and 1993, in particular, this housing sector lost nearly three million units (JCHS 1995, 31).[30] Another 1.7 million units were lost between 1993 and 2002 (JCHS 2003, 20). Most likely to be lost have been rental units affordable to very-low-income households, losses that are seldom offset by new construction. Even in cities where the production of new rental housing has been robust, there may be little benefit for lower-income tenants, since the "new multi-unit family apartments being built are substantially more expensive on average than the ones being lost" (JCHS 2003, 20).

UNSUBSIDIZED OWNER-OCCUPIED HOUSING. Nearly one-half of all very-low-income households in the United States own their homes. Over one-half of these very-low-income homeowners pay more than 30 percent of their income for the fixed costs of their housing—a third pay more than 50 percent (JCHS 2000, 36)—leaving little for maintenance or replacement.[31] Among all homeowners, there has been a dramatic jump in the number of households spending more than one-half their incomes on housing, a financial burden described by HUD as "severe." About 7.3 million homeowners reported severe cost burdens in 2001, up from 5.8 million in 1997, the "first time on record that homeowners have outnumbered renters with severe affordability problems" (JCHS 2003, 26). For these homeowners, especially those in the bottom two income quintiles where 84 percent of the severely cost-burdened households are to be found, there is no margin of safety. Any unexpected expense or disruption in income can dislodge the precarious hold they have on their homes.

More precarious still is the security of those low-income households who own manufactured housing—popularly known as "mobile homes." Outside of metropolitan areas, mobile homes make up a significant portion of the lower-cost housing stock. They are often in poor repair. Even when the housing is adequate, the "park" in which the housing is located often is not. Decrepit water and sewer systems, dangerous electrical service, nonexistent open space, and unpaved, unplowed and unmaintained roads create conditions in many mobile home parks that are barely adequate. Adequate or not, many parks are at risk of being sold and shut down, leaving the owners of homes that turn out to be less mobile than advertised to abandon ship or to search for another space in another park, frequently in vain.

A comprehensive policy of preservation should prevent the loss—and upgrade the condition—of all three categories of lower-cost housing. Such a policy should embody two other principles as well: long-term affordability and resident empowerment. A premium should be placed on methods of saving and improving lower-cost housing that maintain units, retain subsidies and sustain affordability for as long as possible. A premium should also be placed on methods that give residents a personal stake in that housing, whether a stake in ownership, a stake in control or merely a stake in longevity—that is, some assurance of remaining in homes that they have come to regard as "theirs."

Cities and states that commit themselves to preventing the loss of lower-cost housing, while incorporating the principles of long-term affordability and resident empowerment, intervene in four basic ways: (1) they use their regulatory powers to prevent the deterioration, demolition or conversion of lower-cost units; (2) they provide public funding to transfer into nonspeculative ownership many market-rate units at risk of being lost; (3) they provide public funding to stabilize subsidized units already under nonspeculative ownership; and (4) they ensure that whenever units are lost, any persons displaced will be provided with the means to relocate, securely and satisfactorily.

Preserving housing through regulation has a rich pedigree, stretching back to the earliest municipal efforts to set minimum requirements for ventilation, sanitation and safety in tenement housing. By the end of the 20th century, over 3,000 municipalities were using health and building codes to regulate the construction and maintenance of housing; most states had enacted plumbing, electrical, boiler or elevator codes; and over 15 had enacted state-wide building codes (Nenno 1997, 10–11). Several other states have acted aggressively, in recent years, to remove lead, asbestos and other dangerous materials from residential structures. Such minimum requirements for the health, safety and habitability of housing help to prevent the loss of residential units from shoddy construction, deferred maintenance, condemnation or fire—if they are vigorously enforced and if the costs of compliance are not simply heaped onto the shoulders of the present occupants, rendering their housing unaffordable.[32]

Going far beyond code enforcement, some cities and states have sought to preserve their existing stock of lower-cost housing by using the regulatory powers at their disposal to impede the demolition or conversion of housing. Demolition of rental housing—or its conversion to a nonresidential use—is made more difficult when a city requires developers who wish to remove rental units to replace those units on a unit-for-unit basis, either by constructing replacement units or by making an in-lieu-of-production payment into a housing trust fund.[33] Housing preservation ordinances, with or without a replacement obligation, have been pioneered by Hartford, Atlanta, Los Angeles, San Francisco, Seattle and Burlington. New York City has closely regulated the demolition or conversion of single-room-occupancy buildings and is also one of several cities that use rent control to regulate demolitions. Portland, Oregon has a preservation ordinance preventing the loss of any housing subsidized by the municipality. The affordability of such housing must be maintained for a minimum of 60 years.

Looming as a greater threat than demolition in many parts of the country has been the large-scale conversion of lower-cost rental units to condominium ownership. To prevent the loss of these units, a number of cities (and a few states) have enacted strict controls over condo conversions. Most condo conversion ordinances require the owners of rental housing to notify tenants in advance of the planned conversion of their units, a notice period that may stretch into several years. Evictions and rent increases during this notice period are tightly regulated to prevent the premature displacement of the current occupants. Many ordinances give tenants not only security of tenure during the notice period, but the first right to purchase converted units once the notice period has elapsed. Conversion ordinances in Washington, DC and Burlington, Vermont go beyond these individual rights. Upon being notified of their landlord's intent to convert their building into condominiums, tenants are given a collective right to purchase the building before its conversion and are offered assistance by the municipality in making this buy-out a reality.

Another regulatory tactic occasionally used by municipal governments to prevent the loss of lower-cost housing is "receivership." Under a receivership action, municipal officials petition a court to order a building that has become a hazard to its occupants and neighbors to be placed under the control of a court-ordered receiver. Rents from the building and loans from the city (secured by a lien on the property) are then used to bring the building into compliance with local health and safety codes (Listokin 1985; Morrissy 1987). Typically, the owner regains control upon repayment of the costs incurred by the receiver in managing and repairing the building. Michael Stone (1993, 246–247), however, has urged cities to view receivership as "a transitional step" toward social ownership, one that "enables the housing to be physically salvaged before it is too late, while working simultaneously to effect transfer of title to more responsible owners, including residents, community-based organizations, nonprofits, and public agencies."

Most of these regulatory measures may be used not only to prevent the loss of units but also to complement preservation efforts aimed at transferring units into the hands of more responsible owners.[34] With or without this regulatory shove, transferring at-risk housing into the hands of individuals and organizations oriented toward nonspeculative ownership has become the focus of many state and local programs aimed at preserving affordable housing. These programs have been targeted to both subsidized and unsubsidized housing, especially projects with checkered histories and irresponsible owners. Putting troubled projects under the control of either their residents or a private, nonprofit organization has proven to be an effective way of securing the affordability of these projects, while improving their livability and prospects for survival.[35]

Programs to prevent the loss of owner-occupied housing tend to focus either on protecting low-income homeowners against rising costs (discussed below) or preventing the physical deterioration of their units through grants or low-interest loans for rehabilitation.[36] Saving such housing by transferring it to nonspeculative ownership has rarely been tried—with four laudable exceptions.

First, some municipal programs that provide grants or loans for the rehabilitation of owner-occupied housing contain antispeculation provisions. The homeowner is required to return the public subsidy (with interest) upon resale if the house is not sold to another low-income homebuyer. Alternatively, a nonprofit organization is given an option to purchase the house at a below-market price, one that reflects the continued presence of the public subsidy.

Second, several municipalities have attempted to replicate the now-defunct Home Equity Living Plan (HELP) of Buffalo, New York. In these programs, the equity contained in the houses of elderly homeowners is "unlocked" to pay for maintenance or improvements, preventing both the deterioration of the housing and the displacement of its occupants. The drawback,

in Buffalo and elsewhere, is that once the houses are vacated they are resold, usually for a price beyond the reach of another low-income homebuyer (in order to replenish the HELP account). For each elderly homeowner helped in the short run, a lower-cost home is lost in the long run. Only in Madison, Wisconsin has an attempt been made to add an antispeculative twist. The Madison Area Community Land Trust, with the City's support, has explored the feasibility of an equity conversion program that would provide an annuity and life estate for elderly homeowners, but transfer their houses into the price-restricted domain of the community land trust upon the elders' death or departure (Davis, McKenzie and Carminati 1993). To date, however, this program has not been implemented.

Another approach to converting owner-occupied housing into nonspeculative ownership is under development in Massachusetts. The towns of Bedford and Hingham are considering adoption of an Equity Conversion & Homeownership Opportunity (ECHO) program, employing a model proposed by Michael Stone. This program would use public funds to provide both an upfront grant and a multiyear annuity to lower-income homeowners, allowing them to make necessary repairs and to meet their ongoing housing costs. In exchange for this public subsidy, homeowners would accept an affordability covenant, restricting the resale price of their homes and ensuring their future affordability for homebuyers earning below 80 percent of area median.[37]

Finally, a number of state programs facilitate and subsidize the transfer of owner-occupied mobile home parks into nonspeculative ownership. Florida, New Jersey, New Hampshire and Vermont, for example, have enacted state laws requiring lengthy notification and giving current mobile home owners the first right to purchase their parks if they are put up for sale. In Vermont, the State Housing Authority established a special-purpose nonprofit in 1990 to acquire mobile home parks on behalf of current residents and to manage these parks until they can be turned over to resident-controlled cooperatives. Similarly, New York's Mobile Home Cooperative Fund Program, started in 1988, provides low-interest loans to acquire land, complete infrastructure improvements and cover the costs of converting parks to cooperative ownership.

Quick though cities and states have sometimes been to use their own powers and resources to preserve unsubsidized housing, rental and owner-occupied, only a few have accepted responsibility for saving at-risk projects that are publicly owned or publicly subsidized—housing that is already outside of the speculative market. Many municipal officials have, in fact, regarded the threatened loss of subsidized housing as a welcome relief from rent-regulated properties they would prefer to tax at a higher rate, from older projects they would prefer to bulldoze, and from low-income people they would prefer to move somewhere else. Many other officials bemoan the possible loss of these units, but treat this threat as a problem belonging to someone else: the tenants, the private owners, the public housing authority or the federal government.

This has not been true everywhere. A number of cities and states have considered the preservation of subsidized housing to be a high priority. State agencies and municipal governments in Vermont and Massachusetts, for example, played major roles in supporting two of the first tenant-led buy-outs of privately owned, publicly subsidized housing projects in the nation: Northgate Apartments in Burlington, Vermont and Clarendon Hill Homes in Somerville, Massachusetts (see Chapter 7). Ownership of these projects was transferred from absentee investors to partnerships controlled by the project's residents. Similar transfers to nonprofit ownership have occurred with municipal support in Providence and Chicago. In Colorado, the City of Denver and the Colorado Housing Finance Agency played leading roles in transferring ten multiunit rental projects from the Resolution Trust Corporation to nonprofit, nonspeculative ownership (Atlas and Shoshkes 1997). In California, the state has appropriated funds to preserve subsidized projects and has supported their transfer to nonspeculative ownership by exempting from state taxes 50 percent of the gain on the sale of subsidized housing if it is sold to a nonprofit organization, a public entity or a limited-equity cooperative.

Any program for preserving lower-cost housing must make provision not only for preventing the loss of units but also for relocating people when units are lost. Even when a city does everything in its power to preserve the existing stock of lower-cost housing, hundreds of units may still be lost to dilapidation, condemnation, abandonment, demolition or conversion; hundreds of households may still be displaced. Where the removal of housing is directly attributable to the action (or inaction) of the property's owner, the cost of relocating and rehousing persons displaced from this housing should be borne neither by the persons displaced nor by society at large. These costs should be "internalized" within the project's budget, paid by the property's owner.

Many cities and states, accordingly, build into their condemnation, conversion or antidemolition laws a provision requiring property owners to pay for their tenants' costs of moving to another unit, plus any differential between the rent they paid before the move and the rent they must pay for the new unit.[38] This rent subsidy is typically required for a period of three to five years. Owners may also be allowed to meet these costs indirectly by paying "impact fees" into a municipally administered housing trust fund. Better, of course, to save the housing in the first place, but when that proves impossible, displacees should receive adequate assistance in relocating to housing at least as affordable as the units they are being forced to leave.[39]

Protecting against Eviction. Protecting against the loss of units and the eviction of occupants are sometimes combined in the same measure, as in the case of a condo conversion ordinance that stabilizes rents and inhibits evictions in units slated for conversion. Protecting against eviction can take other forms as well. Most federally assisted rental housing, for example, is governed by "just-cause" or "good cause" eviction statutes, where income-eligible tenants may be removed from their units only for damaging a unit, threatening the peace or safety of other tenants, conducting illegal activities, failing to pay rent or refusing to allow the landlord reasonable access to do repairs (see Chapter 9 and Hartman and Robinson 2003). Some cities and states have extended this protection to tenants residing in privately owned rental housing that is not publicly assisted. New Jersey, New Hampshire, New York and California are a few of the states with "just cause" statutes. Similar protections against "unjust" evictions have been enacted by a number of cities, including Seattle, Berkeley, Santa Monica, Oakland, San Jose, New York and Washington, DC.[40]

Tenants may also be forced out of housing not because a landlord has evicted them but because a utility company has shut off their gas, water or electricity. This is sometimes the fault of a landlord, who has stopped paying utility bills to milk a property prior to abandonment or to empty a building prior to demolition or conversion. It is sometimes the tenant's fault. Either way, it is vital to a strategy protecting security of tenure that utility companies not be allowed to terminate service without providing affected tenants with prior notice and due process. In cases where threatened shutoffs are the result of the landlord's negligence, tenants should also have the right to pay for the utilities themselves and to deduct that sum from their rents.[41] Finally, in cases where utility shut-offs may result in immediate harm to the occupants—loss of heat in the dead of winter, for instance—utility companies should be temporarily barred from shutting off utilities at all, regardless of who is at fault. Pennsylvania, Massachusetts and Washington, DC are a few of the places where one or more of these protections against utility shut-offs have been enacted.

Tenants may also be forced out simply because their units have become so dilapidated that they can no longer remain there. To prevent such "eviction by dilapidation" tenants have been given the right to ensure the repair of substandard units under so-called "repair and deduct" laws. If their landlord refuses to correct unsafe or unsanitary conditions after being notified of these defects, tenants may hire their own contractors to correct the defects and deduct the cost of these repairs from rent payments. Some cities take "repair and deduct" much further. In cases where tenants cannot afford the out-of-pocket expense of doing the necessary repairs, a municipal agency pays to correct the building's defects and then puts a lien on the repaired property to ensure that the city is eventually repaid.[42]

Although security of tenure is typically higher for homeowners than for tenants, homeowners are not immune from displacement.[43] The most common way they lose their homes, especially during downturns in the economy, is by mortgage foreclosure. This is often the result of a low-income homeowner losing a job or experiencing some other financial disruption, forcing the homeowner into default.[44] The 2001 recession and the weak recovery that followed, for example, sent mortgage delinquency rates soaring and pushed foreclosures toward record levels. By the end of 2002, between 400,000 and 450,000 homeowners were in the process of foreclosure (JCHS 2003, 18). Most state laws require financial institutions to provide a lengthy redemption period before seizing owner-occupied property, thus granting the homeowner an opportunity to cure the default and retain possession. Many state laws also give homeowners considerable protection against the loss of their "homestead" in the face of bankruptcy or adverse legal claims.[45]

A number of states—and a few cities—have responded to the rising threat to homeowner security that is posed by predatory lending. Equity can be stripped and homes forced into foreclosure through subprime loans charging exorbitant front-end fees, back-end penalties and interest rates much higher than the borrower's income can support, and through abusive practices like inflated appraisals, financed single-premium credit insurance and repeated refinancing with no benefit to the homeowner (Hurd and Kest 2003). Not all subprime lending can be characterized as "predatory," but it is this segment of the mortgage market where the highest rates of default and the worst abuses of borrowers are found. Low-income communities are especially vulnerable. Between 1993 and 2001, the subprime share of home purchase loans in low-income, predominantly minority communities shot up from 2.4 percent to 13.4 percent; the subprime share of refinances soared from 6.8 percent to 27.5 percent (JCHS 2003, 19). Nonfederal interventions to prevent predatory lending have been gathering momentum since 1999, when North Carolina passed the nation's first antipredatory lending law. Within the next two years, sixteen other states had adopted laws of their own, some weak and some strong, for restricting predatory lending. Several cities had done the same, including Atlanta, Chicago, Dayton, Oakland, Philadelphia and Washington, DC.

While such measures provide residents of owner-occupied housing with far more protection against eviction than is usually afforded the residents of rental housing, they adjust only slightly the imbalance of power between the struggling homeowner and the foreclosing lender. Cities and states have, in fact, been reluctant to interfere with a lender's right to repossess properties with mortgages in arrears. One of the few exceptions is Pennsylvania's Homeowners' Emergency Mortgage Assistance Program (HEMAP), enacted in 1983 after an intense grassroots campaign by a coalition of unions, churches and community organizations. HEMAP provides up to 24 months of mortgage payments for homeowners threatened with the loss of their homes. What this laudable program does not do, however, but should, is to require a quid pro quo for such public assistance. For example, assisted homeowners could grant a public or nonprofit organization an option to purchase their property at a below-market price whenever a homeowner decides to vacate. Adding this requirement would turn a simple program for preventing the displacement of financially strapped mortgagors into a dual-goal strategy of preserving lower-cost housing for present homeowners while expanding nonspeculative housing for future homeowners (cf. Stone 1993, 238–239).

Protecting against Rising Costs. "Affordability remains America's most widespread housing challenge," a problem that has "worsened over the past 25 years" (JCHS 2003, 25). Between 1975 and 2002, the inflation-adjusted incomes of households in the bottom two quintiles remained nearly flat, while rents and home prices outpaced general price inflation. Rising costs are leaving millions of lower-income people with precarious housing, inadequate housing or no housing.

One of the most effective methods for protecting tenants against rising costs over the long run, as suggested above, has been to transfer property currently owned by private landlords into the hands of public-sector or third-sector organizations committed to operating such housing on a price-restricted basis in perpetuity. Permanent affordability can be made a reality for owner-occupied housing, as well, through resale controls appended to deeds or ground leases (cf. Davis and Demetrowitz 2003). A number of cities and states have, in fact, dedicated major resources to developing such a stock of nonspeculative housing.

Many other cities have attempted to protect tenants against arbitrary and inflationary rent increases, not by expanding the domain of nonspeculative housing, but by regulating the operation of market housing.[46] Approximately 200 U.S. cities and counties have used some form of rent control over the past 25 years, including those in New Jersey, Alaska, California, Connecticut, Maryland, Massachusetts, New York and Virginia (Gilderbloom and Appelbaum 1988, 27; Keating 1998). Nearly all municipalities with rent control, moreover, not only regulate rents but protect tenants against arbitrary evictions.

The most serious affordability threat facing many low-income homeowners is rising property taxes, especially in neighborhoods where gentrification has caused a precipitous increase in property values. While such an increase may be welcomed by homeowners who plan someday soon to sell and relocate, it can be calamitous for those who have no intention (or means) of moving and who find it increasingly difficult to pay the rising cost of staying. To ease this tax burden, many states have adopted some sort of "circuit breaker" law, limiting (or rebating) property taxes that certain classes of homeowners must pay—for example, homeowners who are poor, elderly or disabled. Only a few of these states—Iowa, Maryland, Vermont, New York and Pennsylvania being prime examples—have offered similar relief to renters who are low-income, elderly or disabled.[47]

Finally, it is worth noting that a major component of rising residential costs, for homeowners and renters alike, is energy. The cost of heat and power can put enormous pressure on households of limited means, especially those who live in older, less energy-efficient dwellings. Recognizing this problem, while coping with a decline in federal funding for residential weatherization, a number of cities and states have used revenues of their own, discretionary funds from other federal sources or exactions from regulated utilities to subsidize energy efficiency improvements in residential buildings.[48] A few have gone further. The state of Wisconsin and several cities, including San Francisco, Sacramento, Minneapolis and Burlington, have used energy conservation codes and time-of-sale ordinances to mandate greater energy efficiency in rental housing.

Enabling Residential Mobility

The "right to stay put" should be combined with the "right to move." It is not enough for persons of modest means to have security of tenure in accommodations that match their current resources and needs. They should also have the ability to secure other housing when their circumstances change and to secure better housing when their circumstances improve. A complement to preservationist strategies protecting residents against the pressure to move are mobility strategies removing barriers, penetrating enclaves and promoting choice for residents who desire to move.

Removing Barriers. Fair housing is not only the first mobility strategy but also the sine qua non for every mobility strategy. Although federal prohibitions against discriminatory practices in the renting, selling or financing of housing play the leading role nationally in removing barriers to entry, all but a handful of states—and dozens of cities—have adopted fair housing laws of their own.[49] The protected classes covered by these state and municipal laws tend to duplicate federal definitions forbidding discrimination on the basis of race, color, religion, national origin, age, sex, familial status or disability. Many states and cities go further than the federal government, however, broadening the pool of "protected classes" to prohibit discrimination on account of marital status, sexual orientation, or past or present service in the armed forces.

Chicago's fair housing ordinance lists "sources of income" among its protections. Massachusetts extends fair housing protections to persons receiving rental housing subsidies like Section 8.

Some municipalities have gone beyond federal fair housing laws in another way as well. To prevent racial discrimination and to promote integration, they have attempted to regulate the practices of key sectors of the housing industry, especially the brokers and agents in private real estate firms. According to Keating (1994, 201), these regulations take three typical forms. The first is regulation of "for sale" signs to prevent blockbusting or panic selling in areas undergoing racial transition. The second is regulation of realtor solicitations, prohibiting brokers from contacting potential homesellers who have placed their names on a do-not-call list maintained by the municipal government. The third requires realty firms who wish to do business with the city to register with the city and to pledge their cooperation with municipal policies promoting fair housing.

In the case of populations with special needs, a number of states have combined "negative" sanctions prohibiting discrimination with "affirmative" incentives promoting the development of barrier-free housing. California's Special User Housing Rehabilitation Program, for example, provides low-interest deferred payment loans for the acquisition and rehabilitation of group homes and apartments for persons with disabilities. Connecticut has provided grants and low-interest loans to create congregate housing for the frail elderly. Florida subsidizes rents in congregate living facilities for low-income adults who are elderly, disabled or blind. Similar state-funded programs, targeted specifically to persons with special needs, have been developed by Maine, Maryland, Massachusetts, Michigan, New York, Ohio, Oregon and Rhode Island.[50]

A few cities and states have attempted to remove another barrier that frequently faces low-income persons who try to move from one apartment to another—or who try, if homeless, to gain access to any housing at all. This class-based impediment is exorbitant security deposits, demanded either by landlords or by utilities. Burlington, for example, enacted an ordinance in 1985 limiting the size of security deposits to the equivalent of one month's rent and requiring the return of those deposits, with interest, if tenants depart without damaging apartments. Massachusetts has a similar law. Connecticut briefly operated, in the mid-1980s, a revolving loan fund that provided low-interest loans for security deposits to homeless households seeking emergency housing. Several other states and cities have done the same, offering grants or loans to the homeless to cover rental and utility deposits that would otherwise bar the door to permanent housing.

Penetrating Enclaves. A second mobility strategy is "fair share": opening up areas from which subsidized housing, rental housing or lower-cost housing of any kind has been excluded; and making every locality participate more equally in meeting a regional responsibility for providing such housing.

Nowhere has fair share been taken more seriously than in New Jersey, where two decisions of the state's Supreme Court and an act of the legislature have promoted the doctrine that every municipality has an affirmative obligation to provide low- and moderate-income housing. In its *Mount Laurel* decision of 1975, the New Jersey Supreme Court declared that every municipality must eliminate illegal barriers to low-income housing and must "by its land use regulations, make realistically possible an appropriate variety and choice of housing." What the Court soon realized, however, was that removing exclusionary barriers might make low-income housing "possible" but does not make it probable. Low-income housing will actually be created in communities that have historically contained little (or none) only if those communities are obligated to provide such housing.

In 1983, in "Mount Laurel II," the Court endorsed a strategy of "mandatory set-asides" to ensure this obligation would be met. The Court encouraged municipalities to require the developers of market-rate housing to make a specified percentage of their units available at an affordable price (rent or sale) for low- and moderate-income households. Complementing this explicit endorsement of inclusionary zoning was the Court's creation of what became known as

the "builder's remedy." If a municipality failed to meet its fair share obligation, "any builder with a reasonable site denied approval by the municipality—and who was willing to provide lower-income housing in his development—would be awarded his approvals by the courts, over whatever objections the town might raise" (Mallach 1988, 12).

In 1985, the New Jersey legislature created a state agency, the Council on Affordable Housing (COAH), to standardize and oversee the inclusionary practices emerging out of Mount Laurel I and II.[51] It also funded a Neighborhood Preservation Balanced Housing Program through a realty transfer tax to assist local governments in meeting their fair share obligations. By September 2004, COAH was able to report that 66,600 "affordable units" had resulted from these court-ordered policies and state-funded programs, including 34,900 units newly built or under construction, 13,800 units rehabilitated, 9,100 units with "realistic zoning in place" and 8,800 units provided through "regional contribution agreements" (COAH 2005).[52]

A number of other states have made quiet progress in opening up suburbia to low- and moderate-income housing. Some have used their housing trust funds or other state and federal monies to promote the production of such housing where it was never available before.[53] Some have used their powers to remove regulatory barriers erected by local jurisdictions. Others have used land use planning laws to require a mix of housing types, tenures and costs.

A few examples: Florida's State Apartment Incentive Loan Program, initiated in 1988, provides low-interest loans to developers who build rental housing for very-low-income persons in "a mixed-income setting." The state of Washington requires all cities with more than 20,000 residents to adopt ordinances allowing the development of accessory rental units in existing single-family homes (Nelson 2003, 5). Minnesota's Livable Communities program, created in 1995, provides grants and loans to "first tier" suburbs surrounding the Twin Cities as incentives to increase the production of lower-cost housing and to eliminate regulatory barriers to such housing (Meck, Retzlaff and Schwab 2003, 88).

Massachusetts, Rhode Island and Connecticut have attempted to accomplish similar results by regulatory measures similar to New Jersey's "builder's remedy." Massachusetts adopted Chapter 40B in 1969, a statute that quickly became known as "Anti-snob Zoning." Chapter 40B gave a state-wide Housing Appeals Committee the power to override local zoning boards in cases where communities with little subsidized housing reject an application from a developer to construct such housing. Developers may pursue this remedy in any town where less than 10 percent of the year-round housing stock is made up of units subsidized for low- and moderate-income households or where less than 1 1/2 percent of the town's buildable land is already developed for subsidized housing. Nearly 30,000 housing units in more than 200 communities have been built using the provisions of Chapter 40B (Heudorfer 2003).[54] Rhode Island's Chapter 45-53, enacted in 1991, and Connecticut's Section 8-30g, enacted in 1989, are similar in structure and procedure to the Massachusetts law, although appeals in Connecticut are made to a court rather than to a special state-wide housing committee (Meck, Retzlaff and Schwab 2003, 141–158).

Oregon has been the nation's leader in attempting to use state-wide land use planning and growth management laws to promote fair share. Since 1973, State Planning Goal 10 has required every city and county to adopt comprehensive plans that "encourage the availability of adequate numbers of housing units at price ranges and rent levels which are commensurate with the financial capabilities of Oregon households." Despite numerous attempts by local governments to circumvent or challenge this requirement, Oregon's courts have not only upheld Planning Goal 10, but interpreted it to mean that local governments have an affirmative duty to facilitate production of the kinds of housing that lower-income people can afford (Toulan 1994; Abbott 2002).

Oregon is not alone. Florida and Washington, like Oregon, require municipalities to adopt affordable housing plans. Connecticut's Fair Housing Compact Pilot, enacted in 1988, encourages municipalities to enter into "regional compacts," setting fair share goals by consensus.

California established a procedure for setting fair share housing goals through regional councils of government in 1980 and has required a "housing element" in all municipal plans since 1989. Vermont has required all municipalities to plan for low- and moderate-income housing since 1988.[55]

At the municipal level, fair share housing has usually been pursued through voluntary compacts negotiated among multiple jurisdictions or through regional housing plans promulgated by a regional planning commission or a council of governments (COG). The nation's first fair share plan, the Dayton Plan, was formulated by the Miami Valley [Ohio] Regional Planning Commission in 1970. Other fair share plans include those developed by the Denver Regional COG, the Metropolitan Washington COG, the Metropolitan Council for the seven-county region surrounding Minneapolis–St. Paul, and the Portland Metro Council for the three counties surrounding Portland, Oregon (Listokin 1976; Abbott 2002; Meck, Retzlaff and Schwab 2003). These plans set numerical targets for allocating subsidized housing, low-cost housing or new housing of any kind among all the municipalities of a specified region. Rarely, however, have these allocations been backed by incentives sufficient to reward a willing municipality for meeting its fair share responsibility or by penalties sufficient to force a reluctant municipality into accepting its responsibility.

Some state and local programs, by contrast, have attempted to promote residential mobility, not by producing lower-cost housing in places where little has existed, but by putting into the hands of low-income households the financial resources that will enable them to move wherever they want to go. San Diego, for example, created a relocation fund in 2001, providing money for security deposits, loan closings and moving costs in order to help low-income minority families relocate to neighborhoods with lower concentrations of poverty. At least five states (California, Connecticut, Maryland, Massachusetts and New York), one city (Seattle) and one county (Montgomery County, Maryland) have operated programs providing tenant-based rental assistance for low-income households, using nonfederal funds.

Many of these subsidized tenants soon discover, however, that their new-found ability to pay for a market-rate apartment does not guarantee access to many suburban enclaves. Pervasive restrictions on the construction of multifamily rental housing, the unavailability of public transportation and the suspicion (or outright hostility) of long-time residents toward newcomers with lower incomes and darker skins tend to keep the doors of many suburbs firmly shut.[56] In recognition of the harsh reality that penetrating enclaves is going to take more than subsidizing demand through the provision of tenant-based rental assistance, some cities and states have begun using their powers and resources to subsidize supply, promoting choice by stimulating the production of below-market housing in areas outside of central city neighborhoods.

Promoting Choice. The final mobility strategy can be called "fair choice." While this might be regarded as merely a minor variation on the previous strategy, promoting choice goes beyond "opening up the 'burbs." If mobility is to be real for persons at every level of income, there must not only be enough below-market housing but also enough diversity of housing tenure, type and locale to accommodate the variety of needs that people bring with them when they go looking for a place to live.

Promoting multiple models of housing as a matter of public policy has been rare, especially when the intended beneficiaries are households with very low incomes. As a moral judgment, the poor are commonly believed not to deserve, at public expense, anything much better than modest flats in large rental complexes. As a practical judgment, the poor are widely believed not to possess the financial or personal wherewithal to manage, much less own, the housing that is "theirs." As a political expedient, the poor are systematically excluded from areas where their very presence is believed to threaten the value of adjoining properties. The customary result, despite some experimentation here and there with scattered-site projects, shared living arrangements, tenant management and suburban development of below-market housing, has been a cookie-cutter approach to subsidized housing

offering neither a choice of accommodation nor a chance to move.

Catherine Bauer was one of the first housing advocates to warn against this anti-mobility mindset. As early as 1957, while lamenting the "dreary deadlock" of public housing, she argued that "what is primarily needed, not only for low-income slum dwellers and minority groups but for the great mass of middle-income families in all their infinite variety of taste and need, is more choice in location, dwelling type, and neighborhood character" (Bauer 1985, 284). A number of cities have heeded her advice. They have attempted to diversify their stock of low- and moderate-income housing, creating an integrated system of lower-cost market housing and nonmarket housing offering more diversity and more mobility than is typically available to persons of modest means. In market housing, they have enacted zoning changes supporting the production of smaller houses (through relaxed "floor-size minimums") and the creation of accessory dwelling units (Nelson 2003). In public housing, they have supported lower densities, scattered sites, townhouse designs and tenant management. In third-sector housing, they have supported a multitude of housing tenures and types, including multiple forms of private, nonmarket homeownership like cooperatives, limited-equity condominiums and community land trusts. In partnership with neighboring towns, they have shared information, expertise and revenues to promote regional solutions that disperse, rather than concentrate, the supply of housing that is affordable to low- and moderate-income households (Rusk 1999; Orfield 1997).

Another sort of residential mobility—another sort of choice—is made possible in some cities by the creation of multiple forms of housing in neighborhoods with a preponderance of low-income renters. Although most municipal programs promoting inner-city homeownership are focused on drawing middle-income homebuyers into inner-city neighborhoods, raising reasonable fears among present residents of gentrification and their own displacement (Varady and Raffel 1995; Lutton 1997), such programs need not be aimed exclusively at attracting affluent newcomers. They can also be designed to help a neighborhood's own sons and daughters to stay put (or to return). Many low-income neighborhoods lack any diversity in the type or tenure of their housing stock, giving present residents little choice but to leave the neighborhood, should they have the means and desire to improve their housing situations (cf. Davis 1991, 165). A comprehensive mobility strategy should not only help low-income people to "move to the 'burbs'" but help those who seek better housing to "stay in the 'hood'," if that is truly where they prefer to be.

When multiple models of housing are developed within the same locale, the transition from one to another is made less difficult than before. People of modest means are provided not only with a choice of housing but also with a chance to move. When multiple models are developed within the same region—penetrating, in particular, suburban enclaves that have long been hostile to any diversity in housing tenure, type or price—people of modest means are provided not only with a chance to move but with a choice of place.[57] These are opportunities too rarely provided by either public policy or the private market.

CONCLUSIONS

Recent interventions by cities and states to address the housing needs of lower-income populations have been plentiful, innovative and frequently progressive, lending credence to the notion that devolution may allow more room for maneuver than is commonly feared. Indeed, with so much good having happened at these lower levels of government during the last two decades, it may be fair to ask whether we should stop worrying about devolution and focus, instead, on seizing those opportunities that devolution presents for redistributing the benefits of growth, expanding nonspeculative housing, preserving lower-cost housing and enabling residential mobility.

I would answer that worry—even fear—remains a reasonable response to devolution. Yes, there are things that cities and states can do to make housing more abundant, affordable, decent and secure. But the dangers are real. Devolution is resulting in less money for

lower-income housing, less targeting for lower-income people and lower-income communities, and more political clout for interests inimical to both. These dangers have been magnified, moreover, by changes occurring over the past two decades that weaken the ability of cities and states to respond creatively and effectively to whatever opportunities devolution may present.

- Economic restructuring, accompanied by corporate downsizing and the accelerated flight of jobs to suburbs, Sunbelt and Third World, has left many urban centers bereft of jobs and made growth more elusive for municipalities that might otherwise consider redistributing the benefits of growth.
- Concentration and centralization in the banking industry has made local activism around community reinvestment more difficult than in days when there were more banks and smaller banks controlled closer to home. CRA activism has been undermined, as well, by the growing proportion of mortgages and other financial services being handled by institutions not subject to the Community Reinvestment Act.[58]
- The stagnation (or decline) in annual earnings for every income group with exception of the top quintile has made households just above the poverty line more precarious—and harder to house (see Chapter 1).
- The de-funding of General Relief programs at the state and county level, combined with "welfare reform" at the federal level, have punched holes in a safety net that already provided only bare-bones protection for households below the poverty line.
- The restructuring of federal housing assistance, including the deregulation of public housing authorities, the substitution of tenant-based subsidies for project-based subsidies, the replacement of long-term subsidy contracts by those with annual extensions and the production of a million tax-credit units with affordability controls of short duration, have all made a dwindling supply of subsidized housing less secure.
- The reallocation of federal spending toward national security after September 11, 2001, the massive cost of invading, occupying and

rebuilding Afghanistan and Iraq, and massive cutbacks in federal taxes (including a ten-year phase-out of the estate tax) have darkened the prospects for funding any new programs for housing and community development while threatening the funding of programs that already exist.

- The consolidation and downsizing of state agencies charged with the administration of housing and community development programs has made many states less able and agile in handling new responsibilities devolved from above.[59] Furthermore, as the budgetary surpluses of the 1990s have been replaced by soaring deficits, many states have not only been cutting deeply into their own bureaucracies but have begun cutting services and benefits for their own citizens.

These changing conditions make coping with the dangers and demands of devolution more difficult than ever before. Might anything make it easier? Probably not. Yet there are things that can be done to improve the odds that cities and states will actively pursue those opportunities that still exist and will actually succeed, on occasion, in making housing more abundant, affordable, decent and secure for those who need it the most.

The most important thing to do is for housing advocates inside and outside of government to devote more attention not only to the kinds of muscular interventions described in this chapter but also to the connective tissue among them. This is partially a matter of tying together multiple strategies—and multiple constituencies—into a single, comprehensive policy. But connecting one housing strategy to another does not go far enough. Housing itself must be linked to issues, interests and constituencies outside its immediate domain. There are many possibilities here, though three hold special promise for helping housing to weather the storm of devolution.

First, the connection between housing development and community development should be strengthened, not abandoned. Housing has long been a bellwether of neighborhood well-being or, conversely, of neighborhood decline. Many public and private interventions aimed at

stabilizing or revitalizing residential neighborhoods have focused, accordingly, on improving the local housing stock. Combining the two has made for good projects—and for good politics—at both the state and local level. Of late, however, the centrality of housing to community development has come under attack.[60] This crescendo of criticism is a useful reminder that jobs, schools, safety and services play as large a role in determining a neighborhood's fate as does the condition and affordability of its housing. But it runs the risk of pushing the pendulum too far the other way, where housing is removed from the mix of strategies for rebuilding community and where nonprofits are badgered or bribed into retreating from tasks that they do well in pursuit of more elusive (and dubious) objectives like seeding fragile economic enterprises in the rocky soils of the inner city.[61] If nonhousing aspects of community development have been slighted in the past, the solution lies not in ignoring housing, but in enhancing the links between housing and services, housing and transportation, housing and jobs, housing and schools, and the like.[62] These issues—and their scattered constituencies—must be joined together if either housing or community development is to have much hope of adequate funding from state and municipal governments in the years ahead.[63]

Second, connections between the preservation of lower-cost housing and the preservation of historical, natural and cultural resources should be strengthened. Those who fight for the stewardship of residential affordability often share many of the same values, supporters, funders—and *enemies*—as those who fight for the stewardship of historic structures, open spaces, forests, farmlands, wetlands and other natural resources. Admittedly, there are issues of development, class and race that often divide these groups. At the state and local level, however, housing, conservation and preservation organizations are discovering new ways of working together for common ends, combining their clout for mutual gain.[64] The fight against sprawl, in particular, is beginning to produce some surprising alliances, with considerable potential for advancing the cause of low- and moderate-income housing.[65]

Finally, the connection between housing and organizing should be strengthened—not in the spirit of embracing something new, but of reviving something old, getting the housing movement "back to its roots" (see Chapter 10). It is true that many cities and states have been pioneers in supporting lower-cost housing, most recently in response to Washington's unilateral withdrawal. It is also true, however, that few of them plunged into the deep blue sea without a vigorous push. As Goetz (1996, 177) has noted, cities and states were "prodded into that response by a community-based housing movement that has combined long-standing neighborhood concerns about disinvestment and gentrification with the interests of tenant organizations, community-based social service agencies, and affordable housing developers." Many cities and states have community reinvestment associations, established to force local lenders into complying with the CRA.[66] Dozens of cities have low-income housing advocacy organizations. Over thirty states have statewide affordable housing coalitions. Across the country, over 2,000 community-based nonprofits struggle daily to provide housing that low- and moderate-income people can afford. Not all of them combine organizing with development; not all of them join willingly with residents, activists and other nonprofits to pressure the public sector into continuing its support for below-market housing. But many do. Nonprofit housers, in a number of locales, have become a significant political force with capacity, credibility and clout.[67]

What cities and states did right for housing during the recent past happened, in large measure, because organizations and coalitions like these organized and mobilized city by city and state by state to make it happen. The current wave of devolution will demand more of the same. If safe, decent, affordable housing for low- and moderate-income people is to remain a priority of cities and states that have been innovators in the past, if it is to become a priority of cities and states likely to inherit even more responsibilities from the federal government in the future, the officials who lead those cities and states must be pushed in that direction. There is much they *can* do. There is little they *will* do

without an organized, mobilized constituency peering in their windows and pounding on their doors.

NOTES

1. For a sample of the kinds of extravagant claims that have been made for "devolving" money, missions and authority to the states—and, to a much lesser extent, to cities—see Gold (1996), Weaver (1996), Caraley (1996), Engler (1997) and Norquist (1996).

2. Quigley and Rubinfeld (1996, 300) discover "no systematic evidence suggesting a better management capacity by local government." Downs (1997) suggests that Congress "is shifting a lot of power to the wrong levels." Caraley (1996, 8) concludes that "there is no evidence to support a proposition that all state governors, legislatures and bureaucracies are more efficient and dedicated than the organs of the federal government." Etzioni (1995) puts it more bluntly: "If the large-scale transfer of monies and missions from Washington to 50 state capitols is the way to curb government, then copy machines are a way to cut paperwork."

3. The Community Development Block Grant Program is a perfect example. Given the flexibility to design their own programs, cities and states have tended to spread housing and community development monies more widely, instead of concentrating CDBG funds in areas most in need; they have tended to shift funds from affordable housing to economic development and public facilities; and they have favored homebuyer assistance over tenant assistance (Goetz 1995; Hayes 1995, 211–215, 242–243; Davis, Wasserman and Staudinger 2000).

4. Part of the solicitude shown by state legislatures to developers, landlords, bankers and other well-heeled private interests is no doubt engendered by many legislators' personal ties to these interests. In far too many state legislatures, conflicts of interest are both rampant and undisclosed (see Center for Public Integrity 1999).

5. Pennsylvania is not the only state to preempt local regulation of condo conversions. During the late 1970s and early 1980s, preemption was used to rescind municipal moratoriums in New Jersey and Maryland, to terminate local condo conversion ordinances in Massachusetts and Maryland, and to prevent the passage of such ordinances in Wisconsin and Virginia. A state preemption bill failed in California only because of strong opposition from tenants and local governments (Lauber 1984, 292–293).

6. As Yeoman (1997, 21) has pointed out, the real estate industry is hardly alone in enlisting sympathetic state legislatures to curtail the regulatory impulses of

cities and counties. Business groups of many kinds "are going to state legislators, with whom they have more pull, and asking them to pre-empt local ordinances." A significant exception to the business sector's preference for state-level law is land use control. The private real estate industry has historically opposed state-level planning and zoning, preferring to deal with local ordinances and local officials.

7. Even in the case of many categorical programs like public housing, urban renewal and Model Cities, municipal (and state) governments were granted an extraordinary degree of discretion and control over these federally funded programs. It is arguable, in fact, that many of the failings usually attributed to these programs were due not to a centralized structure of federal control but to a decentralized ("devolved") structure of local control—a heresy seldom heard above the rising drumbeat for turning over most federal monies and missions to lower levels of government.

8. As Donahue (1997) has observed, the wisdom of transferring power away from Washington and toward lower levels of government (especially toward the states) enjoys "something as close to consensus" as ever occurs in American politics. Eisinger (1998, 316) has made a similar point. On the other hand, while there continues to be widespread support for devolution in the case of housing, community development and social services, the September 11, 2001 terrorist attacks on New York City and Washington shattered whatever consensus may have once existed for devolving federal responsibilities for law enforcement, airline security and public health. The centralizing tendencies of national security have a way of trumping the decentralist proclivities of devolution.

9. It is well to remember that, despite the fulsome rhetoric about "returning" responsibilities to lower levels of government, many cities and states never enacted—and never would have enacted—many of the programs that Congress is now commending into their care. Left to their own devices, many cities and states use their financial resources and regulatory powers to make housing less plentiful, less affordable, less desirable and less available to nonelderly households of limited means. Relaxing federal oversight for these cities and states is a recipe not for innovation but for the diversion of resources away from neighborhoods, tenures and people most in need.

10. I do not mean to suggest that every public intervention reviewed in this chapter was instituted in the last 25 years or instigated in direct response to devolution. Many were, but some—like building codes and fair housing protections—have a much longer pedigree. Devolution has provided not only an occasion for innovation, but an impetus to revive and strengthen earlier interventions.

11. This is not to say that every municipal regime is equally and unequivocally pro-growth. There are many, in fact, that are quite ambivalent about further growth, especially in their own populations. Even when pursued under the guise of "sustainable development" or "smart growth," however, few regimes have been able to avoid entirely the competition with neighboring municipalities for their "rightful" share of a region's economic activity and investment.

12. The origins of inclusionary zoning in New Jersey are rooted in two decisions of the New Jersey Supreme Court: *Southern Burlington County NAACP et al. v. Township of Mount Laurel,* 67 NJ 151 (1975) and *Southern Burlington County NAACP et al. v. Township of Mount Laurel,* 92 NJ 158 (1983). They have come to be known more simply as "Mt. Laurel I" and "Mt. Laurel II."

13. Madison, Wisconsin considered a "reverse-linkage" policy in the early 1990s that would have extracted fees from new commercial development outside of the downtown to support the development of lower-cost housing in central city neighborhoods. This mandatory measure was voted down by the city council.

14. The first states to enact their own CRA laws regulating state-chartered financial institutions were Iowa, Massachusetts, Missouri, New York, Ohio, Washington and West Virginia (National Center for Policy Alternatives 1988, 15–78). Access to insurance can be as much of a problem as access to credit in low-income areas containing large numbers of minority residents (Squires 1995, 1997; Luquetta and Goldberg 2001). Illinois, Minnesota, Missouri, Wisconsin, California and Massachusetts require geographic disclosure of insurance policies. In 1988, Massachusetts became the first state to impose reinvestment requirements for residential insurance that are comparable to CRA requirements for residential lending.

15. This list of states is found in Stone (1993:248). Antispeculation efforts have been focused more narrowly in Montgomery County, Maryland and Burlington, Vermont. They have slowed the speculative conversion of rental housing to condominiums by assessing an "impact fee" against the sales price of each converted unit. These fees are deposited into a housing trust fund to be used later to create lower-cost housing.

16. Monroe County, Florida has funded low-income housing not with a tax on the transfer of properties but with a tax on the turnover of short-term occupants. A "bed tax," collected from hotels and motels in the Florida Keys, is used by the Monroe County Land Authority to purchase lands either for conservation or for the development of below-market housing.

17. Thirty percent of the units subsidized through Florida's collection of real estate transfer taxes serve households earning less than 50 percent of the area median income (AMI); 30 percent serve households earning 50 to 80 percent of AMI; and forty percent serve households earning 80 to 120 percent of AMI.

18. For example, the inclusionary zoning ordinance adopted by Montgomery County, Maryland in 1975 is often cited as a model by proponents of inclusionary zoning. This ordinance has a fatal flaw, however: affordability requirements lasting only 10 years for homeownership units and 20 years for rental units. More than 11,000 units of housing made initially affordable to households earning under 65 percent of AMI have been produced through Montgomery's inclusionary zoning ordinance; by 2003, only 3,800 of these inclusionary units remained affordable (Axel-Lute 2003, 9).

19. More detailed discussions of the rationale for increased municipal and state support of "third sector housing" can be found in Davis (1994, 2000), Davis and Demetrowitz (2003), and Barton (1996).

20. Another type of support for nonspeculative housing is less common but still noteworthy: the granting of regulatory preferences or exemptions. Projects that combine initial affordability with lasting affordability have been granted zoning bonuses for density, height or coverage. For example, some of the projects developed by BRIDGE, a nonprofit housing developer in San Francisco, have been allowed higher densities in areas where such "up-zoning" would never have been granted to a for-profit developer (Wheeler 1990:217). Projects with lasting affordability have also been exempted from impact fees or transfer taxes. Vermont, for example, exempts housing that is permanently affordable from the payment of real estate transfer taxes. The City of Burlington waives 50 percent of required impact fees for projects serving persons below 75 percent of median income—if such affordability is made permanent.

21. State support for the nonmarket housing developed by nonprofit organizations can be provided not only directly in the form of grants or loans but also indirectly in the form of tax credits or tax exemptions. Florida's "community contribution tax incentive program," for example, provides tax credits for private corporations that donate resources to community development projects sponsored by nonprofits. The "affordable housing tax credit" enacted in Illinois in 2001 allows corporations and individuals a 50-cent credit toward their state income tax for every dollar in cash, land or property donated for the creation of affordable housing. Connecticut and California operate their own low-income housing tax credit programs, funded with state dollars. California also exempts from taxation one-half of the capital gain on certain low-income housing projects if sold to a nonprofit corporation, a public entity or a limited-equity cooperative. Important here as well is the states' use of the federal Low Income Housing Tax Credit. Although most states have invested the bulk of their tax credit allocation in projects produced by for-profit developers, Oregon and Vermont are two states that have targeted most of their credits to projects sponsored by nonprofit corporations.

22. Both quotes appear in a widely distributed brochure published by Connecticut's Department of Housing, circa 1987, describing the state's Forever Housing programs.

23. These permanent reductions in property taxes are quite different from the PILOT (payment in lieu of taxes) agreements established in earlier years for public housing and Section 202 elderly housing. Tax assessors are slowly coming to accept, often because they have been forced to do so by a state court ruling, that privately owned housing with a legally recorded, long-term restriction on rents and resales has a taxable market value that is less than a comparable property with no such encumbrance. Two examples where a state court has considered this question are in New Jersey, *Prowitz v. Ridgefield Park Village*, 584 A.2d 782 (1991); 568 A.2d 114 (1989); in Oregon, *Bayridge Assoc. Ltd. Partnership v. Department of Revenue*, 321 Oregon Reports 21 (1995).

24. Massachusetts began subsidizing the operations of approximately 30 CDCs in 1976 through its Community Enterprise Economic Development Program. This program was defunded in 2003. New York has annually subsidized the operations of more than 100 Neighborhood Preservation Companies and about 40 Rural Preservation Companies since 1978. The North Carolina Community Development Initiative provides operational funding for "mature" CDCs, using a mix of public and private monies. New Hampshire provides operating support for a network of twelve nonprofit housing developers via its Housing Futures Fund, capitalized through a one-time tax credit for banks investing in the Fund. "Capacity grants" for Vermont's nonprofit housing delivery system are provided by the Vermont Housing and Conservation Board.

25. Although a nonprofit preference for disposing of surplus public property is typically handled through administrative rules, it may also be enshrined in law. For example, Chapter 440 was incorporated into Oregon's statutes in 1989 (ORS 440.2812). This law declares that "it will further the public interest to put unused state-owned real property at the disposal of nonprofit housing providers and housing authorities to address the housing needs of low-income individuals and families." State agencies are given authority to "sell, convey, or lease" such unused property for the purpose of providing "low-income housing options," including emergency housing, transitional housing and "permanent low-income housing units."

26. Other notable municipal programs for transferring tax-foreclosed property into the hands of nonprofits and cooperatives are Cleveland's Land Bank and the Washington, DC Homestead Program. Often, the biggest hurdle faced by local governments in dealing

with tax-delinquent properties are state laws that create a cumbersome foreclosure process and a lengthy redemption period. A number of states have amended their laws in recent years, however, to make it easier and faster for cities to foreclose on tax-delinquent properties. Florida's amendment is worth special note; there, legislation was enacted that permits community development corporations to purchase tax liens from the county in which a tax-delinquent property is located and prevents the former owner from making claims at a later date (Fannie Mae Foundation 2001).

27. Vermont's statute authorizing "housing subsidy covenants" (27 V.S.A. 610) was enacted in 1989. Maine's statute authorizing "affordable housing covenants" (33-A M.R.S.A. 121) and the Massachusetts statute authorizing "affordable housing restrictions" (Chapter 184, Section 26) were both enacted in 1991.

28. These cooperative housing statutes—found at M.G.L. 157B (Massachusetts), 14 V.S.A. 1598 (Vermont), Section 2002.273.11, Subdivision 8 of the Minnesota Statutes, and Section 33007.5 of the California Health and Safety Code—make special provision for limited-equity cooperatives, sanctioning the use of perpetual restrictions on the transfer of member shares in order to preserve the affordability of housing for low- and moderate-income households.

29. I am not saying that preserving affordability and preserving historically significant features are always incompatible, nor that the latter must necessarily be sacrificed to the former. I am asserting that preserving affordability should have a prior claim over public resources.

30. Between 1974 and 1993, an especially dark period in the federal retreat from subsidized housing, the addition of new subsidized housing for poverty-level renters offset the removal of unsubsidized, low-cost rentals only in the Midwest. In the rest of the country, the number of low-cost rentals subtracted from the affordable housing inventory exceeded the number of subsidized rentals that were added by 36 percent—a net decrease of 902,000 affordable units (JCHS 1995, 31).

31. According to Retsinas (1999), lower-income homeowners tend to live in older homes with more physical problems than do higher-income homeowners. They repair their homes less often and spend less when performing repairs. Nearly 2 million lower-income households live in homes in such poor repair that their homes may pose health and safety hazards. (See also JCHS 2003.)

32. Code enforcement is seldom sufficient, however, in preventing the loss of units from fire when the culprit is arson. Stone (1993:247) suggests that, in cases of arson, code enforcement and criminal investigation be combined with municipal laws requiring insurance proceeds to be used to rebuild fire-damaged housing (for current residents), with the municipality as additional loss payee. He also suggests

that landlords be required "to pay displaced tenants' relocation expenses and housing costs in excess of their pre-fire rents for a period of at least one year."

33. A serious loophole exists in many of these ordinances. They allow landlords to avoid housing preservation requirements by slowly emptying their buildings and holding them vacant. To plug this loophole, Hartford enacted an Anti-blight Ordinance that fines landlords for each housing unit that remains empty for over 60 days and that also presents a fire hazard, attracts illegal activity or becomes dilapidated. San Diego, Seattle, Cincinnati and Burlington have enacted similar ordinances, imposing stiff fines on landlords who leave residential buildings vacant for long periods of time without any movement toward improving, renting or selling them.

34. Although usually targeted to the preservation of unsubsidized rental housing, regulatory measures like antidemolition and anticonversion ordinances can also serve as powerful deterrents to the loss of publicly subsidized, privately owned rental housing. For instance, an overlooked aspect of the often-told story of saving Northgate Apartments, an expiring-use Section 221(d)(3) project in Burlington, Vermont, is the enactment of a condo conversion ordinance in 1987, two years prior to the date when the project's affordability controls were set to expire. This ordinance moderated Northgate's market value and made its owners more willing to sell to a consortium of third-sector and public-sector organizations acting under the direction of Northgate's tenants.

35. Mention should be made here of a common preservation strategy employed by city and state governments: granting or loaning money to private, profit-oriented landlords for the rehabilitation of their rental property. Although such rental rehab programs can be effective in preserving the physical structures, most of them do little (or nothing) to preserve affordability, preserve subsidies or enhance tenant security. Rental rehab programs can be made more effective and fair, however, by targeting eligibility, preventing displacement, maintaining affordability and giving nonprofits, a public housing authority or residents themselves the first right to purchase assisted properties.

36. Rehabilitation programs for low-income homeowners are probably the most common and most popular municipal housing programs. Less common are homeowner rehab programs that are operated by a state agency. Maine provides a good example, however. Maine's housing finance agency contracts directly with community action agencies to close and monitor approximately 1,200 home improvement loans each year, targeted to low-income homeowners.

37. Unpublished description of the ECHO Program drafted by Michael E. Stone on May 27, 2002.

38. The model for most state and municipal laws governing the relocation of tenants is the federal

Uniform Relocation Assistance and Real Property Acquisition Policies Act of 1970 (URA). Federal agencies are required by the URA to pay moving expenses and to assist in paying for replacement housing for homeowners or tenants who lose their homes because of actions initiated or dollars administered by a federal agency (see Hartman 1998). Similar laws at the state or municipal level require relocation assistance for persons displaced by state agencies, by municipal agencies or, in some cases, by private parties, even those who are not using public funds.

39. Hartman, Keating and LeGates (1982, 42) pointed out long ago a problem with preservation ordinances that contain only relocation assistance: "If the only barrier to demolition is dollar penalties and relocation assistance payments, developers will probably absorb these as a cost of business and will continue to demolish lower-rent housing because alternative uses are so profitable."

40. A prohibition against a particular type of unjust eviction, known as a "retaliatory eviction," has been enacted by some cities and states that otherwise do little to interfere with the landlord's right to evict. Under such a measure, tenants may not be removed from their units as a punishment for complaining to a public agency about health or safety violations in their building; for deducting money from their rent to pay utility bills that the landlord should have paid; or for joining a tenants' organization. Massachusetts, for example, has never enacted "just cause" eviction, but its laws against retaliatory eviction are quite strict.

41. Under Pennsylvania's Utility Services Tenants' Rights Act, for example, tenants must be notified if their landlord is seriously delinquent in paying utility bills. Tenants may assume these utility payments themselves and deduct them from their rent. Landlords may have gas, electric or water service terminated, moreover, only after submitting a sworn, notarized statement to the utility certifying that the units are vacant or that tenants have consented to the shut-off.

42. Cities typically use liens that are repaid upon sale of the property. Zarembka (1990, 134), however, has recommended using tax liens that must be repaid within one year of the city's repair of the property. At the end of this period, the municipality would have the right to acquire the property by eminent domain if the landlord has refused to reimburse the city for its work.

43. There is one class of homeowners whose security is just as precarious as tenants: the owner-occupants of mobile homes. Because they lease spaces for their manufactured housing, these homeowners are as vulnerable as any tenant to rising rents and arbitrary evictions. (It is arguable that these homeowners are more vulnerable than the typical tenant, since most mobile homes are not "mobile" at all, fixed as they are to a permanent foundation. Even when they can be moved, their owners often find that no

other park will accept a used mobile home into its midst.) Nearly every state with a substantial number of mobile home parks has laws governing their rental practices and evictions. The strongest protections are to be found in Florida and California. See Barr (1997, 1998). Florida law allows courts to overturn rent increases that are "unreasonable." California law allows municipalities to enact rent control ordinances for mobile home park spaces and, as of 1997, about 100 jurisdictions had done so. In both states, residents of mobile homes can be evicted only for "just cause." In Maryland, park owners who decide to sell their acreage for more lucrative development must give mobile home owners in their parks a minimum of 12 months before eviction and must produce a relocation plan (Hartman and Robinson 2003, 489).

44. It is not only financial institutions that force homeowners into default. Some 20 million homes—nearly one-fifth of the nation's total stock of owner-occupied housing—are governed by homeowner associations. As Hartman and Robinson have pointed out (2003, 482), many of these associations have the "power (used frequently and often capriciously or vindictively) to evict homeowners via the foreclosure process, often without due process."

45. Less common nationally, but a serious problem in some locales, have been various schemes for wresting title away from unsuspecting homeowners, including land contract sales, sale-lease option plans and lien sale contracts. A number of cities and states have been moved to enact fraud prevention measures when such scams have come to light (see, for example, PRRAC 1992).

46. These strategies need not be mutually exclusive. Santa Monica's housing policy in the 1980s, for example, combined rent control with public support for social housing (Capek and Gilderbloom 1992, 261). In Berkeley, on the other hand, Barton (1998, 108) contends that it was "only with the demise of rent control" that progressive and moderate city officials began to support a social housing agenda in earnest.

47. An innovative variation on this theme, combining tax relief with rent stabilization, is the Community Stability Small Homeowners Tax Credit, introduced in the New York legislature in January 2003. Owners of 1–3-unit buildings would receive a real estate tax abatement equal to 50 percent of the difference between the rent they are currently being paid and the "fair market rent," determined by the state, for each apartment. Owners of 4–5-unit buildings would receive a 60 percent abatement. (See http://www.fifthave.org/cstc/cstc.html).

48. State housing finance agencies, in particular, have a chance to play a critical role in promoting energy efficiency in the housing they finance, whether that housing is newly constructed or newly purchased, owner-occupied or renter-occupied. Although HFAs

have done much to expand the supply of low-cost housing (cf. Terner and Cook 1990), few have made energy efficiency a high priority. Sachs and Hunt (1992) tell the story of one that has.

49. State and municipal fair housing laws, similar in structure to federal law, first appeared in the 1960s. California was the first state to enact a fair housing law of its own. Oberlin, Ohio, was the first municipality (Keating 1994, 197).

50. State programs providing financial assistance for special housing needs are described in Chapter Six of the *1990 Compendium of State Housing Initiatives*, published by the Council of State Community Affairs Agencies (Thompson and Sidor 1991). Unfortunately, this excellent state-by-state synopsis has never been updated.

51. New Jersey's Fair Housing Act of 1985 also encouraged municipalities to submit to the Council detailed plans for how they intended to comply voluntarily with the Mount Laurel doctrine. Any municipality with a plan approved by the Council is protected from Mount Laurel II lawsuits and shielded from the builders remedy. By September 2004, according to the Council, 286 of the state's 566 municipalities were participating in this planning and compliance process (COAH 2005).

52. Although New Jersey's Fair Housing Act of 1985 was aimed at opening up suburban enclaves to all income and racial groups, the Act's original intent was undermined by a legislative provision allowing "regional contribution agreements." This provision allows a municipality to "buy out" up to one-half of its fair share obligation by paying another municipality to build below-market housing within its boundaries. As a result, many of New Jersey's inclusionary units have been built in urban—not suburban—neighborhoods. Another disappointment has been the low number of black and Latino households that have actually crossed the urban-suburban boundary, even when inclusionary units have been sited in suburbia (cf. Wish and Eisdorfer 1997; Boger 1997).

53. Five state-supported housing trust funds that have promoted housing on a regional basis are described in Meck, Retzlaff and Schwab 2003, 107–140.

54. Massachusetts may also be the only state to have linked all discretionary state funding for community development to a municipality's willingness to allow housing development in general—and the development of housing for low- and moderate-income families in particular. Executive Order 215, issued by Governor Edward King in 1982, instructed all state agencies to withhold grants for economic development, infrastructure improvements and other projects from "cities or towns which have been determined to be unreasonably restrictive of new housing growth." This executive order has seldom been invoked or enforced by the state, however, since the administra-

tion of Governor Michael Dukakis, who left office in 1990.

55. Good intentions and good planning notwithstanding, it must also be said that none of these states, not even Oregon, has committed the financial resources that are necessary to turn fair share pronouncements into fair share production. The limitations of land use planning as a means of promoting fair share housing are illustrated in the case of Minnesota, discussed by Goetz, Chapple and Luckermann (2001).

56. My focus here is primarily on economic integration: state and municipal efforts to open up affluent suburbs to persons of limited means, whatever their race. It should be noted, however, that a number of public programs for "penetrating enclaves" have been focused primarily on racial integration. State agencies in Ohio, Wisconsin and Washington, for example, have long offered below-market mortgages to first-time, moderate-income homebuyers who are willing to make a "pro-integrative move" into an area where minority homeowners are currently underrepresented (Keating 1994, 202–206; Orfield 1996, 326–327).

57. Cooperatives, community land trusts and other models of private, nonmarket homeownership have proven to be particularly effective in "opening the 'burbs" to classes and races who have long been excluded. Resistant planning commissions and suspicious neighbors often find it easier to accept below-market housing when it is to be occupied by "responsible" homeowners and overseen by a "responsible" nonprofit. More importantly, when mutual aid and social supports are incorporated into the very fabric of the housing that is theirs, lower-income households moving into inhospitable suburban settings can find it easier to weather the chilly reception that too often awaits them. The "social capital" engendered by social housing can help to ensure that "moving to opportunity" is a realized dream, not an empty promise. For evaluations of the HUD-sponsored social experiment known as Moving to Opportunity, see Goering and Feins 2003; Goetz 2003.

58. In 1984, there were 3,418 savings and loan associations (S&L) and 14,496 commercial banks in the United States; by 2000, there were 1,590 S&Ls and 8,315 banks (Colton 2003, 194–197). CRA requirements for smaller banks (those with assets below $250 million) were weakened by the 1999 Gramm-Leach-Bliley Financial Modernization Act. Banks of all sizes, moreover, have been losing business to institutions like private mortgage companies that are not covered by the CRA.

59. In a number of states, the housing finance agency or some other public (or quasi-public) "super-agency" has been given control over the allocation of nearly all grant money for housing (federal and state), all below-market financing for single-family and multifamily housing, all Low Income Housing Tax Credits

and the preparation of all housing statistics, assessments and plans. Whatever efficiencies are presumably gained by placing so many resources and responsibilities under a single organizational umbrella, there are also losses of creativity, flexibility and accountability that cannot be denied. These super-agencies often combine the worst elements of both a risk-averse private bank and a change-averse public bureaucracy.

60. From the right, there has been a long-standing animosity toward place-oriented programs, perceived as discouraging the mobility of people and the movement of capital. From the left, there has been mounting criticism of what is believed to be too narrow a focus on affordable housing by CDCs and other community-based development organizations that are said to have become so devoted to providing housing that they no longer have time for organizing residents of the neighborhoods in which they work (cf. Stoecker 1995). From the center, there is a belief that economic development should become the primary focus of efforts to revitalize impoverished locales. The key to neighborhood revitalization, according to this viewpoint, lies less in rehabilitating the built environment than in resuscitating the local economy, creating jobs within the neighborhood. A competing position contends that human development should hold center stage (cf. Sidor 1995, 1996).

61. Nicholas Lemann (1994) made precisely this argument in his criticism of the Clinton Administration's Empowerment Zone/Enterprise Community Program. He feared that scarce resources would be diverted from housing-related activities that have been the cornerstone of success for many CDCs and directed, instead, toward activities like ghetto-based job creation that have a relatively dismal record. It is also frequently forgotten that housing development is itself a powerful economic engine, providing jobs and multipliers that greatly benefit a local economy (cf. Davis and Knodell 1999).

62. One example of the housing/schools linkage is the problem of high classroom turnover, a damaging form of educational instability that is largely a function of residential instability. See Hartman and Franke (2003).

63. Such connections should be a two-way street. As Cushing Dolbeare (2000, 15) has pointed out: "Ask almost all educators, employment counselors, or health care or social service providers whether they can succeed in their own missions if their clients are homeless or do not have stable housing. The answer is that decent housing is a major requirement for their success. But we do not hear their voices raised in housing advocacy. That is left primarily to 'housers.'" But "housing is too important to be left to housers," she continues, "we need to encourage everyone who recognizes the importance of a decent home and suitable living environment to say so."

64. One of the oldest and most successful of these state-wide coalitions, combining advocates for housing with advocates for conservation, farmland preservation and historic preservation, is the one created in Vermont in 1987 to secure state funding for a housing and conservation trust fund (Libby and Bradley 2000; Axel-Lute 1999; Harmon 1992). A similar mixing of interests and agendas led to the passage of the Massachusetts Community Preservation Act in 2000, a measure that uses a 3 percent surcharge on local property taxes and matching grants from the state for open space, historic preservation and "community housing." Across the country, conservation groups affiliated with the Land Trust Alliance, the Trust for Public Land and the Nature Conservancy have displayed a growing willingness to discuss common agendas with housing and community development groups. Likewise, affiliates of the National Trust for Historic Preservation, once in the vanguard of many efforts to gentrify inner-city neighborhoods, have begun to display a new sensitivity to preventing displacement and preserving affordability.

65. One of the most surprising alliances to have emerged from the fight against sprawl is the consortium of the Bank of America, the California Resources Agency, the Greenbelt Alliance and the Low Income Housing Fund that produced the 1995 report *Beyond Sprawl* (Bank of America et al, 1995). Forging and sustaining such alliances can be a tricky business, however, as Axel-Lute (1999) has noted in her review of attempts to fuse affordable housing and "smart growth" agendas in Vermont, New Jersey, Rhode Island and Maryland. Other attempts to forge multi-issue, multi-jurisdictional coalitions around growth management, tax sharing and affordable housing can be found in Arigoni (2001), Rose and Silas (2001), the Smart Growth Network (2001), Harmon (1998), Rusk (1999) and Orfield (1997).

66. The CRA movement has been especially aware of both the need for organizing and the wisdom of linking grassroots advocacy with community-based development. Bradford and Cincotta (1992, 269), for example, noted that two of the keys to reinvestment are "a strong local base of community organizing complemented by activities that build the capacity of local communities to engage in development activities themselves." Similarly, Taylor and Silver (2003) speak to the "essential role of activism" in community reinvestment.

67. An argument for the growing political sophistication, interconnectedness and clout of nonprofit, community-based developers can be found in Clavel, Pitt and Yin (1997). By contrast, Krumholz (1997) has noted the criticism by local activists in Cleveland that nonprofit developers there have become less political over time as they have become more dependent upon city and state funding, a charge that Stoecker (1995)

has leveled against the entire "CDC model of urban development."

REFERENCES

Abbot, Carl. 2002. Planning a sustainable city: The promise and performance of Portland's urban growth boundary. In *Urban sprawl: Causes, consequences & policy responses*, ed. Gregory D. Squires, 207–235. Washington, DC: The Urban Institute Press.

Apgar, William C. 1991. Preservation of existing housing: A key element in a revitalized national housing policy. *Housing Policy Debate*, 2(2):187–210.

Apgar, William C., and Mark Duda. 2003. The twenty-fifth anniversary of the Community Reinvestment Act: Past accomplishments and future regulatory challenges. *FRBNY Economic Policy Review*, 169–191, June.

Arigoni, Danielle. 2001. Common ground: Smart growth and affordable housing advocates start a dialogue. *Shelterforce*, 23:16–18, November/December.

Atlas, John, and Ellen Shoshkes. 1997. *Saving affordable housing*. Orange, NJ: National Housing Institute.

Avault, John, and Geoff Lewis. 2000. *Survey of linkage programs in other U.S. cities with comparisons to Boston*. Boston: Boston Redevelopment Authority.

Axel-Lute, Miriam. 1999. A meeting of movements. *Shelterforce*, 21(1):10–14.

———. 2003. Zoning for housing justice. *Shelterforce*, 25(5):8–11.

Bank of America, California Resources Agency, Greenbelt Alliance, and Low Income Housing Fund. 1995. *Beyond sprawl: New patterns of growth to fit the new California*, San Francisco.

Barr, Kenneth K. 1997. Laws protecting mobile home park residents. *Land Use and Zoning Digest*, 49:3–7, November.

———. 1998. Controlling 'Im' mobile home space rents. In *Rent control: Regulation and the rental housing market*, eds. W. Dennis Keating, Michael Tertz and Andrejs Skaburskis, 193–203. New Brunswick, NJ: Rutgers Center for Urban Policy Research.

Barton, Stephen E. 1996. Social housing versus housing allowances: Choosing between two forms of housing subsidy at the local level. *APA Journal* 62:108–119.

———. 1998. The success and failure of strong rent control in the city of Berkeley, 1978 to 1995. In *Rent control: Regulation and the rental housing market*, eds. W. Dennis Keating, Michael Tertz and Andrejs Skaburskis, 88–109.New Brunswick, NJ: Rutgers University Center for Urban Policy Research.

Bauer, Catherine. 1985. The dreary deadlock of public housing. In *Federal housing policy and programs: Past and present*, ed. J. Paul Mitchell, 277–285. New Brunswick, NJ: Rutgers University Center for Urban Policy Research.

Bodaken, Michael. 2002. The increasing shortage of affordable rental housing in America: Action items for preservation. *Housing Facts & Findings*, 4(4):1, 4–7.

Boger, John Charles. 1997. Mount Laurel at 21 years: Reflections on the power of courts and legislatures to shape social change. *Seton Hall Law Review*, 27(4):1450–1470.

Bradford, Calvin and Gail Cincotta. 1992. The legacy, the promise, and the unfinished agenda. In *From redlining to reinvestment*, ed. Gregory D. Squires, 228–286. Philadelphia: Temple University Press.

Bratt, Rachel G. 1989. *Rebuilding a low-income housing policy*. Philadelphia: Temple University Press.

Brooks, Mary E. 2002. *Housing Trust Fund Progress Report 2002: Local responses to America's housing needs*. Washington, DC: Center for Community Change.

———. 1994. Housing trust funds. In *The affordable city: Toward a third sector housing policy*, ed. John Emmeus Davis, 245–264. Philadelphia: Temple University Press.

Browning, Rufus, Dale Marshall, and David Tabb. 1984. *Protest is not enough*. Berkeley: University of California Press.

Calavita, Nico, Kenneth Grimes and Alan Mallach. 1997. Inclusionary housing in California and New Jersey: A comparative analysis. *Housing Policy Debate*, 8(1):109–142.

Capek, Stella M., and John I. Gilderbloom. 1992. *Community versus commodity: Tenants and the American city*. Albany: State University of New York Press.

Caraley, Demetrios. 1996. Separating fiction from reality: A case against dismantling and devolving the federal safety net. Working Paper. New York: Russell Sage Foundation.

Center for Public Integrity. 1999. *Hidden agendas: How state legislatures keep conflicts of interest under wraps*. Washington, DC: The Center.

Chen, David W. 2003. One housing woe gives way to another. *New York Times*, December 21, Section 1:49.

Citizens' Housing and Planning Association (CHAPA). 2001. *The homes of 40B: Case studies of affordable housing using the comprehensive permit*. Boston: CHAPA.

Clavel, Pierre, Jessica Pitt and Jordan Yin. 1997. The community option in urban policy. *Urban Affairs Review*, 32:435–458, March.

Collins, Chuck, and Kirby White. 1994. Boston in the 1980s: Toward a social housing policy. In *The affordable city: Toward a third sector housing policy*, ed.

John Emmeus Davis, 201–225. Philadelphia: Temple University Press.

Colton, Kent W. 2003. *Housing in the twentieth-first century: Achieving common ground.* Cambridge, MA: Harvard University Press.

Council on Affordable Housing (COAH). 2005. About COAH. Available on the website of the New Jersey Department of Community Affairs: http://www.state.nj.us/dca/coah/about.shtml.

Davidoff, Paul. 1978. The redistributive function in planning: Creating greater equity among citizens of communities. In *Planning theory in the 1980s,* eds. Robert W. Burchell and George Sternlieb, 69–72. New Brunswick, NJ: Rutgers University Center for Urban Policy Research.

Davis, John Emmeus. 1991. *Contested ground: Collective action and the urban neighborhood.* Ithaca, NY: Cornell University Press.

———. 2000. Homemaking: The pragmatic politics of third sector housing. In *Property and values,* eds. Charles Geisler and Gail Daneker, 233–258. Washington, DC: Island Press.

———. ed. 1994. *The affordable city: Toward a third sector housing policy.* Philadelphia: Temple University Press.

Davis, John Emmeus, and Amy Demetrowitz. 2003. *Permanently affordable homeownership: Does the community land trust deliver on its promises?* Burlington, VT: Burlington Community Land Trust.

Davis, John Emmeus, Nancy Wasserman and Jeff Staudinger. 2000. *Research into the Small Cities CDBG programs of twenty-two states: Community Development Redesign Report II.* Montpelier, VT: Department of Housing and Community Affairs, State of Vermont.

Davis, John Emmeus, and Jane Knodell. 1999. *Economic benefits of public investment in affordable housing and land conservation: A review of arguments and evidence.* Montpelier, VT: Vermont Housing and Conservation Board.

Davis, John Emmeus, Tim McKenzie and Diana Carminati. 1993. *Designing a home equity living plan for Madison, Wisconsin: A pre-feasibility study.* Unpublished report prepared for the Madison Area Community Land Trust, Independent Living, Inc. and the City of Madison.

Dedman, Bill. 1988. The color of money. *Atlanta Journal/Constitution,* May 1–16.

———. 1989. Blacks turned down for home loans from S&Ls twice as often as whites. *Atlanta Journal/Constitution,* January 22.

Dolbeare, Cushing. 2000. Shifting fortunes. *Shelterforce,* 110:14–15, March/April.

Donahue, John D. 1997. The disunited states. *The Atlantic Monthly,* 279:18–22, May.

Downs, Anthony. 1997. The Devolution Revolution: Why Congress is shifting a lot of power to the wrong levels. *Brookings Policy Brief No. 3.* Washington, DC: Brookings Institution, February 21.

Eisinger, Peter. 1998. City politics in an era of federal devolution. *Urban Affairs Review,* 33(3):308–325.

Engler, John. 1997. The liberal rout. *Policy Review,* 81:44–48, January/February.

Etzioni, Amitai. 1995. Devolution is not exactly a household word. Pray that it never will be. *USA Today,* May 25.

Everett, David. 1992. Confrontation, negotiation, and collaboration: Detroit's multi billion dollar agreement. In *From redlining to reinvestment,* ed. Gregory D. Squires, 109–132. Philadelphia: Temple University Press.

Fannie Mae Foundation. 2001. State policies are critical to local responses on tax delinquent properties. *Housing Facts & Findings,* 3(1).

Federal Financial Institutions Examination Council (FFIEC). 1992. *A citizen's guide to the CRA.* Washington, DC: FFIEC.

Gilderbloom, John I., and Richard P. Appelbaum. 1988. *Rethinking rental housing.* Philadelphia: Temple University Press.

Goering, John, and Judith D. Feins, eds. 2003. *Choosing a better life? Evaluating the moving to opportunity social experiment.* Washington, DC: The Urban Institute Press.

Goetz, Edward G. 1995. Potential effects of federal policy devolution on local housing expenditures. *Publius,* 25(3):99–116.

———. 1996. The community-based housing movement and progressive local politics. In *Revitalizing urban neighborhoods,* eds. W. Dennis Keating, Norman Krumholz and Philip Star, 164–178. Lawrence, KS: The University of Kansas Press.

———. 2003. *Clearing the way: Deconstructing the poor in urban America.* Washington, DC: The Urban Institute Press.

Goetz, Edward G., Karen Chapple and Barbara Luckermann. 2001. Enabling exclusion: The retreat from fair share housing in the implementation of the Minnesota Land Use Planning Act. Paper presented at the annual meeting of the Association of Collegiate Schools of Planning, November 7–11.

Gold, Steven G. 1996. Issues raised by the new federalism. *National Tax Journal,* symposium on the Devolution Revolution, 49(2):273–287.

Harmon, Tasha R. 1998. Who pays the price for regional planning? How to link growth management and affordable housing. *Planners Network,* 128, March/April.

———. 1992. *Affordable housing: The Vermont model.* Amherst: Center for Rural Massachusetts, University of Massachusetts.

Hartman, Chester. 1998. Uniform Relocation Assistance and Real Property Acquisition Policies Act of 1970. In *The encyclopedia of housing*, ed. Willem van Vliet, 599–600. Thousand Oaks, CA: Sage Publications.

———. 1984. The right to stay put. In *Land reform, American style*, eds. Charles C. Geisler and Frank J. Popper, 302–318. Totowa, NJ: Rowman and Allanheld.

Hartman, Chester, and David Robinson. 2003. Evictions: The hidden housing problem.*Housing Policy Debate*, 14(4):461–501.

Hartman, Chester, and Todd Franke. 2003. Student mobility: How some children get left behind.*Journal of Negro Education*, Vol. 72., No. 1, Winter.

Hartman, Chester, Dennis Keating and Richard LeGates. 1982. *Displacement: How to fight it.* Berkeley, CA: Legal Services Anti-displacement Project.

Hayes, R. Allen. 1995. *The federal government and urban housing,* Second Edition. Albany: State University of New York Press.

Heudorfer, Bonnie. 2003. *The record on 40B: The effectiveness of the Massachusetts affordable housing zoning law.* Boston: Citizen's Housing and Planning Association.

Hite, James C.1979. *Room and situation: The political economy of land-use policy.* Chicago: Nelson-Hall.

Hurd, Maude, and Steven Kest. 2003. Fighting predatory lending from the ground up. In *Organizing access to capital: Advocacy and the democratization of financial institutions*, ed. Gregory D. Squires, 119–134. Philadelphia: Temple University Press.

Joint Center for Housing Studies (JCHS). 1995. *The state of the nation's housing 1995.* Cambridge, MA: Joint Center for Housing Studies of Harvard University.

———. 2000. *The state of the nation's housing 2000.* Cambridge, MA: Joint Center for Housing Studies of Harvard University.

———. 2003. *The state of the nation's housing 2003.* Cambridge, MA: Joint Center for Housing Studies of Harvard University.

Keating, W. Dennis. 1989. Linkage: Tying downtown development to community housing needs. In *Housing issues of the 1990s*, eds. Sara Rosenberry and Chester Hartman, 211–222. New York: Praeger.

———. 1994. *The suburban racial dilemma.* Philadelphia: Temple University Press.

———. 1998. Rent control: Its origins, history, and controversies. In *Rent control: Regulation and the rental housing market*, ed. W. Dennis Keating, Michael Teitz and Andrejs Skaburskis, 1–14. New

Brunswick, NJ: Rutgers Center for Urban Policy Research.

———. 2003. Comment on Chester Hartman and David Robinson's 'Evictions: The hidden housing problem'. *Housing Policy Debate*, 14(4):517–528.

Krumholz, Norman. 1996. Making a difference with equity planning. In *Planners on planning*, eds. Bruce McClendon and Anthony James Catanese. San Francisco: Jossey-Bass Publishers.

———. 1997. The provision of affordable housing in Cleveland: Patterns of organizational and financial support. In *Affordable housing and urban redevelopment in the United States*, ed. Willem van Vliet, 52–72. Thousand Oaks, CA: Sage Publications.

Lauber, Daniel. 1984. Condominium conversions: A reform in need of reform. In *Land reform, American style*, eds. Charles C. Geisler and Frank J. Popper, 273–301. Totowa, NJ: Rowman and Allanheld.

Leavitt, Jacqueline, and Susan Saegert.1990. *From abandonment to hope.* New York: Columbia University Press.

Lemann, Nicholas. 1994. The myth of community development: Rebuilding the ghetto doesn't work. *New York Times Magazine*, January 9, 27–31, 50, 54, 60.

Libby, James M., and Darby Bradley. 2000. Vermont Housing and Conservation Board: A conspiracy of good will among land trusts and housing trusts. In *Property and values*, eds. Charles Geisler and Gail Daneker, 261–281. Washington, DC: Island Press.

Listokin, David. 1976. *Fair share housing allocation.* New Brunswick, NJ: Rutgers University Center for Urban Policy Research.

Listokin, David, with Lizabeth Allewelt and James J. Nemeth. 1985. *Housing receivership and self-help neighborhood revitalization.* New Brunswick, NJ: Rutgers University Center for Urban Policy Research.

Logan, John R., and Harvey L. Molotch. 1987. *Urban fortunes.* Berkeley: University of California Press.

Luquetta, Andrea Caliz, and Deborah Goldberg. 2001. Insuring reinvestment. *Shelterforce*, 23:12–15, November/December.

Lutton, Linda. 1997. There goes the neighborhood. *The Neighborhood Works*, 20:16-23, July/August.

Mallach, Alan. 1994. The legacy of Mt. Laurel: Maintaining affordability in New Jersey's inclusionary developments. In *The affordable city: Toward a third sector housing policy*, ed. John Emmeus Davis, 226–244. Philadelphia: Temple University Press.

———. 1988. Opening the suburbs: New Jersey's Mount Laurel experience. *Shelterforce*, 11:12–15, August/September.

Meck, Stuart, Rebecca Retzlaff and James Schwab. 2003. *Regional approaches to affordable housing.* Chicago: American Planning Association.

Medoff, Peter, and Holly Sklar. 1994. *Streets of hope: The fall and rise of an urban neighborhood.* Boston: South End Press.

Morrissy, Patrick. 1987. Housing receivership: A step toward community control. *Shelterforce,* 10:8–10, January/February.

National Center for Policy Alternatives. 1988. *Legislative sourcebook on financial deregulation.* Washington, DC: The Center.

Nelson, Arthur C. 2003. Top ten state and local strategies to increase affordable housing supply. *Housing Facts & Findings,* 5(1):1, 4–7.

Nenno, Mary K. 1997. Changes and challenges in affordable housing and urban development. In *Affordable housing and urban redevelopment in the United States,* ed. Willem van Vliet, 1–21. Thousand Oaks, CA: Sage Publications.

Non-Profit Housing Association of Northern California and California Coalition for Rural Housing (NPH/CCRH). 2003. *Inclusionary housing in California: 30 years of innovation,* San Francisco.

Norquist, Grover. 1996. The Spirit of '96. *Policy Review,* 77:24–32, May/June.

Nye, Nancy, and Norman J. Glickman. 2000. Working together: Building capacity for community development. *Housing Policy Debate,* 11(1):163–198.

Orfield, Gary. 1996. Segregated housing and school resegregation. In *Dismantling desegregation: The quiet reversal of Brown v. Board of Education,* eds. Gary Orfield and Susan E. Eaton, 291–332. New York: The New Press.

Orfield, Myron. 1997. *Metropolitics: A regional agenda for community and stability.* Washington, DC: Brookings Institution Press.

Poverty and Race Research Action Council (PRRAC). 1992. Boston bank agrees to precedent-setting settlement to aid victims of home improvement loan scams. *Poverty and race,* 1(2):5–6.

Qadeer, M. A. 1981. The nature of urban land. *American Journal of Economics and Sociology,* 40(2):165–182.

Quigley, John M., and Daniel L. Rubinfeld. 1996. Federalism and reductions in the federal budget. *National Tax Journal,* Symposium on the Devolution Revolution, 49(2):289–301.

Retsinas, Nicholas P. 1999. Lower-income homeowners: Struggling to keep the dream alive. *Housing Facts & Findings,* 1(3).

Rose, Kalima, and Julie Silas. 2001. *Achieving equity through smart growth: Perspectives from philanthropy.* Oakland, CA: Policy Link and the Funders' Network for Smart Growth and Livable Communities.

Rusk, David. 1999. *Inside game/Outside game: Winning strategies for saving urban America.* Washington, DC: Brookings Institution Press.

Sachs, Beth, and Allan S. Hunt. 1992. The critical role of state housing finance agencies in promoting energy efficiency in buildings. American Council for an Energy Efficient Economy, conference proceedings from summer study on energy efficiency in buildings.

Sidor, John. 1995. Transforming community development policy and practice. Washington, DC: Council of State Community Development Agencies, September.

———. 1996. The CDBG program, empowerment, and welfare reform. Washington, DC: Council of State Community Development Agencies, May.

Smart Growth Network. 2001. *Affordable housing and smart growth: Making the connection.* Washington, DC: Smart Growth Network and the National Neighborhood Coalition.

Smith, Steven R., and Michael Lipsky. 1993. *Nonprofits for hire: The welfare state in the age of contracting.* Cambridge, MA: Harvard University Press.

Squires, Gregory D. 1994. *Capital and communities in black and white.* Philadelphia: Temple University Press.

———. 1995. Insurance redlining: Still fact, not fiction." *Shelterforce,* 17:17–19, January/February.

———. 1997. *Insurance redlining: Disinvestment, reinvestment, and the evolving role of financial institutions.* Washington, DC: The Urban Institute Press.

———. 2003. Introduction: The rough road to reinvestment. In *Organizing access to capital: Advocacy and the democratization of financial institutions,* ed. Gregory D. Squires, 1–26. Philadelphia: Temple University Press.

Stoecker, Randy. 1995. The CDC model of urban redevelopment: A critique and an alternative. *Journal of Urban Affairs,* 19(1):1–22.

Stone, Michael. 1993. *Shelter poverty: New ideas on housing affordability.* Philadelphia: Temple University Press.

Taylor, John, and Josh Silver. 2003. The essential role of activism in community reinvestment. In *Organizing access to capital: Advocacy and the democratization of financial institutions,* ed. Gregory D. Squires, 169–187. Philadelphia: Temple University Press.

Terner, Ian Donald, and Thomas B. Cook. 1990. New directions for federal housing policy: The role of the states. In *Building foundations: Housing and federal policy,* eds. Denise DiPasquale and Langley C. Keyes, 113–135. Philadelphia: University of Pennsylvania Press.

Thompson, Ellen Bowyer, and John Sidor. 1991. *State housing initiatives: The 1990 Compendium.* Washington, DC: Council of State Community Affairs Agencies (COSCAA).

Toulan, Nohad A. 1994. Housing as a state planning goal. In *Planning the Oregon way: A twenty-year evaluation*, eds. Carl Abbot, Deborah Howe and Sy Adler, 91–120. Corvallis: Oregon State University Press.

Vale, Lawrence J. 1997. The revitalization of Boston's Commonwealth Public Housing Development. In *Affordable housing and urban redevelopment in the United States*, ed. Willem van Vliet, 100–134. Thousand Oaks, CA: Sage Publications.

———. 2002. *Reclaiming public housing*. Cambridge, MA: Harvard University Press.

Varady, David, and Jeffrey Raffel. 1995. *Selling cities: Attracting homebuyers through schools and housing programs*. Albany: State University of New York Press.

Weaver, R. Kent. 1996. Deficits and devolution in the 104th Congress. *Publius*, 26(3):45–85.

Wheeler, Michael. 1990. Resolving local regulatory disputes and building consensus for affordable housing. In *Building foundations: Housing and federal policy*, eds. Denise DiPasquale and Langley C. Keyes, 209–239. Philadelphia: University of Pennsylvania Press.

White, Andrew, and Susan Saegert. 1997. Return from abandonment: The tenant interim lease program and the development of low-income cooperatives in New York's most neglected neighborhoods. In *Affordable housing and urban redevelopment in the United States*, ed. Willem van Vliet, 158–180. Thousand Oaks, CA: Sage Publications, Inc.

Wish, Naomi Bailin, and Stephen Eisdorfer. 1997. The impact of Mt. Laurel initiatives: An analysis of the characteristics of applicants and occupants. *Seton Hall Law Review*, 27(4):1268–1337.

Yeoman, Barry. 1997. The real state takeover. *The Nation*, 264:21–24, February 24.

Zarembka, Arlene. 1990. *The urban housing crisis*. Westport, CT: Greenwood Press.

Rachel G. Bratt

18   Housing and Economic Security

THE GOAL OF social policies should be to promote individual, family and community well-being. However, housing and other social policies, while often appearing to be benevolently motivated are, instead, generally aimed at promoting political agendas and the economic objectives of private businesses (Marcuse 1986). In addition, housing policy is often seen as apart from, rather than integral to, larger social welfare concerns, such as economic security. Writing with a European perspective, but one that also has validity for the United States, Kemeny has noted:

> Ultimately, the problem comes down to the way in which housing has been defined as a residual area divorced from the central policy-making area of social security. Once the far-reaching ramifications of housing for the whole of social structure are understood, it becomes possible to appreciate how crucial housing policy is to the viability of a welfare state. (1986, 275–276)

Housing analysts and policymakers have often focused on the details and processes of specific programs, such as the changes in the relative severity of different aspects of housing problems (like housing quality, overcrowding and affordability); and the relative costs and benefits of various housing strategies. Further, questions of implementing housing programs often revolve around where housing should be built, who should own and manage it, what types of subsidies are needed, how long the housing will be available to low-income households and who should be eligible to live in it.

While such issues are obviously critical, this chapter, and indeed this entire book, argues that housing policies must be explicitly focused on a more fundamental issue: the well-being of individuals, families and communities. Further, they must also been seen as integrally connected to a larger social policy agenda.[1] Such an agenda should involve the creation of a new social contract between individuals and government to encompass a series of rights and responsibilities to which both would adhere. Key to this discussion is our view that among the rights that should be guaranteed by government to all individuals is a Right to Housing.

A better understanding of the ways in which housing can be seen as part of a larger social agenda is particularly important in the present political context. During the 1990s, under the Clinton Administration, housing began to be viewed as an explicit vehicle to promote "self-sufficiency."[2] And, at the start of the 21st century, the bipartisan Millennial Housing Commission began its report with the following:

> Decent, affordable, and accessible housing fosters self-sufficiency, brings stability to families and new vitality to distressed communities, and supports overall economic growth. Very particularly, it improves life outcomes for children. In the process, it reduces a host of costly social and economic problems that place enormous strains on the nation's education, public health, social service, law enforcement, criminal justice, and welfare systems. (2002:10)

Thus, we have clearly begun the larger discussion about how housing could and should be aimed at promoting economic security, a critical component of individual and family well-being. This chapter examines how housing policies can promote "self-sufficiency" in a larger context—as part of a stream of initiatives aimed at promoting economic security. In fact, the goal of promoting "economic security," rather than "self-sufficiency," would go a long way to advancing the level of dialogue since, as discussed below, nobody in society is truly "self-sufficient" nor should they be.

As background to this discussion, it is important to question whether the provision of housing enhances or thwarts the ability of households to attain economic security. Advocates argue that without adequate housing workers have a difficult or impossible time finding and sustaining employment and parents are stretched to the limit in trying to care for themselves and their children. Often, families cannot stay together without a secure, stable home[3] In addition, attaining decent housing that is affordable in relation to the household's income is essential in order to have sufficient money available to cover the other necessities of life (see Chapter 2). For example, a study that tracked a group of children whose families received housing assistance at some point between 1968 and 1982 concluded that public housing may have positive effects on a child's long-term self-sufficiency (Newman and Harkness 2002).[4]

However, a second view holds that if housing is guaranteed, the motivation to seek employment and to work toward economic security will be undermined. Why work if housing, the single largest expenditure that a household must cover, is given, rather than something that must, with effort, be secured and maintained? In answer to these questions, the weight of existing empirical evidence indicates that if people are provided housing, there are not negative impacts on the motivation levels of workers, or would-be workers.[5] Further, given the evidence to the contrary—that housing is a critical element for families who are striving to achieve economic security and that it is essential in both promoting family well-being and in providing a springboard from which other career and income-enhancing initiatives can be launched—this chapter embraces the view that

providing housing results in positive outcomes for people, rather than serving as a disincentive. The logic of this position is far more compelling, believable and consistent with psychological views on the importance of work to personal self-actualization than the notion that the provision of housing encourages complacency and laziness.

At the heart of economic security is adequate income. Income may be derived from wages, inherited wealth, interest on investments, contributions from family members, property ownership or from income supports provided by the government. (A variety of noncash benefits can also be provided in the form of health care, education, food or even housing.) Public assistance initiatives directly boost income or enhance assets so that households can better afford housing and other necessities. However, for many households, the road to economic security is more complex than "simply" finding and keeping a job or supplementing income with public assistance. Obviously, for some people, holding a steady job is beyond their physical or mental capacity. In addition, substance abuse or other family problems or illness can significantly impede one's ability to maintain employment.

For those who have the capacity to work, achieving economic security also depends on personal attributes and skills, such as the motivation to work and ability to perform in the workplace. Initiatives that focus on providing assistance in this area are often called "self-sufficiency" programs.

Two additional key factors contributing to one's ability to work are the availability of decent-paying jobs as well as accessibility to both jobs and educational programs that prepare children, teens and adults to assume roles in the workforce. There are also numerous job-training programs and other types of initiatives that are aimed at job creation such as economic incentives aimed at the private sector and the direct provision of public sector jobs.

Finally, when wages and other income supports do not provide enough cash to assist households achieve economic security, there are a host of direct benefit programs that provide additional assistance. These benefits may be in the form of subsidized housing or they may assist with other critical needs (food stamps and Medicaid) and thereby free up available cash income to pay for housing as well as other necessities.

This chapter is aimed at broadening the conversation in which housing policy analysts frequently engage. It attempts to place housing in the context of how economic security for the entire population can be achieved, and it explores the role that housing can play in fulfilling that mission. Since adequate income is the essential ingredient of economic security and, indeed, the most direct means to that end, the chapter begins with an overview of the ways in which income enhancement initiatives contribute to economic security. If individuals and families had sufficient income to cover housing and other costs, less direct approaches to achieving economic security would be unnecessary. However, as discussed in Chapter 8, a right to income is almost certainly less achievable than a Right to Housing. And, even if incomes for all were adequate to cover the costs of housing and other necessities, we also know that the housing market is far from perfect and that discrimination, for example, would still create obstacles for large numbers of households, and that speculative profits could swallow up much of the income with little housing improvement. The chapter then examines three key approaches that connect housing with other broad social policy concerns and together relate to the goal of economic security. It focuses on the connections between housing and:

- *Welfare reform*—How is the welfare reform agenda, specifically the "work first" requirement, making it easier or more difficult for households to afford housing and other necessities of life?
- *"Self-sufficiency" programs*—How are housing-based "self-sufficiency" programs being utilized as a vehicle to promote economic security?
- *Programs aimed at increasing access to educational and job opportunities*—How does access to these opportunities create a higher likelihood of an individual attaining a good paying job?

The chapter concludes with a series of recommendations concerning how housing can be used to better promote economic security. The final section also explores how a Right to Housing would fit into a new social contract between individuals and government. The central argument is that current strategies that allegedly promote economic security fall way short of the mark and that, indeed, a Right to Housing would dramatically advance that agenda.

INCOME ENHANCEMENTS

Wages comprise about three-fourths of total family income (Bernstein et al. 2000, 34) and therefore are the most critical source of funds to cover living expenses, including the costs of housing for most households. For some segments of the population, however, wages alone have not been sufficient to provide decent levels of living and economic security. This has always been true, but the situation has worsened over the past two decades. As discussed in Chapter 1, since the late 1970s, average wages have fallen, after controlling for inflation, and wage inequality has increased. In order to supplement wages for households unable to work or whose earnings are inadequate to cover the necessities of life, a variety of strategies aimed at providing income support and benefits have been created. In this context, "income enhancements" include three major sets of initiatives that have the most impact on families with children: the federal income tax system, federal and state minimum wage laws/living wage programs and welfare payments. This section does not examine Social Security, since those benefits are aimed primarily at retired workers, and unemployment compensation, since that is available only to formerly employed workers whose employers contribute to that program.

Federal Income Tax System

The federal income tax system is a potential vehicle for enhancing economic security. Through a truly progressive tax system, families at the highest income levels would always pay the highest percent of income in taxes, and those at the lowest end would always pay the lowest percent or no tax at all. In addition, a negative income tax could provide direct cash payments to households, thereby enabling them to attain incomes that would be life-supporting.

Our current tax system does have progressive elements. The Earned Income Tax Credit (EITC) provides a means to supplement income for low- and moderate-income working households. In 2003, the federal EITC provided a maximum of $4,204 for a married couple with two or more children and with incomes of no more than $34,692 (Berube 2004). More than 19 million families and individuals claim the tax credit, and it lifts about 4.8 million people in working families above the poverty level, more than other means-tested initiatives (Johnson, Llobrera and Zahradnik 2003). In addition, seventeen states plus the District of Columbia offer their own income tax credits, modeled on the federal program and ranging from 4 to 43 percent of the federal EITC (Llobrera and Zahradnik 2004). While this is an important measure, it does not fully provide economic security to all poor and working poor households, based on a realistic measure of "self-sufficiency," as noted below.

A second key progressive aspect of the federal tax system is the different marginal tax brackets, based on income. The higher one's income, the higher the overall percentage of income that is generally paid. Furthermore, a variety of deductions are phased out for higher-income taxpayers. Overall, the highest income quintile (top 20 percent of the population) both earns more than one-half of total national income (Shapiro and Greenstein 1999, 2) as well as pays more than one-half (about 59 percent) of federal taxes (Lav and Greenstein 1999, 8–9).

Despite the progressive aspects of the tax code, the system is most kind to extremely high-income taxpayers. For example, capital gains (based on profits from the sale of stocks, bonds and other assets, which not surprisingly are predominantly held by high-income households) are taxed at a much lower rate than income from salaries, interest, dividends and self-employment. The capital gains tax rate is 20 percent, about one-half the top marginal tax rate for very-high-income households (39.5 percent), and is slated to go down to 18 percent in 2006. In addition, a variety of tax deductions and tax credits enable higher-income taxpayers to shelter portions of their income. Also, wage earners' taxes are deducted from their paychecks, whereas affluent business owners often are able to hide portions of their income, thereby reducing their tax liability. As a result of measures such as these, the more progressive features of the Internal Revenue Code are undermined, and some higher-income households end up paying a lower percentage of their income in taxes than some households with very low incomes. Indeed, there are always a number of very-high-income households who pay no taxes at all, despite a federally mandated alternative minimum tax.[6]

The tax system has also fostered ever-widening income disparities between the wealthiest and poorest citizens. Between 1977 and 1999, the after-tax income received by the top 1 percent of U.S. households rose from 7.3 percent to about 12.9 percent—a higher percentage than in any other year examined by the Congressional Budget Office. Moreover, the after-tax income of the richest 1 percent equaled the total after-tax income of the bottom 38 percent. This translates into 2.7 million Americans with the largest incomes receiving as much after-tax income as the 100 million Americans with the lowest incomes (Shapiro and Greenstein 1999, 2–3; see also Krugman 2002.)

The major way that the tax system relates to housing is through homeowners' deductions. These deductions enable middle- and upper-income families to enjoy significant savings. As noted in the Editors' Introduction, in 2004, about $84 billion was saved by taxpayers (which means lost revenues to the U.S. Treasury) due to the deductibility of mortgage interest and property tax payments from homeowners' incomes. The majority of these benefits went to households in the top two-fifths of the income distribution. Other tax benefits connected to housing, which also accrue disproportionately to higher-income households, amounted to an additional $36 billion in lost revenues (Dolbeare, Saraf and Crowley 2004; see also Chapter 5).

What are the short-term possibilities that the tax system will become more progressive and thereby provide greater economic security to the lowest-income households? Poor to nonexistent. Under President George W. Bush's tax cut, enacted within six months after his taking office and in effect through 2011, the top 20 percent of the income distribution was expected to receive some 70.6 percent of the benefits, while it was anticipated that the bottom 80 percent would receive 29 percent (Shapiro, Greenstein and Sly 2001, 1). More recent estimates of the impacts of these tax cuts have been even more troubling: In 2005 the wealthiest 0.2 percent of the population—households with incomes of more than $1 million per year—enjoyed a tax cut averaging over $100,000. Moreover, tax cut measures slated to take place will result in another $20,000 per year in tax savings for this group. Overall, 54 percent of the new tax cuts will go to those earning more than $1 million per year and 97 percent of the tax cuts will go to the 3.7 percent of the population earning over $200,000 (Greenstein, Friedman and Shapiro 2005).

In summary, the federal income tax system has not significantly altered the ability of low-income households to achieve economic security. While the tax code has some progressive elements and even attempts to modestly redistribute income to low-income wage-earners through the EITC, overall, it does not provide enough preferential treatment to low-income households.

Federal and State Minimum Wage Laws/Living Wage Programs

As of 2005, the federal minimum wage was $5.15 per hour, set in 1997. Prior to the 2000 election, there was considerable debate about raising the minimum wage; however, no such increase was enacted.[7] After accounting for inflation, the value of the minimum wage in 2004 was 26 percent less than in 1979 (Economic Policy Institute 2005). A full-time wage earner working 40 hours per week, 52 weeks per year, would earn $10,712. This is $8,638 less than the federally established poverty level for a family of four, which was $19,350 in 2005. Even if a family were able to reach the poverty-level threshold with wage income, it still would not have achieved

economic security. Indeed, the poverty level, while a useful and consistent benchmark, has little relationship to what it actually costs a family to live in decent housing, eat adequate food, buy appropriate clothes, pay for health insurance and meet the myriad other expenses households face.[8]

Data on wages and housing costs demonstrate how much more than the federal minimum wage households need to earn in order to afford rental units, using the U.S. Department of Housing and Urban Development's (HUD) "Fair Market Rent" (FMR)[9] levels, while paying no more than 30 percent of income for rent. In no locale in the United States is the federal minimum wage sufficient to cover the costs of renting either a one- or two-bedroom unit at an affordable level (National Low Income Housing Coalition 2004).

There is an obvious policy disconnect here. On the one hand, we have a minimum wage. But the income derived from such a wage is completely unrelated to an already unrealistically low poverty level, and to HUD's own assessment of what it costs to rent a decent housing unit. The minimum wage does little to promote economic security. It neither lifts a household with a single minimum wage earner above the poverty level, nor does it provide enough income to support a family.

In contrast to the inadequacy of the poverty level, "market basket" approaches provide much more accurate methods to determine how much income is needed to cover basic expenditures. Michael Stone (1993, 75, Appendix A) provides an overview of such efforts, which are based on actual living costs and expert opinion. In addition, Stone's concept of "shelter poverty" is actually an income-adequacy standard based on such a market basket approach (see Chapter 2).

Building on the "market basket" idea, a "Self-Sufficiency Standard" has been calculated for thirty-four states plus the District of Columbia (Wider Opportunities for Women 2003). Acknowledging that costs vary even within states, "self sufficiency" standards are developed for various locales. For example, in Wilmington, Delaware, a four-person household of two working adults and two children would need nearly $44,000 per year, which translates into an hourly wage of $10.36 for each adult worker (Pearce and Brooks 2003).

In further recognition of the inadequacy of the minimum wage, some 117 city and county governments have mandated that a "living wage" be paid by all private business that benefit from public money (such as through service contracts, grants, loans, bond financing tax abatements or other economic development subsidies—[ACORN 2004]). At the very least, such a wage should boost a wage earner trying to support a four-person household above the poverty level (Albelda and Tilly 1997, 153). Based on the four-person poverty level of $19,350, a worker would need to earn about $9.25 per hour, or about 80 percent more than the 2005 federal minimum wage. Even with this large an increase, in no state would a $9.25 per hour wage earner be able to afford a two-bedroom FMR unit. West Virginia comes the closest, with a worker earning $9.31 per hour able to afford a two-bedroom FMR unit. Other relatively affordable states, where a wage of under $10 per hour translates into a worker able to afford a 2-bedroom FMR are: North Dakota, Arkansas, Mississippi and Alabama (National Low Income Housing Coalition 2004).

Given Congressional reluctance to boost the minimum wage, particularly to levels that would result in a truly livable income, it seems reasonable to surmise that initiatives to enhance economic security through this mechanism are likely to fall way short of the mark. And while living wage campaigns appear to be successful in boosting wages in scores of locales, they still only cover a small percentage of the country.

Welfare Payments

The U.S. government has always had a mixed attitude, at best, toward providing direct cash supplements to the poor. As Katz (1989) has pointed out, "the undeserving poor" are viewed with a combination of contempt and pity, and public policies aimed at assisting them are never generous enough to fully cover the costs needed to maintain a decent standard of living. It is telling that welfare payments are not even pegged to bring a household above the official, woefully inadequate poverty line. Although there is considerable variation in Temporary Assistance for Needy Families (TANF) payments from state to state, no state provides sufficient benefits to lift a household out of poverty.[10] Further, in the typical state, "the purchasing power of the maximum welfare benefit (adjusted for inflation) fell by half between 1970 and 1997" (Sweeney et al. 2000, 31).

The extent to which all government transfer programs lift people out of poverty presents a mixed picture. In 1995, nearly one-half of the 57.6 million people who would have been poor without government benefits were moved out of poverty with the assistance of these programs (Primus 1996). While this was the highest percentage of people who were moved out of poverty with the aid of government assistance for any year since 1980, more than one-half of the poor were not boosted above the poverty level. There are also signs that the trend began to reverse almost immediately. Between 1995 and 1998, contractions in the food stamp program and cash assistance for poor families with children resulted in a reduction in the number of children served, with an overall reduction in the effectiveness of the safety net at reducing child poverty (Porter and Primus 1999).

Although welfare payments provide a straightforward and potentially efficient mechanism for promoting economic security, the record of this type of support, as well as our historical aversion to providing "too much" government assistance to the needy, suggests that this is not a viable solution. Indeed, as discussed below, "welfare reform" has meant that far fewer households are receiving direct income transfers, and more stringent requirements are being placed on eligibility than ever before. The "bottom line" is that poverty has been increasing. The U.S. Census reported that the number of poor people stood at 37 million in 2004, an increase of 4.1 million since 2001. Moreover, the overall poverty rate rose from 11.7 percent in 2001 to 12.7 percent in 2004. And the severity of poverty (the average amount by which the incomes of those who are poor fall below the poverty line) matched the highest on record, dating back to 1975 (Center on Budget and Policy Priorities 2005).

IMPLICATIONS OF WELFARE REFORM FOR HOUSING AND ECONOMIC SECURITY

The welfare debate of the 1990s, which resulted in passage of the Personal Responsibility and Work Opportunity Reconciliation Act of 1996, assumed, in part, that there was a better way to provide public assistance that would enable poor households to move out of poverty. Much of the criticism lodged against welfare revolved around the perception of a permanent welfare population and the seeming inability of these households to move up the economic ladder.[11] Indeed, it has often been argued that the old welfare system's rules undermined the ability of recipients to become independent.[12]

The new law was aimed at ending "the dependence of needy parents on government benefits by promoting job preparedness, work, and marriage" (quoted in Loprest 1999, 1). Specifically, the 1996 act eliminated the 61-year old guarantee, through the old Aid to Families with Dependent Children (AFDC) program, that all children meeting federal eligibility standards could receive assistance. The new system, TANF, mandates states to impose limitations on the length of time that recipients may receive benefits. Most households can rely on public assistance for two consecutive years and a total of five years over a lifetime. Recipients are generally expected to work at least 30 hours per week. If a household does not comply with this requirement, benefits are progressively cut. Further, under the 1996 law most parents are only able to count 10 hours of participation in job skills training, education related to employment and attendance in secondary school or participation in a General Equivalency Diploma (GED) program as part of the work requirement (Economic Success Clearinghouse 2005).

Without belaboring the validity of the arguments behind the 1996 welfare reform act, this section explores the connections between welfare reform, housing and economic security. After a review of the connections (and lack of connections) between the housing and welfare systems, the following questions are addressed: What do early evaluations tell us about the likelihood that welfare reform will promote economic security and enable families to cover their costs, including the cost of housing? To what extent will any shortfalls impact the assisted housing stock?

Housing and Welfare—the Connections

Both the housing and welfare systems are large and complex.[13] The housing system includes dozens of programs funded by HUD (see HUD 1999). In addition, a host of other public and private initiatives have a direct bearing on housing affordable to low-income households. The welfare system is equally complex. A 1995 U.S. General Accounting Office report noted that Congress had created about 80 separate programs providing cash and noncash assistance to low-income individuals and families. "These myriad welfare programs—each with its own rules and requirements—are difficult for families in need to access and cumbersome for program administrators to operate" (GAO 1995, 2).

In view of the difficulties involved in coordinating and rationalizing each of the discrete systems, it is hardly surprising that coordination between the two has been problematic.[14] Newman and Schnare have been in the vanguard of articulating the importance of viewing the two systems as part of a whole, rather than as two separate bundles of services. They argue that "If providing adequate housing to all in need is the goal, the combined system is unfair, ineffective, and inefficient. If fostering economic independence is the goal, the system is even more deeply flawed" (1992, 7). They further point out that the amount of money earmarked for housing through welfare does not come with the requirement that housing meet quality standards, and welfare shelter grants typically fall far short of the cost of decent housing; nearly one-third of welfare recipients live in substandard conditions. Also, housing assistance has typically reached only a small fraction of those who qualify for such assistance, but those who do receive such subsidies are generally adequately housed (Newman and Schnare 1992, 6–7). Pines has astutely observed that:

> Although there is ample documentation of the interlocking nature of the problems of

poor families...the disparate systems operating service programs often exacerbate the problems by dealing with each "symptom" as an unrelated part of the whole. Rather than working to build a strong viable family unit, this fragmented approach seems to pull fragile families farther apart.... Families do not care whether help comes [from one program or another]. They do care if they are funneled from one intake office to another, and if they have to undergo multiple eligibility determinations.... The nation can no longer afford "stand alone" social service systems. They are inefficient and far from user friendly. We must pursue a more rational, coherent family investment system characterized by integrated service delivery at the local level. (1991:112)

The great majority of those who receive HUD housing assistance and those who receive welfare benefit do so from only one type of aid, not both. Nationwide, only about 25 percent of families receiving welfare payments through TANF also receive federal housing assistance (Khadduri, Shroder and Steffen 2003).

One of the problems in coordinating the housing and welfare systems is that each has a somewhat different mission. In the case of housing, the overall concern is that the developments function smoothly and that they provide an optimum living environment for residents. Welfare officials are typically less involved with the housing per se and more concerned with the individual well-being of clients (see, for example, Council of State Community Development Agencies and the American Public Welfare Association 1991, 6–7).

The conflict between the housing and welfare systems first surfaced in the 1930s when the financing formula for public housing required tenants to pay rent based on a percentage of income. As a result, Newman and Schnare note:

[M]any of the poorest households, including those on welfare, were excluded from public housing.... It is unfortunate that this first formal connection between the housing and welfare systems was contentious. It is also disturbing that the earliest frustrations that each system voiced with the other are essentially the same today as they were then. (1992, 14–15)[15]

During the 1950s, the federal government went so far as to explicitly prohibit public housing authorities from hiring staff to provide social or community services. In something of a turn-around, during the 1960s, official administrative guidelines and legislative initiatives encouraged public housing managers to include social and economic goals for tenants, although funds were not appropriated for such activities (Newman and Schnare 1992, 15–16). Newman and Schnare (1992, 18–20) further point out that the history of welfare initiatives includes an emphasis on the importance of housing, particularly for families with young children. And, in 1969 the old Department of Health, Education and Welfare (HEW—predecessor to the Department of Health and Human Services) noted that decent housing was a route to independence and was essential to enable poor people to move toward "self-support, self-care, and a better quality of life" (cited in Newman and Schnare 1992:20).

The Council of State Community Development Agencies and the American Public Welfare Association (the latter is now known as the American Public Human Services Association) have underscored the ways in which the housing and welfare systems provide opportunities for enhanced coordination (1991, 9). However, despite the rhetoric suggesting logical links between the housing and welfare systems, the two continue to function virtually autonomously.

Termination of Welfare Benefits and Employment

A key question about welfare reform is, Will households whose benefits terminate be able to find jobs that will enable them to cover their costs of living, including paying rent? The answer appears to be mixed. But on balance welfare reform is creating vast problems for welfare and former welfare recipients who are facing complete loss of payments due to time limits or sanctions due to noncompliance with the work requirement. The Center for Community Change (1999b) went so far as to call the law "an unmitigated disaster in its impact on poor people."

Concerning the much-touted positive outcomes of welfare reform, the number of households on welfare has gone down dramatically, and many former recipients have found jobs. Some 2 million households received welfare cash assistance in 2003 compared with about 5 million in early 1994 (Lazere 2000, 1; U.S. Department of Health and Human Services 2003). President George W. Bush's former Health and Human Services secretary Tommy Thompson heralded this decline by noting that "Americans are demonstrating that they want to be self-sufficient and economically independent for the benefit of themselves and their children" (U.S. Department of Health and Human Services 2003).

More negatively, however, at least 20 percent of the "families that have left welfare have boomeranged back, and rolls started climbing again [in 2001] in 30 states.... More than half of those who return to welfare... originally left with a job. They soon either got laid off, lost their jobs for other reasons, or found they could not earn enough to stay afloat" (Loprest 2002, 1). Moreover, as the economy cooled in the early years of the 21st century, the percentage of people who left welfare with jobs (or found them shortly thereafter) was significantly lower than the corresponding percentage in the late 1990s, dropping 8 percentage points, from 50 to 42 percent. Not surprisingly, then, a higher percentage of people who left welfare in 2002 compared with 1999 had returned to welfare (Loprest 2003a). Moreover, those jobs that former recipients have been able to secure are likely to pay low wages (Loprest 2003a). Also problematic is that these jobs often do not come with employment-related benefits, such as paid vacation, sick leave and health insurance (Parrott 1998, 17, 18).

As one might expect, the loss of welfare, uncertain employment, low wages and weak benefits translate into a high degree of economic instability and human suffering, including inadequate income to cover rent or mortgage costs, utilities, food and medical care.[16] But researchers have found that those who leave welfare with housing assistance are generally better off than those who do not have this help (Loprest 2002; Zedlewski 2002; Sard 2003).

In summary, the results of welfare reform appear problematic from all but a public relations or budgetary perspective.[17] Welfare reform set out to reduce welfare rolls and to reduce the government's expenditures for welfare payments. It has achieved this. But it has not furthered the goal of providing poor families with a decent standard of living and with sufficient income to pay for rent. If anything, it appears that economic instability has increased for the poorest members of the population.

Welfare Reform and the Assisted Housing Stock

Experiences with welfare reform emphatically underscore just how interconnected the housing and welfare systems are. First, concerning public housing, if the incomes of a substantial number of these residents are reduced due to loss of welfare income, and if equivalent income is not derived from wages, the revenues collected by public housing authorities, which are based on a percentage of income, will be reduced. To make matters worse, "public housing authorities do not generally receive any additional federal subsidy during a year in which they experience a net decrease in revenue, and recent experience suggests that there is no guarantee that their subsidy will increase the following year to compensate for reduced revenue" (Sard 2003, 112–113). In that case, public housing authorities are forced to operate with fewer funds, thereby creating additional stresses on management.

Second, for owners of Section 8 housing, there is less concern about losses in revenues, since federal subsidies increase to offset reduced rental income (Sard 2003). In that case, however, "If HUD payments to the project-based owners rise substantially due to declining tenant incomes as families hit time limits, HUD may have to reduce spending on other housing programs to remain within budgetary limits" (Sard and Daskal 1998).

Little concrete evidence is available about the actual impacts of welfare reform on subsidized housing. As of the late 1990s, the U.S. General Accounting Office concluded that the "impact of welfare reform on the revenue, employment status of tenants, and roles of selected housing agencies is uncertain" (1998b, 27). In a study of developments financed by the Massachusetts Housing Finance Agency (now known as MassHousing), site managers were asked a series of questions about how they anticipated welfare reform would impact their properties. About one-third predicted that the quality of life at the developments would be adversely impacted and that a variety of management problems would increase, including more cases of rent arrearages (Massachusetts Housing Finance Agency 1999, 27). Although difficult to quantify, if welfare creates more stress for housing managers, the quality of maintenance will likely suffer.

The post-welfare reform era provides a good opportunity for the housing and welfare systems to develop more collaborative relationships. Emphasizing the need and importance of such cooperation, Sard and Waller (2002) provide a series of suggestions for how housing assistance and welfare payments can be better coordinated to optimize outcomes for families.

The U.S. General Accounting Office study cited above also urged HUD to pay closer attention to issues of coordination. While acknowledging that "HUD has provided guidance on welfare reform," the report noted that HUD had "not ensured that all of the field offices and public housing agencies received and understood the guidance." The GAO called on HUD to "develop a comprehensive strategy" and to direct its field offices to work closely with federal, state and local welfare reform efforts (U.S. General Accounting Office 1998b, 58, 60).

Despite the lack of data on the impacts of welfare reform on the assisted housing stock, at the very least the issue serves to highlight the importance of seeing the two systems as part of an overall mechanism for promoting greater economic security for residents. So far, however, such coordination seems still to be at the level of opportunity, rather than action. And this lack of a consistent set of policies oriented at optimizing the economic security of those in need will likely create adverse impacts on this population.

HOUSING-BASED "SELF-SUFFICIENCY" PROGRAMS

Historically, housing programs have promoted production and subsidization of housing affordable to low- and moderate-income households.

Measures of success typically include numbers of units produced or rehabilitated and accessibility of those units to households with serious housing needs. But, increasingly, the housing agenda is evolving to include a more expansive set of goals. Now, as noted at the outset of this chapter, it is not enough for housing programs to provide decent, affordable housing—which, of course, is no small feat in itself. Housing must also promote a household's ability to achieve economic independence, or to become "self-sufficient."[18] But what is "self-sufficiency," and why is the term problematic? What have we learned from prior self-sufficiency programs, and to what extent do current initiatives appear to be promoting economic security?

Multiple Meanings of "Self-Sufficiency"

"Self-sufficiency" is a frequently used phrase that defies precise definition. For purposes of this chapter, self-sufficiency refers to individuals and households who are managing their lives without any direct subsidy. Using this strict and simple definition, a self-sufficient household would not be receiving income assistance, housing subsidies or other direct supports.

However, as discussed more fully in Bratt and Keyes (1997), various studies and reports on self-sufficiency have argued that a variety of additional concerns should be considered and factored into a definition: Acquisition of new skills and abilities could enable the person to function without assistance in the future; there can be positive movement toward self-sufficiency, as opposed to total independence and it is important to recognize that for some individuals and households self-sufficiency may not have an economic meaning at all. Instead, it may connote a greater capacity for an individual with serious mental, emotional or physical limitations to cope with life's challenges. In addition, challenges presented by the global economy (such as domestic job losses, deindustrialization) as well as social constraints (like discrimination) make it more difficult for unskilled and uneducated workers to find employment that provides sustainable wages.

Elaborating on the complexities of defining self-sufficiency, Bratt and Keyes reported that a number of respondents (who were heads of nonprofit housing organizations that were implementing some form of a self-sufficiency program) articulated:

> [S]erious objections to the term "self-sufficiency," even while they referred [the researchers] to noteworthy efforts or while they, themselves, readily described their programs as focused on promoting the concept. "Self-sufficiency" invokes criticism for a number of reasons, some of which can be traced to strong, possibly conflicting cultural strands in our society—an infatuation with individual independence embedded within widespread support for collaboration and a strengthening of community.

On one level, many people interviewed raised serious questions about the usefulness of the term "self-sufficiency" because it evokes an image of "rugged individualism," which is no more or less applicable to low-income people than it is to the rest of society. "Self-sufficiency" implies that people who participate in such programs will, at some point, no longer need any outside supports and instead will be totally able care for themselves. In contrast, almost no one in our society is truly self-sufficient. Virtually all citizens receive some form of "special assistance," whether because of low incomes (means-tested) or, mostly, through one of our many entitlement programs that are available either to anyone, regardless of income, or to certain groups, such as veterans, the elderly, homeowners, etc.[19]

Thus, the goal that the poor should somehow become "self-sufficient" is contrary to the way in which almost all U.S. citizens actually live. Yet, at the same time, interviewees acknowledged that society is increasingly articulating a strong desire for poor people to be less dependent on public resources. This was expressed most explicitly in the 1996 welfare reform legislation, which, for the first time, placed a lifetime cap on the receipt of public assistance.

On a second level, several people interviewed indicated that they were uncomfortable with the phrase "self-sufficiency" because it can suggest that until you achieve "self-sufficiency," you are somehow insufficient, clearly a negative connotation.

A third critique is that whether or not someone becomes "self-sufficient" may be less a matter of their own commitment and actions, and more a result of the contextual challenges that

often stand in the way of gaining some measure of economic independence. . . . Although individuals may be working hard to overcome economic dependency, external pressures, such as low-wage jobs or high housing costs, constantly present challenges and roadblocks. (1997, 9)

Despite the problematic nature of the term, "self-sufficiency" has become a popular phrase, denoting a greater, if not complete, level of economic independence from public subsidy.

Since the 1960s, various local programs have provided social services to public housing residents (Newman and Schnare 1992), although the major housing-based self-sufficiency programs began in the mid-1980s. These programs have generally been aimed at providing incentives to create a sense of responsibility among participants in terms of expectations placed on them and countering traditional criticisms of welfare programs, particularly the disincentive to work due to a loss of income and benefits. The largest and best-known self-sufficiency program was created by the federal government in 1990. The "Family Self Sufficiency program"[20] (FSS) directs localities to provide a high level of social services as well as to coordinate these services. While this program "can succeed in leveraging the provision of services only if there is sufficient funding from other sources to support those services" (Shlay 1993, 486), no additional funds are provided for the actual services (Center on Budget and Policy Priorities 1999, 6). In addition, according to Sard, fewer than one-half of all public housing authorities offer the FSS program to residents and, among those that do, the number of participants is restricted. This results in less than 5 percent of families with children living in public housing or utilizing a housing choice voucher involved with FSS (Sard 2001), despite the fact that all such households are eligible to participate.

Based on a series of studies that have investigated the experiences of participants in local and federal programs, some clear policy implications emerge.[21] First, it is impossible to devise a "one size fits all" initiative; participants' assets and deficits (including physical and mental limitations and the particular family's situation) must all be taken into account when creating a self-sufficiency program. As a result, programs must be tailor-made to meet the diverse needs of the population being served. And they must offer a variety of services as a whole package, rather than as a series of separate initiatives, each with its own set of rules and requirements (Rohe and Stegman 1991; Pines 1991; Bratt and Keyes 1997). In order to achieve this type of program coordination, individuals are needed who have significant authority to bring diverse agencies together to discuss how to streamline procedures and provide a full complement of services. This needs to occur both at the national level, in better coordinating the housing and welfare systems, as well as at the local level, where programs get implemented.

Second, whatever the objectives are for helping an individual or family to enhance their economic security, it is important to recognize that long time frames are important; quick fixes are highly unlikely and goals must be set that can be achieved "one step at a time" (Shlay and Holupka 1992; Rohe 1995; Bratt and Keyes 1997). However, the steps are not necessarily linear; for many households, there are invariably many moves forward and backward, and job loss or a family illness can plunge the family back into an insecure economic situation (Sweeney et al. 2000).

Third, programs aimed at promoting economic security should be infused with a respect for clients. Programmatic approaches that promote responsibility and a sense of choice among program participants can be as important as the actual services being offered (Bratt and Keyes 1997).

Fourth, motivating people to participate in a self-sufficiency program can be a challenge, at least in part because many people have given up on themselves, lacking the self-confidence and self-esteem to undertake education and job training programs (Rohe and Stegman 1991; Bryson and Youmans 1991). The use of escrow accounts (accounts that enable households to save the portion of their rent that would be charged under HUD's standard guidelines for increasing rent contributions when incomes rise) may be an important attraction for recruiting participants to such programs (Rohe and Kleit 1999).

Fifth, and in sharp contrast to the FSS program, programs aimed at promoting economic security should be well funded, and housing subsidies should be a critical component of the supports provided. Financial resources are needed to pay for at least three distinct components of a self-sufficiency program: the services themselves, coordinating the services, and paying personnel to do case management and referrals. Housing subsidies are a critical, if not the first, "service" needed in self-sufficiency programs (Bratt and Keyes 1997). In addition, a housing subsidy may be needed even after a household has begun to make progress toward self-sufficiency (Shlay 1993).

Housing-based self-sufficiency initiatives certainly hold promise for promoting economic security. However, since only about one-third of all eligible households actually receive rental housing assistance (Millennial Housing Commission 2002, 14), thereby making them candidates for FSS programs, combined with the relatively small scale of these programs, makes them marginal at best.

HOUSING AND ACCESS TO OPPORTUNITIES

Beyond the effects of housing itself, where people live, in terms of neighborhood setting and locational advantage, may have an impact on access to both educational opportunities and employment and social networks. For example, Wilson's The Truly Disadvantaged (1987) argues persuasively that isolation of poor and nonwhite populations creates its own set of problems, placing barriers in the path of those struggling to move out of poverty. Summarizing the extent of income and race segregation, Downs has noted that "Poor blacks and Hispanics remain far more concentrated in inner-city and other high-poverty neighborhoods than do poor non-Hispanic whites" (1994, 73). Until 1990, the trend had not been encouraging, as the concentration of poor blacks in high-poverty and distressed neighborhoods steadily increased (Kasarda 1993, 283; see also Chapter 3). While recent research points to a reversal of this trend in virtually all neighborhoods except for older, inner-ring suburbs (Jargowsky 2003), the change may not be permanent. In fact, some of the gains may already have been lost due to the downturn in the economy during the early years of the 21st century. Moreover:

> [T]he long-run picture is far from sanguine.... If the inner-ring suburbs provide any indication, then the underlying development pattern that leads to greater neighborhood stratification was still at work in the 1990s, and is likely to have continued in the considerably weaker economic climate of [2000–2003]. If so, greater concentration of poverty and more geographically stratified metropolitan areas could exacerbate social problems in a host of areas.... [W]e should not ignore the warning signs that our society is still vulnerable to increasing concentration of poverty. (Jargowsky 2003,13)

One of the ways that planners and policymakers have attempted to reduce concentrations of poor and nonwhite households has been through a strategy known as mixed-income housing. While the public housing program, when it was created in 1937, was not structured to be occupied exclusively by very-low-income people, by the 1960s and 1970s, income mixing began to disappear as demographic shifts transformed a majority of public housing developments into low-income enclaves, in most of which nonwhite residents were the majority. This trend was exacerbated through legislation enacted in 1981 that directed local housing authorities to target Section 8 and public housing units to households with incomes below 50 percent of area median income.

As public housing was becoming home to more and more very-low-income, nonwhite households, buildings continued to age, police protection of the developments often slackened and quality of management frequently declined. The net result was that the image of public housing worsened, often being referred to as government-supported slum housing. It is little surprise that concentrated poverty was seen as the cause of adverse social conditions, and the notion that subsidized housing should include a mix of incomes became a widely accepted doctrine.

And so, by the 1970s, several state housing finance agencies, notably those in Massachusetts

and New York, explicitly required multifamily developments receiving their financing to rent at least 20 percent of the units to low-income tenants. A portion of the funding to achieve this goal came through the federal Mortgage Revenue Bond Program, which gives local governments and state housing finance agencies the authority to sell tax-exempt bonds, the proceeds of which can be loaned to developers who commit to set aside at least 20 percent of the units for households at or below 80 percent of area median income.[22]

Two other major federal programs that explicitly encourage mixed-income housing are the Low Income Housing Tax Credit (LIHTC) and the HOPE VI program.[23] Enacted in 1986, the LIHTC provides attractive tax credit opportunities to private investors in developments with set-asides for households earning at or below 50 or 60 percent of area median income.[24] The HOPE VI program, created in 1992 to produce physical and social rejuvenation of distressed public housing, has as a key objective a mixed-income approach.

While mixed-income housing has continued to gain popularity and is often accepted as a pillar of a sound housing policy, there are many questions about the extent to which income mixing, as opposed to other aspects of the housing (such as location, quality of construction, amenities and management) is the critical ingredient (two thoughtful critiques of mixed-income housing are Schwartz and Tajbakhsh 1997, and Smith 2002). While there is continued interest in creating housing in cities (as well as in the suburbs) that includes residents with a mix of incomes, there is also a strong sentiment that low-income households will have greater opportunities if they are able to leave the cities, following the trend of their higher-income counterparts.

Although many people love what the city offers—in terms of jobs, recreational and cultural facilities and educational opportunities—demographic data reveal that, during the decades following World War II, millions of households with the financial means to leave their urban homes exercised their option to do so. Those with few or no choices remained in the cities (Goldsmith and Blakely 1992; Downs 1994).

There are a number of reasons why low-income people and people of color have been unable to follow the more affluent and non-minority populations to the suburbs. As manufacturing jobs have left the cities, the lack of education among many inner-city residents has prevented them from competing for better-paying jobs that often are located outside the cities. In addition, discrimination on the part of employers, as well as by the real estate, banking and insurance sectors, has limited the ability of nonwhite households to move to suburban locales. Furthermore, large-lot zoning requirements in many suburban communities effectively bar the production of small, low-cost homes; many suburban towns' zoning ordinances prohibit the development of multifamily housing and mobile homes, which, in turn, prevents access to these locales by lower-income groups. In addition, all of these factors are either fueled or exacerbated by NIMBY (not in my back yard) attitudes of existing suburban residents.

Also important is the fact that the majority of housing developments built with public subsidies are located in central cities, as opposed to the suburbs or outside metropolitan statistical areas (McGough 1997). This is primarily due to the structure of the public housing program, which gives local governmental bodies discretion concerning whether or not to create a local public housing authority (the entity responsible for the production of public housing), as well as to community opposition to siting subsidized housing developments in suburban locations, noted above. Although the criteria for locating public and other types of subsidized housing changed in the 1970s, with attempts to direct the location of new projects outside areas of minority concentration (Vernarelli 1986), ambiguities in the way these criteria were articulated and reductions in federal funding for new construction over the past two decades have meant that the overall pattern of racial segregation in the subsidized housing stock still prevails.

Finally, although housing choice vouchers can be used in suburban locales, the relative scarcity of rental units in these areas makes it difficult, if not impossible, for recipients to find suitable housing outside the cities. While vouchers are much less likely to concentrate welfare families in high-poverty areas than is true of either public housing or Section 8 projects, they do not appear to assist welfare families escape from high concentrations of poverty (Khadduri, Shroder and Steffen 2003, 36).

The outcome has been an increasing trend toward two societies, divided along racial and class lines that are, for the most part, separate and unequal. Harrington's *The Other America*, written in 1962, was one of the first, and certainly among the most powerful, portrayals of our bifurcated society—a trend that worsened throughout the second half of the 20th century. Although the problem of how to measure the effects of neighborhoods on individuals and families is complex and unresolved (Galster 2003, 909), it is still relevant to question what we know about neighborhood effects: To what extent are poor inner-city households who are able to move to nonpoor locales able to attain economic security through improved educational and employment opportunities?

Educational Opportunities

The educational performance of poor, predominantly nonwhite students is far from adequate (Downs 1994; Rusk 1998; Orfield et al. 2004). The reasons are subject to debate and revolve around whether poor educational outcomes among this group are due to the quality of the schools or to the concentration of an impoverished population in those schools.

One view is that "if blacks were able to obtain housing throughout the metropolitan area on the same basis as whites, the problem of racial segregation in schools would largely disappear" (Kain 1992, 452). And, further, the continuing discrimination in housing and the resulting segregated neighborhoods may be important factors contributing to our educational problems (Turner 1998).

A number of initiatives have been aimed at assisting low-income, predominantly nonwhite households move out of inner-city locations and into neighborhoods with lower concentrations of poverty. The first, known as the Gautreaux program, was carried out in the metropolitan Chicago area.[25] Results reveal that a move to the suburbs improved youths' education prospects, although gains were neither immediate nor easy, and significant additional housing and counseling services were required (Rosenbaum 1995, 263–264). To summarize:

> Positive changes were also reported for small samples of children who had been living in less segregated neighborhoods. Although they had initially experienced declines in school performance, in the long run (7 to 10 years) such children were less likely to drop out of school and were more likely to take college-track classes than their peers in a comparison group who moved to city neighborhoods, which were both poorer and more racially segregated than the suburban locations. After graduating from high school, the Gautreaux children were also more likely than their city peers to attend a 4-year college or become employed full-time. (Orr et al. 2003, v)

However, there were significant limitations inherent in the Gautreaux research because of the nonexperimental nature of the study, specifically:

> The causal link between the new residential locations and the improvement was not certain: The observed differences might reflect differences between the kinds of people who moved to the suburbs through Gautreaux and those who moved within the city rather than reflecting the effects of the different residential locations. (Orr et al. 2003, v)

The Gautreaux program was followed by a federal demonstration program, known as Moving to Opportunity (MTO), which incorporated an experimental design, thereby providing a better mechanism for understanding whether moves from high- to low-poverty areas can result in positive changes. Initiated in 1992, MTO was aimed at "assist(ing) very low-income families with children who reside in public housing to move out of areas of high concentrations of persons living in poverty areas to areas with low concentrations of such persons."[26] An evaluation of the MTO program provided some important insights into the benefits to families who had moved to low-poverty areas. Specifically, families reported substantial improvements in housing and neighborhood conditions and enhanced feelings of safety.[27] However, concerning one of the major goals of the program—to improve educational performance—no "convincing evidence" of the effects of the program were found (Orr et al. 2003, xv).[28]

Since all such dispersal programs are likely to remain quite small in the years ahead, due to limited housing supply in suburban locales, discrimination among realtors and rental agents, and NIMBY attitudes on the part of current residents, it is extremely unlikely that significant numbers of inner-city poor households could participate in such an initiative (Yinger 1998; Varady and Walker 2003). Moreover, many inner-city households with that option would strongly prefer to remain in their own neighborhoods under improved conditions. The problem remains of how to provide improved educational opportunities for city dwellers. Charter schools, school voucher programs and general efforts to improve inner-city school systems are some of the approaches being pursued.[29] Wholesale moves to the suburbs, even assuming the best results, do not present a viable approach for most people.

Employment and Social Networks

Where low-income housing is located and where poor people live likely has a great deal to do with the ease or difficulty that many potential workers have in locating employment. Since at least 1968, with publication of the report by the National Advisory Commission on Civil Disorders (the Kerner Commission), the physical separation between jobs and where workers live has been widely acknowledged. The "spatial-mismatch hypothesis," which has been attributed to John Kain, argues that jobs with low educational requirements are disappearing with the decline of traditional manufacturing industries, especially in the city, and that central-city minority residents have been particularly dependent on these declining industries for work. At the same time, city residents lack access to suburban jobs, since they often do not have access to private or public transportation. And since minority workers are often unskilled, they are poorly matched with the high-skill jobs in the service and high-tech industries, which are generally closer to their homes, often in the central business district (Goldsmith and Blakely 1992, 132).

Although Kain (1992) and other researchers (for a summary of studies, see Ihlanfeldt and Sjoquist 1998) conclude that the spatial-mismatch hypothesis is sound, there is considerable controversy about the extent to which a lack of physical access to jobs is the cause of high unemployment among poor inner-city, particularly nonwhite, residents.

Taking a somewhat different view, that social isolation is the most compelling issue, Wilson explains the problem as follows:

> Unlike poor urban whites or even inner-city blacks of earlier years, the residents of highly concentrated poverty neighborhoods in the inner city today not only infrequently interact with those individuals or families who have had a stable work history and have had little involvement with welfare or public assistance, they also seldom have sustained contact with friends or relatives in the more stable areas of the city or in the suburbs.... The net result is that the degree of social isolation—defined in this context as the lack of contact or of sustained interaction with individuals and institutions that represent mainstream society—in these highly concentrated poverty areas has become far greater than we had previously assumed.... Inner-city social isolation makes it much more difficult for those who are looking for jobs to be tied into the job network. (1987, 60)

Following Wilson's analysis, Goldsmith and Blakely present a compelling picture of how ghetto residents are deprived of a host of social contacts which, for many other job seekers, often result in finding employment. They conclude that "ghetto residence is, indeed, an inhibitor to job access " (1992, 136).

Both Gautreaux and MTO, by relocating households to low-poverty areas, attempt to provide better physical access to jobs as well as to increase opportunities to network with neighbors concerning employment opportunities. In the Gautreaux program, whether it was the change in physical proximity or in the social environment, those who moved to the suburbs were more likely to find employment than their counterparts who remained in the city (Rosenbaum 1995, 239). Less positively, however, more recent research did not find any convincing evidence that employment and earnings or household income, food security and self-sufficiency were positively impacted by the MTO program (Orr et al. 2003, xv).

Despite the limited encouraging results of Gautreaux and MTO, vouchers are a key element of a comprehensive housing policy, not the only such strategy. Whether one believes that employment opportunities are constrained due to a lack of available jobs in inner-city areas or because of weak social networks and role models, unemployment among inner-city poor populations is unacceptably high. Despite the mixed results, programs that assist families to move out of high-poverty areas may continue to provide attractive opportunities for some families. However, they will not, in the foreseeable future, be able to accommodate the number of people who might be eligible or interested in participating. The challenge still remains of how to promote better employment and educational opportunities for all low-income people, and the question of what role housing should play in such efforts remains unresolved.

RECOMMENDATIONS

Housing security and economic security are closely intertwined and must be the basis for a new social agenda. The cost of housing, as the single largest expenditure most households must cover, is a constant worry to families that can threaten their economic well-being. The following recommendations are presented at two levels. The first provides concrete guidelines for how current policies, such as the ones discussed throughout this chapter, could be improved in order to enhance economic security. The second outlines a new social contract between government and individuals that would encompass a series of rights and responsibilities for both. A Right to Housing would be a centerpiece of this new contract.

Changes in Current Programs

Income

1. Create a truly progressive income tax system by eliminating preferential tax treatment for the wealthy and reducing or eliminating the homeowners' deduction (see Chapter 5). All additional revenues gained from elimination or reduction in the homeowners' deduction should be earmarked for housing affordable to low-income households.

2. Expand the Earned Income Tax Credit, and encourage all states to adopt their own such programs.

3. Adopt an economic security standard that makes sense, in place of an unrealistic poverty level. A "market basket" approach would provide a clearer basis for determining the minimum amount of money a household needs to achieve economic security and the number of households falling below this level.

4. Encourage state and local governments to adopt living wage policies for all employees of firms that that do business with that locale or that receive subsidies or other kinds of special consideration from the governmental entity.

5. Raise the minimum wage, and make certain that it is indexed to inflation rather than being dependent on renewed Congressional action. The real value of the minimum wage should never fall. The minimum wage should be set in relation to the cost of housing (HUD's Fair Market Rent) and representative of a true poverty level, such as the "market basket" approach noted above.

6. Create a comprehensive employment program offering good jobs that pay a living wage. These could include a range of public sector jobs, including public works improvements and social service delivery.

Welfare

7. Provide welfare payments to qualifying households that enable them to support a decent level of living. Such payments should, at the very least, lift families out of poverty, using realistic definitions and benchmarks, as noted above.

8. Create a welfare system that better integrates the "work first" ideology of the present system with training and education programs. The importance of using the two strategies together is outlined by the U.S. General Accounting Office (1999).

9. Count all participation in training and education programs as work to satisfy the work requirement under the 1996 welfare reform act; such involvement should protect the individual from loss of welfare benefits for not working within the prescribed time limits.

10. Adopt a comprehensive set of "safety net" programs that support families and children. In comparison with western Europe, for example, the United States is far behind in offering quality programs that enable poor families to maintain decent standards of living. Albelda and Tilly (1997), for example, offer a rich set of proposals that would comprise a true "safety net," including financial support for full-time child care, expansion of unemployment insurance and temporary disability insurance and provision of education and training for all.

11. Coordinate the welfare and housing systems so that, at minimum, housing and welfare agencies work together to create welfare reform guidelines that do not conflict with those of various housing programs. Several key provisions are noted above; for a complete set of these proposals, see Sard and Waller (2002).

12. Do not label welfare reform a success until the impacts on former recipients are well understood, in terms of their overall well-being and economic security.

Housing-Based "Self-Sufficiency" Programs

13. Continue to underscore that there is no such thing as "self-sufficiency"; the goal is better stated as one of economic security. Everyone needs (and receives) a certain amount of assistance and support from the government. Poor people may need more of certain types of such assistance than others, although they often receive the least aid.

14. View housing as a baseline ingredient in enabling households to move toward greater economic security. Rather than a

"work first" ideology, we should promote a "housing first" campaign. One of the first critical steps in a family's efforts to promote its well-being involves stabilizing its housing situation.

15. Develop "self-sufficiency"/economic security programs that are of high quality, are well funded and that assume long time frames. They should also involve participants as active change agents, and mechanisms such as escrow accounts should be incorporated.

Access to Opportunities

16. Continue to assess "Moving to Opportunity" and other initiatives aimed at enabling families to move to locales with greater educational and employment opportunities. In view of the overall needs, the ability of this strategy to become the centerpiece of an antipoverty effort is unlikely.

HOUSING AS THE BASIS OF A NEW SOCIAL CONTRACT[30]

Adoption of the above measures would go a long way toward promoting economic security. Another bolder, bigger approach would involve creation of a new social contract between government and individuals. This contract would include a series of rights and responsibilities that each party would be committed to fulfill.

This chapter, and this entire book, argues that housing must be viewed as central to individual and family well-being. Until everyone is guaranteed a decent, affordable place to call home, moves toward economic security will be piecemeal and incomplete. Incorporating a Right to Housing into a new social contract would mean that, for the first time, individuals and families would be guaranteed a stable environment in which to carry out the tasks of daily living—child-rearing, pursuing and maintaining jobs, and participating in education/training programs. In exchange, individuals would be expected to meet core responsibilities, including working to maximize their family's well-being and optimizing their own productivity.

The sense of reciprocity underlying this contract is embraced in the "communitarian" philosophy. According to Etzioni, who has been central to this movement:

> At the heart of the communitarian understanding of social justice is the idea of reciprocity: each member of the community owes something to all the rest, and the community owes something to each of its members. Justice requires responsible individuals in a responsive community. (1995, 19)

There is some precedent for explicitly articulating the expectation that recipients of government assistance also provide something in return. In the 1996 welfare reform legislation, for example, there was a realization on the part of lawmakers that some kind of social contract was needed so that the government and its citizens would each have a clear set of rights and responsibilities. However, this legislation created an arbitrary, "one size fits all" set of government expectations for welfare recipients. At the same time, it did not incorporate sufficiently substantial supports, or guarantees, for those in need. Even for households that still receive welfare benefits, the income provided does not come close to meeting family needs, and again, no single strategy or uniform time limits can be expected to work for everyone. Finally, and in direct contradiction to what is being proposed here, the 1996 law also allows only ten hours of education or training programs to count as part of the 30 hours per week work requirement. And specifically concerning public housing (but not other types of subsidized housing), the Quality Housing and Work Responsibility Act of 1998 included a provision that requires each adult resident to perform community service or participate in an economic "self-sufficiency" program for at least eight hours per month.

Despite these work/service requirements, up to now, the government's expectations for what individuals will contribute as part of their responsibilities have been insufficient and incomplete. Government should not be content with an individual simply finding a job, any job; and a specific minimum hourly work or community service requirement may be far too little (or too much) for a given person. An editorial in the

Boston Globe eloquently summed up the essence of this argument:

> Since welfare reform was signed in 1996, the federal government's mandate to the poor has been simple: Get a job.... It's meager advice. Jobs do keep families afloat, but the battle against poverty needs a better script. The president could say ... go to college ... look for jobs with career paths ... and brave the road to self-sufficiency, but know, whether you fail or succeed, that the United States government will not let your children go hungry or unprotected. (2004)

Instead of an across-the-board work/service requirement, the program being proposed here would involve caseworkers assisting individuals to develop a course of action that would both provide family supports as well as an assessment about how productivity and contributions to society could be maximized. This plan would embrace guarantees while engendering a sense of responsibility. But doing the two simultaneously is, admittedly, not easy, and we have little information about how an outside entity, such as a governmental or nonprofit organization, can stimulate the internal motivation necessary for an individual to commit to education, training or other initiatives that could promote economic security. Indeed, is this something that can be mandated by a federal program, which is essentially what the Welfare Reform Act of 1996 aimed to do? How can we develop a program that stimulates motivation without creating perverse threats and sanctions about possible loss of benefits, housing or food? And how can service to one's family, such as child-rearing or care for an elderly household member be factored into the work/service requirement? These and many other critical and difficult questions would need to be addressed. For the present, however, the following key elements should be considered in the program being proposed.

First, a comprehensive family support system would be developed that would operate as a true and meaningful safety net. It would respect clients, and it would provide needed services. And participation in this support program could be viewed as the initial way that a household could meet the responsibilities expected in exchange for housing assistance. The rationale

for treating participation in a family support program as a responsibility is based on the assumption that if such an initiative can help individuals to develop their own capacities, society at large will benefit. After receiving these high-quality and comprehensive supports for a period of time, the hope is that people would want to move toward realizing their personal development goals.

Second, and integral to the new system of family supports, individuals would be assisted to assess and maximize their skills and productivity. Programs would be devised that would build on the assets and capabilities of each individual, with the long-term goal of greatly enhancing economic security and, ultimately, enabling the household to function comfortably without federal housing subsidies.

The *third* aspect of the program may be the most controversial. It is proposed that *all* households who receive government-sponsored or -supported housing participate in the family support program, including those who take the homeowners' deduction. All recipients of housing subsidies should be treated more or less the same. For example, if low-income public housing recipients and housing choice voucher holders are expected to participate in family support and skills assessment programs, so too should higher-income recipients. This recommendation recognizes that, while it would be most desirable for the homeowners' deduction to be eliminated (as noted above), this may be a long while in coming.

Incorporating higher-income families in the programs outlined here would achieve at least four goals. First, it would provide real supports and services to all families, regardless of income, thereby acknowledging that family assistance and career development guidance are necessary more broadly, not just for the poor.[31] Second, such a far-reaching program would be nonstigmatizing for the poorer participants. Third, it would make explicit how many people do, in fact, receive some form of housing subsidy in the form of the homeowners' deduction. And, fourth, for those homeowners who do not want to participate in the dual programs, the homeowners' deduction would be forfeited, thereby whittling away, and perhaps contributing to the elimination altogether of a regressive subsidy that disproportionately benefits the wealthy.

This proposal is premised on the notion that development of human capital should be at the heart of what government expects of its citizens. This is quite different from the work and community service requirements contained in recent legislation mentioned earlier, which are essentially punitive. The first set of responsibilities that everyone must accept is the responsibility for one's self and his or her family's physical needs and safety. At the most basic level, housing and other family supports would be provided, and recipients would be expected to demonstrate responsibility for moving toward greater productivity and participation in social and economic life. If people were guaranteed decent places to live, with the worry of deprivation and humiliation removed, much human potential could be unleashed.

Some individuals may need to work on literacy or substance abuse issues. Others may need to develop and hone parenting skills. And, as family life is stabilized, education and job-training programs would be provided. A revitalized social service and public works program could be part of this initiative as well. As bridges and other parts of our infrastructure continue to age, workers would be enlisted to assist in such projects. In addition, more one-on-one assistance is needed in a variety of sectors, from schools to hospitals to the kind of casework proposed here. These jobs may be temporary, or they may turn into permanent positions. The key point is that the stability housing provides would go a long way toward enabling individuals to fulfill their responsibilities to their families and to work toward realizing their potential as productive members of society.

The program outlined here would require three major kinds of funding. The first would go to the direct support of a new housing production and rehabilitation program as well as a greatly expanded housing choice voucher program.[32] While it is beyond the scope of this chapter to delve into the specific types of housing that would be created, my strong recommendation would be for an expanded commitment to various forms of social housing—housing owned by the public and nonprofit sectors—as

well as to increasing homeownership opportunities (with permanent nonspeculative resale restrictions). At the very least, in order for housing to promote feelings of self-worth and empowerment, it is likely that a new housing program would embrace ownership forms and management arrangements that would enable residents to maximize control over their living environments.

The second funding stream would go to the family support initiative outlined above. Enough well-trained and competent caseworkers would need to be hired to make sure that case loads are low and to ensure that each participant receives the needed attention. Clearly, the task of caseworkers to assess not only immediate needs but also the potential of family members to reach their capacity in terms of productivity would present huge challenges and a high level of skill. One of the secondary goals of the program might also be to help develop caseworker expertise among those who, themselves, have participated in (or still are actively participating in) the family support program.

Finally, funding would be needed to support the public works and community service jobs that would be created. These kinds of jobs would not only enable workers to develop skills and expertise, but they would also provide needed services to the larger community.

For those who believe that instead we would be inviting a lazy and complacent society, I suggest that we embark on a new social experiment. This new initiative would be significantly bigger and more far-reaching than any other such initiatives to date,[33] and it would allow us to explore different ways of providing basic human needs. Also, key to this experiment would be an opportunity to evaluate how the new rights could be balanced with individual responsibilities.

The costs of implementing a Right to Housing would not be low. But the benefits, hopefully, are apparent in view of the evidence presented throughout this chapter and the entire book. While this book was conceptualized long before the September 11 terrorist attacks, we acknowledge that the recommendations presented here may seem even less plausible, with significant resources being spent on the fight against terrorism, homeland security and military incursions.

It is far from certain when our country will embrace a full and robust domestic agenda. Perhaps the hurricane-stimulated crises along the Gulf Coast will prove to be an important wake-up call about the depth and seriousness of the problems facing poor citizens, particularly poor citizens of color. At the same time, the costs of dealing with the rebuilding of New Orleans and its surroundings may reduce the already depleted funds available for domestic spending. But when our country is finally and fully prepared to confront the range of problems our residents face, we hope these ideas will help chart that course.

NOTES

Acknowledgments: I am indebted to Barbara Sard as well as the co-editors of this book for their careful reading of earlier drafts of this chapter and for their many helpful comments.

1. The view that housing should be seen as part of a larger social policy agenda has been embraced by a number of analysts. (See, for example, Bratt and Keyes 1998; Newman and Schnare 1993; Rohe and Kleit 1997, 1999; Sard 2003; Shlay 1993, 1995.)

2. In charting a new course for HUD's programs, the department's sweeping 1994 proposals, known as the "Reinvention Blueprint," argued that many past HUD initiatives ran counter to the goal of promoting "self-sufficiency." "Low- and moderate-income families should have greater power to make decisions about their lives, and government should support their quest for self-sufficiency [underline in original]. Public and assisted housing rules that have locked families into substandard housing have impeded their ability to move to self-sufficiency.... [Thus, one of HUD's key goals is to m]ake affordable housing serve as a starting point for families working toward stability and self-sufficiency by emphasizing work, education and security" (HUD 1994, 1, 4).

3. Based on a study of 21 nonprofit housing organizations' approaches to "self-sufficiency," Bratt and Keyes (1997) "underscored the importance of housing being secured first, before people could pay serious attention to non-housing issues." They further note that: "Housing is at the core of family stability" (77, n. 3). See Sard and Lubell (2000a, 6–7) for additional support for this view. The National Coalition for the Homeless has stated that "A recent longitudinal study of poor and homeless families in New York City found that regardless of social disorders, 80% of formerly homeless families who received subsidized housing stayed stably housed, i.e. lived in their own

residence for the previous 12 months. In contrast, only 18% of the families who did not receive subsidized housing were stable at the end of the study. As this study and others demonstrate, affordable housing is a key component to resolving family homelessness" (1999, 4).

4. For additional documentation on the extent and ways in which living in assisted housing produces positive impacts, or no negative impacts, see Currie and Yelowitz 2000; Meyers et al. 1993, cited in Currie, 1995; Center for Community Change 1999a; Newman and Harkness, 2000; 2002; Williams et al. 1997; Li et al. 1997. These studies are summarized in Bratt 2003.

5. Newman (1999) has examined a series of studies pertaining to the question of whether housing is an incentive or disincentive to achieving a high level of economic security. She has stated that "most observers take it as self-evident that being homeless increases the difficulty of pursuing education or job training, or getting and keeping a job" (3–4). She also notes that there may be some modest positive effects among residents in assisted housing, such as greater labor force participation or educational attainment; and that findings indicating that "welfare recipients who also receive housing assistance have lower employment rates than those who do not receive assistance" may be due to "administrative decisions, such as preference rules for housing programs that gave priority to the most disadvantaged—not the result of the disincentive effect of housing assistance, per se" (8, 10).

In addition, a study of California residents living in Section 8 housing provides support for the view that the provision of housing does not negatively impact motivation to work. According to the author, "a well-designed housing program can help welfare recipients form a greater attachment to the labor market" (Ong 1998, 791).

Sard and Lubell (2000a) cite a study by Manpower Development Research Corporation of welfare reform in Minnesota that found that "most of the gains in employment and earnings attributable to the state's welfare reform initiative were concentrated among residents of public or subsidized housing. In other words, welfare reform was found to have a larger effect on employment and earnings among families receiving housing subsidies than among other families in the study." They further note that "Preliminary findings from studies in Atlanta, Georgia and Columbus, Ohio, indicate the same may be true of different initiatives undertaken in those cities" (3). See also Freeman (1998) and Reingold (1997). These studies are summarized in Bratt (2003).

In contrast to the above findings, Miller and Riccio (2002) cite two unpublished studies and note that "housing subsidies tend to reduce employment among single mothers" (13).

6. According to a 1998 report by the Internal Revenue Service, based on 1994 tax returns, 1,137 taxpayers who earned more than $200,000 paid no taxes (Online Athens 1998). In California, in 2000, 784 individuals with incomes of $200,000 or more paid no income tax (Smith 2003). Concerning taxation of corporations, the U.S. General Accounting Office reported that from 1996 through 2000, a majority of all corporations reported paying no taxes. And, in 2000, about 94 percent of U.S.-controlled corporations and 89 percent of foreign-controlled corporations reported less than 5 percent in tax liability (2004, 6,7).

7. The minimum wage is not indexed to inflation; increases must be approved by Congress. In 2005, sixteen states and the District of Columbia had minimum wages higher than the federal minimum of $5.15 per hour, with Alaska, Oregon, and Washington leading at $7.15, $7.25 and $7.35 per hour, respectively (U.S. Department of Labor 2005).

8. The federal poverty line was set in the 1960s and was based on a minimum adequate diet for different types of families, multiplied by three. The multiplier is based on the assumption that food constitutes one-third of a household's budget. The poverty line for a family of four is simply the original poverty line, $3,100 (set in 1963), adjusted for inflation and changes in consumer prices (Albelda and Tilly 1997, 20–21). Poverty levels for families of different sizes are set in a similar manner. At least since the early 1990s, the mechanism for determining the poverty level has been viewed as inadequate. In 1999, the Census Bureau analyzed the effects of specific experimental poverty measures, but no changes have been adopted. (See U.S. General Accounting Office 1997 and Porter 1999).

9. The HUD-established Fair Market Rent is the amount of money required to cover the rental costs for physically standard 1-, 2-, 3- and 4-bedroom housing units. HUD calculates these rents for each metropolitan area in the country; they are adjusted annually to keep pace with inflation. However, in many market areas, FMRs are below the real costs of attaining a decent unit of housing. Section 8 subsidies (now known as housing choice vouchers) are based on the difference between what a household can pay, contributing 30 percent of their income for rent, and the Fair Market Rent in that locale.

10. This is based on figures provided by the U.S. Department of Health and Human Services (2002) on TANF benefits provided to three-person families in 2003. The poverty level for this size family in 2003 was $15,260.

11. A report by the U.S. General Accounting Office (Congress changed the name of this office to the Government Accountability Office in July 2004) summarized a series of studies concerned with the length of time recipients stay on welfare and concluded that "relatively few families are long-term welfare recipi-

ents" (1993, 41). Nevertheless, the image of long-term welfare dependency as the norm helped to fuel welfare reform.

12. For example, the U.S. General Accounting Office reported that "As earnings rise, families who receive AFDC, food stamps, and housing subsidies may initially have reduced total incomes, making them financially worse off than if they had not worked.... When heads of families earned at the rate of $10 an hour and worked as many as 80 hours a month, there was still only a small gain in income from employment compared with not working and receiving AFDC, food stamps, and housing subsidies" (1993, 31).

13. This section is revised from Bratt and Keyes 1997, Appendix B, 101–104.

14. Nevertheless, Newman and Schnare point out that "the principle that housing assistance should be a vehicle for independence is not new to either the welfare system or the housing system. As early as the 1920s, the welfare system recognized that adequate housing was one of the most important needs for mothers and their children." And one of the tenets guiding the first national housing act in 1937 was that "subsidized housing should be a vehicle for human development" (1992, 8).

15. For example, housing managers are generally forced to take steps to evict a household if the lease has been violated for cause. However, welfare caseworkers counter that if the family is forced to leave their subsidized unit, they would have no place else to go.

16. Data on the negative impacts of welfare reform can be found in a number of studies of post-welfare experiences. More than one-half of the respondents in a survey conducted by the Urban Institute reported that often or sometimes food did not last until the end of the month, and they did not have money for more; 46 percent reported a time during the previous year when they were unable to pay rent, mortgage or utility bills. Nine percent indicated they had to move in with others because they were unable to pay their bills (Loprest 2001, 5). A Children's Defense Fund and National Coalition for the Homeless study noted that "Many families leaving welfare report struggling to get food, shelter, or needed medical care; many are suffering even more hardships than before" (Sherman et al. 1998, 2). The Institute for Women's Policy Research has reported that the "threat of eviction can be a particularly serious problem for welfare recipients who lose benefits" and that, in the aftermath of welfare reform, there has been an increase in the number of homeless people seeking shelter. Many researchers attributed these changes to the new policies (Nichols and Gault 1999). Further, researchers at the Center on Budget and Policy Priorities, using Census data, reported that "the average disposable income of a significant percentage of the poorest single-mother families was lower in 1997 than in 1995. Of particular

concern, progress in reducing the depth and severity of child poverty . . . halted between 1995 and 1997 despite continued improvement in the economy. The number of poor children declined only slightly during this period, and children who remained poor became poorer, on average. Among many low-income single-mother families with significant earnings gains, the gains were offset entirely by losses in means-tested benefits, leaving the families no better off economically" (Primus et al. 1999, xv).

17. Lazere notes that "As caseloads have fallen, so has spending on cash assistance. Federal and state expenditures for cash assistance benefits in fiscal year 1999 totaled $12.4 billion, or $10.6 billion less than in fiscal year 1994 (2000, 1). For a discussion of the excess funds that were made available to states due to the savings in welfare payments, see U.S. General Accounting Office (1998a). Despite the view that there have been significant reductions in the amount the federal government is paying in welfare payments, other data reveal that these savings may be illusory. Loprest (2003b) reports an increase in other forms of government assistance, such as food stamps and adult Medicaid payments.

18. In addition to housing becoming intertwined with the "self-sufficiency" agenda, since at least the 1960s, housing has also played an important role in neighborhood revitalization efforts. Community development, community-building and, most recently, comprehensive community initiatives all include a central role for housing. However, an examination of the connections between housing and these types of programs is beyond the scope of this chapter.

19. The perspective that even those who profess to have "made it on their own" are instead the recipients of some form of federal largesse is captured in an anecdote involving Vernon Jordan, former Executive Director of the Urban League. During an in-flight conversation between Jordan and a successful white businessman the following transpired:

"After his first martini the businessman observed that black people had to pull themselves up by their own bootstraps. After the third martini the businessman acknowledged that he went to an elite Eastern private college on the GI bill, started his business with a loan from the U.S. Small Business Administration, and purchased his Scarsdale home with an FHA loan. As Jordan concluded, 'So much for lifting yourself up by your own bootstraps.'" (quoted in Squires 1994, 9)

20. The Family Self-Sufficiency program was authorized in Section 504 of the National Affordable Housing Act of 1990 and has been required since 1993. The program is aimed at promoting the development of local strategies to coordinate federal housing assistance with public and private resources to enable low-income families work toward economic independence and "self-sufficiency." Participants include current housing choice voucher holders, as well as public housing residents, and are expected to carry out their self-sufficiency programs within five years.

21. The material presented is drawn from two types of sources: (1) studies of the major "self-sufficiency" programs, including Project Self-Sufficiency, Operation Bootstrap, Family Self-Sufficiency Program, Family Investment Centers, Mixed-Income New Community Strategy Demonstration, Family Support Centers and the Gateway Program (for a complete description of these programs, see Bratt and Keyes 1997; Bogdon 1999) and (2) observations based on field visits to twenty-one nonprofit housing organizations that were implementing some form of "self-sufficiency" program, as presented in Bratt and Keyes 1997. Bogdon has noted a variety of methodological problems with the studies of the three major programs (the first three noted above), which led her to observe that "The most fundamental conclusion is that the potential role of housing assistance in the long-term process of attaining self-sufficiency still needs to be addressed" (1999, 169).

22. The federal government first authorized the use of tax-exempt housing bonds in 1968 through amendments to Section 103 of the Internal Revenue Code. The Tax Reform Act of 1986 added various requirements associated with the issuance of these mortgage revenue bonds (which could be used to support homeownership for qualified first-time homebuyers as well as for multifamily rental housing) and capped each state's bonding authority and instituted more stringent targeting standards to low-income households (National Low Income Housing Coalition 1986).

23. HOPE VI is a component of the Home Ownership for People Everywhere legislation, enacted by Congress in 1990, the Cranston-Gonzalez National Affordable Housing Act. The HOPE program was aimed at empowering low-income families to achieve self-sufficiency and to have a stake in their communities by promoting resident management as well as other forms of homeownership. HOPE VI, which was added to the legislation two years later, does not involve homeownership.

24. Tax credit developments aimed at households at or below 50 percent of area median income must set aside at least 20 percent of the units for this group. Developments aimed at households at 60 percent or less of area median income must reserve at least 40 percent of their units for this group.

25. The Gautreaux program was created as a result of a lawsuit filed by tenants of public housing in Chicago against the Chicago Housing Authority and HUD. Gautreaux attempted to remedy the segregation in public housing developments by providing

opportunities for public housing residents to leave and to relocate in predominantly white areas—either in other areas of Chicago or in the suburbs. While there were about 1,700 eligible households, only about one-fifth used their Section 8 certificate and moved (Varady and Walker 2003).

26. P.L. 105-550 42 U.S.C. 3672 Sec. 146.

27. The homes and neighborhoods of people who moved to low-poverty areas were substantially more desirable than those where control group members lived (Orr et al. 2003, xvi). In addition, the evaluation of the MTO program reported significant gains in mental health among adults in the experimental group and the levels of psychological distress and depression were substantially reduced. Further, among the children in these families, girls experienced a number of positive changes, including improved psychological well-being, less engagement in risky behavior and improved perceptions about their future such as the likelihood of going to college and getting a well-paid, stable job as an adult (Orr et al. 2003, xvi; see also Shroder 2001).

28. Despite the overall negative assessment of the Gautreaux program reported by Orr et al. (2003), Varady and Walker (2003) summarize a number of studies in which, at least in specific cities, positive results in terms of educational benefits are reported.

29. Some observers see only limited hope in such interventions. James Traub, writing in the *New York Times Magazine*, makes a compelling argument that school reform is not a panacea. Instead, he argues that deeply entrenched poverty and family and community environments and values are most critical (January 16, 2000). Nevertheless, there are numerous examples of good schools making significant impacts in poor communities (see, for example, Schorr 1997, 232–297).

30. Versions of this proposal also appear in Bratt 2002 and Bratt 2003.

31. The suggestion that a comprehensive set of family supports be offered broadly has been made by a number of social policy analysts. See, for example, Albelda and Tilly 1997, Chapter 9; Skocpol 2000, Chapter 5; and Schorr 1997. Also, there is ample precedence for universal family support programs in many European countries.

32. The other two editors of this book do not agree that the number of rental vouchers should be expanded. They argue that all federal subsidies should go toward social housing. However, my view is that, at least in the short term, it is necessary to create as many opportunities to promote affordability as possible and that in many markets, vouchers make sense.

33. There have been two other significant experiments exploring various approaches to providing housing. The first, the Experimental Housing Allowance Program, was initiated in the 1970s. As the production-based housing programs (public housing and below-market interest rate programs of the 1960s) began losing support, a series of experiments were launched to test the effectiveness of subsidies linked to individual households rather than to specific housing units. These demonstration programs are collectively referred to as the Experimental Housing Allowance Program (EHAP). (See, for example, Bradbury and Downs 1981; Hartman 1983). The second major experiment was the Moving to Opportunity demonstration, discussed earlier.

REFERENCES

ACORN. 2004. "Introduction to ACORN's living wage web site." March 13. http:// livingwagecampaign.org.

Albelda, Randy, and Chris Tilly. 1997. *Glass ceilings and bottomless pits: Women's work, women's poverty.* Boston: South End Press.

Bernstein, Jared, Elizabeth C. McNichol, Lawrence Mishel and Robert Zahradnik. 2000. Pulling apart: A state-by-state analysis of income trends. Washington, DC: Center on Budget and Policy Priorities and Economic Policy Institute.

Berube, Alan. 2004. Making work pay: Building incomes and assets through the Earned Income Tax Credit. *Building Blocks*, Vol. 5., No. 1, Winter. Washington, DC: Fannie Mae Foundation.

Bogdon, Amy S. 1999. What can we learn from previous housing-based self-sufficiency programs? In *The home front: Implications of welfare reform for housing policy*, ed. Sandra J. Newman. 1999. Washington, DC: The Urban Institute Press.

Boston Globe. 2004. "Welfare vision," April 6.

Bradbury, Katharine L., and Anthony Downs, eds. 1981. *Do housing allowances work?* Washington, DC: The Brookings Institution.

Bratt, Rachel G. 2002. Housing and family well-being. *Housing Studies*, 17(1):13–26.

———. 2003. Housing: The foundation of family life. In *Promoting child, adolescent, and family development: A handbook of program and policy innovations*, eds. Richard M. Lerner, Francine Jacobs and Donald Wertlieb. Thousand Oaks, CA: Sage Publications, Inc., 445–468.

Bratt, Rachel G., and Langley C. Keyes. 1997. New perspectives on self-sufficiency: Strategies of nonprofit housing organizations. Medford, MA: Department of Urban and Environmental Policy, Tufts University.

———.1998. Challenges confronting nonprofit housing organizations' self-sufficiency programs. *Housing Policy Debate*, 9(4):795–824.

Bryson, David B., and Roberta L. Youmans. 1991. Passage from poverty: Self-sufficiency policies and federal housing programs. Washington, DC: National

Support Center for Low Income Housing (a joint project of the Low Income Housing Information Service and the National Housing Law Project).

Center for Community Change. 1999a. *Comprehensive services in public housing: Lessons from the field.* Washington, DC: The Center.

———. 1999b. Jobs and welfare reform. Washington, DC. http://www.communitychange.org/jobswelfare.htm.

Center on Budget and Policy Priorities. 1999. The family self-sufficiency program. http://www.cbpp.org.5-5-99hous.htm

———. 2005. "Economic recovery failed to benefit much of the population in 2004." August30.

Council of State Community Development Agencies and the American Public Welfare Association. 1991. Linking housing and human services: Describing the context. Background Paper, Washington, DC.

Currie, Janet M. 1995. *Welfare and the well-being of children.* Chur, Switzerland: Harwood Academic Publishers.

Currie, Janet M., and Aaron Yelowitz. 2000. Are public housing projects good for kids? *Journal of Public Economics,* 75:99–124.

Dolbeare, Cushing N., Irene Basloe Saraf and Sheila Crowley. 2004. Changing priorities: The federal budget and housing assistance, 1976–2005. Washington, DC: National Low Income Housing Coalition.

Downs, Anthony. 1994. *New visions for metropolitan America.* Washington, DC: The Brookings Institution; Cambridge, MA: Lincoln Institute of Land Policy.

Economic Policy Institute. 2005. Minimum wage: Frequently asked questions. http://www.epinet.org/content.cfm/issueguides_minwage_minwagefaq. September 30, 2005.

Economic Success Clearinghouse. 2005. http://www.financeproject.org/irc/win/work.asp. October 1, 2005.

Etzioni, Amitai, ed. 1995. *Rights and the common good.* New York: St. Martin's Press.

Freeman, Lance. 1998. Interpreting the dynamics of public housing: Cultural and rational choice explanations. *Housing Policy Debate,* 9(2):323–353.

Galster, George. 2003. Investigating behavioral impacts of poor neighborhoods: Towards new data and analytic strategies. *Housing Studies,* 18(6):893–914.

Goldsmith, William W., and Edward J. Blakely. 1992. *Separate societies: Poverty and inequality in U.S. cities.* Philadelphia: Temple University Press.

Greenstein, Robert, Joel Friedman and Isaac Shapiro. 2005. New tax cuts primarily benefiting millionaires slated to take effect in January: Should they be implemented while Katrina costs mount?

Washington, DC: Center on Budget and Policy Priorities.

Harrington, Michael. 1962. *The other America: Poverty in the United States.* Baltimore: Penguin Books.

Hartman, Chester. 1983. Housing allowances: A critical look. *Journal of Urban Affairs,* 5(1):41–55.

Ihlanfeldt, Keith R., and David L. Sjoquist. 1998. The spatial mismatch hypothesis: A review of recent studies and their implications for welfare reform. *Housing Policy Debate,* 9(4):849–892.

Jargowsky, Paul A. 2003. Stunning progress, hidden problems: The dramatic decline of concentrated poverty in the 1990s. Washington, DC: The Brookings Institution.

Johnson, Nicholas, Joseph Llobrera and Bob Zahradnik. 2003. A hand up: How state Earned Income Tax Credits help working families escape poverty in 2003. Summary. Washington, DC: Center on Budget and Policy Priorities.

Kain, John F. 1992. The Spatial Mismatch Hypothesis: Three Decades Later. *Housing Policy Debate.* 3(2): 371–460.

Kasarda, John D. 1993. Inner-city concentrated poverty and neighborhood distress: 1970 to 1990. *Housing Policy Debate,* 4(3):253–302.

Katz, Michael B. 1989. *The undeserving poor: From the war on poverty to the war on welfare.* New York: Pantheon.

Kemeny, Jim. 1986. A critique of homeownership. In *Critical Perspectives on Housing,* eds. Rachel G. Bratt, Chester Hartman and Ann Meyerson, 272–276.Philadelphia: Temple University Press.

Khadduri, Jill, Mark Shroder and Barry Steffen. 2003. Can housing assistance support welfare reform? In *A place to live, a means to work: How housing assistance can strengthen welfare policy,* eds. Barbara Sard and Amy S. Bogdon. Washington, DC: Fannie Mae Foundation.

Krugman, Paul. 2002. For richer. *New York Times Magazine,* October 20.

Lav, Iris J., and Greenstein, Robert. 1999. Tax bill contains only modest benefits for middle class despite its high cost. Washington, DC: Center on Budget and Policy Priorities. http://www.cbpp.org/8-20-99tax.htm.

Lazere, Ed. 2000. Welfare balances after three years of TANF block grants: Unspent TANF funds at the end of federal fiscal year 1999. Washington, DC: Center on Budget and Policy Priorities.

Li, Xiaoming, Bonito Stanton, Maureen M. Black, Daniel Roamer, Isabel Ricardo and Linda Killjoy. 1997. Risk behavior and perception among youths residing in urban public housing developments. *Bulletin of the New York Academy of Medicine,* 71(2):252–266.

Llobrera, Joseph and Bob Zahradnik. 2004. A hand up: How state Earned Income Tax Credits help working families escape poverty in 2004. Summary. Washington, DC: Center on Budget and Policy Priorities.

Loprest, Pamela. 1999. Families who left welfare: Who are they and how are they doing? Washington, DC: The Urban Institute.

———. 2001. How are families that left welfare doing? A comparison of early and recent welfare leavers. Washington, DC: The Urban Institute.

———. 2002. The next welfare reform: Counter boomerang effect. *Christian Science Monitor*, Electronic Edition, September 20. http://www.urban.org/urlprint.cfm?ID=7917.

———. 2003a. Fewer welfare leavers employed in weak economy. Washington, DC: The Urban Institute, September. Snapshots of America's families, No. 5.

———. 2003b. Use of government benefits increases among families leaving welfare. Washington, DC: The Urban Institute, September. Snapshots of America's families, No. 6.

Marcuse, Peter. 1986. Housing policy and the myth of the benevolent state. In *Critical Perspectives on Housing*, eds. Rachel G. Bratt, Chester Hartman and Ann Meyerson, 248–258. Philadelphia: Temple University Press.

Massachusetts Housing Finance Agency. 1999. Impact of welfare reform on developments financed by the Massachusetts housing finance agency. Boston: The Agency.

McGough, Duane T. 1997. Characteristics of HUD-assisted renters and their units in 1993. Washington, DC: U.S. Department of Housing and Urban Development.

Meyers, Alan, Dana Rubin, Maria Napoleone and Kevin Nichols. 1993. Public housing subsidies may improve poor children's nutrition. *American Journal of Public Health*, 83(1):115.

Millennial Housing Commission. 2002. *Report of the bipartisan Millennial Housing Commission: Meeting our nation's housing challenges.* Washington, DC: U.S. Government Printing Office.

Miller Cynthia, and James A. Riccio. 2002. Making work pay for public housing residents: Financial incentive designs at six jobs-plus demonstration sites. New York: Manpower Demonstration Research Corporation.

National Advisory Commission on Civil Disorders. 1968. *Report of the National Advisory Commission on Civil Disorders.* New York: Bantam Books.

National Coalition for the Homeless. 1999. Homeless families with children. N.H. Fact Sheet #7. http://nch.ari.net/families.html

National Low Income Housing Coalition. 1986. Tax bill spells victory for low income concerns. *Low Income Housing Round-up*, September.

———. 2004. *Out of Reach 2004.* Washington, DC: The Coalition.

Newman, Sandra J., ed. 1999. *The home front: Implications of welfare reform for housing policy.* Washington, DC: The Urban Institute Press.

Newman, Sandra J., and Ann B. Schnare. 1992. *Beyond bricks and mortar: Reexamining the purpose and effects of housing assistance.* Washington, DC: The Urban Institute Press. Report 92-3.

———. 1993. Last in line: Housing assistance for households with children. *Housing Policy Debate*, 4(3):417–455.

Newman, Sandra J., and Joseph Harkness. 2000. Assisted housing and the educational attainment of children. *Journal of Housing Economics*, 9:40–63.

———. 2002. The long-term effects of housing assistance on self-sufficiency. *Journal of Policy Analysis and Management*, 21(1):21–35.

Nichols, Laura, and Barbara Gault. 1999. The effects of welfare reform on housing stability and homelessness: Current research findings, legislation, and programs. *Welfare Reform Network News*, 2(2), March.

Ong, Paul. 1998. Subsidized housing and work among welfare recipients. *Housing Policy Debate*, 9(4):775–794.

Online Athens. 1998. IRS study finds 1,137 wealthy taxpayers paid no taxes in 1994. March 31. http://www.onlineathens.com/1998/033198/0331.a3tax.html.

Orfield, Gary, Daniel Losen, Johanna Wald and Christopher B. Swanson. 2004. Losing our future: How minority youth are being left behind by the graduation rate crisis. Cambridge, MA: The Civil Rights Project at Harvard University.

Orr, Larry, Judith D. Feins, Robin Jacob, Erik Beecroft, Lisa Sanbonmatsu, Lawrence F. Katz, Jeffrey B. Liebman and Jeffrey R. Kling. 2003. *Moving to opportunity interim impacts evaluation.* Washington, DC: U.S. Department of Housing and Urban Development.

Parrott, Sharon. 1998. Welfare recipients who find jobs: What do we know about their employment and earnings? Washington, DC: Center on Budget and Policy Priorities.

Pearce, Diana, with Jennifer Brooks. 2003. The self-sufficiency standard for Delaware. Washington, DC: Wider Opportunities for Women.

Pines, Marion. 1991. Self-sufficiency: An investment in poor families. *Journal of Housing*, May/June, 110–116.

Porter, Kathryn. 1999. Proposed changes in the official measure of poverty. Washington, DC: Center on Budget and Policy Priorities. http://www.cbpp.org/11-15-99wel.htm.

Porter, Kathryn, and Wendell Primus. 1999. *Changes since 1995 in the safety net's impact on child poverty.* Washington, DC: Center on Budget and Policy Priorities.

Primus, Wendell. 1996. The safety net delivers: The effects of government benefit programs in reducing poverty. Washington, DC: Center on Budget and Policy Priorities. http://www.cbpp.org/SAFETY.htm.

Primus, Wendell, Lynette Rawlings, Kathy Lain and Kathryn Porter. 1999. The initial impacts of welfare reform on the incomes of single-mother families. Washington, DC: Center on Budget and Policy Priorities.

Reingold, David A. 1997. Does inner city public housing exacerbate the employment problems of its tenants? *Journal of Urban Affairs*, 19(4):469–486.

Rohe, William M. 1995. Assisting residents of public housing achieve self-sufficiency: An evaluation of Charlotte's Gateway Families Program. *Journal of Architectural and Planning Research*, 12(3).

Rohe, William M., and Michael A. Stegman. 1991. Coordinating housing and social services: The new imperative. *Carolina Planning*,46–50, Fall.

Rohe, William M., and Rachel Garshick Kleit. 1997. From dependency to self-sufficiency: An appraisal of the Gateway Transitional Families Program. *Housing Policy Debate*, 8(1):75–108.

———. 1999. Housing, welfare reform, and self-sufficiency: An assessment of the Family Self-Sufficiency Program. *Housing Policy Debate*, 10(2): 333–369.

Rosenbaum, James E. 1995. Changing the geography of opportunity by expanding residential choice: Lessons from the Gautreaux Program. *Housing Policy Debate*, 6(1):231–269.

Rusk, David. 1998. Abell Report: To improve poor children's test scores, move poor families. Baltimore: Abell Foundation.

Sard, Barbara. 2001. The Family Self-Sufficiency Program: HUD's best kept secret for promoting employment and asset growth. Washington, DC: Center on Budget and Policy Priorities.

———. 2003. The role of housing providers in an era of welfare reform. In *A place to live, a means to work: How housing assistance can strengthen welfare policy*, eds. Barbara Sard and Amy S. Bogdon. Washington, DC: Fannie Mae Foundation.

Sard, Barbara, and Jennifer Daskal. 1998. Housing and welfare reform: Some background information. Washington, DC: Center on Budget and Policy Priorities.

Sard, Barbara, and Jeff Lubell. 2000a. The increasing use of TANF and state matching funds to provide housing assistance to families moving from welfare to work. Washington, DC: Center on Budget and Policy Priorities.

———. 2000b. The Family Self-Sufficiency Program. Washington, DC: Center on Budget and Policy Priorities.

Sard, Barbara, and Mary Waller. 2002. Housing strategies to strengthen welfare policy and support working families. Washington, DC: The Brookings Institution and Center on Budget and Policy Priorities.

Schorr, Lisbeth B. 1997. *Common purpose: Strengthening families and neighborhoods to rebuild America*. New York: Doubleday.

Schwartz, Alex, and Kian Tajbakhsh. 1997. Mixed-income housing: Unanswered questions. *Cityscape*, 3(2):71–92.

Shapiro, Isaac, and Robert Greenstein. 1999. The widening income gulf. Washington, DC: Center on Budget and Policy Priorities. http://www.cbpp.org/9-4-99tax-rep.htm.

Shapiro, Isaac, Robert Greenstein and James Sly. 2001. Under conference agreement, dollar gains for top one percent essentially the same as under House and Bush packages; share of tax cuts to top fifth basically identical under the different packages. Washington, DC: Center on Budget and Policy Priorities. http://www.cbpp.org/5-26-01tax2.htm

Sherman, Alroc, Cheryl Amey, Barbara Duffield, Nancy Ebb and Deborah Weinstein. 1998. Welfare to what: Early findings on family hardship and well-being. Washington, DC: Children's Defense Fund and National Coalition for the Homeless.

Shlay, Anne B. 1993. Family self-sufficiency and housing. *Housing Policy Debate*, 4(3):457–495.

———. 1995. Housing in the broader context in the United States. *Housing Policy Debate*, 6(3):695–720.

Shlay, Anne B., and C. Scott Holupka. 1992. Steps toward independence: Evaluating an integrated service program for public housing residents. *Evaluation Review*, 16.

Shroder, Mark. 2001. Moving to opportunity: An experiment in social and geographic mobility. *Cityscape: A Journal of Policy Development and Research*, 5(3):57–67.

Skocpol, Theda. 2000. *The missing middle*. New York: W.W. Norton Company.

Smith, Alastair. 2002. Mixed-income housing developments: Promise and reality. Cambridge, MA and Washington, DC: Joint Center for Housing Studies of Harvard University and Neighborhood Reinvestment Corporation.

Smith, Doug. 2003. Some taxpayers don't owe a penny. *Los Angeles Times*, April 15.

Squires, Gregory, D. 1994. *Capital and communities in black and white: The intersections of race, class and uneven development*. Albany: State University of New York Press.

Stone, Michael E. 1993. *Shelter poverty: New ideas on housing affordability*. Philadelphia: Temple University Press.

Sweeney, Eileen, Liz Schott, Ed Lazere, Shawn Fremstad, Heidi Goldberg, Jocelyn Guyer, David

Super and Clifford Johnson. 2000. Windows of opportunity: Strategies to support families receiving welfare and other low-income families in the next stage of welfare reform. Washington, DC: Center on Budget and Policy Priorities.

Traub, James. 2000. What no school can do. *New York Times Magazine*, January 16.

Turner, Margery Austin. 1998. Moving out of poverty: Expanding mobility and choice through tenant-based housing assistance. *Housing Policy Debate*, 9(3):373–394.

United States Department of Health and Human Services. 2002. Benefit levels for family of 3, July 1995–June 2001, March 14, 2004. http://www.acf.dhhs.gov/programs/ofa/annualreport5/1202.htm.

———. 2003. HHS releases data showing continuing decline in number of people receiving temporary assistance. September 3. http://www.hhs.gov/news/press/2003pres/20030903.html

United States Department of Housing and Urban Development. 1994. Reinvention blueprint. Washington, DC. December 19.

———. 1999. Building communities and new markets for the new century: 1998 consolidated report. Washington, DC.

United States Department of Labor. 2005. Minimum wage laws in the states. http://www.dol.gov/esa/minwage/america.htm. September 30, 2005.

United States General Accounting Office. 1993. Self-sufficiency: Opportunities and disincentives on the road to economic independence. GAO/HRD-93-23.

———. 1995. Welfare programs: Opportunities to consolidate and increase program efficiencies. GAO/HEHS-95-139.

———. 1997. Poverty measurement: Issues in revising and updating the official definition. GAO/HEHS-97-38.

———. 1998a. Welfare reform: Early fiscal effects of the TANF Block Grant. GAO/AIMD-98-137.

———. 1998b. Welfare reform: Changes will further shape the roles of housing agencies and HUD. GAO/RCED-98-148.

———. 1999. Welfare reform: Assessing the effectiveness of various welfare-to-work approaches. GAO/HEHS-99-179.

———. 2004. Tax administration: Comparison of the reported tax liabilities of foreign- and U.S.-controlled corporations, 1996–2000. GAO-04-358.

Varady, David, and Carole C. Walker. 2003. Housing vouchers and residential mobility. *Journal of Planning Literature*, 18(1):17–30.

Vernarelli, Michael J. 1986. Where should HUD locate assisted housing? The evolution of fair housing policy. In *Housing Desegregation and Federal Policy*, eds. Barbara Sard and Amy S. Bogdon. Chapel Hill: University of North Carolina Press.

Wider Opportunities for Women. 2003. Setting the standard for American working families: A report on the impact of the Family Economic Self-Sufficiency Project Nationwide. Washington, DC.

Williams, Christopher, Lawrence M. Scheier, Gilbert J. Botvin, Eli Baker and Nicole Miller. 1997. *Journal of Child & Adolescent Substance Abuse*, 6(1):69–89.

Wilson, William Julius. 1987. *The truly disadvantaged: The inner city, the underclass and public policy.* Chicago: University of Chicago Press.

Yinger, John. 1998. Housing discrimination is still worth worrying about. *Housing Policy Debate*, 9(4):893–927.

Zedlewski, Sheila Rafferty. 2002. The importance of housing benefits to welfare success. Survey Series. Washington, DC: Brookings Institution and the Urban Institute.

About the Contributors

EMILY PARADISE ACHTENBERG (ejpa@aol .com) is a housing policy and development consultant and urban planner who specializes in the preservation of federally-assisted housing. She has assisted community-based nonprofit and government organizations in acquiring and preserving more than 3,500 units threatened with expiring use restrictions and subsidy contracts, and she is actively involved in the development of federal, state and local preservation policies and programs. She is the author of *Stemming the Tide: A Handbook on Preserving Subsidized Multifamily Housing* (2002) and has written about strategies to promote social housing ownership, production and finance. She was an original member of the Planners Network Steering Committee and is currently a Board member of Citizens Housing and Planning Association in Boston. She received an MCP from the Massachusetts Institute of Technology.

RACHEL G. BRATT (rachel.bratt@tufts.edu) is professor and chair of the Department of Urban and Environmental Policy and Planning at Tufts University and a Fellow at the Harvard Joint Center for Housing Studies. She is a co-editor of *Critical Perspectives on Housing* (Temple University Press, 1986) and the author of *Rebuilding a Low-Income Housing Policy* (Temple University Press, 1989). She is also the author or co-author of dozens of professional and research reports, articles and book chapters. In addition to her academic work, she was a professional planner in the City of Worcester, Massachusetts, and has served as a board or advisory committee member for a number of public, private and nonprofit

organizations, including the Consumer Advisory Council of the Federal Reserve Bank and the Citizens' Housing and Planning Association in Boston. She received a Ph.D. from the Massachusetts Institute of Technology's Department of Urban Studies and Planning.

DAVID B. BRYSON was a housing attorney at the National Housing Law Project for 27 years, during which he also twice served as its acting director. Through his litigation, training, writings and legislative and administrative advocacy, he influenced almost every progressive development in affordable housing law. He was author or co-author of *Welfare and Housing—How Can the Housing Assistance Programs Help Welfare Recipients?* (2002), *HUD Housing Programs: Tenants' Rights* (in two editions, 1981 and 1994) and *Public Housing in Peril* (1990). His efforts established numerous rights for residents under the federal low-income housing programs. He also litigated or participated in landmark housing cases, including *Wright v. City of Roanoke* (1987), the Supreme Court's decision recognizing that public housing residents could enforce their statutory right to limited rents, and *Geneva Towers Tenants Organization v. Federated Mortgage Investors*, a case establishing the due process rights of federally-subsidized residents in the rent increase process. David died in 1999.

HELÉNE CLARK (hclark@actknowledge.org) is an environmental psychologist and director of ActKnowledge, a research organization that studies and assists social change efforts. Through program evaluation, community development and public policy research, she brings social science research into partnership with program providers and policymakers. Dr. Clark's work in the field of housing policy has been concerned with understanding and supporting efforts to move housing out of the private market into tenant or social ownership. Currently, she works with nonprofit organizations to develop planning and research tools for social change initiatives.

JOHN EMMEUS DAVIS is a partner and co-founder of Burlington Associates in Community Development, LLC (www. burlingtonassociates.com), a national consulting cooperative specializing in the design of public programs and private models that support the development of permanently affordable housing and the revitalization of lower-income neighborhoods. He previously worked for the City of Burlington, Vermont, and at the Institute for Community Economics. He has taught at New Hampshire College, the University of Vermont and Massachusetts Institute of Technology. His publications include *The Community Land Trust Handbook* (1982), *Contested Ground: Collective Action and the Urban Neighborhood* (1991), *The Affordable City: Toward a Third Sector Housing Policy* (1994), *Bridging the Organizational Divide: The Making of a Nonprofit Merger* (2002), and *Permanently Affordable Homeownership: Does the Community Land Trust Deliver on Its Promises?* (2004). He holds an MS and Ph.D. from Cornell.

NANCY A. DENTON (n.denton@albany.edu) is associate professor of sociology and the associate director of the Center for Social and Demographic Analysis at the State University of New York at Albany. She received her MA and Ph.D. in demography from the University of Pennsylvania and an MA in sociology from Fordham University. Her major research interests are race and residential segregation, and she is the author of numerous articles on the topic. She is co-author of *American Apartheid: Segregation and the Making of the Underclass* (1993), winner of the 1995 American Sociological Association Distinguished Publication Award and the 1994 Otis Dudley Duncan award from the Sociology

of Population section of the American Sociological Association.

PETER DREIER (dreier@oxy.edu) is E. P. Clapp Distinguished Professor of Politics and director of the Urban & Environmental Policy Program at Occidental College in Los Angeles. He is co-author of *Place Matters: Metropolitics for the 21st Century* (2005, 2nd edition), *The Next Los Angeles: The Struggle For a Livable City* (2005) and *Regions that Work: How Cities and Suburbs Can Grow Together* (2000) as well as co-editor of *Up Against the Sprawl: Public Policy in the Making of Southern California* (2004). He writes regularly for the *Los Angeles Times, The Nation* and *American Prospect.* From 1984 to 1992, he served as the chief housing policy adviser to Boston Mayor Ray Flynn and as the director of housing for the Boston Redevelopment Authority.

MARIA FOSCARINIS (mfoscarinis@nlchp.org) is founder and executive director of the National Law Center on Homelessness & Poverty, a nonprofit organization established in 1989 as the legal arm of the nationwide effort to end homelessness. She has advocated nationally for solutions to homelessness since 1985 and was a primary architect of the Stewart B. McKinney Homeless Assistance Act. She has litigated to secure the rights of homeless persons and has also written for scholarly and general audience publications. She is a graduate of Columbia Law School and also holds a MA in philosophy.

CHESTER HARTMAN (chartman2@aol.com) is the director of research at the Poverty & Race Research Action Council in Washington, DC—an organization for which he served as executive director and president from its founding in 1990 through 2003. Prior to that, he was a Fellow at the Institute for Policy Studies and founder and chair of the Planners Network, a national organization of progressive urban planners. He has served on the faculty of Harvard, Yale, Cornell, Columbia, UC–Berkeley and the University of North Carolina–Chapel Hill and is an adjunct professor of sociology at George Washington University. Among his recent books are *City for Sale: The Transformation of San Francisco* (2002), *Between Eminence and Notoriety:*

Four Decades of Radical Urban Planning (2002) and *Poverty and Race in America: The Emerging Agendas* (2006).

W. DENNIS KEATING (dennis@wolf.csuohio.edu) is a professor and associate dean with Levin College of Urban Affairs, Cleveland State University, where he also chairs the Department of Urban Studies. His numerous publications are in housing, housing law, neighborhood revitalization and urban policy. His co-edited special issue of the *Journal of Urban Affairs* on "New Perspectives in Community Development" was published in 2004. His current research projects include a national study of intentionally diverse suburban communities and studies of the First Suburbs Consortium of greater Cleveland.

PETER MARCUSE (pm35@columbia.edu) is a professor of urban planning at Columbia University. He is a co-editor of *Globalizing Cities: A New Spatial Order?* (1999) and *Of States and Cities: The Partitioning of Urban Space* (2002). He was majority leader of Waterbury, Connecticut's Board of Aldermen; a member of its City Planning Commission; later president of the Los Angeles Planning Commission; and more recently, a member of Community Board 9 in Manhattan and co-chair of its Housing Committee. Prior to joining the Columbia faculty in 1978, he was on the faculty of UCLA and for 20 years was in a private law practice in Waterbury, Connecticut. He spent two years in Germany, both West and East, and has taught in Australia and South Africa.

CHRISTY M. NISHITA (cnishita@usc.edu) completed her Ph.D. in gerontology from the University of Southern California in 2004 and is currently a post-doctoral research associate at USC's Andrus Gerontology Center. She was a recipient of a National Institute on Aging predoctoral traineeship to conduct research on the role of supportive housing and home modification in long-term care and has published journal articles, book chapters and policy reports on the topic.

JON PYNOOS (pynoos@usc.edu) is the UPS Foundation Professor of Gerontology, Pol-

icy, Planning and Development at the Andrus Gerontology Center of the University of Southern California, where he also directs its National Resource Center on Supportive Housing and Home Modifications. He has written and edited five books on housing and the elderly, including *Housing the Aged: Design Directives and Policy Considerations* (1987); *Housing Frail Elders: International Policies, Perspectives and Prospects* (1995) and *Linking Housing and Services for Older Adults: Obstacles, Options and Opportunities* (2004). He is a founding member of the National Home Modification Action Coalition and has been awarded Guggenheim and Fulbright Fellowships. Before moving to USC in 1979, he was the director of an Area Agency on Aging/Home Care Corporation in Massachusetts that provided a range of services to keep older persons out of institutional settings and allow them to age in place. He holds undergraduate, master's, and Ph.D. degrees from Harvard University.

ROB ROSENTHAL (rrosenthal@wesleyan.edu) is a professor of sociology and director of the Service-Learning Center at Wesleyan University. He writes frequently on homelessness, is the author of *Homeless in Paradise* (Temple University Press 1994) and was a founding member of the Santa Barbara Homeless Coalition. He is working on a book (with Dick Flacks) on how music is used in social movements and is the author of the historical rock opera, "Seattle 1919." He received his Ph.D. from the University of California, Santa Barbara.

SUSAN SAEGERT (ssaegert@gc.cuny.edu) is the director of the Center for Human Environments and a professor of environmental psychology at the CUNY Graduate Center, where she was also the first director of the Center for the Study of Women and Society. She holds a Ph.D. in social psychology from the University of Michigan. She is a co-editor of *Social Capital in Poor Communities* (2001) and co-author of *From Abandonment to Hope: Community Households in Harlem* (1990) and the *Annual Review of Environmental Psychology, 1990.* She has served as president of the division for Environmental and Population Psychology of the

American Psychological Association, co-chair of the Environmental Design Research Association and on the editorial boards of *Environment and Behavior* and the *Journal of Environmental Psychology*.

MICHAEL E. STONE (Michael.Stone@umb.edu) is a professor of community planning and public policy at University of Massachusetts, Boston. For more than 30 years, he has been involved in teaching, research, policy analysis, program development, technical assistance and advocacy on housing, poverty and living standards, and participatory planning. Among his numerous research reports, articles and books is *Shelter Poverty: New Ideas on Housing Affordability* (Temple University Press, 1993). During 2002 to 2003, he was an Atlantic Fellow in Public Policy, based at the Centre for Urban and Community Research, Goldsmiths College, University of London.

MICHAEL SWACK (m.swack@snhu.edu) is the founder and dean of the School of Community Economic Development at Southern New Hampshire University. He was the founding chairman and current board member of the New Hampshire Community Loan fund. He received his doctorate from Columbia University and his master's degree from Harvard University.

CHRIS TILLY (Chris_Tilly@uml.edu), University Professor of Regional Economic and Social Development at the University of Massachusetts at Lowell, specializes in labor, income distribution and local economic development. His books include *Half a Job: Bad and Good Part-Time Jobs in a Changing Labor Market* (Temple University Press, 1996), *Glass Ceilings and Bottomless Pits: Women's Work, Women's Poverty* (with Randy Albelda, 1997), *Work Under Capitalism* (with Charles Tilly, 1998) and *Stories Employers Tell: Race, Skill, and Hiring in America* (with Philip Moss, 2001).

ROBERT WIENER (rob@calruralhousing.org) has been the executive director of the California Coalition for Rural Housing since 1981. As one of the oldest state low-income housing coalitions in the country, CCRH has played a major role in federal and state housing policy and program efforts in rural housing, farm labor housing, housing preservation and other areas of housing provision. He has been on the faculty of the University of California, Davis, Community and Regional Development Program. In 1999, he co-edited (with Joe Belden) *Housing in Rural America* (1998) and is currently working on a book on affordable housing practice in California. He holds a doctorate in urban and regional planning from UCLA.

LARRY LAMAR YATES (llyates@shentel.net), currently an organizer for the Virginia Organizing Project in the Shenandoah Valley of Virginia, served as the field director for the National Low Income Housing Coalition and was the Grassroots Organizing Mentor at the Center for Health, Environment and Justice. He was also the founding executive director of the Virginia Housing Coalition and provided critical early support to the founders of the National Alliance for HUD Tenants (URL: www.user.shentel.net/llyates).

Index